Blanche of Castile, Queen of France

Blanche of Castile

Queen of France

LINDY GRANT

YALE UNIVERSITY PRESS

NEW HAVEN AND LONDON

Printed in China

Library of Congress Cataloging-in-Publication Data

Names: Grant, Lindy, author.

Title: Blanche of Castile, Queen of France : power, religion and culture in
the thirteenth century / Lindy Grant.

Description: New Haven : Yale University Press, 2016. | Includes
bibliographical references and index.

Identifiers: LCCN 2016000559 | ISBN 9780300219265 (cl : alk. paper)

Subjects: LCSH: Blanche, of Castile, Queen, consort of Louis VIII, King of
France, 1188–1252. | Queens–France–Biography. | France–History--Louis
VIII, 1223–1226. | Louis VIII, King of France, 1187–1226.

Classification: LCC DC91.6.B5 .G73 2016 | DDC 944/.023092--dc23

LC record available at http://lccn.loc.gov/2016000559

A catalogue record for this book is available from
The British Library

FRONTISPIECE   Blanche and Louis IX, seated above a cleric directing a scribe producing a bible,
the final folio of the Toledo moralised bible, New York, The Morgan Library and Museum,
MS M240, f. 8.

For my mother,
Mary Grant,
and my godmother,
Miriam Amos,
to celebrate their 90th birthdays,
7 December 2016

Contents

Preface

I HAVE MANY PEOPLE TO THANK for their help and support over the decade that it has taken to write this book. My colleagues in the Department of History at the University of Reading have been supportive throughout, and I have benefited from discussion with medievalist colleagues attached to the Graduate Centre for Medieval Studies at Reading, notably Gill Knight (who helped with some particularly problematical translations from the Latin), Anne Lawrence, Catherine Léglu (who looked over my discussion of medieval poetry and *chanson*), Elizabeth Matthew and Rebecca Rist. Undergraduate students on my Special Subject course have helped me to refine and focus my ideas, as have my postgraduate students, especially three who work on thirteenth-century France: Charlotte Pickard, Katie Phillips (who produced the family trees with exemplary efficiency) and Charlotte Crouch. Beyond the University of Reading, I have benefited from – and enjoyed! – discussion with a host of French, British and American scholars, and the support and encouragement of friends. The two categories are often, of course, overlapping. Both fellow medievalists and non-medievalist friends have offered moral support, practical help and lively and stimulating discussion. They include: Jeremy Ashbee; the late John Baldwin; David Bates; E.A.R. (Peggy) Brown; Caroline Bruzelius; David Carpenter; Alexis Charansonnet; Francois Comte; David Crouch; David d'Avray, who generously provided me with an important text that he had discovered; Marie Dejoux; the late Jean Dufour, who with great kindness gave me copies of his list of Blanche's acts and took me to see the collection of acts of Louis IX at the Institut de France; Wendy Davies; Anne Duggan; Jean Dunbabin; Theodore Evergates; Peter Fergusson; Véronique Gazeau, for lively

discussion and delightful hospitality; Alexandra Gajewski; John Gillingham, who read some key chapters at a stage when I felt very uncertain of my ideas; Rolf Grosse; Xavier Hélary; my godson Dr Max Kelen and Bud Kelen (Rosemary Burch) who discussed the health of Blanche and her family with me; Terryl Kinder; Frédérique Lachaud; Elisabeth Lalou; Jean-Luc Liez; Emmanuel Litoux; John Lowden; Sheila MacBrayne-Poggia and her family for their warm hospitality in Paris; Thérèse Martin; Robert Mills; Pascal Montaubin; Nigel Morgan; Jean-François Moufflet; Jinty Nelson; Kathleen Nolan; Clare Pillman; Daniel Power; David Robinson; Miriam Shadis; Pauline Stafford; Patricia Stirnemann; Mark Studer; Kathy Thompson; Liesbeth Van Houts; Nicholas Vincent; Monique Wabont, who showed me the remains at Maubuisson, and gave me generous access to her research reports on it; Rose Walker; Björn Weiler; Louise Wilkinson; and Michael Wyss. I hope that I have not left anyone out. Clare Pillman, Rose Walker, my niece Laure Grant and Sheila MacBrayne-Poggia made site visits a great pleasure – and not all the sites and monuments connected with Blanche would naturally find themselves on a tourist itinerary, and the weather was not always perfect . . .

I am much indebted to the kindness and help of the staff at several libraries and archives, notably the British Library; the Bibliothèque Nationale; The Arsenal Library – with special thanks to the curator of medieval manuscripts, Nathalie Coilly; The Bibliothèque Mazarine; the Archives Nationales; The Institute of Historical Research; The Society of Antiquaries; The Warburg Institute and the University Library at Reading. Very special thanks are owing to Madame Sylvie Dechavanne and Marie-Hélène Peltier and their staff at Archives Departmental of Val d'Oise at Cergy-Pontoise, not least for providing such wonderful photographs of some of Blanche's acts and her seal. I should like to thank Stuart Whatling for kindly providing me with one of his magnificent photographs of stained glass and Leonello Morandi for drawing the maps.

Four anonymous readers made an invaluable contribution to the final form of the text. One of them revealed himself as Sean Field, on the grounds that I would have guessed who he was from his comments. I am not sure that I would have done – but it is nice to know whom I am thanking. And, apart from his hugely helpful comments, he saved me from two extremely silly mistakes: but I daresay I have managed to incorporate others into the text, for which, of course, I take full responsibility. At Yale University Press, Delia Gaze was an impeccable copy-editor, and Gillian Malpass has provided continual support and encouragement as she has seen the book through to press with her inimitable style and aplomb.

•

I shall finish with a note on names. Total consistency is impossible. I have anglicised where there is an English version (so I have the Empress Mary, rather than Marie, Philip Augustus rather than Philippe Auguste), unless to do so would be silly (we do not talk of Lewis IX). Where there is not an English form, I have tried to do the most sensible thing. Alphonse/Alfonso is a problem. I have called Blanche's father Alfonso of Castile. But all Alphonses/Alfonsos who pursued their career in France have been called Alphonse. This includes Blanche's favourite nephew, Alphonse of Portugal: partly because the Portuguese introduces another variant on the name, and partly because he and Blanche's son were called 'the two Alphonses' in household accounts. It has become fashionable to use the Iberian Berenguela for Blanche's sister. I have stuck with the Latinised version, Berengaria, since that is regularly used for Blanche's cousin, Berengaria of Navarre, and it is the version used in Blanche's own household accounts. Where people are named from a place, I have anglicised, for example, Adam of Beaumont and Stephen of Sancerre rather than Adam de Beaumont or Stephen de Sancerre, except in cases where historians are more accustomed to the 'de' form. This has led to two figures from essentially English history being 'de' something or other: Hubert de Burgh and Simon de Montfort. I have used 'of' for Simon de Montfort's essentially French brother (Amaury) and father (Simon). It does at least mean that one can distinguish between Simons, father and son. I have kept 'de' where a name is derived from a feature rather than a place name, for example, Peter des Fontaines, John de la Cour, rather than Peter of the Fountains or John of the Court. Names could be a problem in the thirteenth century, too: Eleanor of Aquitaine is said to have chosen Blanche, rather than her prettier sister Urraca, as the bride of the future king of France because she thought that the French court would find the name Urraca uncouth. Blanca, or Candida, or Blanche would do just fine.

•

Blanche was many things; among the most important, she was a mother. Her children, St Louis, Robert of Artois, Alphonse of Poitiers, Isabella and Charles of Anjou, found that like most mothers, Blanche was usually right. It seems appropriate to dedicate this book to my mother, Mary Grant, and to my godmother, Miriam Amos.

Map of France in the thirteenth century

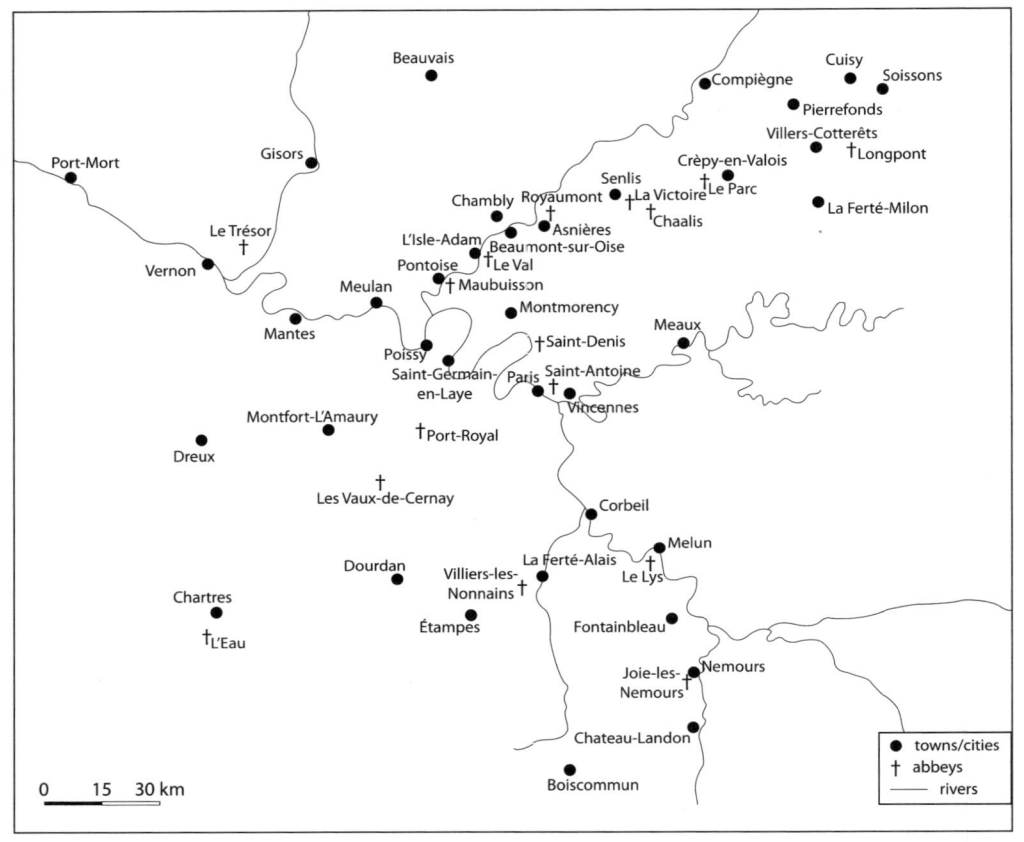

Map of the area around Paris in the thirteenth century

The Anglo-Norman/Angevin family

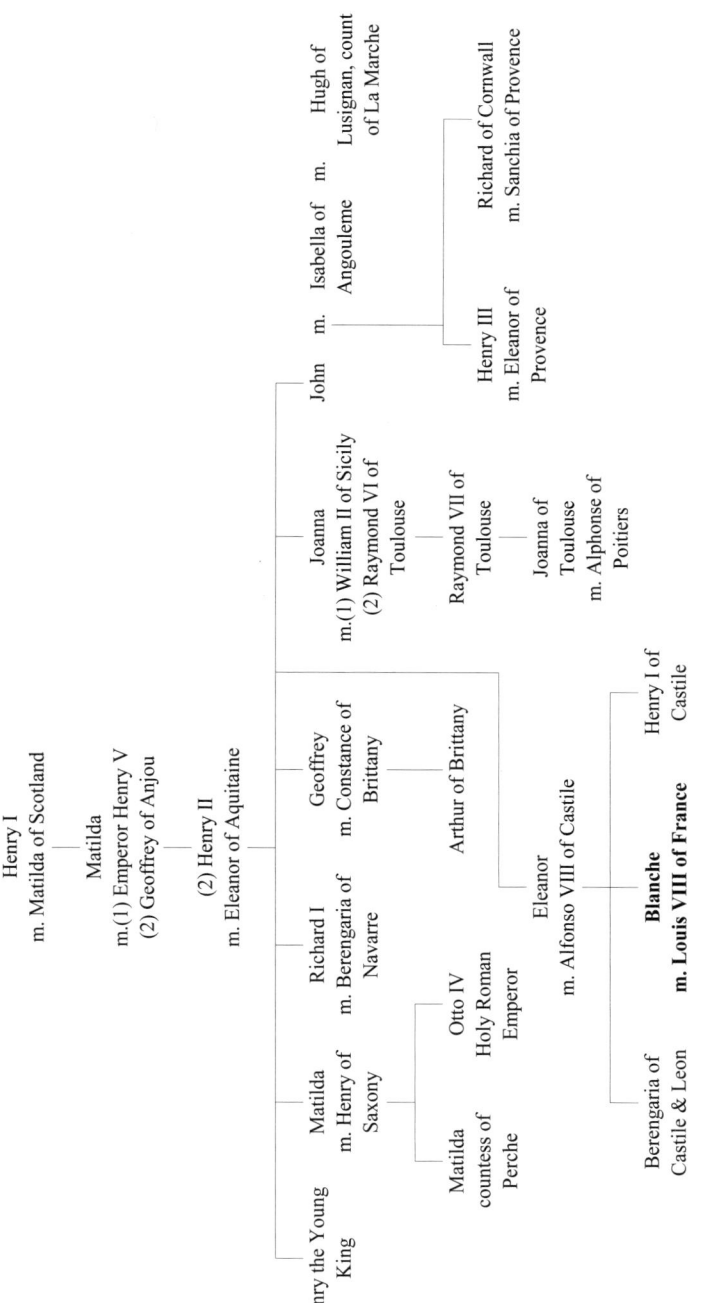

Blanche's Iberian family

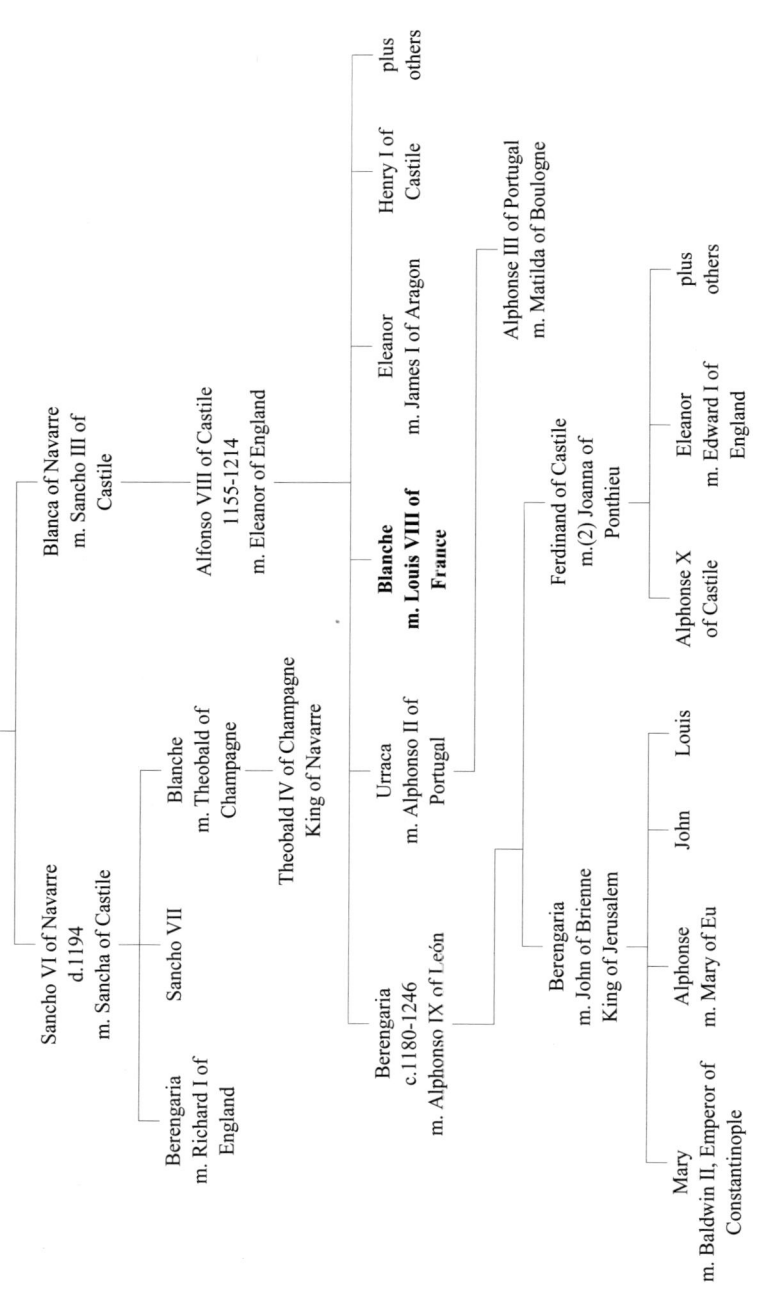

Sancho VI of Navarre
d.1194
m. Sancha of Castile

Blanca of Navarre
m. Sancho III of
Castile

Berengaria
m. Richard I of
England

Sancho VII

Blanche
m. Theobald of
Champagne

Alfonso VIII of Castile
1155-1214
m. Eleanor of England

Theobald IV of Champagne
King of Navarre

Eleanor
m. James I of Aragon

Henry I of
Castile

plus
others

Berengaria
c.1180-1246
m. Alphonso IX of León

Urraca
m. Alphonso II of
Portugal

**Blanche
m. Louis VIII of
France**

Alphonse III of Portugal
m. Matilda of Boulogne

Berengaria
m. John of Brienne
King of Jerusalem

Ferdinand of Castile
m.(2) Joanna of
Ponthieu

Mary
m. Baldwin II, Emperor of
Constantinople

Alphonse
m. Mary of Eu

John

Louis

Alphonse X
of Castile

Eleanor
m. Edward I of
England

plus
others

The Capetian and Champagne families

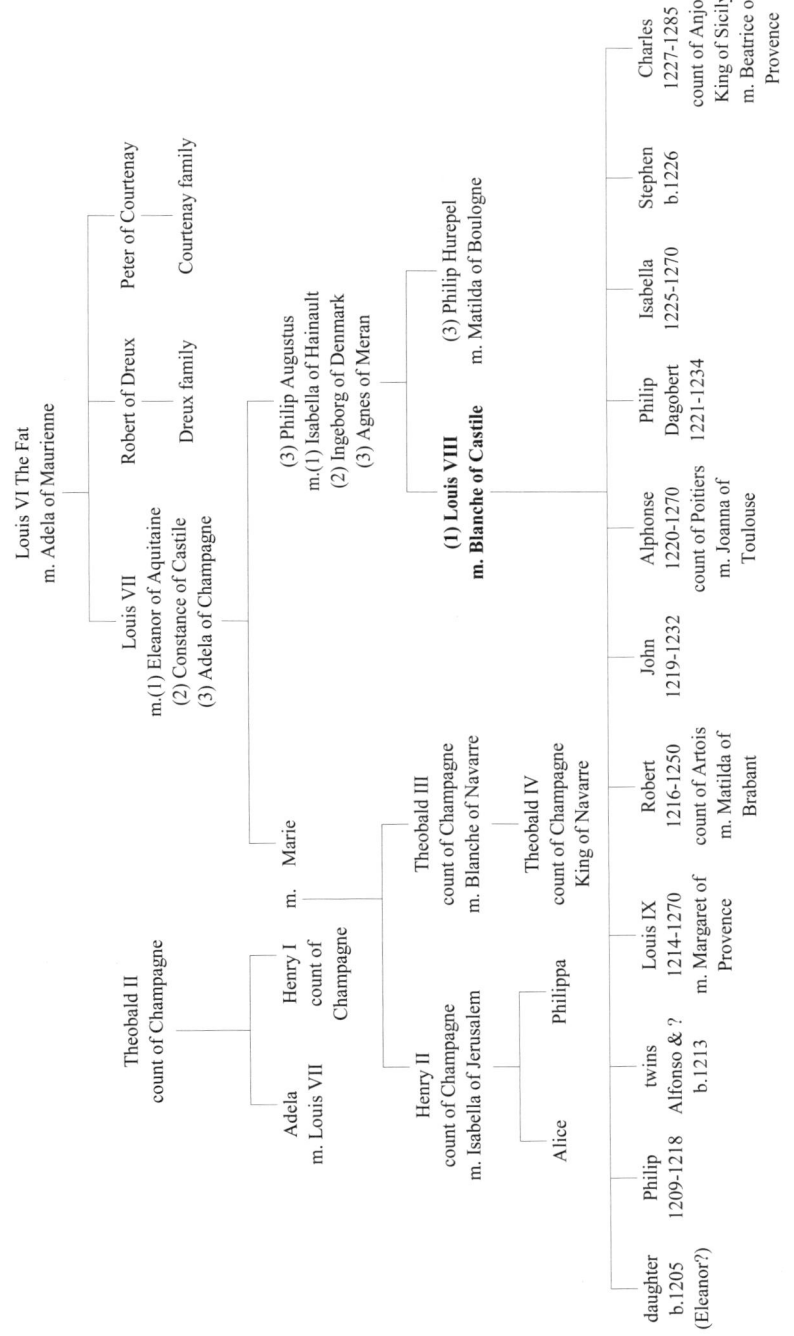

Introduction

THE LAST PAGE OF AN ILLUSTRATED BIBLE painted in Paris around 1230 bears one of the most famous images produced in the Middle Ages (frontispiece). Set against a gorgeous gold ground, a queen sits in conversation with a king; below them, a churchman, a clerk, instructs the craftsman who is making the bible. The clerk sits below the queen, and the craftsman sits below the king. The craftsman does what he is told by the clerk, who points a commanding finger. Above, the king, crowned, enthroned and holding his sceptre, seems to take instruction from the queen, for the king sits passively attentive, while the queen expounds. She does not point, like the clerk, but her gestures have an elegant, yet authoritative eloquence. She is, it seems, counselling the king – and the king is perhaps in need of counsel, for he has no beard: he is young. The queen and the young king are Blanche of Castile, queen of France, and her son, Louis ix of France, the future St Louis.[1]

Blanche of Castile was one of the most imaginative and successful rulers of medieval Europe. The granddaughter of King Henry ii of England and Eleanor of Aquitaine, and the daughter of Alfonso viii of Castile, she was born to pre-eminence. She was the wife and queen of Louis viii of France. When Louis viii died unexpectedly in 1226, after a reign of just three years, he left the kingdom of France and his twelve-year-old son, Louis ix, in the protection of Blanche of Castile. Her influence on her son, canonised as St Louis in 1297, was profound. Blanche ruled France for some eight years, until Louis's majority in 1234. When Louis ix went on Crusade in 1248, he left his mother again in charge of the kingdom of France, which she ruled until her death in 1252. In between the periods

when she ruled France, during the personal rule of her son, Blanche remained an influential political figure. As Robert Fawtier, one of the great historians of medieval France, wrote in the dark days of the Second World War: 'To all intents and purposes she may be counted among the kings of France.'[2]

Fawtier's comment raises the issue of women as rulers. In the Middle Ages, people expected that their ruler would be a man, a figure of natural authority, made in the (male) image of God. They thought that rule by a woman overturned the natural order of things. God had made man first, and then made Eve from Adam's rib. As the thirteenth-century philosopher and theologian Thomas Aquinas put it: 'the female requires the male not only for procreation, but also for governance: because the male excels both in intelligence and strength'.[3] Blanche was not the only woman ruler of the Middle Ages; in fact, there were several. But men often challenged the authority of female rulers. Members of the French baronage tried to challenge Blanche, though they were not successful. When women were strong and effective rulers, like Blanche, contemporaries praised them as viragos, as if they were not womanly.[4] Most, though not all, contemporary commentators were churchmen. Medieval churchmen, most of them supposed to be chaste, were deeply imbued with distrust of women – women, the descendants of Eve, who had been responsible for the Fall of man. But they needed a ruler to be strong and effective; only with peace could the Church flourish. Blanche won their grudging respect. There were, after all, Old Testament precedents for powerful, determined and admirable women leaders, like Deborah and Judith. When Blanche died, the well-informed English monk Matthew Paris praised her as 'feminine in sex, but masculine in counsel'. Churchmen who wrote biographies of her son St Louis praised her as a 'virago, combining feminine intuition with the spirit of the masculine sex' and as having 'the courage of a man in the heart of a woman'.[5]

If men praised effective women rulers as viragos – as not properly womanly – they often also insinuated that a successful woman ruler must have used her sexual charms as a political weapon. Blanche was accused of affairs with her cousin, the poet Count Theobald of Champagne, and with a great churchman, the papal legate, Romanus. The accusations circulated in ribald poetry and churchmen could not resist reporting the innuendos. Effective women rulers still challenge social and political conventions. Commentary on the career of Margaret Thatcher gives an uncanny echo of the way that contemporaries spoke of Blanche: Thatcher was the Iron Lady, with nicely turned ankles, the eyes of Caligula and the mouth of Marilyn Monroe.[6]

•

The last quarter of the twentieth century saw the rise of a new feminist approach to the study of history. An important strand of this new history focused on women and power in the institutionally patriarchal, indeed overtly misogynistic, Middle Ages. How much independent agency did medieval women have? How did women who found themselves wielding power make it effective? How far were they able to wield effective power? How did that power change over the cycle of their lives, from young wife, to mother, to widow? Was the power that women might wield different from the power that men might wield? How did the men around them react? How did contemporaries perceive such women? The result has been a rich seam of studies of medieval queenship. A related group of studies has focused on medieval women who were not queens, but who ruled over important counties or lordships, either as heiress in their own right or as regent for their sons.[7] There are often illuminating parallels in the ways in which queens and countesses or women acting as lord dealt with the practicalities of managing power in a patriarchal world. But a crowned and anointed queen was fundamentally different from a countess, just as a crowned and anointed king differed from even the greatest of his magnates.

These studies of queenship, and to a lesser extent those of other women rulers, provide an invaluable framework for understanding many aspects of Blanche's career – though, as will become apparent, I think that Blanche's career also reveals their limitations. And there are dangers with this focus. There is the danger that the queen, her powers and her activities are seen in isolation from the society in which she operated. If one focuses too much on the limitations on the agency of the queen, one can forget that there were limitations on the agency of kings too. Focus on misogyny can lead one to ignore the prevalence of bitter criticism of power and the powerful in general. Focusing on the cultural and devotional activities of medieval women can lead to the assumption that certain patterns of activity are typical of elite women, when in fact they may be typical of the elite of a generation. A central argument of this book is that Blanche's life story casts light on what it meant to be a ruler and a member of the medieval elite, not 'just' a queen and a medieval elite woman, and that her life story can be told only if one refocuses the lens to look beyond queenship as such.

It is important to note that Blanche occupied three distinct institutional positions as a woman of power: she was a queen consort, a dowager queen – or queen mother – and a regent, a ruler. As queen consort, she was expected to 'participate in the rule' of the king her husband. As regent, she ruled in place of the king her son. For both roles, there were acknowledged powers, privileges, duties and

expectations. The role of queen dowager, the mother of the king, was more uncertain. A queen dowager's ability to continue to have influence or effect the government of the realm depended on her relationship with her son.

Most studies of queenship and female rulership have attempted to define power itself. Pauline Stafford has provided one of the most helpful definitions: 'It is the ability or chance to realise your own will, if necessary against the resistance of others' and 'the ability to take part in events...to have the means of strategic action'.[8] Power meant ensuring that people did as you wanted them to – though while that partly depended on role, status and resources, it also depended on personality. Some people have more natural authority than others. Everything suggests that Blanche had more than her fair share. Many studies of queenship have tended to assume the powerlessness, the lack of agency, of the medieval queen. But throughout her life Blanche was adept at ensuring that people did what she wanted.

An early and influential study of women and power by Erler and Kowalski stressed the difference between power and authority. Authority they defined as legitimately sanctioned; power, by contrast, was that influence that lacked legitimate sanction.[9] Thus, they argued, a man – a king or a count – would have legitimately sanctioned authority; a woman – a queen or countess – might have power and influence if she were capable and/or fortunate. But this heavily gendered distinction between power and authority is misleading. A king did indeed have legally sanctioned authority, but so did his queen, who was anointed and given considerable reserve authority at her coronation.[10] Her coronation prepared her to run the kingdom in the absence or illness of the king. That legally sanctioned authority underpinned her ability to intervene as queen mother, if required by the king, her son. Counts and countesses were not crowned, but it was widely accepted that an aristocratic wife would run her lord's lands for him in his absence, and most customary law accepted the rights of a daughter to succeed to her father's lordships if there were no son. On the other hand, kings were sometimes seen to have exceeded their legally sanctioned authority, most famously, perhaps, Blanche of Castile's uncle, King John of England, whose arbitrary government was checked by Magna Carta in 1215. Legally sanctioned authority was not specific to men. But it can still be useful to distinguish between legally sanctioned authority and the broader category of 'power', which may be informal and may indeed have no legal sanction.

Most historians of female power have seen medieval queens and countesses as wielding a different kind of power from that wielded by male rulers. They see the male ruler as having at his disposal executive government, the imposition of peace

and justice on the realm, backed by the means of coercion. They see his wives, mothers and daughters as more likely to obtain their desired results through influence and perhaps diplomacy. Most historians of queenship have explored the way in which queens and countesses have displayed, signalled and extended the reach of their powers through gesture and ritual, through devotion and religious patronage, and through cultural patronage.

It is true that coercive and magisterial power is the prerogative of the ruler. But it is not gender-specific. Many queens consort and dowager, let alone a queen regent, had to know how to use the more coercive and magisterial registers of power, for they were expected to run the kingdom in the king's absence, and might well, as did Blanche, convene and lead an army. To do so, a queen would work through her officials, sending messages and summonses to those who owed military service – just as a king would. Some aristocrats might feel strong enough to refuse or withdraw their military service – but that happened to kings too. The real difference between queen and king as convenor and leader of a military force was that no one would expect the queen to take part in actual fighting.

And feminist historians have surely gone too far in identifying persuasion, ritual, devotion and religious and cultural patronage as means of both obtaining and signalling power as passive, and as essentially feminine. They have sometimes talked of 'the power of the weak', especially when discussing queenly manifestations of extreme piety or humility.[11] But these powers – the power to influence, to use diplomacy, to charm and to flirt (if one is good at it), to manipulate emotion, to exploit friendship, to use religious and cultural patronage, to display piety, or even humility, to use gesture, ritual and ceremony – are not limited to women rulers. They are part of the wide register of powers that an effective ruler, male or female, is wise to draw upon. Rulers are wise to attend to the image that they project: and these are the tools through which they can do so. It is ironic that while historians of queenship identify these registers of power as particularly queenly, historians of power politics in general are increasingly identifying the use of exactly the same subtle registers of power by male rulers. Geoffrey Koziol and Bernd Schneidmüller have transformed our understanding of early Capetian kingship by recognising the extent to which these kings employed careful manipulation of gesture, ritual and ceremony, of piety and patronage, to enhance their prestige.[12] This should not be surprising. Both Louis vi and Louis vii, only too conscious of their military inadequacy, made useful capital out of their piety and humility – as both famously explained to Walter Map.[13] One might draw an analogy with the distinction made by commentators on twenty-first-century politics in the use of 'hard' and 'soft'

power, and the wide acceptance that all governments will expect to make use of both registers.[14]

Nevertheless, however much these 'softer powers' are in most cases open to exploitation by kings as much as queens, the exploration of them by historians of queenship has been richly illuminating. And some of these 'softer powers' are specific to the queen. Several studies of queenship have explored areas where a queen consort or queen mother was expected to use her influence, with the king and with others. Influence was always susceptible of suspicion. It was seen as informal, insidious, often hidden and absolutely lacking in legal sanction. It could be exercised in private places, notably the bedroom. Queen consorts or queen mothers were regularly accused of too much influence over the king – but so were others in the royal entourage, favourites or ministers of the king. But all medieval contemporaries would have agreed that one of the prime functions of a queen was to use her influence to intercede with the king on behalf of his people. There were religious models for this – the biblical Queen Esther, who obtained mercy for the people of Israel, and above all the Virgin Mary, Queen of Heaven, who intercedes for humanity with her son, Jesus Christ. Historians have argued that a queen's intercession could allow a ruler to show mercy with no trace of weakness.[15]

Historians of queenship have also outlined the role of a queen within dynastic marriage strategies. All royal marriages were diplomatic moves. A queen was expected to make that diplomacy work. Indeed, she was herself a diplomat: she was a channel of communication between her natal and her marital families, who might be allies or enemies. With her personal experience as a channel of communication in a diplomatic marriage, a queen was well placed to prepare younger female members of the family for marriage. Most queens were expected to play an important role in negotiating further dynastic betrothals and marriages.[16]

The most important role of the female consort of a ruler or major lord was the provision of a male heir. Women who failed to do so might find their marriage annulled. Louis VII of France had his marriage to Blanche's grandmother, Eleanor of Aquitaine, annulled in 1152, mainly because she had produced no male heir in fifteen years of marriage. A consort who had not produced an heir was expendable, especially if the diplomatic alliance that her marriage was supposed to cement was no longer useful. Philip II of France threatened to divorce his first wife, Isabella of Hainault, in 1184 because she represented a Flemish faction at court.[17] But once she had given birth to his heir, the future Louis VIII, in 1187, she could not be disposed of so easily. The birth of an heir transformed the queen from the daughter

of an alien and perhaps enemy house into the mother of the future ruler. At the most extreme, it transformed her from expendable to unassailable.

Female consorts must have been intensely aware how much their ability to have political influence depended on their relationship with the heir to the kingdom or polity. The power of the queen through motherhood has been explored by several historians, notably Pauline Stafford in her pioneering work on Anglo-Saxon queens.[18] Most women took care to develop this crucial relationship. Both Eleanor of Aquitaine and Blanche's daughter-in-law, Margaret of Provence, did so at the expense of their relationship with their husbands – in both cases, a miscalculation. Surprisingly, Isabella of Angoulême, queen of King John, preferred to spend her widowhood as countess of Angoulême in her own right rather than remain in England as mother to the young Henry III.[19] Blanche had a particularly close relationship with her son and heir, the future Louis IX, and on that close relationship the effectiveness of her power and influence depended. It meant that she could not be dislodged as regent during his minority; that she was named as sole regent during his Crusade; and that she played an important role in the governance of the kingdom during his personal rule. She is in many ways a classic case of a queen who knew how to extend her power long after the death of her husband through her son.

Considerations of influence over the king and of the role of the queen as wife and mother within a family have led historians to distinguish between public and private roles, and public and private spaces. If the queen uses the intimacy of the marriage bed to influence the king, she is using the private sphere of the family to play a public role. Historians have often been tempted to see public and private spheres as gendered spaces – the private sphere, the sphere of the family, the chamber and the household as identified with women, and the public sphere, the sphere of the great hall, the court, as identified with men.[20] It was expected, of course, that the queen, as a woman, would play the nurturing and caring role within the family unit, and earlier medieval queens had been expected to oversee the king's household. But overseeing the king's household had involved overseeing his hospitality and his gift giving; the household was never a fully private sphere.[21] By the thirteenth century the royal household was such a massive operation that its running was delegated to administrators, perhaps leaving less opportunity for direct intervention by a queen. Moreover, the king and the queen had separate households. This certainly raised the potential, if the king or the queen so wished, for the queen's chamber and the queen's household to be cut off or insulated from

the king, the source of power, and thus rendered private and impotent. That is probably what happened with Blanche's predecessor as queen of France, Ingeborg of Denmark. Blanche of Castile is the first queen of France for whom there is the sort of evidence, especially household accounts, that allows the historian insight into what one might think of as the private life of a queen. But these dry lists of expenditure are in themselves enough to dispel any clear distinction between public and private roles, spheres and spaces, let alone the gendering of public and private space and sphere. Spaces, for the medieval ruler, might be intimate, but were rarely truly private.

•

Unless a woman was a ruler in her own right, she would generally have power through her influence on men or on account of the prestige of the men she was connected with or might influence. The tombstone of Blanche's great-grandmother, the Empress Matilda, expressed this succinctly: 'Great by birth, greater in her marriage, greatest in her offspring'. Her father, her husband and her son were all named Henry: Henry I of England, the Emperor Henry V of Germany and Henry II of England.[22] Some women did rule in their own right. The Empress Matilda spent many years trying to take the English throne as the sole legitimate direct heir of Henry I, though she did not in the end succeed. Blanche's eldest sister, Berengaria, was for some time the designated heiress to the throne of Castile, and did succeed as queen briefly. There were many queens regnant in the medieval Spanish kingdoms.[23] During most of Blanche's lifetime the county of Flanders, as rich and important as some kingdoms, was ruled by female heiresses, Countess Joanna and then her sister, Countess Margaret.[24] Blanche never ruled a kingdom as legitimate heiress herself, though she and her husband attempted to capture the English throne on those grounds.

But Blanche is an example of a medieval queen who had not just influence through her father, her husband and her son, but who also had direct executive agency as a ruler. During the short reign of her husband, she acted as a queen consort should, ruling in his place when he was away on campaign, during his campaign against English forces in 1224 and again during the Albigensian Crusade of 1226. Twice, she acted as regent, when Louis IX was too young to rule himself, and again when he was absent on Crusade. In both cases, her rule was officially sanctioned by, respectively, Louis VIII on his deathbed and Louis IX.

She also had some direct executive agency, as well as considerable influence, during the period of Louis IX's personal rule, between 1234, when Louis attained

his majority, and his departure on Crusade in 1248. During this time, she sat in judgement; she took securities for good behaviour from great barons; she organised great court feasts; she was a major diplomatic figure on the European stage; and she took control of the kingdom when Louis was desperately ill in 1244–5. Her role was so prominent during this period that Jacques Le Goff has called it a co-rulership – a period of double rule, with the still-young king ruling alongside the queen mother.[25]

The extent of Blanche's involvement in Louis IX's personal rule has been seen as exceptional. In a French context, it undoubtedly was. Louis VIII's mother had died during his infancy; Philip Augustus and Louis VII had good reason not to trust their mothers. But I shall argue that Blanche did nothing during the period of her son's personal rule that would have been unexpected within her maternal family. There are close parallels with the activities of her grandmother, Eleanor of Aquitaine, during the reigns of her sons, Richard the Lionheart and King John, and her great-grandmother, the Empress Matilda, during that of her son, Henry II.

Many historians of queenly power have argued that that power diminished between the early and late Middle Ages. In the very personal kingship of the early medieval period, the queen was expected to play her role running the king's house-hold and advising the king openly in hall, alongside the great nobles and prelates. Where royal government was run like a family business, the queen's role had evident importance. But the twelfth century saw the rise of administrative kingship. Government became more complex, and could be made to work only by keeping written records of what the king was owed in revenues or military aid; what the king had given as gifts; and what he had agreed in treaties. Government was no longer a matter of a ruler taking counsel in his hall, but of a ruler working with and dependent on a small group of literate and numerate administrators. These were usually 'new men', men from modest, knightly backgrounds, who were totally dependent on the favour of the ruler. A king like Philip Augustus (1179–1223) ruled with a small coterie of trusted servants. The closest was described as 'second to the king'. Philip did not seek advice from either his mother or his wives.[26]

The theory of the erosion of the queen's power in France in the twelfth century was outlined in an article by Marion Facinger in 1968.[27] Facinger was writing in an almost pre-feminist age, so her article was ground-breaking, and has been very influential. She traced the steady diminution in power between the queenship of Adela of Maurienne, consort of Louis VI, through the three successive queens of Louis VII – Eleanor of Aquitaine, Constance of Castile and Adela of Champagne – and

the two queens of Philip Augustus – Isabelle of Hainault and Ingeborg of
Denmark – to Blanche as queen of Louis VIII. Adela of Maurienne was an able
and active politician. Louis VI mentions her counsel in his charters, which are often
issued in their joint names. He marked her importance by dating charters by her
regnal years as well as his own. In contrast, there is no record of Blanche's involvement in her husband's government in any of the documents issued in his name.
But more recently, historians, notably Miriam Shadis, have challenged Facinger's
thesis.[28] Like them, I shall argue that Blanche was no less powerful a queen consort
than her predecessor a century earlier, and that the apparent contrasts between the
reginal powers of Blanche and Adela of Maurienne are the results of changes in
governmental and administrative practice. Moreover, the problem in identifying a
steady diminution of reginal power in France over the century is that too many of
the queens between Adela of Maurienne and Blanche are special cases. Eleanor of
Aquitaine failed to produce a male heir for France; Constance of Castile and
Isabella of Hainault both died after a few years of marriage; Ingeborg of Denmark's
relationship with Philip Augustus was disastrous from the night of their marriage.
Indeed, there was no real queen of France for most of Philip Augustus's reign.
When Blanche became queen in 1223, she was the first properly reigning queen
consort of France for thirty-four years. In fact, the rise of administrative kingship
made government far too complex for a ruler to manage alone. A queen might
find herself excluded from this new government, but its complexities could also
offer new opportunities to a literate and intelligent consort. Here, too, it is illuminating to set Blanche's career in the context of twelfth- and thirteenth-century
queens of England as well as those of France.

   Blanche's career certainly provides a case study in queenship. In many respects
she emerges as a classic example – of the power of the queen as mother, of the
queen as exponent of marriage diplomacy, for instance. But the extent and range
of her political agency was enormous. Because she was, during the two regencies,
not just a consort, but also the fount of legitimate rule, and because she was
someone who enjoyed power and had the political aptitude to wield it, her career
provides much more than a study in queenship and the power of medieval women.
Her career is a study in power *tout court*. She was a major player in international
politics and the politics of France from her marriage until her death. Her career
casts light on the realities of rulership and government and ideas about legitimacy
and governance in the first half of the thirteenth century. She was also, I will argue,
an innovative politician, who brought to the traditions of Capetian rulership a new

understanding of the importance of cultural diplomacy and of the importance of image and ceremony in the communication of power.

Most medieval queens left light political footprints, so that the traces of their power can be found only in their motherhood, their religious devotion or their cultural patronage, the areas of queenship on which most recent historians have concentrated. This is not the case with Blanche. Motherhood, religious devotion and cultural patronage were hugely important to her, both personally and as aspects of the fulfilment of her role as queen. But Blanche was an exponent of political manipulation as well as cultural influence, and so her story cannot be told without an understanding of the broader political narratives in which she lived and worked. Her career demands the sort of political biography that is more usually provided for medieval male rulers or other 'great men' – a type of biography very different from those that explore queenly power in its more passive or shadowy forms. There are parallels here with Blanche's equally politically active and astute sister Berengaria, queen of Castile-León, the reality of whose power base has been explored by Janna Bianchini.[29] The full range and reach of Blanche's activities, her agency, is best served by what is sometimes now called 'thickened political narrative'. Indeed, her career, her exploitation of both overt executive political powers and the more indirect powers of cultural influence, is ideally suited to the 'new political history', a political history that reflects the importance of ritual and ceremony, and accepts as potent cultural signifiers what used to be dismissed as 'the trappings of power'.

Moreover, kingship and queenship were still very personal at this period, and Blanche was remarkably adept at ensuring that people did what she wanted. Understanding how she achieved this, how her power worked in practice, requires a more detailed analysis of those who made up her household, her entourage and her networks, those who depended on her patronage or her influence, than has previously been attempted. The web of her networks was expansive. It included family, both natal and marital; great princes and minor knights; men and women; laity and clergy; popes, great secular prelates and local holy women. Her networks were familial, cultural, religious and political.

•

Blanche's political life was dominated by the long conflict between the Capetian kings of France and the Angevin kings of England; by an uneasy relationship between rulers and the greater aristocracy; and by a sometimes fruitful, but often difficult relationship between rulers and the Church. These political strands run

throughout the first six chapters, Part I, of this book – the chapters that narrate Blanche's life and career.

When in 1200 Blanche was married to the heir to the French throne, it was a marriage of political enemies. Blanche was an Angevin princess, the granddaughter of Henry II of England. Between 1154 and 1204 the Angevin kings of England – Henry II, Richard the Lionheart and John – were also dukes of Normandy, counts of Anjou and Poitou, and dukes of Aquitaine. As such, they controlled almost half of modern France, to the understandable chagrin of the Capetian kings. Only in 1204 did Philip Augustus break the power of the Angevins, capturing Normandy and Anjou. The slow collapse of the Angevin empire, and the Capetians' attempts to bring its lands under their rule, provided the political and diplomatic matrix in which Blanche and her family, both marital and natal, had to operate throughout her lifetime. Only finally in 1259, after Blanche's death, did Henry III accept that he had no claim to the bulk of the Angevin empire.[30]

Blanche's rulership and political actions, together with those of her husband and her son Louis, must be placed in the context of a long, often covert, conflict of interests between the ruler and the greater aristocracy. Adminstrative kingship tended to sharpen the distinction between the ruling and the ruled. The greater aristocracy, like the queen, found their traditional role as counsellor to the king eroded by the new royal administrators. A queen like Blanche might redefine her role within the new administrative kingship, but the great nobility found themselves excluded from power, reduced to playing a merely decorative role at feasts, hunts and tournaments. At the same time, they found kings were better equipped than ever with the information to demand, and the officials to extract, the dues and duties that the great nobility owed them. Great lords tended to see this as an invasion or destruction of their rights. Moreover, there was an inherent contradiction between the ruler's duty to impose peace on the realm and the aristocracy's long-established right to resolve disputes by private war.[31] But it was all the more difficult for the greatest counts and dukes – the great princes – of France to challenge the grip and reach of administrative kingship, since they themselves had developed their own administrative rulerships.

This sharpening conflict of interest between ruler and magnates was happening everywhere, not just in France. During the thirteenth century there were magnate revolts in Spain, France and England. The English magnates famously forced King John to recognise their disaffection in the Great Charter of Liberties – Magna Carta – in 1215. Attempts to limit the powers of the king and to increase the

influence of the magnates in the governance of the kingdom of England did not end there.[32] Blanche's career was played out against the background of continual aristocratic disaffection. Castilian magnates revolting against her sister Berengaria invited Blanche to send her son to rule them. English magnates revolting against King John invited Blanche's husband to take the English throne; he attempted to do so in her name.[33] A minority government in the thirteenth century almost invariably led to opportunistic magnate unrest, and Blanche's first regency was no exception. But historians have overplayed the magnate unrest in the first regency, and have presented it as exceptional in France. I shall argue that magnate disaffection in France was as endemic throughout the thirteenth century as it was in England, though it manifested itself rather differently. A full study of the French aristocracy in the thirteenth century is still to be written. But this book will attempt to define who 'the barons' – for that is what they called themselves – were, to analyse the different factions among them, and thus to illuminate Blanche's dealings with them.[34] In fact, the most problematic members of the aristocracy from Blanche's point of view were members of the extended Capetian family.

The relationship of the kings of France and the Church was complex too.[35] The kings of France developed a reputation for piety and knew how to make good political use of it. They gave refuge to popes chased from Rome by the emperors; they gave refuge to churchmen who fell out with the kings of England – notably Thomas Becket and his supporters. But they expected to have bishops of whom they approved and who they would find useful, without exerting overt control over the Church in the way that the English kings did. They expected the Church to play its role in the governance of the kingdom. Bishops were often royal administrators or diplomats – indeed, a bishopric was the hoped-for reward for able royal administrators. Kings also expected the Church to contribute financially to the running of the kingdom, for only the ruler could impose the peace in which the Church could flourish. But by the thirteenth century the relationship between the Capetians and the French Church was coming under strain. The newly complex government was both more costly and more effective. The Church, like the great nobles, resented the government's increasing financial demands. Blanche, along with her husband and her son, found herself having to manage these conflicting interests.

The newly complex administrative government put another strain on the relations of Church and State. The government was largely staffed by clergy educated in the Paris schools. Most of them hoped to be rewarded with rich livings or

prebends in cathedral or collegiate chapters, and ultimately with a bishopric. The Capetians had to have enough control over these ecclesiastical positions to be able to reward their faithful clerks. But that went counter to a strong reformist current in the thirteenth-century Church that both issued in, and was reinforced and informed by, the canons of the Fourth Lateran Council of 1215. Again, the Capetians, and the churchmen who served them, had to deal with conflicting demands and expectations. Because the working of Capetian government was so dependent on educated churchmen, the Capetian household and court, through which and within which Blanche operated, were profoundly influenced by religious ideas and by conflicts within the Church and the Paris schools between those who took a strong reformist line and those who did not.[36]

Blanche lived much of her life at the centre of the French royal entourage. The king and queen, and adult members of the royal family, would have their own household to look after their domestic arrangements and their religious life, as they moved from residence to residence. Most of the time, they would be surrounded by a penumbra of friends, relatives, courtiers and supporters both religious and lay, and general hangers-on, who were not part of the official household, but were often used for diplomatic, administrative or military duties. Periodically, the ruler would hold plenary courts, which most of the great churchmen and barons would be expected to attend. Relatively little work has been done on the French royal household and entourage in the thirteenth century. But these were the people through whom Blanche exercised her power, as princess, queen, queen mother and regent, and I have tried to extract some of these people from the shadows of the sources. Courts and courtiers have always had a bad name; they are seen as places of faction and people of ambition and spite. There has, I think, been a general assumption that the court and entourage of Louis IX – St Louis – and his pious mother cannot possibly have been such a nest of vipers, and historians have not tried to disentangle the constituent snakes.[37] I think there is evidence that St Louis's court and entourage was as faction-ridden and politically vicious as any other. As for Blanche, I hope to show not only that she was at home amidst courtly faction, but also that she, like other people of power, knew how to achieve her ends through it.

For Blanche was not just a figure of formidable power; she was the mother of a saint. Louis IX was canonised in 1297, within twenty-seven years of his death. Her only surviving daughter, Isabella, was also a candidate for sainthood. During the canonisation process for Louis, Blanche's youngest son, Charles of Anjou, insisted that his mother was the 'sacred root' – the *sancta radix* – of the family, that her piety and firm moral guidance were the source of the familial sanctity.[38]

The extent to which Blanche's own story is entwined with that of her canonised son is problematic. Since the 1990s historians, notably Jacques le Goff and Cecilia Gaposchkin, have emphasised how far the image of Louis IX is a construct of hagiographers who wrote in order to have him declared a saint, or in the knowledge that the king they described had been canonised. Famously, Le Goff suggested that St Louis was merely a textual mirage, asking: 'St Louis – in the end, did he exist?' It is certainly difficult to understand the man behind the hagiographers' image.[39] Blanche is an important presence in that image. St Louis's hagiographers present her as the perfect mother of the ascetic saintly king, as a strict, humourless, intensely pious moralist, who would rather her son were dead than that he commit a mortal sin.[40] I have tried to reach behind this image to the Blanche who emerges from chronicles and household accounts produced before Louis was regarded as a potential saint. The woman who emerges was less self-abnegatory in her piety than St Louis. Unlike him, she seems to have enjoyed the things of this world and revelled in courtly life. I shall argue that in this Blanche resembled her other children, Robert of Artois, Alphonse of Poitiers and Charles of Anjou – members of the family who are too often forgotten in the construction of the image of a saint-king and his mother.

Blanche's piety was undoubted. She is rightly known as a hugely generous patron of the Cistercian order, especially nuns. She founded three Cistercian abbeys, two of which were nunneries. But her religious interests ran wider than that. Fontevraudine nuns, Victorine canons, Dominican friars and hospital foundations were all specially favoured by her. Her devotional choices, especially her patronage of Cistercian nuns, have usually been seen as typical of elite women of the thirteenth century; in fact, it must be put in the broader context of the devotional choices of a generation, elite men as well as elite women. Her piety was not passive. She was well educated, with a good command of Latin. As I hope to demonstrate, she was a questioning and intellectually involved religious patron, who enjoyed discussion about religion and surrounded herself with men and women who could provide that. She was close to those involved in the Church reform agenda, which came to a head in the statutes of the Fourth Lateran Council of 1215 – however much that agenda might conflict with the requirements of administrative kingship. Along with her husband, Louis VIII, she was close to churchmen who were interested in the new Aristotelian ideas and texts that were arriving in Paris from Arab and Hebrew scholars in Toledo in her homeland of Castile. But many within the Church saw the new Aristotelian texts as dangerous. Blanche knew the great intellectual conflicts within the early thirteenth-century Church at close hand.

Blanche is famous, not just as a successful ruler of France and the pious mother of a saint, but also as a great patron of the arts. Indeed, it is this aspect of Blanche's career that has attracted most attention in the recent past. Terryl Kinder and Alexandra Gajewski have assessed her patronage of architecture, particularly her Cistercian foundations.[41] The extent of her architectural patronage, however, was much wider than is usually realised. Kathleen Nolan included Blanche in her rich study of the seals and tombs of the Capetian queens.[42] Blanche, Louis VIII and Louis IX were almost certainly the commissioning patrons of the first three moralised bibles (*bibles moralisées*), which, with their long cycles of lively gilded images illustrating biblical verses, and moralisations of them, are among the most lavish books produced in the Middle Ages. As such, they have attracted the interest of many scholars, notably John Lowden, Gerald Guest and Sarah Lipton.[43] But almost all assessments of Blanche's role in the commissioning of the moralised bibles have started from the assumption that she could not read Latin well: this, as I hope to show, was not the case. She also enjoyed vernacular poetry, and may even have composed some herself. She loved music, and revelled in the feasting, the ceremonial and the hunting of courtly life.

There has been much discussion among historians as to what it really meant to be a patron – much of it focused on what it meant to be a female patron.[44] The extent of any patron's involvement in a commission varied according to inclination and circumstances. All great patrons, whether male or female, would have had to hand the organisation of large commissions over to trusted members of their entourage. My analysis of the personnel of Blanche's entourage thus throws light on her artistic and cultural patronage, just as it does on her political agency and activities. Indeed, Blanche's architectural and cultural patronage cannot be disassociated from her political agency and actions. However much they might reflect her personal tastes, they were also a means by which she constructed an image of herself as queen of France, and an image of the kingdom of France and its rulers.

•

Blanche of Castile was involved in every facet of political, diplomatic, courtly, cultural and religious life in France in the first half of the thirteenth century. Surprisingly, there has been no major study of her life since the pioneering biography by Elie Berger in 1895. A series of useful biographies have been published in France since then, though most are essentially dependent on Berger. The most substantial is that by Gérard Sivéry. The only one to have been translated into

English is that by Régine Pernoud, who wrote for the 'broader public'. Her biography is a colourful and effective retelling of Blanche's story, based on Berger, but it does not pretend to be a piece of research. The most thoughtful recent analysis of Blanche as a politician and diplomat has been developed by Miriam Shadis, but in most cases she has treated Blanche as a comparison for her true subject, Blanche's sister, Berengaria of Castile and León.[45] Most serious recent work on Blanche has, as I have suggested above, been done by art historians.

It is even more surprising that Blanche has attracted such little attention from biographers in view of the substantial interest in queenship, women and power discussed above. Perhaps this is because historians have often been ambivalent about biography, lurking as it does in 'the interface between narrative and analysis'.[46] Doubtless, this book strays where angels (in which Blanche was rather interested) would fear to tread. It is not a book about queenship. It does not just try to understand Blanche as representative of a particular, if small, group of medieval persons – though I hope that it does illuminate what it meant to be a queen in the High Middle Ages.[47] It is a biography of a person of power, authority and agency who happened to be a woman. It is a biography of a major figure on the European stage in the first half of the thirteenth century, a figure whose life was shaped by, and who sometimes shaped, the great political, cultural, religious and intellectual currents of her time.

I have structured the book in two parts – reflecting, indeed, that uncertain position of biography at the 'interface between narrative and analysis'. Part I, the first six chapters, is a narrative of Blanche's life. Blanche was a woman of action, and action can be told only through narrative. Much of her life must have seemed like 'one damn thing after another'; establishing a chronology for these 'damn things' is essential. From time to time the narrative has to focus on the actions of her husband, and to a lesser extent on those of her eldest son, Louis IX; but her own actions cannot be understood without doing so. The political narrative is often detailed; but that, of course, is where the devil lies. Only in the detail of political networks and events can one see quite how Blanche operated the levers of power.

Part II is a study of important themes that run through her life. Chapter Seven examines the personal and intimate aspects of her life – her natal and marital families, her friendships, and those who served her in her own and the royal households. There is ample evidence for strong affective relationships – she was, as one chronicler put it, 'a woman who knew how to love and how to hate'; but as for any ruler, political imperatives could not be ignored, even in the most

intimate family relationships. Chapter Eight deals with her relationships with the clergy and her interactions with religion – and not just orthodox Catholic Christianity, for heresy, Islam and the Jews were seen as ever-present threats to society. Chapter Nine explores her piety and devotion. Chapter Ten discusses her role as a cultural patron. Chapters Eleven and Twelve examine the way in which her political career casts light on the theory and practice of governance in the thirteenth century and consider her rulership, power and authority, and her contribution to the development of the image of Capetian kingship. Chapter Twelve, on Blanche as Ruler and Counsellor, acts almost as a conclusion, in that it pulls together various threads from the narrative chapters in Part I and from the other thematic chapters in Part II. A short epilogue looks at the image that she projected of herself, and how she herself was perceived by contemporaries. There is inevitable overlap and repetition, but these issues could not be addressed in all their complexity in the context of a biographical narrative.

Some of the chapters in Part II discuss areas that historians have identified as those in which a queen can display and exert her power – her position within the family, her power as a mother, her religious devotion and patronage, her cultural patronage. But, as I have argued, these 'softer powers' are not – apart from motherhood – really gender-specific. Male rulers used family relationships, religious devotion, patronage and cultural patronage, and the crafting and manipulation of image as political tools, too. Blanche, a consummate politician, exploited the full register of power. For that reason, this section of the book leads towards, and culminates in, the chapters on governance and government. Blanche, like other rulers, male or female, might express rulership through family, piety and the arts. Indeed, they could hardly avoid doing so, since these were the principal means through which their subjects and contemporaries perceived their rulership. But one must not forget that medieval rulers were human too, and their family relationships, friendships, their piety and their cultural patronage also express their cares, passions, fears, devices and desires. Sometimes, they were prepared to let those passions, fears, devices and desires override political imperatives.

•

The sources for Blanche's life are both numerous and various. I have already referred to the hagiographical Lives of St Louis. They are problematical in that they were written to construct the image of a saint. But they cannot be disregarded. They were written by people who knew St Louis well. Geoffrey of Beaulieu had

been his confessor. He wrote his account of Louis – the 'Vita et sancta conversatione' – between 1272 and 1275. William of Chartres had been Louis's chaplain during his first Crusade in 1248. His account of Louis, the 'De vita et actibus', was written a few years later. Both works were written to prepare the ground for Louis's canonisation. The account by William of Saint-Pathus, who had been confessor to Louis's wife, Margaret of Provence, was written around 1303, a few years after his canonisation in 1297. It incorporates evidence given for the canonisation process by a large number of barons, courtiers and clergy who knew the king well.[48] Together with the Life of Blanche's pious daughter, Isabella, by her lady, Agnes of Harcourt, the Lives of St Louis often provide an insight into the intimate life of the Capetian family.[49] But all these Lives were written towards the end of the thirteenth century or at the beginning of the fourteenth. Although the writers knew St Louis and his immediate family well, most of them would have known Blanche only in her last years. They were all religious of one form or another – Geoffrey of Beaulieu and William of Chartres were Dominicans, William of Saint-Pathus a Franciscan, Agnes of Harcourt a Franciscan nun.

Their accounts of Louis and his family are complemented by the Life of St Louis by John of Joinville. Joinville was a layman and a soldier, the seneschal of the count of Champagne. He accompanied Louis on the Crusade of 1248, and came often to the Capetian court. He produced his account of Louis's life in the early fourteenth century as a model – a mirror, as contemporaries would have said – for the young Capetian princes to follow. Much of it is eyewitness accounts of Louis's actions on Crusade and his dealings with his entourage and those who came to court. Joinville gave an account of the king to the canonisation commission. He himself used some of the material from the depositions to expand his own work. Like the Life by William of Saint-Pathus, it was put together when Louis was already a saint, though some sections may have been written earlier.[50] But the perspective is that of a knightly aristocrat, not a churchman. Joinville was interested in the sort of worldly details that escaped the hagiographers. From time to time he thought that Louis took his evident piety too far, and behaved in ways that did not become a king. Joinville, who was extremely long-lived (he died in 1317), first came to the Capetian court in 1241. He had met Blanche and gives a vibrant and convincing account of her.

Fortunately, there are many chronicles and contemporary histories produced during Blanche's lifetime, or shortly after her death. Some try to provide general histories of their own times; some aim to record the deeds and lives of kings. Many

were written before Louis IX became king, let alone before there was any suggestion that he might become a saint. Two chroniclers wrote accounts of the life and deeds of Philip Augustus: Rigord, a monk of Saint-Denis, and William the Breton, Philip's chaplain. Rigord died in 1206. William the Breton incorporated Rigord's work into his own 'Gesta Philippi Augusti', and then produced a version in heroic verse, the 'Philippide', which was completed during the reign of Blanche's husband, Louis VIII (1223–6), to whom it was dedicated.[51] Between them, Rigord and William the Breton provide an account of the Capetian court, and the political context in which Blanche lived, between 1200 and her accession as queen in 1223. Inspired, perhaps, by the 'Philippide', the churchman Nicholas of Braie produced a poetic account of the short reign and deeds of Louis VIII. Well-informed French clerical chroniclers included a canon of Saint-Martin at Tours ('Chronique de Tours'), and the Champenois Cistercian monk Aubri of Trois-Fontaines.[52] Two histories of the Albigensian Crusades cast light on aspects of Capetian government and on the French baronage: the 'Hystoria Albigensis' by a Cistercian monk, Peter of Les Vaux-de-Cernay, and the 'Chronique' of William of Puylaurens, chaplain of Count Raymond VII of Toulouse.[53]

Although Blanche never returned to Spain after she left it at the age of twelve, she remained in close contact with her Spanish relatives. Rodrigo Jiménez de Rada, archbishop of Toledo, and Juan, bishop of Osma and then Burgos, recorded the often unstable political context in which Blanche's Castilian family operated in their works, respectively the 'Historia de rebus Hispaniae' and the 'Chronica latina regum Castellae'.[54] English clerical and monastic chroniclers were often very well informed about events in France, even about French court gossip. The Capetians and the Angevins were cousins, linked by Blanche herself; and English politics through much of the first half of the thirteenth century was driven by attempts to reclaim or revive the old Angevin empire after 1204. The Cistercian Ralph of Coggeshall, and in particular the Benedictine monks of St Albans, Roger of Wendover and Matthew Paris, provide a continual and usually informed commentary on French politics in the first half of the thirteenth century.[55] Most of the clerical chroniclers were writing for other members of the clergy, for other canons or other monks. As I have said, clergy, monks especially, were likely to take a misogynistic view of women in general and powerful women in particular. In fact, monks took a dyspeptic view of the powerful in general, and Matthew Paris became in the end a great admirer of Blanche.[56]

There are three important histories of their own times produced in French for the entertainment of laymen and women. The 'Histoire des ducs de Normandie' was composed around 1220 by an author known as the Anonymous of Béthune, who was probably a clerk at the court of Robert VII, lord of Béthune and advocate of Arras. The same author produced a related history of the kings of France, the 'Chronique des Rois de France'.[57] His works are major sources for the battles between the Capetians and the Angevins after 1204, in particular for the future Louis VIII's and Blanche's ill-fated attempt to take the English throne in 1216–17. It is evident that the Anonymous of Béthune knew both Louis VIII and Blanche personally. He refers to her always as '*ma* dame Blanche' – *my* Lady Blanche.[58] Both Louis VIII and Blanche held substantial property in the area of north-east France near Béthune in French Flanders. Much of the fighting before 1214 took place in this area, and the lords of Béthune had to decide which side to support.

The rhymed chronicle of Philip Mousquès and the chronicle of the so-called Ménestrel of Reims appear to have been produced for a less aristocratic audience. Philip Mousquès (Mouskes or Mousket) belonged to a family of wealthy merchants of Tournai in Flanders. Members of the family were involved in city politics. Where his veracity can be tested, Philip often turns out to be well informed. There was a close relationship between the Flemish cities and the counts of Flanders, and Mousquès probably had good access to the Flemish court. Like the Anonymous of Béthune, he lived and worked in an area where Louis VIII and Blanche had strong connections. He could not resist colourful – but not necessarily untrue – court gossip. He is an important source, though an execrable poet. His poem, an epic history of the kings of France, was written around 1240–45.[59] The Ménestrel of Reims produced his history around 1262. He may have used some of Mousquès' work, or he may have used similar Flemish or Champenois sources. While Philip Mousquès attempted to purvey history in verse form, the Ménestrel of Reims sought to entertain his hearers or readers with good stories about the great figures of the present or of the recent past. The Ménestrel is the first to tell the tale of the discovery of the imprisoned troubadour king Richard the Lionheart by his minstrel, Blondel. He conjures up an affair between Eleanor of Aquitaine and Saladin. But within his garbled fantasies, there are often nuggets of court gossip. If neither Philip Mousquès nor the Ménestrel of Reims can be relied on for the truth, they often tell us what contemporaries thought the truth to be.[60]

A remarkable source of political commentary survives in the form of political songs. These were collected in contemporary or near-contemporary manuscripts,

alongside the other songs of love and war of the famous northern *trouvères*. The collections appear to have been put together for baronial enjoyment: at all events, all the surviving political songs give a baronial rather than a royal perspective on politics. There are parallels with the great songs inspired by the struggles between the king and his barons in England, including the Song of Lewes of *circa* 1264. The French baronial songs do not aspire to the same level of political idealism; they are petulant and often scabrous. But they provide an invaluable insight into the baronial perspective, and a revealing commentary on political events.[61]

Blanche is the first French queen for whom detailed household accounts exist. Several survive from her lifetime, but they are all fragmentary. Some are partly illegible, and none shows a full year. Furthermore, the information about income and expenditure that they record is often slightly different, so that they are not strictly comparable. Some are the accounts rendered by the local administrators, the *prévôts* and *baillis*; some are the records of the everyday expenditure of the household; some record expenditure for specific events.[62] The young Blanche and her husband, Lord Louis, receive brief mention in the royal household account for 1203.[63] Accounts for the term of Purification 1213 for their own princely household survive.[64] Louis VIII's reign has left only a very fragmentary account for 1226,[65] but from Louis IX's reign the rate of survival is much higher. Expenditure on robes for the knights, clerks and officials supported by the king for Pentecost term 1231 is recorded.[66] General accounts, or fragments of them, for royal expenses and receipts survive for Candlemas to Ascension, and Ascension term 1234;[67] for the accounts of the royal officials for summer 1234;[68] for the knighting of Blanche's younger sons, Robert of Artois at Pentecost 1237 and Alphonse of Poitou in 1241;[69] for Ascension term 1238;[70] for Ascension and All Saints terms for 1239;[71] and for the accounts of royal officials for Ascension term 1248.[72] The accounts of 1234 cover the year of Louis's marriage, the year when most contemporaries would have considered that his personal rule began. The Ascension term of 1248 covers the period just before Louis's departure on the Crusade, when Blanche was about to take up her second regency. An account survives for Blanche's own household for Annunciation (25 March) 1241 to Ascension (29 May) 1242.[73] There is also an audit of her income and expenditure at the treasury at the Temple, the headquarters of the French Knights Templar in Paris, where all the royal money was stored, dated 2 February 1243.[74]

In spite of their fragmentary and incomplete nature, these accounts are often remarkably illuminating, and they have not yet received the full study they deserve.

It has become clear to me, as I have worked on them, that large sections of the account of 1239 include expenditure made directly by, or at the behest of, Blanche herself. Little use has been made of the unpublished half-year account of Blanche's own household accounts in previous work on her; often it complements or explains information found in the other accounts. In addition to the household accounts, the accounts for Blanche's foundation of the abbey of Maubuisson survive. They were copied into the thirteenth-century book recording the purchase of the lands on which the abbey was built and which provided its endowment, known as the *Achatz d'heritage*.[75]

A complete catalogue of Blanche's charters and letters has never been made, although various letters to her, and sent in her name, survive.[76] I have not attempted to produce a catalogue of her acts here – that work remains to be done. Fortunately, much documentation for her principal foundation of Maubuisson remains in the Archives of the Val d'Oise, including original charters, a seventeenth-century copy of the cartulary and the *Achatz d'heritage*. The charters and other documents from the abbey were published by Dutilleux and Depoin.[77] Documents for Blanche's foundation of Le Lys, again including several seventeenth-century transcriptions of documents, remain in the archives of Seine-et-Marne and the Archives Nationales.[78] A fine cartulary was produced at the abbey in the late thirteenth century and is now Paris, Bibliothèque Nationale de France, MS lat. 13892. The documents for her third major foundation, Royaumont, are more scattered, largely surviving in seventeenth-century copies.[79]

A useful catalogue of the acts of Blanche's husband was produced by Petit-Dutaillis as an appendix to his biography of the king.[80] A catalogue of the acts of St Louis remains in the making. It was Louis Carolus-Barré's life's work; but at his death in 1993 it was and remains a large number of transcriptions and photocopies kept at the Académie des Inscriptions et Belles-Lettres at the Institut de France. Jean-Francois Moufflet has taken on the massive task of producing an edition of the acts of St Louis. When published, it will undoubtedly transform our understanding of thirteenth-century France. For Blanche's father-in-law, Philip Augustus, there is a plethora of published documents, not least the invaluable edition of his Registers – the core government records – by John Baldwin. Baldwin's work on the Registers underpins his magisterial analysis of the workings of Philip's royal administration, *The Government of Philip Augustus*. There is much in the Registers that throws light on Capetian government into the mid-thirteenth century, since Register E remained the main record for the Capetian government until the 1240s.[81]

Fortunately, many of the relevant documents from the archives of Capetian government, now in the Archives Nationales, have been printed in the volumes of *Layettes du trésor des chartes*.

In addition to this rich collection of archival and literary sources, an impressive amount of material culture associated with Blanche has survived. Much is very splendid, though little is undamaged. Fine books include several psalters and the moralised bibles. Two astounding rock crystal crosiers, given to Maubuisson and Le Lys, though much remade and restored, give some impression of the magnificence of the objects that Blanche had made for herself or as gifts.[82] Stained glass commissioned by her survives at Chartres Cathedral (pl. 1) and at the Sainte-Chapelle. Some of her architectural commissions have vanished without trace, but something survives of all three of her Cistercian foundations, Royaumont, Maubuisson and Le Lys, and her great castle at Angers is almost intact.

•

Blanche was born in 1188, married in 1200, crowned queen in 1223, widowed in 1226 and died in 1252. Times are always changing, but as the twelfth century gave way to the thirteenth it must have seemed that times were changing faster than usual. The new administrative government became more efficient, more far-reaching. Everywhere, wealth seemed to accumulate as the economy ran faster than ever. Cities like Paris expanded, were paved and lit. The cathedrals of Bourges and Chartres ushered in a new gigantism in building. The theological debates of the twelfth century were pursued with a new conviction and intellectual confidence, with those that prevailed enshrined in the statutes of the Fourth Lateran Council in 1215.

But the new wealth, new efficiency and new intellectual confidence were offset by a sense that all was not well. It was not just churchmen who knew that it was more difficult for a rich man or woman to get into heaven than for a camel to get through the eye of a needle. The expanding cities contained conspicuous poverty as well as conspicuous wealth, and this was the context that drove the young Italian merchant Francis of Assisi to embrace poverty. In 1209 Pope Innocent III recognised Francis and his followers as a new order of mendicant friars. At the upper levels of society, debt became a serious problem. Many members of the nobility could afford the courtly lifestyle only by taking on heavy levels of debt, and the Church could fund its lavish building campaigns only by raising loans. In response to these problems, the Fourth Lateran Council forbad usury – the lending of money at interest.[83]

Western society seemed hedged with enemies. There was growing distrust of the Jews, partly because they specialised in money lending, and many found themselves in debt to them. Islam had revived at the end of the twelfth century, and in 1188 Saladin captured Jerusalem. In 1195 Blanche's father, Alfonso VIII of Castile, and the other kingdoms of Spain suffered a crushing defeat at Muslim hands at the battle of Alarcos, almost losing Toledo, the ecclesiastical capital of Castile and Iberia. The Church became increasingly concerned about Cathar heresies in Italy and southern France. In 1208 Innocent III instigated a Crusade against them; in 1215 the Castilian preacher Dominic of Osma received papal blessing for his new order of preaching friars to combat heresy. In the mid-1230s news began to seep into Western Europe of a new threat from the east, as the Mongol hordes swept out of the steppes of Central Asia.

Perhaps it was not surprising that there were renewed concerns, as the twelfth century drew to a close, that the Last Times, the end of the world, were imminent. The vivid accounts of the End of Time in the bible – in the Book of Daniel, in passages in St Matthew's Gospel, and above all in the Revelation of St John – created confusion as to what would happen when, but left no doubt as to the terrors to come, as even the good must experience the horrors of the reign of Antichrist, before Christ would come again to judge the living and the dead. A Cistercian abbot from southern Italy, Joachim of Fiore, thought that the age of the Holy Spirit, which would herald the Last Judgement, would begin around 1230; many, including Innocent III, believed his prophecies. There was widespread panic in Paris just before 1200 that the end of the world had come.[84] It was in this edgy, nervous religious atmosphere, in a world of wealth, uncertainty and instability, that Blanche of Castile grew to womanhood, lived and died.

PART I

I

Daughter of the King of Castile, Niece of the King of England

BLANCHE OF CASTILE'S FIRST APPEARANCE in the record of history was not auspicious – a hapless pawn in the diplomatic manoeuvres of her uncles, Richard the Lionheart and John, kings of England, in their conflict with the French king, Philip II Augustus. In the diplomacy and the treaty that sealed her fate, she remained nameless, just a daughter of the king of Castile. She became a child hostage for peace between enemies, far from her homeland. But the treaty was between two of the greatest kings of Christendom, and both had expectations of her ability to mediate between them. She was asked, at the age of twelve, to become, as one French chronicler put it, 'as if herself the guarantee of peace'.[1]

King Richard had returned from Crusade in 1194, to discover that Philip Augustus had taken advantage of his absence to invade Richard's French lands, especially eastern Normandy, and to conspire against him with Richard's younger brother, John. From Philip's perspective, this was an obvious move. Theoretically, Richard held his enormous clutch of French duchies and counties – almost half of modern France – from the French king. The problem was that Richard, like his father, Henry II, and his ancestors, Henry I and William the Conqueror, tended to behave as if he were king in his French lands, to treat his French lands as if they were, as one chronicler wrote, 'almost a kingdom'.[2]

Philip was called 'Augustus' by those around him, partly because it sounded so resonantly Roman, but mainly because he, more than any previous king of France, had increased – the Latin verb for increase was *augere* – the area of France under the real control of the French king.[3] He had made the largest gains so far by marriage, and the failure of great noble families, rather than by war. Together this had brought him control of huge areas of north-eastern France, including Artois and Vermandois. Enriched by these new territories, and encouraged by Richard's absence, Philip had turned his attention to the lands of the English kings in France. But when he returned from the Crusade, Richard rapidly reversed Philip's gains in eastern Normandy. Now, in 1199, both kings had to come to a truce over the disputed lands in the border zones of the Vexin and the Evreçin. Richard agreed to cede to Philip the much-fought-over castle of Gisors, but it would be given only as the marriage gift of one of Richard's nieces, who would marry the heir to the French throne. The niece in question would be one of the daughters of Richard's sister, the queen of Castile.[4]

Before the treaty could be implemented, Richard was dead, killed by a crossbow as he tried to resolve a quarrel in the Limousin. The negotiations were taken up by Richard's younger brother and successor, King John. But now they focused not just on disputed border territories, but also on the very status of the English king's French lands. For John was not the only possible heir. He was the sole surviving son of Henry II; but his nephew, Arthur of Brittany, the son of an older brother, had almost as strong a claim. John had to persuade Philip Augustus to accept him rather than Arthur as the rightful heir to the French territories of the Angevin empire. Philip duly confirmed John as Richard's heir for all the territories, for which he was to be Philip's man, in return for a huge sum of money. The French king would hold the counties of Evreux and the Vexin, except Les Andelys, and the borders were to be non-fortification zones. In celebration, and as surety, a Castilian niece of the king of England would be married to the heir to the French throne, and the French king would receive Issoudun and various fiefs in Berry as her *maritagium*.[5]

The terms of the treaty were finalised at a meeting between Philip and John in January 1200, after which John dispatched his mother, Eleanor of Aquitaine, now nearly eighty, to Castile, to collect the Castilian niece.[6] Blanche was the niece selected. She was twelve. Her grandmother brought her slowly from the Castilian court through northern Spain, then over the Pyrenees to France. They celebrated Easter at Bordeaux, before the retinue carried on towards the Loire. They stopped

at the great abbey of Fontevraud, where Henry II and Richard, and Blanche's aunt Joanna, queen of Sicily and countess of Toulouse, were buried. Probably Blanche was taken to pray at their tombs in the abbey choir. But at Fontevraud the aged Eleanor felt she could go no further. She committed her young granddaughter to the care of the archbishop of Bordeaux, who had accompanied them thus far. He took Blanche on to her uncle in Normandy. Her arrival precipitated the ratification of the treaty at the castle of Le Goulet on 22 May 1200. On the 23rd Blanche and Louis, the heir to the French throne, were married by the archbishop of Bordeaux in the church of Portmort on the Norman side of the border. It was a small and undistinguished church for such a politically portentous marriage, but France was under interdict owing to Philip Augustus's marital irregularities. Immediately after the marriage, amid general rejoicing, Louis took his new wife back to Paris.[7]

Becoming 'as if herself the guarantee of the treaty' was a heavy burden for a child of twelve. Philip had insisted on the marriage of his heir with a niece of the king of England from the very start of the long negotiations. When these began, the succession to the childless Richard was at best unclear; at the time of the treaty, John was childless and unmarried – though he lost no time in remedying the latter issue.

Roger of Howden, the Angevin administrator who is our best source for the negotiation of Blanche and Louis's marriage, did not know the bride's name. For him she was 'the niece of the king, daughter of the king of Castile'; once, he left a blank space in his manuscript to fill in the name later.[8] The king and queen of Castile had two available daughters, and Eleanor of Aquitaine must have been sent to select the one who would be most appropriate. The fact that Eleanor was sent such a long distance at such an advanced age reflects the importance, and the demanding nature, of the role required of the young girl. Eleanor's own experiences left her well qualified to judge which of her granddaughters would best fulfil the role as 'guarantee of the peace'. As heiress to the vast duchy of Aquitaine, she had been married in her own youth to the heir to the French throne, the future Louis VII. In 1152, after fifteen years of increasingly fractious marriage, which failed to produce the desired male heir, Eleanor left Louis for the young Henry, duke of Normandy, count of Anjou and, shortly thereafter, king of England. She played an important role in the governance of Aquitaine for Henry, but in 1173–4 she took the part of their sons in the rebellion against him. After some fifteen years as her husband's prisoner, she resumed a crucial role as adviser to and, when necessary, executrix of both Richard and John in the governance of the huge Angevin

dominions. She knew what it would take to be a 'guarantee of peace', perhaps even better than her daughter, also called Eleanor, who had been married to Alfonso VIII of Castile in 1170. Young Eleanor and Alfonso's marriage was much more successful than Eleanor of Aquitaine's, with both partners united in politically fruitful co-operation and mutual respect and affection.[9]

Eleanor of Aquitaine did not choose the eldest available daughter. By the sixteenth century Spanish chroniclers had an explanation. The most beautiful and oldest unmarried daughter was called Urraca, a name long favoured in the royal family of Castile. The chroniclers claimed that Eleanor thought the name would seem barbaric and unpronounceable in France, and took the younger daughter, with the blander name of Blanca instead.[10] Blanche would grow up to be a woman whom men found very attractive, but she may not have been regarded as a great beauty. Chroniclers tend to talk about her beauty in terms of convention and restraint, or not at all.[11] Her youngest son, Charles, was large and olive-skinned – a colouring he must have derived from his mother, not his blond father, so Blanche was probably olive-skinned too, despite her name.[12]

Blanca was certainly not an old Castilian name. Blanca/Blanche was named after her maternal grandmother, Blanca of Navarre, queen of Sancho III of Castile. Blanca of Navarre herself not only introduced the name to the family of the kings of Castile, but was also perhaps the first woman in Spain to be given what was, in the early twelfth century, a very unusual name, which seems to have emerged in southern France rather than Spain from the low Latin for 'white' or 'pale'. Blanca of Navarre's mother had come from Normandy, and she may have been given her name just because she was strikingly pale.[13] A niece of the dynasty of Navarre, who had married Theobald III of Champagne in 1199, had also been named after her. Now, in 1200, Blanca of Castile was married to the future king of France. So French court circles were already used to the name, though they transformed it into 'Blanche'. Some court chroniclers found it slightly too vernacular: they often named Blanche after the high Latin for 'white', and called her Candida.[14]

Like her mother and her grandmother, her sisters and her cousin Blanche of Navarre, Blanche had been brought up to expect to make a political marriage in her early teens, to travel to a distant land, with an alien culture and language, and to have limited contact with her family thereafter. She never returned to Spain, but throughout her life she kept in close touch with her Castilian family, exchanging gifts and letters, and entertaining Iberian nieces and nephews at the French court.

Little is known of Blanche's childhood. She was born in the wintry early months of 1188, one of ten or eleven siblings, of whom six survived beyond infancy: Berengaria (born 1180), Urraca (1187–1220), Blanche herself, Ferdinand (November 1189–1211), Constance (1199–1243), Eleanor (1200–1246) and Henry (1204–1217).[15] When Blanche's marriage was arranged, her younger brother Ferdinand was heir to their father's throne. In the event Ferdinand pre-deceased his parents, and Alfonso was succeeded by her much younger brother Henry. The oldest daughter, Berengaria, was married in 1197 to Alfonso IX of León. The rejected Urraca was soon married to Alfonso II of Portugal; in 1220 Eleanor was married to James I of Aragón. The youngest sister, Constance, became a nun at the family foundation of Las Huelgas.[16] Their mother, Queen Eleanor, seems to have played a leading role in the negotiations for her daughters' marriages; this would have been all the easier in Blanche's case, where negotiations were with her own brothers and mother.[17]

Where Blanche and her siblings spent their youth is unclear. All high medieval kings were peripatetic, moving continually from palace to palace, monastery to monastery, but Castile was vast, and the kings of Castile were more peripatetic than most. Twelfth-century Castile had nowhere that was emerging as the stable centre of royal administration and court ceremony, in the manner of Paris and Westminster in France and England.[18] The children may have moved around with their father's court; probably they spent time at the royal palace beside the new Cistercian nunnery of Las Huelgas, founded by their parents just outside Burgos.[19] Blanche would have been used at least to travelling long distances. The royal children would have been educated either by court chaplains or perhaps within monastic houses if they stayed long enough in any of them. Blanche, like other royal or high-born girls of the late twelfth century, was probably taught to read some Latin, and perhaps to read in the vernacular too. The language of the court was presumably Castilian, but Queen Eleanor probably ensured that her children could speak some French.

Blanche's father had a long reign, succeeding to the Castilian throne in 1158 at the age of three and retaining it until he died in 1214. The early years of his reign were difficult, since the Castilian aristocracy, and in particular the rulers of the neighbouring kingdoms of León and Navarre, took advantage of his long minority. The adult Alfonso proved an impressive ruler, imposing effective control on his kingdom, which grew increasingly wealthy on trade with the Muslim territories to the south, but also, through the ports of the northern coast, with England, France

and Flanders.[20] At the very end of his reign, in 1212, Alfonso, at the head of a coalition of Iberian and French knights, defeated the Muslim Almohads at the decisive victory of Las Navas de Tolosa – a victory that brought him immense prestige throughout Christendom. But if his reign ended in triumph, the 1190s, the decade in which Blanche grew up, were difficult years for Castile. Indeed, one contemporary chronicler, the bishop of Osma, recorded that the whole kingdom felt unsafe at the time.[21]

In 1195 the Almohad caliph of the southern Muslim lands defeated Alfonso at the battle of Alarcos, and threatened to take Toledo, which Alfonso VI had captured from the Almoravids in 1085. It was regarded as the ecclesiastical 'capital' of Iberia, and its loss would have been a profound setback. The Christian kingdoms of Iberia failed to unite against the Muslim threat; instead, they spent much of the 1190s fighting among themselves. Under Alfonso's grandfather, Alfonso VII, Castile had been indisputably the most powerful of the Iberian kingdoms, and Alfonso VII had called himself emperor of all the Spains. But the later twelfth century saw a strengthening of other Iberian kingdoms, especially Aragón, now united with Barcelona, Navarre, León and the newly emerged kingdom of Portugal. Border conflict between them became increasingly acrimonious in the last decade of the twelfth century.[22] In addition, Castile and Navarre had potentially conflicting claims to the Aquitanean county of Gascony. Gascony had been Eleanor of England's dowry when she married Alfonso VIII in 1170; it would come to her on the death of her mother, Eleanor of Aquitaine. When Richard I married Berengaria of Navarre in 1190, however, he gave Gascony to his bride as a dower, while his mother was still alive. Berengaria held Gascony as queen of England, but Eleanor and Alfonso of Castile must have felt that Eleanor's dowry was now altogether too close to falling into the hands of their enemy, Sancho VII of Navarre, Berengaria's brother. After the death of Eleanor of Aquitaine in 1204, Alfonso tried to invade Navarre twice in order to take control of Gascony, though without success.[23]

Blanche and her siblings must have been aware of these troubles, especially the border conflict with León and Navarre, for the Iberian royal dynasties were so closely linked by marriage that this was almost feuding within an extended family. Blanche herself was named after her grandmother, who was a princess of Navarre. Richard's queen, Berengaria, was Blanche's second cousin. Three years before her own marriage, Blanche's oldest sister, Berengaria, had been betrothed to Alfonso IX of León, in an attempt to arrange a truce between the two kingdoms. From the start, it was unclear whether the Church would consider the marriage valid, for

Berengaria and Alfonso of León were second cousins, well within the prohibited degrees of relationship.[24] The later marriage of Urraca to Alfonso II of the new kingdom of Portugal was intended to secure the Portuguese as allies, and as counterweights to León, in the ever-shifting patterns of conflict between the Iberian kingdoms; this too was a marriage of cousins.[25] The marriage of Eleanor and King James of Aragón was arranged with political intent. So apart from Constance, who entered Las Huelgas, all the sisters were married as 'guarantees of peace', though only Blanche had to guarantee a peace so far from home.

The issue of Gascony underlines the extent to which these inter-cousin rivalries and conflicts were played out on a European stage, because of the importance of Iberia in Franco-Angevin politics. The border between Catalonia and south-western France was not finally agreed until the Treaty of Corbeil in 1258. More pertinent from the Castilian point of view, the duchy of Aquitaine, and thus the territories of the Angevin kings, reached right down to the Pyrenees, where it shared a border with Navarre. The kingdom of Navarre, astride the Pyrenees, controlled the important crossings from the north into the Iberian peninsula. It was to protect the southern reaches of Aquitaine, and Aquitanean trade in the Bay of Biscay, that Henry II had married his daughter Eleanor to the king of Castile; it was to protect Aquitaine against the count of Toulouse that Richard I had allied with Sancho VII of Navarre and married his sister Berengaria. By 1199 Richard had neutralised Count Raymond VI of Toulouse (by marrying him to Joanna, the last of his available sisters), had no need of the alliance with Navarre, and could usefully revitalise cordial relationships with his sister Eleanor, the queen of Castile, by offering the prospect of a highly attractive marriage arrangement for one of her daughters.[26] And so, in 1200, the twelve-year-old Castilian princess made the journey her mother had made thirty years earlier, but in reverse, from Castile to Normandy, and thence to Paris.

•

Blanche and Louis's young married life would be dominated by the long struggle of Louis's father, Philip Augustus, against Blanche's uncle, King John, and Blanche can never have forgotten her role as 'guarantee of peace' – but whose peace? Philip entertained John lavishly in Paris in 1201 – when he was able to dispose of bad wine on the undiscriminating English barons – but he was always determined to bring John's French lands under his effective overlordship, and he undoubtedly aimed to bring some, particularly Normandy, under direct control. Indeed, it was

claimed that he used Blanche to ask for the Vexin during John's visit (see p. ••).[27] At Le Goulet, John had had to accept Philip's overlordship, far more explicitly than had any of his Anglo-Norman predecessors. Philip had insisted on the marriage of the Castilian princess with his heir, Lord Louis, from the start of the negotiations. At the time of the treaty, John was a divorcee without legitimate children. During the negotiations with Richard I, Richard's lack of a son meant that the entire Anglo-Norman/Angevin succession was at issue, for Anglo-Norman succession custom had developed to leave the designation of the new king by the old, usually on his deathbed, and increasingly by written testament, as the principal element of legitimacy.[28] The treaty agreed that if John died without an heir, huge tracts of eastern Normandy would come to Lord Louis through Blanche. The monk Rigord claimed that this covered all John's French lands.[29] It is clear that from the start Philip saw the marriage as a strategy with potential to bring more of the Angevin lands under direct royal control.

It was not his only strategy. Philip was aware that Arthur of Brittany could claim a stronger right than John to succeed to the lands of the Angevin empire. For Arthur was the son of an older brother, and both canon and civil lawyers were divided over whether the claims of the son of an older son should take precedence (or be reserved, as the lawyers put it) over the claims of an uncle. Philip supported Arthur's claims to the Angevin lands when it suited him, and took the precaution of marrying his daughter Mary to Arthur in 1202.[30] But Arthur was captured by John in 1202, and disappeared. Rumours about his fate circulated, but the French court did not have reliable evidence that he was dead until 1211.[31]

In the end, Philip had no need of these careful dynastic preparations to acquire John's French lands. In 1202 two of John's Poitevin vassals, the Lusignan brothers, complained to Philip about John's treatment of them. Philip summoned John to appear before his court in Paris to defend himself; John refused, whereupon Philip declared him forfeit of the lands he held of the French king. In 1203 Philip and his forces attacked Normandy and Greater Anjou. John had alienated too many members of both aristocracy and Church in all his realms, and Normandy in particular had been heavily taxed. Such support as there might have been melted away, and Normandy and Greater Anjou had surrendered to Philip by 1204. Although Blanche and Lord Louis had stood to gain substantial parts of eastern Normandy by the terms of Le Goulet, Philip, in victory, took all of Normandy under his direct control.

•

Blanche's youth as the wife of the heir to the French throne must be constructed from the briefest of mentions in royal accounts, or inferred from indirect evidence that really concerned her husband. But one short, direct account of the young princess exists, and it leaves an indelible image. Bishop Hugh of Lincoln was an austere but humane Carthusian, who had caught the attention and admiration of Henry II and his sons, to whom he acted as both spiritual and political adviser. It was Bishop Hugh who comforted Blanche's cousin, Berengaria of Navarre, after Richard the Lionheart's death; and John had asked Hugh to be present at Le Goulet – and thus presumably also at Blanche's marriage on the following day.[32] Hugh set off from Le Goulet for a visit to his homeland in Burgundy, arriving in Paris a few weeks after the wedding. There he was visited by Blanche's new husband, Louis. At Louis's request, Hugh went to visit her. He found her 'saddened by a recent loss (*afflictamque quodam recenti casu*), and sunk for several days in grief and depression (*merore…quo diebus aliquot lugubris incedebat*)'. Hugh was adept at dealing with downhearted princes and princesses: with a 'few words, he cheered her up so much that her happiness was reflected in her face (*verbis paucis in tantum exhilaravit ut…vultum de cetero et animum gereret letissimum*)'.[33]

The account is brief but revealing. Blanche had been married for less than a month. The loss from which she suffered is not identified. Most likely a favourite nurse, or lady-in-waiting, or trusted member of her parents' court, who had accompanied her to France, had to return to Castile. The profound misery of a lonely twelve-year-old in a distant land is palpable. What Hugh said to cheer her up is not revealed. Perhaps he reminded her of her duty, and that she had a caring husband. In some of the late thirteenth-century hagiographical accounts of St Louis, Blanche is noted for her steely self-possession. But earlier accounts of her, before she was transformed into the mother of a saint, show a woman of powerful emotions, who displayed those emotions without inhibition.

Her young husband comes out of the story rather well, for it implies that he was concerned at her unhappiness, and had some idea as to how it might be lifted. Louis was only six months older than Blanche – he was born on 3 September 1187. The 'Magna vita' of St Hugh describes him as a youth naturally imbued with brightness who listened intently to Hugh's advice.[34] Philip Mousquès says that Louis was blond and handsome, inheriting his fair good looks from his mother, Isabella of Hainault.[35] The Cistercian chronicler Peter of Les Vaux-de-Cernay described him as the 'most gentle of young men, of excellent disposition', 'kindly and benevolent'.[36] In his chronicle, the canon of Tours noted Louis's equability, his

devotion to his wife and his learning.[37] Louis's early childhood cannot have been very happy. His mother had died in 1190 while giving birth to still-born twins; Louis was then two-and-a-half years old. He was regarded as a delicate child: he was desperately ill with dysentery in 1191, and his survival was regarded as a miracle; in 1206 he fell seriously ill at Orléans.[38] The Ménestrel of Reims claimed that Louis was never without pain and sickness:[39] certainly, when his body was exhumed from its grave in 1793, it was reported as being small by the standards of his day, which is all the more surprising given that his mother was unusually tall.[40] As a small child Louis had no siblings. Whereas Blanche grew up in the context of a large family, with parents whose marriage was one of affection and mutual admiration, Louis was brought up as the only child of a father who was often in overt political conflict with his mother's family. When his father departed on Crusade in 1190, a few months after his mother's death, Louis was left in the care of his paternal grandmother, Adela of Champagne.[41]

The young Philip Augustus had married Louis's mother, Isabella of Hainault, in 1180, almost immediately after succeeding to the throne of France. The marriage was brokered by Philip, count of Flanders, the bride's uncle and Philip's guardian and tutor. The marriage would bring substantial territories in north-eastern France under the direct rule of the French king for the first time. But Philip Augustus had no intention of remaining beholden to either Philip of Flanders or his maternal family of the counts of Champagne. Within a couple of years he had emancipated himself from both, and set the counts of Flanders and Champagne at war with each other. His mother, Adela of Champagne, fled the court. In 1184 Philip announced, at a court held at Senlis, that he intended to divorce Isabella.[42] His wife, still in her early teens, revealed an unexpected steel core and sharp political acumen. She appeared barefoot in the streets of Senlis in a loose under-garment, or chemise, and appealed to the people and clergy of the city against her husband's demand for a divorce. They took her side and Philip decided it would be unwise to gainsay them. Isabella's position was strengthened when, in 1187, she gave birth to Louis, for although she might be the niece of the count of Flanders, she was also now the mother of the heir to the throne. There may have been a rapprochement between Philip and Isabella, but her position at court must always have been politically uncomfortable.[43] When she died in March 1190 she was buried, as she had chosen, in the choir of the new cathedral of Notre-Dame in Paris. When her coffin was opened in the nineteenth century, she was found to be remarkably tall – and all contemporary commentators were agreed on her blond beauty.[44] Had

she lived, she would have developed into a formidable queen. After Isabella's death, Philip's attempts to remarry, not least to provide a reserve heir in the face of Louis's fragile health, were little short of disastrous.

In 1193 Philip Augustus married Ingeborg, sister of King Knut VI of Denmark. She too was universally described as beautiful. Nevertheless, on the day after the wedding Philip announced that he could not live with her as man and wife. No one has ever understood why, and Philip could give no reason that convinced contemporary churchmen, let alone historians. The king spent the next twenty years trying to divorce Ingeborg. He could not use the standard method for an annulment – that he and Ingeborg were too closely related – because he had been far more closely related to Isabella of Hainault, and he could not risk having his only surviving heir branded illegitimate. Instead, he claimed that she had poisoned him, or made him impotent by magic. The papacy, and the bulk of the Church, apart from a set of compliant bishops closely linked with the French court, took Ingeborg's part. The case dragged on, and during much of the time Philip kept Ingeborg locked away in a nunnery at Cysoing in the very north-east of France, or imprisoned in the castle of Etampes. He did not improve his credit with the Church when he married Agnes, daughter of the count of Meran. The Church accused him of bigamy, and the pope put France under interdict. (It was on account of the interdict that Blanche and Louis had to be married in Normandy rather than France.) Philip seems to have been genuinely attached to Agnes of Meran, and it was not until after her death in 1201 that he was prepared to consider taking back Ingeborg as queen. Agnes's two children, Philip Hurepel – the 'tousle-haired' – and Mary, were declared legitimate in 1201. Eventually, Ingeborg was reinstated as queen in 1213, though the couple never lived as man and wife.[45]

It was a long and unedifying episode. It revealed Ingeborg as a woman of courage and determination, prepared to withstand real hardship and some danger for an institutional principal. It put Philip Augustus at odds with much of the French Church for a long stretch of his reign. Even two authors who had set out to write admiring lives of the king – Rigord, a monk of Saint-Denis, and Giles of Paris, a master in the Paris schools – were unable to refrain from criticising a king whose matrimonial irregularities left France under interdict.[46] It did little for Philip's reputation then, and has done little for it since. He emerges as stubborn rather than determined, and vicious when thwarted. All marriages were political alliances. Philip's inability to go through with this one and, more positively, his determination to keep and protect Agnes suggest both a strain of neurosis and a need for

affection in this most politically and coldly calculating of kings. For Philip was undoubtedly calculating, and usually coldly so. Everything, including any feeling he might have had for his mother, Adela of Champagne, was subordinated to the growing power of the French crown.

Thus the young Lord Louis, unlike his new Castilian wife, was brought up in a court that was focused and structured around a king, not around a king and a queen. It is unclear whether there was any real affection between father and son. They were, as contemporaries noted, very different. The English monk and chronicler Matthew Paris characterised Philip as 'very wise', but observed that Louis, unlike his father, was 'fond of his wife and tender, over-fond of delights, very articulate – too slippery – with words', and 'pusillanimous and unfaithful in actions'.[47] It is not a flattering description, but Matthew's abbey of St Albans had suffered from Louis's troops during the wars of 1216–17, and he was not unbiased. But the verbal fluency, and the fondness for courtly delights, does reflect the fact that Philip had made sure his son was well educated. Philip was apparently self-conscious that he was unable to read Latin, at a stage when the written documentation of government was burgeoning.[48] Louis had two recorded tutors, Bishop Stephen of Tournai and Master Amaury of Bène, both masters in the schools of Paris and both impressive intellectuals who took an active part in the religious debates of the day.[49] In 1194 Stephen took Queen Ingeborg's side in the marriage dispute, writing to the pope on her behalf; it is unclear whether this caused any tension when Stephen arrived at court to fulfil his tutorial duties.

A contemporary noted that Louis much admired his other tutor, Amaury of Bène, believing him to be a man of 'good conversation and harmless opinion'.[50] Amaury became another contentious character. William the Breton, chaplain to Philip Augustus and his admiring biographer, wrote that Amaury was too attracted by a neo-platonic spiritualism prevalent in the late twelfth century, and had been reading too many of the Aristotelian texts on natural science, most of which were then arriving in Paris from Islamic Spain via Castile. Whatever Amaury's precise beliefs, he was accused of heresy, forced to recant his ideas and burn his writings. That Amaury himself was not burnt too was perhaps owing to the protection that he received from Lord Louis. He was silenced, and probably dead, by 1206. But he had a group of followers, who were known as the Amauricians. They were among those who were convinced of the imminence of the End of Time and the Last Judgement. At a Church council held in Paris in 1210, Amaury's followers were accused of various heresies, including a belief in spiritual rather than bodily

resurrection. Most of them were burnt, and Amaury's body was dug from its grave and thrown into a field. For young Louis, the vicious hounding of his admired tutor must have been traumatic. A member of the papal curia later complained that Amaury's followers could not be extirpated because they had powerful protectors – and it is usually assumed that they had Louis in mind. The Amauricians were certainly at the very centre of court circles. One of them was a canon of the collegiate church in the royal castle of Corbeil. Another, Master Walter of Mussy, was accused of trying to seduce Blanche's cousin, Countess Blanche of Champagne, in both mind and body.[51] But Philip Augustus and his great administrator Brother Guérin, bishop of Senlis, joined the attack on Amaury and his followers, as, clearly, did William the Breton. The grim events must have shaken and split court circles.[52]

As a result of his impressive education, Louis could read Latin with ease – even complex poetic Latin. Several authors, including Giles of Paris, Rigord and William the Breton, dedicated works to him, and Gerald of Wales did his best to do so. Giles at least gave him presentation copies (pl. 2). A luxury moralised bible (Vienna, Österreichische Nationalbibliothek, Codex Vindobonensis 1179), which is generally agreed to have been produced for Louis, has a Latin text with a complex and often sophisticated commentary imbued with the religious debates then current in the Paris schools and nascent university (pl. 3).[53]

Presumably education was a major concern of those members of the French royal household who now had care of Blanche. The dowager queen, Adela of Champagne, may have had some duty of care before her death in 1206, though she was not always at court. Hugh of Lincoln was able to communicate with Blanche; since he is unlikely to have spoken Castilian, Blanche must have been able to speak some French at the time of her marriage, learnt from her mother. Nevertheless, teaching her to be fluent in the language of her new family and new court must have been a priority. There is no evidence of specific tutors. Perhaps masters from the Paris schools were brought in to teach her, as they were for Louis; perhaps she too was taught by Amaury of Bène. It may have been felt that the royal chaplains would be adequate for the task. There is no evidence that she was sent, as was sometimes the case with young princesses, to a nunnery for her education.

All high-born ladies were taught to read Latin well enough to follow a church service, and to use psalms and prayers in private devotion, but there is evidence that the adult Blanche's command of Latin was impressive. A devotional work in Latin, known as 'Audi domina' – 'Listen Lady', or the 'Speculum anime' – the 'Mirror of the Soul', was written for her when she was queen.[54] In a psalter

produced for her around 1216, now called the Psalter of Blanche of Castile, each psalm is introduced by an explicatory Latin sentence of some complexity – a very unusual, indeed, unique addition to the psalter text (pl. 4).[55] She was competent to teach her children to read Latin from another of her psalters, according to a note in it from her grandchildren's time.[56] Many correspondents wrote letters to her in Latin. Historians have usually assumed that letters sent from popes or senior ecclesiastics would be read for her by chaplains, who would tell her what they said. Undoubtedly that sometimes happened, but because Blanche was busy, not because she was illiterate. In a letter sent to her in 1241 by one of her agents in La Rochelle – someone who knew her well – the writer apologises for the length of the letter and recognises that she may have to get someone to read it for her if she does not have time to read it herself. The sender was a layman, not a highly edu-cated churchman, and his Latin is vivid if occasionally slightly incoherent, and includes quotes from Horace. There was no point in decorating one's letters with classical poetry if the recipient could not appreciate it.[57]

In the early years of the thirteenth century the Capetian court found itself housing several young people. Blanche's cousin, Arthur of Brittany, who was also in his mid-teens, was at court between 1200 and 1202, when he left on an ill-advised attempt to attack King John and claim Brittany, resulting in his own capture and death. Louis and Arthur went together to meet Hugh of Lincoln. Philip Augustus found it expedient to support Arthur's claims to the Breton parts of the Angevin lands. In the past, he had built a close alliance with Arthur's father, Geoffrey of Brittany, against Geoffrey's father, Henry II, so it was not surprising that the young count sought refuge at the Capetian court.[58] The young Countess Joanna of Flanders and her sister Margaret were also held at the court, as wards of King Philip until Joanna's marriage in 1212.[59]

There was a group of much younger children too. The two children of Agnes of Meran, Philip Hurepel and Mary, who had spent much of their time with their mother at the royal castle of Poissy, and were often known as the children of Poissy, joined the main court after Agnes's death in July 1201. Philip had them both legitimised by the pope, and in 1202 betrothed young Mary to Arthur of Brittany.[60] In 1209 the son and daughter of Blanche of Navarre, countess of Champagne (and Blanche of Castile's cousin), joined the French court. The unexpected death of their father, Count Theobald III, in 1201 had left Blanche of Navarre pregnant with the young count Theobald IV, and in a politically precarious position, ruling the county of Champagne for what was bound to be a long minority. In 1209 young

Theobald and his sister were old enough to leave their mother's care. They were now effectively hostages, like Joanna of Flanders and her sister Margaret.[61]

One says 'joined the court'; but an early thirteenth-century royal court was a fluid and moving object. The kings of France were less itinerant than the kings of Castile or the Angevin kings – they had a much smaller realm – but still the court moved from residence to residence. Hugh of Lincoln went to see Blanche at the royal palace on the Ile de la Cité in Paris, which was undoubtedly by now, as Rigord insists, the main palace in their capital city.[62] But she would have moved with the court to their other houses and castles too – to the old palace built into the Roman wall at Senlis, where Louis's mother had saved her marriage; to the residence favoured long ago by the Carolingian kings at Compiègne; to the houses in the hills just outside Paris, at Saint-Germain-en-Laye and Pontoise; to the new hunting lodge built by Philip's father, Louis VII, at Fontainebleau to the south-west.

Contemporaries would probably have thought that the phrase 'the king in his court' implied the king sitting either in judgement or taking counsel from the great men of his kingdom – the dukes, counts and other aristocracy, and the great prelates, the archbishops, bishops and a few important and trusted abbots – and perhaps the queen, though Philip did not have an active queen for much of his reign. But they would also have recognised it in a less formal, more intimate sense: the court formed of the group of the king's intimate and trusted advisers, both lay and ecclesiastical; of his household – the officers who supervised the chamber or the chapel or the stables, or the writing office; and of the hangers-on, who hoped to join the ranks of the trusted advisers. And it was not just the king who would have had a court in this sense. Others – the queen, counts, bishops and the heir to the throne and his wife – would have had their own, smaller 'court' establishments. A great man's, or woman's, court did not have a healthy reputation in the late twelfth and early thirteenth centuries. Many writers, especially those in the Angevin sphere, wrote dismissively, often satirically, of the venality and vicious vacuity of court life, and a new genre of literature of 'courtiers' trifles' emerged. But as Walter Map, one of the most famous of these authors, observed, while the court might be hell, there were plenty prepared to enter in the hopes of preferment.[63]

Little is known about the households of Blanche and her young husband, at least before Louis was knighted by his father in 1209. From time to time, royal accounts reveal the expenditure on clothes for them, or the loan or gift of jewels

from the royal treasury. Both would have been expected to look duly splendid on great courtly occasions, for instance, when Blanche's uncle, King John, came to Paris and was lavishly entertained in the royal palace by Philip.[64] An account of royal expenditure exists from November 1202 to February 1203. Blanche's expenses are mentioned only in conjunction with Louis's, which suggests that at this stage they had a joint household. Most of their expenses were defrayed though the *prévôté* (the administrative unit) of Paris, which indicates that the palace on the Ile de la Cité was their main home. Louis had far higher expenses than Blanche, especially for robes, leaving the superficial impression of a peacock prince with his Cinderella princess. But some of the robes and fabrics were not presumably for Louis himself, but for him to provide robes for members of their joint household. Total expenditure on their household was relatively high, at 1,840 *livres parisis*, at least in comparison to the 9 *livres* 17 *solidi* spent in the same period on the 'children of Poissy'.[65] An account of the king's jewels exists for 1206. Both Blanche and Louis received emerald brooches, and Louis was given an extra sapphire.[66]

Almost immediately, both were required to play adult roles. The 'Histoire des ducs de Normandie' claims that when John came to Paris in 1201, Philip Augustus forced Blanche to ask her uncle to hand over the Vexin, in a disturbing image of a wicked father-in-law playing off an innocent princess against her own wicked uncle. It may be true: the author of the 'Histoire' was well informed, though he could never resist a good story.[67] Louis's training in the arts of war continued. He spent part of 1202–3 with his household knights based at the castle of Le Goulet on the Norman border, and in 1206 he accompanied his father on an expedition to Angers.[68]

Blanche's principal role, of course, was to be the mother of a future king. Their first child was born in 1205 when she was seventeen – a daughter, who died at or soon after birth. But in 1209, at the age of twenty-one, Blanche gave birth to her first surviving child, a son to assure the continuation of the Capetian line, named Philip after his formidable grandfather.[69] In her later twenties and thirties she delivered healthy children at frequent and regular intervals: twins – though they died young – in 1213; then Louis in 1214, Robert in 1216, John in 1219, Alphonse in 1220, Philip Dagobert in 1222, Isabella in 1225, Stephen in 1226 and Charles, probably in March 1227 – which suggests there were more unrecorded still births between 1205 and 1213.[70] Unlike her husband, Blanche had a strong constitution.

So in 1209 Blanche had fulfilled her role in ensuring the continuation of the Capetian line. A court poet produced a poem in celebration, rather optimistically

invoking Blanche's role as the 'guarantee of peace' between the Angevins and the Capetians, in the hope that her son would come to rule over the united kingdoms of England and France. Philip Augustus's clerks copied it into the Registers, his official records of government.[71] In the same year, perhaps in recognition that the future of the dynasty was now assured, Philip Augustus knighted Louis, marking his transition from adolescent to young adult. It was a magnificent ceremony, held at a great court at Compiègne, on the feast of Pentecost, 17 May. Many other young men were knighted, including Louis's cousins, Count Robert of Dreux and his 'vallans et preu' younger brother, Peter of Dreux.[72] Following the ceremonies, many of the barons and knights set off to fight in the war in Languedoc against the Cathars.[73] Now Louis and Blanche must maintain their own household, funded from their own revenues, and Philip conferred on them the revenues from Poissy, Lorris, Château-Landon, Fay-aux-Loges, Vitry-aux-Loges and Boiscommun.[74]

But it was rather late. Louis was pushing twenty-two, and it was traditional to confer knighthood at twenty at the latest. Philip Augustus had knighted Arthur of Brittany in 1202, when he was fifteen.[75] Moreover, the knighthood, and the revenues, came with conditions attached. Philip insisted Louis promise that he would not go to fight in tournaments; that he would not attack the king's towns or townsmen; and that his household would consist only of those who had sworn fidelity to the king.[76] It is the first surviving indication that Philip did not fully trust his son and his ambitious young wife; it would not be the last.

Blanche herself might now be the mother of an heir to the throne of France, but she was also the niece of the great enemy of the Capetians. One can only speculate as to what she thought as she watched the defeat of her uncle and the collapse of his French realm, as the peace she was supposed to guarantee disintegrated into war. Her position as the wife of the immediate heir to the French throne must have been difficult, and may have been precarious, until she managed to give birth to a surviving male child – which she did at a relatively late age. Perhaps the court poet's vision of that son as the king who would unite the crowns of France and England reflected Blanche's hopes and aspirations, and her careful positioning of herself within the family of the enemy, into which she had married. She was fortunate to have the love and support of her husband.

2

The Lord Louis and
the Lady Blanche

IN 1209 LOUIS WAS KNIGHTED, Blanche was the mother of a future king, and they had their own establishment. But Philip Augustus did not die until 1223, so they had a long wait before they could attain the power for which both had been raised. The Capetians had not had an adult king and queen in waiting, with their own households, own court and own power base, which might rival that of the king, for as long as anyone could remember. Both Louis VII and Philip had succeeded to the throne while still in their mid-teens. But everyone would have been aware of the travails of the rival Angevin family. Henry II's sons had rebelled against him in 1173, and were thereafter in continual competition with each other and their father for dominance and dominion. Philip had found this very useful, and support for disaffected members of the Angevin family was a major aspect of his diplomacy. He knew, more than most, how destabilising the rival power base of an heir could be. This, presumably, was why he would give Blanche and Louis their own revenues only on tight conditions. And Philip was the first Capetian king who did not have his son and heir associated with him in kingship. Louis was never crowned and anointed as the young king in his father's lifetime, as both Louis VII and Philip had been; he was never even made king-designate, as Louis VI had been. The early Capetians had had their sons made king-associate in their lifetimes because their hold on the throne was so tenuous, and historians have

often interpreted Philip's failure to do so as a sign of strength, of the now unchallengeable succession rights of the Capetians.[1] But the real reason may have been fear of his son's rival power.

Philip had ensured that Blanche and Louis were well provided for. A fragmentary account for the final third of 1213 casts glimmers of light on the life they led, and reveals how wealthy they were. Louis, as heir in 1213, has recorded spending of 3,844 *livres parisis* 6 *solidi* for a third of the year; as king in 1226, he spent only double that.[2] The account of 1213 records only expenditure, not receipts, but there is no suggestion of revenues connected with the lands that Blanche had been given as her dowry. She may have had her own financial office, in which case the couple would have been richer still. The account does reveal that Blanche had a separate household with her own 'clerks' – the clergy who staffed her chapel and ministered to her spiritual needs, but who also provided her writing office and administration.[3] Blanche and Louis based themselves at the properties that provided his revenues, especially Poissy on the Seine, and Lorris and Boiscommun in the Gâtinais, though they were sometimes at other royal residences too, including Mantes and Melun.[4] At Lorris, there were works to provide a pathway to the rooms of Blanche's clerks, and Master James, their physician, was paid expenses for the time he spent in the Gâtinais, presumably at Lorris or Boiscommun, with Blanche and Louis's children.[5] Blanche had given birth to twins at the beginning of 1213, but one did not survive long into childhood. Master James's ministrations were presumably required primarily for them, and for young Philip who was still under five. Blanche herself, having recovered from the birth of the twins in January, was, by late 1213, pregnant with Louis, who was born in the following April.[6]

They ran a lavish, princely court. They hunted enthusiastically, with their dogs and falcons kept by their main huntsmen, William, Robin and John, and William the Falconer. Their horses were well cared for – they were vital for war and travel, as well as hunting. Members of their households were rewarded with expensive robes.[7] Louis ordered the purchase of onyx chalices and ginger, nutmeg, cloves and other spices and wines. Their staff went to Paris and Orléans to buy provisions. The account covers the end of the year: fine table linens and an expensive robe for Louis ensured a princely Christmas.[8] They entertained princely guests, including Louis's younger brother, Philip Hurepel, Robert of Courtenay and his sister, Matilda of Courtenay, countess of Nevers, Stephen of Sancerre and Guichard of Beaujeu, who was married to Louis's maternal aunt. Adam of Beaumont came to hunt, bringing his own dogs. They loaned money to the countess of Saint-Pol, and

corresponded with Blanche's cousin, Blanche of Navarre, countess of Champagne.[9] They themselves were entertained by Passerele, the singer of Stephen of Sancerre; by Garner of Château-Neuf, the viol player of Robert of Courtenay; by the actor or minstrel Tornebeffe; and the famous troubadour Gace Brulée.[10] The aristocratic Poitevin poet Theobald of Blaison sent letters to Louis at Boiscommun. These letters were carried by a Spanish knight, for Theobald was in Spain with Blanche's father, Alfonso VIII. Theobald was partly Castilian, and probably related to Blanche.[11] He would remain a close associate of Blanche and Louis; Blanche appointed him seneschal of Poitou in 1227 and of Limousin in 1229.[12] The young and lively court must have contrasted with that of Philip Augustus, who hated hunting and, to the delight of the Paris clergy and the disgust of the troubadour fraternity, had no time for minstrels and actors.[13]

But Blanche and Louis had plenty of clergy around them too. Blanche, as already mentioned, had her own clerks, though it is not clear how many. Most royal houses probably had a resident chaplain – there is payment to the chaplain at Poissy.[14] They must have had a close relationship with Walter Cornut, Philip's chaplain, an important clerk in the royal administration and later archbishop of Sens, because they gave a gift to his sister Regina, so that she could arrange the marriage of her daughter.[15] Regina Cornut was probably one of Blanche's ladies. A Master Martin and William the clerk are mentioned in Blanche and Louis's entourage, as are two more famous clergy, Simon Langton, the brother of Stephen Langton, archbishop of Canterbury, and Robert of Saint-Germain, the clerk of the king of Scotland.[16] Both Simon and Robert accompanied Louis on his attempt to take the English throne in 1216, and Simon was still a pensioner of the Capetian court in 1234. Simon Langton's presence in the entourage is telling. He was almost as distinguished a master at the Paris schools as his brother Stephen, who was the leader of the reform-minded moralists at Paris, the churchmen whose ideas about pastoral care, the right way to salvation and, indeed, secular morality – just war, just price, usury and good governance – informed the canons of the Fourth Lateran Council in 1215. One of Stephen's students, a Master Garin, was among those condemned and burnt in 1210 as a heretical follower of Amaury of Bène.[17] Intellectual discussion of morality could be a dangerous business, but Blanche and Louis encouraged it, along with the poetry and song. The influence of the reform-minded moralists is visible in the magnificent psalter produced for Blanche, around 1216 (Paris, Bibliothèque de l'Arsenal, MS lat. 1186), which has imagery of unusual intellectual sophistication (pls 5–7, 25).[18]

Louis and Blanche looked after their household well, whether lay or clerical, making several payments in case of sickness.[19] As a result, household staff and knights were loyal to them. They accompanied Louis on his military adventures, and served Blanche long after Louis's death.

But if Louis and Blanche had to be kept at a distance from royal power, they also had to be kept occupied. Blanche, of course, was expected to produce reserve heirs and marriageable daughters. By the time she had produced a second son in 1214, she had proved satisfactorily fertile. She also gained hugely in prestige when her father defeated the Almohad Muslim forces in Spain at Las Navas de Tolosa in July 1212. She was no longer the niece of the defeated King John, but the daughter of the saviour of Christendom. Her position in French royal circles was transformed.

Letters in praise of Alfonso VIII's great victory were sent throughout Christendom. Blanche herself wrote to inform her cousin, Blanche of Navarre, of the almost miraculous news. Her letter largely relayed the text that Blanche had received from a messenger from Spain, but she chose the sections praising the role of Blanche of Navarre's brother, King Sancho.[20] Blanche heard more from her sister, Berengaria, queen of León. One partially surviving letter, copied into a thirteenth-century collection of letters and texts, seems to be part of an ongoing correspondence between the two sisters. In it, Berengaria advises Blanche to 'make note of this [Alfonso's victory] to the king of France and our lord [presumably Lord Louis] and all whom you think proper': an intriguing phrase, in which she seems to encourage Blanche to use her new status as the daughter of the hero of Christendom to her advantage at the French court.[21]

Louis himself exploited his new knighthood on behalf of the realm. Although many chroniclers commented on his gentle nature, he enjoyed war, and defended his interests with determination and occasional violence. He played an important role in his father's diplomatic manoeuvres too, enough to suggest that he was a gifted political negotiator. King John was continually plotting to regain his lost French territories. In the west, Anjou and, in particular, Poitou were not yet securely under French control. Some of the most important nobles in north-east France, notably the counts of Boulogne and Flanders, were aware that their economic interests at least were best served by an alliance with England, so that Philip faced potential threats to both the north-east and the south-west of his kingdom. The north-eastern alliance was all the more potent a threat because the emperor, Otto of Brunswick, was King John's nephew.

Louis worked with his father against John in both east and west. He had inherited substantial lands in the north-east from his mother, including Lens, Bapaume and Saint-Omer – all towns sharing in the wealth of north-east France and Flanders – and he and Blanche had no intention of losing them. He invested heavily in their defence in 1213, particularly on a new castle and associated fortifications at Lens.[22] And perhaps because both Philip and Louis were aware just how important the trade links to England were for north-eastern France, Philip toyed with, and then allowed Louis to pursue, a claim to the English throne too. That claim was pursued most effectively through Blanche, as the granddaughter of Henry II. The claim had already been adumbrated in the poem to celebrate the birth of Blanche's son Philip in 1209.

In 1205 Philip Augustus had tried to persuade Count Renaud of Boulogne and the duke of Louvain, who had both married heiresses to the great trans-Channel honour of Boulogne, to invade England in order to claim, not just the English lands of the counts of Boulogne, but also the crown worn by their wives' grandfather, King Stephen.[23] John and his advisers took the danger seriously, though it sounds more like a distraction for a pair of potentially fractious barons than a serious invasion plan. For Philip was well aware that Renaud of Boulogne was a problem. Renaud's cross-Channel wealth had been badly affected by the collapse of the Angevin empire in 1204. In 1210 Philip tried to tie Renaud to the Capetian cause by a marriage between Renaud's daughter and heiress, Matilda, to Philip Hurepel. But by the following year it was clear that Renaud was conspiring with King John. Philip forced Renaud to give up the town of Boulogne to Louis, and by May 1212 Renaud had joined John.[24]

The count of Flanders vacillated between Philip and John. The county had been inherited by a woman, Joanna, who had been brought up at Philip's court alongside Blanche and Louis. In 1212 she was married to one of Blanche's Iberian cousins, Ferdinand of Portugal, who was 'handsome, dark, and large-nosed'.[25] Blanche may have been involved in the negotiations for the marriage; two other Iberian princesses in France certainly were – Blanche's cousins Blanche of Navarre, countess of Champagne, who was Joanna's aunt, and Matilda of Portugal, widow of Count Philip of Flanders, who was Ferdinand's aunt.[26] In February 1212 Louis ceded to Joanna and Ferdinand rights to areas of Flanders brought to him as part of his mother's dowry, apart from Saint-Omer and Aire-sur-la-Lys, which he seized from their control in one of his moments of decisive aggression. The seizure of these two towns alienated Joanna and Ferdinand.[27]

Meanwhile, in 1212, as relations between John and his subjects worsened, a group of English barons offered the crown to Philip, on the grounds of John's unsuitability as a ruler. Stephen Langton, archbishop of Canterbury and brother of Master Simon, led a deputation of bishops to put the case before Innocent III.[28] The pope agreed that John should be dethroned, but insisted that he, Innocent, would procure another king – though his chosen king too was Philip Augustus. Innocent was in the final stages of persuading Philip to take back Ingeborg of Denmark as his wife and queen, and the gracious offer of the English throne was a useful diplomatic lever. Perhaps Philip and his advisers thought that a higher authority was needed to justify taking the English throne. The Anonymous of Béthune describes Philip waking suddenly at night and exclaiming: 'Dex! K'atenc-jou, qui ne vois Engletierre conquerre?' – God! I hear you, who is it that you wish to conquer England?'[29]

Through late 1212 and early 1213 Philip assembled a fleet and an army and prepared the diplomatic ground, sending Louis to Toul in November 1212 to negotiate an alliance with the future emperor Frederick II against Otto of Brunswick.[30] In April 1213 Philip convened a great council at Soissons.[31] He agreed to reinstate Ingeborg as queen, and announced that the invasion of England would be led by Lord Louis. Evidently, father and son had agreed that Louis rather than Philip should take the English throne, but it is unclear on whose initiative. Philip insisted that his son sign a document agreeing that if Louis, through the grace of God, acquired the kingdom of England, he would in no way act to the detriment of his father.[32] Once again, it seems, Philip did not fully trust his son.

Then in early May 1213 John, in a masterly move, handed himself and his kingdom into the protection of the pope. Philip and Louis's plans were stymied. They were already in the north-east of France, on the verge of invading. They attacked Flanders instead – though this drove Ferdinand and Joanna into alliance with John; and Anglo-Flemish forces, under Renaud of Boulogne, defeated and scuppered the French invasion fleet at Damme.[33] Philip and Louis were now on the defensive. Philip retired to Paris, leaving Louis to defend his north-eastern territories from Lille, with the help of his north-eastern vassals and the count of Saint-Pol and Henry Clément, the elderly marshal of France.[34] That Louis and Blanche were also involved in countering John's increasingly effective diplomatic initiatives in Flanders, Lorraine and the Empire is clear from their household accounts of 1213. They sent Adam, their *panetarius*, twice to Flanders, and rewarded

a messenger from the duchess of Louvain warning of her son's involvement in John's coalition.[35]

In early 1214 John himself invaded Poitou. Marching north, he took Angers and captured Count Robert of Dreux, a Capetian cousin.[36] Louis was sent to secure Chinon. By the summer of 1214 the military threat from both east and west was serious. Philip dispatched Louis with the marshal, Henry Clément, to deal with King John's troops in the west. Apart from Clément, who fell ill and died during the campaign, Louis's men were 'the young knights of France', the young men of his own generation.[37] Louis captured La Roche-aux-Moines on 23 July, and John's troops fled.[38] Two days later, at Bouvines, Philip himself led a massive French army against Emperor Otto and the Anglo-Flemish alliance, in one of the most decisive great battles of the Middle Ages. William the Breton claimed that Philip had sent the best of the army with Louis.[39] But Philip's men delivered an overwhelming victory. Both Ferdinand of Flanders and Renaud of Boulogne were captured. Ferdinand was kept in secure but honourable confinement; Renaud, who had changed sides once too often, was kept in conditions so grim that eventually he killed himself by banging his head against the wall. Philip and Louis made a great ceremonial victory entrance into Paris. Tight-fisted Philip founded an abbey, called La Victoire, in commemoration. John agreed a six-year truce.[40]

With John defeated, Philip was prepared to let Louis respond to the papal call for help against the Cathar heretics of southern France, the Albigensians. In 1208 Innocent III had launched a full-blown crusade against the Cathars. The pope tried in vain to persuade Philip Augustus to join the Crusade, but Philip had more immediate concerns.[41] Several members of the north French aristocracy did respond to the papal summons. They were led by Simon of Montfort, a brilliant and charismatic soldier, one of the few who had distinguished himself on the Fourth Crusade. The Montfort family, originally castellans of the Capetian heartlands, had, by a succession of clever marriages, become one of the great trans-Channel aristocratic dynasties of the Angevin world; they now found themselves, after 1204, reduced to almost what they had been in the eleventh century – lords of a reasonably extensive sweep of heavily forested lands to the west of Paris. Philip was probably glad to see Simon set off to expend his energy and ambition in the Languedoc. Before long, Simon had defeated Raymond VI, count of Toulouse, who was suspected of supporting the Cathar heretics. Pope Innocent conferred the county of Toulouse on Simon.[42]

Louis took the Cross against the heretics in 1213, but not until John was dealt with did Philip allow him to respond to the papal call.[43] Now in spring 1215 Louis led an army down through Lyon to the south to join Simon of Montfort.[44] He was accompanied by several of the younger members of the aristocracy – the men of his own generation – including Guichard of Beaujeu and Adam of Melun, and by his own household knights, many of whom came from his lands in the Gâtinais or in the north-east of France. In many cases these men had been part of his campaign to La Roche-aux-Moines; many would join him in his English adventure. Simon was concerned that the young prince would try to impose Capetian power, though Simon had the support of the papacy.[45] Louis did not, it seems, try to challenge Simon's authority as count, but fought alongside him. Their success, however, was very limited. After besieging Toulouse twice and fulfilling the terms of their forty days' service, Louis and his companions negotiated a truce and returned to the north.[46]

With Louis safely back in the Ile-de-France, he and Blanche once more found themselves working with Philip for the stability of the realm. Their son Philip was now six, and in July 1215 a marriage was arranged between him and Agnes, the heiress to the Burgundian counties of Nevers, Auxerre and Tonnerre. The arrangement was guaranteed by Blanche's cousin, the countess of Champagne.[47] Agnes's maternal uncle was Robert of Courtenay, a close associate of Louis and Blanche and indeed a Capetian cousin, for the Courtenays were descended from a younger son of Louis VI. Like Isabella of Hainault, Agnes of Nevers was a great heiress, and the proposed marriage would bring most of northern Burgundy under the control of the French kings.

After the defeats of Bouvines and La Roche-aux-Moines, King John bought himself time by assenting to Magna Carta. But by the end of 1215 the English barons, the 'community of the realm', now thoroughly disaffected with a man unsuitable for kingship, had elected Louis as king of England. And this time, Louis was elected specifically in right of the claims of his wife, Blanche, to succeed to the English throne as the granddaughter of Henry II.[48]

Innocent III forbade this, since John was a papal vassal and England belonged to the pope.[49] Louis and Blanche ignored him. Louis assembled a great force in his north-eastern territories and sent advance parties to London and southern England in January 1216.[50] The advance party, deprived of good French wine and forced to drink English beer, behaved atrociously, even by medieval military standards.[51] Louis's methods of raising forces were not above reproach either. He sent a

contingent of men to pressurise Blanche of Navarre into sending knights. They burst rudely into her palace and confronted her as she sat dining with her young son, Theobald. The countess took refuge in her chamber, refused to supply the troops demanded and complained to Philip Augustus. Philip was furious with his son. 'I thought I was the only king in France', he is reported to have growled.[52]

Indeed, Philip Augustus did not support Louis and Blanche's project at all. His motives were mixed. Finally back in good favour with Church and papacy after his long matrimonial travails, he was unprepared to challenge the Church again. William the Breton claimed that he did not want to break his truce with John.[53] Besides, Louis and Blanche were more formidable now than in the spring of 1213. They had two sons to ensure the succession, and had built a coterie of younger nobility, knights and clergy around themselves. They had played their part in international diplomacy; Louis had triumphed with his young knights at La Roche-aux-Moines; and, during 1213, he had deepened his hold on the north-eastern territories. Blanche presumably had taken her sister's advice, and made much of her status as the daughter of the Alfonso VIII, the hero of Christendom. Philip probably thought they had power enough. But he was ageing too, and may have feared that the judgement of the Church in this world would be upheld in the next.[54]

Louis and Blanche defied both Philip and the Church. Their lawyers argued the justice of their claim to the English throne with the papal legate at Melun in April 1216 and then at Rome with Innocent himself. Louis sent a letter explaining their case to the abbey of St Augustine in Canterbury.[55] At Melun, the French produced five arguments as to why Louis should take the English crown. First, John had never been a true and legitimate king, because he had conspired against Richard I during the king's imprisonment, had been accused of treason by Richard, and deprived of all rights of succession. (Richard had certainly been tempted, but the two brothers had been reconciled at the last minute.) Second, since John had never been truly king, the kingdom was not in his gift to hand over to the pope. Their next line of attack was that John had been judged forfeit of the kingdom in Philip's court for the murder of Arthur – this is the first mention of this doubtless fabricated judgement. The fourth and fifth reasons concerned the role of the barons, the 'community of the Realm'. No king, they claimed, could give away his kingdom without the assent of his barons, whose role was to defend the realm. Finally, the English barons had elected Louis 'by reason of his wife', for her mother was the only sibling of King John, male or female, alive at the election in 1213.

It was perhaps unwise to challenge the greatest canon lawyer of the day, and Innocent III squashed all their propositions. On the issue of the condemnation of John for the murder of Arthur, Innocent replied that John, as an anointed king, could be judged only by his peers – which the French barons were not; that even had such a court been legitimate, at the worst, in his absence John could be deprived only of the fiefs that he held of the French king; he could certainly not be sentenced to death or to the loss of his kingdom. Finally, Innocent observed robustly that Arthur was not an innocent victim, but had been captured when revolting against his rightful lord. Moreover, the pope insisted that John's proper successor was his son Henry; and that in the notional absence of young Henry, the heir was not Blanche, but the children of John's older siblings, that is, Eleanor of Brittany and Otto of Brunswick. Here the French contingent appealed to their own specific inheritance customs: at the moment of the sentence against John and the election of Louis, Blanche's mother, the queen of Castile, was John's only living sibling. The pope had an answer for this too: in that case, the rightful king of England was Blanche's younger brother Henry, now king of Castile after the death of Alfonso VIII in 1214, or, failing that, her elder sister Berengaria, queen of León – not Louis through Blanche.

But in the face of papal intransigence, Louis went ahead, landing in England on 21 May 1216.[56] He brought with him most of his important vassals from his north-eastern territories, including Michael of Harnes, Arnold of Guines, Baldwin of Lens and the Advocate of Béthune; knights associated with his household, like Renaud of Amiens; and an impressive number of the younger members of the French aristocracy, including Robert of Courtenay, Hervé of Nevers – whose daughter and heiress was betrothed to Blanche and Louis's heir – Guichard of Beaujeu, Stephen of Sancerre and Enguerrand of Coucy.[57] The household account of 1213 shows many of these men, or their families, as already part of Blanche and Louis's circle.[58] Two days later the papal legate, Guala Bicchieri, excommunicated Louis.[59] But Louis seemed unstoppable. On 2 June he was welcomed into London almost as a conquering hero. Most of the great magnates of England came to join him; in the summer, the king of Scots came to do homage. Soon Louis had captured Reigate, which he gave to Robert of Courtenay, and Farnham, Guildford and Winchester, which he gave to Hervé of Nevers.[60]

With London secured, Louis turned back to besiege Henry II's great castle at Dover. Henry II had built the new tower at Dover around 1180 as a status symbol rather than a fortress; it was intended to impress foreign princes and ambassadors,

rather than to keep them out. But things had changed since then. The French, English and Flemish had all become used to requisitioning, if not so much building, fleets; and since Philip Augustus's ill-fated attempt to attack Damme in 1213, maritime warfare in the Dover Straits had played a surprisingly important role in Angevin–Capetian relations.[61] The castle at Dover could and did prevent Louis's ships landing in Dover harbour,[62] and Dover was increasingly seen to be – as its defender, Hubert de Burgh, is supposed to have said – 'The key to England'.[63] But Dover held out, and Louis himself almost came to grief at Sandwich as he tried to control Rye and Winchelsea.[64] Then, in October 1216, John died. Louis was no longer trying to depose a tyrant who was unsuitable to rule, but, in Henry III, an innocent child who was widely seen as the legitimate heir to the English throne. A significant number of the great magnates defected and some of the French contingent left. Louis himself returned to France to raise reinforcements.[65]

Philip continued to distance himself from his excommunicate son. They did not even talk, according to both William the Breton and the Anonymous of Béthune.[66] Nevertheless, Louis managed to raise funds and persuade a new influx of French knights and nobles to join him, and in late March 1217 he returned to England. London held firm for him, and he retook Canterbury and Winchester.[67] But in May a substantial contingent of his men, under the command of the count of Perche and Simon of Poissy, was routed at Lincoln. Many were captured, and the count of Perche was killed.[68]

Now Louis's need for reinforcements was urgent. Philip, once again, refused to provide them. It was Blanche, with the help of Robert of Courtenay, who came to his aid.[69] She based herself in Louis's north-eastern towns of Saint-Omer and Boulogne, and drew on all the potential support there, working closely with Louis's officials in the area, to use the considerable revenues from these northern territories to raise an army and a fleet. Some of the fleet was requisitioned, but some was built new. As admiral of her fleet, she commissioned the most notorious and feared sea dog of his day, Eustace the Monk. It was a huge logistical enterprise, and she worked fast, for the fleet was ready by mid-August.[70]

Even the most sober accounts agree that Blanche did this against the wishes of her formidable father-in-law.[71] Her challenge to Philip quickly became legendary. The Ménestrel of Reims' highly coloured version of recent history features a dramatic scene in which Blanche confronts Philip over his lack of support for Louis: when Philip continues to refuse help, Blanche threatens to pawn her children to provide the money for the fleet to rescue her husband's desperate battle for the – for

her – English throne.[72] It would be nice to think it really happened. But at the least it reflects that fact that contemporaries thought that Blanche gave her full support to the English adventure, to the extent that she might almost be described as a driving force in the enterprise; and that she was prepared to give such support against her father-in-law's wishes, and against the insistence of the Church. Both Blanche and Louis were notably pious; nevertheless, they were prepared to accept Louis's excommunication in order to pursue the English crown.

Blanche's efforts had no more success than Louis's. On 24 August her fleet was dispersed in a storm and defeated outside Calais. The ships were burnt and scattered; forty of them, according to the English chronicler Ralph of Coggeshall, sunk like lead in the sea.[73] Robert of Courtenay was captured, and the ferocious Eustace the Monk was decapitated.[74] Louis had to accept humiliating, and expensive, terms of defeat. The abbots of Cîteaux, Clairvaux and Pontigny arrived to negotiate – perhaps to make things easier for him.[75] But Louis had to present himself as a penitent; then the papal legate absolved him of his sins and welcomed him back into the body of the Church. Louis was unable to persuade the legate to absolve a group of clergy who had all preached publicly against his excommunication. They were either members of his household or seen to be particularly close to him, and they included Simon Langton and Robert of Saint-Germain, both of whom were associated with Louis in 1213, and the artist or purveyor of the arts Elias of Dereham. Eventually, the papal penitentiary agreed that they could be received back into the Church after a ritual whipping.[76] Peace was made on 11 September 1217 at Lambeth; at the end of September Louis returned to France.[77]

There is little sign of activity from either Louis or Blanche for the next year. Relations with Philip probably remained tense. In November 1217 the king insisted that their close associate Robert of Courtenay give undertakings to return the fortresses of Conches and Nonancourt in Normandy to Philip, whenever required. Philip required securities, too, and they were given by others from Louis and Blanche's court circle, including Adam of Beaumont and Gaucher of Châtillon, count of Saint-Pol.[78] In July 1218 Louis and Blanche drew up the dower arrangements for the marriage between Robert's niece, Agnes of Nevers, and the young heir, Philip, at Lorris. Agnes's father, Hervé of Nevers, had played a spirited role in the English invasion. The marriage never happened. By December 1219 young Philip was dead, and King Philip himself had taken control of Agnes's marital prospects, insisting that she could be married only with his permission. Blanche and Louis must have mourned the death of the hopeful young heir, whom they

had buried alongside Louis's mother, Isabella of Hainault, in the cathedral of Notre-Dame in Paris.[79] But there were other sons. Louis, born in 1214, now became his father's heir; Robert had been born in 1216. Time together after Louis's prolonged absences in England produced John in 1219, then Alphonse in 1220.

Finally, Philip found another role for Louis. Simon of Montfort had been killed in the summer of 1218. His son, Count Amaury, continued the fight but, lacking his father's killer instinct, without much success. The pope increased his pressure for northern participation in the Albigensian Crusade. Since Philip was lukewarm, the papacy turned to young Count Theobald of Champagne, now just twenty. The prospect of Theobald adding to his immensely rich county of Champagne a substantial lordship in south-west France, strategically adjacent to the lands of his cousins of Navarre, was enough to make Philip turn to Louis.[80] Once again, in the spring of 1219, Louis set off for a summer campaign against the Cathar heretics of Languedoc. He was accompanied by Philip's right-hand man, Brother Guérin, bishop of Senlis; by Arnold of Audenarde from Louis's north-eastern lands; and by his cousin Peter of Dreux, count of Brittany. The campaign was not much more successful than his previous expedition, though he probably found the young, pious and good-hearted Amaury of Montfort much easier to work with than the redoubtable Count Simon.[81]

Beyond that, Louis and Blanche must have spent the last years of Philip's reign immersed in the life of their young family, in courtly pursuits – in hunting, in commissioning magnificent manuscripts, in listening to musicians and poets, and in discussion with the intellectual clergy around them, like Simon Langton. In July 1220 Simon's brother, Stephen, archbishop of Canterbury, translated the remains of Thomas Becket into a magnificent new shrine in the choir of Canterbury Cathedral. Elias of Dereham, who had been excommunicated along with Simon Langton for his support of Louis during the English invasion, designed and oversaw the construction of the new shrine. Several members of French courtly circles attended this great event, including Blanche's cousin Berengaria of Navarre (the widow of Richard the Lionheart) and Louis's companions, Guy of Châtillon, now count of Saint-Pol, and Count Robert of Dreux.[82] Both Blanche and Louis showed continual devotion to St Thomas. In 1224, when he captured La Rochelle, Louis gave one of its inhabitants to Archbishop Stephen because of his reverence for St Thomas; Blanche would found an altar dedicated to the saint in the great hospital, the Hôtel-Dieu, in Paris.[83] In 1232 Canterbury Cathedral agreed to offer Masses as splendid as those for an archbishop for Blanche and for the deceased Louis, on

account of her well-known devotion to St Thomas.[84] But in 1220 they must have known that it would be politically impossible, after their recent English debacle, for them to attend the translation of the saint.

Philip's suspicions about the younger aristocracy, especially those in his son's circle, persisted. He often insisted that a group of nobles would guarantee, often with substantial financial pledges, the loyalty of any one of their number he suspected. In 1221 Agnes of Nevers, with all her north Burgundian inheritance, was married to Guy of Châtillon, count of Saint-Pol. The marriage had Philip's permission, but still he insisted on large numbers of pledges, especially for the future good behaviour of Agnes's mother, Countess Matilda. It looks as though Robert of Courtenay, Matilda's brother, played a large role in the negotiations.[85] He played a similar role the following year in the provisions of securities for the good behaviour of Count Theobald of Champagne. In spite of his distrust of Theobald, Philip knighted him, along with his young son Philip Hurepel, at Etampes in 1222.[86] In the following summer, June 1223, at Melun, Philip insisted on pledges from the aristocracy for Count Philip of Namur, a younger brother of Robert of Courtenay.[87] At the same time, Philip made Count Robert of Dreux agree that he would hand over Dreux to the king on demand.[88] It was during a court convened at Anet, to deal with the latest suspected baronial conspiracy against him – according to Ralph of Coggeshall – that Philip fell seriously ill.[89]

Philip was taken back to Paris. They halted at Mantes. The king knew he was dying. There was no need to make a will. He had been ill in September 1222 – ill enough to dictate his testament. Technically, this was a codicil, for he had made a will in 1190, before he left on Crusade, leaving the kingdom to his son, Louis. In the will of 1222 he had left monies to Louis to defend the kingdom of France. He bequeathed 10,000 *livres* to Ingeborg and to his younger son, Philip Hurepel. He made generous provision for the poor and sick of his realm, and ordered that an abbey of the order of St Victor be founded at Charenton. He left his jewels and regalia to the abbey of Saint-Denis, so that twenty monks should pray each day for his soul, and the huge sum of 3,000 marks of silver to aid John of Brienne, king of Jerusalem, in regaining the city from the Muslims.[90] Philip called for Louis and told him to love and fear God, to protect his people and do justice.[91] On 14 July 1223 he died, after a momentous reign of forty-four years.

Louis and Blanche were now, finally, king and queen of France. Their long period of waiting had been frustrating. The determination with which both of them pursued the English crown shows how much they wanted to exercise real

power. But it had given them time to build a family life marked by ties of devotion between husband and wife and parents and children – a family life that contrasted markedly with that of Philip Augustus. It had given them the time too to develop a court with its own culture – young, vibrant, chivalric, but also intensely and questioningly religious. Between them, they created around them an atmosphere that was both courtly and devotional, and highly cultured. Again, the contrast with the court of Philip Augustus was striking.

3

Louis VIII and Blanche: King and Queen Consort

Philip Augustus received a magnificent burial in the abbey church of Saint-Denis, with Louis, Blanche and Philip Hurepel in attendance. He had left his jewels to the abbey; in a gesture of filial devotion, Louis redeemed them, for the considerable sum of 11,600 *livres*, using the money to establish elaborate anniversary commemorations at the abbey for the repose of his father's soul.[1] Meanwhile, Louis and his household turned their attention to his coronation.

The king's coronation would take place at the cathedral of Reims, as had Philip's coronation in 1179 and Louis VII's in 1131. Both Philip and Louis VII had been crowned and anointed king of France during their own father's lifetime. So this time, for the first time in as long as anyone could remember, the coronation would mark and celebrate the assumption of power by a new king. Moreover, neither Philip nor Louis VII had been married when they were crowned and anointed at Reims. Their marriages came later, so there were separate coronations for their queens. Famously, during the coronation of Isabella of Hainault at Saint-Denis, hot oil from lamps burning before the high altar splashed over the king and queen. Fortunately, no one was injured, and Rigord managed to present a potential social disaster as a miraculous blessing with sacred oil.[2] So this time, again for the first time, there would be a full double coronation and anointing of a king and his queen.

The clergy of the cathedral of Reims had been preparing for this occasion for some time, it seems. There were several attempts to refine and extend the

coronation service in the early thirteenth century. All these early thirteenth-century variants introduced new, specifically French, elements into the coronation order – an order derived ultimately, like most other European coronation orders, from Carolingian prototypes.[3] The most important of these specifically French elements was the oil with which the new king was anointed. Almost all European rulers were anointed, for the ceremony of king making was based on biblical precedents, especially the first three canonical kings of the Israelites, Saul, David and Solomon. The crucial element in the Bible was not crowning – that element of ruler making was borrowed by Carolingian rulers from Roman custom – but the anointing with oil consecrated at the altar. The French kings had for some time claimed that they were anointed with sacred oil brought from heaven in a small ampulla by a dove at the baptism of Clovis, the first Christian king of France, in the fifth century. The holy oil, in its sacred ampulla, was kept at the abbey of Saint-Remi at Reims, and much was now made, in the new, early thirteenth-century coronation orders, of the ceremonial bringing of the holy oil to the cathedral, where the coronation itself took place. As queen, Blanche, too, would be anointed as well as crowned, but with ordinary consecrated oil, like any other European ruler; not with the holy oil reserved for the kings of France. But at least one contemporary, the Ménestrel of Reims, thought that she was anointed with the same holy oil as her husband.[4]

The coronation took place on 6 August 1223, three weeks after Philip's death. It was a magnificent occasion. Louis, Blanche and the extended Capetian family, together with their households, the great prelates and the great magnates of France with their own households, descended on the city of Reims. John of Brienne, the king of Jerusalem who had lost his kingdom, was there to lend his indigent prestige, and Louis invited Countess Joanna of Flanders.[5] The abbot and monks of Saint-Remi brought the holy oil in solemn procession. The abbot and monks of Saint-Denis brought the regalia – the crowns, sceptre and rods and robes for both king and queen – all the way from their abbey just to the north of Paris, for this, the burial house of most kings of France, was also the holder of the French regalia. Louis and Blanche stayed in the archbishop's palace, next to the cathedral. After the ceremony itself, preceded by Philip Hurepel, holding the sword that represented the king's active power, and having changed their heavy coronation crowns for lighter ones, Louis and Blanche led the way back to the palace and the great celebratory feast to follow.[6] It must have been difficult to arrange with appropriate ceremony, for the archbishop's palace and, more importantly, the cathedral itself

were in the midst of major rebuilding campaigns. The new choir was still under construction in 1223, and the coronation probably took place in the nave of the old cathedral. The richest cloths in the cathedral's treasury must have been deployed to disguise the temporary wooden walls and other scars of construction, and Blanche and Louis must have been crowned in a cocoon of exotic Islamic and Byzantine silks. It was certainly expensive, and there was the question of who should pay for it. Louis himself insisted that the townspeople of Reims should cover the costs, but towards the end of 1223 the archbishop, William of Joinville, complained to the king that he himself had spent 4,000 *livres* on it.[7]

As king and queen, Louis and Blanche no longer based themselves at Poissy or the residences in the Gâtinais. Their principal residence now was the palace on the Ile de la Cité in the middle of Paris, where they had spent their early teens. They also favoured the palace at Saint-Germain-en-Laye, on the hills above the Seine just to the west of Paris, perhaps because of the excellent hunting in the surrounding woods. Their old residence of Lorris in the Gâtinais still featured in the court itinerary, reflecting, perhaps, its importance to them during their long wait for the throne.[8] Blanche was now a mature thirty-five, but she was still giving birth at regular intervals. Philip Dagobert had been born in the year before they came to the throne. Their only surviving daughter, Isabella, was born in March 1225 and a short-lived son, Stephen, in 1226. Their youngest son, Charles, was probably born in March 1227, or perhaps in late 1226, after his father's death.[9] Even as queen, Blanche was a mother of young children, and she spent a large proportion of her short reign as queen consort pregnant.

Historians have been struck by the lack of references to Blanche in contemporary sources during her husband's reign. It is not really surprising. Queens no longer subscribed to royal charters or gave their consent to them in the way that they might have done in the early twelfth century, but then neither did other close advisers of the king. Official documents were now dry, short, and issued by the royal administrators, quite unlike the narrative acts issued by the chancellery of Louis VI, which might mention the presence or consent of the queen.[10] The fragmentary household accounts for one term of 1226 cast little light on Blanche's role as queen. They merely record her total expenditure for that third of the year at 1,852 *livres* 13 *solidi* 4 *deniers*, out of a total expenditure of 37,480 *livres*.[11] But there are other indications of the importance of her role as queen consort. According to Philip Mousquès, Blanche, to general acclaim at a plenary royal court, gave her consent to her husband's departure on his final Crusade against the Albigensians.[12]

Louis would have assumed that his queen consort would take charge while he was away on Crusade and on his campaign against the Angevins in 1224. Indeed, in 1224, at a stage when Louis's campaign against the Angevins was in trouble, Blanche organised a penitential procession of the citizens of Paris to pray for victory. Her dower certainly, and dowry perhaps, brought her the possibility of developing her own networks of patronage of ambitious churchmen or minor nobles who owed their position and advancement to her. She insisted that Louis confirm her possession of substantial dower lands in the north-east – the rich towns of Lens, Bapaume and Hesdin, carved out of the territories that Louis had inherited from his mother – though it is unclear whether she could draw revenues from them while her husband was still alive.[13] She probably enjoyed revenues from her dowry lands, including Issoudun; they were certainly in her hands in the 1230s.[14]

Despite her pregnancies, Blanche provided a queenly focus for Louis's court, so that it was very different in tone from Philip's. The two earliest moralised bibles were almost certainly produced during their reign, commissioned presumably by Louis and Blanche. What they were used for is unclear, but their lavish magnificence established the image of the court.[15] As queen, Blanche was able to give a new level of patronage, protection and encouragement to religious groups that she favoured. Along with Bishop Bartholomew of Paris, she lent particular support to the new Dominican preaching friars as they established themselves in the city. Writing in 1226, the head of the order, Master Jordan of Saxony, spoke of her tender care for the brothers, and how 'she would talk to me about their business in her own words with considerable familiarity'.[16] This suggests that Blanche enjoyed discussion with this most intellectual of religious orders. She may also have been drawn to them on account of their Spanish origins and connections, though most of the Paris brothers were recruits from the university. Their Paris house was dedicated to St James of Compostela.

News of her Iberian relatives must sometimes have been disturbing. Blanche's sister Berengaria was now ruling Castile in conjunction with her son Ferdinand of León, but the country had been plagued by baronial insurgency and disaffection since the death of Alfonso VIII in 1214. In 1223 there was a new revolt led by the count of Molina. Molina and six of his colleagues wrote to Blanche and Louis, complaining of the inadequacy of their rulers, and inviting Blanche and Louis to send their son Louis, who was now eleven, to be crowned king in their place. It must have provided an unwelcome echo of the appeals of the English baronage to Louis himself. Blanche and Louis had no intention of sending their young heir on

such a wild adventure, though they had the letters filed carefully in the French royal archive.[17]

More happily, in early 1224 the elderly John of Brienne, king of Jerusalem, married Queen Berengaria's twenty-year-old daughter, Berengaria of León, as he passed through Castile on return from a pilgrimage to Santiago de Compostela. The marriage was arranged on the initiative of Queen Berengaria, though there may have been some connivance with her sister, the queen of France.[18] John of Brienne brought his wife, now queen of Jerusalem, back to Paris, where she was welcomed warmly by her aunt. John and Berengaria named their first, but sadly short-lived, child after Blanche.[19] In later years, Blanche would show particular affection for John's and Berengaria's children: Mary, empress of Constantinople, and her three young brothers, Alphonse, John and Louis, who were brought up at the Capetian court.[20]

Members of Blanche and Louis's princely households now found themselves part of the royal household, but, despite the lack of trust between Louis and Blanche and Philip Augustus, Louis kept in place the most significant members of Philip's government, Brother Guérin, bishop of Senlis, Bartholomew of Roye, the chamberlain, and Matthew of Montmorency as constable.[21] Philip had tended to keep the great traditional household offices vacant. His father, Louis VII, had already found that the chancellor, who controlled the king's writing office, and hence much of the effective work of government, could become too powerful: the role had been vacant for a long time. The great magnates expected to hold the more ceremonial offices of seneschal or butler. Philip had ensured that they remained vacant, or filled with men, like Bartholomew of Roye, from the lesser, knightly families of the Ile-de-France who owed their position, not to their own high lineage, but to royal favour. Louis VIII took a more traditional approach. Brother Guérin had been de facto chancellor for some years; Louis gave him the chancellorship. And he made his trusted cousin and companion Robert of Courtenay butler.[22]

•

After the ceremonies, the realities of power crowded in on Louis and Blanche. Normandy had been absorbed into the royal domain with remarkably little resistance. Brittany had been given to Louis's cousin, Peter, younger brother of Robert of Dreux – the two brothers had been knighted along with Louis in 1209.[23] The barons of Maine and northern Anjou had accepted Capetian dominion. But Poitou was certainly not under Capetian control; indeed, by the end of Philip's reign it

was coming under increasing Angevin pressure. No attempt had been made to dislodge the Angevins any further south; it had been enough to hold the line at the Loire. Pope Honorius was protective of the rights of the young Henry III, and often intervened on his behalf.[24] Henry III himself was now coming of age, and beginning to consider reclaiming his lost French territories. When he heard that the old king had died, he immediately sent ambassadors, including Stephen Langton, archbishop of Canterbury, and brother of Louis's clerk Simon, to Paris to ask for the return of the Angevin lands. Henry claimed that Louis had sworn on the Bible, as part of the conditions of the treaty of 1217, that he would do everything in his power to see Henry's rightful inheritance returned to him; now was Louis's opportunity. Louis had not been in a strong position in 1217, and may well have sworn this oath; but he had no memory of it now. He and his lawyers replied that John and his successors had been judged forfeit of his lands in the court of the king of France; if Henry III wished to challenge the judgement, the court of the king of France was the appropriate place to do so. Stephen Langton and his colleagues retired – probably not very surprised.[25]

Henry III's new focus on the Angevin territories in France brought a new element, too, to the Albigensian issue. The Crusade had lost momentum with the death of Simon of Montfort. The brief expedition of Louis and Peter of Brittany in the spring and summer of 1219 had done little to revive it, though Count Simon's sons, especially Amaury, continued the fight. The young and energetic Raymond VII had succeeded his father as count of Toulouse in 1222. The Church saw Raymond VII as less complaisant towards Cathar heresy than his father had been. Moreover, Raymond was Henry III's first cousin – as indeed he was Blanche of Castile's, for Raymond's mother, Joanna, was another daughter of Henry II. Raymond and Henry used the family relationship to develop a political one. It must have become obvious to Louis and Blanche that the Albigensian issue was no longer a distant and essentially local problem: now it had the potential to lead to a great south-western alliance, between Languedoc and Aquitaine, against Capetian suzerainty. Most of Louis's short reign was spent planning and then leading a major Crusade against the Albigensians, and fighting off or neutralising Angevin incursions in Poitou, Saintonge and eastern Aquitaine.

If the rump of the Angevin empire still presented the same problems in the west, in the east the battle of Bouvines of 1214 had been decisive. With Count Ferdinand of Flanders still a prisoner, the countess, Joanna, was in a very weak position. Although they had not got England, Louis and Blanche had spent much time and

expense in developing the Flemish lands inherited from Isabella of Hainault, fortifying its towns and cultivating the support of the aristocracy and the urban patriciate there. In 1225 Countess Joanna's authority was challenged by an imposter purporting to be her aged father, Count Baldwin, who had disappeared in battle in the Latin empire in the east in 1206. Louis gave Joanna his full support, for which she was profoundly grateful.[26] While the count – and the county – of Flanders was at Louis's mercy, the count of Champagne was increasingly escaping Capetian control, since Theobald had attained his majority in 1222 and had entered into full enjoyment of his inheritance.

Theobald IV of Champagne had been born posthumously to his father Theobald III, leaving his mother, Blanche of Navarre, to rule the county during the long minority. Blanche had had to pay an enormous relief to Philip Augustus to allow her son to succeed, and Philip had insisted that the young man and his sister be brought up at the Capetian court from 1209, when Theobald was about eight.[27] When Theobald attained his majority in 1222, Philip knighted him, alongside Philip Hurepel.[28] Theobald received a good education. Like his uncle, Richard the Lionheart, he became a renowned troubadour poet.[29] Blanche of Navarre decided that the interests of the county of Champagne were best served by close co-operation with Philip Augustus. Although Philip drained off huge revenues, she was almost certainly right. She played an important role at court, and Philip seems to have trusted her and recognised her competence. When young Theobald's succession to Champagne was challenged by a cousin, Blanche was able to rely on the king's protection.[30] But now that Theobald had reached his majority, Louis and Blanche were no longer dealing with a woman ruling for a son who was effectively a hostage at the royal court, but with a lively, independent and cultivated young man.

The county of Champagne was worth ruling. It stretched from the plateau of Langres in the south to the river Vesle in the north, from the Brie, very close to Paris, in the west to Joinville in the east, though it was never a fully consolidated territory in the way that the duchy of Normandy was. The counts of Champagne held most of their lands from the king of France, but they held some from the archbishop of Reims, some from the duke of Burgundy and some from the emperor. In spite of this lack of territorial cohesion, the counts of Champagne were enormously wealthy, their riches garnered from the Champagne fairs, the most important trading fairs in twelfth- and early thirteenth-century Europe, which took place in their towns of Lagny, Provins and Troyes, and from the dues taken from the merchants who traversed the county as they traded between England, Flanders

and Italy. From the second half of the twelfth century the counts of Champagne had concentrated on developing the economic potential of their lands, on developing the administrative machinery that would enable them to realise that potential, and on establishing a court renowned for its generosity and literary sophistication. They had proved supporters rather than enemies of the kings of France – indeed, Philip's mother was a member of the family. But Philip was not sentimental, and did not pass up the opportunity offered by the minority of Theobald IV.

Ralph of Coggeshall had talked about baronial disaffection under Philip Augustus.[31] He may have had Theobald of Champagne in mind. Philip's viciously decisive handling of Ferdinand of Flanders and, in particular, of Renaud of Boulogne after Bouvines left his baronage unprepared to challenge him. But younger members of the aristocracy – men such as Robert of Dreux and his brothers, Peter of Brittany and Count John of Mâcon; Guy of Châtillon, count of Saint-Pol, and his brother, Hugh; Robert of Courtenay and his brother-in-law, Count Hervé of Nevers; and Enguerrand of Coucy – had begun to revolve around Lord Louis and Blanche rather than the old king. These were the 'young knights of France', who accompanied Louis on his various campaigns, to western France, to England and against the Cathars in the south, or set off on Crusades on their own account. They felt that the old king did too much governing without them; that he relied instead far too much on a set of relatively low-born administrators. Peter of Dreux had already proved difficult. Philip had arranged a splendid marriage for him – to the heiress to Brittany. Peter was a clever and educated man. He had been intended for the Church, and that, combined with his evident ambition for worldly power and influence, earned him the nickname 'Mauclerc' – the wicked clerk. He had already tried to fulfil some of those ambitions by conspiring with the circle of the young Henry III of England before the death of King Philip.[32]

The others were not actively conspiring with the enemy. But they must have assumed that it would be different when their companion-in-arms and his wife came to the throne. Louis had baronial expectations to manage. And there was already the potential for a rival centre of power for the disaffected in Louis's younger brother, Philip Hurepel. In the event, Philip Hurepel proved a loyal companion-in-arms to Louis, but Philip Augustus, on his deathbed, is said to have told the two of them to keep the peace.[33] Philip Hurepel had married a great heiress, Matilda, daughter of the unfortunate Renaud of Boulogne, and was due to inherit many of Renaud's great honours. His territories were one of the first things that Louis dealt with when he came to the throne. He gave Philip Hurepel

a slightly less generous arrangement than Philip Augustus had done. Philip was given lands in the Seine valley in Normandy, which had once belonged to Renaud of Boulogne; but in exchange, Louis took areas of western Normandy, especially Coutances, into his own control.[34]

The Church also had expectations of Louis and Blanche as king and queen. Philip Augustus had managed to rebuild a reputation for piety in the last ten years of his life, but many would remember his twenty-year battle with the Church over his marriage. Louis and Blanche, unlike Philip, had developed close relationships with churchmen who were renowned as scholars in the Paris schools, and who were sympathetic to the reformist agenda that lay behind the Fourth Lateran Council in 1215. Louis had been taught by Amaury of Bène and Stephen of Tournai, and their household had included Simon Langton. Louis and, particularly, Blanche were already renowned for their deep personal piety. But in fact the Church was to discover that Louis, and Blanche after his death, were happy to challenge any ecclesiastical demands that might damage the rights, revenues or authority of the kings of France.

Louis's first major legislation was the statute, or *stabilimentum*, on the Jews, issued in November 1223.[35] The statute prevented the payment of interest on all existing debts to Jews. The payment of interest due after the date of the statute would not be enforced; instead, the principal of those loans was to be be repaid over three years, not to the Jewish creditors, but to the lord who owned the Jews. The king had many Jews on his lands, and much of that money would fill the royal coffers. The statute also withdrew the administrative machinery whereby royal Jews had been able to have their loan agreements authenticated and sealed by royal officials – in short, their arrangements would no longer have the overt protection of the king. Louis persuaded most of the north French magnates who owned Jews to subscribe to the statute – and the statute forbad any lord to keep and profit from any Jews who belonged to, and had fled from, another lord, thus ensuring that none of them would offer refuge to royal Jews. The only great magnate who did not subscribe was Theobald of Champagne. The wealthy counts of Champagne had – and exploited – a very large number of Jews, and Louis had to deal with Theobald in two separate agreements.[36]

Louis was as concerned as his father had been to ensure the receipt of all potential revenue, and the intention and effect of this statute were partly financial. But there was much more to it than that. The intense study of the Bible that had dominated twelfth-century intellectual endeavour had led to a deepening hatred of

the Jews within the Church, particularly among the moralists of the Paris schools. Early in his reign, Philip Augustus had expelled the Jews from France, earning the approbation of the Church; later, in 1198, realising the financial disadvantages, he had reversed the decision, allowing the Jews to return under close royal control. For Rigord, this was almost as reprehensible as his bigamous marriage.[37] The Parisian moralists were also increasingly concerned about usury, culminating in Robert Courson's tract against it, and the forbidding of usury at the Fourth Lateran Council. This reinforced anti-Jewish sentiment, since in northern Europe the provision of loans was dominated by Jews.[38] Louis's statute was driven by an abhorrence of usury. Above all, it removed royal authentication from instruments of Jewish usury, and forbad the enforcement of payments of interest to Jewish creditors. The influence of the Parisian moralist churchmen in Louis's entourage is clear.

There was a new political perspective too – a strikingly broad one. Philip Augustus had indeed already had agreements, especially with the wealthy county of Champagne, over the control and exploitation of each other's Jews. But now Louis's statute declared that the provision preventing the reception and exploitation of another's Jews applied equally to those magnates who had subscribed to the statute and to those who had not.[39] In short, Louis saw this statute as applying throughout his realm, the kingdom of the French. That was not quite the reality, of course. Theobald of Champagne did not subscribe to it, instead negotiating separate agreements that went no further in principle than his agreements with Philip Augustus, agreements between one ruler of a polity and another. The statute for the Jews reflects not just the moral views of the Church reformers, but also the political perspectives on the integrity of the kingdom absorbed from the Langtonians who had persuaded Louis to aim for the English crown.

But even before he had issued the statute on the Jews, Louis was dealing with the stability of his realm. In September 1223 he went to the Loire; in November and December he went to the north-east; in January 1224 he went to Normandy. In the west, he assured himself of the loyalty of Amaury of Craon, the seneschal of Anjou, and arranged truces with Aimery of Thouars and Hugh of Lusignan, count of La Marche.[40] In 1220 Hugh of Lusignan had married Isabella of Angoulême, King John's widowed queen. Not only did Hugh and Isabella control a huge and strategically important area of Poitou, but they were also potential allies of Isabella's son, Henry III. From a Capetian point of view, it was fortunate that Isabella's relationships with her Angevin children were chilly, and that she was one of the Courtenay clan – Robert of Courtenay was her uncle.[41]

Already, at the very start of his reign, Louis was trying to detach the men of the Perigord from the English allegiance.[42] For the pressures, and the potential, of another Crusade against the Cathars was there from the start. In January 1224 the archbishop of Narbonne and his suffragan bishops wrote to ask Louis to lead a new Crusade; a few weeks later, Amaury of Montfort came to Paris to cede to Louis all rights that the Church had given to his father, Count Simon, to the county of Toulouse.[43] Meanwhile, in spite of Louis's careful diplomacy in Poitou, Henry III had sent a force there. In May 1224 Louis sent a crisp response to the demand that he lead a Crusade; first he had to ensure the stability of the realm.[44] He negotiated a treaty with Hugh of La Marche against the English in Poitou; received the homage of Hugh's brother, Geoffrey of Lusignan; and renewed the truce with Aimery of Thouars.[45] Then, in summer 1224, he himself led a great French army out to the west. Members of the Capetian household and entourage such as Brother Guérin, Bartholomew of Roye, Ours the Chamberlain, Walter Cornut, archbishop of Sens, the constable Matthew of Montmorency, Adam of Beaumont and Guy of Méréville came, as did many of the great magnates – Philip Hurepel, Theobald of Champagne, Robert of Dreux and Peter Mauclerc, the counts of Blois and Chartres, Guy of Saint-Pol, Enguerrand of Coucy and Archibald of Bourbon – together with a large number of bishops. John of Brienne, king of Jerusalem, who had just brought Blanche's niece, Berengaria of Castile-León, back to Paris as his wife, lent additional heroic lustre to Louis's forces.[46]

Perhaps Louis had in mind a great victory in battle to set alongside his father's victory at Bouvines. The English forces were too wily for that, and Louis had some difficulty in holding his great army together. At Tours, the Norman bishops of Coutances, Avranches and Lisieux left, taking their contingents with them: they had fulfilled their allotted forty days service, and were under no obligation to continue.[47] Later, Theobald of Champagne, too, pointed out that he and his troops had fulfilled their obligations; but Louis managed to persuade Theobald to stay.[48] Indeed, Theobald helped Louis to develop an anti-English alliance with his cousin, the king of Navarre.[49]

In July Louis invested the great port city of La Rochelle. It was, as English chroniclers like Matthew Paris acknowledged, the key to English control of Poitou, so had great strategic importance.[50] The Angevins, especially Richard the Lionheart, had expended much on its economic development and its fortification. It began to look as though the fortifications would hold against Louis's impotent attacks. It

was at this point that Theobald of Champagne announced his intention to go home.

Louis, as he once again confronted military disaster, looked to his wife for help. Blanche did not try to raise more troops: this time she tried to enlist God's help, staging a great performance of public penitential theatre in Paris. She was accompanied by her niece, Berengaria of Castile-León, queen of Jerusalem, and by Queen Ingeborg. The three queens walked in solemn procession with the citizens of Paris, praying and weeping, from the cathedral of Notre-Dame on the Ile de la Cité to the Cistercian nunnery of Saint-Antoine-des-Champs outside the walls of Paris, in the fields to the east. There, they prostrated themselves before the high altar, praying that God would bring victory to Louis, as He had to his father. It worked. The next day Louis took La Rochelle.[51]

Perhaps Blanche had taken to heart chroniclers' comments that the destruction of the great fleet she had assembled in 1217 was the judgement of God. Perhaps this time, she took care to pre-empt that judgement. If her prayers for divine intervention failed to work, a display of penitence for sins that involved the people of Paris meant that that failure could be recast, not as Louis's lack of ability as a military leader, but as the judgement of God on the people of Capetian France. And here was the queen of France, supported by her fellow queens, interceding with God for her people, as the Queen of Heaven intercedes with God for all people. Blanche was fulfilling her role as queen consort. In the absence of the king, it fell to her to lead their people. The assurance with which she fulfilled that role is striking. So is the sophisticated inventiveness of the ceremony. The emphasis on penitence was in tune with reformist theology and the canons of Lateran iv. There are close parallels with the penitential ceremonies that marked the reception of the Crown of Thorns in 1239 – which was displayed to the people at Saint-Antoine before it was carried into the city of Paris. Blanche played a pivotal role in its acquisition, and those ceremonies were almost certainly inspired by the intercession of 1224.[52]

Louis returned in triumph. In thanks for his victory, he gave a wealthy citizen of La Rochelle to Stephen Langton, the archbishop of Canterbury, on account of Louis's deep devotion to Thomas Becket.[53] Perhaps to thank his wife for her support, in late 1224 or early 1225 he confirmed, at Blanche's request, the lands that she had been given as dower at her marriage, Bapaume, Lens and Hesdin.[54]

Around the same time, Blanche and Louis made arrangements to support chaplains to celebrate anniversary Masses for their eldest son, Philip, whom they had

had buried in Notre-Dame in Paris, alongside Louis's mother, Isabella of Hainault. Young Philip had been dead for at least six years, but the altar at which he would be commemorated was in the nave of the great cathedral, which had emerged from the scaffolding of construction only recently. Louis and Blanche would choose the chaplain during their lifetimes; after their deaths, the appointment would be made by the cathedral chapter. The altar was dedicated to St John the Baptist and St Thomas Becket.[55]

In June 1225 Louis made a will.[56] It is possible that an unrecorded illness precipitated this. More likely, he was already planning the Crusade against the Albigensians; and, in spite of his triumph at La Rochelle, Henry III and his allies had not given up. Moreover, Louis and Blanche now had a large number of young sons, all of whom would need providing for. Louis left 30,000 *livres* to Blanche and 20,000 to their only surviving daughter, Isabella, then aged three months. To his oldest son (Louis), he left the kingdom, with the riches to rule it. For his other sons, he established territories to support them, out of some of the new lands that had come to the French crown in the last forty years. The second son (Robert) was to have Artois and the other lands inherited from Isabella of Hainault, apart from those lands reserved for Blanche's dower during her lifetime. The third son (at this point, John) was to hold the counties of Anjou and Maine; the fourth son (at this point, Alphonse) was to have the counties of Poitou and Auvergne; other sons were to enter the Church. As was expected, Louis left substantial amounts of money to the Church, particularly to hospitals and leper houses, to Premonstratensian and Victorine canons, and to the Cistercians. He commanded that his own crowns and jewels should be sold to found a new Victorine house, like his father's foundation of La Victoire.

It was all very well to leave Poitou and Auvergne to his fourth son in his will. The triumph of La Rochelle had not secured Poitou for France. In April 1225 Louis wrote to the pope to complain about the English in Poitou, and he had to spend much of that summer campaigning, once again, in the Loire, keeping his anti-Angevin alliances intact.[57] Henry III had made his energetic younger brother, Richard of Cornwall, count of Poitou, and had sent him to Gascony. Louis dispatched Hugh of Lusignan against him, but Richard defeated Hugh at La Réole.[58]

The careful provision for his sons in his will may have reflected the problems of providing for his younger brother, Philip Hurepel, and some of the Capetian cousins. Louis had appointed Robert of Courtenay to the great household office of butler, and with that Robert was content. He had given Philip Hurepel control

of the lands that he inherited through Matilda of Boulogne, except for certain castles, soon after his accession to the throne. Robert of Dreux and, in particular, Peter of Dreux were causes for concern. Both had married heiresses to Anglo-French territories, so both could reasonably claim to have lost out on English lands that would, pre-1204, have been theirs. Henry III gave both of them money fiefs in recompense, and made particular efforts to cultivate Peter of Dreux, who had married the heiress to Brittany, once a part of the Angevin world and adjacent to the old Angevin heartland of Normandy. By October 1225 Peter of Dreux had secretly betrothed his daughter, Yolande, to Henry III.[59] Louis was sufficiently concerned in June 1225 to buy Robert of Dreux's loyalty with some extra properties – but to forbid him to fortify them.[60] In February 1226 he gave Peter of Dreux lands along the southern edge of Normandy: Bellême, La Perrière and Saint-James. But then, in April 1226, Louis discovered that Peter, now a widower and now merely guardian of Brittany during the minority of his young son, was negotiating to marry Countess Joanna of Flanders. Peter had tried to persuade the pope to annul Joanna's marriage to Ferdinand of Flanders, who had been languishing now for twelve years in Capetian prisons.[61]

Louis was horrified. If possession of Brittany gave Peter of Dreux reason and opportunity to toy with alliances with Henry III, possession of the county of Flanders, with its close economic links to England, would do so all the more. Two years earlier Louis had rejected papal suggestions that he should free Ferdinand of Flanders.[62] But now he drew up a convention with Countess Joanna, agreeing to release him. Joanna had to agree to remain married to Ferdinand, and to pay a huge sum in relief to Louis. She had little choice: she already owed a substantial debt, both actual and metaphorical, to Louis, who had supported her the previous year, when the false Baldwin threatened her rights to the county of Flanders.[63] And so, in April 1226 the complex convention, with all its accompanying securities, was ratified at Melun.[64] As one of Ferdinand's Iberian cousins, with material interests in the Franco-Flemish border zones, Blanche probably played a role in the negotiations, perhaps encouraging Joanna to agree to the heavy demands of the treaty.

With the stability of the realm assured, Louis could apply all his energies and determination to the organisation of the Crusade against the Albigensians. He drove a hard bargain with the Church to fund it. He took care to ensure that potentially fractious magnates came too, and that his lands had Church protection against outside attack while he was on Crusade. He also ensured that territories gained in the course of a successful campaign would come to the king of France.[65]

Louis used people he trusted, such as Bishop Walter of Chartres and John of Brienne, king of Jerusalem, to argue his case in Rome.[66] This was very different from the two knightly *chevauchées* Louis had led south as prince. The careful diplomatic and logistical preparation is reminiscent of Philip Augustus's campaigns against the Angevins and their allies. Louis's pursuit of the Crusade was not just motivated by concerns about heresy. He knew that Raymond VII of Toulouse was apt to ally himself with his cousin, Henry III. Control of the county of Toulouse would strengthen Louis's position against the Angevins.[67]

Nevertheless, the pope had realised that Louis would undertake the Crusade only if all his demands for protection and funding were met, and that the French Church could be persuaded to fund it only by a seasoned and sophisticated papal negotiator. In spring 1225 he dispatched Romanus Frangipani, cardinal of Sant'Angelo, as papal legate to France. Cardinal Romanus was in many ways an inspired choice. He was said to be a distant relation of Louis himself. He had been educated at the Paris schools. He was cultured, sophisticated and deeply interested in the new Aristotelian knowledge of the natural world emerging from Toledo. He had commissioned the great scholar Michael Scot to translate into Latin the works of the Arab-influenced Jewish philosopher and scientist Maimonides.[68] Along with Blanche and Bishop Bartholomew of Paris, Romanus was a supporter of the new house of Dominicans in the city. Both Louis and Blanche found him sympathetic: after Louis's death there were rumours that Blanche found him too sympathetic. His Achilles heel was his arrogance.[69]

The first clear indication of Louis's commitment to the Crusade project came as late as November 1225, when he asked Theobald of Champagne to bring Count Raymond VII of Toulouse, under safe conduct, to a planned Church council at Bourges;[70] by implication, planning had already reached an advanced stage. In early 1226 Louis and Romanus's diplomacy brought the desired results. With Blanche's consent, Louis took the Cross at Paris on 30 January.[71] As Simon of Montfort's son, Amaury of Montfort once again resigned all his lands and rights to the county of Toulouse to the king of France.[72] The conditions on which Louis would undertake the Crusade were agreed by the Church. The French Church voted him a tithe to fund the Crusade, and the pope promised protection for the king and the kingdom of France.[73] The magnates of France formally asked the king to attack the southern heretics, and promised their support in doing so. In April 1226 Louis issued an ordinance against the heretics.[74] In May Romanus convened the great ecclesiastical council at Bourges.[75] Raymond VII of Toulouse was declared forfeit

of his lands, for failing to extirpate heresy within them. Accompanied by the bulk of the great prelates, and all the important magnates of France, Louis set off directly from Bourges for the south. The Crusaders included Philip Hurepel and Louis's cousins, Robert of Courtenay, Philip of Namur, Peter of Brittany and Imbert of Beaujeu; Louis's close associates such as Guy of Saint-Pol, Stephen of Sancerre, Brother Guérin, Walter Cornut, archbishop of Sens, and Amaury of Montfort, Matthew of Montmorency and his cousin, Bouchard of Marly; barons like Enguerrand of Coucy and Archibald of Bourbon; and several prelates including the archbishop of Reims, the bishops of Beauvais and Chartres and the abbot of Saint-Denis. Blanche watched Louis go in deep distress.[76] Matthew Paris, always well informed about English court gossip, claimed that Henry III, frustrated that Louis's lands were now under papal protection, was heartened by the predictions of his court astrologer, William of Pierrepont: if Louis set out for the south of France, he would never return alive.[77]

The Crusade travelled through Lyon and then down the Rhône valley. Louis wrote to inform his ally, Emperor Frederick II, that he would be traversing imperial territory. Once in the south, Louis spent three months besieging the city of Avignon, which he finally took on 9 September 1226. The city, divided between the counts of Toulouse and the counts of Provence, had become an easy refuge for Cathars.[78] There, Louis's close companion Guy of Châtillon, count of Saint-Pol, was killed, hit on the head by a stone. Louis mourned his friend, and swore to carry his heart back for burial in his north French homelands.[79] After the fall of Avignon, the southern nobles began to join Louis, and he moved south-west through the Cathar heartlands of Béziers, Carcassonne, Pamiers, Castelnaudary and Puylaurens to the south of Toulouse. But it was now too late in the year to invest Toulouse itself, and Louis turned his army north to return to Capetian territories.[80]

There was already trouble with some of the greater magnates. Peter of Brittany had come to an agreement with Hugh of Lusignan in the high summer, and was still pursuing his negotiations with Henry III, including the betrothal to him of his daughter Yolande. Theobald of Champagne may have been involved in the conspiracy with Peter and Hugh. Both Theobald and Peter arrived late at the siege of Avignon.[81] Theobald was certainly disaffected. At Avignon, he declared that he had fulfilled the demands of his military obligations towards the king, and that he would retire, with his troops, back to Champagne.[82] King and count had a furious argument. Soon, there were rumours that Theobald was trying to poison the

king – and that the two men hated each other, because Theobald was having an affair with Blanche. The wild rumours travelled widely and fast, and were picked up by English chroniclers, though Matthew Paris, to his credit, did not really believe them.[83]

Many in Louis's army were certainly ill; dysentery spread easily among the northern troops in the hot southern summer weather, especially during the lengthy siege of Avignon.[84] As the army marched north, William of Joinville, archbishop of Reims, Philip of Courtenay, count of Namur, and Bouchard of Marly all died of it. Then Louis himself sickened. When the army reached Montpensier, it was clear that Louis was very ill indeed. He called his magnates and prelates before him. In his presence, they witnessed and sealed a charter in which they undertook, should he die, that for the stability of the kingdom they would have his young son and heir, Louis, crowned king, as stipulated in Louis VIII's will.[85] As he worsened, he called three of his closest allies in the Church, Walter Cornut, archbishop of Sens, Walter, bishop of Chartres, and Miles, bishop of Beauvais, a cousin of Guy of Châtillon. With the three as witnesses, he consigned the control and wardship – the *ballia* and *tutela* – of his son, the future king, and of the kingdom itself, to his wife, Blanche of Castile.[86] On 8 November 1226 he died. His companions carried his body, salted for preservation, back towards Paris. Blanche, unaware of his death, set out with her children to greet a king returning in victory, and found herself faced with his funeral cortège. Louis was taken on to Saint-Denis, where he was buried next to his father.[87]

4

Queen Regent

BLANCHE WAS DEVASTATED BY LOUIS'S DEATH. She wept so much it was feared she might go mad.[1] She was thirty-eight, and pregnant with her youngest son, Charles. But she could not afford the luxury of grief. The first priority was the coronation of her oldest surviving son, Louis, which was to take place on the vigil of the feast of St Andrew, 29 November 1226, the first Sunday in Advent. A group of twelve bishops and barons of France sent out letters summoning the magnates and prelates of the kingdom to the ceremony. The letters to the bishops of Burgundy and Normandy, and the administrators and lords of Normandy and Anjou, survive.[2] On their way to Reims, the royal party stopped at Soissons, where Louis was knighted.[3]

As the court returned to Reims, Blanche must have remembered her own, still-recent and notoriously expensive coronation. Her son's coronation must have been less magnificent, for the king was very young, and there was no queen to crown. The English chronicler Matthew Paris claims that Blanche had to rush it through to avoid danger to the crown.[4] In fact, it was no more rushed than the previous coronation, since both took place three weeks after the death of the previous king. The cathedral was still a building site. The archbishop of Reims had also died on the return from the Albigensian Crusade, so Louis IX was crowned and anointed by the bishop of Soissons, James of Bazoches, the senior suffragan bishop of the province of Reims, assisted by the cardinal legate. The patriarch of Jerusalem enhanced the ecclesiastical contingent; King John and Queen Berengaria of Jerusalem were present too. The countesses of Flanders and Champagne squabbled

over the honour of carrying the sword before the king; in the event the sword was carried, as it had been three years earlier, by Philip of Boulogne. Some of the magnates did not attend, notably Theobald of Champagne and Peter Mauclerc – though Peter's brother, Count Robert of Dreux, was present. In Peter's case, this was clearly a snub. Theobald, according to Philip Mousquès, had every intention of taking his place, but Blanche could not face seeing the man who was said to have poisoned her husband so soon after his death. She ordered the officials of the city to close their gates to the count and throw out his advance entourage with the comital baggage.[5] Those who had issued the summonses to the coronation – Walter Cornut, archbishop of Sens, the archbishop of Bourges, and the bishops of Beauvais, Noyon and Chartres, together with Philip Hurepel, the counts of Blois and Montfort, Enguerrand of Coucy, Archibald of Bourbon, John of Nesle and Stephen of Sancerre – all attended. Walter Cornut, together with bishops Miles of Beauvais and Walter of Chartres, had witnessed Louis VIII's assignment of the control and wardship of king and kingdom to Blanche, and most of the lay signatories of the coronation summons had been longstanding companions-in-arms of Louis VIII.

There was no real threat or challenge to the status of young Louis as king. He had been designated by his father in his will, and the Capetian line had descended from father to son since 987. But when power was personal, minority government was always contested government. Magnates like Theobald of Champagne and Peter Mauclerc, who had been chafing under the heavy fists of Philip Augustus and Louis VIII, would certainly take advantage of the minority to push claims to additional land and power as far as they could, and protect themselves against what they saw as royal encroachment on their lordships. Others who were fundamentally loyal to the Capetians would still see a minority as an opportunity to bolster their positions. Peter Mauclerc was already exploiting Henry III's desires to regain the Angevin lands as a lever of personal power: he would not let slip the opportunity offered by a minority. All this could be expected.

Blanche's status as guardian and custodian of king and kingdom was another matter. There were no established norms for regency, whether in the case of a minority or when the king was out of the country on Crusade. The only previous Capetian to have succeeded as a minor was Philip I in 1060. The realm was ruled during his minority by his uncle by marriage, Count Baldwin of Flanders, probably with some assistance from Philip's mother, Anna of Kiev.[6] Arrangements for Crusading regencies had varied. Philip Augustus had left the country in the

guardianship of his mother, Adela of Champagne, her brother, the archbishop of Reims, and six prominent Paris merchants, who supervised the financial accounts.[7] During the Second Crusade, the regents, 'elected' under the influence of Bernard of Clairvaux, were an unlikely, and not very successful triumvirate: Abbot Suger of Saint-Denis, the archbishop of Reims and Louis VII's cousin Ralph of Vermandois.[8] No powers were vested in Louis VII's mother, Queen Adela of Maurienne. The great principalities had a stronger tradition of leaving power in the hands of an absent prince's wife or a minor prince's mother. Recent notable examples were the successive countesses of Champagne, Mary of France and Blanche of Navarre. But leaving the kingdom in the hands of the queen alone was novel. (At least in France, though there was the recent example of Margaret of Navarre in Sicily.) At the very least, one might have expected her to hold power jointly with a prominent churchman. The archbishop of Reims was the traditional choice – but William of Joinville had died shortly before Louis, on the return from the Albigensian Crusade. It is surprising that Walter Cornut was not appointed joint regent.

Walter Cornut was, of course, one of the three episcopal witnesses of Louis VIII's appointment of Blanche as sole regent.[9] It is difficult to know how far this document can be taken at face value. Was Louis VIII well enough to make his intentions clear or was the letter concocted by the three bishops? Either way, it suggests that Louis and/or the bishops thought that there might be more challenge to Walter Cornut than to Blanche as regent. It also suggests that Louis and/or the bishops had considerable confidence in Blanche's ability to handle the challenges of power.

There certainly were challenges to the regency from the French baronage. Political songs of the day accused Blanche of sending money to Spain, and accused both Blanche and Walter Cornut of preferring the men of Spain to the barons of France.[10] They accused Blanche of keeping young Louis unmarried so that she could remain in power, and accused her of being the mistress of, variously, Theobald of Champagne and Cardinal Romanus Frangipani.[11] Like most regents, Blanche would have to make concessions and obtain by diplomacy what a king would have obtained by command.

The narrative of Louis's minority produced by all his biographers, Geoffrey of Beaulieu, William of Nangis and Joinville, is a dramatic one, of terrible threat to Blanche's rule, and even to the king himself. All of them were writing long after the events, but all of them knew many of the protagonists, and reported first-hand accounts from Louis himself. The same dramatic story is told by the contemporary

chroniclers, the Flemish Philip Mousquès, the English Roger of Wendover and Matthew Paris, and the slightly later Ménestrel of Reims. But there are problems with all these sources. Their chronology of events is unclear and sometimes contradictory. Wendover may have had some information from those who campaigned with Richard Marshall alongside the most fractious of the French barons, Peter Mauclerc; at all events, Wendover's account, while a splendid source of French 'baronial' gossip, is not always reliable as to facts.[12] Matthew Paris, reworking Wendover's text, could not resist the baronial gossip, though he often dismissed it as lurid rumour. Of the contemporary French chroniclers, Philip Mousquès was well informed on French court gossip from a Flemish perspective, but his chronology is confused. The Ménestrel of Reims' court gossip was more second-hand, and his main aim was to entertain: his chronology is more even more confused. St Louis's biographers tend to collapse together events that happened over a long time span, while Joinville, as seneschal of Champagne, was particularly concerned with events in and affecting that county. For all these sources, the narrative of the valiant widowed queen protecting her young son against the powerful wicked barons of France was irresistible. Indeed, it is clear from Louis's reminiscences, as reported by his biographers, that it had become the family's own narrative.

But it is a dramatization and an oversimplification. Many French magnates remained loyal. Those who proved particularly fractious had already been so under Louis VIII. The most consistent plotter of all, Peter Mauclerc, count of Brittany, continued his conspiracies long after St Louis had reached his majority; and Theobald of Champagne's major revolt occurred under Louis's personal kingship. Private war remained endemic in France, though Louis tried to outlaw it, to the disgust of his barons, in 1258.[13] Blanche faced a continual need to control marriage alliances that might lead to dangerous power blocs – but that had been true in the previous two reigns, and continued to be an issue after Louis attained his majority. Much of the worst trouble was not aimed at toppling Blanche's status as guardian of the realm; it was a series of attacks against Theobald of Champagne. The succession to Champagne had long been an issue, as had the border zone between Champagne and Burgundy. Blanche and Louis intervened, for the king (or his regent) should ensure peace within his realm, and they did so with reasonable success.[14] The exact chronology of the troubles is difficult to establish, but it seems that, after a difficult few months, stability had been restored by March 1227. In summer 1229 came the major attack on Champagne by members of the Burgundian aristocracy together with various related allies – though the fact that their relations

included Peter of Brittany gave it a dangerous edge, for Peter was also plotting an
invasion from England with Henry III. By summer 1230 it was clear that had failed,
and although Peter of Brittany made war in western Normandy and the western
Loire in most subsequent campaigning seasons until 1236, he was increasingly
isolated. After 1230 he was an irritant rather than a threat to the Capetian
kingship.

Joinville makes much of Blanche being a foreigner, from Spain, 'who had neither
relatives nor friends in all the kingdom of France'.[15] This was untrue. She had both
friends and relatives on whom she could depend. The friendship and patronage
networks that she had developed since her arrival in France, as the Lady Blanche
and as queen consort, now supported her. The administrators, both lay and ecclesiastical, who had worked so closely with her husband, and who were in many
cases inherited from Philip Augustus, notably Bishop Guérin of Senlis (until his
death in April 1227), Walter Cornut, archbishop of Sens, and his relations, the
Clément family, Bartholomew of Roye, the chamberlain, and Matthew of
Montmorency, the constable, proved intensely loyal.[16] It was in their interests to
support the Capetian crown, from which they derived their power and prestige.
They might have been slightly cool in support of a queen regent, but they were
not. Like her husband, Blanche could rely on the support of the aristocracy of the
north-east, where her dower lands lay, such as Michael of Harnes, Arnold of
Audenarde and John of Nesle, and on some of the most important reformist
churchmen, notably the Cistercian bishop Walter of Chartres.[17] She made the loyal,
and partly Spanish, Theobald of Blaison seneschal of the politically sensitive
Poitou.[18] The important Angevin families of Craon and Des Roches supported the
Capetians, as did the rich city of La Rochelle.[19] Many of the great barons, too,
were faithful, notably Stephen of Sancerre, John of Nesle, Amaury of Montfort
and the counts of Blois and Chartres. The last two held their counties through
their wives, the sister countesses Margaret of Blois and Isabella of Chartres, who
were members of the Capetian family and cousins of Blanche herself.

Although control of the baronage, and thus the imposition of peace in the realm,
was vitally important, it was by no means Blanche's only concern as guardian of
the kingdom. She developed her husband's initiatives against usury with statutes
to regulate Jewish lending. The settlement of Languedoc, the cause in which her
husband had died, was also profoundly important for her. For the funding to
pursue the Albigensian Crusade, she was prepared to challenge the north French

Church. Despite her piety, she was, like her husband, conscious of the importance of royal rights, and would not brook their infringement. Much of her time and energy was absorbed by a series of clashes with the Church in protection of royal rights, and she was never afraid that her firmness might alienate ecclesiastical support. She was unafraid of alienating important sections of the Church community when there were clashes within that community; unlike Philip Augustus, she took on the University of Paris. The standard narrative of her regency as dominated by baronial revolt is much in need of revision. Nevertheless, dealing with the magnates, and ensuring the peace of the realm, must have been her first concern, and so this will be discussed first, before returning to her relations with the Church.

•

Although Philip Hurepel played an important role in ensuring the coronation of his nephew, he, more than any other great magnate, might have expected to be appointed a joint regent. Capetian cousins, especially the family of the counts of Dreux, might also hold such pretensions. Baronial opposition to Blanche quickly crystallised around Philip Hurepel and the ever-intriguing Peter of Dreux, count of Brittany.[20] In December 1226 Blanche tried to buy the support of Philip and Robert of Dreux, giving some Norman lands to Robert and not only confirming the extensive honours of Philip Hurepel, but also conferring on him the fief of the county of Saint-Pol.[21] But many barons felt that their claims to lands were not satisfied by Blanche. They assembled at Corbeil, acclaimed Philip Hurepel as their leader, and plotted a rebellion led by Peter of Brittany.[22] As the barons plotted at Corbeil, Blanche and young Louis took refuge in the castle of Montlhéry, safe on its precipitous hill between Corbeil and Paris. Many years later, Louis told Joinville that the royal party had been too terrified to return to Paris, until the people of Paris came out to Montlhéry to save them and escorted them back to the city. Louis recalled the road thronged with people, many armed, calling on God to protect the king.[23]

Doubtless Blanche knew that Philip Hurepel and Peter of Dreux would always look to their own interests. It was to her advantage that the two great barons did not really have the same aims. Philip must have wanted the regency, but his interests would not be served by a weakening of the Capetian family. Peter of Dreux, however, as count of Brittany in right of his wife, and thus potential lord of

extensive Anglo-Norman honours, stood to gain considerably if Henry III were able to reconquer the old Angevin lands of Normandy, Anjou, Maine and northern Poitou lost in 1204–6.

Louis VIII had initiated the release of Count Ferdinand of Flanders to prevent the marriage of Countess Joanna with Peter of Brittany.[24] Immediately she took control of the realm, Blanche pushed through the complex set of treaties and securities ratifying the release, though on slightly more generous terms than had been negotiated under Louis VIII, which reflected the relative weakness of a minority government. She made sure that the sureties preceded the release, and Ferdinand paid the high price of 5,000 marks for his liberty.[25] Many of the initial sureties were provided by the men and towns of Artois and the north-east, from the areas with which both Louis VIII and Blanche had had long connections, thus reinforcing Blanche's power networks in this area. Heavy ecclesiastical sanctions against Ferdinand and Joanna, should they break the treaty, had been arranged by Louis; Blanche insisted that Joanna got papal recognition of them. Amaury of Montfort, standing pledge for this aspect of the arrangement, announced that the ecclesiastical sanctions arranged by Blanche were better in form than those produced by Louis VIII, though the meaning of this elliptical phrase is unclear.[26] Ferdinand was Blanche's cousin, a fellow Iberian, and he and Joanna proved loyal to Blanche.

Support came too, perhaps unexpectedly, from Theobald of Champagne. Again, Theobald was a close relation of Blanche's, son of her cousin, Blanche of Navarre. Indeed, far from being a lone Spanish woman in France, as Joinville claimed, Blanche made active use of her Iberian cousins, as the baronial political songs complained.[27] English chroniclers like Wendover and Matthew Paris had ascribed Theobald's quarrel with Louis to his illicit passion for Blanche, but even they seem to have realised that this was really no more than a courtly game. Contemporaries thought that he openly addressed some of his *chansons*, his courtly poems, to her.[28] Theobald probably did admire Blanche, and she, as a consummate politician, was doubtless prepared to exploit his affection for her. Theobald's actions were dictated – from his point of view, justifiably – by the interests of his county of Champagne. Occasionally, he judged those best served by an alliance with Peter of Brittany; later, in the mid-1230s, he would rebel outright against Louis IX. Theobald's political judgement was uncertain, and he suffered from a growing reputation for vacillation. He was not a reliable ally, but he was often a needy and thus a malleable one, since he alienated most of his fellow magnates.[29]

It was Theobald's forces that enabled Blanche to force Peter of Brittany and Philip Hurepel to terms at the Treaty of Vendôme in March 1227. Blanche mustered a large force, and moved through Tours, Chinon and Loudun. The diplomacy, according to the Tours chronicler, took twenty days; in the end Peter came to terms because he thought everyone was laughing at him. Blanche was clearly an enterprising diplomat.[30] The self-interested Philip Hurepel was bought off with a gratifyingly large annual income.[31] Peter of Brittany was forced to depend on 'la merci le roi' – the king's mercy, according to Joinville.[32] The crucial issue was the prevention of the projected marriage alliance between Peter and Henry III. The marriage of Peter's daughter, Yolande, to Henry III was expressly forbidden by the treaty; instead, Yolande would be affianced to Blanche's young son John, count of Maine and Anjou. Philip Hurepel would hold Yolande as ward, until the children were old enough to marry. At the same time, a settlement was negotiated for Hugh of Lusignan, count of La Marche, and his wife, Isabella of Angoulême, Henry III's mother.[33] To ensure their continuing adherence to the Capetian side, Blanche was prepared to offer another of her children as a marriage pawn, in this case, her infant daughter Isabella, who would be affianced to the son and heir of Hugh and Isabella of Angoulême.[34] Soon Hugh of Thouars, an associate of the Lusignans, came to do homage to young Louis, and Richard of Cornwall, Henry III's brother, agreed to a truce.[35] The English threat was, for the moment, neutralised. Blanche's counsellor, Bishop Walter of Chartres, played, alongside Walter Cornut, a prominent role in the negotiations behind the Treaty of Vendôme, and it is likely that this rare coming together of Blanche and Louis, Philip Hurepel and Peter of Brittany as an extended Capetian family was celebrated in the great glass windows in the north and south transepts of Chartres Cathedral (pl. 1).[36]

Some of Bishop Walter's lands and fortresses had been seized by the viscountess of Châteaudun during the revolt. In May 1227 Blanche ordered the viscountess to return them. The act in which she does so survives; it gives a vivid insight as to how Blanche ruled. Blanche reminds the viscountess that she has already ordered the return of the properties, both by written mandate and 'also by speaking *viva voce*'. Since that has had no effect, Blanche and her son have held a council with the barons of France. It is now agreed that Blanche will make the viscountess return the properties by force, unless she does so immediately.[37] Two things are striking. One is the personal nature of power: there have been face-to-face confrontations. The other is that Blanche used the barons in council to give extra

legitimacy to her use of coercive force. She always had enough baronial support to be able to make this use of them – she would do so to drive Peter Mauclerc into a corner in 1230. But the fact that she felt the need to have the counsel of the barons probably reflects her relative weakness at the start of her regency.

Theobald IV of Champagne had almost as much need of Blanche's support as she had of his. His own right to the county of Champagne remained open to challenge. Theobald's father was a younger brother, who had succeeded as count of Champagne after the elder brother, Count Henry, went on Crusade and married the queen of Jerusalem. Count Henry had two daughters from his second marriage: Alice, queen of Cyprus, and Philippine, married to a Champenois noble, Everard of Brienne. Both women advanced claims to the county of Champagne from time to time. Philip Augustus had held the claim at bay during Theobald's minority, in return for a substantial payment. The claims of Philippine and Everard of Brienne were provisionally settled in July 1227, doubtless helped by the fact that Everard's brother was John, the king of Jerusalem and a close ally of Louis VIII, and the husband of Blanche's niece, Berengaria.[38]

After the treaties of Vendôme, Blanche had a couple of years of respite from problems with the barons. Henry III of England had troubles of his own, and a truce was arranged with him in June 1228.[39] The Poitevin nobility, including Hugh of La Marche and Hugh of Thouars, continued to see their interests best served by Capetian alliance, and came to do homage periodically.[40] Blanche was able to focus instead on pursuing her husband's aims in south-western France. By June 1228 Pope Gregory IX had agreed to the clearly consanguineous marriage of Blanche's son Alphonse with Joanna, heiress to the county of Toulouse.[41] South-western lords and cities, like the lord of Comminges and the city of Limoges, came to do homage to young Louis.[42] A small French force remained in the south-west, under the command of Louis VIII's highly effective cousin Imbert of Beaujeu.[43] But a new impetus was required, and would be as costly as the last had been. The north French Church was no keener to provide a Crusade tithe for Blanche than it had been for her husband. Blanche's demands for a new Crusade were actively supported by the papacy. The papal legate, Cardinal Romanus, who had played such an important role in implementing Louis VIII's last Crusade, quickly became one of Blanche's most trusted advisers. Soon rumours of an inappropriate relationship between the queen and the cardinal were circulating, to join those of her illicit romance with Theobald of Champagne.[44]

The north French Church regarded the demands for the Crusading tithe as papal greed. Romanus himself was widely perceived as arrogant. But Blanche was every bit as determined as Romanus to press for the new Crusade: she must fulfil her husband's unfinished business; besides, the Crusade chimed with her own athletic faith. Like her husband, she saw the political advantages of ensuring that Toulouse was attached to Capetian France rather than Angevin Gascony. However, it placed her on a collision course with the north French Church, at a time when she could have done with their friendship, and it took all the political acumen of Walter Cornut and Bishop Walter of Chartres to reconcile the Church and the queen in late summer 1227.[45] The bishop of Mâcon did not pay his contribution towards the expedition until March 1229.[46] Matthew Paris claimed that the expedition to the south was a failure; but it succeeded well enough to persuade Raymond of Toulouse to sue for peace.[47]

In April 1229 terms of peace with Raymond of Toulouse were agreed, and the marriage of Alphonse and Joanna of Toulouse arranged, in the Treaty of Paris. In June Raymond himself came to ratify the treaty, at Blanche and Louis's favoured old residence at Lorris.[48] Romanus played a role in the negotiations, as did Peter of Collemezzo, chaplain of Pope Gregory IX, who was probably already well known to Louis VIII and to Blanche, since he was a canon of their town of Saint-Omer. Theobald of Champagne, who was a cousin of Raymond's, was also involved.[49] Apart from the marriage of his daughter, Raymond agreed to compensate southern monasteries for damage, to set up at his own expense a new university at Toulouse to teach the true faith, and to do liege homage and fidelity to the king, 'according to the customs of the barons of France'.[50]

The treaty with Raymond proved remarkably resilient. It was an excellent settlement for Blanche's son Alphonse; Raymond may have felt it was equally appropriate for his daughter, Joanna. The counts of Toulouse had tended to ally with the Angevins, not least because the trade routes of the rivers Lot and Garonne reached the sea through Angevin Gascony. But trade routes to the north and Paris had developed; besides, thirteenth-century England had to get its wine from somewhere. Raymond was Blanche's first cousin, as well as Henry III's; perhaps he found more in common with his Spanish cousin than his English one. At all events he came quite often to the Capetian court, where his daughter Joanna now lived, and developed a close friendship with Blanche.[51]

Toulouse was adjacent to Gascony, and Henry III of England cannot have regarded the alliance of Capetians and Toulouse with equanimity. There was already

some disaffection in the former Angevin lands in France. In December 1228 the archbishop of Bordeaux and a handful of Normans, most from western Normandy – an area that had not gained obviously from the Capetian conquest – invited Henry III to invade.[52] This was too tempting for Peter of Brittany. By summer 1229 he himself was encouraging Henry to recapture Normandy and the old Angevin lands, and by the end of the year Peter was in open revolt, supported by a small group of lords from south-west Normandy, led by Fulk Paynel.[53] But before trouble in the west escalated, the peace of the kingdom was shattered by war in the east – a concerted attack on the unloved Theobald of Champagne.

Theobald had agreed to marry Peter of Brittany's daughter, Yolande, in a secret ceremony at the aptly named Premonstratensian abbey of Le Val-Secret. Yolande was held in wardship by Philip Hurepel in preparation for her eventual marriage to Blanche's younger son, John, according to the terms of the Treaty of Vendôme, and Philip was presumably complicit in the secret marriage. Somehow Blanche and her advisers heard. A loyal and able court official, Geoffrey de la Chapelle, was sent to intercept Theobald with a letter from the king forbidding the marriage. It would have been open rebellion to disobey.[54] But Peter of Brittany felt that he and his daughter had been humiliated. Peter had relations in Burgundy, where his brother John was count of Mâcon and his niece was married to Hugh IV, duke of Burgundy. It was easy to persuade them to attack in the border zone between Champagne and Burgundy, and in the summer of 1229 a coalition of Peter, his brother, Robert of Dreux, and his powerful Burgundian relatives, together with Philip Hurepel and several other members of the aristocracy who thought they might take advantage of Theobald's often ill-defined frontiers, invaded Champagne. The magnates invoked once again the festering issue of the Champagne succession – this time pressing the claims of Alice, queen of Cyprus. Indeed, Peter of Brittany toyed with the possibility of marrying Alice, and thus adding the county of Champagne to his portfolio of possessions.[55]

Theobald seemed powerless to repel the invasion, and turned in despair to Blanche and young Louis, who went to Troyes to impose peace, and did indeed stabilise the southern, Burgundian border zone.[56] Meanwhile, Pope Gregory IX, presumably at Blanche's behest, issued papal letters forbidding the marriage of Peter of Brittany and Alice of Cyprus.[57] War in the east of the kingdom continued in a desultory fashion for the rest of the year, with the duke of Lorraine and Ferdinand of Flanders supporting Theobald against Peter Mauclerc's extended family coalition. In March 1230 Theobald was still at war with the duke of Burgundy.[58]

Archibald of Bourbon helped to stabilise the areas to the west of Burgundy, ostensibly on behalf of the king, though doubtless to his own advantage.[59] Eventually, Alice of Cyprus was bought off, with the help of Blanche and Louis, in a complex set of treaties that transferred the counties of Blois, Chartres and Sancerre and the viscounty of Châteaudun from Theobald's overlordship to that of the king.[60]

Blanche cannot have welcomed the war against Champagne. Inter-baronial squabbles were endemic, but war on this scale threatened to undermine the fundamental royal duty to enforce peace in the realm. The English chronicler Wendover saw it as a direct attack on Blanche herself, and reported that it was said that the invaders of Champagne – he names the duke of Burgundy, Robert of Dreux, the count of Mâcon, the count of Saint-Pol, the count of Bar, Enguerrand of Coucy and Robert Courtenay – were allied with Peter of Brittany and the king of England.[61] Most of them were related to Peter of Brittany, and were indeed happy to side with him against Count Theobald. The count of Bar, Enguerrand of Coucy and Robert of Courtenay all stood to make gains from inroads into Champagne's soft borders. But the count of Saint-Pol, brother of Guy of Châtillon, had changed sides by February 1230.[62] And there is no evidence that they attacked royal lands, and none that they were prepared to support Peter in his intrigues with Henry III.

Peter of Brittany had in fact over-extended himself. Nevertheless, his intrigues with Henry III were maturing. In October 1229 Henry gathered an invasion fleet at Portsmouth. Blanche summoned Peter to answer for his infidelity at a great court at Melun on 30 December 1229. Peter sent representatives and a letter protesting his innocence, but refused to come himself. It was tantamount to a declaration of rebellion.[63]

Blanche wasted no time. January was hardly a good month for campaigning, but she and young Louis invested and took Peter's castle of Bellême on the border of Normandy and Perche, and then occupied Angers, Baugé and Beaufort in the Loire.[64] In May 1230 Henry III landed at Saint-Malo, then marched down to establish himself on the Loire at Nantes, where Peter Mauclerc joined him. Blanche and Louis's forces advanced as far as Clisson. There, with the support of their allies, Hugh of La Marche and the Maine noble Andrew of Vitry, they boxed Peter and Henry into the flat lands at the mouth of the Loire.[65] At a plenary court at Ancenis, in June, Blanche and Louis persuaded an impressive set of magnates, including Ferdinand of Flanders, Theobald of Champagne, Guy of Nevers, the counts of Blois, Chartres, Roucy and Vendôme, Amaury of Montfort and Stephen of Sancerre, to issue a judgement against Peter of Brittany. Other signatories included

Walter Cornut, Bishop Walter of Chartres, Bishop William of Paris, Matthew of Montmorency, John of Nesle, John of Beaumont and the northern lords of Audenarde and Béthune.[66] By late June Peter and Henry were suing for peace; by August the terms of peace were established, and Philip Hurepel had fallen into line; by October Henry had sailed for England.[67] As usual, there was not just one treaty, but a series of interrelated treaties that dealt with the various interested parties, including Hugh of La Marche and his wife, Isabella of Angoulême, with further discussion of the terms of the projected marriage between their heir and Princess Isabella.[68] As at earlier treaties, Blanche used the considerable wealth at her disposal creatively; there was quite a lot of buying off.[69]

Peter had been contained rather than crushed. As Wendover observed, Blanche and Louis were not strong enough to invade Brittany.[70] The settlement was expensive. Most of the treaties of 1230 have a provisional air. They were valid with the queen until Louis reached his majority and could take power into his own hands.[71] Louis was now sixteen, and quite old enough to play an active role in campaigns and negotiations. The accords with Andrew of Vitry and Hugh and Isabella of La Marche were conventions with subjects who could demand a high price for their co-operation. The French kings – and Blanche – were used to making subjects swear on holy relics to do what their ruler required of them. In both these cases Blanche and Louis were required to swear on sacred relics to keep their side of the bargain. In both cases, they refused to do the swearing themselves. It was done for them by the constable, Matthew of Montmorency.[72] He swore, too, on behalf of the king for the marriage of the little princess Isabella: Blanche and Louis made Matthew swear this time on his own soul.[73] The faithful Matthew was rewarded with the lordship of the substantial town of Laval in Maine.[74]

Three of Henry's barons, Ranulf of Chester and Richard and William Marshall – all of whom had claims to Norman lands lost in 1204 – remained in Brittany with Peter, and wreaked havoc in Maine and western Normandy with a series of *chevauchées*.[75] It merely persuaded the lords of the area, including some who had backed an English invasion, such as Fulk Paynel and Ralph of Fougères, to go over to the Capetian side.[76] In summer 1231 Blanche and Louis led another campaign to invade Brittany via western Normandy. Peter again came to terms quite quickly, and a three-year-truce, the Truce of Saint-Aubin, by which Peter was confined to Brittany, was arranged. It was negotiated by Peter's brother Henry, archbishop of Reims, and by Philip Hurepel; and Philip was to be responsible for its enforcement.[77]

It must have been clear to Philip Hurepel by now that his own interests were no longer served by an alliance with Peter of Brittany. Philip's own lands around Mortain in western Normandy had probably suffered from Peter's raids, and the events of the previous year had revealed how limited was support for Peter among the French baronage. In his intrigues with Henry III, Peter had gone too far. Young Louis was now at an age at which many kings would rule in their own right. There was no longer much point in Philip angling for the wardship of his nephew; he would do better, as the new king reached maturity, to develop a role as a dependable uncle.

Indeed, it must by now have been clear to most of the French baronage that the instabilities – and possibilities – of the late 1220s were over. Much of southern Poitou, Saintonge and Gascony were in English hands, but Normandy and the Loire had signally failed to respond to Peter and Henry III's call to arms. Blanche and Louis IX now transformed the city of Angers into a great fortress, with a huge new citadel and great city walls on both sides of the Loire (pl. 9). Most of the religious institutions of the city put in substantial claims for damages inflicted on them by the fortifications, but the citadel and the city walls were a magnificent demonstration of royal power and wealth. The new citadel was built very fast. Its walls were massive, and its towers 130 feet (40m) high. Blanche's masons commandeered ready-cut stone from the cathedral workshop.[78]

Blanche and Louis were now strong enough to allow the great magnates some licence, though they insisted, as Philip Augustus had done, on substantial securities from fellow magnates against bad behaviour. In March 1231 they had settled the extent of the county of Ponthieu, allowing the exiled count, Simon of Dammartin, uncle of Matilda of Boulogne, to return to France. The two daughters – the heirs – of the count and countess of Ponthieu were only to be married with the licence of Louis or Blanche.[79] Robert of Courtenay, who had not attacked Louis or Blanche, but had been unable to resist the potential for expansion offered by the war against Theobald of Champagne, was given permission to fortify his town of Château-Renard, strategically placed between the Capetian lands and the disputed north Burgundian border – but again, with sureties.[80] Early in 1234 Philip Hurepel died of wounds from a tournament, leaving a daughter, Joanna, as sole heir. His widow, Matilda of Boulogne, did homage, but Blanche and Louis kept as much control over Matilda and Joanna as Philip Augustus would have done. Both could be married only with their express agreement.[81]

In January 1234 Pope Gregory IX granted licence for Louis's own marriage to Margaret of Provence. Gregory stated that he was responding to Blanche's personal request. There was a question of consanguinity, but Gregory felt it could be overlooked 'for the good of a kingdom where so much blood has flowed'.[82] Strategically, it was an astute match, which would buttress the Capetian position in the south of the kingdom. It reveals just how important the 'conquest' and settlement of the south was to Blanche. For Philip Augustus, the south was another country, and he had been content to leave it in the hands of Simon of Montfort. Louis VIII had been drawn gradually into the fight against the Cathars. Whatever his initial level of enthusiasm, he had planned his last Crusade as a final conquest, and had done so with relentless focus. He had also, as papal letters and Capetian documents often pointed out, given his life for it. For it was in the south, not the north, of the kingdom that 'so much blood had flowed'. For Blanche, the settlement of the south-west, the inheritance of it by her son Alphonse, had become almost a sacred trust. Now, as part of the marriage arrangement between Louis and Margaret, the bride's parents, the count and countess of Provence, agreed that all disputes with the counts of Toulouse would be brought before the courts of Louis as king of France or before Blanche of Castile.[83] Blanche negotiated patiently to ensure Raymond of Toulouse's assent. Raymond came to ratify the agreement at Blanche and Louis VIII's favoured residence at Lorris. Blanche rewarded him with a vermilion mantle.[84]

Baronial revolt did not distract Blanche from her most important act of regal piety, the foundation of a new abbey in memory of her husband, as he had directed in his will. Louis VIII had left a substantial endowment for the new abbey: it was to be funded by the sale of the jewels and molten gold extracted from his crowns and regalia. He had specified too the type of abbey – it was to be Augustinian, founded from the abbey of Saint-Victor in Paris, just like the abbey of La Victoire founded by Philip Augustus to celebrate the victory of Bouvines.[85]

It is unclear whether Blanche used Louis's crown and jewels to buy lands for the abbey and its endowment. She certainly did not honour his request for a Victorine house. In December 1227, with help from Walter Cornut, she obtained papal dispensation to overturn a vow,[86] and she turned to her own favourite religious order, the Cistercians, for the new foundation. Founded at Cuimont, beside the Oise, not far from Senlis, it soon became known, from its royal connections, as Royaumont. The foundation charter insisted that the new abbey had been founded in response to Louis VIII's will, 'with the counsel of good men and with

the will and assent of the Louis VIII's executors'. The executors were bishops Bartholomew of Paris (who died in October 1227), Walter of Chartres and Guérin of Senlis (who died in April 1227), together with Abbot John of Saint-Victor. All were close associates of Blanche, and presumably did as she asked them.[87] The new abbey benefited from rich lands and the rights to grain from the king's granges along the Oise. Construction must have begun almost immediately, and the high altar was dedicated in 1232. Bishop Walter of Chartres led the services, and it was a great court occasion. The church was consecrated in April 1235 (pls 8, 16).[88] Loyal courtiers, like Amaury of Montfort and Matthew of Montmorency, made gifts.[89] Blanche seems to have used it as a place of retreat for her still-young family. In later life Louis IX recalled how he and his younger brothers had helped the monks with the building of the church, carrying stones and mortar in wheelbarrows. Blanche had her son Philip Dagobert buried at Royaumont when he died in 1234, perhaps because this younger son, intended for the Church, was receiving his education there. Royaumont soon became an accepted burial place for the royal children.[90]

•

In her attitude to the Crusade on which he had died, Blanche was more faithful to her dead husband's wishes. She knew that Louis VIII had been on the point of bringing Raymond of Toulouse to terms, and knew that the Church had voted a substantial Crusade tithe, the Albigensian tenth, at the Council of Bourges. She had every intention of sending another army down to the south-west in the summer of 1227. In this she was supported by Romanus, cardinal of Sant'Angelo, and the papacy.[91]

The Albigensian tenth became an issue almost immediately after Louis VIII's death. The French Church had voted the tenth, with reluctance, to Louis for the Crusade: the Crusade had returned, and Louis was now dead. The Church had fulfilled its obligations. Some chapters stopped paying the first instalment, due in November 1226, as soon as they heard of Louis's death; there was even more recalcitrance over the payment of the second instalment, due at Easter 1227. But the Crusade had made perceptible progress in the Languedoc, and northern reinforcements were required to maintain momentum. Blanche and the papal legate, Romanus, insisted that the French Church should pay the voted tenth; Romanus authorized the seizure of chapter properties by royal administrators to enforce payment.

On 27 May 1227 the chapters of Reims, Sens, Tours and Rouen wrote to Gregory IX to complain. By the time Gregory could respond, Romanus and Blanche had already confiscated properties from the chapter of Paris, which appealed separately to the pope against this outrage. Gregory insisted that chapter properties be restored, though he reserved judgement as to whether the French Church should pay the tenth or not.[92] In the late summer the stand-off between Blanche and Romanus on the one hand and the French Church on the other was resolved by her ever-dependable episcopal supporters, Walter of Sens and Walter of Chartres. Between them, they promised Blanche and young Louis that they would each pay 1,500 *livres parisis* each year for five years to the king for the Albigensian business on behalf of the chapters of the Sens archdiocese, unless it could be collected directly from the chapters.[93] The amount was substantial as a 'gift' from the two bishops – though it perhaps indicates just how wealthy both bishops were; but it was a huge reduction in what the crown might hope to draw from the full tenth from the archdiocese.[94] Perhaps Romanus and Blanche correctly calculated that the complaint of the chapters would collapse once the province of Sens was detached. Romanus and Archbishop Walter then went to argue the royal case in Rome. By November 1227 Gregory IX ordered the French Church to pay. Blanche was fortunate that many French churchmen saw this as papal interference, and focused much of their disaffection on Romanus.[95]

In the end, Gregory IX supported the French crown's claims to the Albigensian tenth. But it was a bitter conflict. Both Blanche and Romanus were heavy-handed – or were certainly perceived as being so by the French chapters. They must have felt that they were in the right – and in effect they received papal vindication. But Blanche had only just, in March 1227, defeated Peter Mauclerc's first rebellion, and had benefited from the support of the secular Church in doing so. Many churchmen must have felt that this was not the thanks they expected. Moreover, the chapters of several of the sees in the Sens archdiocese, Sens itself, Orléans, Senlis, Chartres and, perhaps above all, Paris, had substantial numbers of canons who worked, or had worked, in royal administration, or were related to the families that did. The appeal to the pope from the Church of Paris was written by the dean, Philip of Nemours, who was himself as closely related to the Capetian court as a churchman could be. His uncle, Ours de la Chapelle, had been Louis VIII's chamberlain.[96] Blanche and Romanus had no hesitation in alienating them. Both, one a woman and the other a representative of the papacy, fulfilled, in their different ways, all the negative expectations of provincial secular churchmen.

Mainly, the clergy blamed the legate. But salacious gossip about the queen and the cardinal spread quickly among the cathedral chapters and schoolrooms of the university. Even Philip of Nemours, dean of Paris, could not quite resist a few suggestive phrases about the queen and the legate in his letter to the pope:

> Once the king was dead, whatever the legate did with the queen, whatever the legate established, whatever he promised, was not done with the requisite will of the chapters...the legate, as was being said, wished to compel them to pay, as he had promised the queen, even saying that he would give her our capes.[97]

Blanche did not allow such comments to distract her from pursuing her husband's legacy in the south.

Although the French chapters did not wish to pay for it, the Church and Pope Gregory would have seen Blanche's settlement of Languedoc as a great success for orthodoxy. They approved, too, of her handling of the Jews. Here, too, the queen continued the work of her husband, who had used his statute of 1223 to try to suppress usury. She issued an ordinance of the Jews in June 1227, and then a new ordinance, with some clarifications, in May 1228. It is possible that this indicates discussion within the administration as to how to deal with the Jews. Walter Cornut had Jews working for him in his own episcopal administration, and may have had more appreciation of the economic advantages of Jewish finance than did the harder-line Parisian moralists. But the reasons for clarification were largely practical. As Jordan has shown, Blanche's administration was faced with the results of Louis viii's withdrawal of the seal from Jewish transactions, and had to organise a new register of debts before the new measures could be implemented.[98]

Blanche's ordinances, like Louis viii's, would bring a helpful influx of revenue to the royal treasury, but like his, they had wider ambitions. Even more than her husband, Blanche focused on the issue of usury; that was why it was necessary to keep records of the debts. Interest was not to be paid on debts incurred since Blanche's first ordinance, or on any future debts. But it is notable that the loans themselves taken out between June 1227 and May 1228 were to be repaid to the Jews, not to the king. This reflects the influence of those who followed the Augustinian precept that the Jews should not be left unable to live, but should be sustained within society as witnesses of Christ's life and death.

In December 1230, at a great court at Melun, Blanche, in Louis ix's name, issued a new statute of the Jews.[99] Usury was tightly defined as 'anything beyond the principal'. Christians must pay their debts, but not interest on them. The Jews

must present their records of debt, and debtors must pay them off over three years. As with her earlier legislation, a nice balance was struck. Usury was proscribed, but the Jews must take their place within society. Like Louis VIII, Blanche included clauses preventing the reception and retention of another lord's Jews. But now, any lord who did that, or resisted the other provisions, would be regarded as a rebel, and would face legal action and, if necessary, royal military coercion. Some provisions of the new ordinance expressly extended throughout the kingdom of France. Moreover, Blanche was able to persuade most of the great magnates to subscribe, including Philip Hurepel, Hugh of La Marche and Theobald of Champagne, who was now heavily dependent on Blanche's political support.[100]

Blanche's confrontation with the University of Paris, like her determination to enforce the Albigensian tenth, brought her plaudits from some sections of the ecclesiastical community, and execration from others. The university had been given a charter as a corporate institution as recently as 1215; until then, education in Paris had been delivered by masters at a large number of independent and competitive schools. By 1200 Paris had become the undisputed centre for the study of philosophy, theology and canon law, and attracted students from all over Europe. The students were a mixed blessing. They brought wealth and prestige to the city, which was lauded as the new Athens; and since most contemporary writers of commentary or chronicle, or even romance, had spent a blissful and inebriated youth studying in the Capetian capital, the Capetians tended to benefit from a generosity denied to the Angevins, the emperors or other fellow rulers. But the students took advantage of their clerical immunity from secular authority; the citizens of Paris cannot have forgotten the drunken and fatal student riots of 1200, when Philip Augustus had taken the side of the totally guilty students.[101]

And there were divisions and problems within the scholarly community of Paris itself. Debate about many of the great theological issues became increasingly bitter as the twelfth century drew on, driven perhaps by the Joachimite fears about the imminence of the End of Time, and by fears about the Cathar heresies now established in the Languedoc. The new Aristotelian works emerging from Spain at the same time added to the theological hysteria. Louis VIII's tutor, the Paris master Amaury of Bène, had found himself on the wrong side of these arguments in 1206; in 1210 his followers were prosecuted and burnt for heresy, accused, among other things, of denying the bodily resurrection, just as the Cathars did. There were still concerns about Amaurician ideas at the University of Paris as late as 1225.[102] Study of the new Aristotelian works was forbidden, and neo-platonic works, such as

Eriugena's *On the Nature of Things*, were ordered to be burnt. In 1228 Gregory IX forbade the study of either philosophy or natural science at the university.[103]

So the intellectual atmosphere in early thirteenth-century Paris was explosive. There were institutional jealousies too. When the university was set up, it was agreed that only the chancellor of the cathedral of Notre-Dame, and in some cases the dean of Saint-Geneviève, could confer the degree of master. The masters of the university chafed under what they saw as their subjection to the chancellor of the cathedral. This had come to a head in 1225, during the Council of Bourges, when Cardinal Romanus took the side of Notre-Dame and broke the seal of the university. The students rioted, and Romanus was nearly lynched. He had to be rescued by Louis VIII's soldiers.[104] Romanus was still trying to resolve arguments about the giving of licences to teach between the bishop and the cathedral chancellor on the one hand, and the masters on the other, in June 1228.[105]

At Carnival in 1229 another student riot flared.[106] On Shrove Tuesday, a group of students got into a fight over the price of wine in a tavern on the lands of the priory of Saint-Marcel. The students went back the next day with reinforcements to attack the landlord and his neighbours, destroying the tavern, cracking open all his flagons of wine. The prior of Saint-Marcel complained of this wanton damage to his tenants to William of Auvergne, bishop of Paris, to Cardinal Romanus and to Blanche herself as holder of the guardianship of the kingdom. William had been a great master of the Paris schools and Romanus had been a student there himself, but William was now bishop and Romanus had his own recent experience of student riots. Both were inclined to side with the prior of Saint-Marcel. Blanche – at least according to the English monk Matthew Paris, who provides the most vivid account of the incidents – took a stronger line. 'Stirred', says Matthew, 'with womanly shamelessness and violence of mind', Blanche ordered that the students should be punished. In the resulting violence, two rich and important clerics, one from Flanders and one from Normandy, were killed. Again the students complained to Blanche, Romanus and Bishop William of Paris; again they received scant sympathy.

The scholars of Paris announced that they would leave the city. Most went to those older centres of scholarship that had been overshadowed by Paris – Angers, Reims and Orléans. Peter of Brittany, whose relationship with his own Breton clergy had been highly confrontational, tried to persuade some to come to his court at Nantes.[107] Some went to the new university just established at Toulouse – ironically, given that the foundation of a university at Toulouse had been one of

the provisions of the Treaty of Paris of 1229 imposed on Raymond of Toulouse by Blanche and Romanus. Henry III saw an opportunity here too, and wrote from Reading Abbey offering attractive terms to any scholars who wished to establish themselves in England.[108] Several congregated in Oxford, effectively founding the university there. Matthew Paris must have got his account – detailed, circumstantial and very inimical to Blanche – from one of them.

Not everyone was sorry to see them go. Philip de Grève, the chancellor of Notre-Dame in Paris, attacked the university masters in a sermon as 'fighting cocks'.[109] Not everyone left. The monastic scholars of Les Val-des-Ecoliers returned to Paris. Bishop William established them with a new church, Sainte-Catherine-de-la-Couture, where they would pray particularly for the souls of Philip Augustus and Louis VIII. Blanche contributed 300 *livres* for its construction, and young Louis laid the foundation stone in 1229.[110] The absence of the students gave the scholars of the Dominican house at Saint-Jacques, to whose foundation Blanche had been so sympathetic, the opportunity to establish themselves firmly within Paris. Bishop William gave the Dominicans their first chair at the university. By the mid-thirteenth century rivalry between the Dominicans and the seculars would threaten to destroy the University of Paris, and the secular masters looked back on this as the start of that problem.[111]

By November 1229 Gregory IX had become involved.[112] Often intemperate and not always well informed, the pope took the side of the scholars against Blanche, presumably to the surprise of his legate, Romanus, and Bishop William of Paris. He wrote with inappropriate firmness to Blanche and young Louis, and to the legate and bishop. He refused to listen to the case presented by Blanche's messengers, Master William of Auxerre and Stephen Baatel, and commissioned Bishop Maurice of Le Mans, the new bishop of Senlis, Master Adam de Chambly, and Master John, archdeacon of Châlons, to bring both sides to a compromise. Meanwhile, he encouraged more masters to move to Toulouse, by permitting the study there of subjects such as philosophy and natural science that he had himself, a year or so earlier, forbidden at Paris.[113]

The impasse was resolved by 'discreet men', as Matthew Paris coyly put it. Perhaps the papal commission turned out to be unexpectedly effective. At all events, by 1231 most of the scholars had returned, and the university functioned once more. William of Nangis, in his world chronicle, written around 1290, is the first to suggest that it was the young Louis IX who persuaded the scholars to return. Louis, he says, was profoundly distressed to see the 'treasury of knowledge', the

study of letters and philosophy, disappear from Paris; finally, the young king persuaded the scholars to return, and punished the townspeople. For Louis saw that God had formed the kingdom of France like a lily, with three petals, one representing chivalry and the other two wisdom and faith – which, it might be hoped, the students would gain by their studies.[114] This was incorporated into other accounts of the saintly young man, and fed an emerging portrait of a wise and thoughtful king, a young Solomon, who recognised, and could mediate, the intemperance of his courageous but intransigent mother, who, as a woman, could not be expected to understand the importance of scholars and learning. But there is no earlier evidence that Louis took any independent action, or thought any differently from his mother on this issue.

For the displaced scholars, and Matthew Paris, Blanche fulfilled all their misogynistic stereotypes of womanly pride, intemperance and lack of sympathy for learning. It was not just misogynistic. The scholars hated the legate almost as much. In Latin satirical songs, they claimed the queen was his mistress: 'Alas, we die... defeated...and despoiled: the legate's whore makes us suffer this.' The same slur appeared in verses produced at more or less the same time by trouvères who supported Peter Mauclerc.[115] The more dispassionate might observe that Blanche had acted decisively and fairly, and with courage, for she must have known that even her redoubtable father-in-law had backed down in his confrontation with the drunken students of Paris. She had the full support of both Romanus and Bishop William – distinguished scholars both: all three of them were pioneering supporters of the newly established Dominican scholars in Paris. If anyone was intemperate, it was surely Gregory IX. Someone on the side of the Paris scholars had managed to influence him: probably English envoys at the papal court played a role. Gregory saw this as an issue of clerical immunity, as the riots of 1200 had been. This case was more complex, for the students had damaged the property of the Church. Blanche, Romanus and Bishop William acted to protect the property of the prior and priory of Saint-Marcel. It was a bitter struggle, as the satiric verses attest, at a stage when the threat from Peter Mauclerc and Henry III was at its most acute. Even in those circumstances, Blanche had firm belief in the rectitude of her position, and did not give in.

•

The landed wealth of the Church, and the regalian rights of the crown, were bound to lead to conflicts between Church and State. The sharpest, and most

extended, confrontation between Blanche and the Church was with successive archbishops of Rouen.[116] She clashed with Archbishop Theobald in spring 1227, over rights in the forest of Louviers. This was shortly after the Treaty of Vendôme, and at more or less the same time that Romanus and Blanche were pressurising French chapters to pay their second instalment of the Albigensian tithe. The archbishop excommunicated the royal bailiff of Verneuil for taking timber from the forest of Louviers. Blanche summoned the archbishop, in her son's name, to the king's court at Vernon, for he had failed to answer to the Norman exchequer court, as bishops and barons of Normandy should do. Blanche asserted that the excommunication of the royal officer injured the king, and that the archbishop's rights to timber in the forest of Louviers were limited. Theobald was also accused of excommunicating the dean and chapter of Saint-Hilaire of Gournay, who were under royal protection.[117] The archbishop came to court, but proved recalcitrant. These were spiritual issues, he claimed, and since he did not hold anything 'feodale' from the king, there was no reason why he should be summoned before the king's court. Blanche, on her son's behalf, was furious.[118] Theobald was again called to answer in the royal court – a full court with all the king's barons. He remained implacable, insisting that he held his lands not as fiefs, but in pure alms. No secular ruler would, or could, agree. With the counsel and consent of the barons, Blanche and Louis confiscated the archiepiscopal rents and secular possessions. The archbishop, in return, cast an interdict over the royal demesne lands and castles in his vast archdiocese, and appealed to Rome. Blanche and Louis also put their case to Gregory IX, claiming that their actions were in line with royal precedent. Gregory commissioned Romanus to resolve the conflict, in a letter that suggested that he had listened with sympathy to the representations from both sides.[119] The outcome is unclear; presumably Romanus did indeed effect a temporary compromise.

But the forest rights remained an issue, and there were other, often unnamed, disputes. In 1233 Louis, presumably directed by Blanche, rejected the abbess supported by the archbishop of Rouen after a disputed election at the nunnery of Montivilliers. The archbishop excommunicated the nuns who took part, and this unhappy situation was only resolved three years later, by the new archbishop, Peter of Collemezzo, who brought in an abbess from the Brie.[120] Trust between the archbishop and the crown collapsed. In the summer of 1232 Theobald had been succeeded as archbishop by Bishop Maurice of Le Mans, the bishop appointed to the papal commission into the student riots. Blanche and Louis refused to return the regalia of the see. Archbishop Maurice retaliated by placing the archdiocese

under interdict. It was not lifted until October 1234.[121] The interdict affected the royal bailiffs, their families and chaplains, and the royal chapels, though it was to be suspended if the king or queen happened to be in residence. This was a serious consideration. Louis and Blanche were not often at the residences within the duchy of Normandy, but the archdiocese of Rouen extended beyond the duchy to cover their much-used castle at Pontoise. To register his fury more powerfully, the archbishop ordered that images of the Virgin should be taken from the altar, placed on the floor in front of it, and surrounded by thorns until the king and queen should be moved to concede.[122] More practically, the archbishop appealed to Rome. Gregory IX took the archbishop's side, more firmly than he had done in the previous altercation. He wrote firmly to Louis himself, and separately to those who should advise the king to come to his senses, that is to Blanche, Walter Cornut, Bishop Walter of Chartres and the chamberlain, Bartholomew of Roye.[123] He commissioned Bishop William of Paris, Bishop Adam of Senlis and John of Montmirail, archdeacon of Paris, who was just on the point of joining the Paris Dominicans, to intervene.[124]

Gregory could hardly have chosen three churchmen who were closer to the court and, unsurprisingly, nothing happened. In August 1233 an exasperated pope sent a volley of letters, altogether more minatory in tone, to Louis, to Blanche and to the counsellors of the king; to the ineffective commission, who had clearly suspected that Gregory was ill informed; and to the bishop of Tournai, the abbots of the Cistercian houses of Pontigny and Savigny, and the prior of the Dominican house in Paris, who should act if his original committee failed to do so.[125] Presumably, this impressive clutch of churchmen succeeded in bringing about an accommodation during the summer of 1234, when Blanche and Louis spent much time in Normandy, dealing with Peter of Dreux.

It is unclear why these disputes became so fractious. Indeed, it is unclear what the issues at dispute were – apart from the initial quarrel over rights to wood. It may be that they arose from the untidy and ill-tempered exchange of archiepiscopal and ducal lands forced through by Richard the Lionheart in 1196.[126] Both archbishops Theobald and Maurice insisted that they were protecting the liberties of the Norman Church, and there is evidence in the disputed elections that followed both their deaths that a 'Norman' party was growing among the canons of the cathedral.[127] But neither man was Norman. Theobald was from Amiens, and Maurice a reform-minded French Benedictine monk, moved from the bishopric of Le Mans to Rouen on the initiative of Gregory IX. But relations certainly became

easier when Maurice was succeeded by a series of churchmen who had good connections with the Capetian court – Peter of Collemezzo, followed by Eudes
Clément, abbot of Saint-Denis, then the Franciscan Eudes Rigaud. Peter resolved
the Montivilliers election; and Blanche worked closely and productively with Eudes
Rigaud while Louis was on Crusade. Indeed, in 1250 Blanche and Eudes Rigaud
came to an accord over 'the long contention between the archbishop and the
king'.[128]

Blanche and Louis's fundamental position is clearer. They were enraged by
Theobald's refusal to accept that he held anything 'feodale' – as a fief, from the
crown. It was a strange claim; most bishops, along with all contemporary laymen,
accepted that the properties that supported a bishop existed in the temporal world,
and could not be separated from its demands and responsibilities. Gregory himself,
in his letter to Blanche and Louis, seems at best uncertain about Theobald's claims.
The essentially temporal nature of a bishop's temporalities, and the responsibilities
attendant on them, was something on which Louis insisted in 1247, when he
complained to the pope about aspects of the behaviour of the French Church in
his famous 'Protest'.[129] The liberality with excommunication and interdict, with
which both archbishops met any move to which they objected, was also unaccep-
table to both Blanche and Louis. Excommunication and interdict had wide social
implications, as well as spiritual ones. Interdicts could lead to problems with
unburied and unshriven dead, especially in towns. In a society that feared the tor-
ments of hell, and where the End of Time could seem very close, the comforts of
religion mattered; and the well-being of the realm quite rightly mattered to the
king or queen. Excommunication put people at a disadvantage at law, and meant
that, in theory, they were outcasts from society. The wholesale excommunication
of the king's officers – as practised by the archbishops of Rouen – meant that the
ordinary business of government was, theoretically, impossible. Again, the indis-
criminate use of ecclesiastical censures featured in Louis's complaint to the pope
in 1247, and both Louis and Blanche regularly persuaded the popes to accord them
personal immunity from any excommunications that were launched.[130]

What precisely was Blanche's role in this confrontation with the archbishops of
Rouen, and what was young Louis's? Undoubtedly, she was the leading royal actor
in the initial clash in 1229, when Louis was still relatively young. The account in
the Rouen Chronicle emphasises her participation, and Gregory's letter to Romanus
reveals that the king and the queen had written to the pope to put their side of
the dispute, where a letter could easily have been sent in the name of the young

king. Because Blanche's involvement in 1229 is so evident, historians have tended to assume that she remained the leading agent of royal confrontation in 1232–4. Involved, she undoubtedly was. But the Rouen Chronicle is less specific about her role at this stage, and Gregory addressed his primary letters of admonition to Louis himself, writing to Blanche as someone who would have influence with the king – as Gregory continued to do for the rest of his life, long after Louis had attained full majority. By 1232 Louis was eighteen – not yet at the age of official majority, but certainly at an age at which kings and magnates would expect to act as a full adult. During his personal rule, Louis proved every bit as inflexible over royal rights over Church temporalities and ecclesiastical censures as Blanche was.[131]

The second stage of the confrontation with the archbishop of Rouen coincided with an equally bitter quarrel with the Miles of Nanteuil, bishop of Beauvais. There was friction within the city over a disputed mayoral election. Louis appointed a mayor from outside the city; the result was a riot. Louis arrived, claiming he had the right to punish the malefactors; the bishop responded that Louis did not have rights of justice within the city. Louis then demanded the right of *gîte*, the right of the king to stay in episcopal properties at the bishop's expense, to 'eat him out of house and home'. When Bishop Miles played for time, Louis seized the temporalities of the see, including the episcopal palace. Miles appealed to his metropolitan, Archbishop Henry of Reims. At the Council of Noyon, in February 1233, the bishops agreed to place the province under interdict, though the extent to which this would discommode the king and the court was undermined by the refusal of the loyal Adam of Chambly, bishop of Senlis, and the bishop of Noyon, who was a nephew of Bartholomew of Roye, to take part. Bishop Miles set off to make his case to the pope in person, but died on the way in late 1234. An inquiry into the riots was commissioned in 1235. The rights of *gîte* were finally settled in May 1238, largely in favour of the king, but full peace between the king and the bishop of Beauvais was made as late as 1248.[132]

It is usually assumed that the responsibility for this confrontation between Church and State lay not with Louis, but with his mother, and that the reason should be sought in her hatred of Bishop Miles. By the 1260s gossip, as purveyed by the Ménestrel of Reims, had cast Miles as one of Blanche's enemies, and the source of the rumours that she slept with the cardinal legate. According to the Ménestrel, Blanche scotched the rumours by throwing off her clothes in the midst of a council meeting to show that she was not pregnant.[133] The rumours are more likely to have been invented by disaffected wandering scholars from Paris. And

there is no firm evidence that Miles had done anything to earn Blanche's hatred, and thus inspire this attack on his episcopal rights. Miles had been a close adherent of her husband, Louis VIII, and was one of the three bishops who swore that Louis had left the charge of the young king and the kingdom to Blanche in 1226. He showed his support for the queen by joining Blanche and Walter of Chartres at the consecration of Longpont in October 1227, and he undertook diplomatic missions for her in the early years of the regency. He then concentrated on rebuilding his cathedral on a gigantic scale, which left him heavily in debt.[134] The inquiry of 1235 into the dispute emphasises Louis's role, though Blanche is recorded as supporting the king's determination to deal with the riot.[135] In fact, in April 1234 Gregory IX wrote to Blanche, asking her to persuade her son to make peace with the bishop, as if Blanche might be a moderating influence here.[136] And the problems between the king and successive bishops of Beauvais continued long after Miles's death, and Louis's official majority.

The Rouen and Beauvais confrontations of Church and State have established Blanche's reputation as a person apt to react swiftly and furiously, who might allow herself to be influenced by personal hatred, and who would then hold that position tenaciously and inflexibly. Matthew Paris, in accusing her of behaving thus over the university of Paris, put it down to the fact that she was a woman, and this was womanly behaviour. Set alongside the confrontation with the Paris scholars, these incidents have contributed to an impression that Blanche's confrontational stance might be mitigated by her more emollient son. But young Louis's intervention in the scholars' strike seems to be a charming fantasy of William of Nangis. Over the Beauvais dispute, Gregory IX regarded Blanche as the potential peacemaker and Louis as the intransigent figure. As for Rouen, Blanche was certainly responsible for the bitter explosion in 1229. But Louis VIII had been in dispute with the archbishop of Rouen in 1224, so problems of royal and episcopal rights had been festering for some time. Young Louis appears to have been as keen as Blanche to insist on royal rights by the mid-1230s. In the end, it was Blanche, working with the trusted Eudes Rigaud, who was able to come to a final accord in 1250.[137]

•

Throughout the regency, Blanche had fully justified her husband's faith in her ability to rule the kingdom. She reacted courageously to challenge and opposition, whether from the Church, Paris masters or the barons. She used the full range of coercive powers available to the ruler. She raised armies; she sat in judgement; she

issued at least one kingdom-wide ordinance, the statute on the Jews; and she was a determined negotiator. Occasionally, commentators accused her of intemperance, where they might perhaps have written of the righteous anger of a king; but monastic chroniclers like Matthew Paris often described kings as intemperate too. Like any good ruler, Blanche exploited also the power of diplomacy, cultural and religious patronage, gesture and ritual. Although her negotiations were determined, she was flexible, prepared to buy peace, and not usually vengeful. She made networks and friendships work for her. She used every advantage that her gender brought her: she gave rein to powerful emotion as broken-hearted widow; presented herself as a brave mother protecting her orphaned children; she flirted where appropriate. It is tempting to suggest that only a woman could have had the patience and perspicacity to force her principal opponent to come to terms because he thought that everyone was beginning to laugh at him.

The precise nature of the balance of power between Blanche and Louis IX as the young man approached his majority is difficult to assess. All acts were issued in his name, from the very beginning of his reign. Young Louis came with Blanche on all the great armed expeditions out to the west to deal with Peter Mauclerc, and on the expedition to settle the borders of Champagne in 1229. The Rouen and Beauvais confrontations suggest that by 1233, even perhaps 1232, Blanche was encouraging her son to ease himself into royal authority, with some independence from herself. In November 1232 her friends, John of Nesle and his wife, gave her their fine house in Paris; perhaps she was beginning to consider some retirement from active life as her son reached his majority.[138] But that is hardly the impression given by the terms of the arrangement with Margaret of Provence's parents: that disputes between the counts of Provence and the counts of Toulouse should come before either Louis or Blanche. The balance of power between mother and son would remain delicate, shifting and uncertain throughout the years of Louis's personal rule.

5

Queen Dowager

I N MAY 1234 LOUIS IX WAS MARRIED TO Margaret of Provence. Blanche organised a magnificent wedding in the cathedral of Sens, with the aid of the ever-dependable Walter Cornut. Various members of the household, including Blanche's lady, Odelina, and her clerk, Thomas Touquin, were sent on ahead to ensure that all was prepared. Blanche provided her family, her ladies and the royal household with appropriate robes. The men wore purple, and Blanche's ladies wore scarlet. Jewels were purchased from the goldsmith of Countess Joanna of Flanders. Blanche had a fine seat with painted cushions, and she and her family, surrounded by rich cloths, cushions and carpets, sat beneath silk canopies. She was accompanied by six trumpeters. Minstrels, paid for by Louis's younger brother Robert, were much in evidence. After the marriage ceremony, Margaret was crowned queen of France, while Louis wore full royal regalia. The household accounts recording the lavish expenditure refer to the entire event as 'the coronation'. Margaret was only thirteen, and Blanche had a new, small, gold crown made for her. It was a long journey to Sens, and the aged Bartholomew of Roye was provided with a cushion.[1] The royal party travelled down towards that uncertain zone between Champagne and Burgundy that had seen the worst of the baronial private wars; it was a vivid demonstration of royal authority imposed on a peaceful realm.

Margaret's beauty and charm were lauded by most chroniclers.[2] She was for some time brought up at court alongside Princess Isabella, to whom she was close in

age. The marriage would not be consummated immediately, but before long there would be expectations of pregnancy. Margaret was nineteen before her first child was born in 1240 or 1241, and there were concerns about her fertility.[3] The first child was a daughter, named Blanche, as might be expected. Bishop William of Paris managed to turn the family's inevitable disappointment in the sex of the long-awaited child to joy at the arrival of a daughter by a gentle jocularity, according to a contemporary anecdote.[4] The desired heir, called Louis after his grandfather and his father, was born in 1244.

Joinville, who knew both Louis and Margaret well, paints a picture of love and tenderness between the king and his young queen, at least early in their marriage.[5] But by the time they were on Crusade, Joinville suggests that early affection had given way on Louis's part to a certain distance. He noticed that Louis rarely mentioned his wife. Margaret described her husband as 'contrary', and insistent that she consult him first in all her actions.[6] It cannot have helped that Blanche was not a sympathetic mother-in-law. Joinville gives a compelling account of her consistent demeaning of the young queen. Blanche insisted that Louis leave the bedside of Margaret, who was screaming in agony during a difficult and dangerous birth. Louis and Margaret particularly liked the castle of Pontoise, because their chambers were linked by a staircase where they could make love before the arrival of the queen mother to make sure that they were both tucked up in their separate beds.[7] When Margaret cried over the news of Blanche's death, Joinville asked her why she should cry at the death of her worst enemy; Margaret replied that she cried for Louis, for she knew how distraught he was at the news of his mother's death.[8]

Louis's marriage marked his majority, the point at which he should shoulder the full, weighty, responsibilities of kingship. It was probably to mark his majority that Blanche had a third moralised bible completed. This is the magnificent three-volume Toledo Bible, with the final image of Blanche instructing her beardless son in the business of government (see frontispiece). It is impossible to tell from official documents when Louis's minority ended, since all acts had been issued in his name from the start of his reign. No regency seal had been used. Long after Louis's marriage and majority, Blanche continued to play a major and overt role in his administration. Most of the time, both mother and son seemed content with this arrangement. Blanche was forty-six, had given birth to her last child a mere seven years previously, and was the mother of two children under ten. Contemporary gossip still talked of her as a sexually attractive woman. She was healthy, energetic, capable and enjoyed power.

Louis is an enigmatic figure. He was capable of great energy. As a young man, he could be impetuous and assertive of his royal authority, as the clashes with the bishop of Beauvais show; and he often revelled in knightly accomplishments, including war. As a king, he was likely to intervene in everything, and insist that things were done as he wanted. But his attitude to royal power was ambivalent. He believed in it, as God-given; but perhaps did not always enjoy wielding it. He was often unwell and tired. His initial delight in his marriage, and even more, his growing sympathy for mendicant devotion, particularly for a life of Franciscan abnegation, may have distracted Louis from the administration of the realm. Undoubtedly these predilections induced a distaste for the showy aspects of thirteenth-century kingship – the courtly feasts, entertainments, hunts and tournaments.[9]

Blanche had a more robust attitude to royal power, to its Realpolitik and necessary compromises, and to the uses of its showier manifestations. Papal letters continued to be addressed to Louis and Blanche; if the pope wanted to influence Louis, he wrote to Blanche. Treaties and arrangements with the great feudatories, like Peter Mauclerc and Matilda of Boulogne, were negotiated by and often issued in the names of Louis and Blanche. Letters to keep Blanche informed about events within the realm, written with the understanding that she remained politically engaged and active, survive from agents in Carcassonne and La Rochelle; presumably, there were other letters from other agents. Blanche often sat in court with or for her son. In 1238, for instance, judgement in a case about the rights of the cathedral of Notre-Dame in Paris had to be put off because both Louis and Blanche were ill.[10] Jacques Le Goff has called this a co-royalty.[11] William Jordan has argued that only in early 1245, when Louis, recovering from a dangerous illness, resolved to go on Crusade, did he really emerge from the influence of his mother, and take full kingly powers to himself.[12] But Louis had shown occasional determination to assert his own authority as king as early as 1233. From the late 1230s there is evidence that he became more concerned to assert that authority. Sometimes this was at the expense of his mother's power and influence. He loved, revered and trusted his mother, as he loved, revered and trusted no one else, but that did not stop him chafing against her influence as he developed his own, sometimes rather different approach to rulership. Louis did not, perhaps, have her formidable natural authority. He had to learn how to exploit his physical frailty, his fastidiousness, his intense piety and humility, and transform these into a highly effective Christo-mimetic kingship. But it took time to do so, and this very personal interpretation of

kingship became fully effective only after his suffering and courage on Crusade. In the meantime, he was fortunate that he could rely on his mother's authority and experience when he needed to do so.

•

As I have stressed, baronial disaffection was not confined to Blanche's regency. The barons who had been fractious during Blanche's wardship continued to be so now that Louis had reached his majority. But there could be no excuse now. A baron might complain about maternal influence, but defiance now was rebellion against the king. Nevertheless, this was an area of Louis's kingship where he tended to rely heavily on his mother's experience and her diplomatic acumen.

Blanche and Louis knew that the three-year truce with Peter of Brittany was drawing to an end. In the summer of 1234 Peter, backed by substantial money from Henry III, but no promise of invasion, ravaged the lands of his Breton enemies and territories along the Breton border.[13] Blanche and Louis had planned carefully against this. In the previous year, and now again in the early summer of 1234, they made sure that Peter's principal Breton enemy, Henry of Avaugour, and lords of the Breton border zones, notably the Fougères, were firmly attached to the Capetian camp. This was done by treaties before the Capetian court at Beaumont-sur-Oise and Fontainebleau, with the help of Bishop Walter of Chartres.[14] Blanche also used more indirect methods. She arranged the marriage of one of her ladies, Odelina, to Robert of Montfort-sur-Risle, a cousin of the Fougères clan.[15] The host was summoned in April, and Louis, with Blanche, led a formidable army out to the great new fortress at Angers.[16] The French lands of Peter's accomplice, Richard Marshall, who had just died, were seized.[17] Peter was once again forced to sue for peace. Large numbers of the baronage, including his brother, Count John of Mâcon, Hugh, duke of Burgundy and Hugh, count of Saint-Pol, stood expensive security for him.[18] In November Peter came to Paris, and in the presence of Blanche and Louis renounced his claims to lands in the Norman border zones at Saint-James-de-Beuvron, La Perrière and Bellême. On sacred relics, he swore to serve faithfully both the king and the queen, his mother.[19] As usual, interlinked treaties protected the interests of the count of La Marche and his wife, Isabella of Angoulême.[20]

The summer of 1234 saw the final resolution, with papal support, of the Champagne succession question that had been left hanging in the air after the war of the invasion of Champagne in 1229.[21] The uncertainty had doubtless served to

keep Theobald loyal to Blanche and Louis, who had come to his rescue. Alice of Cyprus came first to a 'parlamentum' held at Saint-Germain-en-Laye shortly before Easter 1234. Then in September, before Louis and Blanche, she renounced all her claims against Theobald in return for a substantial annual income of 2,000 *livres*. In addition, Louis gave her a pay-off of 40,000 *livres* on Theobald's behalf, representing the sum for the fiefs of the counties of Blois, Chartres, Sancerre and the viscounty of Châteaudun, which Theobald sold to the king.[22] In March 1233 Theobald had married the daughter of Archibald of Bourbon, one of the magnates who had pursued private wars, but had not been unfaithful to the Capetians.[23] The marriage alliance helped Theobald to stabilise his southern border against pressure from the duke of Burgundy. In July 1234 Theobald succeeded his uncle as king of Navarre.[24] His new kingdom, new wealth and new security had provided him with the money and the lands to pay off Alice of Cyprus.

Peter of Brittany was unable to resist the opening of the summer campaigning season of 1235, but had no real support. Blanche and Louis once again assured themselves of the loyalty of Ralph of Fougères and Peter's other enemies from the Breton borders. A distracting quarrel had broken out between Ralph and Guy Mauvoisin, a member of the prominent family from the French Vexin who had been given lands in western Normandy. Blanche and Louis insisted that all parties come for arbitration before a court held jointly by the king and his mother at Crépy-en-Valois.[25] By July Peter himself had yet again come to terms.[26]

Peter continued to plot for his own advantage. There was no likelihood now of Henry III taking Normandy and lower Anjou, and no prospect whatsoever of destabilising Louis IX. But Peter exploited the limited possibilities of conspiracy. Surprisingly, he now developed another alliance with Theobald of Champagne. Theobald, now confirmed as count of Champagne and king of Navarre, had been indulging in private war from early 1235, when he entered into a confederacy with Hugh, duke of Burgundy, and his father-in-law, Archibald of Bourbon, against the count of Nevers, 'saving their fidelity to Louis and the lady queen his mother'.[27] In January 1236 Theobald's daughter, Blanche, married Peter's son, John of Brittany.[28] This was handled more efficiently than the bungled attempted secret marriage between Theobald himself and Peter's daughter. But Louis and Blanche were furious, not least because Blanche had arranged a prestigious marriage for young Blanche of Champagne with the heir to her nephew, Ferdinand III, king of Castile.[29] But they had to accept Theobald's fait accompli, and agreed to the marriage provided sufficient securities for good behaviour were made by fellow

magnates and prelates, including Walter Cornut.[30] In April 1236 the unlikely trio of Peter, Theobald of Champagne and Hugh of La Marche entered into an accord of mutual protection.[31]

Soon Theobald was in open revolt against his king. It is unclear what he thought he might gain by it. His motives, too, are unclear. Perhaps he resented Louis's anger that royal permission had not been sought for the Champagne–Brittany marriage. Matthew Paris suggests that Theobald, along with Peter Mauclerc, still resented the fact that the kingdom was ruled by 'womanly counsel'.[32] Perhaps Theobald hoped, as the grandest of the French princes, and now a king himself, to supplant Blanche as the young king's principal counsellor. If so, as so often, Theobald miscalculated. He was forgiven by Louis, according to both Mousquès and the Ménestrel of Reims, only because Blanche asked Louis to do so. Blanche invited Theobald to the palace to discuss peace terms. Her second son, Robert, disliked Theobald intensely, resenting the undoubtedly flirtatious friendship with his mother. Robert also possessed a raucous and earthy sense of humour. On Robert's orders, as Theobald stood on the threshold of the queen's chamber in the palace on the Ile de la Cité for his interview, he was struck full in the face with a runny cheese, in the manner of a custard pie, according to the Ménestrel, or was drenched in dung-filled rotten animal intestines, according to Mousquès. Dripping cheese, or something more putrid still, the discomfited count faced the queen, on whose magnanimity his forgiveness depended. To compound Theobald's humiliation, Robert cut off the tail of his palfrey.[33]

Louis and Blanche kept Peter and his family under observation and in check. In December 1235, as Peter's son, John, reached his majority, and took over as count of Brittany, Louis instituted an inquisition into the rights of the counts.[34] In spring 1238 Count John and his father came to the court at Pontoise to promise to hand over any of their castles to Louis or to Blanche, on demand.[35] Peter's brother John, count of Mâcon, admitted in 1236 that he held the county of Mâcon from the king;[36] three years later he sold the county to Louis. Robert, the oldest of the Dreux brothers, had died in 1234, leaving a minor heir and a complex inheritance, which put the honour of Dreux itself at the king's mercy, and left the countess, Eleanor, swearing fidelity and good behaviour to Louis.[37]

In the second half of the 1230s Louis, often with the overt intervention of Blanche, was more concerned with the north-east of France and Flanders than with Brittany and its marches. This was a rich area, with its short sea passage to England and important ports for English trade: Boulogne; Montreuil; and Abbeville at the

mouth of the Somme, the main port of the county of Ponthieu. Blanche's own most valuable dower lands, at Lens, Bapaume and Hesdin, lay within this area. She had long established close relations with the aristocracy of the area; men like Michael of Harnes, Arnold of Audenarde and John of Nesle had been close associates of both Blanche and her husband.[38] Perhaps this accounts for the extent of her involvement in north-eastern and Flemish affairs throughout Louis's personal rule. Besides, the counties of Flanders, Boulogne and Ponthieu had all been inherited by women by the early thirteenth century. In all three cases, by the 1230s the county would be inherited in the next generation by daughters. In these circumstances, marriage broking, so often the preserve of a queen, was an essential lever in the maintenance of the balance of power and the peace of the realm.

The death of Philip of Boulogne in 1234, leaving his wife, the countess Matilda, and daughter, Joanna, as heir, had enhanced royal control in the area.[39] Matilda of Boulogne could not marry off her daughter, or remarry herself, without the express permission of Louis and Blanche, though the countess could keep her daughter with her rather than surrendering her to the crown.[40] Before long, Blanche found the ideal husband for Matilda in one of her Iberian nephews, Alphonse of Portugal – though Alphonse turned out to be less than ideal from Matilda's point of view, deserting his wife to take the throne of Portugal when it became vacant in 1245. By late 1236 Joanna of Boulogne had been married to the loyal Gaucher of Châtillon, son of the count of Saint-Pol.[41]

Countess Mary of Ponthieu was Matilda of Boulogne's aunt by marriage. Ponthieu was a much less wealthy inheritance than the vast Boulogne honours, but the county controlled the mouth of the Somme, from which William the Conqueror had invaded England, and its strategic importance, both naval and commercial, was widely appreciated on both sides of the English Channel. Indeed, it was reflected in the fact that Countess Mary's mother was a daughter of Louis VII. Blanche had already prevented a marriage between the heiress, Joanna, and Henry III, and had ensured that Joanna could be married only with her permission.[42] Now, in late 1237, Blanche arranged a brilliant match for Joanna of Ponthieu with her nephew Ferdinand, king of Castile.[43] For the time being, the mouth of the Somme was secured against the English, though ironically King Ferdinand gave Ponthieu as dowry when their daughter, Eleanor, married the future Edward I of England in 1254.

Blanche's cousin, the loyal Ferdinand of Portugal, count of Flanders in right of his wife, died in 1233. In the summer of 1235 a marriage was arranged between

Blanche's second surviving son, Robert, designated by his father as count of Artois, and Mary, daughter of Ferdinand and Countess Joanna, and the heiress to Flanders. The dower and dowry arrangements were complex, but this marriage would bring the county of Flanders into Capetian family control.[44] In early 1237 Countess Joanna considered marrying Simon de Montfort. Blanche and Louis moved together to prevent the marriage. Mousquès thought their motivation was simply Blanche's personal hatred for the ambitious adventurer, but there was more to it than that. Simon's brother, Amaury, was a conspicuously loyal member of her entourage. But Simon had by now committed himself to the English inheritance of the Montfort clan, and the disastrous attempt to take the English throne in 1216–18 may have been too raw a remembrance.[45] Besides, if Countess Joanna remarried there was the danger that she would have a son, thus threatening her daughter Mary and young Robert's prospects of inheriting Flanders. Surprisingly, Blanche and Louis took that risk, finding a more suitable husband for Countess Joanna in Thomas of Savoy, an uncle of Margaret of Provence. Substantial securities were demanded from the aristocracy and the towns of Flanders. In all cases, the securities were addressed to Blanche as well as Louis, and the convention they secured is specified as between Countess Joanna on the one hand and Louis and 'Blanchia Regina' on the other.[46] Joanna and her new husband did homage to Louis, and swore fidelity to the king, his heirs, his brothers and his mother, at a great court held jointly by Louis and Blanche at Compiègne in December 1237.[47]

In summer 1237 Blanche's high-spirited son Robert reached his majority. Louis knighted his younger brother along with 140 other knights at Compiègne, and Robert was formally endowed with the great fief, or *apanage*, of Artois, as Louis VIII had prescribed in his will more than twenty years previously. Blanche's rich northern dower lands of Hesdin, Bapaume and Lens were now given to Robert; Blanche was given in exchange a clutch of equally wealthy towns and lands around Paris, including Melun, Etampes, Corbeil and Pontoise.[48] Mary of Flanders had died in the meantime, so Robert was married instead to Matilda of Brabant, this marriage also reinforcing the Capetian position in the broader Flemish and imperial world. The knighting and marriage were celebrated with a magnificent feast. Louis and Robert wore vermilion and purple and sat on painted cushions. There were gifts of emeralds for the royal cousin, Margaret, countess of Blois, and the wife of Enguerrand of Coucy. The entertainments reflected Robert's fondness for minstrels and acrobats; the king was served his meal by minstrels riding two great horned oxen in scarlet trappings.[49]

Two years later, at Pentecost 1239, there was another great knighting ceremony, this time for Blanche's nephew, Alphonse of Portugal, closely followed by his marriage to Matilda of Boulogne. The knighting was held at Blanche's new dower castle of Melun, and the wedding at Beaumont-sur-Oise, close to her new dower town of Pontoise. The two ceremonies were managed under her aegis. Among those knighted with Alphonse were a son-in-law of her lady Matilda of Lorris and Baldwin, the Latin emperor of Constantinople, husband of Blanche's great-niece Mary.[50] Blanche gave Matilda of Boulogne a robe of fine green samite, and had her nephew Alphonse and his household splendidly attired.[51] Both the knighting and the wedding, like those for Robert of Artois, were entertained by large numbers of minstrels. Wolves were brought to the park at Beaumont-sur-Oise for a great hunt after the wedding.[52]

Papal politics impinged increasingly on France from the late 1230s, for Gregory IX was an energetic and interfering pope. He clearly had great respect for Blanche's abilities. He wrote to ask for Louis's help in his projects; but in most cases he wrote, usually separately, to Blanche too. Evidently Gregory thought that the best way to persuade Louis to act was through the influence of his mother. The pope's belief in Blanche's political efficacy both reflected her position at the centre of political life in France and served to reinforce it.

Gregory continued to pressurise Raymond of Toulouse, launching inquisitions against heresy in the Languedoc. From the Capetian point of view the arrangements of Blanche's Treaty of Paris of 1229 were satisfactory. Raymond was largely loyal, and came quite frequently to court, where his daughter, Joanna, betrothed to young Alphonse, was brought up with the other royal children. In May 1237, though, Gregory wrote to Raymond insisting that he go to the Holy Land for the good of his soul, claiming that this was at the request of Louis and Blanche.[53] In 1238, and then again in 1239, Gregory tried to persuade Blanche to do all in her power, for the remission of her sins, to help the pope unseat the emperor Frederick II.[54] Gregory proposed that Robert of Artois should become emperor instead; the proposal was firmly rejected – by Louis, according to Matthew Paris; by the advice and prudence of Blanche, according to Aubri of Trois-Fontaines.[55] Capetian policy had tended to be pro-Swabian. Neither Blanche nor Louis would have seen the unseating of the emperor as the business of the king of France.

Gregory's other great project was the launch of a new Crusade. Frederick II had brought Jerusalem itself under Christian control by treaty, but its position was perceived as vulnerable. The Latin kingdom of Constantinople was threatened by

both Turks and dispossessed Greeks. Baldwin of Courtenay, the emperor of Constantinople, came to France in 1236 to raise interest in the plight of his threatened realm. Baldwin's connection with the French royal family was very close. Through his mother, he was a first cousin of Louis VIII; as a Courtenay, he was a member of the extended Capetian clan. And he was married to Mary, daughter of Blanche's niece, Berengaria of Castile-León, and John of Brienne. Indeed, Baldwin was dispatched to France by John and Berengaria. At the same time, they sent their three small sons, Alphonse, John and Louis, to the French court, in the hopes that the princes would be well cared for there.[56] Blanche seems to have felt a close affinity with Berengaria's children, and they were absorbed into the nursery at the court. Alphonse in particular was a favourite with the family.[57] But neither Blanche nor Louis responded to Baldwin's pleas for direct military help for Constantinople. Nor did Blanche respond to Gregory IX's plea in 1237 that she send 'suitable knights or other appropriate subsidy' to help the emperor Baldwin against the Greeks, and certainly not to Gregory's invitation that she herself should go to the Holy Land in exchange for an indulgence.[58]

But Baldwin's visit and Gregory's attempts to organise another Crusade did bear fruit. Several members of the French aristocracy left for the East in 1239. Louis sent the loyal Amaury of Montfort in his stead, supported to the tune of 32,000 *livres parisis*.[59] Several members of the royal household received gifts to go, including Rousellus from Blanche's stable and the valet who looked after Princess Isabella's palfrey.[60] Conveniently for the king and his mother, the group included many who had pursued private wars, or toyed with an Angevin alliance in the previous decade, notably Peter Mauclerc, but also his relation, Hugh of Burgundy and his brother, John of Mâcon. The Crusade was led by Theobald of Champagne.[61] Crusading was an expensive business, and in many cases the magnates could raise the sums required only by selling important rights and properties to the crown. Hugh of Burgundy came to an arrangement with Louis, and John of Mâcon sold the county of Mâcon to the crown.[62] Peter Mauclerc and his son, Count John of Brittany, made their peace with Louis and Blanche before leaving. They came to court at Pontoise; Count John handed over all his Norman border castles to Louis, and swore that he would hand over anything to the king, or the queen, his mother, on their demand. Peter Mauclerc agreed to this abject concession as plain Peter of Braine.[63]

The French crown was able to help the emperor Baldwin with what must have been accounted 'an appropriate subsidy'. The palace chapel at Constantinople

contained some of the most important relics in Christendom. Pre-eminent among them was the Crown of Thorns: John of Brienne had told Louis and Blanche about it on one of his visits to Paris.[64] But Baldwin, desperate for money, had already pawned it to the Venetians. In 1238 Louis redeemed it for him, and arranged for the precious relic to be brought to France, for keeping in his chapel in the palace on the Ile de la Cité in Paris.[65] Finally, in August of the following year, the Crown of Thorns arrived in Capetian France. It had been brought through Italy, over the Alps, through Burgundy and Theobald of Champagne's capital of Troyes. Louis, with Blanche and his brothers, and the court, received it at Villeneuve-l'Archevêque, halfway between Troyes and Sens, on the very border of Champagne and the royal lands. The royal family met the relic as penitents, barefoot and dressed in their chemises. Thus attired, in imitation of the sufferings of Christ, Louis and his brothers carried the Crown of Thorns to Sens. From there it was taken to Paris, and deposited in the chapel of St Nicholas in the palace on the Ile de la Cité.[66]

The arrival of the relics was carefully choreographed. The organisation was entrusted to Blanche's adviser, Walter Cornut, archbishop of Sens. Walter wrote a short celebratory account of it, presumably for members of the Capetian family. His account insists on Blanche's prominent role in the project. He pointed out that she was the 'prudentissima' aunt of the empress Mary. At all stages of Walter's account, decisions are made by, and the progress of negotiations reported to, both Blanche and Louis. Walter ensured that the initial ceremonies occurred in places that he controlled. Sens itself, the metropolitan city of the Capetian lands, was a natural choice for the first major ceremonies; but the selection of the small town of Villeneuve-l'Archevêque, built and run in parity by the archbishops of Sens and the counts of Champagne, reflects Walter's controlling hand. The town had been founded in the late twelfth century, laid out with the neat grid pattern that it still, 800 years later, retains. Its church – the scene of the reception of the relics by Louis – was undistinguished. Walter, or perhaps Blanche, felt that it required embellishment, and dispatched a group of sculptors to create an incongruously magnificent new portal, featuring the *Coronation of the Virgin*, with an unusually prominent crown for Christ himself (pl. 12).[67] The transport of the Crown of Thorns mainly by boat from Sens to the Paris area was arranged by Denis the Scutifer. Before the final entrance into the city of Paris, the Crown of Thorns was displayed on scaffolding swathed in silks beside the Cistercian nunnery of Saint-Antoine-des-Champs. The construction of this tabernacle was entrusted to Peter Pig-Flesh. Both Denis and Peter were trusted members of Blanche's

household. From there, Louis and Robert of Artois, barefoot and penitential in their chemises, carried the relic into the city, first to the cathedral of Notre-Dame and thence to the palace chapel. The final stage of the penitential journey, from Saint-Antoine to the mother church of the city of Paris, was a reverse echo of that made by Blanche and the queens Ingeborg and Berengaria of Jerusalem in 1224 to pray for victory for Louis VIII. Blanche was deeply involved with Saint-Antoine-des-Champs at this stage: she was founding a new nunnery of her own, with nuns drawn from Saint-Antoine, and the abbess, Agnes Mauvoisin, was often in her entourage. Everything suggests that the ceremonial reception of the Crown of Thorns was organised by Blanche and Walter Cornut.[68]

In 1239 Louis acquired even more relics from Baldwin, including substantial portions of the True Cross.[69] He decided that the relic collection needed a new palace chapel to house them. By the early 1240s the building of the Sainte-Chapelle was under way; in April 1248 the finished chapel was consecrated.[70] One of the stained-glass windows tells the story of the redemption of the Crown of Thorns, clearly based on Walter's account. The Capetian family, including Blanche, are shown receiving and venerating the Crown of Thorns (pl. 13). It is unclear how much Walter contributed to the imagery of Sainte-Chapelle, for he died in spring 1241. Blanche must have mourned the cleric who had been an unwavering support to her.

•

Blanche by now had her own building and development plans. She had probably always ensured that her dower and dowry lands were well administered, and thus as productive as they could be. By 1236 she had the time to concentrate on the dowry lands in Berry, given to her by her uncle, King John, especially the fortress town of Issoudun. Here she bought up houses and redeveloped the centre of the town, building new stone market halls – to the discomfort of several local abbeys, who found their mercantile opportunities curtailed.[71] In 1237 her northern dower towns had been exchanged for an impressive portfolio of towns in the Ile-de-France, including Meulan and Pontoise on the Seine and Dourdan, Etampes, Corbeil and Melun to the south of Paris. In 1240 Louis augmented these with Pierrefonds, Crépy-en-Valois and La Ferté-Milon to the north-east of Paris. At the same time, Blanche resigned her dowry lands in Berry, including Issoudun, to Louis himself.[72] The new arrangements exchanged distant holdings for properties closer to Paris, a wise move as Blanche aged. All her new towns were on major roads or

rivers into Paris; all of them were flourishing; all of them already possessed fine castles, and Pontoise and Melun had long been favoured centres of royal power. These two castles became Blanche's favoured homes for the last twelve years of her life. Outside both she founded Cistercian nunneries.

The earliest and most substantial of the two nunneries was Maubuisson, or the abbey of Mary, Queen of Heaven, founded in the fields below the castle at Pontoise. Blanche was buying properties to prepare for its building and endowment from 1236, which suggests that the decision to give Pontoise to her as part of a new dower settlement had already been made. The site was ready to receive the nuns, with a church, chapter house, dormitory and refectory, by 1241. In 1244 the abbey church was consecrated. The new nuns came from the nunnery of Saint-Antoine-des-Champs. Blanche had a house built for her use at Maubuisson and spent increasing amounts of time there. Louis and his court came there from time to time too. Younger women from the court circle with spiritual leanings were encouraged to join the community, such as Blanche's great-great niece Blanche of Eu-Brienne, who became the second abbess. Louis IX had his daughter Blanche educated there, and hoped she would take the veil there, though in the end she was destined for a dynastic marriage. Blanche herself intended it as her burial place.[73]

She put the implementation of the establishing and construction of the house into the hands of a trusted royal official, Master Richard of Tourny, who was based in her castle at Pontoise. Master Richard often acted to attest royal household expenditures, in particular those associated with Blanche.[74] Blanche took a keen interest in every detail. Master Richard discussed both the funding and the progress with her, and produced a set of detailed accounts, which the nuns had copied into a book about the foundation of their abbey, called the *Achatz d'heritage*.[75] The abbesses of Saint-Antoine – Agnes Mauvoisin was abbess until 1240, when she was succeeded by Amicia Briard – are frequently recorded in Blanche's entourage at this time, and both must have sat with the queen and Master Richard to ensure that all the requirements of the nuns would be met.[76]

Master Richard's accounts show that Blanche spent 24,431 *livres* on the foundation between 1236 and 1242.[77] Like most women founders, she did not alienate lands for the foundation, for neither her dower nor her dowry was really hers to give away. Instead, she assigned funds from her own revenues, mainly from the issues of the *prévôtés* of Mantes and Meulan, and used them to buy out those whose

lands lay in her way. Meulan was one of the towns given to her in 1237; Mantes was not part of the dower exchange, and its issues may have been supporting her for some time. The Meulan and Mantes revenues are first recorded in the abbey accounts for 1239, but some 4,912 *livres* derived from Blanche's other sources of revenue were spent in the first year of operations.[78] The *Achatz d'heritage* records the joy that various men and women felt in confirming that their lands had been bought by the queen for the furtherance of God's work: it is impossible to tell whether they felt amply rewarded or the victims of compulsory purchase. Land surveyors were employed to assess the compensations they should receive.[79] There is evidence that some who lived on abbey lands resented paying their tithes.[80] On some of these lands, the abbey itself was built. Others, a little further away, would provide both produce and revenues once the nuns had moved into their new home. In the meantime, Master Richard could sell the produce – the area was clearly richly productive of leeks – to provide yet more revenue for the building and stocking of the house.[81]

The *Achatz d'heritage* says that the abbey was founded in May 1236, in the first week after Pentecost. Purchase of lands and building began at once, though lands were still being obtained in 1239.[82] The dormitory, the chapter house, the church and the queen's house were all built with speed but finesse. The chapter house and the east claustral range, fragments of the church, a fine barn and a magnificent range of latrines still stand (pls 10, 11). The church was ready for its dedication on 26 June 1244 by Bishop William of Paris.[83] Elaborate provision for water was put in place, and the cloister provided with an elegant towered lavabo, revealed in excavations between 1978 and 1983 (pl. 17). In 1239 compensation was paid for damage to a house during the works to supply spring water to the abbey.[84] Cut stone was brought from quarries along the Oise, and huge amounts of wood for scaffolding, for roofs and for wainscoting from the queen's lands around the Oise, from the forests of the Evreçin in eastern Normandy, and from the woods at Cuisy, near Soissons. Paving stones were cut and laid, and huge numbers of tiles were fired, some in green and red, for roofs, floors and the essential water pipes. A group of trusted purveyors were used, including Master Geoffrey the Norman. No architect as such is named in the accounts, though a major role was played by Master Robert the carpenter. By 1240 Master Richard was ordering white cloth for nuns' habits, and stocking the abbey farm with chickens and cows. Cloths, keys and cooking pots were bought – usually at the Lendit Fair at Saint-Denis.[85] Blanche

ensured that the nuns at her new foundation were well provided with books: she left them one of her illustrated psalters, and another 'joly livre bien escript', probably a devotional text of some kind.[86]

In 1241 the abbey was ready for occupation, and the nuns were brought from Saint-Antoine. Now Blanche issued the foundation charter (pl. 21). In it, she names her new abbey Santa Maria Regalis – St Mary, Queen of Heaven, the name that her parents had chosen for Las Huelgas. It is founded for the sake of the souls of her beloved parents, Eleanor and Alfonso, and her beloved husband, and of her children.[87] The abbess of the new house, Guillemette, must have been chosen by the abbess of Saint-Antoine, with Blanche's consent. Guillemette was relatively young, for she did not die until 1275, and the new house flourished under her guidance. By 1260 it had attracted at least 120 nuns, and was much favoured by the French aristocratic women who wished to take the veil. Blanche and the abbess Agnes or Amicia had clearly chosen well. But it was a surprising choice in that Guillemette appears to have had no aristocratic connections, in an age when most abbesses of prestigious foundations did. Agnes and Amicia of Saint-Antoine, for instance, were both from established aristocratic families of the old Capetian heartlands; the first abbess of Blanche's other foundation, Le Lys, was Alice of Vienne, countess of Mâcon, and the second abbess of Maubuisson was Blanche of Eu-Brienne, niece of the empress Mary of Constantinople.[88]

Slightly less imposing, and less central to the spiritual – and political – life of the court was Blanche's other Cistercian nunnery founded close to her castle of Melun. She began to accumulate the requisite lands for both the abbey itself and its supporting revenues in the late 1230s. Works began in 1244, and the abbey was ready for occupation by the nuns in 1246.[89] The foundation charter was issued in 1248. No detailed accounts survive for this abbey, but there is a late thirteenth-century cartulary (Paris, Bibliothèque Nationale, MS lat. 13892), and the substantial, if ruined, remains of the abbey church bear witness to the courtly elegance and fine workmanship that Blanche demanded in her commissions (pls 18, 20). Maubuisson was essentially Blanche's foundation. Louis IX probably had more active involvement in the foundation of Le Lys. Its 'foundation' charter was issued by the king, with two other charters, as he set off on Crusade, and both it, and other charters, given by him claim the foundation as his own.[90] Nevertheless, his charters confirm sales of land arranged by Blanche and the provision of revenues from her dower lands; and one of them refers to the abbey that Blanche has 'de novo construxit'.[91] The initiative for the foundation was hers, but she may have

required a level of financial help from her son that was unnecessary at Maubuisson – probably because she was spending so much on the latter. And Blanche herself, in a charter of October 1250 issued at Maubuisson, confirming some of her gifts, specifies that she has founded the abbey along with her son. In this charter, she gives the new nunnery its name. Louis just refers to it as the abbey dedicated to the Virgin; Blanche calls it Le Lys – the lily, in subtle double reference to the flower associated with the Virgin at the Annunciation, which provided also the arms of France.[92]

The first abbess was a friend and distant cousin, Alice of Vienne. Alice had already made a substantial gift of revenues drawn from Rouen to Maubuisson.[93] Now, as the intended first abbess, she must have overseen the foundation of Le Lys with Blanche in the way that the abbess of Saint-Antoine would have helped with Maubuisson. Countess Alice came from a distinguished family, descended from the dukes of Burgundy; her grandmother Scholastica of Champagne was Philip Augustus's cousin. Heiress in her own right to the Burgundian county of Mâcon, she had been married to Peter and Robert of Dreux's brother, John – probably as a result of Philip Augustus's attempts to stabilise Burgundy and bring it within the Capetian sphere. In the event, Count John had often been involved in the anti-Champagne plots of his Dreux brothers. He died on Crusade in 1239, leaving Countess Alice to sell the county to the French crown, and decide to retire from the world. Alice of Vienne was the sort of woman that one might expect to see heading a royal foundation, but most abbesses would have worked their way through the ranks of a nunnery: Alice had been a nun for seven years at the most. Perhaps Blanche and Alice thought that a woman who could govern a county would have no difficulty in running a convent. The rest of the nuns were presumably drawn from Maubuisson or Saint-Antoine. When Alice died in 1253, she was succeeded by her niece Matilda.[94]

•

Blanche's new dower arrangements certainly gave her easy and frequent access to Louis's court. But they perhaps indicated that she was henceforth expected to base herself in her own dower castles rather than at the centre of the king's court itself. In the first years of Louis's personal rule, much government business had been done in court before both Blanche and Louis, and many documents associated her with that government. From late 1238 this began to change. Where it is specified that business has been done before the king's court, other counsellors are mentioned,

but not Blanche.[95] This is also the case where the business concerns heiresses or widows: since control of their marriage was always an issue, this was an area where Blanche had usually played a substantial role.[96] It may be that this corresponds to a stage at which Blanche herself had withdrawn slightly from court to concentrate on her monastic foundations. She was ill around the feast of St Martha (29 July) in 1238, and it is possible that the illness was sufficiently serious to cause her withdrawal.[97] But her absence from court procedures and business also suggests that Louis was now determined to be seen as the ruler of France.

It was only a partial distancing. Judgement between the town and chapter of Saint-Quentin was rendered by Louis at Blanche's castle of Pontoise in March 1244 'in the court of the king…in the wardrobe of the Queen, at the back, towards the garden below'. Robert of Artois and Alphonse of Poitiers were there too, so perhaps advantage was taken of a family gathering.[98] When regal majesty was required, Louis might turn to Blanche. She, not Margaret, played the role of female ruler at the great feast when Alphonse was made count of Poitou in 1241; she, not Louis, presided at the show trial of the Talmud in 1240. Where what mattered was courtly ceremonial or chivalric festivity, Louis clearly turned to Blanche, as he did for the reception of the Crown of Thorns. The knightings of Alphonse of Portugal and Charles of Anjou both took place at Blanche's castle of Melun. She was probably much involved in the great feast for Alphonse of Poitiers. With a matriarchal air, she organised the family in its courtly interactions with the Church. In October 1240 she swept her sons off to Senlis to receive the archbishop of Canterbury, Edmund of Abingdon, then in flight from England. It was Blanche, not Louis, who offered Edmund refuge in France. The refuge would be at Louis's expense, but he and his brothers concurred.[99] In September 1244 the royal family, with a substantial courtly entourage, went to Burgundy to visit both Vézelay and Cîteaux to seek prayers and commemorations. With her family and their entourage, Blanche attended chapter at both institutions.[100] At Cîteaux, it was the general chapter of the order. The Cistercians did not expect lay men to attend: the idea that the queen of France, her daughter, daughter-in-law and their ladies might do so left the Cistercian high command aghast. It is clear from the anguished discussions as to how the order would cope with the influx of a monstrous regiment that the entire visit was Blanche's initiative. The order, like Louis and his brothers, accommodated themselves to Blanche's commands.[101]

Louis may have resented the fact that it was widely believed that it was due to the influence of his mother that he had forgiven Theobald of Champagne. He may

have begun to resent the fact that Gregory IX regularly appealed to Blanche's influence over her son. Raymond of Toulouse was another who depended on Blanche's influence on Louis. In 1242 he wrote to Blanche asking her to intercede with the king for him. Raymond's letter contains some intriguing phrases. Stressing his relationship to her, and the fact that she has long shown affection for him, he expresses his profound regrets that he 'might have given material to those detractors to produce rumours against the renown of your goodness, purity and discretion'.[102] He mentions her detractors more than once in the letter. The chronicler William of Puylaurens, who was Raymond's chaplain, also knew that certain persons at court had denounced Blanche for showing too much favour to Raymond.[103]

Raymond's letter is not the only evidence that the atmosphere at court had become poisonous as Louis tried to assert himself as king. In April 1241 at the palace of Saint-Germain-en-Laye, Louis and a small group of ecclesiastical counsellors forced Margaret of Provence to swear on the sacred Gospels that she would never do anything contrary to the ordinances and the testament of the king. The churchmen in question were all men who were personally close to the royal family, and in particular to Blanche herself – Bishop William of Paris, Adam of Chambly, bishop of Senlis, Eudes Clément, abbot of Saint-Denis, and Ralph, abbot of Saint-Victor.[104] Margaret's oath-taking occurred shortly after the death of Walter Cornut, to whom the smooth running of Capetian government for the last two decades owed so much. It is possible that his death led to a realignment of factions at court.

The event must have been a deep political humiliation for Margaret. Since the magnificence of her marriage and coronation, Margaret had lived quietly at court with the companionship of Blanche's daughter Isabella. Margaret had not yet provided Louis with an heir – their first son was not born until 1244 – and she was not in a strong position to enter into intrigues. There was no attempt to annul the marriage, but Louis never recovered trust in Margaret's integrity, judgement or competence.

It is not certain what Margaret had done. Perhaps she had been involved in attempts to reconcile Louis and Henry III of England through her sister, Eleanor, who was Henry's queen. Probably, she had attempted to play high politics as Henry III tried yet again to build a coalition to reclaim the Angevin lands. Henry may have found that the sisterly closeness between Eleanor and Margaret of Provence provided him with useful information from the French court.

Henry's old ally Peter Mauclerc had returned from the undistinguished and unsuccessful Barons' Crusade of 1239–40, but Peter now found his interests best served by supporting his Capetian cousins rather than the unreliable English king. Instead, Henry sought an ally even more intimately linked to the Capetian family. Raymond of Toulouse was eased away from his alliance with Blanche and Louis, and drawn into Henry's orbit. Raymond gave his tacit support to attacks on the king's lands in Carcassonne and Narbonne in 1240. William des Ormes, the royal agent in Carcassonne, sent Blanche a lively account of the siege. It is full of technical details of mines, countermines and trebuchets, including 'a really good Turkish stone-thrower'. Blanche seems to have sent some knights of her own to relieve the defenders. William tells Blanche that he will tell her more when he sees her in person. The letter makes no reference to the king, and leaves the distinct impression that Blanche has been pursuing her own policy, with her own networks, in Languedoc.[105]

Blanche's third surviving son, Alphonse, had now reached the age of majority, and, doubtless with a view to countering Henry III's clumsy diplomacy, he was knighted by Louis and given possession of the county of Poitou, the *apanage* prescribed for the third surviving son by Louis VIII. The entire court ambled off to the Loire in summer 1241. The knighting and great feasting that followed were held in the great hall built by Blanche's grandfather, Henry II, at Saumur.[106] The young John of Joinville was there as the seneschal of Count Theobald of Champagne. It may have been the first time that Joinville had met Louis and his family, and he wrote a vivid account of the scene, a litany of baronial names, and silken robes and tabards. Peter Mauclerc, now resigned to his role as elderly uncle, sat at the king's table. Count Theobald had his own table. Great bishops and abbots were there, as well as the barons. The presence of only one woman is mentioned. Blanche of Castile headed her own table, opposite that of the king, as if she were the queen consort.[107] The young queen herself is conspicuous by her absence in Joinville's account. Blanche's inclusion reflects her still substantial political weight.

It is Joinville who relates that the hall at Saumur was built by the great king Henry; and that it was built, moreover, to the design of a Cistercian cloister. Joinville's interest in buildings and their patrons was limited, and this striking claim has caught the attention of many architectural historians. Presumably, Joinville repeats this information because it was much discussed at the occasion itself. Blanche's devotion to, and Louis's strong favour towards, the Cistercians was well known in court circles. The choice of the great hall at Saumur by one or the other

of them must have been deliberate. For it had been built by Henry II, and now within it Alphonse, as his great-grandson, was taking possession of the county of Poitou, which had once been Henry's in right of his wife, Eleanor of Aquitaine.

The dry lists of household expenditure show that Joinville did not exaggerate the magnificence of the occasion. Substantial works to the royal residence and park at Saumur were required. Vast tents were brought from beyond the seas – presumably from the Middle East. There were three types of wine – from Berry, Saumur and Saint-Porcien. The cooks and sauce makers of both Louis's and Blanche's kitchens came to provide the food. There were gold plates, and a great new silver-gilt plate costing 68 *livres* for alms, and painted cushions for the king to sit on. Those who were knighted along with Alphonse were given robes and horses. They included the courtier Adam of Melun, to whom Blanche gave a robe of samite. The young queen – for Margaret was undoubtedly present – Princess Isabella, Countess Joanna of Toulouse and the countess of Artois wore purple of Spain; Alphonse himself wore a particularly fine robe of purple of Spain given to him by his mother.[108] Louis too was attired in regal magnificence, but chose to offset this with a simple cotton cap on his head, which Joinville for one thought unsuitable for the occasion.[109] Louis did not have to face having his meal served by minstrels balancing on scarlet-draped oxen as at Robert's knighting. Blanche's robes are not specifically mentioned, but doubtless she was not outshone by the younger royal women. Perhaps she wished she had an extra cushion, since a young knight was compensated for the tabard that he lost beneath her at the feast.[110] After this great chivalric display, the royal court moved on to Alphonse's new capital, the city of Poitiers itself.[111] Blanche herself, with her entourage, travelled back to her castle of Etampes via her old haunt at Lorris.[112]

At Poitiers, Hugh of La Marche and his wife, Isabella of Angoulême, came to do homage to Alphonse.[113] Isabella had an audience with Louis in the king's chamber. Louis was accompanied by the young queen, by Countess Isabella of Chartres and Isabella's sister, the abbess of Fontevraud. The details of the meeting, and their dramatic outcome, are known from a letter written in a vivid and chatty Latin to Blanche by a Capetian official based at La Rochelle.[114] Isabella of Angoulême, wrote the official, felt she was not treated according to her proper status as queen of England. She was kept waiting, not asked to sit down, while the French royal party lounged on Louis's bed, and was not given an opportunity to speak in confidence. She was, it seems, deliberately humiliated. Blanche, with her keen understanding of the importance of image and of political realities, might

have handled the situation differently – she had, after all, spent many years and much diplomatic effort to keep Hugh and Isabella detached from the Angevins. Isabella's reaction, though, was hardly balanced. She rushed back to her husband's castle at Lusignan, where Hugh had entertained Louis and Alphonse, and threw all her 'utensils and ornaments great and small', even a precious image of the Virgin, out of the castle. Then she locked herself and her possessions in her own castle of Angoulême. Eventually, her husband managed to calm her down. But the price of her acquiescence was that Count Hugh should break his fidelity to the Capetians, and join with Isabella's son, Henry III, in his attempt to regain Poitou.[115]

For Henry III had not been put off by the show of Capetian courtly magnificence and wealth in the Loire. The letter to Blanche warns her of the developing anti-Capetian alliance building in Gascony and Poitou, and of threats to blockade the strategically important port of La Rochelle, captured by Louis VIII in 1224.[116] The author of the letter clearly feels that it is important to keep the queen mother abreast of events, and suggests that she may be able to intervene to useful diplomatic effect. But he warns Blanche against being too soft on Hugh and Isabella of Angoulême.[117] Raymond of Toulouse, now on the Angevin side, was attempting to arrange a marriage with their daughter, though in the end the papacy, possibly at Blanche's urging, judged the marriage consanguineous.[118] Blanche visited Alphonse in Poitiers in late spring 1242, doubtless bringing her diplomatic experience. It is probably in this context that she lent the lord of Mirabeau, a member of the Blaison family, 1,000 *livres tournois*.[119] By the summer of 1242 Henry III had his alliances in place, and he and his allies invaded southern Poitou. Louis and his brothers gathered together a large army to repel the invader. They defeated Henry's forces at Taillebourg, on the Gironde, in July.[120] The battle was decisive. Henry fled, and although he did not formally renounce his claims to the Angevin lands, except Guyenne, until 1259, he made no further attempts to recapture them. Hugh and Isabella of La Marche made their peace with Louis and Alphonse of Poitiers, on humiliating terms.[121]

Raymond of Toulouse, in joining Henry's alliance, had also miscalculated badly. As always under pressure from the papacy, he was now desperate to make peace with Louis and his son-in-law, and eventual successor, Alphonse of Poitiers. Raymond turned to Blanche. He wrote a long and ingratiating letter, begging her to intercede with the king on his behalf.[122] Raymond made much of the fact that his mother and Blanche's mother were sisters, knowing, perhaps, that such appeals to family ties would move her. Raymond's letter proved effective. He was given

safe conducts, and came before Louis to throw himself on the king's mercy in January 1243. He undertook to uphold the terms of the Treaty of Paris, and to extirpate heresy from his lands. Blanche had done more than intercede: Raymond's reconciliation shows clear signs of her intervention throughout. It took place at Lorris, which, though it was no longer one of her own residences, had been her principal home for so long. Besides, although Raymond swore to keep the Treaty of Paris to Louis, it was to Blanche herself, 'because of her special grace and love', that he swore to destroy the heretics.[123]

Raymond's letter is the one in which he refers to Blanche's long-standing affection for him, and regrets that his recent adventures have given ammunition to her detractors at court. He promises to support the Church in its attacks on heresy, 'so that both your detractors, and all those who will hear of your circumspection, because you supported our dealings, will bless [you]'.[124] Blanche was indeed a strong advocate for Raymond at court. His daughter, Joanna, was at the Capetian court as Alphonse's wife, as Raymond observed in his letter, and Blanche may have had a closer bond with that daughter-in-law than with Margaret.

For Raymond, as for Theobald of Champagne, Blanche had asked for forgiveness and reinstatement. The official at La Rochelle thought that she might harbour too much sympathy towards Isabella of Angoulême and Hugh of La Marche. As argued above, it was often Louis rather than Blanche in the mid-1230s who insisted on pursuing a harder line when dealing with his prelates or his magnates. There can be no doubt that in the late 1230s and the 1240s Louis was determined to establish his royal authority and impose himself as king – and as his treatment of Isabella of Angoulême showed, he could do so with a certain casual cruelty.

Another area where Louis took a stronger line than his mother was in their approach to the Jews. Nevertheless, Louis asked Blanche to preside in his place at court in an inquisition on Jewish rabbinical tradition, the so-called trial of the Talmud, in 1240. Other members of the presiding bench included Blanche's episcopal friends Walter Cornut, archbishop of Sens, Adam of Chambly, bishop of Senlis, and William of Auvergne, bishop of Paris.[125] A Jew who had converted to Christianity, called Nicholas Donin, had persuaded Gregory IX that the corpus of rabbinical learning, brought together in the Talmud, contained material that was injurious to Christ and his mother, the Virgin, and potentially to Christians. Gregory wrote to the rulers of Christendom asking them to investigate these claims, and to destroy the Talmud if the claims were upheld. Louis IX was the only ruler to accept Gregory's challenge. In 1240 the books of the Jews of France were seized

and handed over into the temporary keeping, as Gregory had suggested, of the Dominican and Franciscan friars of Paris. Some of the most distinguished of the Jewish scholars, particularly their leader, the Rabbi Yehiel, were called to the palace to answer the charges against the Talmud, which were made by Donin himself. Rabbi Yehiel wrote an account of the proceedings, called the Vikkuah, which was later copied into a book on the problems faced by the Jews by Joseph ben Nathan Official. Joseph Official himself, and his father, owed their name 'Official' to the fact that they staffed Walter Cornut's episcopal administration, presumably because, with a Jewish financial background, they were excellent keepers of accounts.[126] From Rabbi Yehiel's account, it is clear that the trial was presided over, not by the king, but by the queen.[127]

The queen is not named, and could conceivably have been Margaret, though that is unlikely. Margaret was still young, and Yehiel's queen has formidable political and intellectual authority. When Yehiel tells the queen he fears the mob, her response shows that she is familiar with Augustine's stance on the Jews: 'It is our intention to protect you and all that is yours. All who do harm to you incur sin and iniquity. Thus we find in our books and from the Pope.'[128] When Yehiel refuses to take a Christian oath, the queen silences those who object: 'Since this is a difficult act for him, and as much as he has never taken a false oath, let him be.'[129] Much of the theological discussion is abstruse, and occasionally obscene, with a brilliant display of scholastic exegesis of what Christians called the Old Testament by Yehiel. The queen is engaged by the arguments, equal to the exegesis and unfazed by the obscenities – for much of the discussion circles around Yehiel's defence that the Jesus punished by boiling in excrement was not the Jesus whom Christians regard as Christ. When the argument becomes too vicious, she intervenes:

> Why do you [Donin and the assembled clergy] make yourselves so odious. See, it is to your own honour that he [Yehiel] said that it does not mention your god sentenced to excrement. They did not speak of him thus, that he was sentenced to boil in excrement. But you seek to draw out your shame from his mouth. It is your shame that you draw out of his mouth.

Turning to Yehiel, she asks: 'On your honour, are you telling the truth?'[130]

Yehiel's account suggests that he thought he had won his battle in front of the queen. Certainly, no immediate action was taken against the Jewish books. If

Blanche defended the Talmud, she was not alone. Walter Cornut defended the Jews and their books to St Louis's face, and some of their books were returned. The Dominican Thomas of Cantimpré, who gives this anecdote, says that the archbishop had been bribed; when Walter died in April 1241, Thomas said it was the judgement of God.[131] Louis was much less sympathetic towards the Jews than Blanche and Archbishop Walter, and he had the books of the royal Jews publicly burnt in 1242 and then again in 1244.

•

In December 1244, while he was staying at Blanche's castle of Pontoise, Louis fell desperately ill. It was a long illness – he did not recover until the end of January. Although Blanche had often been kept slightly distanced from Louis's government during the last few years, she immediately took charge. Countess Joanna of Flanders had just died, and her successor, her sister Margaret, must swear fidelity and do homage to the king. Louis was far too ill to deal with this; indeed, the family thought that he was too ill to be told of Countess Joanna's death, which might distress him too much. So Margaret swore provisional fidelity and did provisional homage to Blanche, as queen of France, and to Louis's brothers.[132] The documents were drafted with great care to ensure the fidelity of Margaret, while at the same time protecting the rights of the incapacitated king. They make clear the centrality of Blanche's role in the crisis. Moreover, it was Blanche who took the lead in organising the swearing of securities for Margaret of Flanders.[133] There were others who could have taken charge. Queen Margaret was now in her mid-twenties, and the mother of the heir to the throne. As queen consort, it was in effect her duty to act in place of her husband in cases where he was absent or incapacitated. But Queen Margaret is not mentioned. Two of Louis's brothers, Robert and Alphonse, were fully adult, knighted and running their own substantial administrations, but their role as receivers of the countess's fidelity is clearly secondary to that of Blanche.

Louis's illness was severe as well as long. He was given up for dead, but as one of the nurses pulled up the sheet to cover his face, it was clear that he was still, just, breathing. As soon as he regained consciousness, Louis vowed to go on Crusade. Blanche's reaction, according to Joinville, was powerful. Overcome with joy at the news that her beloved son had escaped death, she was all the more devastated to hear that he had taken the Cross. She mourned, said Joinville, just

as if he had died (pl. 14).[134] She tried desperately hard to dissuade him. She argued that the kingdom could still benefit from the stabilising power of the presence of the reigning king – and she had deep understanding of that power. Moreover, her husband had died on Crusade. But Louis was adamant, and would not be deflected. This time, his mother was unable to influence him.[135]

6

The Crusade Regency

B Y MARCH 1245 LOUIS HAD FULLY RECOVERED. In thanks, he gave
gifts to Royaumont.[1] He was able to receive the homage of Margaret of
Flanders.[2] He must have realised how far the stability of the realm during the crisis
of his illness had depended on his mother. Now once again he associated her closely
with the governance of the land. It was acknowledged, for instance, that the succession to Margaret of Flanders – a complex issue, for she had sons from two
marriages – was established in a convention between Margaret on the one hand
and Louis and Blanche on the other.[3] Dispositions for the Lusignan succession in
June 1246, as a result of the recent death of Isabella of Angoulême, were finalised
at Maubuisson; although Blanche is not named in the act recording the arrangement, the fact that it was settled at her house in the abbey at Maubuisson shows
that it was done in her presence. Her experience, and her relative sympathy for
Isabella and Count Hugh, perhaps ensured an effective resolution.[4] Besides, in the
previous year, Raymond of Toulouse had attempted to marry one of Hugh and
Isabella's daughters. The Church put a stop to that, producing a formidable dossier
to demonstrate the consanguinity of the potential spouses.[5] It was not in Capetian
interests for Raymond to produce a male heir. Managing Raymond was clearly
Blanche's business within the family.

In May Louis and Queen Margaret's second son, the future Philip III, was born.
Blanche's own youngest son, Charles, was now reaching adulthood. In June 1245
his marriage was arranged, with Beatrice, a younger sister of Margaret and Eleanor
of Provence. Since her older sisters were so well provided for, as, respectively, queens

of France and England, it was agreed that Beatrice should inherit the county of Provence, so that this marriage would bring an area of the Empire under the rule of a member of the Capetian family. In the following year, young Charles was knighted at a great court at Blanche's castle of Melun; presumably, like the knighting of Alphonse of Portugal, the ceremony and festivities were organised by Blanche. Charles was formally invested with the *apanage* of Anjou, inheriting the lands that had been destined for his older brother John.[6]

From now until his departure in late 1248 Louis IX's focus was on preparations for the Crusade to the Holy Land, which he was determined to undertake. It was not an easy task.[7] Blanche supported her son's endeavour, but had reservations about its wisdom. Pope Innocent IV was determined to launch a Crusade within Europe against the emperor Frederick II. Innocent wanted money from the French Church, and French knights, for this purpose. Louis refused his demands.[8] Louis and Blanche, together with the younger princes, met Innocent himself at Cluny in November 1245. Louis and his mother hoped to reconcile Innocent with the emperor, as well as reinforcing papal support for his own Crusade to the east.[9] They continued to work together towards the reconciliation of pope and emperor, even while Louis's Crusade was under way: in 1249 Louis sent an embassy to the emperor from Cyprus, while Blanche wrote to Innocent.[10]

Although he remained obsessed with his quarrel with Frederick II, Innocent gave Louis his support. He dispatched Cardinal Eudes of Tusculum – the French master, Eudes of Châteauroux – to preach the Crusade to the East in France. Both Louis and Innocent saw the completion of the Sainte-Chapelle, the house to hold the precious Crown of Thorns, as a prerequisite for a successful Crusade. Innocent issued indulgences for those who contributed to its completion in November 1246; on the same day he issued bulls of protection for French Crusaders.[11] After the consecration of the completed building by Eudes of Tusculum in April 1248, further papal indulgences were issued for visitors to the chapel and its relics.[12] The household accounts of 1248 show the expenditure on the finishing touches in the chapel, especially works by the two goldsmiths, Robert and John of Bur.[13]

In mid-Lent 1247 Louis held a great court to persuade his prelates, magnates and knights to join him. A letter from the king of the Tartars was read out to impress upon them the peril that threatened the Holy Land.[14] Money was raised, troops were assembled and ships commissioned.[15] Louis had a new town built on the Rhône delta at Aigues-Mortes, so that he could sail directly from a French port. He tried to ensure the safety of the realm, for while Henry III might be

ineffective, he was still not to be trusted. Margaret of Flanders had to provide large numbers of securities for her succession to Flanders. Henry III's brother, Richard of Cornwall, came to Paris in the autumn of 1247 to ask for the return of his territories – the county of Poitou. His request was refused.[16] It helped that Alphonse was proving an astute and capable administrator of Poitou. For Louis, the good governance of the realm, as well as its safety, mattered. Perhaps because he was so focused on the need to raise all potential revenues, he observed more closely the activities of his agents of local government, the *baillis* and *prévôts*. He found their integrity wanting. He was struck by the number who had been in place for a long time, and who had integrated themselves into local society, arranging advantageous marriages for their daughters and influential ecclesiastical positions for their sons. He tackled the problems fully only after he had returned from Crusade, but he started before his departure, moving officials around, and establishing commissions of inquiry into abuses of government. For these inquisitions he mainly used Dominicans and Franciscans, like Eudes Rigaud.[17]

Louis decided at an early stage that Blanche should once again have the governance of the country in his absence. Provision for Blanche's rule was incorporated into arrangements with his subjects. When the Latin emperor Baldwin was in Paris in June 1247, he drew up a protocol whereby his staff would hand over all his castles in French territories, including Namur, on demand, to the king, or to Blanche, or to the king's brothers.[18] Robert, Alphonse and Charles had all taken the Cross with Louis. In the event, Alphonse and Charles left later than Louis, and returned well before him. They were not formally associated in the regency with Blanche. But Blanche was no longer young, and the protocol with the emperor Baldwin shows that Louis was prepared to contemplate a future where his own death, and that of his mother, might bring the wardship of his young heir into his brothers' hands.[19] There was no suggestion that Queen Margaret should have any involvement in the governance of the country; instead, Louis took her with him. She was not the only great lady to go; Alphonse took his wife, Joanna of Toulouse, too. And Louis was following precedent: Louis VII had taken his wife, Eleanor of Aquitaine. In the event, Blanche governed with the support of an informal group of higher clergy, including John de la Cour, bishop of Evreux, William of Bussy, bishop of Orléans, Adam of Chambly, bishop of Senlis, Renaud of Corbeil, bishop of Paris (for her old friend Bishop William had died in 1248), and, less regularly, Philip Berruyer, archbishop of Bourges, and Eudes Rigaud, archbishop of Rouen. All of them had a background in royal administration, so

that they were in theory well placed to take over as a regency council in the event of her death.[20] But Louis gave all executive power to Blanche. At the very start of his journey to the south, in June 1248, he held a court in the hospital of Corbeil – chosen, perhaps, because Blanche had funded, with considerable generosity, its recent construction.[21] There he conferred on her the full power to choose, appoint and remove administrators and officers who undertook the business of the kingdom, as she saw fit; the power to appoint or remove the *baillis* and *prévôts*, the agents of local government; and full regal powers in relation to the Church, including the giving of the licence to elect prelates, the giving or withholding of regalia, and the receiving of fidelity from elected prelates.[22] It seems a thin provision for the governance of the realm, but the powers were wider than they appear at first glance, and the very lack of prescription gave Blanche room for manoeuvre. The accounts for the spring of 1248 show a flurry of works to the queen's quarters and chapels in various royal palaces – Fontainebleau, Montargis and Villeneuve-sur-Yonne. This may be no more than standard maintenance; but the works were substantial, and suggest a determination to fit the royal houses for the itinerary of a ruling queen.[23]

Like Louis, Blanche sought God's help and blessing for her son's projected Crusade. She occupied herself with her new foundations of Maubuisson and Le Lys. Maubuisson was now fully functional, and she spent much time living in the fine house she had had built within the precinct wall. Le Lys was still under construction. Louis confirmed her gifts to them both, and made generous gifts of his own before his departure.[24] Perhaps moved by Blanche's special sympathies for Cistercian nuns, Louis also made gifts to Porret (often known as Port-Royal) for the sake of his soul, and for the souls of Blanche and Louis VIII.[25] Along with her sons, Blanche attended the translation of the remains of the now-canonised St Edmund of Abingdon at Pontigny in northern Burgundy in early 1247. As an archbishop of Canterbury who took refuge in France, Edmund reminded Blanche of his predecessors who had done the same – Stephen Langton, brother of Master Simon, and Thomas Becket, to whom Blanche and Louis VIII had been so devoted. Blanche and her husband had not been able to attend the great translation of Becket's remains in 1220; perhaps she drew some comfort, as her son prepared his journey to the East, from her presence on this occasion. Matthew Paris, often well informed on court gossip, clearly thought so. Blanche held a vigil at the shrine, and Matthew imagines her prayer: 'O saintly master confessor, who had blessed myself, a supplicant, and my sons . . . and through me by your grace made transit

in France, confirm what has been begun by us, and confirm the kingdom of France in stable and triumphant peace.'[26] She still had profound reservations about Louis's adventure. Early in 1248 she and the bishop of Paris (at that stage, probably still William of Auvergne) made one belated bid to stop Louis going. His health was fragile, and his kingdom needed his presence. Blanche applied maternal pressure: 'Remember how much it pleases God if you obey your mother.' It was enough to make Louis waver, but not enough to stop him.[27]

The preparation of the soul for Crusade culminated in the consecration of the completed Sainte-Chapelle, and the translation into it of the Crown of Thorns on 26 April 1248. It was one of the great courtly occasions of Louis's reign, but an occasion that showed the king, and his mother and brothers, caring for the poor and the hungry of the kingdom in a great donation of alms. On 12 June Louis left Paris for the south. At Corbeil, he held his plenary court in the hospital that Blanche had built. There he resolved his long battle with the bishops of Beauvais. There, too, he conferred the full powers to rule the kingdom on Blanche. Perhaps it was at Corbeil that Louis and his mother parted. The Ménestrel of Reims says that Blanche walked with Louis for three days after he left Paris. When he left her, she collapsed in despair.[28] On 28 August Louis sailed from Aigues-Mortes. Robert of Artois and Queen Margaret went with Louis, though Alphonse and Countess Joanna, and Charles of Anjou, did not set off until the late summer of 1249. Alphonse and Charles returned a year later, but Blanche never saw Louis or Robert again.

From the moment that Louis left, Blanche was once again the ruler of the kingdom of France, and guardian of the young heir to the throne. She dealt with the day-to-day business of government – settling disputes between the bishop and burghers of Châlons-sur-Marne, between the countess of Artois and the advocate of Béthune, between the lord of Nesle and the bishop of Noyon, between the drapers of Paris and the abbey of Saint-Denis. She ordered inquests into the rights at issue, and often, though not always, sat in judgement where issues were referred to the king's court. Mindful of the scholars' strike during her last regency, she insisted that the scholars and citizens of Paris swear in solemn council to keep the peace.[29] Alphonse and Charles provided some support. Both before they left and after their return, in the late summer of 1250, they concentrated on ruling their own territories, but that in itself must have been a huge relief to their ageing mother. Alphonse, for instance, took steps to ensure the stability of Poitou and the good behaviour of the Lusignan clan.[30] Raymond of Toulouse was now ailing. He

had taken the Cross in Paris in 1247, but had put off his departure. Now, he came to see Alphonse and his daughter Joanna as they left for the East from Aigues-Mortes, to discuss the affairs of the county of Toulouse with them. In October 1249 he died.[31] Joanna and Alphonse now inherited the county of Toulouse, to set alongside Poitou. Charles had been married to Beatrice, heiress to the county of Provence in early 1246, and was intent on imposing his authority there, probably because Anjou was fairly stable.[32] Since Charles held Anjou, and Alphonse held Poitou and Toulouse, the two of them, when they were present, formed a formidable barrier to any pretensions that Henry III might have harboured to the old Angevin lands south of the Loire.

Blanche had been in her late thirties when she took control after the death of Louis VIII; now she was sixty. Fortunately, the political situation was calmer. Louis was a Crusader, and his lands were thus under papal protection. Nevertheless, Henry III threatened war with France, though Matthew Paris thought this was merely an expedient to raise money from his barons.[33] Henry had himself taken the Cross, and Blanche wrote to Pope Innocent IV asking that Henry should be excommunicated if he did not honour his Crusade vow. Henry's brother, Richard of Cornwall, and Simon de Montfort visited Blanche to negotiate a truce with Henry until the end of the year. Blanche received Richard surprisingly warmly – 'like a mother to a son', said Matthew Paris, when Richard stayed with her at Melun over Easter 1249.[34]

As for the barons, Philip Hurepel was long dead, though the French court was still settling his debts;[35] Hugh of Lusignan died in 1249; Peter of Brittany and Theobald of Champagne and Navarre, together with most of the younger genera-tion of greater barons, had joined the Crusade. The Ménestrel of Reims mourned that 'France was emptied of its nobility and still has not recovered.'[36] Blanche is unlikely to have shared his regrets. She took care to ensure that those who did remain were firmly controlled, insisting that they came to her at Paris or Pontoise to swear fidelity or to ratify previous agreements, especially if death brought a new successor to a lordship. Where she deemed it necessary, she demanded substantial pledges, and sometimes hostages. Isabella of Craon, the hereditary seneschal of Anjou, agreed to hand over a set of important fortresses on request.[37] The death of Philip and Matilda of Boulogne's daughter and heiress, Joanna, in early 1252 precipitated a reconsideration of the rich Boulogne heritage. Many had claims, including both Alphonse and Charles. On 23 February Blanche issued a letter in council that dealt with the situation in the short term. The liquid assets were

returned to Countess Matilda, who was still alive; otherwise Blanche was careful to preserve any rights or interests that the king might have. She left the final resolution until the king should return.[38]

The future succession to the county of Flanders was a potential problem. The Countess Margaret had been married twice: first, when very young, to Bouchard of Avesnes; the second time to Guy of Dampierre. Margaret had been advised against marriage to Bouchard of Avesnes; in the end she had their marriage annulled, and her two sons by him declared illegitimate. When Margaret had merely been a younger sister, this had not mattered too much. But the death, in quick succession, of Countess Joanna and her daughter made Margaret sole heir to the rich and strategic counties of Flanders and Hainault. The Avesnes brothers successfully challenged their status as illegitimate. Margaret, her husband, Count Guy, and her two Dampierre sons were forced to come to an arrangement with the Avesnes brothers. The Avesnes brothers would inherit Hainault, and the Dampierre would inherit Flanders itself. The Avesnes brothers came to Blanche's court in November 1248 to conclude the agreement over the division of their Flemish inheritance. In early 1252 Count Guy of Flanders confirmed all arrangements made with his predecessors as count, all of which tended to the advantage of the king of France. But neither party was truly satisfied. Margaret came to Paris to ask for Blanche's help, and then offered the county of Hainault to Charles, who had returned from the Crusade. Charles was tempted, but for the sake of peace Blanche persuaded him to desist.[39]

The gradual increase of royal authority in Burgundy over the previous half century, together with the control of the Languedoc, meant that Blanche was very conscious of control of the Massif Central. The lords of Turenne and Castelnau in the upper reaches of the Dordogne swore fidelity to her at Pontoise in late 1251.[40] She was particularly determined to ensure Bourbon fidelity. In the twelfth century the lords of Bourbon, while distinguished, were of local importance, lords of an unproductive mountainous wilderness on the edge of the Massif Central. Now they and their lands had great strategic importance, reflected in their marriages. One of Archibald of Bourbon's daughters was married to Theobald of Champagne and Navarre. Another was married to Eudes, son of the duke of Burgundy. When Eudes succeeded his father-in-law to the lordship of Bourbon in late 1249, Blanche ensured that he came to Paris to swear fidelity to her, and homage to Alphonse, from whom the lands in question were held. It was unclear whether a relief should be paid for the lands or how much it should be, but Blanche demanded and got

substantial securities and potential hostages against the eventual payment should it be required.[41] In February 1252 she insisted that some of the younger relations of the Bourbons, both clergy, swore fidelity to the crown.[42] Blanche's determination to ensure the Bourbons' fidelity is unsurprising.

When Raymond of Toulouse had died in October 1249, he had asked to be buried at the feet of his mother Joanna, and alongside his uncle Richard the Lionheart and grandfather Henry II at Fontevraud, and left substantial gifts to Fontevraud and to Cistercian nuns. Blanche gave her permission for Raymond's body to taken for burial as he desired.[43] In death, Raymond acknowledged his Angevin heritage. Although Blanche had become close to her cousin, his death must have come as a relief from the political point of view. Raymond had too often been tempted to ally with his other cousin, Henry III of England, and if Raymond married, as he clearly would have liked, there was the ever-present threat of a male heir. Now, there was no question that the county of Toulouse would come through Raymond's daughter to Alphonse. For the first time, this huge, rich and strategically important county would come under direct Capetian control. Blanche sent trusted officials, the knights Guy and Hervé of Chevreuse, with Philip, the treasurer of Saint-Hilaire in Poitiers, to get oaths of allegiance to Alphonse from Raymond's lands, as had been agreed at the Treaty of Paris which she had negotiated twenty years earlier.[44] Most of the southern lords and cities complied, though the consuls of the city of Agen insisted on coming to Paris to negotiate a slightly different form of oath with Blanche.[45] She gave Philip the Treasurer authority to work with Simon de Montfort, then in charge of Gascony for Henry III, to protect Alphonse's eastern borders.[46] Wisely, she left Raymond's experienced official Sicard Aleman in place as vice-gerent in the county for Alphonse, as he had been for Raymond.[47] Raymond's death reopened potential disputes between Alphonse, who as count of Toulouse was also marquis of Provence, and the count of Provence – who was Charles of Anjou in right of his wife. The relationship of the cities of Arles and Avignon to the counts and marquises of Provence was also unclear. This would have to be resolved between the two brothers on their return, when indeed they worked together to mutual advantage.[48] In the meantime, the local lord, Barral of Baux, assured Blanche that the city of Avignon would be subject to Alphonse, and the city of Arles to Charles.[49]

Blanche dealt with ecclesiastical issues with the determination to protect the proper rights and privileges of the crown that she, and Louis IX, had always shown. Abbeys and cathedral chapters wrote to her to ask for the right to elect, and to

ask for the return of the regalia when a new bishop, abbot or abbess was in place. If she felt that this had not been done properly, or that there were other outstanding issues, she refused. The election of Peter of Lamballe as archbishop of Tours in January 1252 was settled amicably, but the election of Guy de la Tour as bishop of Clermont in 1250 and Nivelon as bishop of Soissons in late 1251 brought conflict.[50] In neither case did Blanche have any objections to the choice of bishop. Guy de la Tour was a Dominican. But the chapter at Clermont had failed to apply for the licence to elect.[51] In both cases, there were outstanding issues with provisions to prebends in the chapters, which Blanche and her advisers considered to be royal privileges, and she refused to return the regalia to the bishops elect until these issues were resolved. The chapter of Soissons, which had been foolish enough to challenge her decision in the royal court, quaked before her righteous anger.[52] But she could be more flexible than her son where royal rights were less clear-cut. In March 1250 she and Eudes Rigaud, the archbishop of Rouen, resolved a dispute between Louis and the archbishop over the patronage of a church near Eu; in June 1252 they resolved another one, over rights to hold prisoners. Both disputes had, it seems, been festering for a long time.[53]

Blanche arranged money for the payment of the Crusade. She had money sent out to Louis at Damietta and to Alphonse in early 1250.[54] From Innocent IV she extracted a two-year extension of the Crusade tithe; though Innocent, knowing that its collection was unpopular, as Blanche herself was probably only too aware, suggested she should appoint suitable collectors.[55] Baldwin and Mary of Constantinople were, as ever, desperately in need of funds. Baldwin came to ask Blanche for money in 1247, but Blanche did not think much of him: she 'found his words childish . . . he much displeased her, because she said a wise man is needed to rule an Empire', according to the Ménestrel of Reims. She asked Baldwin to send his wife, her great-niece, whom she did want to see.[56] Blanche did in the end pay off one set of Baldwin's debts, mainly to Constantinopolitan and Italian merchants, in response to desperate pleading letters from Mary.[57] The payments were made by Blanche's clerk, Stephen of Montfort, the treasurer of Pontoise, at the Hôtel-Dieu, the great hospital next to Notre-Dame in Paris, presumably in the great hall that she had had built in memory of her husband, almost as if it were a distribution of alms. The merchants were made to feel that this was money dispensed in the work of Crusade rather than for secular services rendered.[58] Mary left Constantinople in 1248 and met Louis's Crusade at Cyprus; they had to provide her with decent clothes to wear as she made her way to Paris. When she reached

Pontoise, Blanche was overjoyed to see her, and Mary remained with her until Blanche's death.[59] At some point, the empress Mary must have confessed to her formidable great-aunt that her feckless and childish husband Baldwin had managed to raise some money by pawning their only son Philip to the merchants of Venice.[60]

•

The Crusade had started quite well. The Crusaders took the Egyptian port of Damietta with ease. Robert of Artois sent a chatty and deeply affectionate letter to his mother to tell her of the success. All members of the family were well, and a son had been born to Beatrice and Charles of Anjou in Cyprus.[61] Blanche herself wrote to Henry III to convey the news, for she knew that Queen Eleanor of England would want to know that her sisters, Margaret and Beatrice, were both in good health. Blanche expanded, in a way that Robert had not, on the fact that a church previously in the hands of the Muslims was now a place of Christian worship.[62] But the successes did not continue. Several Crusaders died, including the bishops of Noyon and Soissons, Hugh of Châtillon, count of Saint-Pol and Blois, and the old warrior Peter Mauclerc.[63] Relations between English and French Crusaders were uneasy. Robert of Artois's boisterous sense of humour alienated the Hospitallers, the Templars and the English, whom he teased for having tails between their legs.[64]

In February 1250 the Crusaders suffered a crushing defeat at the Battle of Mansurah. Robert of Artois had led an attack against the advice of the Templars and Hospitallers. Matthew Paris blamed Robert's arrogance for the defeat; Joinville found himself trying to explain why Robert had pushed rudely through the Templar ranks. Robert died on the battlefield, drowned in the waters of the Nile under the weight of his armour; his body was never found.[65] Shortly thereafter, Alphonse was captured by the Egyptians. In April 1250 Louis himself was captured. He and Alphonse, and the many prominent French barons and knights captured with them, were released on the payment of a huge ransom raised by Queen Margaret, who took command of the disorganised and disheartened Crusaders in Damietta, although she had just given birth to a child.[66]

It is not clear how fast news travelled between Paris and the Nile delta, and how soon Blanche knew about the unfolding disasters. But the French court was horrified at the losses; some, according to Matthew Paris, began to question their faith in God. Blanche's faith was too robust for that; but the queen who loved music and song so much forbade its performance at court.[67] When she heard that Louis

and his brothers were free, she issued a vidimus of his letter, to be published throughout the realm.[68] She wrote to Louis begging him and his brothers to return as soon as possible: she was ill, and his realm was in danger from the king of England. The danger to the realm is not obvious, but it may have been her perception, and she may have felt that any argument was justified if it would bring her sons back to her. Alphonse and Charles heeded their mother's demands, and announced their intention to return home. Many of the Crusaders agreed with them, but Louis decided to stay.[69]

The patriarch of Jerusalem wrote to Blanche to reassure her that Louis, Margaret and their two young sons were safe.[70] Louis himself kept in touch with his family with affectionate letters. When he wrote to Alphonse in August 1251 he asked for news of Blanche and his siblings, Charles and Isabella.[71] Louis also wrote to Blanche directly, sending her a list of the monies that he had lent to his barons overseas and asking her to add them to the royal registers, so that the debts could be reclaimed on his return.[72]

While there was no obvious threat to the peace of the realm when Blanche wrote begging Louis to return in 1250, in the following spring a serious crisis developed. Groups of peasants and townspeople gathered in Flanders and north-eastern France, determined on undertaking their own Crusade. They were poor and dispossessed. Contemporaries called them the *pastoreaux* – the shepherds, which many of them may have been.[73] Led by a charismatic preacher called the Master of Hungary, they exhibited the uninhibited religious fervour of the age. Initially, many were impressed by their fervour and their poverty. The Master of Hungary promised that they, the shepherds, would bring aid to the king on his Crusade; for it was to shepherds, not knights, that the arrival of Christ on earth had first been revealed. Blanche herself welcomed them as they arrived in Paris at the beginning of June 1251. Doubtless she felt that any additions to her son's shrunken forces in Egypt would be welcome; she certainly thought that the Church, as ever, showed little enthusiasm to contribute. She had just finished persuading Innocent IV to extend the two-year Crusading tithe.[74] But almost immediately it was clear that this was an uncontrolled rabble, not a potential Crusade army. The riches of the city of Paris were too tempting to them. There were riots, during which foodstuffs and goods were stolen or despoiled, and clergy and churches attacked. Some clergy were thrown into the Seine, and the Church accused the rioters of heresy. By 11 and 12 June break-away groups of *pastoreaux* had attacked Rouen, where they chased Eudes Rigaud from his cathedral, and Orléans; other groups went to Tours and Bourges.

Blanche waited until the *pastoreaux* had deserted Paris for the countryside around it; then she dispatched troops to confront them. The Master of Hungary was killed at Bourges.[75]

Blanche has been accused of responding slowly to this attack at the very heart of the Capetian realm. Some historians have argued that she was prepared to encourage a rabble that clearly verged on the heretical because they might provide reinforcements for Louis in Egypt, though this is surely going too far. Certainly, she was initially taken in by the *pastoreaux*, but she may not have been the only person. Once they started attacking churches, they were, of course, accused of heresy. Some of the strongest condemnations came from the Franciscans; perhaps they too had initially found the poverty, fervour and rootlessness of the *pastoreaux* sympathetic. Blanche's apparent hesitation in dealing with them was probably an astute assessment of what was possible. She may have decided that confronting them in Paris itself was unwise. They were evidently numerous, violent, and had nothing to lose. They were disorganised, but also fluid, perhaps attracting recruits from the local dispossessed and disaffected as they went, and may have been quite difficult to repress.

The *pastoreaux* were not the only peasants to challenge the authority of the Church in the summer of 1251. Peasants from estates at Orly that belonged to the chapter of Notre-Dame in Paris were in the process of negotiating their freedom from serfdom – their manumission. They were wealthy peasants, quite unlike the dispossessed *pastoreaux*. The chapter, or at least some members of it, took the opportunity to make the manumission conditional on the payment of an additional arbitrary tax. When the peasants objected, the chapter imprisoned some of their wives and children in the gaol within the cloister precinct. The peasants appealed to the queen, who went along with a troop of soldiers and court officials to rescue them. By the time the Grandes Chroniques were written in the early fourteenth century, this incident had acquired the status of legend. Blanche herself was depicted hammering at the entrance to the cloister to defend the poor and innocent from the greed of the Church. The reality, more interesting still, emerges from an inquisition into the episode in March 1252. Breaking into the cloister was to infringe the immunities of the cathedral. Nevertheless, Blanche ensured that it happened. She gave orders. She herself 'went into the cathedral church, and lingered there for a bit'; meanwhile, her officials were left to their own devices. Nobody questioned in the inquiry could remember very clearly hearing the crash of the splintering of the cloister door. After her vigil in the church, Blanche went

to the chapter house, where with apparent surprise she encountered some profoundly grateful released prisoners in the care of her castellan. The queen asked the castellan how they had been liberated. Her castellan duly delivered the response she required: 'Don't worry, my Lady, St Leonard – [the patron saint of prisoners] – freed them.' 'What have you done with the others?' she asked. 'Don't worry, my Lady, they are safe at the palace.' Blanche was aware that there was more to rule of the realm than managing the aristocracy; and the legend constructed around this event built on her real generosity towards the poor.[76]

Blanche's health was no longer as robust as it had been. She was seriously ill in early 1251. Innocent IV wrote to tell her to take good care of her health, for her 'life was the safeguard for so many'.[77] Fortunately, she appears to have made a good recovery. There was no indication that she was unwell in late July 1252, when she and Eudes Rigaud negotiated the agreement over prisoners; she seemed as focused as ever. She and her court moved as usual between Pontoise and Maubuisson, Paris and Melun over that summer.[78] In fact, it was Alphonse of Poitiers who fell desperately ill. He was partly paralysed, and temporarily blind. By May 1252 he was recovering, and had decided to return to support Louis in the East when he was well enough.[79] Alphonse's illness, and his determination to return to the Crusade, must have been bitter blows for his mother, still recovering from Robert's dreadful death. Her nephew, King Ferdinand of Castile, had just died too.[80]

By 15 November 1252 there is evidence that Blanche was no longer able to act as queen regent. The churchmen of the Sens archdiocese held a council at which they attacked Theobald of Champagne's attempts to uphold his comital rights against what Theobald would have seen as ecclesiastical encroachment.[81] Blanche would undoubtedly have agreed with Theobald, for he was being censured for behaving exactly as the queen did as ruler of the French realm. The Sens clergy were too closely dependent on the queen for them to attack her. Indeed, among those who signed the deposition against Theobald were her close advisers, the bishops Renaud of Paris, William of Orléans and Adam of Senlis. The fact that they felt they could censure Theobald suggests that Blanche was not party to the council, or was not available to give advice. By 22 November she was undoubtedly ill. The prior of Saint-Martin-des-Champs came to settle a case at the court; the resultant charter makes it clear that Blanche was not there; that she was, on the 22nd, still living, but was now dead.[82]

Blanche fell ill at Melun. She was taken to Paris, presumably to the palace on the Ile de la Cité where she had been taken after her marriage half a century ago.

She realised she was dying and set her affairs in order. She named Renaud of Corbeil, bishop of Paris, the abbot of Saint-Victor, and her clerk, Stephen of Montfort, now dean of Saint-Aignan at Orléans, as executors of her testament.[83] After receiving Holy Communion from Renaud of Corbeil, she had herself dressed in the plain habit of a Cistercian nun, becoming on her deathbed a humble member of the community of Maubuisson, where her body would be buried. Blanche insisted that, even if she recovered, she would retire into the nunnery; but she must have known that she would not recover. The abbess, Guillemette, and other members of the community were presumably present. Alice of Mâcon, the abbess of Le Lys, is said to have asked Blanche to allow her heart to be buried at Le Lys. The queen presumably assented. When she seemed close to death, those who were caring for her carried her from the bed and laid her on a monastic straw mattress on the floor, covered in plain rough sheets, according to the monastic customs for the dying. They thought she had died, but softly she began to murmur the words of the prayer of the suffering: 'Subvenite sancti Dei' – 'Come to my aid, saints of God'. After a few verses, her voice stopped. Blanche was dead.[84]

She died in the afternoon of either 26 or 27 November. Her heart, perhaps with her viscera, was cut out of her body. Embalming was not necessary, for her remains did not have to travel far. Her ladies covered her Cistercian habit in royal vestments, and placed a crown on her veiled head. As queen of France, she was carried on a bier in stately procession, followed by her sons, Alphonse and Charles, and the great prelates and magnates of the kingdom, to the abbey of Saint-Denis. Her body rested overnight in the choir of the great abbey church, in which were buried her husband and most of his predecessors as kings of France.[85] But Blanche had made it clear that she wanted to be buried at Maubuisson, and on the following day the sad cortège moved on. Thus on 29 November she was buried in the centre of the nuns' choir of her new foundation. Renaud of Corbeil, bishop of Paris, and Eudes Rigaud officiated.[86]

The news of his mother's death took a long time to reach Louis in the Holy Land. He was devastated. He had lost, he said, the mother whom he loved more than anyone else in the world. He shut himself in his room for two days.[87] Queen Margaret, who had, as Joinville told her, lost her worst enemy, wept piteously because she could hardly bear the thought of her husband's grief. The news of the queen's death, and the news that with her death royal authority in France had collapsed, finally persuaded Louis that he should return home.[88]

•

The group of clergy who had worked closely with Blanche formed an ad hoc regency council.[89] Acts were issued in the name of the ten-year-old heir to the throne, Louis. The council included gifted administrators, like John de la Cour, bishop of Evreux, Renaud of Corbeil, bishop of Paris, and Adam of Chambly, bishop of Senlis. But the council were unable to exert their authority, perhaps because all of them were churchmen. They ought to have been able to turn to the king's brothers, Alphonse and Charles, to provide support if necessary. Alphonse and Charles were able, as they were when their mother was alive, to control their own extensive territories, but that tended to absorb their attention. Moreover, Alphonse probably took some time to recover fully from his illness, and was planning to return to the Holy Land. The ever-opportunistic Charles took advantage of the Flemish succession problems to pursue ambitions in Hainault, which Blanche, when alive, had been able to prevent him from doing.[90]

The Flemish succession war escalated. Trouble broke out at the University of Paris in 1253, in a vicious battle between the secular masters and the mendicants. The regency council – bishops all – failed to uphold royal and lay rights against ecclesiastical, especially papal pressure, often to the dismay of the urban elites. They either failed to support, or actually dismissed, some of the most efficient royal officials, those put in place in Louis's recent reforms, for much of the officials' work involved what the Church saw as encroachment on their privileges. The aristocracy became restive, some apparently calling for Simon de Montfort, who was running Gascony for Henry III with brutal efficiency, to be installed as regent.[91] Henry III saw his opportunity. Although he knew he should not attack the lands of a Crusader, he began to gather an expedition to Gascony with a view to repossessing territories that he regarded as rightfully his. The monastic chronicler at Saint-Denis did not mince his words: 'The realm was in great danger.'[92] When Louis finally arrived back in France, nearly two years after his mother's death, he realised he had much to do. The extent and depth of the troubles that emerged or broke out after Blanche's death reveal just how formidably effective a regent the ageing and possibly ailing queen had been.

PART II

7

Family, Friends and *Familia*

BLANCHE WAS A WOMAN OF POWERFUL emotions and affections. She cared deeply about members of her family. She enjoyed the company of her Iberian relatives, and dealt sympathetically with her politically wayward cousins, Theobald of Champagne and Raymond of Toulouse, despite criticism for doing so. She had, too, a gift for friendship with both men and women. People remained in her service for a long time, and Blanche took good care of her household, her extended family and her friends. This chapter explores these relationships and friendship networks. They provided, of course, an important constituent of her political effectiveness. Blanche's relationships with family and friends might be intimate, but they were rarely private, rarely free from the demands of public life. Apparently private spaces, like her wardrobe tucked away by the lower garden at Pontoise, might be appropriated for the business of government.[1] And while marriage might create and sustain the family unit, it was also always at the heart of political strategy. A queen was traditionally expected to play an important role in implementing marital strategy, exploiting her familial and friendship networks to do so. Blanche, of course, not only implemented the Capetian family's marital strategies, but also often initiated and drove them.

Most of the evidence for Blanche's family and familial relationships is drawn from two very different sources: the intimate scenes from family life in the hagiographies of Blanche's saintly children, Louis and Isabella, and the household accounts of the royal court and of Blanche's own household. I discussed the various – and they are various – household accounts in the Introduction.[2] They

show how the households, whether princely, royal or Blanche's own, were run; they provide evidence for the personnel of the royal entourages, and frequent visitors to the court; they indicate who was favoured by gifts and patronage; they reveal the constant travel between royal houses and castles; and they give insight into the clothes Blanche and her family wore, the food they ate and the way they entertained themselves. They will be used often in this and the following chapters. But I repeat my caveat that nothing like a complete run of household accounts survives, just 'snapshots' for the years 1203, 1213, 1226, 1231, 1234, 1237, 1238, 1239 and 1248, and for Blanche's own household in 1241–2 and 1243.

On the royal accounts, it is often difficult to tell which expenditure was by or for Blanche herself, but there are some clues. Household expenditure was carefully controlled and accounted by the various clerks who ran the royal administration. For much of the 1230s the controlling mind was probably Master John de la Cour, who was then dean of Saint-Martin of Tours. Expenditure was authorised, or 'testified to' (*teste*), by various members of the household, usually by the clerical administrators, but sometimes by lay people, and often, especially in 1234 when she was still regent, by Blanche herself. Blanche's ladies authorised spending on her own account of 1241–2: some of them authorised her expenses on the main royal accounts.[3] Blanche's almsgiving in the account of 1239 was often authorised by the abbess of Saint-Antoine.[4] In 1234 certain clerks, especially Master Thomas Pignus, Master Thomas Touquin and Master Peter, tended to authorise expenditure for Blanche, though they did not work exclusively for her.[5] Master Peter was probably the Master Peter of Lissy who was responsible for Blanche's own household account for 1241–2. He accounted for Blanche's income and expenditure at the Temple in 1243.[6] Master Richard of Tourny may have been one of the general household clerks, but he worked almost exclusively for Blanche. He was supported by a prebend in the college of Saint-Mellon, in the castle at Pontoise, and by other rich prebends in the royal gift in Normandy and Rouen.[7] When Blanche founded Maubuisson, she put him in charge of the works. His meticulous accounts were incorporated into the abbey's book of foundation documents, the *Achatz d'heritage*.[8]

The household accounts of the 1230s and 1248 do not distinguish clearly between the households of the king, Blanche and the young queen. The year 1234 was the last of Blanche's regency, so that her expenditure was central to the royal account; nevertheless, she had her own household and kitchens. By 1239 the young queen, too, had her own kitchen.[9] Both women were presumably supported by some revenues from their dowries and dower, independent of the royal household

revenues, but there is no reflection of that in the accounts. Once Louis and Margaret were married in 1234, one might have expected a clearer distinction to emerge between the accounts of the king and queen and the accounts of the dowager queen and the other royal children, but it is not apparent. Margaret was still very young, and in 1238 her expenses were lumped in with those of the royal children.[10] Blanche's expenditure on clothes or alms, or favoured Spanish knights or clergy, is often regarded as an integral part of the expenditure of the royal household, especially in the account of 1239, though this may reflect periods when she had joined the king's court. This is all the more striking in that, in their youth, Blanche and Lord Louis had had their own household, separately accounted from that of the king. The accounts treat the royal family and their households as one great extended family. Perhaps that is how Blanche saw them.

It may be that when Robert of Artois and Alphonse of Poitiers reached maturity and took control of their counties, there were suggestions that the dowager queen should also have her own, separate accounts. The account of 1239 sets aside 1,378 *livres* 19 *solidi* 3 *deniers* to pay the debts of the queen, by whom they mean Blanche.[11] This suggests some division between the queen's expenditure and royal expenditure. But a large proportion of the expenditure on the rest of this long account is due to Blanche, though this may reflect the fact that it includes expenditure for two ceremonies for which she was the driving force – the reception of the Crown of Thorns, and the knighting and wedding of Alphonse of Portugal. From 1237 Louis's generous settlement in exchange for Blanche's dower and dowry lands established her in her own houses close to Paris, easing her away from the itinerant king's court. By early 1241 she had her own household accounts.[12]

The household accounts do not distinguish clearly between family expenditure and what might be called 'state expenditure'. Blanche's – and Louis's – personal gifts to minstrels or lepers or close friends are listed alongside gifts to ambassadors or household knights and clerks setting off on the business of the realm. The knightings and weddings of Robert and Alphonse, and the magnificent wedding of Louis and Margaret, were both family occasions and state occasions. Only in 1261 did St Louis issue an ordinance that established clear divisions between the departments of the royal household, and thus imposed some order on its accounting systems.[13]

A medieval queen's power and influence depended heavily on marriage and mother-hood.[14] Everything suggests that Blanche's own marriage was one of mutual respect, even love, despite its inauspicious start. All contemporary sources agree that she was devastated at Louis VIII's death – and not just because of the political difficul-ties it brought. She and her husband were well matched intellectually, both enjoy-ing the company of the scholarly and reformist clergy in Paris or at court. Both enjoyed too more courtly, chivalric, pursuits. Louis himself had a reputation for faithfulness to his wife. Both William of Puylaurens and Gerald of Wales tell vari-ants of tales that Louis would not have casual sex, even if it were apparently for the good of his health.[15] Blanche herself held strong views on the importance of marital fidelity: she impressed upon Louis IX that she would prefer he were dead than deceiving his wife with concubines.[16] Frequent sex is not necessarily an indica-tion of a happy marriage, but Blanche and Louis VIII's steady production of chil-dren after 1209 suggests that they spent a great deal of time together until Louis left for his final crusade. By 1220 the future succession was well assured, but Blanche's pregnancies became if anything more frequent. She was pregnant with Charles when Louis departed. Perhaps they enjoyed sex.

Their conjugal happiness was reminiscent of the relationship of Blanche's parents, but distinguished them from her Angevin relations, and even more from the old king, Philip Augustus. Philip had tried to divorce Louis's mother, Isabella of Hainault, though he was more accepting of her once she delivered an heir. After Isabella's death in childbirth in 1190, Philip's undignified and unsuccessful attempts to have his marriage with Ingeborg annulled left him excommunicated and France under interdict. Philip seems to have been genuinely attached to Agnes of Meran, and was not prepared to set her aside. Perhaps he saw himself, in his own light, as a devoted husband. But the Church was outraged, and Philip's reputation suf-fered severely, even from those, like Rigord, who set out to praise him.[17] Philip's marriages were all the more problematic in that the Church was in the throes of reformulating its approach to marriage. Reformist theologians insisted that mar-riage was a sacrament: this was confirmed in the canons of the Fourth Lateran Council. To infringe the rules of marriage would be henceforth to infringe a sacra-ment. Churchmen increasingly defined marriage as a relationship based on mutual consent and marital affection.[18] Lord Louis and his young wife presented an image of the perfect modern marriage to the churchmen of northern France, and provided hope to those who despaired of the bigamous old king. There are strong parallels with the striking portrait of an ideal marriage in the 'Hystoria Albigensis', the

chronicle of the Albigensian Crusade by the Cistercian monk Peter of Les Vaux-de-Cernay: the marriage of Simon of Montfort, count of Toulouse, and Alice of Montmorency. Count Simon depends on Alice to raise troops for him, and the two are shown as having a relationship based on love and trust, a relationship of strong mutual support.[19]

Blanche and Louis were too young to consummate their marriage immediately, and the account of Hugh of Lincoln's visit to the unhappy princess in 1200 shows them living separately at the French court. However, the 1203 budget accounts for the two of them together, which suggests that by then they were living as man and wife. They were fourteen or fifteen, an acceptable age for the full married life. Blanche had her first recorded child, a daughter, who did not survive, in 1205, when she was seventeen.

Blanche and Louis had twelve recorded children. The intervals at which the births occurred are surprising. One would expect that Blanche would have been at her most fecund, and strongest, in her late teens and early twenties. But she was twenty-one when her first surviving child, Philip, was born in 1209; after that there are no recorded births until twins, who died in infancy in 1213. In 1214, at the rather advanced age of twenty-six, Blanche gave birth to Louis. In the twelve years between 1214 and her husband's death in 1226, she delivered seven children who survived, at least into childhood.[20] It may be that Louis spent much of his teens with Philip's troops, learning the arts of war with the marshal, Henry Clément: Louis was certainly absent on campaign quite frequently, against the forces of the Angevin alliance in France or England, and the Albigensians, until his return from the second Albigensian Crusade. But perhaps there were other births, unsuccessful and unrecorded, between 1205 and 1213.

If there were concerns that an heir was taking some time to materialise, they are not recorded. Concerns there undoubtedly were about the fertility of Margaret of Provence, who gave birth to her first surviving child at nineteen; to the intense disappointment of the family, it was a girl.[21] The birth of Blanche and Louis's first son, Philip, the heir to the Capetian throne, was greeted with rejoicing and celebratory verse anticipating the union of the crowns of France and England in the person of the newborn prince, implicitly through Blanche as granddaughter of Henry II.[22] A queen's status, prestige and power rested on her position as the mother of the heir to the throne.[23]

The naming of children was an opportunity to remember and honour grandparents, and to draw carefully chosen people into the family circle with the

responsibility of godparent. The first male child was named after his paternal grandfather. One of the twins born in 1213 was named after Blanche's father, Alfonso.[24] Since both children died young, the grandparental names were deployed again for younger sons. The only daughter to reach adulthood was named Isabella after her paternal grandmother, Isabella of Hainault. Given Blanche's reverence and affection for her parents, it is likely that her first child, the daughter born in 1205, was named after her mother, Eleanor. Young Louis was named after his father. Robert was a traditional Capetian name, slightly old-fashioned within the main royal line, though popular within the Capetian cousin dynasties of Dreux and Courtenay. Perhaps Robert of Courtenay stood as godparent. John was neither a Capetian nor a Castilian name. It seems unlikely that the child was named after Blanche's uncle, the king of England, whose kingdom Lord Louis had just failed to capture. Perhaps John of Nesle or John of Brienne acted as godparent.

Their last three sons were all given names with royal resonance. The name Stephen, given to the son born in 1225, had not been used previously in the Capetian, Angevin or Hispanic families. Perhaps it was simply used because Stephen of Sancerre was a godparent. But St Stephen the Deacon was a frequent dedicatee of French cathedrals, and had long been seen as, if not quite a patron saint in the manner of St Denis, a saint with a special protective role for France. Moreover, the name Stephen came from the Greek for crown, and Louis VI had chosen the feast of the Invention of the Relics of St Stephen for his coronation.[25] The names of Philip Dagobert and Charles, born in 1222 and 1226 respectively, commemorate great historical, and almost legendary, kings of France: King Dagobert, the great Merovingian founder of the abbey of Saint-Denis, and Charles the Great – Charlemagne. Charles must have been Blanche's own choice, for the child was born after Louis VIII's death. It gave a powerful signal as to how she saw the prestige of the Capetian family. Charlemagne was not only revered as king and emperor of the Franks. He was also, according to romance epics, such as the Song of Roland and the hugely popular Turpin legends, the ruler who first defeated the forces of Islam in Spain.[26] The name would have had special resonance for the mother of the king of France and the daughter of the victor of Las Navas de Tolosa.

Alphonse, John and Charles, like her own name, Blanche, were new introductions to the repertoire of Capetian family names; all three were used frequently among her successors. Members of the local aristocracy, such as Bouchard of Marly and Agnes of Beaumont, or the lord of Villers-Saint-Paul, a donor to Royaumont, began to call their sons Alphonse, to signal their loyalty to the Capetian family.[27]

Historians have often questioned how much time an active queen consort, let alone a queen regent, would have spent with her children. Eleanor of Aquitaine saw relatively little of some of her children: this may have accounted for the poor relations between her sons.[28] It is clear, however, from Charles of Anjou's account of the family and the hagiographical accounts that Blanche made sure that she saw a great deal of her children, that she and her husband cared deeply for them, and that there were strong affective relationships between the siblings.[29]

When they were very young, Blanche and Louis's children were spared some of the incessant travelling of the royal entourage. The fragile, newly born twins, and perhaps young Philip, stayed at one of the residences in the Gâtinais, probably Lorris or Boiscommun, in 1213, while their parents moved between those residences and Poissy, Mantes and Melun.[30] In the early 1230s the children had their own household.[31] A gift to the chaplain 'who was with' Philip Dagobert suggests that he had not been travelling with the court, perhaps because of poor health: he may have been living at Royaumont, where he was buried.[32] In 1239 Charles fell ill at Vincennes while Blanche was at Melun; she rushed back to be with her sick child.[33] Blanche herself had probably spent some of her youth in Castile in the palace attached to her parents' new Cistercian nunnery of Las Huelgas: after her husband's death, she used Royaumont to provide stability, refuge and fresh air for her young family, though they stayed at the nearby residence at Asnières rather than at the abbey itself. Louis and his younger brothers, Robert, John, Alphonse and even young Charles, helped in the building, bringing stones in wheelbarrows to the masons.[34] Young Isabella spent much time visiting a sick and distressed gentlewoman in the hospital at Méru, which suggests that she stayed often at Asnières, Pontoise or Maubuisson in the 1240s.[35] Even the small children joined the main court for great celebratory occasions like Louis and Margaret's wedding in 1234, for which they were provided with new gloves and new robes.[36] But if the children travelled less than Blanche herself, and the king's court, they were used to an itinerant life. Agnes of Harcourt has a story of the young Princess Isabella being so deeply involved in her devotions that she was almost wrapped up in her own bedding, as the chamber staff hurried to pack up.[37]

The names of some of the children's staff are recorded. Robert's wet-nurse was Aalita of Paris; Denis 'looked after' Charles, in the 1230s, and Perriau of Lorris and Hallez also served the young prince.[38] Isabella's nurse, Helen Buisemont, remained with Isabella throughout her life. There was a deep bond of trust between them; it was Lady Helen whom Isabella asked to beat her for her sins.[39] Lady Helen is

known only from Agnes of Harcourt's Life of the saintly princess. There is no trace
of her in the household accounts – which underlines the fragmentary nature of
the evidence.

Blanche and Louis ensured that all their children, including Princess Isabella,
were well educated. Presumably, as with Louis VIII, the finest intellectuals of the
day were commissioned to teach the royal children, but there is no record of their
names. A Master William Escouz may have taught Charles.[40] In 1234 the 'Magistra'
of Etampes was rewarded with a robe: was this a female teacher employed to teach
the girls and the younger children of the household?[41] The education was strict:
Louis, at fourteen and already king, was beaten by his master if he failed at his
lessons.[42] They were better educated than many of the clerks in the royal entourage:
both Isabella and Charles corrected their clerks' inadequate Latin.[43] Family tradition held that Blanche herself saw to their earliest education, teaching St Louis,
and presumably the rest of her children, to read from the illustrated psalters that
she and the family owned. In the early fourteenth century, still within the lifetime
of those who would have known Blanche personally, one of the royal entourage
inscribed 'This psalter belonged to my Lord Saint Louis, who was king of France,
in which he learned [to read] in his childhood' in one of the psalters that Blanche
owned – the Leiden Psalter.[44] In his deposition for the canonisation of St Louis,
Charles of Anjou insisted on the pivotal role that Blanche had played in the religious and moral education of all her children.[45]

They grew up less fast than Blanche, her husband and her father-in-law had
done. Philip Augustus was sole ruler by the age of fifteen. The future Louis VIII
was concentrating on his military training by the time he was thirteen, spending
time in camp in the Vexin and soon taking part in major campaigns.[46] But the
young Louis IX was fifteen before he played any serious military role. Blanche and
Louis had been married at the age of twelve. Their children were much more
mature before marriage. All the sons who survived into adulthood – Louis IX,
Robert of Artois, Alphonse of Poitou and Charles of Anjou – were around twenty
when they married. For the three younger princes, marriage coincided with the
conferring of knighthood and of their inheritance, though Louis was knighted on
the way to his coronation. Serious marriage arrangements were made for Princess
Isabella when she was eighteen. Historians have argued that Blanche, together with
her contemporaries, her sister Berengaria of Castile and Eleanor of Provence, queen
of England, deliberately ensured that marriage took place at a relatively late age,
much later than had been the case in earlier centuries.[47] But Blanche arranged

Louis's marriage to Margaret of Provence when Margaret was thirteen. Age at marriage depended primarily on the availability or otherwise of suitable marriage partners.

Much as she loved her children, Blanche knew that the children of a king or a great prince were pawns on the chessboard of diplomacy, as she herself had been. The French crown had acquired control of large areas of north-eastern France through the inheritance of Isabella of Hainault. The betrothal in 1215 of Philip, Blanche and Louis's eldest son and heir, to Agnes, the heiress to the county of Nevers, was designed to bring a substantial and strategically placed swathe of northern Burgundy into the direct control of the crown. Young Philip's death by 1219 meant that this marriage strategy was never implemented.[48] Blanche had more success with her determination to arrange the marriage of Joanna, heiress to the county of Toulouse, to her younger son Alphonse. After her betrothal, young Joanna was kept at the Capetian court and was brought up alongside the princess Isabella, so that she became absorbed into the Capetian family.[49] Blanche made sure that Joanna's father, Raymond of Toulouse, did not threaten his daughter's status as sole heiress by another marriage.[50]

Betrothals were useful political bargaining tools. Blanche and Louis VIII used them to neutralise, control or retain the adherence of powerful French barons and princes. They could be arranged when the children were much too young for marriage. The set of treaties of March 1227, with which Blanche stabilised the kingdom, were based on the betrothals of her children. John, then aged eight or nine, was betrothed to Peter Mauclerc's daughter, Yolande, while Isabella and Alphonse were betrothed to offspring of the count of La Marche: Alphonse was seven, and Isabella two.[51] Blanche and Louis's eldest son, Philip, was betrothed at the age of six. All these betrothals were hedged around with complex pre-nuptial agreements, with clauses that allowed for the failure of the betrothal, for the death of one of the young couple or both, before or after the birth of heirs. There was a long way between betrothal and marriage, and several betrothals, particularly those of March 1227, seemed designed to fail. By 1229 Blanche had extracted Alphonse from his betrothal to the daughter of the count of La Marche, and had betrothed him instead to the daughter of the count of Toulouse – a far more advantageous match from every point of view.[52]

Blanche had only one daughter – Isabella – who survived long enough to become a part of her mother's marriage strategy.[53] Isabella's betrothal to the son of Hugh of La Marche and Isabella of Angoulême in 1227 was part of the

arrangements around the Treaty of Vendôme. It was agreed that, if the marriage did not take place, the French king would pay the count a substantial financial penalty. In the political crisis of 1230 the implementation of the betrothal was clarified.[54] Blanche and Louis IX were expected to allow young Isabella to live at Isabella and Hugh's court – the handing over of a young bride to live with her future family was standard practice in royal and aristocratic marriage arrangements. If they did not send her to live at the Lusignan court, and the young princess then refused to go through with the marriage, they would have to pay 5,000 silver marks to the Lusignans in compensation. But Blanche did not hand over her daughter. She preferred to keep her at court and risk paying the substantial penalty, though by the time Isabella was of marriageable age the proposed Lusignan marriage was no longer useful for either party. Blanche was even prepared to allow her daughter to veto the marriage if she wanted to.

In 1243 a far grander marriage was proposed for Princess Isabella, this time with Conrad, son and heir of the emperor Frederick II. She was now eighteen, of fully marriageable age. Relationships with the Empire were always important to the Capetian kings, and Blanche and Louis IX were well aware of how damaging an alliance between the emperor and the king of England could be to French interests. Pope Innocent IV too saw the political advantages of the marriage, and wrote to Isabella to persuade her into it.[55]

But Isabella refused. She had grown into an intensely religious young woman, who wished to live, if not a monastic life, then certainly a chaste life as a virgin devoted to God. Presumably, Pope Innocent had been asked, either by Blanche or Louis IX, to write to persuade Isabella into the marriage because the family were finding it difficult to persuade her themselves. Isabella was adamant, but seems to have fallen ill under the pressure – so ill that, while the court moved on, she had to be left at Saint-Germain-en-Laye with Margaret of Provence, who had recently given birth to her first child. Isabella's illness worsened, so that her life seemed in danger. Blanche, with Louis, rushed back to her bedside. The queen, evidently deeply distressed, turned to a religious woman at Nanterre. The woman told Blanche that her daughter would recover, but that 'her heart would never be in the world, nor in the things of this world': Isabella must be allowed to pursue the religious life, not political marriage to the heir to the Empire. Blanche, Isabella's family and Pope Innocent all accepted that, henceforth, Isabella was to be a bride of Christ.[56]

Isabella, like her brother Louis, became a candidate for canonisation, and thus the object of a hagiography. Agnes of Harcourt's 'Life of Isabella', like the various Lives of St Louis, by Joinville, Geoffrey of Beaulieu, William of Chartres and William of Saint-Pathus, provide an intimate portrait of the deep love that Blanche felt and displayed for these two, overtly religious children, and of its reciprocation. This kind of evidence does not exist for Blanche's relationships with her other children – the young heir, Philip, who must have been so precious but died before he was ten; John and Philip Dagobert, who both died in the early 1230s, John a youth of thirteen, Philip Dagobert not yet ten; the daughter, the twins Alphonse and his sibling, and Stephen, all of whom died in infancy; and Robert, Alphonse and Charles, the sons who grew to manhood.

Robert, Alphonse and Charles were in many ways very different in character from St Louis and Isabella. They all shared the strong piety inculcated, as Charles of Anjou said, by Blanche of Castile.[57] Charles founded two Cistercian abbeys, Realvalle and Vittoria; Alphonse's recorded almsgiving is generous, and often reflects his mother's devotional preferences. Like their parents, these two brothers were interested in faith and religious discussion, but they did not wish to enter religious life themselves.[58] They both had a strong sense of the duties of the ruler, but had none of the difficulties with the trappings of power, or the furs, silks, jewels and feasts of courtly life, that afflicted Louis and Isabella. They enjoyed the hunting, minstrelsy and gambling of courtly life, though Charles could be unsmiling.[59] They, far more than Louis and Isabella, resembled their mother.

Robert of Artois appears different again. He did not have the long, successful, well-documented rule that provides such an insight into the characters of his brothers. Charles of Anjou stressed Robert's piety, and his burning desire to die in battle fighting against the infidel.[60] Joinville and Matthew Paris paint a vivid portrait of him on Crusade, and it is not entirely positive. Robert emerges as a strong but impulsive knight, heedlessly brave. It was Robert who advised Louis to make straight for Cairo, against the advice of the king's more experienced captains; it was Robert who was responsible for the rout of Mansurah, in which he himself perished.[61] Robert, like Charles and Blanche, loved music and song.[62] He also possessed a bawdy sense of humour. He dowsed Theobald of Champagne in runny cheese or worse as the count tried to make a dignified entry into Blanche's presence. He could not resist teasing his English companions on the Crusade about the tails that the English were supposed to hide beneath their hose, and he made sardonic

comments on the Hospitallers and Templars.[63] At his knighting feast, he had his fastidious older brother served his food by minstrels balancing on the horns of oxen. No wonder Louis wore a cotton cap at the knighting feast for Alphonse. And yet of all the brothers, it was Robert who was most loved by the saintly Louis.[64]

The popular image of Blanche as a mother is based on her relationship with Louis and Isabella. Her relationship with her other adult children must have been different, given their very different characters. The Lives of St Louis present him as her favourite child. He was undoubtedly the most important – he was the king, and on him her status and power depended. At both a personal and a political level, the relationship between Blanche and Louis was very interdependent, perhaps unhealthily so. Her oldest son and her only daughter emerged as very different personalities from their siblings, perhaps because as heir to the throne and as only daughter they did receive a different level of attention from their mother. Robert, Alphonse and Charles may have benefited from a less intense mothering.[65]

Louis's and Isabella's relationships with Blanche appear to possess a charge that those of their siblings do not. Joinville could see the corrosive effect of Blanche's possessive love for her son on his marriage to Margaret of Provence. He admired Blanche, but his portrait of the over-dependent love between mother and son is Freudian *avant la lettre*. There is no evidence that Blanche had such unfortunate relationships with her other daughters-in-law. Moreover, Louis and Isabella possessed an emotional intensity that found its outlet in religious fervour, in a way that their siblings did not. Both rejected the luxuries – the rich clothes, jewels and foods – of courtly life. Both imposed heavy penances on themselves – rough clothing, attempts to keep silence, beatings until blood was drawn. St Louis would not laugh or have his hair done on a Friday. In both cases, their religious fervour was seen as excessive and inappropriate by contemporaries; it was even seen as excessive by their respective hagiographers.[66] Both had to challenge their mother's authority, Isabella to adopt the religious life, Louis to go on Crusade against Blanche's wishes. In both cases, serious illness persuaded their mother to accept their decisions.[67] Louis's illness in 1244–5 was unquestionably dangerous, but there may have been a more psychological element in Isabella's case. Her mother had already resorted to giving alms to persuade her daughter to make conversation and to eat enough for her health, for Isabella refused to eat bread, and lived on soup and split peas.[68] It is impossible to avoid the suspicion that both Louis and Isabella were in some sense damaged by the intensity of their mother's love and care for them: that they

became too dependent on it, but that at the same time knew instinctively how to use their fragility to get what they wanted from their mother. Their siblings, on the other hand, fulfilled all the contemporary expectations of the well-brought-up prince.

Isabella and Louis influenced each other in their religious practices and were devoted to each other. But Louis also had great affection for his slightly younger sibling, Robert, however different their characters. He wept bitterly over Robert's death, and missed the support that Robert had always given him. The Crusade brought out a certain distance between Louis and his younger brothers, Alphonse and Charles. After his imprisonment by the Muslims, Louis, unwell and depressed, bemoaned the fact that neither Alphonse nor Charles had bothered to come to comfort and reassure him, as Robert would have done.[69] Louis took the Crusade as a sacred trust, and did not want to return home, even though Blanche begged him to return for the good of his country. Alphonse and Charles, like many of the Crusaders, took a more practical view of the enterprise. Both, sensibly, advised returning to France, since the king was required there and his forces in Egypt were decimated: advice that Louis himself spurned, though he sent them back.[70] In the intervals of peace, both enjoyed courtly pastimes, especially gaming and gambling. Joinville, a courtier himself, describes Alphonse as 'such a courteous player . . . who handed over fistfuls of money'.[71] Louis disapproved, and threw Charles of Anjou's dice and gaming board overboard.[72] And yet, Louis was deeply concerned about Alphonse when the Muslims appeared to be keeping him hostage after Louis's ransom had been paid; and Charles, according to Joinville, was almost in tears as he sailed for France, leaving his older brother behind in the East.[73] And family solidarity tended to override these sibling differences. Alphonse was, like Louis, a generous patron of Isabella's foundation of Longchamp. In later life Charles played an important role in establishing both Louis and Isabella as candidates for canonisation, commissioning Agnes of Harcourt's 'Life of Isabella' and remembering his brother, his siblings and the commanding influence of his mother with deep affection and respect in his deposition in the cause for Louis.[74]

Famously, Charles identified Blanche as the 'holy root', the *sancta radix*, of the noted personal piety of all her children, and the saintly character of Louis and Isabella.[75] In this he was followed by others who wrote hagiographies of Louis. Charles himself was born after his father's death, but little was made of any pious influence that Louis VIII might have had on the older children. This is surprising, since Louis VIII had died, as popes were keen to remind his family, as a martyr

fighting heresy, and until his death in 1226 the religious tone within the family probably owed as much to him as to Blanche. But this was forgotten by the time that the hagiographies of Louis IX and his sister were being written in the late thirteenth century and the early fourteenth. Much of the information and the family anecdotes contained in them came from those, especially Charles of Anjou and Margaret of Provence, who were too young to have known about the first quarter of the thirteenth century.[76] But they all had powerful memories of Blanche. Moreover, Louis's biographers found the story of the serious child king educated and protected by his strong and pious mother irresistible. Geoffrey of Beaulieu drew an analogy between Louis and Blanche and the biblical king Josiah and his mother Idida.[77]

Louis's biographers show Blanche inculcating an austere Christian ethos of good behaviour into her children, especially Louis himself. She is stern and unforgiving. When she hears that Louis may have been unfaithful to his young wife, she announces that she would prefer him to die rather than commit the sin of adultery.[78] Blanche's personal piety must have been influenced by her psalter and the devotional work, the 'Audi domina', written for her. Both are minatory, both stressing the loneliness of the penitent soul before the judgement of God at death and at the End of Time. The impact on her children may have been two candidates for canonisation; but while Louis's and Isabella's fervid piety was much admired, it was also seen as excessive by some contemporaries. Their morbid aversion to the things of this world was not quite what Blanche had intended. It was certainly not what she practised. She was deeply concerned about Isabella's refusal of food, and was always trying to dress her much-loved daughter in beautiful clothes and glimmering jewels.[79] One is not told what she thought of their use of discipline; or whether Blanche herself, or any of her other children, took mortification of the flesh that far. Louis's and Isabella's piety was in fact very different from their mother's, both in its demonstrative quality and in its focus on Franciscan ideals of the poverty of Christ. Blanche's piety was more restrained and internalised; it must have given edge to, but could not extinguish, her evident savouring of the things of this world. Here again, it was her other sons who reflected her own practices and temperament. But perhaps Louis's and Isabella's religious morbidity reflects the inner contradiction at the heart of Blanche's intense response to the things of this world and the things of the world to come.

•

Matthew Paris has a powerful drawing of a distraught Blanche at the bedside of her beloved son Louis, holding a cross over his apparently dead body (pl. 22). It illustrates the moment when Louis recovered enough from the illness that nearly killed him in the winter of 1244–5 to determine to go on Crusade – to the horror of Blanche, who had just seen him restored to her. Blanche sat at many bedsides, for illness and death surrounded her.

Blanche herself must have been fundamentally robust, or she would not have survived at least eleven births, including one set of twins. She remained active throughout her forties and early fifties, though she may have felt herself to be ageing when she founded Maubuisson and Le Lys in the late 1230s and 1240s. She was sixty-four when she died – a respectable age, similar to her sister Berengaria – though elite women who survived childbirth often lived into their seventies or eighties, as did Margaret of Provence and Eleanor of Aquitaine.[80] Blanche probably believed strongly in the benefits of blood-letting. The household accounts show that in 1234 she had her own blood-letter, Geoffrey Miniaz, suggesting that she was bled frequently, unlike anyone else in the household; and the two blood-letters at Pontoise and Anet in 1213 may have been called on Blanche's account, since she had recently given birth to twins.[81] But there is no other indication of any kind of chronic ill health. Indeed, there is little mention of any serious illness until her final two years, though both she and Louis were ill in 1238.[82] She was very unwell in the spring of 1251, and took some time to convalesce. The illness that killed her was mercifully short. It may have been heart failure or perhaps an infection like pneumonia, though the sudden flare up of a hidden cancer cannot be ruled out.[83]

Her husband was notoriously sickly; he had nearly died as a child, and was dangerously ill again in 1206, shortly after the birth, and death, of their first daughter.[84] Their children may have inherited some of Louis VIII's fragility. Five of their children died before the age of eleven. Within two years, in 1232 to 1234, Blanche had to cope with the deaths of both John and Philip Dagobert. Less than a year before St Louis's famous brush with death, Isabella's life had been despaired of, bringing Blanche and Louis dashing to her bedside at Saint-Germain-en-Laye. Alphonse of Poitiers fell ill with temporary paralysis on his return from the Crusade. Even Charles of Anjou, who otherwise seems to have inherited his mother's physical robustness, was seriously ill in 1239. Again, Blanche rushed from Melun to his bedside at Vincennes, giving 25 *livres* to the paupers of Paris for prayers for his recovery on the way.[85] For St Louis, illness was a way of life and a

manifestation of a devotion to Christ by imitation of His suffering. He probably suffered chronic migraine, and took to his bed in intense pain for a few days every few months. He was less able to support the heat and insanitary conditions of the Crusade than his stronger brothers. But he was unhealthily fascinated by the illness of others, too, especially where that illness, as with leprosy, was gruesome to behold.[86]

Not surprisingly, several doctors were maintained at court. Master James, *phisicus*, looked after the sickly twins in 1213. He was probably still a valued member of the household in 1234, when he was given robes for the wedding of Louis and Margaret.[87] His name, still relatively unusual in France in the early thirteenth century, suggests that he may have been Spanish, as does the surname of Geoffrey Miniaz. Perhaps both men had learnt their skills from Arab physicians in the rich cultural melting pot of Toledo, as surely had the physician Louis the convert, presumably a Jewish, or even a Muslim convert, given a robe along with the other court physicians in 1239.[88]

Chronicles and documents record the illnesses that were terminal or threatened to be so, or at least serious enough to impinge on the business of government. Minor illnesses passed unmarked. There was little in the way of pain-deadening drugs available. Childbirth, even when both mother and child survived, must have been grim. There was no relief from what to us are minor ailments and injuries – toothache, earache, broken limbs, arthritic joints. The living of everyday life required a level of stoical acceptance that most of us can hardly contemplate.

•

Blanche was taken away from her family when she was twelve. She never saw her parents or her brothers and sisters again. But she retained a profound affection for them, and reverence for her parents. Her seal showed her as queen of France, but her counterseal proclaimed her the daughter of the king of Castile (pls 22, 23).[89] Her parents, Alfonso VIII and Eleanor of England, were the principal focus of the prayers of the nuns of Maubuisson, though there were many other members of her family, not least her many dead children, who might have held that position. Blanche and Lord Louis, probably in consultation with Bishop Walter of Chartres, had windows dedicated to Alfonso and Eleanor placed in the choir clerestory at Chartres Cathedral.[90]

Knights and clergy – usually Spanish, but occasionally French – went backwards and forwards between the French court and the Castilian, bearing messages, letters

and gifts.[91] The gifts exchanged by Blanche and her Spanish relatives were rich and exotic. In late 1241 she received horses and pomegranates.[92] Earlier that year she had sent a jewelled belt and rich fabrics to her sister Eleanor, queen of Aragón, now repudiated by her husband and living with their sister Berengaria at Las Huelgas. She dispatched 'to Spain', which doubtless means Castile, considerable quantities of fine cloths and furs, as well as furnishings for a personal chapel – an image, perhaps of the Virgin, silver chalices and a 'hanap' – a goblet.[93] She sent rich cloths to Spain in 1239.[94] Probably in the 1240s, in conjunction with Louis, she sent to her sister, the queen of Castile, an entire personal chapel, with rich robes for the chaplains, ivory pyxes, a rock crystal cross, a missal in two volumes and a breviary in one.[95] Blanche's conspicuous generosity to her Spanish relatives was criticised in baronial songs.[96]

Blanche and her older sister Berengaria had much in common. Berengaria also found herself ruling for a young son, against baronial opposition. She was already married before Blanche left for France, to her second cousin, Alfonso ix of León, in an attempt to end conflict between the two contiguous Iberian kingdoms. When the marriage was annulled in 1204 Berengaria retreated to Castile, with her young son, Ferdinand, taking refuge at Las Huelgas. When Alfonso viii and Eleanor of Castile's only surviving son, Henry, died in 1217, after only three years as king of Castile, Berengaria, as the oldest daughter, inherited the throne. Aware that there were many difficulties in her way as queen regnant, Berengaria had Ferdinand declared king of Castile. Ferdinand iii was sixteen at his accession, slightly older than Louis ix, but young enough for Berengaria to play a full queenly role alongside him. Her position as queen differed from Blanche's in that she was the heir to the kingdom in her own right. Her son owed his powers as king to her, whereas Blanche owed her powers as queen to her son.[97]

The accounts of 1234 and 1241–2 indicate that Blanche and Berengaria corresponded with some frequency.[98] The one surviving letter, from Berengaria to Blanche, describing the great victory of their father at Las Navas de Tolosa in 1212, has an intimate, familial quality that suggests real affection between the two sisters. It implies that they were used to exchanging letters. Nevertheless, historians have been wary of taking this letter at face value. It survives in a thirteenth-century manuscript from the Cistercian abbey of Cambron in Flanders, but does not conform to Castilian chancery practice, or to the formalities of contemporary letter writing, and it contains some old French words. Theresa Vann has argued convincingly that it was confected for Mary, empress of Constantinople, granddaughter of

Berengaria and one of Blanche's favoured nieces, perhaps by Blanche herself, to remind her of Alfonso VIII's great triumph over the Muslims. As empress, Mary was only too aware of the challenge of Islam.[99] An element of confection there may be, but there is evidence that it is based on a real letter between the sisters, for the confecting scribe included an unnecessary last line praising Theobald of Blaison. This must have been inadvertently copied from a letter written at the time of the battle. Theobald had been close to Lord Louis and Blanche, but he had died in 1229, long before this version of the letter was produced for Mary of Constantinople.[100]

It has been argued that the letter suggests not closeness, but coolness between Blanche and Berengaria. Berengaria gives herself a queenly title, but addresses Blanche only as 'her beloved and esteemed sister, Blanca, wife of Lord Louis, first born of France'. But in 1212 or 1213 that was correct. Blanche was not queen of France, and did not become so until she was crowned with Louis in 1223. It is true that the French court retained the letters from Berengaria's enemies in Spain, who wrote to Blanche and Louis VIII in 1223 asking them to send a son to become king of Castile in place of Berengaria and her young son Ferdinand; but there is no evidence that either Blanche or Louis considered acting upon them.[101]

Whatever the precise state of their sisterly feelings, the two sisters co-operated in the arrangement of inter-familial marriages. Berengaria organised the marriage in 1224 between her daughter Berengaria and John of Brienne, king of Jerusalem, contracted as John returned to France from a pilgrimage to Santiago de Compostela; but it is difficult to believe that Blanche played no part in the marriage of her niece with one of her husband's close friends. The sisters played a more equal role in the marriage of Ferdinand III, in 1237, to Joanna, heiress to the strategically placed French county of Ponthieu, and in the abortive attempt to arrange the marriage of Theobald of Champagne's daughter, Blanche, and Berengaria's grandson Alfonso in 1235.[102]

As for Blanche's other sisters, her generous gifts to Eleanor of Aragón in 1241–2 are recorded, and she ensured that Eleanor and the nun Constance, and indeed all her sisters, were remembered in prayers throughout the Cistercian order. In 1243 full services were held in memory of the recently deceased Eleanor and Constance, the first clearly at Blanche's request, the latter probably. In 1251 Blanche asked for a special commemoration for her parents and her sisters.[103] She was an indulgent aunt to her sisters' children. In 1252 she requested prayers from the Cistercian order for her recently deceased nephews, Ferdinand, king of Castile, and Alfonso, son of

Eleanor of Aragón.[104] In 1248 the French court provided, and repaired, a house at Chauny for one of Eleanor of Aragón's sons.[105] In the early 1230s Blanche's older sister Urraca, queen of Portugal, sent her younger son, Alphonse, to Blanche's court. Alphonse appears in the accounts as 'Alphonse the Nephew', and as a close companion to Blanche's son Alphonse. Alphonse the nephew was provided with his own household, with Maundy money, with robes – purple silk for Louis's wedding – and horses for himself and his household.[106] At Pentecost 1239 Blanche had him knighted, and arranged a brilliant marriage for him, with Matilda of Boulogne, a great heiress in her own right, but also the rich widow of Philip Hurepel. Blanche herself gave Alphonse a robe made partly of Spanish purple silk for the occasion.[107]

Queen Berengaria's daughter, Berengaria of Jerusalem, became a favoured niece. With her husband, John of Brienne, Berengaria of Jerusalem spent much of 1224 at the French court. She accompanied Blanche and Ingeborg on their pilgrimage to Saint-Antoine in 1224 to pray for Louis VIII's victory at La Rochelle. Both John and Berengaria were prayed for by the nuns at Maubuisson,[108] and Blanche took their children under her wing. Their daughter, Mary, married the emperor Baldwin of Constantinople, who was related to Louis VIII through the Courtenay clan and through Isabella of Hainault. Empress Mary wrote to Blanche in French, and her letters to her 'douce tante' – her sweet aunt – have a touchingly intimate tone. Mary left Constantinople for Paris in 1249. Blanche was overjoyed to see her, and Mary stayed with her great-aunt until Blanche's death.[109] For Mary, Blanche produced the confected version of the letter about Las Navas de Tolosa from Berengaria.[110] Mary retired to her county of Namur after Blanche's death. There, in 1255, she probably commissioned and dispatched a tomb of Tournai marble for Blanche, perhaps for her heart burial at Le Lys (pl. 29).[111] Mary's brothers, Alphonse, John and Louis, were sent to live at the French court, where they were known as the children of Acre.[112] Blanche arranged a brilliant marriage for Alphonse, to Mary, heiress to the county of Eu. Alphonse of Eu-Brienne had the same subversive sense of humour as Robert of Artois: on Crusade he amused himself by smashing Joinville's crockery with a small catapult, and sent his pet bear to eat Joinville's chickens.[113] Alphonse of Eu-Brienne's daughter, Blanche, named after the queen, became a nun at Maubuisson, and eventually its second abbess. From one of her well-travelled relations, the abbess Blanche acquired a coconut, which became a treasured item in the abbey treasury and survives to this day. Empress Mary and

her brother John of Brienne were buried alongside their great-aunt in her abbey of Maubuisson.[114]

A lesser member of Queen Berengaria's extended family, Lady Mincia, or Mencía, a niece of Berengaria's son, King Ferdinand, and daughter of his steward, Lope Díaz de Haro, resided at the French court in the early 1230s. Mincia was provided with clothes and horses and her own household, with a splendid new robe for Louis and Margaret's wedding, and finally, in late 1234, with the means to return to Spain, at Capetian expense.[115] She returned to marry a Castilian noble, Álvaro Pérez de Castro. Both her father and her husband were involved in growing baronial disaffection against Ferdinand III. Fortunately, Queen Berengaria managed to negotiate a rapprochement between Ferdinand and Álvaro Pérez and his wife.[116] Berengaria probably saw the French court as providing a sort of finishing school for favoured members of the Castilian aristocracy, like the lord April Garcia who had his own cook and clerk, and was given rich gifts for his return to Spain in 1234.[117]

In Iberia, the kingdoms of Castile, León, Portugal, Navarre and Aragón struggled for power and resources within the peninsular. But the ruling families of the Iberian kingdoms were all closely related, and when they found themselves in France the offspring of the warring dynasties treated each other with surprising affection. Blanche and Lord Louis corresponded with Blanche of Navarre, countess of Champagne, though Blanche of Navarre had to complain to Philip Augustus about Lord Louis's unmannerly demands for troops.[118] Both women were named after Blanca of Navarre, queen of Sancho III of Castile, grandmother of Blanche of Castile and aunt of Blanche of Navarre. When Blanche passed on to her cousin the glorious news about the great victory of Las Navas de Tolosa, she addressed her as her dear sister, and included much about the contribution of Sancho of Navarre.[119] Blanche of Navarre underwrote the planned marriage of the young prince Philip with Agnes of Nevers in 1216.[120] The sympathy evident between Blanche of Castile and Theobald of Champagne, which led to rumours of scandal, may have been due to a shared Iberian background – perhaps simply an ability to converse in Spanish. Ferdinand of Portugal, who proved a loyal supporter of Blanche after his release from prison, was a cousin. Both men were unpopular with many of the barons because they were perceived as Spanish. Baronial songs accused Walter Cornut of loving Spanish men more than he loved the barons.[121]

Blanche's relations with her mother's Angevin family were more problematic, in that they were the enemies of the Capetians. The only Angevin name among her

large brood of children is John. In general, she treated her cousin Henry III as the enemy that events had made him. She could never trust him – with good reason: Henry wanted the return of his French lands. In 1252 she refused to allow him passage through France to visit Gascony.[122] But she received his brother Richard of Cornwall graciously in Paris; she was gracious too when she wrote to tell Henry that his two sisters-in-law were in good health on Crusade. She addressed him affectionately as her very dear cousin, and it is a warm and thoughtful letter.[123] Blanche shared the Capetians' implacable enmity to another cousin, the emperor, Otto of Brunswick. But she developed a warm friendship with her cousin Raymond VII of Toulouse, who made much of their close family links in his letters to her. She played an important role in the mediation of his relations with the papacy as well as the French crown, ignoring the resultant criticism. As with Count Theobald, she could probably enjoy a shared meridional culture with him.

Like other rulers, Blanche could never view her family as a private domain. Sons and daughters were to be married off to political advantage. Relationships with cousins – especially Angevin cousins – were subject to political imperatives. But it is clear that Blanche's relationships within her family were affective and intensely human – distressingly so in the relationship with Margaret of Provence. Occasionally, she allowed personal feelings to override political considerations – in her indulgence towards her Iberian relatives, and above all in her sympathetic treatment of her determinedly devout daughter.

•

The royal household – the *familia* – was both an extended family and the epicentre of the governance of the realm. Here, too, what might be thought to be private was always political. Members of the royal household might attend to the most private needs – emotional, physical and spiritual – of the royal family; but just because they were so deeply trusted, they were often used as diplomats, administrators and agents of government. Two things stand out in the membership of Blanche's households over her long career from princess to queen dowager: the continuity of staff, and of the families who formed that staff, and the number of Iberians. The number of clergy was high, but probably no higher than in any other contemporary household, for the clergy did not just provide spiritual services. Highly educated as they were, they ran most of the written administration, and doubtless provided the education on which Blanche insisted for her children.[124]

The accounts for 1231 give an indication of the size of the household. There were forty-three knights, twenty-seven clerks, nineteen sommeliers (officials in charge of provisions and pack animals), eleven esquires, two marshals, twenty-seven valets of horse, twelve archers, four huntsmen with five valets, two falconers, two fureters (ferreters), six sommeliers of the pantry, six sommeliers of the *échansonnerie* (which dealt with drink and drinking vessels), sixteen runners, four fruiterers (who dealt with lighting by torch and candle as well as the provision of fruit), seven huissiers (ushers), six valets of the dogs, eighty crossbowmen and twenty-one sergeants-at-arms. Out of this chaos, Louis IX established six household departments in 1261 – the pantry, the *échansonnerie*, the kitchen, the fruiterers, the stable and the chamber of the king.[125]

The great offices of court had once been filled by magnates, but Philip Augustus had long since ensured that if they were filled at all, it was by men beholden to him, from knightly or, at most, the old castellan families of the Capetian lands. Louis VIII and Blanche inherited Philip's grand chamberlain, Bartholomew of Roye, and his constable, Matthew of Montmorency.[126] Surprisingly, Louis VIII gave the butlership to one of his baronial friends: his cousin Robert of Courtenay. When Robert died in 1240, he was succeeded by the equally baronial Stephen of Sancerre. The butlers were often at court and of course present at great occasions, but were not permanent members of the household.

The hierarchy within the household – between those who were knights or held important named offices, and managed large numbers of staff, and those who did the menial work – must have been very obvious, not least in the wages and in the quality of the robes distributed to them. Nevertheless, those who made the royal family's beds, or helped them bathe and dress, or nursed them when they were ill, or cooked their favourite food, or knew how to make clothes that flattered them, could become very close to them, and deeply trusted. The master cook, Gervaise of Escrennes, for instance, undertook diplomatic roles in the early 1240s.[127]

The castellan and knightly families of the Capetian heartlands formed the backbone of the royal entourage and household.[128] Even in the 1240s there were many who had risen to prominence under Philip Augustus, and who had clustered around Lord Louis and Blanche in their youth. Bartholomew of Roye remained the grand chamberlain until he died in 1237. He was given his own embroidered cushioned chair for the coronation of the young queen in 1234.[129] Although his origins were relatively lowly, marriage to a member of the Montfort dynasty and years of royal service had left him rich enough to behave like a member of higher

aristocracy, founding the Premonstratensian house of Joyenval as his family mauso-leum. Members of the extended family of Ours the Chamberlain, who had served the young Lord Louis and had acquired the lordship of Nemours, continued to serve in the royal entourage, as did members of the extended Cornut-Clément clan. In most cases, members of the same family served both as lay courtiers and as secular clergy in the household.[130]

Bartholomew of Roye probably ran the household on a regular basis as grand chamberlain. John of Beaumont succeeded him after his death.[131] There were several subsidiary knightly chamberlains. Those who did the menial work involved in arranging the chambers of the royal family are rarely named, though Blanche's own chambermaid (*chambellana*) around 1240 was called Mary.[132] A substantial staff ensured that the royal family and their entourage were well fed. The knight Hugh of Athies held the honorary office of the pantler – the provider of bread. Adam the Cook ran the royal kitchens in the early 1230s.[133] It was a demanding job, for the court was so often on the move, and the pots, pans and fine plate must be packed into carriages and provisions ordered ahead. Several fishermen kept the court provided with fish.[134] Blanche had her own kitchen establishment, with its own pots and pans, from 1234, under the command of William, the queen's cook. His high status was recognised in the gift of a palfrey for him to attend the wedding celebrations of 1234.[135] William's staff included four turners of the spits and a sauce maker, Renaud.[136] Blanche had her own stables.[137] Horses were required for transport, warfare and hunting, and horses and their trappings were often given as gifts, both to reward staff and to flatter important visitors. She also had her own *chanteuse* or female singer, called Melana.[138]

Blanche can be seen dealing with various specialist providers to the household. Ivo provided gloves for her and the children in 1234; Gilbert supplied the court with gloves in 1239.[139] Eudes of Cormeilles and John of Ermenonville were the court robe makers.[140] John was still owed 7 *livres* 10 *solidi* for the queen's robes four years after her death.[141] Herbert the Parchmenter provided parchment and illuminated and rebound an ordinary; Blanche provided a dowry for his daughter's marriage in 1242.[142] She often gave members of the household, or those closely associated with it, money to ensure the marriage of daughters or sisters.

Records show certain lay members of the royal household, like some of the clerks, as being particularly close to Blanche – but the evidence is fragmentary, and this does not mean that others were not. Denis the Scutifer and Peter Pig-Flesh were probably part of the general royal household in 1239, but appear to be part

of Blanche's own household in 1241–2, though there may always have been some permeability between the two establishments. Adam of Melun seems to have kept the accounts for the royal robes and fine silks: Blanche gave him a robe of samite from her own clothes chests when he was knighted alongside Alphonse of Poitiers. Adam married rather well for a household official in charge of fine silks. His wife was a daughter of Stephen of Sancerre, and the queen's patronage surely lay behind their marriage.[143] Gerald of Espineul, in charge of the royal hunt, was the son-in-law of one of her ladies, Matilda of Lorris, and Blanche had him knighted alongside her nephew Alphonse of Portugal.[144]

Blanche would have been accompanied by a small group of women attendants when she first arrived from Spain at the age of twelve. They probably included the lady Dorea or Doreta, who was part of Blanche's household in 1213 and still there as late as 1239. She was given gifts and robes, and had her own valet, who organised the robes for the household of the king for the knighting of Robert of Artois. Her wages are recorded in the account of 1239: she received 38 *solidi* for the thirty-eight days from the feast of St Remi to All Saints.[145] Dorea's name, as well as her long service, marks her out as probably Castilian: it was certainly not a current north French name.

Most of the other women recorded as Blanche's ladies in the 1230s and 1240s were French. They provided the queen with permanent subservient companionship, as well as service. Their social status varied, but most were drawn, like the royal administrators, from the castellans, knightly families and lesser aristocracy of the Ile-de-France. They included three women from the Cornut-Clément clan. Walter Cornut's sister, Regina, was given money to marry off her daughter in 1213; Blanche was still lending her money in 1243. By 1239 Isabella and Agnes Cornut had joined the household. Agnes may have been one of Blanche's ladies by 1234, for a Lady Agnes authorized a payment to the Cistercian nuns of La Joie-lès-Nemours then, and both Lady Agnes and her sister were given robes to accompany Blanche at the wedding and coronation of the young queen at Sens.[146] They are probably the Lady Isabella and perhaps the Lady Agnes recorded on Blanche's household account of 1241–2.[147] Odelina de Casteneto – de Chataignes – was given a painted cushion in 1234 and accompanied Blanche to Sens for the wedding and coronation of the young queen.[148] Mary of Champagne probably belonged to a cadet branch of the Beaumont-sur-Oise family: a relation, John, was a household knight.[149] Matilda of Lorris, together, perhaps, with her sister Joanna, may have joined Blanche's household when Blanche and her husband held their princely court at Lorris as they

waited for the old king to die. Matilda was still part of Blanche's household in 1241.[150] In the early 1230s Blanche's ladies included Aveline de Castellario, probably from the family of the castellans of Melun.[151] Agnes de Viriaco (of Vrigny?) had joined the team by 1239, and was active in Blanche's household in the 1240s; a male relation, Peter de Viriaco, was one of the household knights in 1231 and 1239.[152]

Blanche's ladies were trusted to ensure that monies were entered into the queen's coffers, and make dispensations from it.[153] More surprisingly, some of them were allowed to authorize expenditure on the main royal household account. In all such cases, the expenditure was clearly ordered by Blanche, and often reflected her favoured good causes. Thus in 1234 Doreta authorised 20 *solidi* for a Spanish *conversa* – presumably a Jewish convert – in the Maison-Dieu at Poissy, while Lady Agnes authorised 10 *livres* to the Cistercian nuns of La Joie-lès-Nemours at Saint-Germain-en-Laye.[154] In 1239 Matilda of Lorris authorised expenditure on more than one occasion; Agnes Cornut authorised gifts to Juliana of Domfront and her sister; and Agnes de Viriaco authorised gifts to Lady Mabilia of Joigny.[155]

Blanche ensured that her ladies were well provided with fine clothes, especially when they accompanied her on great courtly occasions, like the knighting and marriages of her sons, and the marriage of Louis to Margaret of Provence in 1234.[156] She paid off debts owed by Aveline de Castellario to 'a certain man of Loudun'.[157] In 1241 she bought 17 *livres* worth of jewels from Matilda of Lorris, and in addition gave her 40 *livres* as a gift. It is unclear why the Lady Matilda needed so much money so suddenly: perhaps she had decided to enter Maubuisson.[158] Blanche took a matriarchal interest in her ladies' marriages. In 1234 she organised the marriage of Lady Odelina to a Norman aristocrat, Robert of Montfort-sur-Risle. The marriage was a political one, tying Robert, who had family connections with the Fougères family on the border with Brittany, closely to the Capetian cause.[159] At about the same time, she arranged for another of her ladies to marry William, the son of a less important Norman lord, William of Minières, lord of Corneuil near Damville. Whereas Lady Odelina seems to have left court on her marriage, the wife of William of Minières – her name is unknown – brought William into Blanche's household.[160] In the Norman inquests of 1247 the young man's father, William of Minières senior, complained that he could not afford to provide for the young couple, for his lands had been wasted by royal agents. Blanche had probably tried to help the family, for in 1241, at her abbey of Maubuisson, the

older William sold substantial properties to the great Capetian clerk and adminis-trator John de la Cour.[161]

By the late 1230s the abbess of Saint-Antoine, Agnes Mauvoisin, was so fre-quently at court that she became almost a member of the household. Stephen of Lexington, the reform-minded abbot of Savigny, soon to become abbot of Clairvaux, wrote to Abbess Agnes in 1236 to remind her that neither she nor her nuns should dine or stay the night away from their nunnery – unless they were with the lady queen.[162] Abbess Agnes, sister of one of the great heroes of the Albigensian Crusade, was probably unabashed.[163] Besides, Blanche had frequent need of discussion with her, for she acquired the nuns for Maubuisson from Saint-Antoine. Abbess Agnes acted much like Blanche's most trusted ladies. In 1239 she authorised royal expendi-ture, twice to place women in Cistercian nunneries, and twice for gifts to the Cistercian nuns of Belleau and Penthemont.[164] Her successor as abbess of Saint-Antoine, Amicia Briard, played a similar role, handing over Blanche's monies as a gift to the Cistercian nuns of the Paraclete in 1241. The abbesses of Cistercian La Grâce and L'Eau also distributed Blanche's gifts to religious houses.[165]

Blanche was always surrounded by those who spoke the language of her child-hood. It has already been suggested that Doreta, Master James the physician and Geoffrey Miniaz the blood-letter might have been Castilian. Walter, her pantler was probably Spanish, for Blanche paid for his visit to his home country in 1234. In the early 1240s she was attended by a Lady called Agnes de Argal – a toponymic with a distinctly Iberian tinge; and her household included a 'little Spanish girl'.[166] An unidentified Spaniard did business for Blanche in her dowry town of Issoudun. Martin Alfonsus did business for the queen at La Rochelle. The lords Ferdinand and Roger of Spain were given robes for the wedding of 1234. In 1239 wages were paid to Lord Ferdinand and Peter the knight of Spain.[167] Many of the clergy in Blanche's entourage were also Iberians.[168]

The great princely and baronial families of Capetian France kept their own courts. Nevertheless, on the great courtly occasions – marriages, knighting and the great feasts of Christmas and Easter – members of the grander aristocracy of Capetian France joined the royal family and their household. The very greatest of these families were closely related to the Capetians – Philip Hurepel was Louis VIII's half-brother; the Courtenay and the Dreux were descended from Louis VI. The counts and countesses of Flanders, Champagne and Toulouse, and the coun-tesses of Blois and Chartres, were all related to Blanche or Louis VIII or both. In

spite of political stress between the kings and queens of France and the great aristocracy, there were often close personal friendships.

Blanche enjoyed the friendship of both women and men. In 1251 she petitioned the Cistercian general chapter for special prayers in memory of the dead of her immediate family, but also, more unusually, 'for her other friends'.[169] She was able to depend, throughout her career, on friendships built with her husband in their youthful and chivalric court, or on his campaigns. Theobald of Blaison was one example; and Blanche took good care of Theobald's family after his death.[170] Stephen of Sancerre, a younger member of the sprawling house of Champagne, was part of their entourage in 1213, and often at court thereafter, where he was made butler in 1240. Like Blanche, he enjoyed vernacular music; he often brought his minstrels to court with him. He was a strong supporter of Blanche during the regency. His daughter, Comtesse, was married to Adam of Melun, to whom Blanche gave the robe of red samite from her own coffers in 1241.[171] John of Nesle and his wife, Eustacia, a first cousin of Louis VIII, gave their Paris home to Blanche in 1232. Their nephew and heir, Simon of Nesle, remained devoted to Blanche's service.[172] Simon was married to a daughter of Amaury of Montfort. Amaury, too, had been one of Blanche's strongest supporters during her first regency. When he took the Cross on the ill-fated Barons' Crusade in 1239–40, he went funded by Blanche and Louis IX, as if in their place. Blanche's household accounts reveal her distress as news of Amaury's capture and subsequent death filtered back. She paid 8 *livres* to a servant of Amaury's who brought news of the prisoners, then sent his daughter a fine gold belt in condolence.[173] In 1241 Blanche paid 30 *livres* for the marriage portion of the daughter of Gaucher of Nanteuil, a cousin of Louis VIII's old companion-in-arms, Guy of Châtillon, count of Saint-Pol.[174]

Her relations with most of the women of the extended Capetian family were warm. The countesses Joanna and Margaret of Flanders had been brought up at Philip Augustus's court, so that Blanche would have known them from her youth. She dealt firmly with both women politically. But Joanna sent Blanche a palfrey in 1239, and when the royal family needed jewellery for the wedding of Louis and Margaret, they turned to Countess Joanna to recommend a goldsmith.[175] When Joanna died at the end of 1244, Blanche and her family were devastated. She did not dare tell the sick Louis the news, for fear it would kill him.[176] Blanche had the anniversary of Joanna's death remembered at Maubuisson.[177] Isabella, countess of Chartres, and her sister Margaret, countess of Blois, were, like Blanche, grand-daughters of Eleanor of Aquitaine.[178] Isabella and her daughter Matilda, lady of

Amboise, were provided with robes to attend the wedding of 1234 with Blanche. Isabella was given a fine robe in 1239.[179] She accompanied the royal party to Poitou in 1241, perhaps because her other sister, Alice, was abbess of Fontevraud.[180] Margaret's daughter Mary, countess of Blois, now married to Hugh of Châtillon, was given emeralds at Robert of Artois' knighting and wedding in 1237.[181] Later, Blanche sent her singer, Melana, to soothe Mary in childbirth.[182] When Blanche arranged the apparently advantageous marriage of the widowed Matilda of Boulogne with Alphonse 'the nephew' of Portugal, she gave Matilda a magnificent robe of green samite.[183] For Countess Mary of Ponthieu's daughter, Joanna, Blanche arranged the still more glittering marriage with her other nephew, Ferdinand III of Castile.

Alice, countess of Mâcon and Vienne in her own right, was, like Blanche, descended from Eleanor of Aquitaine, and they described themselves as cousins.[184] Alice had been married to John, the brother of Peter and Robert of Dreux. There were no surviving children, and before Count John left on the Barons' Crusade of 1238 – on which he died – he sold the county of Mâcon to the king, leaving a substantial income to Alice. Alice used this to endow Blanche's new foundation of Maubuisson, into which she presumably retired.[185] When Blanche founded Le Lys, Alice became its first abbess: her speedy elevation to this status undoubtedly reflected Blanche's wishes. Alice's niece Matilda entered the nunnery too, and became the second abbess at a more appropriate speed. At Blanche's death, it was Alice who is said to have asked for, and obtained, the queen's heart for burial at Le Lys.[186]

Blanche did not just cultivate friendships with Capetian cousins. The lady of Audenarde – from the lands that had come to Louis VIII from his mother – came to Paris to venerate the Crown of Thorns in 1239, and appeared in Blanche's entourage in the following year.[187] Some aristocratic women received unexplained gifts, like Juliana of Domfront in 1234 and 1239 and Lady Mabilia of Joigny in 1239 and 1241, almost as if they were in need of royal generosity.[188] There were clearly close friendships with members of the local aristocracy too. When Anselm of L'Isle-Adam made his will in 1252, he wrote that he had taken the advice of the Lady Queen as to how he should dispose of his wealth, and arranged that his executors should also do everything with her counsel. Anselm is not otherwise recorded in Blanche's entourage, though he was closely related to the Mauvoisin, Montmorency and Montfort families, but his will casts a flicker of light on a relationship of affection and trust between a knight and the queen.[189]

Blanche helped out many members of her circle with loans. She lent to ecclesiastics, to members of the household, to minor knights and to the highest aristocracy. In 1213 Blanche and Lord Louis together had advanced loans to Countess Matilda of Nevers, the countess of Saint-Pol, Guy of Beaujeu and Philip Hurepel.[190] Perhaps they were concerned to ensure that those close to them were not beholden to Jewish moneylenders. The audit of Blanche's income and expenditure for Candlemas 1243 shows her acting almost as a bank for the aristocracy. The lady of Beaumont and Lady Beaumont-Bois were loaned 400 *livres* each; Lady Bronnai (perhaps the lady of Braine?) was loaned 200 *livres*; Mary, countess of Eu, owed Blanche 300 *livres*; Countess Joanna of Flanders, 500 *livres*; and the Lord of Mirabel, presumably a descendant of Theobald of Blaison, was loaned 1,000 *livres tournois*.[191]

Undoubtedly, Blanche knew the political value of friendship. Often she addressed quite distant cousins as *consanguineus* or *consanguinea*. In an act of December 1250 dealing with property rights, Blanche calls Countess Philippa of Ramerupt and Mary, lady of Nanteuil, her 'charissimae consanguineae'; in the same act Theobald of Champagne is addressed with more reason as her 'charissimus consangineus'.[192] Often, her reaction to baronial disaffection was to bind the disaffected even closer to Capetian family interests by marriage alliances. It is how she dealt with both Peter Mauclerc and, more successfully, Raymond of Toulouse. Sometimes, her friendship with the wife of a fractious baron must have been helpful. Her cousin Countess Alice of Mâcon, married to Peter Mauclerc's brother John, gave her an opening into the heart of the Dreux family. She continually forgave her politically incontinent cousins, Theobald of Champagne and Raymond of Toulouse, despite the suggestions of impropriety with Theobald, Robert of Artois' disapproval and the gossip of detractors at court. Many of those, male and female, with whom Blanche had close friendships shared her approach to religious devotion, particularly her patronage of female Cistercian or Fontevraudine monasticism.[193]

•

How did Blanche spend her days? The years when she actively and overtly held the wardship of the young king and the country – a substantial period of her adult life – brought the duties of an active ruler. But what was the quotidian for a princess, a queen regnant and a queen dowager?

The centre of Capetian rule was the palace on the Ile de la Cité in Paris. Blanche and her husband had lived there in their youth. How far she used the house near

Les Halles given to her by John of Nesle and his wife as her base in Paris in 1232 is unclear.[194] As ruler, she was itinerant. In the four months between Candlemas and Ascension 1234 she zigzagged back and forth between the houses close to Paris at Beaumont-sur-Oise, Vincennes, Pontoise and Saint-Germain-en-Laye, and undertook expeditions to Bourges and Issoudun, via Lorris, Nemours, and Fontainebleau; to eastern Normandy, including Pont-de-l'Arche, Les Andelys and Gisors; and to Anjou.[195] Even as queen dowager, she travelled incessantly. Her household accounts covering the year from Annunciation 1241 to Ascension 1242 show her moving mainly between her residences at Pontoise, Melun, Etampes, Corbeil and Crépy-en-Valois; sometimes staying at the royal houses of Asnières, Saint-Germain-en-Laye, Vernon and Vincennes, presumably joining Louis at them; and occasionally staying at the Cistercian nunneries of Maubuisson and Le Parc. In the summer of 1241 she went via Beaugency to Chinon, and thence, presumably, to the great feast at Saumur, returning by Bourges, Lorris, Etampes and Dourdan to Pontoise. She spent Christmas 1241 at Pontoise, and Easter with the royal court at Saint-Germain-en-Laye. In summer 1242 she again went to Poitou, travelling via Melun, her old home at Lorris, Châteauneuf-sur-Loire, Orléans and on to Poitiers. She was thus in Poitou when Louis and Alphonse gathered their forces for the campaign that led to the defeat of Henry III at Taillebourg.[196]

Devotion occupied a great deal of an elite woman's time. Beyond that, like any good lady of a household, Blanche kept a close eye on the household accounts. She herself often authorised expenditure of the royal household. When Master Richard of Tourny worked on the project to found and build Maubuisson, he held meetings with the queen, at which he was expected to render clear account of what had been achieved, and how much it had cost, before Blanche would authorise the provision of new funds. She wanted to know, too, what revenues Master Richard had managed to raise from the lands bought to support Maubuisson, from the selling of leeks, for instance.[197] In the 1230s she developed her dowry properties at Issoudun, with the provision of new trading halls.[198] It is easy to see her building a tight working relationship with the men who administered the household and recorded its revenues, the clerks such as John de la Cour, Richard of Tourny and, at an earlier stage in her career, Walter Cornut. These were men she trusted in the domestic sphere, and that trust extended to the wider political world, where they often obtained important bishoprics, like John de la Cour, later bishop of Evreux, or undertook important diplomatic missions.

Blanche was not preoccupied with revenues and expenditure because she was tight-fisted. Her saintly son feared that her almsgiving was too generous, and everything suggests that she kept a lavish court, with no expense spared. But she knew the value of riches: in the difficult days of the minority, she made astute use of the wealth at her disposal to buy time and peace. Her dowry lands in the Berry are not reflected in the account of 1213, and only fleetingly in the accounts of the 1230s, but she must have drawn some revenue from them, and by the 1230s was investing in them. The dower lands in the wealthy north-east, including Hesdin, Lens and the rich trade-route town of Bapaume, must have been immensely productive. The settlements of 1237 and 1240 gave Blanche many of the richest towns of the old royal domain. Her approach to Issoudun and to the lands for Maubuisson suggests that she would have known how to exploit their potential. Along with her dower and dowry, her husband had left her 30,000 *livres* in his will. Blanche was, even for a widowed queen, conspicuously wealthy. Her total income for the Candlemas term of 1243 amounts to some 14,964 *livres*; so her annual income would have been in the region of 45,000 *livres*. That is slightly more than the massive 40,000 *livres* that St Louis is estimated to have spent on the building of the Sainte-Chapelle. She stored her riches, as the Maubuisson accounts and the audit of 1243 show, with the bulk of the royal monies, in the Paris Temple.[199]

Blanche knew she had to set up her stores in heaven, and she was always generous to favoured foundations, favoured orders and favoured good causes, especially the support of converted Jews and the marriage of poor women. But there is no evidence that she felt confined or oppressed by riches as St Louis and Princess Isabella did. Everything suggests that she enjoyed spending them on a richly princely and then royal court, and a great deal of her time must have been spent discussing the provision of food, gowns and jewels, the furnishing, upkeep and reparation of castles, palaces and hunting lodges, the organisation of leisure – hunting and music – and the logistics of ordinary itinerant court life, as well as the great court occasions like the knightings. Of course, Blanche could rely on the experience of staff like the indispensable Batholomew of Roye; but royal will was required to galvanise and direct the activities of household and court. Her continuing importance as queen dowager derived partly from the fact that she was prepared to engage with the details of the things of this world that kept the court and household – the everyday reality of royalty – going, in a way that the unworldly young Louis was not.

Isabella may have hated the furs, silks and jewels in which she was dressed; Louis may have favoured plain cotton hats. But Blanche, her husband and her other sons liked to dress themselves, their households and favoured relations in royal splendour.[200] Eudes of Cormeilles and John of Ermenonville specialised in obtaining the fine woollen cloths – the stanforts – and silks, samites and purple silks of Spain, and creating from them magnificent gowns and tunics.[201] Cupboards were made to store Blanche's rich clothes, which were cared for by an official named Rener.[202] Finely crafted gloves were expensive, but necessary in a life that involved so much riding.

Isabella in particular, and Louis to an extent, found the rich foods of court life too much. Louis ruined delicious sauces with water, to the chagrin of his kitchen staff, and messed with his food so that it looked as though he had eaten it.[203] Blanche, it seems, enjoyed food, and thought others, even those in religion, should too. She sent almonds to her beloved Dominicans at Saint-Jacques in Paris, and expensive cheeses to the nuns at Pontoise.[204] She was fond of salmon, and was prepared to pay 30 *solidi* – the price of a decent psalter – for one brought to her specially.[205] Every year she had pomegranates and pomegranate wine sent specially from Spain.[206] Perhaps it was for Blanche's slightly exotic tastes that ginger, nuts, cloves and spices were provided in 1213, and that sugar – from Spain, or perhaps Sicily – appeared in the household accounts for 1239.[207]

Young Louis and Isabella's idea of leisure was the reading of improving religious literature.[208] Neither enjoyed hunting, which was seen by some clerics as ritualised violence, and Louis hated gambling.[209] Blanche, her husband and her younger sons all read improving religious literature too. But Alphonse and Charles enjoyed gambling and gaming. Alphonse had ivory chess sets bought for his wedding.[210] Hunting featured large in the household accounts of 1213: clearly, much of Blanche's and the future Louis VIII's life revolved around it. There are many references to hunting in the account for 1234, the last year of Louis's minority. The horses, dogs and falcons were carefully groomed; hunting parks were carefully husbanded. Wolves were often brought from the wilder areas of France to enliven the tamer parklands around Paris. The marriage of Alphonse of Portugal, organised by Blanche at Beaumont-sur-Oise in 1239, was celebrated by a wolf hunt the following day. Among those knighted, along with Alphonse, was Gerald of Espineil, who was in charge of the royal hunt. Alphonse of Portugal's knighting was essentially Blanche's affair; and it is significant that Gerald was the son-in-law of Blanche's lady Matilda of Lorris.[211] Later records of hunting expenditure are more restrained,

though they include the wages for the men who coursed hares and the boys looking after the hunting dogs at Vincennes in 1239. By 1256 'hunting' seems to have been a matter of sending out ferreters and partridge hunters to supply the table.[212] The court kept a menagerie, or at least lions, the king of beasts, in the 1230s – something that the hagiographies of Louis never mention.[213]

St Louis would have no 'jolivetez' at court, and forced a young squire who sang worldly songs to learn anthems to the Virgin instead.[214] But the presence of musicians, minstrels and mimers distinguished the household of Blanche and Lord Louis in 1213 from that of Philip Augustus, and they are omnipresent in the household account of 1234. By the late 1230s minstrels were often present at the behest of Blanche, Robert of Artois or Alphonse of Poitiers. Blanche's friends and relations, like Robert of Courtenay, Stephen of Sancerre and the emperor Baldwin, brought their viol players, their singer, Passerelle, and their cornemuse (bagpipe) players to entertain Blanche and her family, and the musicians were generously rewarded.[215] When Blanche appeared at Louis and Margaret's wedding, she was accompanied by a set of trumpeters; and she had her own *chanteuse*, Melana.[216] Alongside religious contemplation and improving reading, Blanche revelled in the vibrant tones of contemporary music and song. She does not seem to have discouraged the wicked schoolboy humour of her younger son Robert, and her loved great-nephew Alphonse of Brienne. She savoured and encouraged the noise and colour of a lively court, as well as the quiet of the pious life.

8

Religion, the Church
and Other Faiths

BLANCHE WAS ALWAYS ENGAGED BY RELIGION and belief. It interested her, as it did her husband; like him, she was sometimes interested in what the Church regarded as unorthodox belief. In common with her husband, her father-in-law, her oldest son and her Angevin family, she held strong views about the role of the institutional Church within the common good of the realm, and she had no hesitation about challenging the Church and churchmen where she thought their position might infringe the rights of the crown, or be damaging to the realm. As has been seen, the relationship of this famously pious queen and the French Church was often one of conflict.

The court and household of Blanche, Louis VIII and Louis IX, like those of all contemporary rulers, crawled with clergy. Some served the overtly religious needs of the king, queen and court. Large numbers of clerks, educated in the schools and proto-universities, were required to run the administration of the royal household and royal government. In addition to the clerks of the household staff, there were several churchmen who held no official role within the court, but whom Blanche and her husband, and later her son, trusted, and with whom they often worked closely, including papal officials, bishops and abbots. These were not, of course, inviolably distinct groups: Walter Cornut, for instance, had been an almoner to Philip Augustus and a gifted administrator for him, Louis VIII and Blanche; once rewarded with the archbishopric of Sens, he was expected to act as one of

the principal advisers of the king of France. Most of these churchmen owed their position in the household or the royal entourage to their administrative, political or diplomatic abilities.[1] One should not assume that the politically adept were inevitably lacking in piety. However they balanced their piety and their politics, they were a numerous and permanent presence in the household and court circles, and they both set and reflected the religious tone of the royal entourage. By the time Blanche was queen, most of the clerks were masters, trained in the Paris schools. There was the potential for sophisticated discussion of matters ecclesiastical and theological within the household and the court.

Most of the household clerks were rewarded, and supported, by positions within the royal gift, or at least subject to royal influence – prebends, deanships and treasurerships within collegiate churches such as Notre-Dame at Etampes, Saint-Aignan at Orléans, Saint-Mellon at Pontoise and, most prestigious of all, Saint-Martin at Tours. The most valued of the household clerks were rewarded with bishoprics, which, while not in the royal gift, were susceptible to royal influence. Thus Master Aubry Cornut became bishop of Chartres and Master John de la Cour became bishop of Evreux, in both cases after holding the deanship of Saint-Martin at Tours.[2] As bishops, they were well known to Blanche and Louis IX, and could be expected to be sympathetic to royal demands – though they did not always turn out to be as accommodating as expected. The names of the clergy serving in one capacity or another within the royal household for 1231 and 1239 are known from the lists of those who were given robes in the traditional ceremony at Pentecost. Twenty-eight were given robes in 1231, twenty in 1239; seven churchmen appear on both lists.[3]

A king would have a substantial personal chapel staff. By 1238 Louis IX's chapel in his palace on the Ile de la Cité was established with five chaplains, each paid 50 *livres* for one term, two matriculars or sacristans and Master Matthew, the king's principal chaplain.[4] The king's principal chaplains, and perhaps his entire chapel staff, would travel with him. Most of the royal residences also had resident chaplains.[5] When Louis IX rebuilt the chapel at the palace of Saint-Germain-en-Laye, he insisted that permanent chaplains should serve there, instead of the monks of Coulombs, who had hitherto provided intermittent religious service in the royal chapel when the court was in residence.[6]

Surprisingly little is known about Blanche's chapel staff. The queen had her own chapels – in the sense of buildings – at the royal houses of both Fontainebleau and Montargis, for both were separately accounted in works for 1248, and she

probably had separate chapels in other major residences too.[7] She also had her own chapel staff. In the early 1230s her chaplain was Peter of Chambly, presumably a relative of Adam, the bishop of Senlis. He travelled with Blanche on the campaign out to the west against Peter Mauclerc in 1231, where he attested gifts to knights along with Blanche herself, Amaury of Montfort and John of Beaumont.[8] Blanche's own household account for 1241–2 names Dom Peter the chaplain; he is probably to be identified with the Master Peter the Chaplain on the general household account for 1239, and perhaps with Peter of Chambly.[9] Brother Geoffrey, chaplain of the queen, was given a robe in 1239. He was probably Blanche's chaplain, though he might have been chaplain to young Queen Margaret instead.[10] His designation as 'brother' suggests that he was a friar, probably a Dominican, or perhaps a Templar. When Blanche's children were young, chaplains from the king's or the queen's households provided for their religious needs; there is reference in 1234 to the chaplain 'who has been with' the young Philip Dagobert.[11] Once Blanche's sons were established with their own households, they had their own chaplains. Alphonse of Poitiers' chaplain, Philip, was supported by the rich living of the treasurership of Saint-Hilaire at Poitiers. Philip was an able diplomat, who helped Blanche rule Alphonse's lands while he was on Crusade. Alphonse named Philip as an executor of his will.[12]

As adults, all Blanche's children had personal confessors in addition to their chaplains. Often, these were friars, like the Dominican Geoffrey of Beaulieu, who became St Louis's confessor, though Princess Isabella made her confessions to Master Haimery, chancellor of the cathedral of Notre-Dame in Paris. Isabella's blameless existence made for such tedious confession that her confessor had trouble keeping awake.[13] The fashion for personal confessors reflected the injunction to frequent confession in the canons of the Fourth Lateran Council. Blanche may have belonged to a generation who confessed to their chaplain, and it is unclear whether she had a personal confessor. None is mentioned in the household accounts, but a collection of *exempla* – edifying anecdotes for use in sermons – compiled by a Dominican of Angers around 1285 claims that the scholarly William of Auvergne, bishop of Paris, acted as her confessor.[14]

Almsgiving was not controlled by the chapel staff, but functioned as a separate department, with its own clerk and staff.[15] The almoner – unnamed – was given robes, along with the other important clergy of the court in 1231 and 1239.[16] Two different almoners are named on the account of 1239, but one may have succeeded the other in that year.[17] The giving of alms was not necessarily authorised by the

almoners or their clerks; it was often attested by the clerks who dealt with general administration, or, in the case of Blanche's alms, by her ladies.[18]

The account of 1213 shows that Blanche had numerous clerks of her own, even as a princess. Surprisingly, only one man, Stephen of Montfort, treasurer of Saint-Mellon at Pontoise, is specified as her own clerk in later surviving records. In 1251 Stephen was rewarded with the more generous royal prebend of the dean-ship of Saint-Aignan at Orléans, and Blanche made him one of the executors of her will.[19] After her death, Stephen worked for the king. His long association with Blanche must have made him well known to the Castilian court, and Stephen played an important role in arranging the projected marriage between the princess Berengaria of Castile and Louis, heir to the French throne, in 1255.[20] For a clergy-man who was so close to Blanche, Stephen of Montfort's character was not impec-cable. He appropriated a psalter worth 25 *solidi* from the college of Saint-Mellon at Pontoise and never returned it, despite continual demands from the archbishop, Eudes Rigaud.[21] The clerks found in the royal household accounts who had joined Blanche's own household by 1241 have already been mentioned, notably Master Richard of Tourny, a colleague of Stephen of Montfort at Saint-Mellon at Pontoise, and Master Peter of Lissy.[22]

The royal entourage was filled with Spanish clergy. One would guess that they were closely associated with Blanche herself, but in what capacity – as chaplain, administrator or diplomat – is rarely specified. Those given robes as members of the household include Dom Vincent, Master Martin, Master James and Master Simon of Spain in 1231, and Master Martin and Master Giles of Spain in 1239.[23] Master Martin appears in the princely household account of 1213, and may have accompanied Blanche to France in 1200. He was still a valued member of the household in 1241. His rewards included a fine robe for Louis's wedding, and a place in the ceremonies to receive the Crown of Thorns. In 1241 he accompanied Blanche when she made a gift to the Dominicans of Paris in their chapter house.[24] Garcia the clerk undertook important diplomatic missions to Spain in 1234 and 1239.[25] Roger or Rodricus the priest of Spain and his colleague Peter joined the household rather later. They were paid wages in 1239. Peter remained as Blanche's chaplain in 1241, while Rodricus returned to Castile.[26] The Master Dominic who appears in 1234 is likely to have been an Iberian too: he is probably the Dom Dominic who saw to payments to two poor Spanish clerks in 1239.[27] By 1239 Master Giles of Spain was well enough established within the royal household to manage the handing out of payments.[28] Master Michael of Spain appears only in the

accounts for 1234, but was clearly highly regarded for he was given robes worth 4 *livres* 8 *solidi* for Louis's wedding.[29] As usual, Blanche advanced the careers of her natal family, establishing her great-nephew Philip of Castile as treasurer of Saint-Martin at Tours in 1243.[30]

There was a small but nebulous group of churchmen who were often to be found in the royal entourage, and often supported by royal gifts, but who were not permanent members of the household. They include Master Simon Langton, the brother of Stephen, archbishop of Canterbury, who had been such an important supporter of Louis VIII during his ill-fated English invasion. Simon was part of Louis and Blanche's court circle in 1213, and was still supported by the French court in 1234.[31] The successive abbots of Saint-Denis, especially, Eudes Clément, cousin of Walter Cornut, were often at court as trusted advisers.[32] Perhaps more surprisingly, abbots of Saint-Victor and members of the new Dominican house of Saint-Jacques in Paris, especially its prior, were frequent members of Blanche's entourage, travelling with her, and recipients of robes and other favours. Among papal officials, the flamboyant legate Cardinal Romanus Frangipani and the diplomatic Peter of Collemezzo, later archbishop of Rouen, were attached to the royal court at various times as representatives of the pope.[33]

All bishops could be expected to give counsel at plenary courts, but some belonged to the inner royal circle. Master Walter Cornut, archbishop of Sens, was Blanche's principal political support when she ruled the kingdom for young Louis and an important adviser until his death in 1241. As Blanche and the royal household moved around in 1234, messengers were sent continually to Walter Cornut, who, with John of Nesle, held together the royal administration.[34] He organised the great liturgical ceremonies of the court – Louis IX's coronation in 1226, Louis's marriage and the coronation of the young queen Margaret at Sens in 1234, and the reception of the Crown of Thorns in 1239. His short book recounting the acquisition and reception of the Crown of Thorns stresses Blanche's role in the event.[35] He was devoted to the queen, and was a donor to her new abbey of Maubuisson.[36] His sisters and nieces belonged to Blanche's innermost circle.[37] The worldly Walter Cornut often worked, for both Louis VIII and Blanche herself, alongside a very different character, Bishop Walter of Chartres. Walter of Chartres was a Cistercian monk, and had been prior of Preuilly and abbot of Pontigny before his elevation to the see of Chartres in 1218.[38] Louis VIII and Blanche found him politically adept: along with Walter Cornut, he oversaw the potentially difficult transition of regnal power to Blanche after Louis's death, and frequently worked with Cornut to

support the queen in her widowhood.[39] He is listed among the clergy of the court who received royal robes in 1231.[40] His relationship with Blanche and her family was intimate. He consecrated the high altar at Royaumont in 1232; he sent a horse as a gift to the young prince Robert in 1234; and he borrowed 1,000 *livres tournois* from Blanche in Brittany in 1230.[41] But he was not a career courtier churchman: rather he was personally austere, as befitted a Cistercian monk. And as a bishop he was inclined towards the pastoral reformist agenda of the Fourth Lateran Council.

The same could be said for the two successive bishops of Paris, Bartholomew, bishop from 1224 until October 1227, and William of Auvergne, bishop from 1228 until his death in 1248. Bartholomew had previously been dean of Chartres, and was closely associated with Bishop Walter. Louis VIII made Bartholomew of Paris and Walter of Chartres executors of his will, alongside his chancellor, Guérin of Senlis, and Abbot John of Saint-Victor.[42] Bartholomew's death must have been a serious blow to Blanche in the early days of her son's minority. His successor as bishop of Paris, William of Orléans or Auvergne, was widely regarded as one of the greatest Paris scholars of the day. His works included translations of Aristotle. He was the dedicatee of Nicholas of Braie's poem on the 'Deeds of Louis VIII'.[43] Blanche supported William in his quarrels with the University of Paris; he negotiated treaties on her behalf with Peter of Brittany.[44] Like Blanche, he was an enthusiastic supporter of the Dominicans in Paris.[45] Dominican *exempla* underlined the intimacy of William's relationship with the French royal family: not only was it Bishop William who extracted Blanche from her inconvenient vow to undertake a pilgrimage to Compostela; it was also Bishop William who was entrusted to give the news to Louis IX that his longed-for first child was, sadly, a girl.[46] Joinville records Bishop William dealing with the religious doubts of a Paris master with wit, charm and humanity.[47]

Adam of Chambly, who became bishop of Senlis in 1229, was less distinguished, but he too was a Paris master, described by a contemporary as 'an adequate preacher and theologian'. Like Walter Cornut, he was regarded as a permanent member of the royal household, receiving robes at Pentecost in 1231 and 1239. He was also a trusted member of Blanche's inner circle, rewarded with remembrance in the Maubuisson calendar.[48] Master John de la Cour – his name, 'de Curia', 'of the court', says it all – belonged to a slightly younger generation. He was one of the most important of the household clerks in the 1230s, probably the most frequent attestor of expenditure in the account of 1234. He had succeeded Aubry

Cornut as dean of Saint-Martin at Tours by 1239. He was rewarded with the
bishopric of Evreux in 1244, which he held until his death in 1256. During Blanche's
Crusade regency, he was one of her principal advisers, and, along with Adam of
Chambly, he served on the regency council that so signally failed to govern effectively after her death.[49]

Most of the household clerks, and those who obtained important Church
positions as a result, were drawn from the faithful families who had served the
Capetians since the late twelfth century – from those families who supplied many
of the lay members of the household and Blanche's ladies. Several churchmen were
drawn from the Nemours dynasty, for instance, Philip of Nemours, bishop of
Châlons from 1227.[50] The preeminent clerical dynasty was the Cornut-Clément
clan, of whom Walter Cornut was the most important figure. His brother, Aubry,
became dean of Tours, then bishop of Chartres from 1236 to 1243. Another brother,
Giles, succeeded him as archbishop of Sens. Another member of the family became
bishop of Nevers, and a younger relative, Henry, succeeded Giles to the archbishopric of Sens, aided no doubt by the large number of Cornut sons and cousins
who had acquired prebends in the cathedral chapter.[51] Walter's cousin Eudes
Clément became abbot of Saint-Denis, and developed the sort of personal closeness
between abbey and royal family that had not been seen since the days of Suger
and Louis the Fat, or Eudes of Deuil and Louis VII. A niece became abbess of the
Cistercian nunnery of La Joie-lès-Nemours.[52]

The grip of the clerical dynasties meant that there was considerable continuity
between the clergy at Louis VIII's and Blanche's court, those at the court that
Blanche ran as regent, and those at the court of Louis IX. There is no obvious
difference between Blanche's household staff in 1231 and St Louis's in 1239, though
marginally more were qualified as 'master' in 1239, and there were probably fewer
Iberians.[53] Nor is there an obvious difference between the household clergy in 1239
and 1256, though the grip of the Cornut-Clément clan had weakened with the
post-Crusade generation. Brother Guérin was a Hospitaller, and Louis VIII had had
a Templar as his almoner. The masters of the Temple continued to act as bankers
for the royal treasure, but men of the military orders were less prominent in the
royal entourage after Louis VIII's death.[54] By the 1230s friars, like the prior of
the Dominicans of Paris, Dom Stephen the Preacher of Paris, Brother Geoffrey,
the queen's chaplain, Brother Roger the almoner of the court, Brother John 'de
Magno Ponte', of the Great Bridge, and Brother Matthew, Louis IX's principal
chaplain, had infiltrated the royal entourage, though most were not supported with

household liveries.[55] Whereas only half of Philip Augustus's clerks were masters, most of the clerks listed in the household accounts of the 1230s were.[56] The arrival of the friars and the increasing predominance in university-trained masters were trends that could be observed in other European courts by the second quarter of the thirteenth century. If the clerks were loyal to the Capetians, the Capetians took good care of them. Many were given generous pensions, and prebends where they were in the royal family's gift; many were given robes and horses; Master Hugh of Athies was given a breviary worth 14 *livres*.[57] They and their families were taken care of when they were ill, and dowries were provided for their nieces.[58]

The churchmen in Blanche's entourage emerge from the records because they were supported by the court, or because they were involved in royal administration or diplomacy. It is easy to gain the impression that Blanche surrounded herself with the sort of career churchman who was much criticised by contemporaries, not least in the pages of the moralised bibles. Some of them undoubtedly were. Stephen of Montfort and Richard of Tourny handled much of Blanche's administration in the early 1240s, both travelling with her when she went to Poitiers in early summer 1242. Both were clearly excellent administrators and financial specialists: Stephen became a master of the Norman exchequer, and Richard ran the Maubuisson project. Neither were model churchmen. Stephen had a light-fingered approach to fine books. Master Richard was a great accumulator of benefices. Both held important positions in the collegiate church of Saint-Mellon at Pontoise: when Eudes Rigaud visited it in 1249 he was scathing in his criticisms.[59] Any ruler or great lord or lady with an administration as large and complex as Blanche's had need of such men. But the most careerist of churchmen may also have been profoundly pious. And most of the churchmen in her entourage had received a Paris school or university education, and were aware of the lively religious debates raging within the schools.

Blanche, like her husband, enjoyed the company of those who engaged in the scholarly questions of the day. Louis VIII had, famously, received his early education from the subtle scholar Stephen of Tournai and the dangerously neo-platonist Amaury of Bène, who was clearly interested in Aristotelian texts as they arrived in Paris at the turn of the century. Simon Langton was well looked after by the Capetian court over at least quarter of a century. He does not appear to have been employed in an administrative capacity, and was perhaps retained as a religious and theological adviser. During her husband's reign, Blanche showed special interest in the small group of Dominican intellectuals establishing themselves in Paris close

to the schools. Her close relationship with William of Auvergne and the highly educated Cardinal Romanus – both distinguished Aristotelians – and their regard for her confirm the impression of a woman at ease among some of the most formidable theologians of the day, and interested, perhaps, in what they had to say.[60]

Like Louis VIII, Blanche could depend on her reputation for personal piety and for her sympathy with the reformist wing of the Church – those who were affected by the moralist teachings of Stephen Langton, and the pastoral reformist agenda of the Fourth Lateran Council. This made it easy for the churchmen of the curial Cornut-Clément and Nemours clans to work with Blanche and Louis VIII; it also attracted to them men like the Cistercian bishop Walter of Chartres. The thrust of the pastoral reforms of Lateran IV is made manifest in many of the images in the moralised bibles produced for Louis VIII and Blanche.[61] Successive popes appreciated her rectitude. Honorius III instructed Romanus, as papal legate, to support the widowed queen. Gregory IX wrote frequently to her, aware of the influence that she exerted over Louis IX, both before and after his majority, and over Raymond of Toulouse; Innocent IV continued the tradition.[62]

Nevertheless, as has been shown, where Blanche felt royal rights were under threat from the Church, she had no hesitation in confrontation. A contemporary commentator like Matthew Paris might ascribe to female intemperance her intransigence in the face of what she saw as ecclesiastical encroachment or exploitation.[63] But Blanche's approach was no different from that of her predecessors as rulers of France, or from other contemporary rulers, both regal and baronial. Her saintly son proved quite as intransigent as she was. In her determination that the French Church should pay the tithe it had voted to support the Crusade against the Albigensians, she was simply implementing what her husband had struggled so hard to extract. During both her regencies, she reacted strongly when she suspected that bishops were infringing royal rights and revenues, and when the papacy exploited rights, especially those to appoint to benefices.[64] She objected to the over-free use of excommunication that the Church had become increasingly apt to use to get its way in cases of dispute: Gregory IX responded to her objections by issuing exemptions for Blanche's and Louis IX's chapels during interdicts.[65] She insisted that the Church observe the proprieties of the licence to elect new bishops or abbots, and upheld the French kings' view that the monarch had the right to appoint canons to prebends while a see was vacant. As regent, Blanche refused to give the licence to elect a new bishop of Soissons in 1251, on the grounds that appointments of canons had been made improperly during the vacancy. The canons

of Soissons complained to the pope and challenged Blanche in the royal court, but in the end they complied with royal custom, and Blanche finally and duly conferred the licence.[66]

These issues continued to plague relations between the king and the French Church during the personal rule of her son. They were outlined in a complaint of St Louis and the barons to the pope in 1235,[67] and then again more forcefully in the complaint or 'protest' of St Louis in 1247. The protest of 1247 set out the position of the kings of France as the founders and protectors of the churches of France, who had endowed them with their temporal goods, which might properly be used for the good of the kingdom.[68] These two complaints to the pope were initiated by groups of nobles. They have often been presented as manifestations of problems between the king and his barons, with Louis adopting the baronial line to avoid confrontation with them. But in both cases baronial complainants included those who were models of loyalty to the crown. In both cases Louis IX was in total agreement with his barons. He took as firm a line against episcopal encroachment on royal rights as did his mother. The conflict with the bishop of Beauvais was driven by Louis rather than Blanche.[69] In 1238 Louis clashed with both William of Auvergne, bishop of Paris, and Aubry Cornut, the new bishop of Chartres, despite the closeness of both men to the king. The clash at Chartres was over the appointments of canons to prebends during the vacancy of the see.[70] The chapter of Notre-Dame in Paris complained that the king and his *baillis* were injuring the rights of the cathedral – presumably demanding too much in impositions. They tried to get judgement on their rights from Louis and Blanche in 1238, but they were both ill. The issue was not resolved until May 1248. There was no mention of Blanche's involvement after 1238 until the final settlement, where her presence is noted. Louis seems to have been unwilling to settle; it is likely that his mother would have acted as mediator.[71] Joinville shows Louis, shortly after his return from the Crusade, teasing Matthew des Champs, bishop of Chartres, and the archbishop of Reims about their failure to render unto Louis that which he held to be rightly his. Matthew des Champs, according to his cathedral obituary, found his battle with the sanctimonious and teasing king a bruising encounter.[72]

The conflict with Bishop Miles of Beauvais has been categorised as a battle between Blanche and Louis and a member of the baronage – a prince bishop of a slightly old-fashioned kind. Miles was indeed succeeded by curial bishops, like William of Grez, whom Alphonse of Poitiers named as one of the executors of his will,[73] and there was an increasing tendency for bishoprics to be filled by clerks

from the royal household and court. But bishops from baronial families did not always cause trouble: James of Bazoches, bishop of Soissons, who crowned Louis IX, was a firm supporter of the minority government. Blanche's own most bitter clash was with successive archbishops of Rouen: neither Theobald of Amiens nor Maurice was from a baronial background. Conversely, as St Louis's attacks on both William of Auvergne and Aubry Cornut show, he had no compunction about challenging curial bishops, or those close to the court, when he saw the Church infringing what he took to be his rights.

In most cases, faction and conflicting interests within the Church itself complicated the issue, but often strengthened the royal, princely or baronial hand. The provincial Church, for instance, often abhorred the growing power of Rome even more than did kings, queens and princes. Increasingly, the papacy exerted its right to appoint to benefices, and to bishoprics in the case of disputed elections. Usually, especially in the case of bishoprics, the popes were careful to make an appointment that would be pleasing to the crown: this was certainly the case when Gregory IX appointed Peter of Collemezzo to the archbishopric of Rouen in 1237. But there was widespread resistance in northern Europe to having benefices filled by absentee Italians. In 1238 an unfortunate and unnamed Italian churchman had to accept, at the request of Louis, Blanche and the pope, that he had not been given a prebend at Saint-Mellon at Pontoise, and that he would revoke all the excommunications he had launched.[74] Presumably Gregory had made an unwise appointment – to Pontoise, where the court stayed so often; and pope and papal appointee were now forced to an undignified climb-down, though only after ample but inappropriate use of ecclesiastical censure by the disappointed Italian.

•

If the Church and Christian faith shaped Blanche's life and her work as queen, so too did its obverse – heresies and the different beliefs of Judaism and Islam. Her earliest childhood must have been shaken by the defeat of her father by Muslim forces at Alarcos in 1195, and she would have grown up aware of the threat of the armies of Islam, while surrounded by Islamic culture. Her father's great victory over the Almohads at Las Navas de Tolosa in 1212 enhanced her prestige as the wife of the heir to the French throne; and in commemoration she and her husband set her parents' images among those of the Crusaders against the Cathars of the Languedoc in the upper windows at Chartres Cathedral.[75] She was continually aware of the pressures to take the fight against Islam to the Holy Land, not least

from the family of Berengaria of Jerusalem, whose sons, Alphonse, John and Louis, were brought up by Blanche with her younger children at the French court. Demands for help from their sister, the empress Mary, and her husband, the ineffectual Baldwin II, were perennial. The popes put pressure on periodically too. Gregory IX tried to persuade Blanche's close adviser, the prior of Saint-Jacques, to negotiate a treaty between Louis IX and Henry III and then organise a Crusade from France.[76] In 1237 Gregory suggested to Blanche that she should go to the Holy Land for the good of her soul, and to help the emperor Baldwin. Gregory suggested she take the advice of Bishop William of Paris. Blanche could think of better ways to help Mary and Baldwin: John of Brienne had already mentioned the Crown of Thorns to her on one of his visits to Paris.[77]

It is surprising that the future Louis VIII did not join any of the Crusades to the East, despite the urgings of John of Brienne. Presumably, Philip Augustus was not prepared to risk losing his only really legitimate heir. Besides, between 1213 and 1219 Louis was taken up with campaigns elsewhere. When Louis IX announced his intention of taking the Cross in 1245, Blanche was passionately opposed to him doing so, for she dreaded losing him. She had already lost her husband to the Crusade against the Cathar heretics. Louis VIII's approach to the early Crusades against the Cathars seems to have been lukewarm, but he planned the Crusade as king with meticulous care, and pursued it with relentless determination. Soon Gregory IX was describing Louis as a martyr to the faith.[78] The two moralised bibles produced during Louis VIII's reign must have been in the making while he planned his final and fatal Crusade against the Cathars. They were full of denunciations of Cathar heretics – often showing the Cathars holding the cat whose anus they were supposed to kiss, and from which they were supposed to take their name.[79] The moralised bibles exhort the good ruler to take firm action against heresy. One image shows the king or prince burning heretics at God's command. Another shows 'the good messengers of Jesus Christ who return from the Albigensians and recount to the princes and to good Christians the evil and miscreance of the Albigensians and all the friends of God take the Cross and say that they will kill and destroy them all'.[80] Perhaps Louis VIII and Blanche instructed the makers of these bibles to include such direct anti-Cathar imagery; perhaps the churchmen around them who worked with the producers of the bible knew they would appreciate them – or thought that they should be always conscious of the threat the heretics presented.

Blanche regarded the pursuit of Louis's unfinished business in the south as a sacred trust, however much her demands for funding antagonised the French Church. As regent, she issued the ordinance *Cupientes* in 1229, which effectively established the Inquisition as a method for dealing with heresy in the Languedoc, and imposed the terms of the Treaty of Paris on Raymond VII. In later life, however, Blanche was seen as slightly too sympathetic to Raymond, who was never totally free from the taint of heresy.[81]

For Blanche and her husband themselves had had an early brush with heresy. Louis's tutor, Amaury of Bène, had been accused of unsound teaching and forced into silence in 1206; in 1210, at a council in Paris, a group of Amaury's followers were accused of heresy, and some of them burnt.[82] What they really believed and taught are known only from the accusations against them.[83] But it seems certain that they were interested in Aristotelian texts, which were just arriving in Paris from Spain, and in neo-platonic, spiritualist works, such as those by John Scotus Eriugena.[84] They were accused of the belief that all earthly hierarchy would finish with the End of Time, and of denying the bodily resurrection. The council of 1210 ordered the burning of Eriugena's *De natura*, which insists that mankind's resurrection is essentially spiritual. Within a short time, the papacy had also forbidden the reading of Aristotelian texts in the schools and the university of Paris. Although many churchmen in court circles were quick to condemn Amaury and his followers – William the Breton was particularly vicious in his condemnation – there was still an uneasy sense that relations between Amaury and Lord Louis had been close. Cardinal Henry of Susa reported that some of Amaury's followers were still being protected at the time of the Fourth Lateran Council – and most historians have taken that to mean that protection came from the Capetian court. It was certainly rumoured that although Amaury's followers believed in the annihilation of all earthly hierarchy when the Last Judgement came – and they thought it was very close – they believed that Philip Augustus and Lord Louis, alone among the inhabitants of this earth, would retain their regal rank in the afterlife.[85] Several images in the two moralised bibles in Vienna reflect these theological quarrels that came so close to the very centre of Capetian kingship. Philosophers are always seen as dangerous, apt to lead unwary students away from true theology, and often equated with 'miscreants' – heretics (pl. 26).[86] Whoever was in charge of commissioning the bibles took a strongly conservative view – the view adumbrated by William the Breton.

Doubtless, Louis and Blanche took care to distance themselves from the more outlandish claims of Amaury's followers. Perhaps they accepted the orthodox Augustinian view that one cannot know when the end of the world will come, and that one should not seek to know it. But perhaps, like Amaury's followers, and many contemporaries, including, briefly, Innocent III, they suspected it might be very near. Interpretations of the present as the Last Times were rife. Rigord condemned popular terrors about the End of Time shortly before 1200, but nevertheless recorded a poetic prophecy written before the Third Crusade of 1189–92 suggesting that Philip Augustus might be the mythical Last Emperor, who would establish peace in Jerusalem and thus set in motion the End of Time.[87] Around 1220, at the request of Brother Guérin, one of Philip's clerks copied a version of the Last Emperor prophecy into the royal administrative record, Register E, suggesting that some around Philip still thought that this new Charlemagne might be the king of the Last Times.[88] It was easy to see the battles against the Muslims in the Holy Land as fulfilling some of the conditions of the End of Time as it was spelt out in the biblical book of Revelation. It was easy to see the Muslims, or the Cathars, or later the frighteningly successful group of warriors beginning to impinge on the Mediterranean – the Mongols – as the forces of Antichrist unleashed upon the world.[89] The luxury manuscripts produced for Blanche and Louis around 1220 – the two moralised bibles now in Vienna and Blanche's psalter – are replete with violent imagery of the Last Times. In the two moralised bibles that is to be expected. Louis's bible ends, as a bible should, with Revelation. The French bible may once have contained it, but no longer does; nevertheless, several images of the Last Times act as moralisations of Old Testament scenes, and the reign of Antichrist in particular is depicted with gruesome enthusiasm. But in the psalter (Paris, Bibliothèque de l'Arsenal, MS lat. 1186), produced for Blanche before she was queen, perhaps around 1215–20, the emphasis on the Last Times is unwonted. Like other luxury psalters for royal or aristocratic laity, it opens with a set of biblical images, ending, as was normal, with an image of the apocalyptic Christ in Majesty. But abnormally, the psalms themselves are followed by another set of images, all concerned with the End of Time, starting with the conversion of the Jews and beginnings of the reign of Antichrist (f. 168r; see pl. 7), then the Last Judgement with St Michael weighing souls, the apocalyptic Christ in Majesty displaying his wounds, with the instruments of the Passion, with the saved and the damned (see pl. 6), then a further image of the saved, in Abraham's bosom, and the damned, in hell.

The eyes of the monster representing hell are painted as thick steely blobs of blackening silver: it is all strikingly minatory in tone (pls 5, 7).[90]

The Last Judgement imagery in Blanche's psalter is closely related to that of the great cathedral portals of the beginning of the thirteenth century, especially those at Chartres, Notre-Dame in Paris and Amiens. The Last Judgement had not been the chosen subject for cathedral portals for the previous half-century, and the renewed popularity of the image must have reflected the edgy fears of the imminence of the end around 1200. As in Blanche's psalter, there is a strong emphasis on the division of the saved and the damned, using the striking image of St Michael weighing souls to drive home the awful consequences of worldly wickedness (f. 169v). In the psalter, as on the portals, the saved and the damned are shown not just as naked souls: they are also individualised and their heads are dressed to reveal their social status, to impress upon the observer that while there are good kings, bishops, merchants and princesses in heaven, there are bad ones in hell (see pl. 6). They are very real figures. In short, this new French Last Judgement imagery stresses the corporeality of the bodily resurrection, in line with canons of the Fourth Lateran Council. The Church had stressed the doctrine of the bodily resurrection at the Council because Amaury of Bène and his followers, in their neo-platonic, spiritualist readings, were seen to challenge it. Amaury and his followers were also accused of denying earthly hierarchy after the End of Time: again, the imagery of the Last Judgement portals, and of Blanche's psalter, seems deliberately framed to counter such thoughts. Whoever gave the orders for the images in Blanche's psalter made sure that they countered any lingering influence that Amaury of Bène's ideas on the bodily resurrection might have had on the princess and her husband.[91]

But in doing so, and in placing such undue emphasis on the End of Time, they kept alive, and placed before the future queen of France, the bitter intellectual struggles over doctrine of the early 1200s. In some ways, an even more potentially subversive image opens Blanche's psalter. Three wise men compute the date of Easter from the stars (see pl. 25). The central figure holds up an astrolabe, and the other two take notes. The writer on the left is shown as writing a Latin script, but the one on the right sits forward of his two companions and holds the pages of his text open to view, showing letters that are manifestly intended to be taken for Hebrew, or perhaps Arabic. It is impossible to see this and not be put in mind of the new Aristotelian texts, translated from Arabic and Hebrew in Spain, which appeared so attractive – to the Amauricians among others – and so dangerous in early thirteenth-century Paris.[92]

At the very end of her life Blanche found herself fleetingly in sympathy with another group that was subsequently condemned by the Church as heretical – the *pastoreaux*, or the shepherds, led by the Master of Hungary.[93] They came from Flanders and from the north-east of France – those lands that had once supported Blanche and her husband and from which her dower lands had been carved, areas where she had always had connections and support. Moreover, the *pastoreaux* presented themselves as Crusaders – *crucesignati* – intending to sail to Egypt to rescue St Louis from Saracen capture. Blanche, and indeed the whole court, was quite used to Crusaders who were not drawn from the flower of chivalry. The accounts of 1239 in particular are full of gifts given to *crucesignati*, many of them menial members of the household, many of them poor Crusaders met along the roads or in the towns through which the court travelled, the indigent recipients of royal generosity along with pauper women with daughters to marry.[94] But it soon became apparent that this was a starving and violent rabble, not an army. The Church declared the *pastoreaux* heretics; and Blanche and the group of churchmen who helped her rule in Louis's absence soon regarded them as a threat to the peace of the realm rather than the latest manifestation of saintly poverty.

If Blanche and her husband might occasionally come too close to heresy for the more rigidly orthodox of the churchmen who surrounded them, on the issue of the Jews they were themselves models of orthodoxy. The Church's position on the Jews had been established by St Augustine. Jews were not to be attacked, because as a people they bore witness to the life of Christ. While conversion was naturally to be encouraged, an essential element of the Last Times would be the mass conversion of good Jews, who would finally understand that Christ had been the messiah for which they still waited – so a substantial number of Jews available for conversion was a necessary pre-condition for the awaited final revelation and the Heavenly Jerusalem.[95] Nevertheless, much ecclesiastical rhetoric was directed towards pointing to the inadequacy of the old law of the Old Testament in the face of the new law of the New, and to the complicity of the Jewish people in the torture and death of Christ.[96] That rhetoric had hardened over the twelfth century. In the middle of the century serious Western theologians, particularly those associated with the school and traditions of the Parisian abbey of Saint-Victor, had worked in fruitful co-operation with Jewish rabbinic scholars to deepen their knowledge and understanding of the Old Testament. That sort of co-operation, and respect for Hebrew learning, continued in some centres, notably Toledo.[97] But it was no longer considered acceptable in the schools of Paris, and in much of the

papal curia. And while the Church never countenanced anti-Jewish pogroms, strong anti-Jewish sentiment was undoubtedly encouraged by Crusading rhetoric, which stressed so strongly the reality, the quiddity, in time and place, of Christ's life and death.

The Jews had long exploited their own widely dispersed connections, and the fact that their rules on the lending of money were more practical and flexible than the Christian equivalent, to establish themselves as merchants and bankers – with great success, so that many were outstandingly wealthy. Most rulers, whether kings or princes, found it convenient to control and protect the Jews working within their lands. The ruler could levy totally arbitrary taxes on them at will, in the name of protection. Success in money lending did not invite sympathy, and by the early thirteenth century many in society, including lords who tried to live above their income, or bishops and abbots who indulged in building campaigns, were deeply in debt to Jewish creditors. The Church had theological objections to society's indebtedness to the Jews. A Christian deeply in debt was almost a slave of the Jew to whom he owed so much. Loans were often advanced against magnificent gold, silver and jewelled liturgical objects, and there were hysterical fears of the desecration of chalices that had held the Blood of Christ. By the late twelfth century Paris scholars had begun to see usury, lending at interest, whoever it was committed by, as against morality. Robert Courson produced an influential tract against usury, 'De usuria', and usury was condemned as contrary to canon law at the Fourth Lateran Council in 1215. Jews were not alone in lending at interest, but the new focus on usury did nothing to improve their reputation in society.[98]

Early in his reign, Philip Augustus had responded to widespread anti-Jewish sentiment by expelling the Jews from France. It earned him the approbation of most of the French Church and the Paris schools. But the king soon recognised the economic importance of the Jews, and in 1198 he invited them back into his lands. Many French churchmen, including Philip's biographer, the monk Rigord at Saint-Denis, were disgusted. They saw it as almost as bad as Philip's bigamous marriage to Agnes of Meran. But Philip persevered, merely attempting to make arrangements with some of the great princes who also maintained Jews on their lands, which were aimed at ensuring that one great prince did not make economic gain at the expense of another by attracting the other's Jews to his lands.[99]

Where Philip Augustus had seen the Jews as an economic necessity, even if a necessary evil, Louis VIII, Blanche and Louis IX saw them as a religious issue. In fact, both Blanche and Louis VIII were good Augustinians in their dealing with the

Jews. In their statutes for the Jews, both ensured that the Jews were repaid moneys that they were owed – though only the principal. Neither set out, in their legislation, to destroy the Jews, or drive them from the kingdom. The Jews should remain as witnesses of Christ, and as those whose conversion would herald the End of Time. Blanche and Louis VIII set out to regulate them, and above all to prevent usury, in line with the provisions of the Fourth Lateran Council. They had no quarrel with the fact that Walter Cornut used a Jewish family, the Officiel dynasty, as crucial staff in his episcopal administration.

St Louis's statutes for the Jews take a much stronger line, increasingly undermining their ability to function as money lenders at all, and forcing them to wear the sign of the Jew on both front and rear of their garments. Each successive statute put more pressure on them to convert to Christianity, or to leave the kingdom.[100] The difference between Blanche and St Louis in their approach to the Jews emerged too in their response to the accusations against the Talmud in 1240. Blanche was fascinated by the discussion, and did not conclude that the Talmud should be condemned. Louis took a more intransigent view. It is not that Blanche wanted to discourage conversion. Converts were much favoured in her almsgiving. Blanche and Louis VIII appear to have abhorred usury, and the damage that it would do to the realm, but had no taste for forced conversion. Louis IX had a stronger sense that Judaism itself would damage the realm. Both William of Chartres and Matthew Paris noted his abhorrence of Jews: William said that he could not even bring himself to look at them.[101]

Blanche's relative – very relative – tolerance for Judaism is not surprising. She was a Castilian princess, and remained throughout her life in close contact with her extended Spanish family. In Spain, Jews played a more integrated role in society, respected as scholars and even acting as royal administrators, though that was beginning to change in the first half of the thirteenth century. Rodrigo Jiménez de Rada, archbishop of Toledo, primate of Castile and a close associate of Blanche's natal family, wrote a dialogue against the Jews that revealed close study of Hebrew biblical exegesis; but, like Walter Cornut, he employed them in his episcopal administration.[102] The difference in approach between Blanche and St Louis was partly a difference of generation. In the second quarter of the thirteenth century anti-Judaic sentiment was undoubtedly ratcheted up by some of the younger mendicants, both Franciscan and Dominican. The attack on the Talmud was orchestrated by them, and there is some evidence that Walter Cornut was not the only bishop who found the new mendicant anti-Judaic zeal slightly distasteful or

inconvenient, or both. Both Gregory IX and Innocent IV had to remind St Louis and the attackers of the Talmud that the Jews must be sustained as witnesses to biblical events.[103]

There was certainly powerful anti-Jewish sentiment in certain quarters at the Capetian court even during Philip Augustus's reign. It is manifest in Rigord's sustained diatribe against the Jews. It is manifest in the psalter produced for Blanche around 1216. This loses no opportunity to show those who oppose King David as Jews in their Jewish hats.[104] Blanche's psalter has a unique feature among psalters for lay devotion: each psalm is introduced by a short explanatory gloss. They are derived from Peter Lombard's Commentary on the psalms, and many of them give an anti-Judaic interpretation. They remind the reader of the proper triumph of the new law over the old; and remind them too of how important will be the conversion of the Jews.[105] Indeed, the extended sequence of images of the End of Time begins with the conversion of Jews (see pl. 7).[106] Nevertheless, Jews are not caricatured, and the issue of conversion, whether in current time or at the end, is handled within an Augustinian framework.

The Vienna and Toledo moralised bibles are much stronger in tone, in both their imagery and their moralisations. The wickedness of the Jews, and the prominence of their role in the death of Christ, their undermining of Christian society by usury and, at an intellectual level, their failure to recognise the displacing of the old law by the new, are perhaps the strongest consistent themes in the moralised bibles, receiving more emphasis than heresy. In fact, heresy in the moralised bibles is often linked to or conflated with the Jews.[107] Where the moralised bibles go far beyond Blanche's psalter is in their vicious visual caricaturing of the Jews – though kings, clergy and scholars are caricatured too. But the impact of the anti-Jewish rhetoric and imagery in the moralised bibles is very powerful. Perhaps St Louis and his generation absorbed the anti-Judaic messages of the moralised bibles in a way that his mother and Walter Cornut did not.

Did Louis VIII and Blanche demand this strong anti-Judaic strain in these costly and precious books? Or does it, especially the vivid, vicious caricaturing in the moralised bibles, reflect what some of the clergy of their entourages thought they ought to think? It is impossible to know. But it is clear that anti-Jewish sentiment was particularly strong in books associated with Blanche and Louis VIII, and that this appears to be new.

However repugnant their attitudes to the Jews might be to modern sensibilities, Blanche and the two Louis undoubtedly thought they were doing God's work. And

they were doing it with the endorsement of the finest theologians of their time. Indeed, Blanche and young Louis evidently thought that their actions were for the good of the Jews of their realm, that they would persuade them to see the errors of the old law and convert to the new. To such converted Jews, both Blanche and her son were conspicuously generous, as the household accounts of the 1230s and 1240s show. Although both knew that humanity should not speculate about the final coming of Christ, they may still have had a lingering sense that the Last Times were not far off, and that they would both play a role in the widespread conversion of the Jews that would be one of the harbingers of the end.

9

Piety and Devotion

ALL KINGS, QUEENS AND PRINCES were expected to protect and support those who prayed, and those who were poor and sick. This was a ruler's duty, though this aspect of rulership was one that was traditionally associated with the queen, as an area where she would manifest her 'participation in kingship' as 'the consort of the king'. Blanche was famed within her lifetime for her piety, which was widely regarded as outstanding even by regal and reginal expectations.[1] This reputation rested partly on the extent of the resources at her disposal. But it rested too on the intelligent, searching and directed quality of her devotional pursuits. She and her husband aligned themselves with the reformist wing of the Church, unless their interests were damaged by doing so, and her devotional preferences consistently reflected that. Piety was for Blanche an integral aspect of her rulership and role as *consors regni* – the consort of the king. It was also intensely personal, informed by what the churchmen around her would have considered proper Christian fear before the only too imminent judgement of God.

Blanche had been brought up to know that a queen should protect and support the churches and religious of her realm; she knew too that riches were a danger to the soul, and that a wealthy woman must offset that danger by using her riches for the good of the Church. Blanche was conspicuously wealthy, even by the standards of a queen, especially in her long widowhood, with her rich dower lands and the 30,000 *livres* that Louis VIII left her in his will.[2] She could afford to commission religious books for her own devotions, for the devotion or religious education of members of her extended family and household, and for the religious

institutions she favoured. She could also afford to advance substantial loans to religious institutions. In 1243 several abbeys, including some Cistercian nunneries, were indebted to her for quite small sums, while Pontigny owed her 1,000 *livres*, Cîteaux 1,500 *livres*, Saint-Denis 2,000 *livres* and Saint-Victor 3,000 *livres*. In 1250 she lent 2,000 marks to the cathedral of Notre-Dame in Paris to rescue the chapter from its debts.[3]

When Louis IX finalised the organisation of Blanche's dower in 1240, he limited the amount that she could permanently alienate in free alms from her lavish dower provision to 800 *livres* in annual revenues, to include the 100 *livres* already assigned to Maubuisson. When he departed on Crusade in 1248, he allowed her to give away an extra 300 *livres*. It restricted her slightly in the foundation of the nunnery of Le Lys – she refers to the limitation in a charter of gifts to the abbey. But it was not unreasonable: dower was not Blanche's to give away; she should live on the revenues from it, and retain it intact to support the next queen mother.[4] Her reaction to the wealth amassed by the French kings, to the riches in which court life cushioned her, was to dispense it with regal largesse. But Louis's limitation on it suggests that even this most deeply pious of kings felt that in Blanche's case it could get out of hand. When Louis issued his Ordinance for the Household in 1261, he imposed very tight limits on Margaret's almsgiving. She could have just 400 *livres* per year for all her 'aumones et oblacions' – alms and oblations – 16 *solidi* for alms when out riding, and the number of poor she could feed at her table was limited to thirteen. Margaret's piety was not in question, but she did not have the resources to demonstrate it in the way that her wealthy mother-in-law had done.[5]

The household accounts record Blanche's almsgiving. As noted earlier, the accounts are fragmentary, occasional and not always easy to interpret. It is not always clear from the accounts of 1234, or from those of the later 1230s, especially 1239, which alms were given on Blanche's initiative or on young Louis's. Often, however, there are strong indications that the initiative was Blanche's. Some disbursements are attested to by Blanche herself, or by court officials, such as Richard of Tourny, who worked closely with her. The large number of indigent Spaniards given alms, and, in several cases, the continuity of interest with Blanche's own household accounts, indicates her involvement. Indeed, royal alms rolls surviving from the fourteenth and fifteenth centuries suggest that Blanche's devotional preferences had a lasting influence on the almsgiving of subsequent French kings.[6] Unfortunately, alms are not recorded in the incomplete account of 1213.

Permanent revenue streams to religious institutions were paid through the administrations of the *prévôts* or *baillis* almost automatically, like direct debit payments at a bank. The accounts for the foundation of Maubuisson, for instance, record revenues from the Meulan and Mantes *prévôtés* from 1237, while the report of the Mantes *prévôtés* for 1248 shows the annual payment of 50 *livres* disbursed to the queen's new abbey.[7] Some disbursements were the result of alms set up by Blanche's and Louis IX's predecessors. This is most easily seen in the alms for Normandy, where Blanche and Louis's provision can be compared with the provisions of the dukes of Normandy on the Norman exchequer rolls. The Capetian almonry was still, in 1234 and 1248, paying towards the roofing of the cathedral of Evreux, long since completed, together with an anniversary Mass for the count of Evreux who had set up the annual payment in the 1130s when the cathedral was being rebuilt.[8] Many of the gifts to religious houses in Anjou and the Loire probably reflect the generosity of Blanche's Angevin forebears and relations rather than her own or her immediate family's predilections.[9] The alms to the abbey of Saint-Josse in the Boulonnais recorded in the Crèpy-en-Valois *prévôté* were established when Crèpy-en-Valois was part of the Vermandois inheritance.[10]

Much largesse was disbursed in a fairly organised fashion through the office of the almoners.[11] Whenever the queen and her entourage arrived at one of her castles or palaces, wherever she held court, a contingent of deserving poor would appear to be handed monies or fed at her table, or in doles and pittances after she had dined. Blanche might hand out alms in a meadow, as she did at Beaumont-sur-Oise in 1234, or she might arrange to feed paupers in her chamber, as she did at the castle of Vernon in 1242.[12] Feast days, such as the Annunciation, Ascension, Christmas and Epiphany, were marked by distributions. On Maundy Thursday 1234 the entire royal family, including Blanche's young children and her indulged nephew, Alphonse of Portugal, were provided with money to take part in the ceremony.[13] Alms were given to commemorate the anniversaries of the deaths of both Louis VIII and his mother, Isabella of Hainault – 20 *livres* for Louis, 10 *livres* for Isabella.[14]

Presumably it was part of the almoners' duty to select, present and dispatch the paupers, this permanent reminder of the poverty of Christ at the heart of the court. The contingents were large, and the stench must sometimes have been overwhelming. Blanche's account of 1241–2 lists groups of 100 paupers at Conflans dealt with by Stephen of Montfort; 200 paupers at Melun, dealt with by her almoner; 100 paupers at Asnières, with 34 the following week; 40 at Etampes; 100 at

Crèpy-en-Valois; and 206 paupers at Corbeil, among whom 10 *livres* 3 *solidi* was distributed by her almonry and Stephen of Montfort.[15] Sometimes, close and trusted associates, such as the abbot of Saint-Victor, the prior of Saint-Jacques and her ladies, were given charge of particular alms distribution.[16] The accounts record little specific provision of food; much expenditure recorded as a cash amount was probably used to buy the required food and drink for the doles. Nevertheless, many disbursements were simply handed out as money.[17]

If many alms were distributed in the established rituals of court life, many were also given on the spur of the moment. Blanche's almoners had to keep account: 'for 10 *solidi* given each day to paupers through the almonry from the Octave of Candlemas to the Octave of Ascension, 48 *livres*'; 'Daily alms for paupers, 10 *solidi* per day, almonry total 428 *livres*'.[18] Whenever the court was in transit, and it was in transit very often, monies would be given to the almoner for dispensing almost indiscriminately along the way: 'Alms for going between Nemours and Fontainebleau'; or 'alms for when the queen went from Melun to Corbeil', as the accounts record it.[19] In 1234 Blanche stayed at the old Angevin palace at Pont-de-l'Arche in the Seine Valley in Normandy. There she handed out 20 *solidi* in alms. She and her entourage moved on to Petit Andely, beneath Château Gaillard; here Herbert the scutifer disbursed 4 *livres* in alms for her. At Portmort, about four miles further on, the village where she had been married so long ago, she gave 10 *livres* to two girls. Soon thereafter, they reached Gisors; here the queen spent 8 *livres* 8 *solidi* on alms.[20] The whole journey from Pont-de-l'Arche to Gisors is a mere 60 miles; they were probably travelling by river, and this was less than a full day's journey. And alms might be given in desperation, too. Blanche offered to give 40 *solidi* in alms to the poor for each mouthful of bread she could persuade Princess Isabella to eat.[21] Young Charles's dangerous illness in the summer of 1239 prompted a frantic outburst of generosity. Twenty-five *livres* were spent on the paupers of Paris in the king's court, while Blanche scattered coins around her as she rushed from Melun to Corbeil on her way to the bedside of her sick child at Vincennes.[22]

Wherever she was, whether on her travels or staying in one of her palaces, houses or castles, the poor and the sick appealed to her generosity. Perhaps she sent many away empty-handed: the accounts record those whose appeals touched her, and there were many of them. Evidently she felt that women should be of particular concern to a queen. Frequently she provided dowries for women to marry, or for those, especially widows, too poor to marry off their daughters.[23] Often she gave to those who needed money or vestments to retire into a religious house.[24] Two

groups were guaranteed success. One was 'the converted', occasionally converted Muslims, or 'saracens', but usually converted Jews, especially, again, if they were women. In April 1234, for instance, 20 *solidi* were given for 'a certain Spanish conversa' at the hospital of the Domus Dei in Paris, the gift attested by Blanche's long-serving lady Dorea or Doreta.[25] The importance of Jewish conversion was a leitmotif throughout Blanche's life. The other favoured group was her countrymen and women. Some of the converts were Spanish.[26] The household accounts are full of gifts to distressed Iberians, including Spanish merchants despoiled of their goods and Spanish clergy who had run into debt while studying in Paris. Doubtless this gave ammunition to her critics at court.[27]

Her patronage of institutions was by its nature more considered. Blanche's gifts were often set up, as with Maubuisson and Le Lys, to be paid regularly out of her revenues. But here too there were many occasional gifts of monies. When the court was in a particular area it was likely to receive specific requests from local religious houses, but abbots and abbesses often found it worth their while to make the substantial journey to petition in person. Thus in 1241 the abbesses of the Cistercian nunneries of Le Verger near Arras and Val-des-Vignes near Bar-sur-Aube were rewarded with gifts of 10 *livres* at Asnières and Corbeil or Melun, respectively.[28] The reasons for most gifts were unspecified. The standard amount given was 10 *livres*.[29] Occasionally, the gifts were specifically intended for building works. In 1234 Blanche and Louis gave monies for building to the parish churches at Jargeau and Andely, to the abbey of Saint-Pierre-des-Ursins in Paris, and to the Dominicans at Chartres.[30] Blanche contributed particularly to the construction of three Cistercian nunneries that had not been founded by her: Le Parc near her town of Crèpy-en-Valois, La Joie-lès-Nemours and Le Trésor in eastern Normandy. She contributed 90 *livres* to the dormitory at La Joie, and then 10 *livres* for windows, presumably in the church.[31]

Blanche's almsgiving was catholic – a queen of France could not be exclusive in her largesse. Nevertheless, she had clear preferences, both in her institutional giving and in her personal alms. There is no doubt that her strongest affection was reserved for the Cistercian order, especially Cistercian nuns, and this is discussed more fully below. Like many of her generation, she supported women religious. She fostered a group of Beguines at her town of Crèpy-en-Valois from 1239 – long before St Louis made support of these lay religious women fashionable.[32] She was committed to the order of Fontevraud. She had stayed at Fontevraud with her grandmother Eleanor of Aquitaine on her long journey from Castile to Normandy

for her marriage in 1200, and she must have been conscious of upholding Angevin family traditions. Her mother was revered as a major benefactress of the order.[33] She was certainly influenced by the fact that the abbess of Fontevraud from 1228 to 1243 was a cousin, the able Alice of Blois.[34] Blanche was remembered in their prayers as a great 'supporter and benefactor' of the order, and especially of Fontevraud itself.[35] Blanche probably asked the order to remember her sister, Queen Berengaria, in their prayers too.[36] Blanche and Louis gave Fontevraud a gift of 500 *livres* around 1241; and she left the abbey a substantial amount in her will.[37]

She was conspicuously generous to hospitals, particularly the kind known as the Hôtel-Dieu or God's House (Domus Dei), usually run by brothers and sisters living under an Augustinian rule, and often under the aegis of cathedrals in cities. Not long after her husband's death, and in his memory, she built a new infirmary hall for the Hôtel-Dieu beside Notre-Dame in Paris, with an altar dedicated to Thomas Becket.[38] She gave alms and gifts to the Hôtels-Dieu at Issoudun (one of her dowry towns), Pont-de-l'Arche, Beaumont-sur-Oise and at her dower towns of Etampes, Dourdan, Corbeil and Crèpy-en-Valois.[39] She often paid to place people in Hôtels-Dieu.[40] Leper houses feature prominently in the accounts of 1234, and this may reflect what in Louis IX became an almost obsessive sympathy for lepers. Blanche's own accounts show her as a frequent patron of lepers.[41]

Much has been made of the fact that, just as she focused the royal family's patronage away from the Augustinians to the Cistercians, so her son St Louis and her daughter, Isabella, refocused family patronage again, this time towards the mendicant orders. There is some truth in the assertion. St Louis tried to live as much like a Franciscan as he could and his confessors were Dominicans. Isabella determined to live the Franciscan life herself, and founded her own order of Franciscan nuns at Longchamp to do so. It was partly a generational shift. In her patronage of Cistercian nuns, Blanche was reflecting the interests of her parent's generation, and her own. By the 1240s in Capetian France, as elsewhere in Europe, the mendicant orders had captured the imagination of the powerful. In fact, Louis, Alphonse and Charles remained active patrons of the Cistercians, as well as the mendicants.[42] Conversely, the household accounts show that Blanche did not desert the Augustinians of Saint-Victor or reject the new mendicant orders.

Blanche did transform her husband's intended house of Victorine canons into Cistercian Royaumont, but evidently the Augustinian canons of Saint-Victor forgave her. They remembered her in their prayers as 'their sister, who showed sincere love and affection for their church, who gave it many and

great benefactions, and who always promoted their interests and looked after their privileges'.[43] She did indeed look after their interests. She lent the abbey 3,000 *livres* in 1243.[44] She gave Saint-Victor a fine bible, and both the incumbent Abbot Ralph and, even more, the retired Abbot John were frequent and trusted members of her entourage. Abbot John appears to have been almost a pensioner in her household. He handled some of the distributions of alms to the poor for her.[45] Abbot Ralph was one of her political supporters at court and helped to restrict Margaret's political activities in 1241.[46] Blanche named the abbot of Saint-Victor, alongside the bishop of Paris and her clerk, Stephen of Montfort, as executors of her will.[47] The necrology of Saint-Victor is replete with anniversary remembrances of those close to Blanche: her clerk, Peter of Spain; Adam of Melun, whose knighting she sponsored; Adam of Chambly, bishop of Senlis; William of Auvergne, bishop of Paris, who was buried at Saint-Victor; and Bartholomew of Roye.[48] Alongside Blanche, the abbey commemorated with particular devotion her husband, Louis VIII, and her son Robert of Artois, 'our brother, killed in battle, aflame with zeal for the faith and devotion'.[49]

As for the friars, Blanche was far from inimical to them. Her veneration of Francis of Assisi was well known enough for his companions to send the saint's pillow to Blanche and Louis in 1228, and she made gifts to the Franciscan houses of Pontoise, Etampes and Poitiers in 1242.[50] There is no evidence that Blanche had Franciscan confessors, as did some of her children and the young queen Margaret.[51] The Franciscan preacher, then archbishop of Rouen, Eudes Rigaud, officiated at her burial, though Eudes' intimacy with St Louis and the royal family really developed after Louis's return from Crusade.[52]

Her own preference was clearly for the preaching Dominicans rather than the mendicant Franciscans. The Dominicans had after all been established to preach against the Cathar heresies in Languedoc, in the fight against which her husband had died. The Albigensian Crusade had strong Cistercian support, and the Dominican order emerged in the same fervent reformist and Crusading atmosphere that led to the foundation of so many female Cistercian houses. Indeed, the first house that St Dominic founded was Prouille, for nuns, in 1206.[53] The early Dominicans received much support from Simon of Montfort and his wife, Alice of Montmorency, both from families that also patronised Cistercian houses, including Cistercian nuns. Simon had St Dominic baptise his daughter Petronilla, and officiate at the marriage of his son and heir, Amaury.[54] In Paris, the Dominicans' earliest aristocratic support came from the heiress Amicia of Breteuil, sister-in-law

of Alice of Montmorency. After the Dominicans decided that they could not hold landed properties, and thus the land she had given them, Amicia founded the Cistercian nunnery of Villiers-aux-Nonnains on it.[55] Blanche may have been introduced to the Dominicans through members of the Montfort and Montmorency families. She may also have been attracted to the Dominicans because Dominic himself and some of his followers were Spanish. Given Blanche's eager cultivation of all Iberian contacts, it is likely that she and her husband had met Dominic on one of his many visits to Paris between 1203 and 1221. Their close associate Theobald of Blaison, who was both an Albigensian Crusader and apparently a member of the Guzmán family, must have known St Dominic.[56] The Dominican house in Paris, reflecting these Iberian origins, was dedicated to St James, the patron saint of Spain.

The Dominicans established themselves in their house of Saint-Jacques in Paris in the early 1220s. From there they could preach and teach orthodox theologies to the students of the newly established university. Blanche supported them from the start. In 1226 Jordan of Saxony, the Master of the order, wrote to inform Pope Honorius III of the progress of the new foundation. He extolled in particular the interest taken in them by the queen, who often came to discuss their plans with them.[57] Jordan found another strong supporter in Cardinal Romanus Frangipani, then in France to establish the terms of Louis VIII's Crusade. When the University of Paris dispersed in 1229, furious at their treatment by Blanche and the cardinal, the Dominicans of Saint-Jacques stayed behind, and prospered. It was Dominicans, Brothers James and Andrew, who were dispatched in 1238 to negotiate the redemption of the Crown of Thorns.[58] The convent of Saint-Jacques in Paris received frequent gifts from the court, some evidently from Blanche herself, including almonds for the friars.[59] In 1241 she was received in their chapter house, where she gave them 40 *livres* for alms.[60] She supported their new priory at Chartres. Her close friend, the Cistercian Bishop Walter, invited the Dominicans to Chartres as early as 1221, but a powerful faction in the cathedral chapter opposed their new house in the city. Blanche contributed to the construction of their new church in Chartres and attended the first Mass celebrated in it in 1232, at which she gave the brothers a great silver cross, incorporating a piece of the True Cross, and altar cloths embroidered with the castles of Castile.[61] The prior of Saint-Jacques accompanied her frequently, receiving robes for special events and authorising the giving of alms. He was probably a Norman, Henry Bruisol, who had previously been dean of Avranches.[62] She may have enjoyed the company of the sub-prior too: he was

Theobald of Sézanne, a converted Jew and biblical scholar, who was involved in the trial of the Talmud.[63]

According to a late thirteenth-century *exemplum* – *exempla* were collected stories that might be suitable for sermons – Blanche had sworn to go on pilgrimage to Santiago de Compostela, but had no time to go. William of Auvergne persuaded her instead to commute her vow to completing the buildings of the convent of Saint-Jacques in Paris, which she did with a mixture of joy and relief. The anecdote was relayed in a collection by a Dominican of Angers around 1285.[64] Such stories usually contained a kernel of truth: at the very least, contemporaries had noticed her support of the institution. And the Dominicans responded to her support with signal generosity. In 1240, for the first time, their general chapter agreed that the order might pray and hold Masses for friends and benefactors. The first to be so honoured, in 1240, was Gregory IX; but the following year, the honour was extended to Blanche of Castile and her son Louis IX.[65]

Prior Jordan's letter suggests that Blanche enjoyed discussion of matters theological with the preaching friars. Although poverty was important to St Dominic, contemplation, study and the salvation of souls through preaching constituted the core of their mission.[66] Blanche's two favourite children, St Louis and Isabella, both responded more to the Franciscan focus on voluntary poverty, extreme abstinence and personal chastisement. Both tried to reject the riches of court life – the rich food, the jewels, silks and furs. Isabella was finally able to persuade her mother to desist from trying to arrange grand marriages for her, and to let her retire from the world. She used Blanche's concern at her rejection of food with a quiet determination to get her way, and she offset the need to wear jewels and garments appropriate to her rank by beatings. Louis knew that as anointed king he could not escape his duties: these included holding court in appropriate fashion and the continuation of the royal line, though he dismayed his young wife with his attempts to remain chaste beyond the necessities of procreation.[67] Blanche herself, like her younger children, Alphonse of Poitiers and Charles of Anjou, seems to have seen extreme poverty as something that it behoved the wealthy to relieve. She knew how to make good use of riches, both for religious motives and to ensure the good of the realm. The Franciscan way was not for her.

That the Cistercians, especially Cistercian nuns, were most dear to Blanche's heart is indisputable. All the new foundations in which she was closely involved – Royaumont, Maubuisson and Le Lys – were Cistercian. She chose Cistercian Maubuisson as her burial house. Disregarding the provisions of her

husband's will for the foundation of a Victorine house, she founded Cistercian Royaumont instead. Several of her loans in 1243 were to Cistercian houses, with small loans to Porret, Villiers-aux-Nonnains, Le Parc and Jouy, and substantial loans to Pontigny and Cîteaux.[68] The preponderance of her occasional gifts to monastic houses was to Cistercian foundations. Many houses of white nuns received her standard gift of 10 *livres*. Her great political supporter Bishop Walter of Chartres was a Cistercian. By the late 1230s the abbess of Cistercian Saint-Antoine-des-Champs had become a frequent member of Blanche's household, often authorising occasional gifts to Cistercian houses.[69] Before she became queen, in 1222, at the request of Abbot Guy of Cîteaux and Bishop Walter of Chartres, the Cistercian general chapter agreed to pray for Blanche in recognition of her devotion to the order.[70] In 1227 the general chapter granted the petition that she submitted, along with Louis IX, for an annual commemoration of her husband, Louis VIII, throughout the order. These were the first of many such petitions by Blanche, or by those who were acting on her behalf.[71]

The foundation of Royaumont was a strange business. Louis VIII had made provision in his will for the foundation of a monastery after his death his gold crown and his jewels were to be sold to found a house of Augustinian canons from Saint-Victor in his memory, reflecting a long tradition of Capetian support for the Victorines, culminating in his father's foundation of La Victoire, in celebration of the victory of Bouvines. Without the slightest discernible compunction, Blanche founded a Cistercian monastery instead, openly contravening the terms of the will. The crown and jewels do not appear to have been sold to buy the land required, for in 1261 the main royal crowns in use were still those commissioned by Philip Augustus.[72] The costs of the foundation were presumably found elsewhere from royal resources. In 1227 Blanche obtained papal dispensation for the overturning of an unidentified vow, probably to clear the way for transmuting Louis's wishes. The foundation charter emphasises the fact that the new foundation was undertaken for the salvation of Louis VIII's soul, with the advice, counsel, will and assent of wise men and the executors of his will.[73] If the foundation charter of 1228 focuses on the soul of Louis VIII, Louis IX's subsequent charters of 1233 and 1247 insist that the abbey was founded for the good of the soul of 'his beloved mother, Blanche, queen of France' too.[74] All royal charters were given in Louis IX's name. But Louis was very young at the inception of the new monastery in 1228, and the decision to turn to the Cistercian order must have been Blanche's. The church's dedication, to God, the Virgin and to All Saints, reflects Blanche's preoccupations.[75] Strangely,

Blanche herself gave no gifts to the abbey – or at least none is recorded.[76] But there were gifts from Robert of Artois in 1248 and from loyal members of Blanche's entourage – Simon of Poissy, Amaury of Montfort and Matthew of Montmorency – in the early 1230s.[77] Blanche's son Philip Dagobert may have been educated there: when he died in 1234, it was where she had him buried.

The women religious of the Cistercian order were the principal focus of Blanche's patronage. The Cistercian order had not been welcoming to women. After a few early experiments, the order refused to accept women religious for most of the years of its greatest expansion in the twelfth century. In these years the orders of Fontevraud and Héloïse's Paraclete provided reformed monasticism for women. But by the end of the twelfth century the foundation of Cistercian houses for women had become fashionable. Largely, this was driven by patrons who were usually rich and powerful. Many important patrons were men. More often they were widowed women. Where they were a couple, the woman was often either an heiress or the daughter of a family with important and long-established ties to the Cistercian order. Often, too, the family had an impressive 'war record', fighting the infidel on Crusade and, especially, heresy in the Languedoc.[78] The Cistercian order usually gave in to patronal pressure and accepted, though often with reluctance and delay, a new house of nuns as a member of the order. Patrons such as Countess Isabella of Chartres and Blanche herself usually got what they wanted. In 1242 the order agreed that Countess Isabella could have a Cistercian lay brother as her almoner, since she had given so much to the order; while Blanche's arrangements for Le Lys were to be a matter of discussion between the abbot of Cîteaux and the queen herself.[79] But there was a backlash. Increasingly, the order tried to clamp down on female houses and to insist that even the abbess should remain enclosed – not what someone like Blanche expected. As Blanche, and the rest of the Albigensian Crusade generation died, the order became ever more hostile to nuns.[80]

By the time that Blanche founded the two Cistercian nunneries of Maubuisson and Le Lys, in 1236 and 1240 respectively, this type of foundation was already well established in Capetian France. She was following, not setting, patterns already established in Capetian court circles.[81] An early group of foundations, around 1200, has been connected with the religious fervour surrounding the Fourth Crusade of 1204. In 1202 Matilda and Geoffrey of Perche founded Les Clairets. Matilda was Blanche's first cousin, another granddaughter of Henry II of England; her son Count Thomas of Perche died fighting for Lord Louis in England in 1217. At the same time, another of Louis's companions, John of Nesle, castellan of Bruges, and

his wife, Eustacia of Saint-Pol, founded L'Abbaye-aux-Bois near Noyon at which both elected to be buried.[82] A couple of years later Matilda of Garlande, widow of Matthew of Montmorency, founded Porret (or Port Royal) in the forest of Rambouillet, to the south-west of Paris: the church was consecrated in 1230. Matilda was a formidable woman who took part in the Albigensian Crusade, where she harried heretic women until they rejoined the Church.[83] In 1204 the great heiress Eleanor of Vermandois founded Parc-aux-Dames near Senlis. All these houses belonged to the filiation of Clairvaux. Often the lay founder worked closely with the bishop in whose diocese the nunnery lay, to the extent that the bishop might be considered a co-founder.

The Cistercian nunnery continued to be a favoured foundation among those with close links to Capetian court circles, though houses of the 'second generation' were more likely to be affiliated to Cîteaux itself rather than Clairvaux. Margaret of Flanders founded Le Pré near Douai in 1218; Countess Joanna of Flanders petitioned the Cistercian general chapter to found a nunnery in 1225.[84] Beaupré near Arras was founded by the lords of Béthune in 1221.[85] In the early 1220s Amicia, the wealthy lady of Breteuil, a relation of both the Montfort and the Dreux families, founded Villiers-aux-Nonnains on lands originally destined for the Dominicans, with the support of Bishop Guérin of Senlis.[86] La Joie-lès-Nemours was founded by the courtier Philip of Nemours in 1230, with the advice of Walter Cornut and the Dominicans of Paris; the second abbess was a member of the Cornut family.[87] Blanche's cousin, Countess Isabella of Chartres, was a particularly active supporter of Cistercian nuns. With the support of Bishop Walter of Chartres, she founded L'Eau in 1218, and established a chaplain there to pray for her soul and that of Blanche.[88] At about the same time, Countess Isabella founded Romorantin on her lands south of Orléans with the support of Walter Cornut; again, she established Masses there for Blanche.[89] Together with her husband, John of Oisy, she founded another nunnery at Le Verger on John's lands in 1225.[90] Blanche's other cousin and namesake, Blanche of Navarre, countess of Champagne, founded the richly endowed nunnery of Argensolles as her burial house in 1221, a substantial foundation for ninety nuns.[91] Blanche of Castile gave generously to most of these houses founded by her friends and relations, and stayed at Parc-aux-Dames in 1241.[92]

One Cistercian nunnery founded around 1200 was undoubtedly linked with Crusading, and indeed to apocalyptic, fervour. Saint-Antoine-des-Champs, just outside the eastern wall of Paris, was founded in 1198 by the charismatic preacher Fulk of Neuilly, whose devastating indictment of the sins of the people of Capetian

France persuaded many to take the Cross. Unlike the other early foundations, it was affiliated to Cîteaux, the official head of the Cistercian order, rather than Clairvaux, which still retained its prestige as the abbey of St Bernard.[93] Saint-Antoine was initially founded for fallen women, but it soon attracted the attention and the patronage of the aristocracy of the Parisis, and of those in court circles. In 1211 Robert Mauvoisin, a close associate of Simon of Montfort on the Albigensian Crusade, and described by the chronicler Peter of Les Vaux-de-Cernay as 'a most noble knight of Christ, accomplished in learning', built a chapel at the nunnery, intended for his burial. Many of his family were buried there too, including his son-in-law, that inveterate courtier Adam of Beaumont.[94] Petronilla of Montfort, sister of Count Simon of Toulouse, was brought up there until she was twelve; her husband, Bartholomew of Roye, was a generous donor.[95] Robert Mauvoisin's widowed sister, Agnes, took the veil there, and in 1233 became the fourth abbess.[96] The house soon became a preferred refuge for the aristocratic ladies of the Parisis. When Agnes died in 1240 she was succeeded by Amicia Briard of Villepècle, a cousin of Amicia of Breteuil, early patron of the Dominicans and foundress of Villiers-aux-Nonnains.[97]

Quite how early direct Capetian patronage of Saint-Antoine began is unclear. Antiquarian sources claim that Lord Louis and Blanche gave a gift to celebrate the birth of a son, though no surviving documentary evidence supports the claim.[98] But Blanche made Saint-Antoine the object of her barefoot penitential procession, together with Ingeborg and Berengaria of Jerusalem, to pray for victory at La Rochelle in 1224, and it was the chosen last station for the Crown of Thorns before its triumphal entry into the city of Paris in 1239.[99] Louis IX confirmed the abbey's possessions in 1228;[100] and both Blanche and Louis attended the dedication of the abbey church by Bishop William of Paris in 1233, in the presence, probably, of Walter of Chartres, James of Soissons, Adam of Chambly, bishop of Senlis, and the bishops of Châlons and Meaux.[101] The abbess of Saint-Antoine – Agnes Mauvoisin, then, after her death, Amicia Briard – spent a great deal of time in Blanche's household, travelling with her and overseeing her alms to other Cistercian nunneries, to the disquiet of Stephen of Lexington, the future abbot of Clairvaux.[102] Perhaps around this time Princess Isabella's first attempt at sewing, a small cap for her brother Louis, was bought by Perronelle of Montfort (probably the daughter of Simon of Montfort, count of Toulouse, who had been baptised by St Dominic and became a nun at Saint-Antoine) and given to Saint-Antoine as a memorial of the saintly princess.[103] When Blanche decided in 1236 to found a Cistercian

nunnery, she drew the nuns, and the first abbess of her foundation, from Saint-Antoine.

So Blanche was surrounded by courtiers, both lay and clerical, male and female, involved in the foundation and patronage of Cistercian nunneries. The clergy who were close to her, such as the bishops Walter of Chartres, William of Paris and Walter Cornut, were active supporters of Cistercian nunneries, as were the inter-related courtier families of Garlande, Montfort, Montmorency, Beaumont and Mauvoisin. Many of the members of these families, both male and female, had taken part in the Albigensian Crusade, and had, like Simon and Alice of Montfort, supported St Dominic's earliest foundation, the nunnery at Prouille. As a young princess, Blanche knew Eleanor of Vermandois and Blanche of Navarre well and must have met her cousin Matilda of Perche; now as a mature widowed queen, she was close to the countesses Isabella of Chartres and Joanna of Flanders.

Blanche was not the first member of the Capetian family to patronise the Cistercians. Louis the Fat had founded Chaalis, and Louis VII had founded Barbeau; but the Capetians' preferred order, as Philip Augustus's foundation of La Victoire and Louis VIII's will suggests, was the Victorines. Nor was she the first queen of France to follow her natal family's predilection for the Cistercians. Adela of Champagne, Philip Augustus's mother, had used her status as the daughter of the great patron of Pontigny and Clairvaux, and as queen of France, to obtain access to the chapter house at Pontigny and ensure burial in the choir there, despite the reservations of the general chapter.[104] Patronage of the Cistercians, including Cistercian women, was part of Blanche's family heritage. The Angevins had been great supporters of the order of Cîteaux from an early stage: the empress Matilda, Henry II, Richard and John had all founded at least one important Cistercian male house. In 1148 the Cistercians absorbed the Norman reformist order of Savigny, which had an established tradition of female houses, and the duchy was always more receptive to the idea of the Cistercian nunnery. The empress Matilda herself founded Saint-Saëns from Clairvaux in 1167.[105] When Blanche's mother, Eleanor of England, and father, Alfonso VIII of Castile, founded a new abbey adjacent to their palace outside Burgos it was a Cistercian nunnery – Las Huelgas. This, above all, must have been the model for Blanche when she founded Maubuisson.

Las Huelgas was occupied by nuns and given its foundation charter in 1187. In 1191 it was accepted as a member of the Cistercian order, dependent, like Saint-Antoine in Paris, on Cîteaux itself.[106] It was in some ways a classic case of the newly fashionable type of Cistercian nunnery of the end of the twelfth century.

Like the French foundations of this period, its foundation reflected Crusading fervour and endeavours – but then what did not in late twelfth-century Castile? But there were many surprising things about it that perhaps reflected Castilian traditions of patronage. Its intimate relationship with the royal family was one. It was constructed next to, and perhaps within, a royal palace, and the Castilian royal family, particularly the women and children, often stayed there. Their daughter Constance took the veil there, and although she never became abbess, she governed the abbey during the vacancy of 1232.[107] There are parallels with major royal Benedictine houses, like Westminster Abbey and Palace, Reading Abbey, where the court stayed frequently, and especially with Fontevraud. But this sort of interrelationship was not encouraged in the Cistercian order. Moreover, from at least 1199 Alfonso and Eleanor intended that they and their son Ferdinand would be buried at La Huelgas; perhaps they always intended it as the mausoleum of the dynasty.[108] They insisted that the abbey be given an unusual dedication – to Santa Maria Regalis – St Mary, Queen of Heaven. To underline the status of the new founda-tion, Alfonso and Eleanor persuaded the Cistercian general chapter to agree that Las Huelgas should be the mother house of all Cistercian abbeys, whether for nuns or for monks, within Castile. Only the great fighter against the enemies of Christendom could have extracted such a concession. In the foundation of Las Huelgas, Eleanor and Alfonso drew on their own, Angevin and Castilian, traditions of Cistercian patronage. Probably the new nunnery at Las Huelgas also reflected some of Eleanor's memories of her family's fondness for Fontevraud. Fontevraud was the principal recipient of her mother's patronage: Henry II and Richard were both major patrons, as was Eleanor herself; Eleanor of Aquitaine had her children John and Joanna brought up there; she lived there in her old age, and probably always intended to be buried there.[109] In 1189 Henry was buried there, as, in 1199, were Richard and his sister Joanna of Toulouse. Members of the family took the veil there, and some became abbess, like Henry II's aunt Matilda of Anjou and Eleanor of Aquitaine's granddaughter Alice of Blois.

Whatever the rich conceptual heritage that had gone into the foundation of Las Huelgas, it undoubtedly served as a model of royal foundation for Blanche. She must have stayed in the palace as a child, and would have watched its construction. Perhaps she was expected to help in it, sewing habits, for instance, as she insisted her sons humble themselves in the construction of Royaumont. Although she never saw Las Huelgas again after she left Castile in 1200, she was in touch with her sisters, Queen Berengaria and Eleanor of Aragon, who lived in semi-retirement

there, as Eleanor of Aquitaine had at Fontevraud.[110] When she set in train the establishment of Maubuisson in 1236, she must have seen it as the place where she would be able to lead a life of semi-retirement, before her death and burial in the house. The new abbey would rise in the valley below the walls of Pontoise, always a favoured haunt of the court, given to Blanche as part of the dower exchange in 1237. From the start, the new nunnery would have a mansion for the queen just within the inner precinct wall, giving easy access to the convent for the queen and her ladies, but equally easy access to the outside world.

The detailed accounts of the foundation, kept by Master Richard of Tourny and copied into the *Achatz d'heritage* of the abbey, reveal the extent of Blanche's largesse – 24,431 *livres* spent between 1236 and 1242.[111] Her old friend William of Auvergne, bishop of Paris, dedicated the abbey church to the Trinity, the Virgin and St John the Baptist in June 1244. When the nuns moved into their abbey in March 1242, Blanche issued the official foundation charter, which still exists, with her seal attached (see pl. 21).[112] It is very personal. Blanche chose the name of the abbey: Santa Maria Regalis – St Mary, Queen of Heaven, the name that her parents had chosen for Las Huelgas. It was founded for the sake of the souls of her beloved parents, Eleanor and Alfonso, of her beloved husband, and of her children. The naming of her parents, where so many such charters say just 'for the souls of my parents', places a striking emphasis upon them, and underlines, along with the abbey's name, the extent to which Las Huelgas was in her thoughts. An unusually long and elaborate prologue gives her reasons for the foundation. 'The doctors of Holy Mother Church assert that the blessed angelic spirits give way to joy if someone is reborn at the baptismal font; [because?] it is difficult in the present worthless age to evade the incursion of sin.' It refers to Luke 15.10: 'There is joy before the angels of God over one sinner who repents', and emphasises the difficulty of avoiding sin in this wicked world.[113] The reference to doctors of the Church – Jerome and Augustine – gives a scholastic gloss. The emphasis on angels, on the importance of the salvation of souls – there is surely a reference to conversion – and on the challenge of living in this world are reminiscent of the unusual and powerfully minatory images in Blanche's surviving psalter, which opens with the Fall of the Rebel Angels (pl. 5). Although the Latin is slightly tangled – created, perhaps, by one of those clerks who would have been corrected by Princess Isabella – this sort of reflective preamble is virtually unique in thirteenth-century lay *acta*. It recalls the elaborate charters created by monastic beneficiaries in the

eleventh century and the very early twelfth. There is nothing like this in the acts for Royaumont – and nothing like it in those for Las Huelgas either.

As Maubuisson took shape, Blanche began the foundation of the Cistercian nunnery of Le Lys below her other dower castle of Melun. St Louis played a significant role in funding the abbey, and he, not Blanche, issued the foundation charter in 1248. This, too, has a reflective preamble. It is the only comparable preamble that I have found in the *acta* of either the royal family or the aristocracy. Although issued by Louis, it presumably reflects Blanche's wishes. This too observes the difficulty of negotiating present time in this lamentable world without sin, and that only with divine help can one attain the delights of Paradise.[114] Blanche issued a charter at Maubuisson in 1250 confirming her gifts to Le Lys, and declaring that she had founded the abbey along with her son. Here she gives the abbey its name: Le Lys, the Lily, the flower that associated the Virgin Mary with the kings and queens of France, for the golden lily on a heavenly blue ground was now well established as their emblem.[115]

How does Blanche's pious patronage compare with that of other contemporary women rulers? Blanche's own household account for Annunciation (25 March) 1241 to Ascension (29 May) 1242 – just over a full year – records roughly 1,409 *livres* spent on 'occasional' alms and religious donations, including donations for building at religious institutions. Her annual income was around 45,000 *livres*, so she spent approximately 3 per cent of it on occasional alms, at a stage when she was also funding her two new foundations of Maubuisson and Le Lys.[116] As a widow, she had immense resources at her disposal, far more than her recent predecessors Ingeborg of Denmark and even Adela of Champagne, who was a far more active patron than she has often been seen to be.[117] Blanche had considerably more resources at her disposal than her successor, Margaret, whose generous impulses were constrained by St Louis. She could afford to be much more lavish than Henry III's queen, Eleanor of Provence. Her great-niece Eleanor of Castile, queen of England, husbanded her resources with sharp business acumen, and was able to make substantial Dominican foundations as a result. But Eleanor had her largesse distributed through chaplains and almoners, rather than making disbursements herself, and ended up with a reputation from contemporary chroniclers for meanness.[118] Among Blanche's near contemporaries, perhaps only her grandmother Eleanor of Aquitaine possessed, as a widow, comparable wealth. Eleanor was a generous patron of Fontevraud. There are no household accounts to provide record of her almsgiving; but equally, there is no suggestion from contemporary

chroniclers that it was in any way or extent exceptional.[119] Some of the other great aristocratic widows or women rulers in Blanche's circle, notably Eleanor of Vermandois, Isabella of Chartres and Blanche of Navarre, countess of Champagne, were probably as lavishly generous, relative to their resources, as Blanche.[120]

The most comparable patron among women rulers was undoubtedly Joanna of Flanders, the ruling countess of a hugely wealthy county. The resources that she could deploy in pious patronage would have outstripped even those available to Blanche. Joanna's devotional choices were not unlike the queen's: Cistercian nuns were evidently her preferred order; and she was an early supporter of the Dominicans. Like Blanche, she built hospitals. She was an important protector of Beguines. It may be that the two women influenced each other, Blanche leading in her support of Dominicans, Joanna in her support of Cistercian nuns and Beguines.[121]

It is illuminating to compare Blanche's largesse with that of her son Louis IX. Blanche's 1,409 *livres* on occasional alms in 1241–2 is nearly a quarter of Louis's expenditure on alms in the year from February 1256 to February 1257, which totalled 6,094 *livres*, though it is a tenth of the massive 14,124 *livres* spent in alms by the king in the nine months from February to November 1257.[122] But the totals for Louis include fixed alms. Besides, Louis was the king of France; in 1241–2 Blanche was a queen dowager in relative retirement.

●

Throughout her life, Blanche surrounded herself with a small group of religious men and women whose spiritual guidance, religious advice and discussion she valued. The women were mostly Cistercian nuns, like the two abbesses of Saint-Antoine and Alice of Vienne, the first abbess of Le Lys. But Blanche also supported an anchoress at Etampes, and the Life of Isabella tells us that she often visited a holy woman at Nanterre, between Pontoise and Paris.[123] When Isabella fell ill, Blanche turned to the woman of Nanterre in despair. It was she who told Blanche that her daughter would recover only if she were able to turn away from the things of the world and the court. The men included the abbots Ralph and John of Saint-Victor, Prior Henry of the Dominicans of Paris, the austere Cistercian bishop Walter of Chartres, and the profound and scholarly William of Auvergne, bishop of Paris. Someone in this group, perhaps Walter of Chartres or William of Auvergne, wrote a tract of spiritual advice, 'Listen Lady' – 'Audi domina' – for Blanche.[124] Based heavily on Cistercian literary traditions, drawn from Bernard of

Clairvaux, the text warns a queen of France how she must act and prepare her soul to meet the final judgement of God. It was written in Latin for Blanche, and the well-educated Isabella owned a copy. A French translation was presented to Blanche for wider dissemination among the great ladies of the Capetian court. A fine early fourteenth-century copy of the French text has an initial showing the presentation of the work to a queen by a Cistercian nun, and it is possible that Blanche commissioned the translation from a nun at Saint-Antoine or Maubuisson (pl. 24).[125]

Like most contemporary royal and aristocratic women, Blanche was devoted to the Virgin Mary, especially in her role as Queen of Heaven, the dedicatee of Las Huelgas and Maubuisson. The Virgin was the *tutrix et patrona* of Castile, and Blanche's father fought beneath a standard bearing her image. At the cathedral of Chartres, the canons prayed for Blanche on account of her well-known devotion to the Virgin. Blanche must have been all the more discomfited when Archbishop Maurice of Rouen tried to persuade her to accept his forest rights by humiliating a statue of the Virgin.[126] The prologue to her foundation charter for Maubuisson and the – rare – imagery of the Fall of the Rebel Angels in her psalter suggest that she was abreast of the new intellectual interest in angels among Paris scholars in the early to mid-thirteenth century (see pl. 5).[127] A devotion to St James of Santiago reflected her Iberian roots.

She was fascinated by contemporary saints, people with whom she herself might have some, if vicarious, contact. Joinville describes Blanche kissing the forehead of the son of St Elizabeth of Hungary at the great court held at Saumur in 1241 – with just a hint that this may be an imposter taking advantage of the queen's pious sensibilities.[128] Elizabeth of Hungary, Landgravine of Thuringia, had died a mere ten years previously. Stories of her Franciscan sympathies and her rejection of the things of this world had a considerable impact on both Louis ix and Princess Isabella, though Elizabeth provided a model for abnegatory queenship that Blanche herself was loathe to follow.[129]

Thomas Becket held great importance for both Blanche and her husband. The Capetians had always capitalised on the political embarrassment that the quarrel with Becket brought for Henry ii. Louis vii offered Becket and his followers refuge in France. In 1179, when the young Philip Augustus fell dangerously ill, Louis vii went on pilgrimage to Canterbury to pray for his son's recovery at Becket's tomb, so that Becket had in effect assured the continuation of the Capetian dynasty. Blanche was herself a granddaughter of the man held responsible for Becket's murder. In fact, the Angevin family had managed to draw almost more advantage

from the rapidly canonised archbishop than did the Capetians. Having done penance, Henry II ascribed victory over the Scots in 1174 to Becket's celestial intervention. Henry's daughters were quick to adopt the new saint. Joanna, queen of Sicily and later countess of Toulouse, commissioned a large image of Thomas Becket in the apse of the new monastic cathedral and royal mausoleum of Monreale in the late 1170s. In 1179 Blanche's mother, Queen Eleanor of Castile, became protector of an altar dedicated to Becket in the cathedral of Toledo, though the altar had been founded by members of the Castilian aristocracy.[130] Blanche may have heard family stories about her grandfather and Becket from her mother, or from her grandmother Eleanor of Aquitaine during the long journey from Castile to the northern Angevin lands in 1200. Just as she could kiss a son of St Elizabeth, she could talk directly to a niece of St Thomas, who visited the court at Vincennes in 1234, and came to see Blanche herself in 1242.[131]

The joint interest of Blanche and the future Louis VIII in St Thomas was heightened by their connections with Thomas's successor as archbishop of Canterbury, Stephen Langton. Langton had played a major role in the offer of the English throne to Philip Augustus and Lord Louis. Several members of his household joined Louis before and during his invasion, while Simon Langton remained a pensioner of Blanche's court until his death. Archbishop Langton had officiated at the translation of Becket into a new shrine in 1220 – the shrine designed by Elias of Dereham, who had joined Lord Louis's household during the English invasion – though neither Blanche nor Louis could attend. When Louis captured La Rochelle in 1224, he gave a wealthy burgher of the town to Canterbury on account of his devotion to Becket.[132] Blanche and Louis founded an altar dedicated to Becket in the cathedral of Notre-Dame in Paris to commemorate their oldest son, Philip; later, Blanche founded another altar to Becket, in memory of her husband, in the great new infirmary hall that she had built at the Hôtel-Dieu, the hospital of the cathedral in Paris.[133] The failure to be present at the translation into the new shrine in 1220 must have been offset by Canterbury Cathedral's agreement in 1232 to offer Masses for Blanche and her husband as if they were archbishops.[134]

In 1240 the current archbishop of Canterbury, Edmund of Abingdon, travelled through France on his way to Rome. Edmund had fallen out with Henry III and with the monks of Canterbury, and he travelled to France in conscious imitation of his sainted predecessor. Edmund was a Paris-educated intellectual – he had studied with Stephen Langton – with Cistercian and Dominican sympathies, just the sort of churchman with whom Blanche liked to surround herself. At Senlis,

Edmund had 'an intimate and lengthy conversation' with the queen, who was, as Edmund's biographer, Matthew Paris, observed, 'known to be a woman of great – but not womanly – counsel'. Blanche, according to Matthew Paris, had 'brought her sons with her', and asked Edmund to bless them, 'because she had heard that [Edmund] had been distinguished by many signs of sanctity, and that he was following unerringly in the footsteps of Thomas the Martyr'. Blanche, seconded by Louis and his brothers, tried to persuade Edmund to stay at the French court at the expense of the king – rather, perhaps, like Simon Langton. Edmund refused graciously, and carried on to the Cistercian abbey of Pontigny, where Becket had sought refuge some eighty years earlier. Perhaps Blanche gave Edmund the magnificent vivid green Andalusian silk chasuble venerated as a relic after his death (pl. 15).[135]

Edmund died near Pontigny, and was buried in the abbey church. There was soon a movement to have him canonised. Simon Langton and Adam of Chambly, bishop of Senlis, were involved in the canonisation process.[136] By early 1247 Edmund was canonised; on 9 June 1247 his remains were translated into a new shrine at Pontigny. This time, there was no question that Blanche would be present. She attended, with Louis and his brothers, along with 'many counts and great persons, two cardinals . . . the cardinal of Albano and the legate of France [Eudes of Châteauroux], with archbishops, bishops, abbots and priors'.[137]

•

Like all her contemporaries, Blanche was profoundly concerned with the proper commemoration of the dead, and with the intercessory prayers and the good works necessary for the salvation of one's soul and the souls of those one loved. She inspired, cajoled or paid several institutions to offer prayers for the salvation of the souls of herself and her family, often special prayers of the level usually offered for founders or major ecclesiastics. Saint-Victor offered her sisterhood, and Robert of Artois, brotherhood; and the order of Fontevraud made much of her in their memorials.[138] Frequently, she insisted that prayers were devoted to the souls of her parents Alfonso and Eleanor, her husband, Louis VIII, and her eldest son, Louis IX, along with her own soul, as she did at Maubuisson. In 1232 the order of Premonstratensian canons agreed to Blanche's and Louis IX's request to make special mention in their prayers of Blanche and her family, including her parents, and her son John, who had just died.[139] She had prayers said for herself and Louis VIII at the altar of Thomas Becket in her new hall in the Hôtel-Dieu in Paris, and her

husband was naturally the focus of commemoration at Royaumont. She was in the vanguard in being assured of the prayers of the Dominican order. She and Louis IX were the first friends for whom the order would offer their prayers, apart from Pope Gregory IX.[140] In 1243 the Dominicans of Rouen promised to remember both Blanche and Louis IX in their prayers, as they remembered no one but their founder saint himself.[141] Two distinguished older Benedictine houses far from the centre of Capetian power also offered extraordinary Masses for the souls of Blanche and her husband. In 1232 and again in 1244 the abbey of Vézelay in Burgundy agreed to celebrate the anniversaries of Blanche and Louis VIII as if they were the founders of the abbey, while in 1232 the monastic cathedral of Canterbury agreed to celebrate the anniversaries of Blanche and Louis VIII in the way that they commemorated their archbishops.[142] It is unclear whether the initial impetus for the Vézelay commemorations came from an abbey seeking royal protection or from a queen aiming to expand royal influence. In September 1244 Blanche, with Louis and the court, went to Vézelay, where she, along with Louis and Margaret, asked in person and in chapter for the abbey's prayers.[143]

As outstanding patrons of Cistercian monasticism, Blanche and her family were commemorated by the order. She first obtained prayers from the order in 1222, before she became queen; in 1227 she petitioned successfully for commemoration for Louis VIII throughout the order.[144] In 1232 the abbot of Cîteaux, probably at Blanche's instigation, petitioned for anniversaries for her parents throughout the order.[145] In asking for Cistercian memorial prayers, Blanche was following a lead set by her cousins Blanche and Berengaria of Navarre, and by Queen Ingeborg, who had already obtained commemoration throughout the order for Philip Augustus.[146]

Although not the first of the powerful women patrons of the early thirteenth century to demand and obtain Cistercian prayers, she was probably the most formidable and the most determined – and the order was in the most material sense heavily indebted to her. In 1244 the general chapter had to make special arrangements so that Blanche, Louis, Margaret and their entourage could attend the general chapter itself. The women could stay and eat meat in the house of the duke and duchess of Burgundy – the founding patrons of Cîteaux – just by the precinct wall. The general chapter, doubtless slightly daunted in the presence of Blanche and the court, agreed to all her petitions. Blanche and Louis were to be held in 'special memory' throughout the order: the anniversaries of her parents, hitherto private, were now to be solemn; full services and anniversary prayers would

also be held for her younger children, Isabella, Robert, Alphonse and their respective wives.[147] She continued to petition for prayers and memorials, on behalf of her Capetian family, her Spanish relations, including her nephew, King Ferdinand of Castile, and her friends.[148]

In most cases where she sought the intercession of religious institutions, Blanche omitted her younger children, unless they were buried there. The exceptions were the Premonstratensian prayers for John, the commemoration of Robert of Artois at Saint-Victor – but there was no body to be prayed over elsewhere – and the very personal Cistercian commemorations, which include her friends as well as her children, sisters and other relations. Otherwise, it is almost as if she saw these intercessory prayers as being reserved for kings and queens, and thus in effect for the good of the realm, rather than purely personal.

The most important place of commemoration and intercession was, of course, the place of burial, all the more important since there was now such emphasis on the bodily resurrection on the Day of Judgement. There was no doubt as to where her husband would be buried. As king of France, he would join his father and most of his Capetian predecessors in the choir of the abbey of Saint-Denis. Blanche's first son, Philip, who died in 1218, was buried in the choir of the cathedral of Notre-Dame in Paris. In 1225 Louis VIII and Blanche established a chaplaincy to pray for his soul at the altar of St John the Baptist and St Thomas Becket, though this altar was in the nave.[149] It is surprising that Philip, who was the first-born and destined to be king of France, was not buried in Saint-Denis. Notre-Dame may have been Louis VIII's choice, for it was the burial place of his mother, Isabella of Hainault, and her dead children, Louis VIII's siblings.[150] Royaumont became the favoured place of burial for the royal children, including Louis and Margaret's small children, Blanche and John, in 1243 and 1248 respectively.[151] The first to be buried there was Philip Dagobert, who died in 1234. Dagobert was intended for the Church, and may have received his education at Royaumont. Clearly, the new abbey church was sufficiently complete for the burial. Dagobert was entombed beneath an effigy that still survives (pl. 28). It has a strikingly tender quality, capturing the vulnerability of his youth. On the tomb chest, a frieze of the castles of Castile and fleur-de-lis proclaims his lineage; beneath them figures of angels and clergy weep and pray for the young prince.[152] John had died in 1232, at a stage when Royaumont was still under construction. Instead, he was buried in the collegiate church at Poissy, beside another of Blanche's dead sons, probably the twin called Alphonse who had died very young. Probably both died when the court was

staying at or near the residence at Poissy. The young princes' grave was marked with a shared tomb (pl. 30). Like the surviving tombs of young Blanche and John from Royaumont, it was made of copper; but unlike them, it was not enamelled. Kathleen Nolan has argued plausibly that it was Blanche who commissioned these elaborate tombs for her dead children and grandchildren; if so, she turned to very different artists to supply them.[153] The burial places of Blanche's other offspring who died in childhood are not known. At the very end of her life, she had to accept that the battered bodily remains of her son Robert of Artois would have no burial at all, but must rise on the Day of Judgement from the silt of the Nile Delta. She could draw some comfort, perhaps, from the fact that Saint-Victor had offered Robert confraternity and celebrated his zeal and devotion to the faith, for which he suffered 'cruel death'.[154]

Blanche herself could probably have been buried in Saint-Denis had she so wished. Most queens were buried elsewhere, but it is not clear that there was an official embargo on the burial of anyone except a reigning king there. Blanche's great-great-aunt Constance of Castile, second queen of Louis VII, was buried there; Ingeborg had expressed a wish to be interred there in her will, though that was disregarded; and Isabella of Aragon, queen of Philip III, was buried in the abbey after her death in 1271. Blanche's body rested there, in regal state, on its way to burial at Maubuisson.[155] But Blanche had probably always intended to follow her parents in consigning the care of her bodily remains and her soul to the Cistercian order. As she lay dying in Paris, she had herself dressed in the coarse white cloth of a Cistercian nun and laid on a bed of ashes on the floor, and was received into the order.[156] She was buried in the choir at Maubuisson. Her burial turned the convent into an alternative mausoleum for members of her family. Alphonse of Poitier's heart and entrails were buried alongside her, as were the bodies of her grandson Robert II of Artois and the children of Berengaria of Jerusalem, the empress Mary of Constantinople and John of Brienne.[157]

One seventeenth-century antiquarian, Charles de Combault, claimed that Blanche's close friend Alice of Mâcon, abbess of Le Lys, asked to have Blanche's heart buried at the abbey. Another, Sebastian de Rouillard, described her heart tomb as a great marble tomb, supported by four pillars, with a statue of the queen, standing in the choir of Le Lys. These claims have always intrigued historians. There is no mention of the extraction or separate burial of Blanche's heart in any of the contemporary accounts of her death and burial.[158] Louis IX makes no mention of the burial of his mother's heart there in his later charters to Le Lys.

Blanche's other surviving children made no gifts to Le Lys that might commemorate her heart buried there. One member of the family, however, did do so: Blanche's grandson Peter, count of Alençon.

Peter never met his grandmother; he was one of the children born to Louis IX and Margaret during the ill-fated Crusade. But he would have been brought up to revere her, and he seems to have taken a special interest in her. When he made his will in July 1282, he made donations to several Cistercian nunneries that Blanche had supported, including Saint-Antoine, Porret, Les Clairets and Villiers-aux-Nonnains – this at a stage when support for Cistercian nunneries was no longer as fashionable as it had been in the first half of the thirteenth century. Two Cistercian nunneries were the focus of his particular devotion: Maubuisson – 'Nostre Dame le Real' – because 'our grandmother the queen Blanche lies there' – 'nostre aeole la raine Blanche . . . laiens gist'; and Le Lys because of 'our grandmother the queen Blanche, whose heart lies there' – 'nostre aeole la raine Blanche don't li cors gist laienz'.[159]

Heart burials were becoming fashionable among the greater aristocracy in the thirteenth century, perhaps to ensure an increase in the prayers said for one's soul. Blanche's Angevin family were to an extent pioneers in this division of the body. Henry I's viscera were buried at Notre-Dame-du-Pré in Rouen, and his body at Reading Abbey. The viscera of Henry the Young King were at Grandmont; his body was at Rouen Cathedral. The body of Richard the Lionheart was buried at Fontevraud, his entrails at Charroux, and his heart was buried alongside his brother Henry at Rouen.

The earliest examples of bodily division on death were practical. It was often done when a great prince or ruler, or an important churchman, died far from home or the intended place of burial – on Crusade, perhaps. Evisceration of the body, usually including the heart, greatly reduced the rate of decomposition of the corpse on its journey to its final resting place. Thus, the heart and viscera of Robert of Arbrissel, the founder of Fontevraud, were buried at the priory of Oursan, where he died in 1116, so that his body could be transported to the mother house for burial. The same method was used in 1240 to ensure that the body of Edmund of Abingdon arrived safely for burial at Pontigny – his heart and entrails remained at Soisy, where he died. There were good practical reasons to remove the brains and the viscera from the corpse of Henry I and bury them at Rouen: he died in Normandy, and shipping his body back across the Channel might – and indeed

did – take some time. The same held true of Henry the Young King; it was a long journey from the Limousin to Rouen.[160]

But Richard the Lionheart was different. On his deathbed, Richard ordered a threefold division of his body, specifying the places of burial for each part, and separating the heart from the viscera.[161] He did not say he wanted thus to be commemorated in three of the polities he had ruled, but that is the unspoken implication. His heart was encased in a silver container. When the new choir of Rouen Cathedral was finished in the 1230s, Richard was provided with a fine effigy.[162] Blanche must have seen her uncle's splendid heart tomb, as she would also have seen the tomb that housed his body in the choir at Fontevraud. Did she introduce an Angevin burial tradition to Capetian France?

Heart burials, with an emphasis on the heart as the seat of the soul, not just the burial of that which might rot, had become fashionable in English court circles by the mid-thirteenth century. The countess of Winchester had a separate heart burial in 1235; Richard of Cornwall's first wife, Isabella, ordered the disposition of her remains between the royal Cistercian abbey of Beaulieu and her natal family's house of Tewkesbury in 1240.[163] Heart burials were more rare in Capetian court circles, but not unknown. The earliest ones are all in the context of death in another country. Noyon Cathedral housed a tomb for the heart and viscera of Ferdinand of Flanders, while his body was buried in Countess Joanna's Cistercian nunnery of Marquette: presumably Ferdinand died on his way between the Capetian court and Flanders in 1233.[164] In Crusading cases, it was not a question of burying the perishable heart and viscera *in situ* and transporting the bones home: rather, the body was interred locally, and the heart brought home. Philip Mousquès claims that Louis VIII had the body of his great friend Guy of Saint-Pol buried in the Alyscamps at Arles, but undertook to take Guy's heart back to France himself.[165] Amaury of Montfort died in Apulia on his way back from Crusade; his body was buried at St John Lateran in Rome, but his heart was brought back to be interred, by Aubry Cornut, bishop of Chartres, at the Montfort mausoleum of Les Hautes-Bruyères in 1241.[166] On the same Crusade, Count John of Dreux died in Nicosia; his heart was returned to the family mausoleum at Braine.[167]

Blanche's heart burial may thus have been the first occasion in France where there was no practical imperative. She was dead and buried within two days. Like T. S. Eliot's Magi, her last journey was short, and in the dead of winter. It established a tradition within the Capetian family. The heart and entrails of one of her younger sons, Alphonse of Poitiers, were buried alongside Blanche in the choir at

Maubuisson after his death on Louis ix's ill-fated Tunis Crusade of 1270. Charles of Anjou ordered that his own heart should be sent to his mother's favoured house of the Dominicans in Paris. The heart of Theobald v of Champagne and Navarre, who died on the 1270 Crusade, was enclosed in an exquisite octagonal heart tomb, still extant, at the Dominican house at Provins. The heart of Peter of Alençon's sister Isabella, the wife of Theobald v, was interred in the choir of Clairvaux. Peter of Alençon himself ordered that his body be buried at house of the Franciscans in Paris, and his 'mauves cuer' – his 'wicked heart' at the Dominican house. If he died too far away for his body to be transported, he asked that his bones and his heart could be taken to the appointed places.[168]

But the practice was controversial. Most of the multiple burials within Blanche's immediate family were the result of death on Crusade. The emphasis on bodily resurrection left the Church with awkward questions to answer about body parts lost on the battlefield, or bodies devoured by fishes – which must have been the presumed fate of Robert of Artois. Many churchmen did not approve of the gratuitous division of the bodies of those who were rich enough to ensure that they were remembered and prayed for in more than one religious institution. In the early fourteenth century Pope Boniface viii tried to forbid the practice, though with little success.[169] St Louis himself was known to share ecclesiastical disapproval of the practice – though dying as he did in the heat of distant Tunis, his corpse was subjected to the most extreme of bodily divisions. Charles of Anjou asked for his heart and his entrails and took them to Monreale, and the boiled bones were finally returned for burial at Saint-Denis.[170]

One might suspect that Blanche's views on the propriety of bodily division would have resembled and informed those of her pious eldest son. Nothing in the foundation of Le Lys suggests that she intended it as the site of her heart burial, and she was not the only patron to make multiple foundations. But she may have been persuaded by Alice of Mâcon, whose husband had died on Crusade, and by Mary of Constantinople, accustomed to the logistics of distant death. It is clear from the anxious discussions of the Cistercian general chapter how important aristocratic and royal burials were to the monastic institutions concerned and how far even Cistercians would go to ensure that they kept control of an illustrious body.[171]

Whoever initiated the double burial of Blanche's body, both graves were soon marked by magnificent memorials. At Maubuisson, her tomb in the centre of the nuns' choir was massive, made of copper, supported on a base of copper with

columns, with a copper effigy showing her in a religious habit, but crowned. It was surrounded by a laudatory inscription commemorating the daughter of King Alfonso and the wife of King Louis, the princess of Castile who took up the governance of France, who now lay here as a poor nun.[172] It was melted down at the Revolution, so its precise form is unknown. Perhaps the effigy resembled those copper effigies, emblazoned with Limoges enamels, made for her small grandchildren at Royaumont. Copper or bronze tombs were fashionable in early to mid-thirteenth-century France: most shared the same fate as Blanche's and are known only from drawings, usually those for the antiquarian Gaignières. Walter Cornut had a tomb of yellow copper at his cathedral of Sens, though the tomb was flat, and his image simply inscribed on its surface. Blanche was commemorated by a bodily effigy in relief. Ironically, the tomb for a contemporary that provides the closest analogy – copper in relief – is that of her old enemy Peter Mauclerc at the abbey of Saint-Yved at Braine. But perhaps the real inspiration for her tomb was the great retrospective tomb in copper relief provided for the Carolingian emperor Charles the Bald at Saint-Denis, presumably in the 1230s for the newly rebuilt choir.[173] It is impossible to know whether the queen ordered her tomb. She is more likely to have left it to her executors, Bishop Renaud of Paris, her clerk, Stephen of Montfort, and the abbot of Saint-Victor, since that would have been usual practice.[174]

Blanche's heart tomb was very different from the copper tomb at Maubuisson. Rouillard, who saw it in the seventeenth century, described it as made from marble, supported by four pillars, above which was an effigy of the queen.[175] It has often been connected with an account of 1255, which shows payment for 'the tomb of queen Blanche bought at Tournai and for its transport'.[176] This was probably ordered by Mary of Constantinople, her great-niece, who had stayed with Blanche since her arrival in France. After Blanche's death, Mary spent much time at her castle of Namur, with easy access to Tournai, until she lost the castle in 1258.[177] Mary was also buried in a tomb made from Tournai stone: it is the tomb now preserved at Saint-Denis that was once at Maubuisson, where Mary had herself buried close to her great-aunt.[178] But Rouillard does not say that Blanche's tomb was made from black marble – and the colour would surely have been striking. It is just possible that the tomb used eventually for Mary was indeed the Tournai marble one that she had originally commissioned and had transported to France in 1255 as a memorial to Blanche herself (see pl. 29).

10

The Culture of the Court

IF THE HOUSEHOLD WAS THE DOMESTIC SPHERE for a ruler, queen or princess, the court was the theatre for their most overtly public role. The two merged into one another, of course: a court occasion was the household in full display. Conversely, important political business was done in the most intimate recesses of the household, or while hunting, or during the incessant hours lumbering over rough roads in heavy carriages. But the court, in its widest sense, was where rulers presented themselves to the people over whom they ruled, and to ambassadors and visitors from other realms. The culture of the court established the tone of rulership.[1]

The courts of Louis VII and Philip Augustus provided little competition for the courts of their greater princes. Louis VII lacked the wealth of the counts of Champagne or Flanders, or the Angevins. In the twelfth century the great princes set the pace in courtly magnificence. They built innovative palaces and castles on a grand scale, such as Philip of Flanders' Ghent, Henry of Champagne's palace quarter at Troyes and Henry II's great hall at Saumur, or his castles at Dover, Chinon and Gisors, and Richard's works at Château-Gaillard. They founded or rebuilt abbeys, hospitals and cathedrals. They provided these foundations with rich gifts of jewelled liturgical furnishings and wonderfully painted bibles and psalters. The Anglo-Normans and Angevins even showered their largesse on institutions in Capetian France. Henry II and Richard gave to Chartres Cathedral; Henry I and Henry II made major contributions to the building of Cluny, not least by the provision of lead for the roof; and the empress Matilda gave jewels to the Capetian

burial house of Saint-Denis. When they died, they had themselves commemorated in ever more elaborate tombs, none more splendidly than the counts Henry and Theobald of Champagne.[2]

Their palaces and castles were as richly furnished as the churches they built. Here much less has survived, and one must depend on contemporary accounts. But it is clear that accoutrements were magnificent, and feasts lavish. The Angevins and the other princes surrounded their palaces with complex and elegant gardens, ensured their parks were well run, firmly enclosed and full of game, and kept menageries. Many of them held great tournaments on their lands, thus attracting some of the finest knights to their courts.[3] They did not just see themselves as knights and hunters. The princes of late twelfth-century France appreciated, encouraged and commissioned sophisticated romances in prose and poetry that reflected back to them the image of their chivalric courts. Arthurian legend – the Matter of Britain – emerged at the Angevin courts; the greatest exponent of it, Chrétien de Troyes, wrote mainly for the court of Champagne, but produced his last great work, *Perceval*, or the Knight of the Grail, for Count Philip of Flanders. The counts of Champagne established an impressive library containing fine copies of devotional books, religious works of various kinds, classical works and modern romances. They commissioned new manuscript copies of established works, commissioned new works from authors such as Chrétien de Troyes – or at least supported them with livings in administrative or religious posts in their gift – and they treasured the fine old volumes that they had inherited. The Champagne family were used to owning fine books, in the way that some of the great bishops did. There is evidence that the Anglo-Norman and Angevin kings had a similar princely library. Henry II had a richly gilded 'textus', perhaps a Gospel book, in his chapel; King John's library was extensive, containing at least two bibles, including an Old Testament in six volumes. The kings themselves and their families were well educated. Throughout the twelfth century a lively literary culture developed at and around the Anglo-Norman and Angevin courts. The princely courts enjoyed too the slighter, often scurrilous love songs, usually focused on hopeless love for an unattainable lady, whether in the Occitan of the south or the Francien of the north.[4]

Most of this rich, chivalric culture bypassed the Capetian court. Louis VII was conscious of his lack of wealth and largesse against that of Henry II, and was perhaps unable to compete had he wished to. By 1200, when Blanche arrived at the French court, Philip was much richer. But he disliked singers, poets and mimes,

to the delight of the French clergy, and did not patronise them in the way that the Angevins and the other French princes did. Rigord thought that other courts were unacceptably frivolous in comparison.[5] Philip's court also lacked a prominent woman to commission, or to receive dedications from, hopeful poets. The queen mother, Adela of Champagne, was often in her homeland and was dead by 1206. Ingeborg was confined away from court until 1213, and then played only a discreet role; and Philip realised that it would not be acceptable to flaunt Agnes of Meran as queen. Without an active queen, there was no need for a queen's household, no need for ladies-in-waiting, or the other noble women who would normally provide a queen with company. The romances and poems of courtly love were written mainly by men, many of them clergy, and some of them distinctly misogynistic. But their subject is love and sexual desire, and the romances and poems gained much of their potency from being performed in a court setting that was always supposed to be a potential marriage market, and thus a natural setting for sexual intrigue. Philip's court must have been colourless and flat when Blanche arrived there in 1200.

The court in which Blanche grew up in Castile in the difficult 1190s was uncomfortable and unstable, and lacked the resources of the courts of Champagne, Flanders and the Angevin empire. But it was linked to the troubadour culture of south-western France, and some aspects of it would have seemed dangerously exotic in northern France. The earliest parts of Blanche's parents' new abbey of Las Huelgas were built by craftsmen working in Arabic styles and stucco traditions, derived from the Islamic kingdom of Córdoba. The best of these craftsmen may have been converted, or even unconverted, Arabs. Toledo in particular was a centre at which Hebrew, Arabic and Christian scholars were used to working together. It was there that the Aristotelian natural science texts were translated from Arabic and transmitted to scholars in Paris and other western centres. Toledo, the ecclesiastical capital of Castile, was much frequented by the Castilian court.[6]

Philip Augustus may have been aware that his court lacked sparkle. Perhaps that was why he insisted that Lord Louis should have such a good education. Those around Philip made valiant attempts to recast him as the new Charlemagne and a Roman emperor in his kingship. By 1200 Rigord had called him Augustus, and Giles of Paris had presented his 'Karolinus', in which Charlemagne and Philip provide a double mirror for kingship, to the young Lord Louis. After 1204, and even more after 1214, these claims carried weight. William the Breton's poetic versions of Philip's deeds openly hail the king as the new Charlemagne and the new

Alexander. Both Rigord and William the Breton, like Giles of Paris, dedicated their works to Lord Louis, and the well-educated prince was probably equal to Giles's and William's convoluted Latin.[7]

Long before they came to the throne, Louis and Blanche had established a very different tone at their court from that of Philip Augustus. The new tone was consciously literary, cultured and chivalric. The younger barons found a ready welcome there; if there were no wars to fight, they could show their prowess out hunting. Blanche and her ladies provided the gender balance that was lacking at Philip's court, and thus the element of sexual excitement without which the courtly love songs and romances could not flourish. The young couple's early tastes for romances and songs owed much to the traditions of the courts of Champagne, for which Gace Brulé, whom they invited, had written and performed. Their close friend Stephen of Sancerre, who brought one of his minstrels along, came from a cadet branch of the family.[8] The current countess of Champagne was Blanche's cousin, Blanche of Navarre, and three youngsters from the dynasty, Count Theobald of Champagne and Joanna and Margaret of Flanders, were brought up at court alongside Blanche and Louis in the first decade of the thirteenth century. So youth and sex, gaiety and song distinguished Blanche and Louis's establishment from Philip's.

But if the French king's court was slightly dull, it was based in Paris, and by 1200 Paris had become the unrivalled centre of the liberal arts, of philosophy and theology – the intellectual centre of northern Europe, 'the new Rome in its poets, the new Athens in its philosophers', as one Paris master called it.[9] If Philip had no *trouvères* in his entourage, he had large numbers of educated clergy as administrators. These were the men who praised his deeds, and whom he called on to educate his son. Lord Louis and Blanche did not push these Paris masters away as they attracted minstrels and troubadours into their orbit. On the contrary, both Louis VIII and Blanche enjoyed the company of clergy who were not just devout but also engaged in the confrontational religious debates of the day, so that their court was not just chivalric, but also conspicuously and combatively intellectual.[10]

Their friendship with the Langtons ensured the influence of reformist and moralist theologians in their entourages. This strain of theological and moral thinking provided the religious orthodoxy of the day. It lay behind the pastoral and moral reformist agenda of Innocent III and the Fourth Lateran Council, and sustained the battle against the heresies of the Albigensians. It tended to attract churchmen with Cistercian sympathies or backgrounds, like Walter of Chartres; and St

Dominic's new order of preaching friars was forged by it. The actions and predilections of Blanche, her husband and her children, continually reflect the influence of the moralists. It is not surprising that when Blanche became queen, she enjoyed discussions with the first Dominicans to arrive in Paris.

There were more contested strains of theological enquiry: the neo-platonism, which could lead to a Catharist spiritualism, and above all the new Aristotelian learning emerging from the Jewish, Muslim and Christian scholars of Toledo. Many churchmen saw Aristotle as explosively dangerous. William the Breton thought the Amauricians had read too much Aristotle.[11] In July 1228 Gregory IX forbad the study of Aristotle in the University of Paris. But many of the churchmen who were closest to Blanche and her husband were open to these strains. Amaury of Bène and his followers, one of whom was a student of Stephen Langton, were clearly interested in the neo-platonism of John Scotus Eriugena and the Pseudo-Dionysius, as well as in Aristotle. Cardinal Romanus was a Paris-educated, questioning intellectual, who commissioned the first translation of Maimonides from Michael Scot, and recommended Scot to Stephen Langton.[12] William of Auvergne, bishop of Paris, worked extensively on the forbidden *Physica* and *Metaphysics* of Aristotle and cited the Arabic scholars Avicenna, Avicebron and Averroës.[13] It was Bishop William who gave the Dominicans their first chair at the University of Paris; he was also the dedicatee of Nicholas of Braie's poem on the deeds of Louis VIII.[14] Indeed, the year before he forbad the study of Aristotle in Paris, the capricious Gregory IX had written to Stephen Langton, asking him to use his connections to find a post for the brilliant scholar Michael Scot, whose training in Toledo had made him fluent in Latin, Hebrew and Arabic. Is the Master Michael of Spain who was richly robed in the household accounts for 1234 evidence that Stephen had turned to Blanche to find a place for him?[15]

Along with Philip's entourage, Blanche and Lord Louis must have been fascinated, and perhaps terrified, by the continual speculations about the imminent End of Time, the coming of Antichrist and the Last Judgement. In theory, the Church's position on the issue of the End of Time was clear: it had been settled by Augustine. Humanity could not know when it would come, and should not speculate. But speculation was inevitable, not least because crucial biblical accounts of the Last Times – the book of Revelation and sections of St Matthew's Gospel – had been written in expectation that the second coming of the Messiah would be very soon. The prophecies of Joachim of Fiore gave new life, and a certain amount of intellectual respectability, to eschatological speculation. Neither Innocent

III nor Stephen Langton could resist. The great Crusade preacher Fulk of Neuilly, founder of the nunnery of Saint-Antoine, drew much of his urgency and inspiration from his sense that the end was near.[16] Rigord recorded and dismissed popular rumours and false prophecies by astrologers of the end of the world around the year 1200.[17] But such speculations did not end in the new century. One of the principal accusations against the Amauricians was that they insisted that the end was imminent.[18] The Church might dismiss these prophecies and speculations as at best misguided, at worst heretical. But an unhealthy fascination with the Last Times ran deep. Various prophecies that had emerged in the late antique and Byzantine world announced that time would end with the fall of the Roman empire. Both Rigord and William of Auvergne discussed one of these prophecies, the so-called Pseudo-Methodius, at length.[19] In late tenth-century France a version of these prophecies emerged in which a king of France would act as the last Roman emperor. He would go to Jerusalem, lay down his crown on the Mount of Olives, and thus initiate the coming of the Antichrist. Around 1220 one of Philip Augustus's clerks copied a garbled version of this prophecy into the king's register of government. Some at Philip's court took this seriously. The sense that the end might be imminent was never far away in the thirteenth century. It permeated the intellectual culture of the court, and sharpened the sense that the delights of courtly life might soon turn to dust in the reign of the Antichrist.[20]

With their engagement with intellectual currents and their enjoyment of courtly display, Blanche and Louis VIII established a lively book culture at the Capetian court. The twelfth-century kings and queens of France must have possessed the necessary devotional books for their chapels; but there is no evidence that they had collected a princely library as the counts of Champagne had done. Both literary endeavours and book production were centred in the Paris schools rather than the court.[21] But Giles of Paris presented an illustrated copy of his 'Karolinus' to the young Lord Louis in 1200, shortly after Louis's marriage to Blanche (see pl. 3). Perhaps the educated Louis was already collecting a small library of his own. Presentation copies of other books dedicated to him have not survived, but presumably his library contained copies of Rigord's account of his father's deeds, and William the Breton's in both prose and poetic form. It would be nice to think that it also contained a copy of Gerald of Wales's 'Instruction for Princes', since Gerald thought Louis the ideal dedicatee.[22] Louis must have had his own fine psalter, and perhaps owned devotional texts or religious commentaries by the clergy to whom he was close. Delisle made the attractive suggestion that the Psalter of Joanna of

Navarre in the John Rylands Library in Manchester was produced for Louis. It must have been produced for court circles – but there is nothing in it to link it conclusively to the future Louis VIII.[23] By 1220 Blanche owned two fine psalters. During Louis and Blanche's short reign, the first two great moralised bibles were added to their collection. The psalters and heavily illustrated moralised bibles were designed to aid their devotions within the relative intimacy of their chapels, but also to display their piety in a wider courtly context. All such books might be – some were – used as diplomatic gifts; all were likely to have been shown to other rulers, princes, great barons, papal legates, ambassadors – to anyone on whom the wealth and piety of the king and queen of France should be impressed. Louis VIII's and Blanche's engagement in the intellectual and religious ferment of the early thirteenth century is made manifest in these religious books.

Blanche acquired one psalter, now known as the Leiden Psalter, from an uncle, Geoffrey, illegitimate son of Henry II and archbishop of York. Geoffrey died in exile in Normandy in 1212, and she may have inherited it then. It might have been a wedding gift from Geoffrey and King John, who had met at Rouen in June 1199, as John was in the process of arranging Blanche's marriage and the Treaty of Le Goulet.[24] Into its calendar, Blanche had entered the death of her beloved father in 1214. A couple of years later, perhaps around 1216, she acquired another psalter, now known as the Psalter of Blanche of Castile (Paris, Bibliothèque de l'Arsenal, MS lat. 1186). She had no family anniversaries entered into the calendar, which remained pristine, but it seems certain that the book was produced for her. The form of the prayers and the image of a praying woman in the initial for psalm 101 (f. 122v) show that it was meant for a woman – but not a queen, hence the assumption that she acquired it before 1223 (see pl. 4). The book was absorbed into the royal chapel, where it was recorded in a fourteenth-century inventory as 'a very beautiful psalter that belonged to Madame Blanche, the mother of my lord St Louis'. A fourteenth-century inscription on folio 191 makes a similar claim.[25]

Blanche's new psalter was more luxurious than the one she had inherited. It is unusually heavily illustrated, with a prefatory cycle before the psalter text, then a short Last Judgement cycle between the psalms and the canticles. The paintings, in rich and vibrant colours, are backed by thick burnished gold. Most of the illustrations are the sort of Old and New Testament scenes that were usual in psalters. Images of Eve and the Virgin are featured, as in other contemporary psalters produced for women, such as that probably given to Countess Joanna of Flanders by Blanche of Champagne in 1212, and the Ingeborg Psalter, owned by Ingeborg

of Denmark after 1213.[26] But there are some very unusual images too. The cycle starts with the 'Fall of the Rebel Angels', who tumble down into the open mouth of a grim bear-like monster with eyes made of thick discs of blackened silver that glimmer like mirrors of iniquity (see pl. 5).[27] The Last Judgement cycle, emphasised by its separate placing between the psalms and the canticles, is an unusually extensive representation of the End of Time and the coming of the New Jerusalem. It incorporates some of the powerful new imagery developed in the Last Judgement portals recently built at Notre-Dame in Paris and Chartres Cathedral, such as the huge figure of St Michael weighing the souls in a balance, and the clear social and bodily differentiation of the dead rising from their tombs and facing the judgement of Christ.[28] The sequence starts with the horrors and confusion of the reign of Antichrist, but also with an image of the final conversion of the Jews. The Jews appear to be converted by an elegant and eloquent woman (see pl. 7).[29] The imagery in Blanche's psalter is a powerful reflection of the fascination with salvation history that pervaded Capetian court circles in the early thirteenth century.

The psalter opens with a magnificent full-page image of three astronomers (see pl. 25). The central figure holds up an astrolabe to the stars; to the right of him, one of the astronomers holds open a book towards the viewer. The writing on the page is clearly designed to look, not like Latin script, but like Hebrew or even Arabic.[30] To the left, a younger astronomer writes down his computations. The scene has been identified as representing Sosigenes of Alexandria and Dionysius Exiguus, the scholars of antiquity who established the Christian calendar and computed the dates for Easter. It seems a fitting subject for a painting that introduces the section of the psalter containing the calendar, with the dates of the major saint's days and feasts of the Church, and the paschal table that allows the computation of the dates of Easter.[31] But three astronomers are shown, not two, and they are not producing tables. Rather, they are using the text of an open book – a Hebrew or Arabic book – and an astrolabe to tell time by the stars. By the late twelfth century computational tables were reserved for psalters for monastic use, apart from this psalter and the Christina Psalter, which was also commissioned by the Capetian family, and possibly by Blanche herself.[32] And no other surviving medieval psalter contains a comparable image. It introduces an exotic note. Udovitch has linked this image to the new Aristotelian scientific learning arriving in Paris from Spain in the early thirteenth century, brought by Michael Scot, among others.[33] Was this image designed to remind Blanche of her Castilian background, to remind her that the Aristotelian ideas that were attractive to so many

of the churchmen around her came from Toledo, where Christian, Jewish and Arabic scholars worked closely together?

It is an exotic and overtly intellectual opening to the princess's psalter. Whoever ordered the image knew that Blanche would be struck by it, and able to understand its significance. The same is true of the extensive cycle of images, which was produced for someone who could take the text of the psalms at more than face value, who was used to sophisticated exegesis of the biblical text. A set of explicatory sentences, written in blue and gold, introduce each psalm (see pl. 4). They are drawn from Peter Lombard's Commentary on the psalms. Produced in the 1160s, this had become the standard gloss on the psalms. Nevertheless, the compiler of the psalter extracted from it phrases and ideas that reflected the spirit of the canons of the Fourth Lateran Council. Many stress the need for penitence and the confession of sins. They stress the humanity of Christ – surely aimed at Cathars and Amauricians who were thought to deny it. They stress the superiority of the New Dispensation and the New Testament over the Old. They rail against the pride and obduracy of the Jews, but look forward to their conversion now or at the End of Time.[34] In effect, Blanche was given a lightly glossed psalter. No other psalter produced for lay devotion is glossed in this way.[35] In short, Blanche's new psalter, luxurious with thick gold and vibrant colour, attests to a princess, and a court culture, finely, almost dangerously, attuned to the intellectual and theological debates among Parisian scholars in the early thirteenth century.

This was not the first richly produced illuminated psalter to be commissioned for a woman in court circles. Blanche of Navarre, countess of Champagne, had presented one to her niece Countess Joanna of Flanders, probably when Joanna married Ferdinand of Portugal in 1212, though there Blanche was acting within Champagne family traditions.[36] Around 1200 someone, probably Eleanor of Vermandois, commissioned a psalter, even more beautiful, even more lavishly gilded than Blanche's, for a princess or a queen of France.[37] This is the psalter that Queen Ingeborg owned by 1214, when the dates of the battle of Bouvines and the anniversaries of the deaths of her parents, and of Countess Eleanor of Vermandois, were added to the calendar. Many scholars have questioned whether this glorious manuscript was made for Ingeborg.[38] Her father's death had occurred in 1184, but was written into the calendar at the same time as that for Eleanor of Vermandois, who died in 1213. For the twenty years after her marriage, Ingeborg was hardly in a position to commission such a luxurious psalter for herself. Nor would it have been politic for her supporters among the French clergy, such as Stephen of

Tournai, to have commissioned it for her, for they stressed the poverty in which Philip was forcing her to live.[39] It has many things in common with Blanche's psalter, especially the choice of several saints in the calendar suitable for a French queen or princess, and many images feature the Virgin as Queen of Heaven. Most scholars agree that this manuscript must have been destined for a woman who was, or would become, queen of France.[40]

Is it possible that the Ingeborg Psalter was in fact commissioned for Blanche when she married Louis in 1200 – and perhaps by Eleanor of Vermandois, who was still close to the court? A striking aspect of both it and the Psalter of Blanche of Castile is the number of English saints, especially English royal saints, in their calendars. There are strong parallels with the English saints in the calendar of the Leiden Psalter, which would be explicable if Blanche arrived with the Leiden Psalter in 1200. No one has explained satisfactorily their relevance for Ingeborg; for Blanche, married as the niece of the king of England, and the means by which the future king of France might also be king of England, their relevance is obvious. Perhaps Blanche commissioned her psalter after she was asked – or perhaps offered – to give this one to Ingeborg when Ingeborg was reinstated as queen in 1213. Ingeborg's reinstatement occurred at the Council of Soissons in 1213 – the council at which Philip agreed that Louis would invade England in a bid to take the English throne. Louis was forced to sign an agreement that, if he acquired the English throne, he would do nothing to the detriment of his father's dominion.[41] Perhaps the glorious golden psalter was another part of the negotiations.

The Ingeborg Psalter lacks the theological complexity of the Blanche Psalter. There are no explicatory sentences to introduce the psalms, and the images are more straightforward. Indeed, the images seem designed to instruct at quite a basic level. Many of them have simple captions in French, and some of the figures in them are labelled in French, as if the recipient needed some help with the French language. That would have been appropriate for Ingeborg, if the psalter were given to her on her marriage in 1193: Ingeborg could certainly read Latin, but did not know French.[42] It would also, of course, have been appropriate for the twelve-year-old Blanche at her marriage in 1200. But by the time Blanche commissioned or was given the Blanche Psalter, she was a well-educated woman, versed in the theological discussions of the day.

Not long after the production of the Psalter of Blanche of Castile, two even more splendid books, two illuminated and moralised bibles, were commissioned at the Capetian court. Both books are now in the Österreichische Nationalbibliothek,

numbered Codex Vindobonensis 1179 and 2554.[43] It is generally agreed that Codex 1179 was produced for Louis VIII, and for Louis as king, since the last page of the book shows a king commanding the making of the book (see pl. 3). A short, now fragmentary, poem alongside the image of the king refers to his illustrious regal ancestry, in phrases that recall Giles of Paris's apostrophe of the future Louis VIII.[44] Codex 2554 has lost its last section, so it is not known whether this too had a portrait of the owner. Both books are picture books. Painted and gilded roundels illustrate verses from the Bible, which are written next to them. Each biblical verse is provided with a corresponding 'moralisation', in the form of a text, and a painted illustration. The texts in Codex 1179 are longer than those in Codex 2554. They are more theologically complex, and are in Latin, whereas those in Codex 2554 are in French. In the Latin bible, the biblical text is usually derived from the Vulgate, and the moralisations make frequent use of the Glossa Ordinaria, as might be expected. The biblical passages in the French bible are loose, often incompetent translations, perhaps done from memory, and the moralisations do not depend on the expected glosses and commentaries. The images are magnificent, but the texts of both bibles, especially the French one, are full of mistakes: major scholars were not in charge here.[45] Nevertheless, the moralisations, particularly those that point a moral from contemporary life, are reminiscent of the moralisations of Peter the Chanter and Stephen Langton.[46] Both bibles open with a magnificent image of God as creator of the macrocosm, the universe. The texts around them give an indication of the directness and simplicity of the French text against the sophisticated complexity of the Latin text. The French text reads: 'Here God creates heaven and earth, the sun and the moon and all the elements.' The Latin text, on the other hand, is couched as a convoluted and cryptic verse: 'Hic orbis figulus disponit singulus solus' – 'Here the sole maker of the universe arranges each separate [element]'.[47]

These two books give suggestive insights into the courtly culture around Blanche and Louis VIII, but they also pose many questions. They are among the most sumptuous manuscripts ever produced, and there is no doubt that they were intended for royal ownership. The presumption must be that the couple commissioned them, perhaps to celebrate their joint coronation in 1223.[48] Indeed, the image of the king in Codex 1179 shows him in the act of commanding the bible from the artist. The fact that Codex 2554 has a French text, with less sophisticated readings than Codex 1179, has led many scholars to argue that Codex 2554 was intended for Blanche. But Blanche was sufficiently proficient in Latin to read

letters, recognise references to Horace and understand the sentences explaining the psalms in her psalter. She could teach her children to read Latin from the psalter, and at least one Latin devotional text, 'Audi domina', was written for her.[49] She had no need of a picture book written entirely in French; the literary Louis had no need of a Latin picture book. Perhaps Blanche and Louis intended to use the bibles as teaching aids for their children, as Blanche did with the psalters – though she would have found some highly unsuitable material had she done so.

These books appear to be the first of their kind. Bibles produced for the clergy were regularly glossed to explain the moral, or the deeper meaning, of the Bible – not least because the biblical text was so full of contradictions and the Old Testament in particular full of incidents where the moral was not easy to draw. But no one had produced a book like this before, with so many biblical illustrations, so many moralisations and with so much emphasis on the pictures rather than the text – or with such defective and unscholarly texts. Most previous bibles had been produced for churchmen, to be kept in their private book collections, or for the libraries of abbeys or cathedrals. These bibles were produced for perusal by royalty, by their entourage and by the highest aristocracy, for display in a courtly context.

Who conceived the idea of such a novel book – Blanche and Louis, or the clergy who surrounded them? Who determined the programme in it – the biblical verses to be illustrated, the moral to be drawn, and how the verses and the morals should be illustrated? Neither Blanche nor Louis would have had time to oversee the content of the books in detail, though they must have given an indication of what they wanted. Did they leave the content and the practicalities of commissioning to their chaplains, to the clerical administrators like Walter Cornut and Master John de la Cour? Did they ask one of the scholars around them, like Simon Langton, to sketch out an overview? If so, the execution of the text was left to very undistinguished clerks – but then there were plenty of clerks at court whose Latin required correction by the young Princess Isabella.[50] Did they place the commission in the hands of one of their trusted household knights – Bartholomew of Roye, perhaps?

The content of both books is sometimes surprising and sometimes shocking, especially in the many moralisations that relate to contemporary life. Certain themes emerge strongly in the books. The influence of the reformist ideas behind the Fourth Lateran Council is pervasive – as one might expect.[51] There is much about how and how not to be a good king and, more occasionally, queen. The

good king should not listen to evil counsellors and wicked barons, but to the good clergy.[52] But the books are not sustained mirrors for princes and princesses. There is quite as much criticism of clergy as there is of kings, especially of clergy who have too much wealth and are too close to the court (pl. 27); and no branch of the clergy, whether Benedictine or Cistercian monks, scholars, hermits or bishops, escapes censure.[53] In fact, issues that exercised the Paris scholars and clergy in the early thirteenth century are omnipresent. Some of those issues were relatively minor: these moralisations were clearly intended to raise a knowing smirk and sometimes a raucous chuckle. One image compares the good scholars who stay in Paris learning theology with the bad scholars who go off to Bologna to study law.[54] More seriously, there are clear warnings against sodomy and pederasty – and the images of both show clergy as the perpetrators.[55] Heresy is frequently invoked. Miscreants (as they are called in the text) are shown holding small tabby cats. The reference to Cathars, who were thought to derive their name from their habit of kissing a cat's bottom, is clear, and would have been very topical as Louis VIII negotiated the terms of the Albigensian Crusade.[56] But some miscreants are connected with wicked scholars, and this is almost certainly a reference to the Amauricians. Both the Cathars and the Amauricians had been accused of sodomy, and the warnings against homoeroticism can probably be placed in that context. Scholars who have strayed from safe theology towards the dangers of philosophy – pseudo-Dionysian, or Aristotelian, perhaps – are often castigated.[57] Dialecticians, philosophers and astronomers are always evil.[58] One striking image in both bibles shows an inversion of the magnificent image of the three astronomers that opens Blanche's psalter. Here the three – the central one holding the astrolabe, his companions writing in books – are struck down by the thunderbolts of God (see pl. 26).[59]

A powerful anti-Judaism informs both books. Synagogue collapses before Ecclesia, and the imperfections of the Old Law, and the Old Testament, which will be made perfect in the New, are continually underlined. Jews are viciously caricatured as the tormentors and murderers of Christ, as usurers and as evildoers who ruin Christians and consort with miscreants.[60] Worldly clergymen are shown taking usurious loans from Jews (see pl. 27).[61] Anti-Judaism is a feature of Blanche's psalter too, in the images and in the texts introducing the psalms. But the anti-Judaic images in the two bibles have a vicious edge of caricature that is not present in Blanche's psalter. It is impossible to tell whether the books respond to Blanche's and Louis VIII's own anti-Judaism, or whether the books were one of the principal

means by which some of the clergy around them persuaded them that here, too, they should behave differently from Philip Augustus.

What did Blanche and Louis think of the coded references to Amauricians and those who toyed with the new Aristotelianism, like William of Auvergne and Cardinal Romanus? Were they supposed to accept these warnings from a disapproving clergy? What did Walter Cornut think of the criticism of clergy who consorted with Jews – Walter whose episcopal administration was run by Jews? Two images suggest that the laity was unable to understand the higher reaches of theology, and should be given only the simplest religious ideas by sensible clergymen.[62] But Blanche and Louis retained Simon Langton and liked to talk with the new Dominicans; Louis was praised by Gerald of Wales and Giles of Paris for the very fact that he was a lettered prince. In fact, it is impossible to make sense of these books unless one accepts that Blanche and Louis, and the clergy around them, possessed a robust and rather earthy sense of humour. The books provide strongly satirical comments on the culture of the court and its often unhealthy intersection with the culture of the Church and the nascent university – though heresy had been no laughing matter for Amaury and his followers. The moralised bibles are not so much mirrors for princes, as illustrated 'Courtiers' Trifles', warning masters and churchmen of the seductive dangers of power and the court in the manner of Walter Map.

After Louis VIII's death, Blanche continued to commission manuscripts, many of them magnificent religious books. Some were intended for her collection; many were intended as gifts. Her own books were well cared for. Goldsmiths' work for the court in 1239 included two heavy clasps, weighing around 3 ounces (85g), for the queen's books.[63] Her psalter served as a model for some of the imagery in a psalter produced for the royal chapel at Saint-Germain-en-Laye, presumably shortly after St Louis re-established and rebuilt it in 1238.[64] She had her own scribe in 1241.[65] The household regularly purchased parchment, some of which may have been used for fine books, though parchment was also required for administrative records, letters and charters.[66] Herbert the Parchmenter, a prominent Parisian book producer, was well enough known to Blanche for her to contribute 100 *solidi* towards his daughter's wedding in 1242 – though that paled beside the 40 *livres* that she gave for the daughter of one of her fishermen; and she gave Master Nicholas the illuminator 100 *solidi* to pay off his debts to John de la Cour, dean of Tours.[67] She bought three psalters from the sons of Guy Cocus in 1221–2: one cost 40 *solidi*, the other two 100 *solidi* between them.[68]

Blanche often gave devotional books as gifts. She ensured that members of the household had the devotional books that they needed: in 1234 a breviary was purchased for Hugh of Athies.[69] The chapel that Blanche sent to her sister, the queen of Castile, included a missal in two volumes and a breviary in one.[70] In the early 1230s someone, possibly Blanche, commissioned a psalter, richly illustrated, and related to if slighter than her own psalter, perhaps for one of her children – Robert of Artois or John – or for her nephew Alphonse of Portugal. Eventually it was given to her great-nephew Philip of Castile, who was in Paris during the 1240s. It takes its name, the Christina Psalter, from Philip's wife, Christina of Norway. The anti-Judaic imagery in this is more negative, and more caricatured, than that in Blanche's psalter, perhaps because it was commissioned from artists who had worked on the moralised bibles, perhaps because anti-Judaic sentiment had hardened between 1215 and 1230. There is no image of the conversion of the good Jews at the End of Time.[71] Blanche presented a large illuminated bible to the abbey of Saint-Victor. It is not as finely crafted as the royal psalters and moralised bibles, and there are signs of haste, but it has a contemporary index at the back of the book.[72]

When she founded Maubuisson, she ordered parchment to make devotional books for the nuns, and paid Herbert the Parchmenter 40 *solidi* for 'illuminating and binding' an ordinary for the new abbey.[73] Richard of Tourny procured a 'psalterio habito' for 45 *solidi* for the nunnery in 1241 – presumably a psalter suitable for those who are habited as nuns.[74] Blanche left Maubuisson fine books of her own, including an illustrated psalter and a devotional text in a 'joly livre bien escript'.[75]

Perhaps for her son's coronation, she commissioned another moralised bible, the Toledo Bible.[76] Begun in the late 1220s, it was finished in the early 1230s, possibly because Blanche and those around her had more immediate political preoccupations in the early years of Louis's minority, and were away from Paris on campaign for long stretches. It may have been completed for presentation to Louis in 1234, as he reached his majority and took full powers as king, marked by his marriage to Margaret and her coronation, at which Louis wore his crown and regalia. Like Louis VIII's bible, this ends with an image showing the patron commanding the work. This is the magnificent double portrait of Blanche with the new young king. Below them, a cleric instructs the scribe what to write and draw in the manuscript (see frontispiece).[77] This bible, a vastly extended version of the earlier ones, in three volumes, had text in both French and Latin. The texts are much

more scholarly than those of the other two bibles, with some influence from the very recent work of the Dominican scholar Hugh of St Cher detectable. Nevertheless, the anti-philosophical and anti-Judaic satirical rhetoric of the first two bibles is retained.[78]

One devotional work, a mirror for the soul beginning 'Audi domina' (Listen Lady), was written for Blanche.[79] It is a minatory work, based on Cistercian devotional tracts, with a grimly vivid emphasis on what would befall one at the Last Judgement if one failed to walk in the path of righteousness. Its tone and its message are reminiscent of Blanche's psalter. The author dares to address the queen of France directly. At the end of time, when all are equal, someone will point at her and say: 'Look, that was once the queen of France' – what will she say in reply?[80] The identity of the author is unknown, and it is not clear when the book was written. The tone suggests that the author was close to her: William of Auvergne is a possibility; so are the Cistercian Walter of Chartres and Simon Langton. Blanche did not object to the warning addressed to a queen. She gave a copy to her daughter, and received a French translation, known as the 'Miroire de l'âme', dedicated to her.[81]

If it is unclear whether Blanche actively commissioned the French translation, she seems to have treasured it. A fine copy was included in a magnificent 'Somme le roi' manuscript made in 1295 for Philip IV's queen, now Paris, Bibliothèque Mazarine, MS 870. The opening initial of the 'Miroire de l'âme' shows the book being presented to a queen by a Cistercian nun or abbess (see pl. 24). If this initial, too, was copied from the book sent to Blanche, it would suggest that the translation was made for her in one of the Cistercian nunneries with which she was closely connected, perhaps Saint-Antoine, or her foundations of Maubuisson or Le Lys.[82]

There is no evidence that Blanche encouraged or was the dedicatee of the writing of contemporary history in the way that her husband had been. No new histories were dedicated to the young princes. Nicholas of Braie dedicated his 'Deeds of Louis VIII' to William of Auvergne.[83] Nor did Blanche commission histories, saints' lives or romances in the vernacular – an area often associated with royal and aristocratic women, especially Eleanor of Castile.[84] Walter Cornut's short account of the reception and display of the Crown of Thorns is not dedicated to Blanche, but Walter stresses her involvement throughout, and she is likely to have asked her loyal supporter to write it. It probably originated as a sermon at one of the events and services for the reception of the relic. Parts of it were soon adapted for reading

at Matins. It is not a work of great literary distinction, though it relays its narrative with commendable pace. It is in Latin, not the vernacular.[85]

Blanche's well-educated children continued the courtly book culture in their subtly different ways. Isabella valued books highly: her library included a copy of the 'Audi domina', a Latin grammar and Walter of Châtillon's Latin romance of Alexander.[86] Alphonse was, perhaps, interested in histories and in texts in the vernacular. In 1245 he had a 'roman' – a romance – and a copy of 'the history of Rencevaux' – the Chronicle of the Pseudo-Turpin – re-bound. An updated history of the Capetian dynasty in French, the 'Chronique des rois', now Paris, Bibliothèque Nationale, MS fr. 5700, was presented to him in the late 1260s.[87] St Louis ordered the establishment of a royal library for the edification of the royal entourage, in emulation of the sultan of Egypt. There was a focus on saints' lives, and surviving manuscripts are plain. This was not a library to rival that of the counts of Champagne. The luxury devotional books were all kept in the royal chapel.[88] It was Charles, questioningly intelligent, power-hungry and visually sophisticated, whose book collecting perhaps most closely reflected his parents' tastes.[89]

Blanche certainly encouraged the more evanescent courtly culture of poetry and song. Minstrels of all kinds are a feature of every household account connected with Blanche from 1213 onwards. In 1213 she and Louis enjoyed the playing of Robert of Courtenay's viol player, Stephen of Sancerre's singer Passerele, the acting of Tornebeffe and the poems of Gace Brulé.[90] Gace Brulé had worked mainly at the court of Champagne, but had contacts too with Blanche's poet uncle, Richard the Lionheart. Blanche and Louis VIII introduced to Capetian court circles the music and poetry of the Angevin and Champenois courts that Philip Augustus had ignored or discouraged. Passerele was still entertaining the court in 1239.[91] As queen dowager, Blanche had her own female singer, Melana, whose name suggests an Iberian.[92]

Robert of Artois shared his mother's love of courtly music and song: he paid for the minstrels for Louis and Margaret's marriage and coronation in 1234.[93] Charles of Anjou was throughout his adult life both a major patron of poetry, music and song and, like Richard the Lionheart, a *trouvère* himself.[94] Louis IX enjoyed devotional music, and one hymn to the Virgin is attributed to him. But he hated secular music – at least, according to his hagiographers. He once made a young squire who sang 'worldly songs' learn anthems to the Virgin instead.[95] Louis would have no 'jolivetez' – which court minstrels often provided.[96] After 1261 he refused to have minstrels and *jongleurs* at his court.[97] The change in taste at court is to an

extent reflected in the household accounts. The account of 1234, when the court was essentially under Blanche's control, shows a court alive with music. Some of it – that purveyed by Robert of Courtenay's minstrel, Four Eggs, or the ill-dressed (or perhaps excessively well-dressed) Malappareillez – was doubtless comic or satiric in tone.[98] Large numbers of minstrels are recorded in the account of 1239, but most took part in the extensive feasting and celebration for the knighting of Blanche's much-loved nephew Alphonse of Portugal and the emperor Baldwin at Melun at Pentecost 1239, and then Alphonse's wedding at Beaumont-sur-Oise. Blanche was undoubtedly the presiding genius of these events.[99] Others were brought to court by her close friends.[100]

Blanche clearly admired the partly Castilian aristocratic poet Theobald of Blaison.[101] He shared her religious sensibilities, giving to reformed monasteries, such as Fontevraud and Cistercian Chaloché and Bonlieu.[102] Blanche invited him to Louis IX's coronation in 1226, and appointed him seneschal of Poitou in 1227 and of the Limousin in 1229, the year in which he died.[103] Theobald of Blaison was a fairly prolific poet in the charming courtly manner. He exchanged poetic banter with Hugh of La Ferté, but did not follow Hugh's urge to associate himself with a baronial, anti-royal party, nor did he produce overtly political songs. He was the dedicatee of a poem by Theobald of Champagne, whose works his own resemble.

Blanche's cousin Theobald of Champagne hardly required her patronage. He was renowned as an accomplished poet, and his love songs must have been performed, perhaps by Theobald himself, at the Capetian court. Blanche may have been the overt object of some of Theobald's love songs – though he always described his longed-for, unattainable mistress as blond, while Blanche, like Charles of Anjou, was probably dark-haired and olive-skinned.[104] Theobald enjoyed toying with the conventions of courtly love, but his songs presumably lay behind the scurrilous gossip, which reached Roger of Wendover and Matthew Paris in England, that Theobald fell out with Louis VIII because he and Blanche were having an affair. That Blanche and Theobald were closer than a queen and a great baron should be, and that Theobald was responsible for the death of Louis VIII, was a recurrent theme in the political songs that circulated in the second quarter of the thirteenth century.[105]

Blanche herself, like Richard the Lionheart and Charles of Anjou, may have written songs. Other aristocratic women in the thirteenth century did so, including the duchess of Lorraine.[106] Two late thirteenth-century French song collections

ascribe songs to Blanche. Whether the attributions are true or not, by 1300 it was widely believed that she had composed songs. One is a song to the Virgin, with music. The writer addresses the Virgin as 'Virge roine, flours de lis' (Virgin Queen, fleur-de-lis); the last verse stresses the role of the Virgin as the 'vessel…where the Holy Spirit was nourished for nine full months'. It is not difficult to see this as the work of the woman who named her two abbey foundations Santa Maria Regalis and Le Lys, and who was intensely conscious of her role as the mother of an earthly king.[107] This poem would have pleased the exigent St Louis. The other would have pleased neither Louis nor Robert of Artois, for it is a two-part courtly flirtation ascribed to 'le roi de Navarre [Theobald of Champagne] a la dame roine blance'.[108]

Many *trouvères* produced songs that referred to contemporary politics. Some were love songs, with covert political subtexts; others were overtly political, and often satirical. The political song emerged as a genre in France, Flanders and England at the very end of the twelfth century, and flourished in the thirteenth. At least, a large number of political songs survive from this period: people felt they were worth inscribing into collections. Many of these songs were produced not in aristocratic circles, but among a rich, educated *bourgeoisie*. The cities of French Flanders, especially Arras, were particularly productive. These were precisely the areas of France that had come to Louis VIII and Blanche through Isabella of Hainault's dowry. The students of Paris had their own traditions, already established in the twelfth century, of the subversive, satirical and often scurrilous 'goliardic', as they were called, songs. It is difficult to know how much overlap there was between court and urban and student culture.

Most of the thirteenth-century political songs from these areas were connected with aristocratic and baronial courts, rather than the royal court.[109] Indeed, they are overtly anti-royal. They express the grievances of the barons and the great lords against a crown that takes their money and their lands, but not their counsel. The composers were often young aristocrats themselves, such as Hugh of La Ferté. Several found willing patrons in the barons who had been fractious under Philip Augustus, Louis VIII and then during the minority of Louis IX. The minority, and the rule of a woman, was an irresistible gift to a political poet, and Blanche, sometimes lightly disguised as Dame Hersent, the formidable housewife from the tales of Reynard the Fox, found herself the subject of many of these songs. She was accused of keeping Louis unmarried, sending money to Spain and being too close to the count of Champagne and Walter Cornut, who was accused of preferring

men of Spain to the barons.[110] But the poets could not quite help admiring her too: as one song said, she knew better how to govern the world than the barons could run a village.[111] After her troubles with the University of Paris, she featured in goliardic songs – songs that accused the queen of an affair with the papal legate, Romanus. The goliardic songs reached Matthew Paris in England.[112] The great barons might revolt periodically – though only Peter of Brittany did so consistently – but many of them were cousins, and most of them came frequently to court. Theobald of Champagne was in many ways typical. He was never a dependable political ally, for he always looked to the interests of Champagne and Navarre; but his relationship with Blanche was that of an affectionate cousin. It is impossible to believe that Blanche did not hear these songs at court. Perhaps she enjoyed them; perhaps they made her laugh. The concatenation of satire, the scurrilous and the profound – or at least serious political criticism – in the political songs is reminiscent of the texts and images in the moralised bibles. They too suggest that Blanche and the clergy and aristocrats around her had a saltier and more robust approach to life and death, religion and politics, than is usually assumed.

•

The castles and palaces where the court stayed provided the theatres in which Blanche's and her family's lives were played out. The building, and the fitting out of them, was an essential part of court culture. Architectural patronage must be extended to the various religious institutions that the queen and her entourage might visit, in which they might stay, and even to those where royal presence was not expected, but where royal architectural patronage would reflect royal magnificence and largesse. Gerald of Wales's 'Instruction for Princes', notionally dedicated to Lord Louis, is one of many texts that make clear that the provision and fitting of great buildings within one's realm was the proper business of a great prince.[113] Blanche and her sons took this aspect of rulership seriously.

Here, too, as with the patronage of romance, poetry and literary culture, Blanche's active architectural patronage seems to reflect her Angevin heritage and the traditions of the princely courts of France, rather than those of the Capetian kings. The Anglo-Norman and Angevin kings had the wealth to build castles and churches on a scale that was not possible for the Capetians in the twelfth century. But by the thirteenth century the Capetians were no longer the poor relation of their great princes. Philip Augustus and his master masons developed a programme of simple but effective castles that demonstrated his power over old Capetian lands

and his domination of the lands he had captured. Philip's castles had rounded
mural towers placed at careful intervals, and tall cylindrical great towers, which
managed to combine elegance with menace. The most famous of his great castles
was his new fortress of the Louvre, guarding the western approaches to Paris, built
in conjunction with the new city wall that he persuaded the citizens to fund. Philip
built fine new market halls for his capital city, and insisted that the streets were
paved.[114] The household accounts for 1213 suggest that Louis VIII shared his father's
passion for castle building. He spent around 1,700 *livres* on Lens, in line with his
father's castle expenditure. Louis's mason was Master Fulk, who worked with his
brother Garin, probably a specialist *fossator* who dug the great ditches around a
castle. Master Robert handled the carpentry.[115] None of these men appears in the
long list of masons, carpenters and *fossatori* who worked for Philip Augustus, so
Lord Louis convened his own construction team.[116] It is just possible that Master
Robert the carpenter was employed some thirty years later by Blanche at her abbey
at Maubuisson.[117]

Both Philip and Louis VIII appear to have been less interested in the patronage
of ecclesiastical architecture, though appearances may be deceptive. Louis left provision for a great new Augustinian abbey in his will, and Philip founded and had
built the abbey of La Victoire. Philip's abbey was effectively rebuilt in the fifteenth
century; had the original survived, historians might have had a different impression
of him as an architectural patron. Shortly before 1220 Louis contributed glass for
the windows in the choir at Chartres Cathedral, commemorating his intervention
in the Albigensian Crusade.[118] Philip's deliberate development of the built environ-
ment of Paris, his conscious development of a city that looked like a capital, suggests an understanding of the potential role of architecture within rulership.
Nevertheless, neither Philip nor Louis VIII demonstrated the architectural largesse
of Henry II or Richard the Lionheart, or Blanche's parents, Eleanor and Alfonso.[119]

The earlier Capetians were fortunate that they did not really need to make much
effort to 'illuminate their kingdom with beautiful abbeys they had built there', as
Joinville thought a king should do, and as Blanche and St Louis did.[120] Since Abbot
Suger's rebuilding of Saint-Denis between 1130 and 1145, the great churchmen of
Capetian France had been in competition to commission ever more magnificent
religious building on an ever larger scale. The bishop of Auxerre in 1215 was quite
open about his need to build a splendid new cathedral to keep up with those of
his episcopal colleagues.[121] In the fifty years between 1190 and 1240 a sequence of
French cathedrals – Chartres, Bourges, Reims, Amiens and Beauvais – were built

to a new, towering scale; art historians call this 'High Gothic'. The high vaults of Beauvais Cathedral were nearly 150 feet (45m) from the ground. It was too ambitious. Beauvais was unstable from the start and was never finished. Subsequent building was more measured in scale, but rich in detail, especially elaborate window tracery. The traceried rosette window patterns typical of building in Capetian France from around 1230 led art historians to call this the Rayonnant style. While the architectural lead in the hundred years between 1130 and 1230 in Capetian France had often been taken by bishops and chapters of cathedrals, the urge to emulate had inspired a large number of deans of colleges, abbots and patrons of abbeys and priories to major rebuilding projects. The France to which Blanche was brought in 1200 was in the throes of one of the most substantial, inventive and brilliant building booms in history.[122]

Blanche challenged the traditional Capetian reticence about involvement in great building projects almost as soon as she found herself in charge of king and country after her husband's early death. Perhaps because of her close interest in the Cistercian order, Blanche, along with the young king and Bishop Walter of Chartres, attended the dedication of the great new church at the abbey of Longpont in 1227. There she saw the first Cistercian church to reflect the High Gothic cathedrals. Four years later she was present at the dedication of the church of Saint-Antoine.[123] She knew at first hand most of the many Cistercian nunneries founded and constructed by her parents, close friends and relations in the first thirty years of the century. When Eudes Clément, abbot of Saint-Denis, decided to rebuild his largely ancient and now tottering great church, he consulted Blanche and young Louis first.[124] He had need of the royal imprimatur, because legend had it that the existing church had been consecrated by Christ himself. Building began in 1231, with rapid construction until 1245. From the start, it was a building of subtle spaces and elegantly clever tracery. The upper levels seemed to be little more than large expanses of stained glass. Saint-Denis is rightly considered the first building in the Rayonnant style, and it was very influential.[125] Blanche was not a patron of the rebuilding, but she must have been very conscious of it. It was the burial place of her husband; besides, Abbot Eudes Clément, cousin of Walter Cornut, was often at court. He knew he must retain her support for the project, and ensured that the choir and south transept portal were liberally ornamented with painted and sculpted lilies of France and castles of Castile.[126]

Stained glass provided the ideal medium to carry the striking image of the gold castle of Castile on its deep red ground. The great transept glazing campaign at

Chartres Cathedral was probably designed to celebrate the Treaty of Vendôme, and the closing of Capetian family ranks after Blanche's first dramatic stand against Peter Mauclerc and Philip Hurepel. Peter was persuaded to pay for the glass of the south transept gable; Philip and Matilda of Boulogne contributed to the glazing of the north transept clerestory, while Blanche and the young king Louis signalled their patronage of the north transept gable with a glowing display of the castles of Castile and lilies of France (see pl. 1). The programme and the execution of the scheme were doubtless overseen by the loyal bishop, Walter, who had himself played a crucial role in the negotiations of the treaty.[127] Again in concert with Bishop Walter, in the early 1230s Blanche contributed to the construction of the new Dominican house in Chartres, providing it with glazing and liturgical objects and fabrics emblazoned with her golden castles.[128]

Blanche's own first two major building projects were in Louis VIII's memory – the Cistercian abbey of Royaumont and a new infirmary hall for the Hôtel-Dieu in Paris. Finished by 1232, the Hôtel-Dieu hall has vanished without trace. It contained within it an altar dedicated to Thomas Becket, and one might surmise that it was designed with an integrated chapel, containing the altar, opening directly off the hall to the east. This had become the standard design for hospital infirmary halls by the late thirteenth century, but most hospitals constructed in France in the twelfth century, including the hospitals at Le Mans and Angers built under the patronage of Henry II and his entourage, had separate halls and chapels. The integrated hall and chapel arrangement was probably inspired by the new emphasis on the Eucharist at the Fourth Lateran and the other reformist councils, and Blanche's infirmary hall may have been been one of the first in France to have reflected the new demands. It must, at all events, have been a fine architectural statement, at the very centre of the Capetian capital.[129]

Royaumont has left substantial traces (see pl. 8). It was built very fast. Work cannot have begun before late 1227, but the high altar of the abbey church was dedicated in 1232 and the church itself in 1236, both important courtly gatherings. Philip Dagobert was buried there in 1234.[130] The abbey buildings must have been constructed almost at the same time, since they were crucial to the monks who staffed the abbey. Building was still under way in 1238, when 300 *livres* were paid 'for works' from the royal coffers.[131] The church was close in size to a cathedral such as Soissons. It had an elaborate east end with ambulatory and radiating chapels, and an elegant elevation with traceried clerestory windows and a traceried triforium (see pl. 17). The plan resembled that of the Cistercian abbey of Longpont.

The delicate tracery reflected approaches to masonry that had emerged and developed in the workshops of the great Gothic cathedrals of Reims and, particularly, Amiens, and had probably begun to appear in smaller abbey churches and larger parish churches in Paris and the Paris area by the late 1220s. The tracery designs feature trilobes or quatrefoils above cusped arches, resembling tracery on the towers and upper levels of Notre-Dame in Paris, which was still in the 1220s in the process of completion. But Royaumont did not have the vast sheets of glass that characterised Saint-Denis, and its tracery forms appear lumpen, heavy and old-fashioned in comparison to the sharp, slender designs in the latter – and marginally later – building.[132]

The other great building campaign undertaken by Blanche of Castile during the minority was the fortification of the town and the castle of Angers. She had had to cede the city to Peter of Dreux at the Treaty of Vendôme in 1227, but she had many loyal supporters in the area, including the Blaison, Craon and des Roches families, and she took it back into royal control in 1230. Fortifying the fine, rich city of her ancestors against the restive Peter and Henry III was an obvious move. But the scale of the work was massive, and the architectural conception magnificent. The walls are 3 metres thick. This castle was built to withstand the latest siege engines and mining techniques. Seventeen huge, evenly spaced mural towers plunge down into a cavernous fosse. They were striped in sandstone, limestone and slate, to recall the land wall at Constantinople, or Richard the Lionheart's Château-Gaillard. Their size – they are 130 feet (40m) high – made Philip Augustus's tower at the Louvre look puny. There was no great tower keep. This was one of the first castles to foreshadow a new trend – the focus on gatehouses rather than principal towers. At Angers, one great gate tower led into the town; the other, the Porte des Champs, opened out into the countryside beyond (see pl. 9). Both great gate towers made impressive entrances, bristling with arrow slits, machicolation and the latest defensive measures; but they were also majestically vaulted above sculpted corbels. The grandeur of the conception – the fortification of the castle was integrated into the fortification of the entire city on both sides of the river – was reminiscent of Château-Gaillard, as was the speed of construction. Houses were compulsorily purchased and destroyed to build the huge wall around the town and the castle in its midst. The lands and properties of the Church were not immune, and Blanche's masons impounded stones worked ready for Angers Cathedral from its workshops. The royal coffers disbursed 500 *livres* to the town in compensation, as well as several separate settlements to individual ecclesiastical institutions. Most

work was done in 1232; by 1234 construction was more or less complete. Blanche had the payments, and probably the organisation of the works, overseen by her trusted clerks, Master P – probably Peter – and Master Thomas Pigris. In 1234 they accounted for 4,422 *livres* on the works on the castle itself. The letter from William des Ormes describing the siege of Carcassonne suggests that Blanche took a close and informed interest in the design of fortifications.[133]

The household accounts reveal the continual work of repair, building and rebuilding at the various royal residences. In 1234 there were works at Vincennes, Crépy-en-Valois, Pierrefonds, Compiègne, Saint-Germain-en-Laye, Melun, Pontoise, Laon, Péronne and other towns in Artois, together with works on Philip Augustus's halls at Paris, all funded from the revenues of the relevant *prévôtés*.[134] Particular efforts were made when it was known that the court would be arriving, especially for one of the great courtly events. A sum of 61 *livres* was spent to prepare the castle of Beaumont-sur-Oise for royal occupation in 1234.[135] The marriage of Louis and Margaret at Sens led to a flurry of work: 106 *livres* was spent on works for the queen at Villeneuve – presumably Villeneuve-sur-Yonne just south of Sens, where Philip Augustus had had one of his high towers built.[136] The accounts of 1248 record works at the royal residences of Fontainebleau, Montargis and Villeneuve, and the king's houses at Sens. The queen's chapel was the focus of attention at Fontainebleau; new windows were inserted in her chapel at Montargis, and the queen's chamber at Villeneuve was panelled.[137] It may be that this was done for Queen Margaret, as she accompanied Louis at the start of the Crusade; but it would mean that a ruling, and thus itinerant, queen regent would find her quarters in the royal houses in good order.

When Louis IX acceded to his personal rule, he developed two new architectural projects, both palace chapels: the chapel at Saint-Germain-en-Laye, then the chapel at the palace on the Ile de la Cité in Paris, built to house the newly acquired Crown of Thorns. Works to the park and the house of the king at Saint-Germain-en-Laye had begun already in 1234.[138] The new chapel there was finished in 1238. The old chapel had been served by monks of Coulombs, when the court was in residence. Now Louis insisted, to some resistance, that it was served by a permanent staff of chaplains.[139] In 1239 it was fitted out with eight candelabra and an image, presumably to place on the altar, purchased at Tours for 12 *livres*.[140]

The new chapel at Saint-Germain-en-Laye has huge windows, divided by delicate tracery lancets surmounted by rosettes, which must have glowed with stained glass. There was no space for a window on the west wall, which abutted the rest

of the palace, but a whirling wheel of elaborate blind tracery filled the blank wall. Here, as elsewhere in the chapel, blank areas of wall, and the slender stone shafts, ribs and arches, would have been delicately picked out in paint. Louis did not use the master masons who had worked at Royaumont for this – perhaps they were still too busy. Instead, he employed a master and team who had designed and were building the new abbey church at Saint-Denis.[141] Perhaps it was Louis himself who asked for the Master of Saint-Denis. Perhaps he left such practical matters to his curial clerks: Walter and Aubry Cornut were after all first cousins of Eudes Clément, the abbot who had launched the works at Saint-Denis.

When the Crown of Thorns arrived in Paris in 1239, it was housed initially in the chapel of Saint-Nicolas, built more than a century earlier by Louis VI, in the palace on the Ile de la Cité. Unsurprisingly, a new chapel to display the precious relic was soon under consideration. Construction probably begun around 1240. The chapel was basically finished when a college of canons was formally established there in 1246; it was dedicated on 26 April 1248. Expensive works in gold, silver and stone for the relics in the chapel, together with the work of a gilder and a goldsmith, are recorded in the accounts of 1248.[142] By 1246 Louis was planning a Crusade, and the dedication of the chapel, and subsequent displays of the relics there, became an important part of the extended ceremonial taking up of the Cross.[143]

For this chapel, Louis and his clerks turned to a different architect. The architect is unknown, but art historians agree that he had worked on the cathedral of Amiens. The Sainte-Chapelle was very different from the intimate family chapel at Saint-Germain-en-Laye. It was the chapel of the king's main palace, the centre of his government and his kingdom, where he would appear with the full court, with ambassadors and fellow rulers. It was designed to house and display relics of profound import, which would be shown to pilgrims. It was a very public building. As a result it was very big. The upper chapel, with its vast windows, has the scale of a cathedral clerestory, and it rises above a lower chapel of considerable size. It is not surprising that those who had charge of the commissioning of the architect should turn to one who had experience of working on one of the gigantic High Gothic cathedrals.

Art historians have often castigated the result as being, from a purely architectural point of view, slightly old-fashioned, a little dull and safe. By the 1240s Parisian architects like Pierre of Montreuil were producing more experimental tracery, with a sharp, linear quality, like a drawing; in fact, the lower chapel at the

Sainte-Chapelle features this sort of work. But size, and a certain bold grandeur of conception, was what mattered at the Sainte-Chapelle. It is often described as a reliquary turned inside out, and to an extent that is true. But it tends to distract attention from the fact that this chapel needed to be, and was, huge in scale.[144]

The architecture provided an imposing frame for the rich sequence of painted images, on wall and window in the upper chapel, which must have mattered more than the stonework to Louis and his entourage. The images, especially the glowing glass, told the history of salvation from the Creation until the End of Time. Old Testament imagery in the side walls flanked the Christological cycle in the apse, which culminated, in the axial bay, with the Crucifixion, with a stress on the Crown of Thorns and the True Cross, which were displayed as relics on the Grande Chasse below. Biblical models of kingship and queenship featured in the windows – David, Solomon and Christ himself, and Queen Esther, who interceded with the king for her people. The Jewish leaders enumerated in the biblical book of Numbers, none of them kings, are here shown in the very act of coronation. Louis, his mother and his brothers are given their place in this history. The west-ernmost window on the south side of the chapel, placed in the sequence just before the Last Judgement on the west wall, shows the story of the acquisition, the reception and the housing of the Crown of Thorns by the king of France and his family (see pl. 13).[145]

There is no evidence as to who, among the curial clerks, was charged with overseeing the building of the Sainte-Chapelle. Louis's principal chaplain, Brother Matthew, together with Brother John of the Great Bridge, organised the payments for the works to display the relics in 1248 and, at the same time, for works at Royaumont, including crosses and various subsidiary buildings.[146] There is no evidence as to who planned the complex iconographic programme of the upper chapel. Walter Cornut organised the reception and initial display of the relics, and his 'Libellus' on the reception of the Crown of Thorns established the overall intel-lectual context in which the iconographic programme was developed. He empha-sised the special position of 'our France' and her king within the history of the world: he emphasised the manner in which the possession of Christ's own crown underlined that; and the appropriateness of France, and the king of France, as guardians of this special relic. The narrative in the window showing the reception of the relic was derived from Walter's 'Libellus'. But Walter died in the spring of 1241, just as works on the chapel were starting.[147]

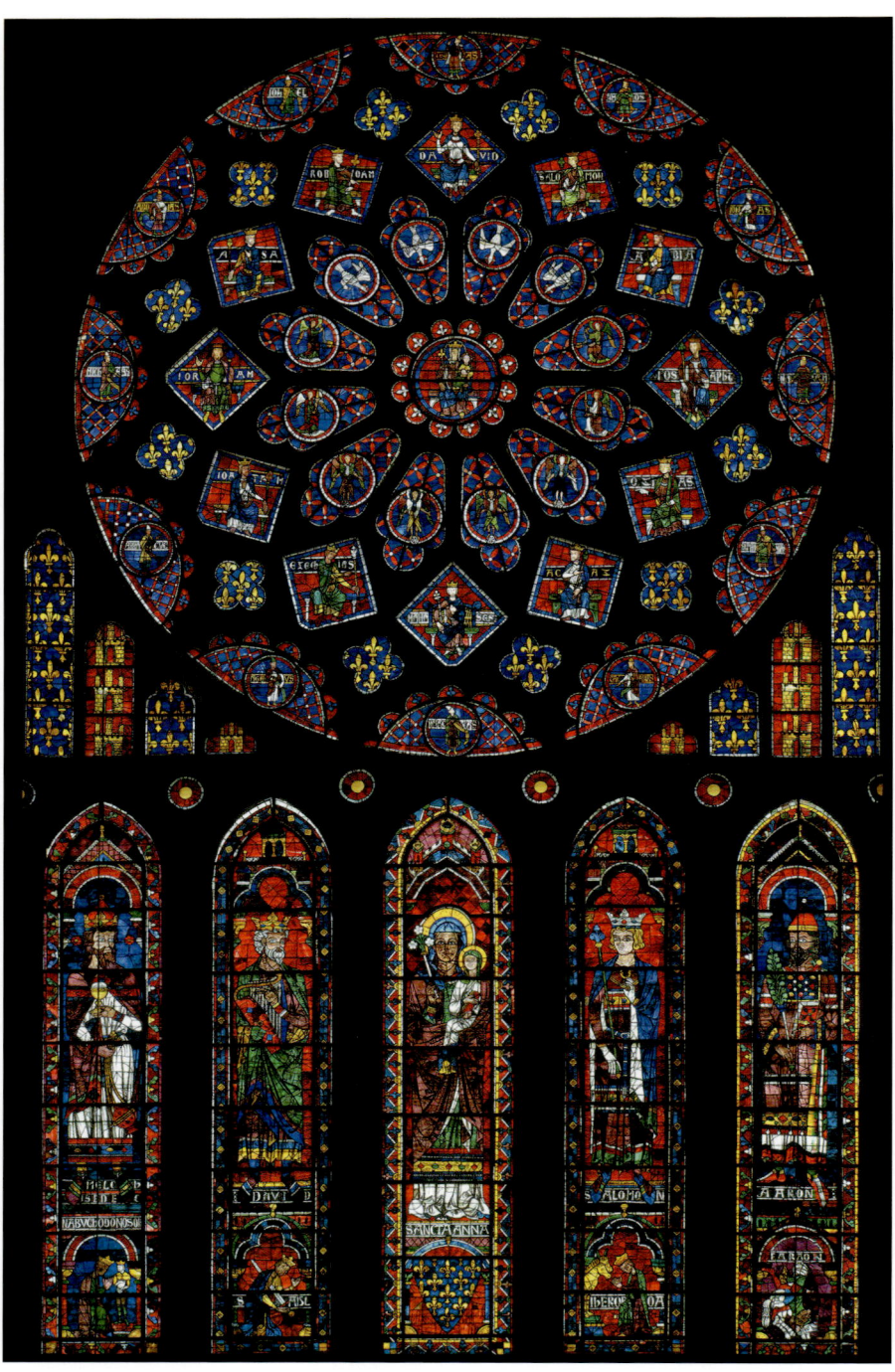

1   The north transept window of Chartres Cathedral, with the arms of France and Castile.

2   Giles of Paris, the 'Karolinus', Paris, Bibliothèque Nationale de France, MS lat. 6191, frontispiece: detail showing Giles presenting his book to the future Louis VIII.

3   Moralised bible, Vienna, Österreichische Nationalbibliothek, Cod. Vindob. 1179, f. 246r, detail showing Louis VIII holding a moralised bible.

ut sedeant mecum: ambulans in uia im
maculata hic michi ministrabat.
Non habitabit in medio domus mee qui
facit superbiam: qui loquitur iniqua
non direxit in conspectu oculorum meorum.
In matutino interficiebam omnes peccato
res terre: ut disperderem de ciuitate domi
ni omnes opantes iniquitatem. Quintus

oracionem meam:
et clamor meus ad
te ueniat.
Non auertas fa
ciem tuam a me in
quacunq; die tribu
lor: inclina ad me
aurem tuam.

In quacunq; die inuocauero

4   Psalter of Blanche of Castile, Paris, Bibliothèque de l'Arsenal, MS lat. 1186, f. 122v, Blanche
at prayer.

5 (ABOVE LEFT)   Psalter of Blanche of Castile, Paris, Bibliothèque de l'Arsenal, MS lat. 1186, f. 9v, 'Fall of the Rebel Angels'.

6 (ABOVE RIGHT)   Psalter of Blanche of Castile, Paris, Bibliothèque de l'Arsenal, MS lat. 1186, f. 170, 'Last Judgement'.

7 (FACING PAGE)   Psalter of Blanche of Castile, Paris, Bibliothèque de l'Arsenal, MS lat. 1186, f. 168, 'Conversion of the Jews and the Beginnings of the Reign of Antichrist'.

8 Abbey of Royaumont: general view from the south-east.

9 Castle of Angers, the Porte des Champs.

10 Abbey of Maubuisson, showing the conventual buildings from the west.

11 Abbey of Maubuisson, showing the conventual buildings from the east.

12 (ABOVE) Villeneuve-l'Archevêque: the north portal added to the parish church, probably in 1239.

13 (LEFT) Detail of the Relic Window from the Sainte-Chapelle, probably showing the ostension of the Crown of Thorns on the temporary scaffolding at Saint-Antoine-des-Champs.

15 (FACING PAGE BOTTOM) The chasuble of St Edmund of Abingdon, now in Provins, Musée de Provins et du Provinois, inv. MP 1173. The chasuble is made from a magnificent green lampas silk from Spain. Blanche gave green silk robes to her cousin Raymond of Toulouse and to Countess Matilda of Boulogne for her marriage to Blanche's nephew Alphonse of Portugal. It is possible that St Edmund was given the silk for this chasuble by Blanche.

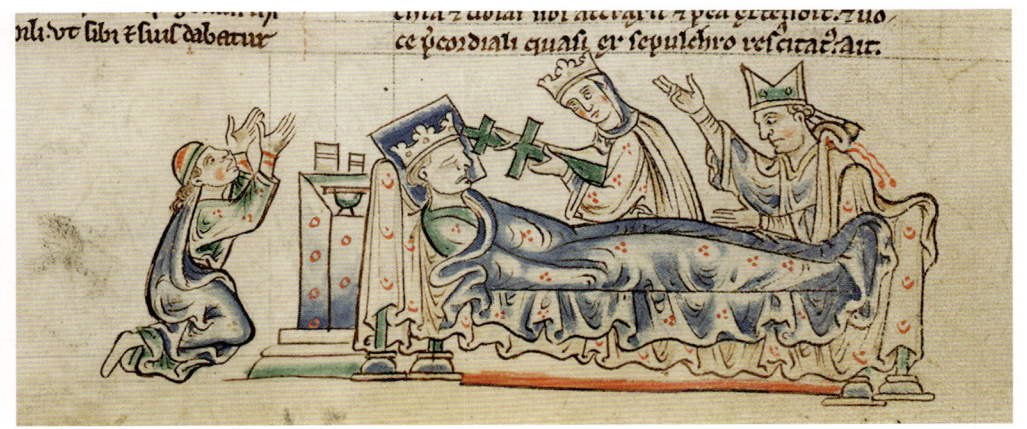

14 Matthew Paris, '*Chronica majora*', Cambridge, Corpus Christi MS 1611, f.183r, detail showing Blanche of Castile at the bedside of St Louis, when he took the Cross on recovering from his illness in winter 1244–5.

17 (ABOVE) Abbey of Maubuisson:
the cloister lavabo, reconstruction drawing of
one of its bays by Monique Wabont.

16 (LEFT) Abbey of Royaumont:
the remains of the north transept.

18 (FACING PAGE TOP LEFT) Abbey of
Le Lys: the east window of the church.

19 (FACING PAGE TOP RIGHT) Le Lys
Crosier, now in the Musée Lambinet,
Versailles, detail of the rock crystal head.

20 (FACING PAGE BOTTOM) Abbey of
Le Lys, showing the remains of the abbey
church.

In nomine sancte et individue Trinitatis Amen. Universis in fide catholica viventibus ad quos presens scriptum pervenerit Blancha dei gratia Regina Francorum Salutem in eo qui est vera Salus...

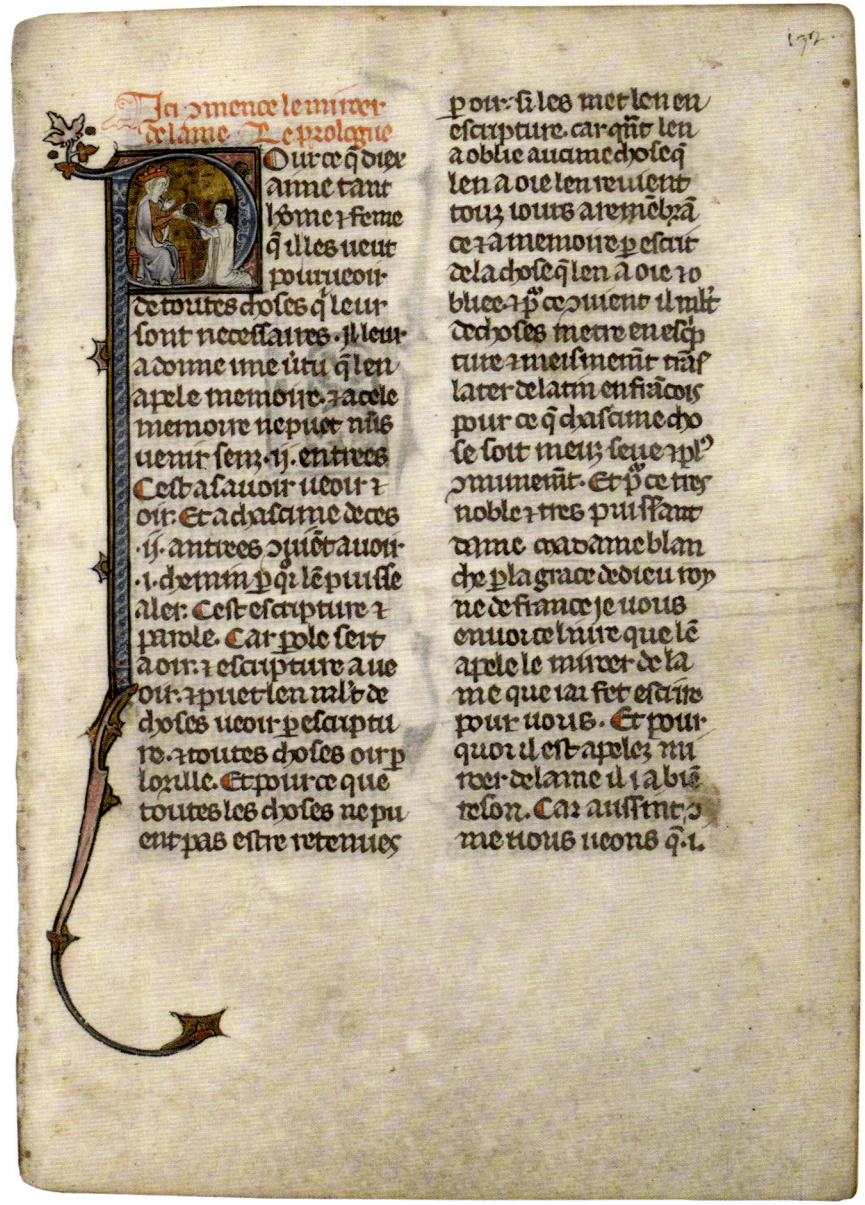

24 (ABOVE) Presentation page of the 'Miroir de l'âme', Paris, Bibliothèque Mazarine, MS 870, f. 192, showing a Cistercian nun presenting the work to a queen of France.

21 (FACING PAGE TOP) The foundation charter for Maubuisson, Archives Départementales du Val d'Oise, 72H115.

22 and 23 (FACING PAGE BOTTOM) Seal and counterseal of Blanche of Castile, from the foundation charter for Maubuisson, Archives Départementales du Val d'Oise, 72H115.

26 (LEFT)   Moralised bible,
Vienna, Österreichische
Nationalbibliothek,
Cod. Vindob. 2554, f. 3v,
detail showing God destroying
astronomers and philosophers,
in the lower roundel.

27 (LEFT)   Moralised bible,
Vienna, Österreichische
Nationalbibliothek,
Cod. Vindob. 1179, f. 82,
detail showing clerks doing
business with Jewish
moneylenders, in the lower
roundel.

25 (FACING PAGE)   Psalter of
Blanche of Castile, Paris,
Bibliothèque de l'Arsenal,
MS lat. 1186, f. IV,
'The Astronomers'.

28 (TOP)   The tomb of Philip Dagobert from Royaumont, now at the abbey of Saint-Denis.

29 (ABOVE LEFT)   The black Tournai marble tomb of Mary, empress of Constantinople, possibly originally intended for Blanche of Castile, from Maubuisson, now at the abbey of Saint-Denis.

30 (ABOVE RIGHT)   Tomb of Alphonse of France and John of Anjou at the collegiate church in Poissy, from the Gaignières Collection 4922, Paris, Bibliothèque Nationale de France, MS Est. Rés. Pe IIC, f. 48.

How far was Blanche involved in these two palace chapel projects? There is nothing to suggest her involvement at Saint-Germain-en-Laye. The Sainte-Chapelle is a different matter. She played a major role in the negotiations, the redemption and the reception of the Crown of Thorns, working closely with Walter Cornut. The staging of the dramatic display of the relic at the Cistercian nunnery of Saint-Antoine before its final triumphal entry into the city of Paris must have been devised by the two of them: it was implemented with the assistance of trusted members of her household, Denis the Scutifer and Peter Pig-Flesh. In the chapel itself, her presence is stamped all over the glass in the form of her personal crest, the castle of Castile that she had engraved on her counterseal. Just before the choirscreen, two private pews are set into the wall on either side of the upper chapel, one presumably for the king, the other for the queen. Above the southern pew, the windows tell the story of the Old Testament heroine Queen Esther, who interceded for her people with queenly grace. Next to this window is that other Old Testament heroine, Judith, who led her people with conspicuous courage. Both women are evoked as models for a queen in the coronation orders. Doubtless many in court circles who saw those windows would have found themselves thinking of Blanche. If they needed reminding, the golden castles of Castile on their rich red ground were there to do so, especially in the Esther window, more forcefully than in any other part of the chapel (see illustration on back of jacket). But Margaret was the reigning queen consort, the woman who might be expected to accompany the king during ceremonies and services within the palace chapel. Yet the pales of Provence are nowhere to be found.

By the late 1230s Blanche had ample building projects of her own.[148] The most significant was the new Cistercian nunnery of Maubuisson, founded and built at a cost of 24,431 *livres* between 1236 and 1242.[149] The dormitory, the chapter house, cloister with fountain, the church and a house for the queen were ready for occupation in 1241. The church was ready for its dedication in June 1244.[150] The project was run by Blanche's trusted official, Master Richard of Tourny, under her close scrutiny.[151] Master Richard's accounts, copied into the *Achatz d'heritage*, reveal much about the building process.[152] They are written in a Latin that frequently slips into French, especially when dealing with building materials. No architect as such is named on the accounts, though a major role was played by Master Robert the Carpenter.[153] A group of trusted purveyors were employed repeatedly, including Master Geoffrey the Norman, John Morier, who provided the timber for the dormitory, Jacob of Soissons and Andrew Sallenbien, all of whom specialised in the

provision of timber.[154] Some providers, like William de la Broce and Walter of Viez-Conches (Vielles-Conches), furnished wood already worked into panelling.[155] Some purveyors, like Robert Racine and John Morier, provided both wood and stone.[156]

Cut stone was brought from quarries along the Oise. Occasionally, it is listed in the accounts as 'corbels', presumably pre-cut in the quarry. The amounts of timber required for scaffolding, for roofs and for panelling and wainscoting, were prodigious. Much of it was supplied by Normans – Master Geoffrey the Norman, Robert of Rouen and Walter of Vielles Conches – probably from the forests of the Evreçin in eastern Normandy. Some of the main cloister walks, and the infirmary cloister, may have been timber.[157] Paving stones were cut and laid. Vast numbers of tiles were fired, some in green and red, for roofs and floors. John the Tiler is, apart from Master Robert the Carpenter, the only named craftsman.

The tile makers also provided tile pipes for drainage. Elaborate provision for water was put in place before the substructures were built, with a sophisticated system of aqueducts to bring fresh water and drainage channels to evacuate used waters. In 1239 compensation was paid for damage to a house during the works to supply spring water to the abbey.[158] The fountain or lavabo in the cloister, at the heart of the water system, was built in 1239, at a cost of 219 *livres*.[159]

The east claustral range, the chapter house, fragments of the church, the great barn and a remarkably intact set of latrines still stand (see pls 10, 11). The plan of the church, with substantial transept and apsidal east end, reflected, not surprisingly, that of Saint-Antoine. The scale of the church was larger than any of the surviving aristocratic foundations within France, but at 60 metres in length is comparable to Joanna of Flanders' Marquette, which it resembles in plan.[160] The cloister lavabo, with a traceried pavilion above a tiered fountain facing the entrance to the refectory, was discovered in excavations between 1978 and 1983 (see pl. 17). Elegance and fine workmanship, with a certain measured magnificence appropriate to a royal Cistercian house, mark the work at Maubuisson.

Building works began on Blanche's other foundation, the Cistercian nunnery of Le Lys, in 1244, just as those at Maubuisson were completed.[161] Unlike Maubuisson, almost no evidence about the building process has survived. Perhaps Blanche asked Richard of Tourny to oversee the project as he had Maubuisson, but Richard was based at Pontoise, and she is more likely to have used a clerk based at Melun, Corbeil or Etampes. In 1248 the new abbey was inspected and found to be ready for the nuns to move in.[162] The foundation charter issued in June 1248 by St Louis

describes the dormitory, refectory and cellar as complete.[163] The choir of the abbey church must have been finished and usable. But works were continuing, for a second charter issued by Louis in July 1248 provides wood for construction purposes.[164] The house was sufficiently complete for Blanche and her entourage to stay there in October 1251.[165]

The church, now ruined and roofless, was slightly smaller than Maubuisson, with a square east end where Maubuisson was apsidal (pls 18, 20). The sophisticated design of triple lancets, triple roses and a trefoil in the tracery of the east window reveals that this too was a building of appropriately restrained elegance. The profile of each element in the tracery at Le Lys is a simple chamfer, and the windows gain elegance from the fact that all their mouldings are continuous – there are no capitals to mark the arch springings within the windows. The elegant simplicity of the Lys windows has been related to other churches, usually parish churches or grand priories, in the Oise and Valois, areas that Blanche knew well, such as Agnetz, Chambly and the Victorine house of Saint-Martin-aux-Bois. Similar approaches to window design are found in slightly later buildings in northern Burgundy: Villeneuve-sur-Yonne, Saint-Urbain at Troyes, Saint-Thibaut-en-Auxois and Mussey-sur-Seine. What the tracery at Le Lys does not resemble is the surviving tracery from Maubuisson, which comes from the cloister fountain (cf. pls 17 and 18). Here profiles are rounded, and the points at which the arch heads spring are clearly marked by capitals. The master mason at the two abbeys was not, it seems, the same man.

As she had her two new foundations built, Blanche seems to have taken over the architectural patronage of three other Cistercian nunneries: Le Parc, La Joie-lès-Nemours and Le Trésor. Le Parc, founded by Eleanor of Vermandois in 1204, lay just outside Blanche's dower town of Crèpy-en-Valois. Blanche stayed at the abbey in 1241; in the following year she gave the nuns 30 *livres* to complete the refectory.[166] La Joie-lès-Nemours had been founded in 1231 by Philip of Nemours, a member of the family of Ours the Chamberlain. In 1236 Blanche supported its affiliation to the order of Cîteaux.[167] In 1239 she gave the nuns 90 *livres* to build their dormitory. In 1241 she paid for windows, presumably in the church, and other works there.[168]

Nemours was very much a Capetian household affair. It is less clear why Blanche took the Norman Cistercian nunnery of Le Trésor, founded in 1227 by a small local lord, under her wing. It was on the very edge of Normandy, above the valley of the Epte, so not far from Pontoise and close to the royal castle at Vernon.

Blanche may have found it a useful staging post on her way to Rouen. Amaury of Montfort supported its affiliation to the order of Cîteaux in 1236, and may have persuaded her to take an interest.[169] At all events, in 1241 and 1242 she gave 100 *livres* for the dormitory, another 100 *livres* for building works and then 20 *livres* to finish the cloister. Master Richard of Tourny dispensed some of those monies.[170] Le Trésor was not far from Maubuisson. Given that much of the wood for Maubuisson was supplied from Normandy, it is likely that works at Le Trésor were undertaken by members of the Maubuisson team. The east claustral range built by Blanche survives. It is much less ambitious than the works at her own two founda- tions, but was perhaps the first building in Normandy to use the Rayonnant style, with Parisian tracery and abaci pointed in the direction of the rib that sprang from them. It resembles surviving work from Maubuisson.[171]

Blanche's household accounts reveal the existence of one other major building project of the early 1240s, though the building itself has disappeared without trace – a new hospital at Corbeil. Master Richard handled some of the funds spent on this project; but Master Robert of Gonesse was charged with organising most of the works. The considerable sums of 190 *livres* are recorded in her accounts but are unlikely to represent the full extent of her expenditure on it.[172]

Blanche's gifts specifically for building works at Le Parc, Le Trésor, La Joie and the hospital at Corbeil are known only from her household accounts. A large number of charters from Le Parc, Le Trésor and La Joie survive, but none of them records Blanche's architectural patronage. They do record the properties and annual revenues that she gave for the running of these abbeys. This has important implica- tions for assessing Blanche as an architectural patron. The surviving accounts for her own household cover little more than a year of her life. The inevitable conclu- sion is that only a fraction of Blanche's architectural and artistic patronage is recorded.

•

How do Blanche's building projects relate to other contemporary royal works? The obvious comparison is Cistercian Royaumont, theoretically a work of the king, though one in which Blanche had a guiding hand. Royaumont was a male house, and thus inevitably grander in scale than Blanche's nunneries. It had an ambulatory with radiating chapels, while Maubuisson had an apsidal and Le Lys a flat east end. But there are parallels. The three-level nave elevation at Le Lys, with columnar piers and a trefoil-headed triforium opening, is a simplified version of the elevation

of Royaumont; Maubuisson was probably similar. Decorative elements such as corbels, capitals and bases, and rib and arch profiles, at Maubuisson are very similar to those at Royaumont. The fragment from the cloister fountain arcade at Maubuisson is almost identical in both pattern and profile to the fragment from the triforium at Royaumont (pls 16 and 17). This is not surprising. The two abbeys were very close, both set just off the Oise. Since some stones were delivered ready cut into corbels at Maubuisson, it is possible that they came from the quarries supplying Royaumont.

Both Royaumont and Maubuisson have similar conspicuously sophisticated and meticulously planned water systems, including magnificent latrine provision. Moreover, excavations in the 1990s revealed a water system at the royal manor house of Vincennes with a central fountain using tile pipes almost identical to those at Maubuisson. Works were under way at Vincennes in 1234, before Louis's majority, and may have been as much on Blanche's initiative as Louis's.[173] It seems certain that the same specialist water engineers were involved on the two abbey sites and the royal manor house. Water provision for Le Lys has never been explored.

The elegantly linear tracery at Le Lys cannot be paralleled at Maubuisson, or in any of the other royal works between 1230 and the early 1250s. The parallel with Victorine Saint-Martin-aux-Bois is intriguing, given Blanche's closeness to the Victorines. Saint-Martin-aux-Bois is the sole surviving Victorine building in the Ile-de-France from this period. The parallels with Villeneuve-sur-Yonne and later north Burgundian churches are suggestive too. Blanche and the court stayed often in the castle at Villeneuve, with works recorded there in 1234 and 1248.[174] The record of works at Villeneuve, and the revelations of the excavations at Vincennes, are reminders of the fact that what survives is a mere fraction of the royal works in Blanche's lifetime, and that much of that work was secular and domestic.

Robert Branner characterised the architecture that most historians have associated with Blanche – Royaumont, Maubuisson and Le Lys – as one of restraint, in comparison to the much more elaborate and courtly works produced for St Louis at Saint-Germain-en-Laye and the Sainte-Chapelle.[175] But the three buildings that Branner assigned to Blanche are all Cistercian abbeys, while the two he assigned to St Louis were palace chapels: one would expect decorous restraint in the former and courtliness in the latter. And as Cistercian abbeys go, Royaumont's restraint is limited. After Blanche's death, the Cistercian general chapter plucked up the courage to censure the abbot of Royaumont for enriching the church with too

much sculpture and colour.[176] Although the new chapel at Saint-Germain-en-Laye was built on Louis's initiative, most historians suspect that Blanche had some involvement in the Sainte-Chapelle, given her ubiquitous castles in the glazing and the crucial role that she played in the acquisition of the Crown of Thorns. Besides, Blanche's other great project of the early 1230s was the great castle and city fortification at Angers. Branner's distinction between Blanche's architectural restraint and Louis's courtliness was based on a view of Blanche's character informed by Geoffrey of Beaulieu. It was Blanche who revelled in the rich texture of courtly life, not the over-fastidious Louis.

St Louis turned, not to architects working for the court at Royaumont, but to architects and masons who had begun working at Saint-Denis in the early 1230s for Saint-Germain-en-Laye, and then to architects from Paris and Amiens for the Sainte-Chapelle. This raises the issue of how the royal works related to other great works of the time. How far did royal works give an architectural lead? Should historians talk, as Branner did, of a 'court style'?[177]

Most historians agree that the building that really established the new 'Rayonnant' style was the abbey church of Saint-Denis, rebuilt by Abbot Eudes Clément from 1231. Major projects at other Parisian abbeys developed the new style, at Saint-Martin-des-Champs, with a fine new refectory, built in the early 1230s, and even more at Saint-Germain-des-Prés, with a new refectory and then a sharply elegant Lady chapel built by the Paris master Pierre of Montreuil in the 1240s. Major works were under way at the cathedral of Notre-Dame in Paris throughout this period, and the workshops there also acted as architectural forcing houses. These projects were not funded by the king, and were clearly not part of the royal works. The new Rayonnant style was as much the style of the vibrant city of Paris as of the court, and St Louis was able to draw on those working in it for his two palace chapels.[178]

If the new work at Saint-Denis was funded by the abbey itself, it was, of course, well known in court circles. The abbey drew its prestige from its place as the burial house of kings and the guardian of the royal regalia. The new church, with its hugely developed transept area, was designed from the start to offer more space for royal tombs and royal ceremonials, such as the elaborate anniversary commemorations of dead kings and the acceptance of the *oriflamme*, Charlemagne's banner, before the king went to war. Blanche and Louis were present at the consecrations that marked the building process, and the abbot, Eudes Clément, sought

their permission before he began the rebuilding. He was Walter Cornut's cousin, and was often at court and on intimate terms with both Blanche and Louis. The new building at Saint-Denis was not part of the royal works, but it was a commission at the very centre of court circles.

The chronology of the new Rayonnant style is in itself suggestive. Whether court projects, or projects initiated by the great ecclesiastical institutions, or adjustments at the north French cathedrals, the elegant and elaborate new traceried architecture emerged in the early 1230s, with Royaumont acting, to an extent, as a precursor. It coincides with Blanche's wardship of the kingdom as regent, once she had dealt with the threats of the start of the reign. The flowering of the Rayonnant style around 1230 may not make it a court style, but it suggests that the queen's preparedness to undertake great projects herself from about 1228 acted as an important architectural stimulus.

•

The court at which Blanche arrived in 1200 was probably the dullest in western Europe; by 1250 it was probably the most brilliant. Philip Augustus had made Paris the administrative capital of Capetian France; Blanche made it the cultural capital not just of France but also of Europe, with wide cultural influence. The architecture associated with the royal court and with Paris was copied throughout Europe. A satirical poem claimed that Henry III wanted to take the Sainte-Chapelle home with him when he saw it in 1258. At least one moralised bible ended up in England, and probably inspired the late thirteenth-century English tradition of illustrated Apocalypse manuscripts.[179]

Blanche did not impose the cultural centrality of the royal court alone, of course. Her literary and knightly husband, Louis VIII, matched her in introducing a book culture, an intellectual culture and a chivalric culture of hunting, poetry and song to the Capetian court. Between them, they encouraged poets, artists and intellectuals who had previously been associated with baronial courts, or the university, to gravitate to the royal court. But Blanche seems to have understood the importance of architecture as the theatre of royal power and the demonstration of royal piety in a way that Louis VIII did not. The complex flavours of the court in the second quarter of the thirteenth century reflected the contribution of Louis IX, determined to express his kingship in fine architecture, the music-loving and jocular Robert of Artois, the cultured and 'courteous player' Alphonse of Poitiers, pious and learned Isabella and clever, poetry-writing Charles, under Blanche's own presiding genius.

Although the young St Louis almost outdid his mother in the brilliance of his architectural patronage, by the time he returned from the Crusade in 1254 he had lost his taste for courtly architecture.[180] He established a royal library on his return, though most of his books were quite plain. After 1261 minstrels and *jongleurs* were no longer allowed at court.[181] The brilliance of Capetian court culture coincided absolutely with Blanche's long dominance as princess and queen. It reflected her own vibrant and enquiring intellect, her understanding of the importance of show in the articulation of power, her intense and questing piety, and her rich sensual enjoyment of colour, texture, conversation, poetry and music.

II

Legitimacy and Authority

Blanche's life and career as niece, wife and mother, as princess, queen consort, queen regent and queen mother, illuminate several aspects of thirteenth-century governance – of the legitimate basis for royal power, of what rulers thought they were trying to do in ruling, and how they might achieve their ends; of how rulers, especially women rulers, were perceived. These issues are explored in this chapter and the next. This chapter situates Blanche's career as a person of power within the theories and practices of rulership of her time. Chapter Twelve assesses Blanche's contribution to the governance of France in the thirteenth century.

In the Introduction, I noted the useful distinction often drawn between power – informal influence – and authority, defined as an 'officially sanctioned right to make decisions binding on others'.[1] I noted too the way that historians have distinguished, often implicitly, between the sort of power that is able to obtain its ends by executive government, supported by the means of coercion, and the sort of power that obtains its ends by the exercise of influence, by the use of gesture or ritual, or by the manipulation of image. As noted in the Introduction, most historians of queenship have given these typologies of power a gendered meaning. They see authority and executive government backed by the means of coercion as pertaining to the king; they see the queen's power deriving from and displayed in influence, intercession, gesture, ritual, religious devotion and cultural patronage. Blanche's life and career, in conjunction with those of her husband and sons, contradict this gendered reading of power. A king has authority, but so does a

female ruler in her own right, or a regent whatever their gender. A queen consort, like Blanche, who was crowned and anointed to office, had fully sanctioned authority from her coronation. On the other hand, the king's brother, or oldest son, unless he had been made associate king, must be content with the power to influence. And Blanche, like her husband and her sons – for one should include Charles of Anjou as well as St Louis – used the full register of powers, coercive, magisterial, through to devotional and cultural patronage, gesture and ritual as appropriate. And the authority of all rulers, whether male or female, was subject to the grubby realities of power politics and the critiques of the Church.

•

The Gregorian reforms of the late eleventh century generated a strong critique of secular power and authority by the Church. Extreme positions were taken on both sides, especially in the Empire. By the second quarter of the twelfth century a workable if uneasy stasis had been reached. The standard ecclesiastical view of kings was clearly articulated by Ivo of Chartres in his *Decretum*. God in his anger had given kings to the people of Israel, because they were not competent to govern themselves. If people found themselves suffering under a bad king, they must put up with it, for a people got the ruler they deserved, and a bad king merely reflected their own sinfulness.[2] In practice, most churchmen found strong royal rule easier to live with than private war between members of the aristocracy. French churchmen like Abbot Suger of Saint-Denis looked with envy on the firm rule of English kings like Henry I or, later, the young Henry II.[3] But Henry II's desire to see equitable justice and peace within his realm conflicted with the Church's insistence that criminous clerks should be subject only to the judgement of the Church. Becket's intransigent defence of the Church's position and his resulting death – his martyrdom, in the Church's view – encouraged a fresh critique of royal power in the late twelfth century, especially in the schools of Paris, for Becket and his party had strong connections there, and spent their exile in or within easy reach of the French capital.[4] Louis VII made considerable political capital out of his support of Becket, and thus, by implication, of Becket's views of the limits of royal authority over churchmen, but it meant that Philip Augustus did not dare to challenge the Paris scholars in 1200.[5] The most viciously spiteful attacks on Blanche came from the Paris scholars, because she did challenge them in 1227.

Even before the Becket controversy, the Paris schools were generating newly sophisticated critiques of royal power. In the late 1150s John of Salisbury, later one

of Becket's great defenders, wrote his book, *Policraticus*, for Becket as he became Henry II's chancellor. John repeated Ivo of Chartres' formulas about kingship, and the need simply to suffer vicious kingship; but then in some passages he contradicted himself, arguing that it might be right, in certain circumstances, to kill a tyrant. In support of this undoubtedly shocking thesis, he cited the biblical example of Judith, among others. Talk of rebelling against a tyrant may have been relatively common in ecclesiastical circles in mid-twelfth-century Paris – one of Suger's letters of 1150 warns Louis VII's younger brother, Bishop Henry of Beauvais, against rebelling against the king without consulting magnates, bishops or the pope; as if with such consent one might rebel against an inadequate king.[6] John of Salisbury also outlined an extended metaphor for the realm as the body politic, with the king as the head. He probably derived it from descriptions of ecclesiastical hierarchies, but his version produced a compelling and highly influential image of the ideal state. John's book was widely read and influential: Helinand of Froidmont used it in his *De bono regimine principis*, written at the request of Philip Augustus.[7]

The ever-increasing bite of administrative kingship, which finally under Philip Augustus began to affect the Capetian realm, hardened attitudes to the powers of kings in the late twelfth- and early thirteenth-century schools.[8] Philip, Louis VIII, Blanche and Louis IX wanted substantial contributions from the Church when they protected it, or did the Church's business in holy war, and they increasingly had the administrative capacity to collect them – as they did to collect regalian rights during ecclesiastical vacancies.[9] Their claims to revenues from ecclesiastical sources were not new, but their administrative powers to take them were. Churchmen used to Capetian kings who could sleep unguarded beneath a tree secure in the love of the happy inhabitants of 'la douce France', as Walter Map found Louis VII, began to find themselves imposed upon almost as firmly as their colleagues in the Angevin realm.[10]

The Bible gave the clergy easy ammunition against bad kingship, and – most vibrantly with Jezebel – bad queenship. Even the biblical kings who were presented as models of kingship in the coronation orders, David and Solomon, had their weaknesses. David lusted after Bathsheba and engineered the death of her husband. Solomon loved too many women, and in the end turned away from God because of his love for 'foreign' wives. Good biblical queens were few and far between, but Queen Esther at least provided an irreproachable model.

Blanche and Louis VIII must have been fully aware of these ecclesiastical critiques of kingship. They were personally close to reformist churchmen, such as Bishop

Walter of Chartres and William of Auvergne, bishop of Paris. Louis and Blanche's attempt on the English throne was launched with the full support of the English churchmen, above all Stephen and Simon Langton, who gave religious and intellectual authority to the movement to depose John for bad kingship, and to place limitations on his rule in Magna Carta. Stephen Langton, indeed, was prepared to invert Ivo's views on kingship and take John of Salisbury's ideas to their logical conclusion: he argued that it was right to punish princes for the sins of their people.[11] Ecclesiastical critiques of kingship and queenship are made manifest throughout the moralised bibles. These hugely expensive courtly commissions told Blanche, her husband and her son that they should not listen to bad counsel and that they should restrain their agents of government, their *prévôts* and *baillis*.[12] From them, Blanche and her family must have absorbed the message that earthly rulers were merely God's expedient to deal with people who could not govern themselves: that before the Fall, there was no need for earthly powers, and at the End of Time all earthly power would cease in the perfect harmony of the Heavenly Jerusalem.

Or would it? The Church was beginning to waver on this. For it was not just kings, princes and counts who held power on earth. So did popes, bishops, abbots, archdeacons and rural deans. Some theologians began to suggest that the hierarchy of ecclesiastical powers would continue in the perfect realm of God after the End of Time. Many found this shocking, including those around Prince Louis's tutor, Amaury of Bène. The denial of the continuation of ecclesiastical hierarchy after the End of Time was one of the accusations levelled against the Amauricians. They were also accused of believing that only two people would retain their earthly powers in the afterlife – not churchmen, but kings, Philip Augustus and his son, the future Louis VIII. But more mainstream churchmen were prepared to accept that all earthly hierarchy and powers, including that of kings and princes, would continue, including Gerald of Wales in his 'Instruction for Princes', the book that he wanted to dedicate to Lord Louis. Surprisingly, it was Franciscan thinkers who developed these ideas most strongly over the course of the thirteenth century.[13]

Moreover, the ecclesiastical critique of kings and their earthly powers should not be seen out of context. All earthly powers, and all manifestations of earthly power, were the object of criticism from the scholars and reformist clergy of the late twelfth and thirteenth centuries. In fact, their most bitter criticism was aimed not at kings and queens, but at bishops, archdeacons and abbots, and at fellow scholars swollen with pride. They condemned the opulent lifestyle of the great prelates,

their desire to build magnificent cathedrals and palaces, their grasping and efficient administrations, and their sexual appetites, whether for women, other men or young boys. The texts and images in the moralised bibles that provide either criticisms of bad kingship or recipes for good are far outweighed by those that satirise bad prelates, or show how the good should behave. Blanche of Castile might have been surprised to find several warnings against sodomy in them. This was almost certainly an obsession of the clergy who produced the books, rather than a warning for Blanche and the Capetian family. John of Salisbury in *Policraticus* attacked churchmen who abused or came too close to power as strongly as he condemned tyrannical lay rulers.[14]

•

The orders for the coronation of kings and their queens provide the fullest statement of the theoretical essential elements of legitimate rule – of what made a ruler legitimate in the eyes of both the Church and the laity.[15] It is a conservative view, for most of the crucial elements were incorporated in the earliest Carolingian orders. But legitimacy rested heavily on custom and precedent, and drew its strength from its conservatism. The king-making, and the kingship of the coronation orders, was based on biblical precedent, especially on those of Saul, David and Solomon. The king is chosen by God; then elected and acclaimed by the people; then finally anointed and crowned by the Church. This is a churchman's view of what makes a king, but all successful usurpers, from the early Carolingians to Hugh Capet in 987, were dependent on the Church to give legitimacy to the power they had grasped from another reigning and anointed king. These fundamental elements remained the basis of legitimate rule for twelfth-and thirteenth-century writers, including John of Salisbury and Gerald of Wales.[16]

God might reveal his choice of king in many ways. His choice of David, greatest of the Old Testament kings, the type for Christ as king and the model for all medieval kings, was revealed by his defeat of the incumbent king, Saul, thus offering a convenient justification to anyone with usurpation in mind. God might reveal his choice through the suitability or worthiness of the future king. As with Saul and David, worthiness became an issue when the incumbent king or ruler was seen to be unsuitable, or unworthy.[17] In 987 Hugh Capet was considered capable of ruling and protecting France, unlike the last Carolingians, so often dismissed as the useless kings – the *reges inutiles*. Worthiness to rule was dangerously open to interpretation. The Capetians had, by 1200, developed a compelling narrative of

themselves as 'the most Christian kings', so that even when they lost battles, usually to their Anglo-Norman or Angevin subject rivals, they remained the most properly worthy of kings, as Walter Map and Gerald of Wales attest.[18] One of the great late twelfth-century Paris masters, Peter the Chanter, had speculated as to whether a minor could be properly worthy to reign. Peter went so far as to wonder whether a bishop who crowned and anointed a minor as king should be censured.[19] Peter was one of the most famous and influential of the Parisian masters, and his writings were well known in the schools and the university. But in 1226 the French bishops ignored his speculations on minority; none of them stayed away from young Louis's coronation. Nor did any of the baronial party try to exploit this.

It was believed that God usually revealed his choice of king by providing the incumbent ruler with a suitable son and heir. The Capetians famously produced a long succession of sons to fathers, from 987 to the early fourteenth century.[20] The biblical model that most neatly prefigured such a succession was that of the Tree of Jesse. But biblical precedent could be tricky. Solomon was not David's oldest son, but the son of his illicit relationship with Bathsheba. Bathsheba ensured Solomon's succession by persuading David to have him anointed king while David was still alive. This provided biblical precedent for the Capetian tradition of anticipatory succession, by having the heir crowned and/or anointed in his father's lifetime, or, if the king did not want to go that far, making his son king-designate. Occasionally, younger sons, or younger sons of second marriages, seem to have hoped that the Solomonic precedent might operate, notably on the death of Philip I in 1108. But by the early thirteenth century Philip Augustus was so sure that his oldest son would succeed him as king of France that he made no move to have Lord Louis made king, or even king-designate, during his lifetime. Joinville was the only contemporary to suggest that Philip Hurepel hoped to take precedence over his nephew, Louis IX, when Louis VIII died. Nevertheless, Louis VIII himself had taken the trouble to spell out in his will that his oldest son should succeed him; and had taken the trouble, too, to provide generously for his younger sons. Those for whom generous landed provision could not be made should go into the Church.

The second crucial element of legitimacy in the coronation orders is that of election and acclamation by the people. It was the essential principle of legitimacy for the Church and was used by the Capetians to justify the accession of Hugh Capet in 987.[21] This too had potential dangers, and those potential dangers for a

royal dynasty were exposed when Philip Augustus, Lord Louis and Blanche made their series of bids for the English throne.

Succession to the English crown had been more complicated than succession to the French. William the Conqueror was one of the most famous and successful of usurper kings; and the subsequent succession to the English throne had included several younger brothers and one nephew. The succession of Henry I and the competing claims of Stephen and Matilda were justified in terms of suitability.[22] Henry II tried the Capetian expedient of anticipatory kingship. Gradually, one powerful legitimising element emerged – the designation of the new king by the old, often on his deathbed and increasingly by written testament. Thus in the end Henry II left everything to Richard; when Richard died, he left everything to John.[23] Louis VIII, indeed, adopted the English method. He did not have young Louis crowned in anticipatory kingship; instead, he named him as king in his will. On his deathbed, he named Blanche as guardian of the king and kingdom.

As early as 1209 Philip and his chancery clerks were speculating on the possibility that the English throne might come to the Capetians through Blanche. On the birth of her firstborn son, Philip, a poem was inscribed in Register A containing the lines 'Blanche in a wished-for birth gives a lord to the French and the English'.[24] King John now had a son and heir, so it was not clear how the Capetians thought they might engineer this. In the event, it was the invitation of the barons of England in 1212, and then again in 1215, that provided the Capetians with their opportunity.

In 1212 some of the barons of England offered the crown to Philip, on the grounds of John's unsuitability as a ruler, while Stephen Langton and a deputation of bishops persuaded Innocent III that John was not worthy to rule and should be dethroned. At the end of 1215 the barons, the 'community of the realm', elected Louis himself, as king of England in right of his wife, in view of the continuing unsuitability of King John.[25] So Philip and Louis had to exploit both suitability to rule and election by the community of the realm and the barons as fundamental principles of legitimacy in their attempts to take the English throne. Philip Augustus went so far as to refute John's claim to have surrendered England into the hands of the pope by saying that this could not be done 'without the assent of the barons who are held to defend the realm'.[26] It was in a sense the ideal view of the body politic, with king and barons working in harmony, and the French court used it to legitimise the original Capetian usurpation in 987. King lists produced for Philip

and Louis in the royal registers in the early thirteenth century claimed that the last Merovingian was deposed 'through the consideration of the barons of France'. Both the king lists and William the Breton stress that Hugh Capet was 'elected by the barons'.[27]

It was a dangerous game to play, though. The Capetians' awareness of the dangers of dependence on one's barons for legitimacy is reflected in their subtle and gradual stressing of the claim through hereditary right: that is, through Blanche. Philip could claim the throne only through election or papal choice, but Louis could claim it through Blanche, which is presumably why, in 1213, Philip prepared for Louis, rather than himself, to take the English crown. Gerald of Wales, taking an ecclesiastical line, emphasises Louis's claims through suitability, but reports Louis himself saying that he would remain faithful to his wife 'because his right to possess the kingdom of England depended on his faith to his legitimate wife'.[28] Certainly, Louis's defence of his claim to the throne in his letter to the English realm, at the council of Melun and in Rome in 1216, culminated in the fact that he had been elected 'by reason of his wife'.[29]

That succession might be through a woman, or that succession should be in right of a wife, or even that a woman should succeed to a kingdom, was accepted by all. The Angevins traced their rights to the English throne through the empress Matilda, daughter of Henry I. Louis claimed his directly through Blanche and her mother, while Philip Augustus's administrators compiled genealogies in Registers C, E and F tracing Louis's rights to the English throne through two avenues – one through Adela, the daughter of the Conqueror, and her granddaughter, Adela of Champagne, the mother of Philip Augustus, and the other through Louis's marriage to Blanche.[30] Innocent III, in response to Blanche's and Louis's claims, stated that if the succession to the English throne went, as the French argued, through Queen Eleanor of Castile, Blanche's older sister Berengaria would have a stronger claim, though he thought that their brother Henry should succeed, because 'the male should be preferred'. Even the pope was prepared here to countenance, at least theoretically, a succession that favoured strict primogeniture irrespective of the sex of the candidate.[31]

•

There is no denying that in the thirteenth century men expected to rule, and people expected rulers to be men. When a woman found herself in a position to rule or command, whether as a hereditary ruler or commander, or as the guardian

of a realm or territory in the absence of her husband, or in the minority of her son, she faced disadvantages that male rulers did not.[32] Moreover, almost all written contemporary comment on her rule would have been made by men – and usually by clergy, who often had their own special problems with women. The rule of a woman in the Middle Ages was always a special case, though Blanche was not the only woman among her close contemporaries to govern substantial territories, especially if the great princedoms of France are taken into account. Contemporaries tended to see the rule of a woman as an opportunity to challenge the authority and power of the ruler; but those very challenges are often revealing about both the realities and the perceptions of power and of government in the medieval period.

Blanche was not just the ruler of a principality, like Blanche of Navarre, countess of Champagne, or Countess Joanna of Flanders; she was a queen, the wife and consort of the king of France. As such, at the coronation, she was crowned and anointed as queen of France. She was not anointed, as her husband was, with the holy oil reputedly sent down from heaven for the baptism of Clovis, but then neither were any kings other than those of France. But she was anointed on the head and the breast with consecrated oil. Innocent III tried in vain to stop the tradition of anointing rulers on the head, as being too close to the ordination of a priest.[33] The consecration gave her, like the king, a special status; she was no longer an ordinary laywoman. That special status was manifest at the end of the coronation, when, together with her husband, she received Communion under both kinds. Like her husband, she was now the Lord's anointed.[34]

She was given regalia that represented not only the responsibilities, but also the authority and powers of her office: a sceptre, smaller than that of the king, and a rod, just like his. The sceptre and the rod represented the authority and the duty to keep the peace, to defend the weak and to do justice within the realm.[35] As in the case of the king, the barons of the kingdom demonstrated their appointed place within the realm by supporting the crown of the queen as she moved from the high altar to her throne. It is true that she was not presented with the sanctified sword of governance, that she made no coronation promises or oaths, and that her hands were not anointed. Nevertheless, at her coronation, the queen of France was invested with the full authority and powers of a reserve ruler; she was made ready to take on the full duties of the rule of the realm, should her husband be unable to fulfil them, owing to illness or absence. She was already invested with full

authority and powers, should her husband die before her son was old enough to take them on himself.

The responsibilities of the king were set out, and spoken out, during the coronation liturgy. The king promised to maintain the peace in his lands, to prevent pillage and other iniquities, and to do justice with equity and mercy. He promised to observe the faith of the Church, and to defend the Church and its ministers. He promised to rule and defend the realm in a just manner.[36] When the queen was invested with the sceptre, the rod and the crown, she was, tacitly, accepting the responsibilities that these represented for the king. Like the biblical Queen Esther, she would be 'consort of the king' and would 'take part in his kingship'.[37] The way in which her coronation affirmed this must have been all the clearer to Blanche and Louis VIII because, for the first time in living memory, they underwent a full double coronation for both king and queen. Besides, Ingeborg's long struggle to be accepted as Philip's queen must have left the entire Capetian court conscious of the role and status of a queen. Ingeborg's legal arguments had centred on the reality of her marriage, but she and her supporters made pointed reference to the fact that she was the anointed queen of France and that she had been, in the words of the coronation orders, 'raised up to the royal throne'.[38]

The coronation orders had been devised and developed by churchmen, and represented a medieval churchman's view of good kingship, of how regal authority and prestige should be translated into active rule over the realm. Doubtless the kings and queens themselves saw nothing to which they might object in the definition of their responsibilities as rulers, or indeed in the rest of the liturgy. The orders impressed upon the ruler that their power came from God, but medieval rulers tended to see the fact that they were king or queen 'by the grace of God' (*gratia dei*) as a reinforcement of their authority, not a limitation. And, of course, the difference between theoretical and actual power could be immense – though that was not only the case for women.

Blanche had limited need for her reserve regal authority during her brief reign as queen consort. Louis VIII did not make any special arrangement for her rule as he set off on the Albigensian Crusade in 1226. He was not leaving the realm, and probably intended to be back before the end of the fighting season. There was no more need for special arrangements than there had been when he campaigned against Henry III's forces at La Rochelle in the summer of 1224. In both cases, in his absence Blanche as queen consort could, if necessary, do justice and preserve peace: in other words, rule.

Before French kings went on Crusade overseas, aware that they would be absent from the realm for some time, they made special arrangements for the governance of the realm. When Louis VII set off in 1147, he took his queen consort, Eleanor of Aquitaine, with him. Surprisingly, he did not give his mother, Adela of Maurienne, guardianship of the kingdom while he was away. Instead, regnal authority was invested, on the advice of Bernard of Clairvaux, in an ill-assorted trio of the archbishop of Reims (the leading prelate of France), Louis's cousin, the seneschal, Ralph of Vermandois, and Suger, abbot of Saint-Denis. Queen Adela was a woman of considerable political adeptness, but she had remarried, and may have been considered to have had divided loyalties. As it was, she used her energy and political acumen to intrigue on behalf of her younger sons during the king's absence.[39] Philip Augustus did appoint his mother, Adela of Champagne, one of the guardians of the realm in 1189, along with her brother William, archbishop of Reims. Adela had not remarried, but Philip was clearly concerned that both Adela and Archbishop William might advance the interests of their natal family of Champagne. To protect against this, he gave control of his great seal to the council of the City of Paris. The arrangement was surprisingly successful – at least, there is no evidence of serious problems within the realm. Before he set out, Philip gave his regents detailed instructions in an ordinance as to how they should run the country. The queen and Archbishop William were to assure the workings of justice in the king's absence: they should hold court in Paris every four months to hear plaintiffs. They should keep an eye on the king's *baillis*, who must report to them frequently. They could not remove *baillis* who might be unsatisfactory, but they must inform the king. The regents were to deal with ecclesiastical vacancies, keeping the regalia during a vacancy as the king would do; collations were to be kept vacant until Philip returned to make his own appointments. The most detailed section concerned the royal revenues. They were to be brought to Paris, stored at the Temple, and accounts rendered three times a year.[40]

So there was no pattern of Crusade 'regencies' for the kingdom of France when St Louis made his arrangements in 1248. The archbishop of Reims was the common factor on both previous occasions, but this time the archbishop was accompanying the king on Crusade. Otherwise, it is possible that Louis would have appointed the archbishop along with his mother. Instead, he turned to Blanche, knowing that he could trust both her integrity and her ability. St Louis followed his grandfather's precedent in outlining the regency powers in an ordinance. But where Philip's ordinance was designed to limit the power of his regents, not least by consigning

the seal to the Paris merchants, St Louis's ordinance of 1248 is breathtaking in its simplicity. The business of government was left to his mother's judgement. He limited her action only in the giving of royal charity.[41]

Precedents for a Capetian minority regency lay back in the mists of the eleventh century. The last had been that of Philip I in 1060.[42] So there was no recent precedent to suggest who should be regent, or at what age the king was deemed to be sufficiently mature to govern by himself. It is true that Philip Augustus was only fifteen when his father died in September 1180. But Philip had already been crowned and anointed as king, in the traditional Capetian manner, in the previous year. Count Philip of Flanders had acted as the young prince's tutor, and had attained huge influence at court in the 1170s. He swore an oath to the ageing Louis VII to protect the young prince, and bore the sword before Philip at his coronation in November 1179. In spring 1180 he organised Philip's marriage with his niece, Isabella of Hainault. But Count Philip was never the official guardian of the king. Nor were any of King Philip's Champenois relatives, his mother or his uncle, the archbishop of Reims. The Flemish and Champenois parties struggled for influence over the young king at court, but neither side played any official guardianship role. In spite of his youth, Philip ruled after the death of his father as king.[43] There were more immediate examples of minor rulers in other European realms: Frederick II had assumed full power in Sicily at the age of fourteen; the eighteen-year-old Henry III of England, on the other hand, had not yet, in 1226, assumed full regnal power.[44]

Attitudes to the age of majority had changed since Philip had come to the throne. This may have been cultural: by the second quarter of the thirteenth century many of the marks of adulthood – the age at which one married, consummated a marriage or was knighted – came later in life. Indeed, the age of majority was usually marked by both marriage and knighting. Blanche had all her sons married about the age of twenty or twenty-one, and the younger ones knighted at the same age, suggesting that she herself favoured that as the age of majority. Canon law set majority at the rather advanced age of twenty-five; but in England the barons and prelates who drew up Magna Carta set the age at twenty-one.[45]

In customary law, the age of majority varied across France, tending to be set at around twenty or twenty-one in the west, and around fifteen in the east.[46] As both canon and customary law were developed and formalised, the age of majority probably became crystallized. Philip Augustus himself and his administrators played a role in this formalisation, and in setting the age of majority at twenty or

twenty-one rather than fifteen. Customary law allowed a lord to take wardship or guardianship of a minor. This was a hugely valuable seigneurial privilege The lord could usually divert most of the revenues from wardship to himself. He could usually control the marriage of the minor heir. If the widow of the dead lord wished to hold the wardship until her son and heir had reached his majority, she would be required to pay a substantial relief to the overlord for the right to do so. No one benefited from this as much as the king. Philip Augustus exploited every opportunity that such minorities presented to him. When Theobald iv of Champagne was born after the death of his father in 1201, Philip took the child and his rich inheritance into guardianship. He allowed Theobald's mother, Blanche of Navarre, the countess of Champagne, to administer the county, but she had to hand over several castles and continual and considerable sums of money to Philip in exchange. In 1209 Theobald himself was handed over to be educated at the Capetian court. He was not permitted to take control of the county himself until he attained his majority in 1221, even though the customary age of majority in eastern France was fifteen. In a similar way, Philip was able to control the county of Flanders after the death of Count Baldwin in 1206. In that case, the heir was not only a minor, but also female. Again, the heiress, Joanna, was handed over to the royal court. Philip, as overlord, exploited the county, appointing Joanna's uncle, Philip of Namur, to administer the county for her until she reached her majority.[47]

When Louis viii died unexpectedly in 1226, the Capetians were hoist by their own petard. Louis ix was only twelve at his father's death, so a regency of some length was inevitable. But some of the curial administrators, like Bartholomew of Roye, must have remembered that Philip Augustus had ruled from the age of fifteen. The fact that neither Blanche nor Louis ix nor any of their administrators marked the point at which the young king attained his majority is always put down to Blanche's determination to hold on to power. But it may be that they found it convenient to try to ensure that the age of royal majority remained undefined. In 1271 Philip iii did fix the date of majority of the heir to the throne – at the age of fourteen.[48]

Just like any other lordship, in the event of a minority a king and a kingdom would be provided with a guardian or guardians until the rightful ruler was old enough to take charge. Unlike any other lordship, a kingdom had no overlord to name the guardian. The issue was who should make the appointment, and who should be appointed. Ideally, the dying king would be able to name the person or

persons who would take wardship of the king and kingdom. Whether Louis VIII himself named Blanche as the guardian of his son and the kingdom, or whether his dying wishes were concocted by Walter Cornut, Walter of Chartres and Miles of Beauvais, will never be known. But no one challenged the bishops' account of Louis's disposition. The words of a dying king had considerable power.

It must have surprised many that Louis, with or without episcopal connivance, named Blanche alone as the guardian of the king and the kingdom. In the only real precedent, the 'tutela' and 'custodia' of the king had been left to Count Baldwin V of Flanders when Philip I succeeded his father in 1060.[49] Count Philip of Flanders had obviously hoped to fulfil the same position for the young Philip Augustus. The closest parallel, which all the French court and baronage would have known, was Blanche's cousin, Henry III. King John dictated a brief will on his deathbed, naming those who should 'ordain' the wardship of his nine-year-old son. A few days later, after the child king had been crowned, the 'ordainers' chose William Marshall as the person who should have the guardianship of the kingdom and the child king, along with the papal legate, Guala Bicchieri. Henry's mother, Isabella of Angoulême, was not given a part in the guardianship of her son, nor was she named as one of the ordainers in her husband's will. When Louis VIII died, England was still effectively ruled by a regency council. Henry assumed full powers, and began to issue charters under his own seal in January 1227, when he was nineteen.[50] Louis VIII, together with Walter Cornut and Walter of Chartres, had observed the vicissitudes of the English minority after the death of William Marshall, as great barons and curial administrators fought for influence and control of the young king. Perhaps that had reinforced their determination to turn to the widowed queen and mother.

Blanche knew what had happened within her family in Castile. In 1204 her father, Alfonso VIII of Castile, issued a testament in which he made his wife, Eleanor of England, guardian of the young king and the realm in the case of his death.[51] In the event, Eleanor did not long survive Alfonso's death in 1214, leaving ten-year-old Henry as the heir to the Castilian throne. Instead, Blanche's sister Berengaria had the tutelage of her young brother, and ruled Castile along with the archbishop of Toledo and the bishop of Palencia, though a powerful group of Castilian nobles, led by Álvaro Núñez de Lara, soon wrested control of the young king from her.[52] In 1217, when young Henry hit his head while playing and died, Berengaria herself inherited the Castilian throne. Conscious of the fragility of her position, she accepted a position of co-ruler with her still under-age son Ferdinand

III, though within two years he had attained his majority.[53] Blanche was well aware of her sister's troubles as guardian of their young brother, and then co-ruler with her minor son. Around 1223 a group of Castilian nobles wrote to Blanche and her husband asking them to send help to overthrow Berengaria and send the young Louis to rule in her place. Blanche and Louis VIII had no intention of dispatching their son and heir to Castile. But they kept the letters of invitation in the Capetian archives.[54]

Berengaria of Castile-León was not a comfortable parallel as a woman holding guardianship of a king and kingdom. But within the great princedoms of France, women had proved successful guardians. Mary of Champagne, who was half-sister to Blanche's mother, had administered the county with efficiency and courtly flair when her husband, Count Henry the Liberal, was on Crusade from 1179 to 1181, then during the minority of her son, Count Henry II, from 1181 to 1187, then again when he was in the Holy Land between 1190 and her death in 1197. Both husband and son had full confidence in entrusting the county to her while they spent long periods Crusading. The unexpected death of Theobald III of Champagne in 1201 left Blanche's cousin Blanche of Navarre as guardian of the county for their posthumous son, Theobald IV, until his majority in 1222. Blanche of Navarre faced more problems than had her mother-in-law. The claims of the daughters of Count Henry II and their husbands were continually destabilising, until finally declared invalid in 1234, and left Blanche of Navarre very dependent on Philip Augustus. By 1201 Philip Augustus was a much more formidable figure than he had been when Mary held guardianship of the county. But Blanche of Navarre was wise enough to work with, rather than against, him, and was able to hand on a flourishing county to her son in 1222.[55]

Within the Anglo-Norman and Angevin family, the kings were long used to leaving the effective governance of parts of their dominions to female members of their family on a regular basis, not because the king was unable to rule in person through youth or absence on Crusade, but because those dominions were so extensive. In this sense 'regency' – acting as vicegerent for the ruler – was an intrinsic feature of the Anglo-Norman and Angevin realm. Matilda of Scotland played a crucial role in the governance of England whenever her husband, Henry I, was away in Normandy. In the first decade of his reign, Henry II, like his grandfather, often left England in the competent rule of his wife, Eleanor of Aquitaine. Henry II left the effective governance of Normandy in the hands of his mother, the empress Matilda, until her death in 1167.[56] Both Richard the Lionheart and John

depended on their mother, Eleanor of Aquitaine, to rule her inheritance of Aquitaine, but also to act with a sort of reserve regnal power anywhere within their realms when any of their designated justiciars or seneschals proved unequal to the task. The barons and prelates of France would have been well aware that it was Eleanor who had intervened in the Longchamp crisis, when Richard was on Crusade, and Eleanor who had ensured the smooth succession of John in 1199.[57]

So the barons and prelates of France may have been surprised when the queen was named by the dying Louis VIII as sole guardian of both king and kingdom, but there were plenty of precedents and parallels. They were not unused to women governing vast territories, even kingdoms, in the absence of the male ruler, or where he was still under-age, or where he was simply acting in another part of a multiple realm. But the fact that there were no established precedents for guardianship of the king and realm undoubtedly left Blanche's rule open to challenge.

There is no evidence that anyone tried to dispute Louis VIII's deathbed wishes. Historians have been suspicious of the letter issued by Walter Cornut and his fellow bishops, but contemporaries appear to have accepted it without demur. Joinville makes it clear that the serious threat to Blanche's guardianship came from Louis VIII's younger brother, Philip Hurepel.[58] As the only adult male member of the immediate royal family, who had carried the sword of Charlemagne before the new king at Louis VIII's coronation, Philip had strong grounds for feeling that he had been denied a role that rightfully should have been his. The initial revolt against Blanche was almost certainly designed to supplant her as guardian of the king, or at least force her to accept Philip Hurepel as principal guardian. Philip tried to emulate Álvaro Núñez de Lara in Castile. Capturing the young king would make him de facto guardian. But Philip miscalculated. The Ile-de-France was not Castile. Blanche was able to depend on an established and substantial curial knighthood, and the urban elite of Paris. Both groups had been amply rewarded for their support of the French crown; both groups had reason to be wary of the greater aristocracy.[59]

Joinville, like all the biographers of St Louis, makes much of the danger that the young Louis and his dauntless mother faced from the baronage, claiming that Philip Hurepel and his co-conspirators intended to capture Louis to make Philip himself king in Louis's place. This is unlikely. Once young Louis was crowned and anointed, he was, as the Lord's anointed, virtually untouchable. One might, as John of Salisbury had suggested, depose a tyrant; but a blameless twelve-year-old child could not be accounted a tyrant. Blanche, the curial administrators and the

prelates ensured that Louis's coronation occurred without delay – though in fact it was arranged no faster than his father's. But even before the coronation, the courtiers and the barons knew that Louis VIII had designated his eldest son as his successor in the will that he made in 1225. Their own entitlement to property was based on the same inheritance customs as the succession to the throne. Controlling a puppet king during his minority was an attractive option; deposing him would undermine the body politic to which they all belonged.

In short, Blanche's authority during her first 'regency' was stronger than is often suggested, and certainly than is suggested by St Louis's hagiographies. The initial threat to her position was very real. Armies had to be dispatched out to the west every summer until the mid-1230s to contain Peter Mauclerc. English attempts to repossess their Continental lands were a continual problem. The various baronial alliances certainly disturbed the peace of the realm, especially in northern Burgundy, Champagne and Flanders, but the object of their attack was Theobald of Champagne, not the queen regent and the young king. And private war, as a means of settling disputes with another baron, was not prohibited in most of France, in the way that it was in England and Normandy. Philip of Beaumanoir, who had been a royal official, devoted an entire chapter to the proper and legitimate pursuit of private war in his late thirteenth-century summation of the customs of the Beauvaisis. But there was, of course, an inherent conflict between a baron's established right to wage private war and the king's (or queen's) duty, made explicit in the coronation orders, to keep the peace of the realm. Hence Blanche's determination to stamp out the Champagne war, and Louis IX's attempt to outlaw private war in 1258.[60]

Surprisingly, perhaps, the way that Blanche was addressed in letters asking her to act during her last guardianship of the kingdom suggests widespread acceptance, indeed welcome, of the authority of a woman in power. During her son's minority, she was careful to issue all acts and letters in his name, under his seal; and letters to ask the young king to return regalia or give permission for episcopal election were, as one would expect, addressed to him. But in her Crusade guardianship, this pretence was forgotten, and in many cases Blanche was addressed in terms that might be thought appropriate for an empress, not just the queen regent of France. She herself issued acts as Blancha, *Dei gratia Francie regina*.[61] Eudes Rigaud asks his most excellent lady Blanche, by the grace of God illustrious queen of the Franks, to act with the serenity of royal majesty, and hopes that the excellence of her authority (*dominacionis* – the word used for an order of angels) will be strong

in Christ.[62] 'May your magnificent authority prosper', hopes the chapter of Coutances.[63] The chapter of Tours writes to her thus to thank her for confirming their new archbishop: 'To our most excellent lady, Blanche, by the grace of God queen of the Franks...salutation and [that she should] obtain the glory of the celestial kingdom through the felicitous rule of the temporal kingdom. We inform your royal majesty (*Majestati vestre regie*)...'.[64] Even the disappointed chapter of Soissons calls her the most excellent and illustrious queen of the Franks, by the grace of God, and refers to her 'royal serenity'. They note that God has chosen her to have rule of the kingdom and the guardianship of the Church – that ecclesiastical epitome of legitimate authority. They remind her that 'royal power is held to reside more in mercy than in tyranny', but they do not question of the fullness of her God-given power.[65]

Clerical chroniclers too, like Matthew Paris, for all his inbred monastic misogyny, seem to have accepted the full regal powers of Blanche's later guardianship of the kingdom of France as the God-given and natural and proper order of things. She was 'dominarum saecularium domina', 'the lady of ladies of this world, the custodian, protector and queen of France...the magnanimous'. Like other contemporary commentators, he noticed that everything fell apart after her death.[66] All chroniclers deployed variants of the cliché used for women who wielded power with conspicuous success – that they had the heart of a man in their fragile women's bodies. But Blanche is described as acting as a ruler. She 'administered vigorously, wisely, strongly and righteously, and guarded the rights of the kingdom', said William of Saint-Pathus.[67] How she ruled will be considered in the next chapter.

●

Kings died, but their queens often lived on after them, crowned, anointed and conscious of their special status, which they might not be able to exploit to the full, but which nevertheless, as Ingeborg's long struggle had reminded everyone, could never be revoked. Isabella of Angoulême insisted on retaining her title as queen of England, though she played no role there: it was why she was so affronted when treated like an ordinary member of the nobility by Louis IX at Poitiers in 1241. In 1206 Adela of Champagne was buried in the choir of Cistercian Pontigny. The Cistercian order accepted that kings and founders might be buried in the choirs of their abbeys. Reluctantly, they accepted that Adela, as queen of France, might have this privilege too.[68]

Blanche undoubtedly perceived herself in this light. It has been observed that the acts that she issued in her 'private' capacity as a great landholder rather than as ruler nevertheless adopt the formulas of the royal chancellery: these are manifestly the acts of someone with royal status.[69] As queen dowager she was, whether regent or not, still the crowned and anointed queen of France with a duty to her people. The clearest evidence of this is the extent of her provision for the poor and the sick in almsgiving and hospital building. The rich must give to the poor, but the scale of Blanche's almsgiving was exceptional – not least in relation to the scale of the almsgiving of the reigning king. Louis limited the amount that Blanche could alienate in free alms to ensure that the value of her dower properties, which would return to the crown after her death, was not dissipated. He could not control what she gave from her huge income. The tight limit that he set on Margaret's almsgiving in 1261 is suggestive. For Blanche and Louis recognised almsgiving on the sort of scale on which Blanche practised it as a fulfilment of rulership, of fulfilling one's duty to one's people, not just an attempt to squeeze through the eye of the metaphorical needle.

But it was an ambivalent position. What was the proper role of a queen during the reign of her son? Should she participate in his kingship as she properly did in her husband's? During the minority of Louis IX, and during his Crusade, Blanche was ruler of France with full and proper authority, given to her by the king (Louis VIII, then Louis IX) in both cases. During his personal rule, the level of her active participation in his government, and the extent of her influence as a counsellor, fluctuated, but were often considerable.

The extent of Blanche's influence on Louis IX and her active participation within his government, after he had attained his majority, led Le Goff to describe their relationship as that of co-royalty.[70] Historians have pointed to the parallels with Blanche's sister Berengaria of Castile and her relationship with her son, King Ferdinand III. It has been suggested that Blanche's knowledge of Iberian traditions of rulership, and of her sister's rule in Castile, may have predisposed her to conceive her role in such terms.

But for considerable periods of her life, Berengaria had no living male sibling, and had been accepted by the Castilian magnates as the legitimate heir to the crown of Castile should her father die without a son to succeed. Berengaria did indeed succeed her young brother Henry as queen of Castile after Henry's premature death in 1217. Castile was already in the throes of disorder, and Berengaria

made the decision to associate Ferdinand, her son from her marriage to the king of León, with her as king, thus establishing a de facto co-rulership, for here it was Berengaria, not Ferdinand, who was the legitimate successor to the kingdom. Co-rulerships, where a queen, usually a mother, ruled in association with the king, appear to have been accepted arrangements within the Spanish kingdoms.[71] Co-rulership was known in Capetian France, in the quite specific sense that most kings, until Philip Augustus, had in some way associated their son and heir in their rule, whether as a crowned and anointed young king, or at least as king-designate.[72]

The issue of Blanche as co-ruler is clouded by the fact that the minority was never officially ended – though nor, in fact, was the minority of Henry III in England.[73] Her status as co-ruler becomes an issue for the historian only in the mid-1230s, when Louis was married and over twenty-one. Should it really be characterised as a 'co-rulership'? Did she absorb more of Louis's regnal authority than contemporaries expected? Did she absorb more of it than he expected or really wanted? Is that why she had detractors – did they accuse her of usurping, appropriating to herself, Louis's regnal authority? Did she behave as contemporaries expected a queen mother to do?

Contemporary expectations in Capetian France were perhaps rather vague. The last active queen mother, Adela of Champagne, had died in 1206. From the start of his reign, Philip Augustus was determined to keep Adela's family at a distance, and thus Adela too, though he made use of her as regent, with tight limitations, when he went on Crusade in 1189. In the absence of a suitable reigning queen, Adela may have played a useful maternal role towards the many youngsters at court as hostages, wards or members of the royal family, like Blanche herself, but her participation in Philip's governance went no further. Adela of Maurienne, a very active queen consort, much trusted by her husband, was less so by her son Louis VII, perhaps because she had remarried. She was certainly politically active during her son's reign, though tended to intrigue with her younger sons. If she was remembered at all at the Capetian court in the early thirteenth century, it was perhaps as an inappropriate model for a dowager queen – but she had been dead since 1154.[74]

Blanche's Angevin family provided stronger, and more positive, models as to how the mother of a king might play an active role in the governance of her sons. The empress Matilda had in effect ruled the duchy of Normandy for Henry II from his accession to the English throne until her death in 1167. One of his letters

instructs the Norman recipient that, 'unless you do it, my Lady and mother the Empress will'; in other words, executive power of governance in the duchy was vested in Matilda.[75] Henry appreciated her wise advice on governance. Walter Map recalls the empress telling Henry that he should keep his courtiers and barons in thrall, as one would keep a hawk on a leash, with occasional reward to encourage their appetite for more. Those on both sides of the Becket dispute realised that Matilda's influence over Henry would be crucial to resolving the issue; she was deeply involved in negotiating a way through this first great crisis of Henry's reign when she died. Matilda, then, advised, interceded and played a central role in royal diplomacy; she upheld the ducal dignity and provided a centre for ducal governance in Normandy.[76]

After her husband's death, Blanche's grandmother, Queen Eleanor, ruled Aquitaine for both Richard I and John. Eleanor issued charters as duchess of Aquitaine, and did homage for the duchy to Philip Augustus after Richard's death in 1199. She did so, of course, in her own right. She was the heiress to the duchy, and her husbands had ruled it only through her. But as queen dowager, she intervened elsewhere in the Angevin dominions, most notably in England itself during Richard's captivity. Both Richard and John employed their mother on the most delicate diplomatic tasks, especially the arrangement of royal marriages – not least her journey to Burgos to collect Blanche. Like Matilda, she advised, interceded and played a central role in royal diplomacy, and assured the governance of one of the constituent dukedoms of the Angevin realm. She also took direct independent executive regnal action in England, as Matilda never needed to do. No one questioned her authority to do so. She had not been commissioned as 'regent' by Richard, but Eleanor retained full powers to act as the crowned and anointed queen of England.[77]

Blanche's actions as queen dowager amount to no more than those of her grandmother and great-grandmother. A wise and experienced mother of a king was expected to advise him. She would intercede with him, and would thus be a natural focus of diplomatic activity. Popes, great churchmen and great laymen would expect to influence the king or gain favour with him through her; thus popes like Gregory IX and Innocent IV, and great princes like Raymond VII of Toulouse, addressed themselves to Blanche. She would be expected to mediate at court. She had the royal authority to intervene in crises to maintain the governance of the realm, as Blanche did during Louis's near-fatal illness in 1244–5, and as Eleanor did in England in 1192.

In short, Blanche's activities after Louis's minority were no more and no less 'co-rule' than those of other queen dowagers. No king could rule on his own. All kings – even Philip Augustus – relied heavily on those they trusted for advice, and often for executive action. William the Breton described Brother Guérin as 'quasi secundus a rege' – 'as if second to the king'; indeed, Jacques Krynen characterised Philip and his administrators as almost co-governors.[78] The vastness of their realms forced the Angevin kings to rely even more on the governance of others, including their mothers and their wives. Blanche's prominent role depended on the consent of her son. Louis trusted her judgement. He may also have found many of the demands of ruling uncongenial. Blanche certainly had her detractors at court, but she was probably criticised, not for playing a role in the execution of government, but for influencing her son in one direction by those who hoped to influence him in another.

The death of a king meant that there was often more than one queen. Blanche herself did not have to deal with an active dowager queen: Ingeborg lived on the edges of court and political life; besides, she was not Louis VIII's mother. Eleanor of Aquitaine did not have to deal with a forceful young queen: Berengaria of Navarre, like Ingeborg, was retiring; Isabella of Angoulême was still a child. But the potential problem of two crowned, anointed and politically engaged queens is made manifest in the relationship between Blanche and St Louis's queen, Margaret of Provence.

At her marriage in 1234 Margaret of Provence was too young to play an active role as queen. The household accounts of 1239 still distinguish between the queen, by which they mean Blanche, and the young queen – Margaret.[79] By 1241 Margaret had decided that she should play the role expected of a reigning queen. She was almost certainly engaging in diplomacy over the continental Angevin territories with her sister, Queen Eleanor of England. Churchmen loyal to Blanche, presumably at the older queen's behest, put a stop to that. It was Blanche rather than Margaret who took the initiative in the crisis of 1245. Although Margaret accompanied the court on the great expedition to Saumur for the knighting of Alphonse in 1241, it was Blanche who headed the queen's table, as if she, not Margaret, were queen consort. In the Sainte-Chapelle, Blanche of Castile's queenship is signified by a blatant scattering of the castles of Castile: the pales of Provence are absent.

Margaret was courageous and spirited. When Louis was captured on Crusade, she kept her nerve and steadied that of the demoralised Crusaders, organised the payment of his ransom and the defence of Damietta, in spite of the fact that she

had given birth to a son a few days previously. She reacted with quick-witted bravery when fire engulfed her cabin, and she accepted the dangers and discomforts of the Crusade with grace and good humour.[80] But her attempt to work towards peace between her husband and her brother-in-law, Henry III, in 1241 lost her the trust of Louis and his close advisers – Blanche, of course, was the closest of them all – and that trust was never regained. That distrust was apparent in 1261, when Louis reorganised the household. There were draconian checks on Margaret's expenditure and almsgiving. She was not to receive gifts, not to give orders to royal *baillis* or *prévôts*, or to undertake building works without the permission of the king. Her choice of members of her household was also subject to his agreement.[81]

Margaret survived her husband by some thirty years, so that she herself was queen mother, to Philip III, and was still a presence at court during the reign of her grandson Philip IV. But Louis did not make her regent on his second, and fatal, Crusade in 1270. In the early 1260s Margaret tried to persuade her young son, the future Philip III, to agree to obey her until he was thirty. When Philip told his father, Louis was horrified. In a strange echo of the events of 1241, he forced Philip to resile from his oath to his mother, and forced Margaret to agree never again to attempt such a move.[82] Margaret had overplayed her hand. It meant that she was specifically prevented from acting with those full and legitimate powers of a crowned queen after the death of her husband that Blanche, like Eleanor of Aquitaine, had been able to deploy for the good of the realm.

Why was Margaret treated so differently from Blanche? Were attitudes to the power of women changing? Not yet. In 1294 Philip IV was prepared to name his queen, Joanna of Champagne-Navarre, as sole regent with full regal powers in the event of his son's succession as a minor. She conducted diplomatic negotiations for him. He often associated her with his kingship in his acts. And Philip IV wanted Joanna buried among the kings of France at Saint-Denis – though she herself chose burial with the Paris Franciscans.[83] The effectiveness and evident importance to their husbands of Eleanor of Provence and Eleanor of Castile in England led David Carpenter to characterise late thirteenth-century England as a period of 'resurgence in queenship'.[84]

The problem for Margaret was personal, rather than institutional. Blanche had had her detractors at court. It is not clear who they were. There were always factions at courts, not least one that centred around Margaret, and anyone who had influence over a king would have detractors. They might have been clerks with

misgivings about women in general, and powerful women in particular, and there
may have been others who believed that the power of a queen should be curtailed.
No one did curtail Blanche's – far from it. By the late thirteenth century the
Capetian family were commissioning and promoting accounts of Louis IX that
praise not just her firm and just rule as regent, but also her role as adviser and
counsellor – her continuing influence – during his personal rule. As William of
Saint-Pathus put it, because she was such a 'sage et preude femme', Louis always
wanted 'sa presence et son conseil'.[85] But where Blanche was seen as the wisest and
best provider of good advice that a king could have, a queen whose advice would
always be for the good of the king and his realm, Margaret was seen by Louis as
a queen at the centre of intrigue, whose advice would not be disinterested.
Surprisingly, such formidable political players at the English court as Simon de
Montfort and her nephew, the future Edward I, felt that it was worthwhile to do
diplomatic business through Margaret. Initially, Henry III and Simon de Montfort
chose Margaret, not Louis, to arbitrate between them. She was a more active diplomat than Joinville and the Lives of Louis suggest, and probably, where her aims
coincided with her husband's, quite effective.[86]

To an extent the difference between Blanche's and Margaret's position and influence simply reflected political reality. Blanche was accused of sending rich gifts to
her family in Spain, and advancing them within the court. But there was no danger
that her cultivation of Castilian family connections could damage the interests of
the Capetian realm. Margaret's Provençal connections could. Her sister Eleanor was
married to Henry III of England. Margaret and Eleanor undoubtedly attempted to
bring about a rapprochement between the two kings. This was helpful once Louis
himself had decided to come to an agreement with Henry in the late 1250s, but
was perceived as meddlesome plotting in the 1240s. Moreover, Margaret's sister
Sanchia was married to Henry's younger brother, Richard of Cornwall, who claimed
the county of Poitou, and her youngest sister, Beatrice, countess of Provence, was
married to Charles of Anjou. Sanchia's interests were in direct conflict with those
of Alphonse of Poitiers; and Margaret herself felt that she had dowry claims in
Provence, and alienated Charles by attempting to pursue them. Indeed, her ill-fated
attempt to tie her son Philip to her included clauses that he would not ally himself
with Charles of Anjou against her.[87]

And, of course, Blanche's status as queen dowager depended, like all power
relationships, on personality. She and Louis IX were very close. When she died,
Louis declared that he had lost what he loved most in the whole world. Moreover,

Louis clearly found certain aspects of royal power challenging. He shrank from the things of this world, becoming increasingly unhappy with the demands of the courtly life. He was content to leave some of the work of governance in the hands of those he trusted, like Walter Cornut, John de la Cour and, above all, his mother. Charles of Anjou trusted, admired – and obeyed – his mother too, but, like her, he enjoyed the realities of power. Had he been the heir to the French throne, Blanche's role would probably have been very different.

It has been observed that Blanche does not fit easily into the thesis proposed many years ago by Marion Facinger, whereby the power of Capetian queens leached away over the twelfth and early thirteenth centuries, as the demands of administrative kingship concentrated real power in the hands of the king and his chancery clerks.[88] In fact, the growth of administrative kingship meant that government became more onerous, as did the growth of the size of the realm administered by the kings of France. Only the king could give his *fiat*, the final say; but he had to rely on others for major executive actions of government. By the 1240s the royal agents who ran the distant territories for Louis IX were described as *vice-gerentes* – vicegerents for the king – that is, those who ran the territory in his stead.[89] Blanche, like the empress Matilda, Eleanor of Aquitaine and Eleanor of Provence, acted as vicegerent – as the demands of the new complex government required. Administrative kingship could deliver more power to a queen who had the qualities to handle it.

But it was all a question of trust. In many cases, his mother or his wife might prove the person the king could, should and did trust more than any other. Blanche was trusted by both her husband and her son. Matilda of Scotland, Matilda of Boulogne, Eleanor of Aquitaine (at first) and, in the thirteenth century, Margaret's sister Eleanor of Provence, were trusted advisers of their respective husbands, the kings of England: Henry I, Stephen, Henry II and Henry III; all four women at some time ruled as vicegerents for their husbands. The empress Matilda and Eleanor of Aquitaine owed their power and agency as dowager queens to the trust they inspired in their sons. The case of Eleanor of Provence is illuminating. Like Blanche of Castile, her career gives the lie to the argument that reginal power faded with the growth of administrative kingship. But it did depend on personal relationships. Eleanor had a long widowhood, but her son Edward I did not depend on her counsel or use her undoubted diplomatic gifts as Henry III had.[90]

Philip Augustus famously distrusted his mother and his first wife, though that was in part because they might have loyalties to their own French princely

dynasties. And it was not necessarily misogyny: he distrusted his heir, Lord Louis, even more. Louis VIII himself, in contrast, placed absolute trust in his wife. Louis IX trusted his mother, though he did not always agree with her. And there are signs that from the late 1230s he occasionally chafed under her powerful influence. Louis had a very high idea of the authority of the king. His quarrels with the Church in the mid-1230s reflected his attempt to assert himself as he reached his majority. As he grew more mature, he wanted to interfere and intervene in everything. Louis's conception of kingship had no real room for 'co-royals', or even vicegerents, except in emergencies like Crusades. But there were many aspects of kingship that he disliked, which did not come naturally to him: he needed his mother's support. Nevertheless, it is surprising that he never really challenged Blanche, except to limit her pious largesse. But it is tempting to suggest that the restrictions he imposed on Margaret's queenship in 1261, on both her largesse and her authority, were a displaced and belated rejection of the power and generosity of his formidable mother.

12

Ruler and Counsellor

Blanche, according to William of Saint-Pathus, was a 'preude femme'. She defended the rights of the kingdom with her foresight; with her manly heart, she administered vigorously, wisely, strongly and righteously. For Geoffrey of Beaulieu, she 'administered, protected and defended the rights of the realm' with force, hard work, justice and power, combining her manly heart with feminine intuition; with faith and prudence, she had 'managed and administered the business of the realm'.[1] Aubri of Trois-Fontaines wrote of the good effects of her 'counsel and providence'.[2] Matthew Paris said that her death left the kingdom of France destitute of all solace.[3] Even the baronial *trouvères* could appreciate that 'she knew how to govern a kingdom better than the barons could rule a village'.[4] A Paris-educated Franciscan, writing in Italy around 1300, was even more effusive in his praise: 'Even today it is said that the Lady Blanche, queen of France, ruled the kingdom of France well and extended its dominion, such that no other person since her has ruled better.'[5] Of Blanche's formidable competence in what contemporary commentators, and most modern historians, cannot help seeing as the masculine role of ruling, including the use of military, magisterial and coercive power, there is no doubt. As has been argued in the previous chapter, and as these contemporary comments make clear, there was remarkable acceptance of the fact of her rule and her role as counsellor and consort of the king, and of the legitimacy of her doing so.

The type and extent of the political agency that she could exercise changed, of course, as her status changed through her lifetime. As wife to the heir to the throne,

she was at the very centre of Capetian court circles, though Blanche and Louis's circle was rather different from that around the old king. Because her husband loved and trusted her, her voice was listened to. Her sister Berengaria knew that she would be able to make political capital of their father's great victory in 1212. When the Cistercian order granted Blanche's request for special prayers in 1222, it signalled its recognition that she was someone whose favour was sought after.[6] She had also some potential political agency as the wife of a great lord, which she used effectively, if in the end in vain, in organising an army and fleet to salvage Louis's English expedition in 1217.

I have already discussed the apparent paradox of Blanche's invisibility in the historical record during her three short years as queen consort and the effectiveness with which she took control immediately after her husband's death.[7] The reason why she seems to play a much less active role as queen consort than that played by Adela of Maurienne, the queen of Louis VI, a century earlier is to be found in the changed format in which royal commands and decisions were recorded. The wordy, narrative formal charters, attested by those who gave the king counsel, including the queen, were instruments of the past. That does not mean that the king did not seek the counsel of his queen. Philip Mousquès shows Louis taking care to have his consort's formal consent, in a plenary court, to his departure on the Albigensian Crusade: even if it is an invention, it is what Mousquès, and his intended audience, thought might or should have happened.[8] Her rapid, efficient and effective organisation of the penitential procession of the three queens in 1224 demonstrated her competence in ruling in her husband's place when he was away fighting. Her mobilisation of the people of the capital city of the kingdom, her leading of the people in procession, demonstrated her conception of her role as 'the consort of the king...who takes part in his kingship', as the coronation orders proclaimed. Louis handed the guardianship of the young king and the kingdom to Blanche alone because he had had ample evidence of her competence to rule. For the same reason, the bishops accepted his decision.

•

All historians and commentators – and that includes St Louis's hagiographers – have seen Blanche's struggle with the great barons as the defining issue of her rule during the minority. I hope I have shown that it did not occupy her to the exclusion of other issues, and that she dealt with the barons from a strong position of legitimate authority. Moreover, her struggle with them must be placed in the much broader

context of the uneasy relationship between kings and their magnates from the later twelfth century to the early fourteenth.

Joinville described her, in her struggle with the great barons, as a woman alone in a foreign country, without friends and supporters.[9] That was not true. Blanche was always able to depend, like Philip Augustus, Louis VIII and Louis IX, on other parts of the body politic. The Capetian bishops supported her, as did the towns and cities, which had flourished under Capetian rule. Louis VI and Philip Augustus had both done much to encourage their economic development. Paris was the fastest growing city in Europe around 1200. The Capetians were seen as great supporters of its nascent university, and Philip Augustus had given his great seal into the care of twelve citizens of Paris when he went on Crusade in 1189. The urban elites needed reasonable peace within the realm to trade effectively.[10] Strong royal or comital rule was always more conducive to trade than baronial *chevauchées*, hence the support of the people of Paris for Blanche and young Louis in the crisis of 1226.

Within Paris itself, relations between the ever-growing community of scholars and the merchants were often difficult. Philip Augustus had taken the part of scholars in 1200; in 1226 Blanche, supported by Cardinal Romanus, was prepared to face down the students. Some students went to join her enemies, Peter Mauclerc and Henry III, and Blanche was excoriated in student songs. But within three years most students had returned to Paris; and in the meantime the Dominican scholars that she favoured had been firmly established in the Capetian capital. The solid support of the citizens more than offset the damage done by the student songs.

Besides, the Capetian court still offered the best opportunities for advancement for the ambitious student or master. Blanche inherited an established corps of clerical administrators from her father and husband. Led by the redoubtable Brother Guérin and Walter Cornut, their support for Blanche was unwavering. Gifted young masters like John de la Cour, Eudes of Lorris and Richard of Tourny joined the household and worked for her loyally.

And her problems were with a very small number of the great aristocrats of France. The lesser aristocracy of the Ile-de-France, the descendants of the knights and castellans who had caused Louis the Fat such grief, had long since realised that their best interests were served by working with the Capetians rather than against them. The grandest of these old castellan families were the Montforts, the Beaumonts and the Montmorency. The Garlandes, Mauvoisin, L'Isle Adam, Mello, Poissy and Montmirail formed a well-established second tier of Capetian

aristocracy. They were all densely intermarried.[11] Into their ranks had married the lesser knightly families, such as the Cléments-Cornuts and Nemours, and Bartholomew of Roye, promoted by Philip Augustus. Their numbers had been swelled by members of families of equivalent status from the north-eastern territories held by the future Louis VIII and Blanche, such as Michael of Harnes, John of Nesle, castellan of Bruges, and the lords of Audenarde. For all of them, the Capetian court was their social cynosure, the place where they glowed in the reflected glory of royal prestige. Many of them held offices at court. Their younger sons provided the royal court with its household knights. Most of Blanche's ladies were drawn from their ranks. The Cléments were the marshals; Amaury of Montfort and Matthew of Montmorency served as constable. This group was absolutely loyal to Blanche; without hesitation they joined the armies she raised to counter Peter of Dreux and his allies. Matthew of Montmorency swore on his soul on behalf of Blanche and young Louis to uphold the treaty to marry Princess Isabella to the Lusignan heir.[12]

Even among the greater aristocracy, there were many who remained loyal. The counts of Blois and Chartres never joined the rebellious barons – perhaps because they held the counties in right of their wives, the joint heiresses of the counties of Blois and Chartres and royal cousins, Margaret and Isabella. The count of Chartres, John of Oisy-Montmirail, was himself a member of the old castellan families. Stephen of Sancerre, a member of the Champagne dynasty, remained a close friend and supporter, as he had been in 1213. Hugh of Châtillon-Saint-Pol could usually be tempted away to a private war between fellow great barons, but he and his brother had been very close to Louis VIII, and he held back from attacking Louis's widow.

Those who caused most difficulties were part of the extended Capetian family – the Dreux and Courtenay. Peter of Dreux, having been given the county of Brittany, was able to operate within the special circumstances of the imploded Angevin empire in western France. Both the Dreux and Courtenay families had interests in Burgundy, especially in the north of the duchy, where it bordered Champagne. Louis VII and Philip Augustus had established them there with the intention of bringing Burgundy back, as it had once been, under Capetian control. The betrothal of Blanche and Louis's son and heir, Philip, to Agnes of Nevers in 1216 was part of this strategy, though it came to nothing with the young prince's death in 1219. In the twelfth century the counts of Champagne had taken advantage

of the weakness of the lords of northern Burgundy to extend their influence in the region. Philip Augustus probably hoped that his Courtenay cousins would counter it. In his unfinished attempt to increase royal control over Burgundy, he had set up a conflagration waiting for a spark to set it off. Blanche had to try to put the conflagration out, for the king, or his guardian, must ensure the peace of the realm. But the war in Champagne and the Burgundian borders was not, as such, an attack on Blanche herself, or the king: it was a private war by the Dreux and Courtenay against Theobald of Champagne.

Those who caused trouble for Blanche identified themselves, and were identified by contemporaries, as 'the barons'. For Joinville, it was 'li baron de France' who tried to take advantage of the fact that the kingdom was in the hands of a woman and a foreigner, and 'tuit...li baron de France' who attacked Theobald of Champagne.[13] Hugh of La Ferté, the aristocrat from Maine who threw in his lot with Peter of Brittany, and whose main contribution to Peter's war efforts was the writing of political songs, appealed to the collective sense of baronial self: 'France is laid low – Lord Barons, listen – when a woman holds it in her control'. 'The other day at Compiègne, when the barons could not obtain their rights, and she didn't deign to look at them or see them', complained a fellow poet.[14]

Who exactly were the barons of France? In the early thirteenth century Philip Augustus's chancery clerks drew up a hierarchy of fiefs, divided into counts and dukes, barons, castellans and vavassors.[15] Philip and his clerks were interested in defining these groups in terms of what was due to the king from them. But for aristocratic and court circles, the term 'baron' covered a wider spectrum of society, including dukes and counts – from whose ranks came the worst offenders against Blanche. In the end the term 'baron' bore little relation to the chancery's social hierarchy. It suggested the higher, richer aristocracy, whether they held the title of count or not. It became an emotive shorthand for an aristocracy that saw itself as independent of the royal court. The barons had their own courts, where they sat in judgement, and enjoyed courtly pleasures. They could raise their own substantial armies, and had their cohorts of household knights, and chanceries staffed by ambitious clerks who would benefit from their patronage. Some of them, notably the counts of Flanders and Champagne, ran administrations of notable efficiency and just governance. If they had grievances against each other, they pursued them by means of private warfare, not by bringing their grievances before the king. Unlike the Garlandes, Mauvoisin, even the Montmorency and Montfort, they

thought that they did not need to derive either their prestige or their power from the royal court. A couple of them signalled their independence by failing to attend Louis IX's coronation.

Some of them saw themselves as not just independent of the royal court, but also as antagonistic towards both the royal court and the royal government. 'The barons could not obtain their rights', sang Hugh of La Ferté. The higher aristocracy, in France as elsewhere, undoubtedly felt themselves under pressure in the thirteenth century. It was becoming ever more expensive to maintain an aristocratic lifestyle. Castles must be stone; good clerical administrators had become essential; armour for one's household knights was heavier and more complex; richer spices and finer poets and minstrels must be found for feasts, and finer jewels and robes for one's wife and her ladies. One's sons must be knighted in ever more elaborate ceremonies, and substantial dowries in either monies or properties must be found for one's daughters. Under Philip Augustus, the French crown had begun to catch up with the Anglo-Norman and Angevin kings in imposing, and recording, their seigneurial rights over the aristocracy of France: rights to fealty – and expensive pledges if that were thought to be in doubt; rights to demand military service; rights to demand monetary reliefs to confirm the succession of a son to his father's fief; rights to wardship in the case of a minority; and rights to control the marriages of daughters and widows of important lordships. Philip's chancery clerks kept careful records of what was owed, and his newly organised local officials, the *baillis* and *prévôts*, proved increasingly effective at extracting it from the aristocracy. And while the barons might think, with the royal official Philip of Beaumanoir, that 'The King is sovereign in his kingdom, but each baron is sovereign in his barony', nevertheless, the king was increasingly attracting justice into his own courts, and away from baronial courts.[16]

At the same time, the greater aristocracy felt that its position at the royal court was being usurped by 'new men, risen from the dust'. These anxieties were not groundless. By the mid-twelfth century kings had realised that the great offices of the household offered an unscrupulous or ambitious appointee the potential for great power. They often kept the seneschalcy, traditionally filled by one of the great nobles of the realm, vacant. They made sure that the offices of marshal, constable and chamberlain were filled by members of the lesser castellan nobility or knightly classes.[17] All these positions offered access to the king and the queen, and the possibility of bringing influence to bear at the centre of royal power. As the greater aristocracy distanced themselves from court circles, they yet complained that the

traditional avenues of access and influence were being denied them. The other traditional role of the greater aristocracy in the governance of the realm was the giving of counsel to the king or queen at the great courts. Great courts were still held – Philip Augustus and Louis VIII held several in which they sought the advice of their barons.[18] But the baronial perception was otherwise, and, as the baronial poet complained at the great court at Compiègne, the barons' voices were not always heard.

It is important to note that baronial disaffection was not confined to Blanche of Castile's guardianship of the kingdom. It was endemic throughout thirteenth-century France. Philip Augustus was lucky in that several potential leaders of disaffection died, leaving daughters or minors as heirs. He took advantage of this, using Capetian cousins, particularly members of the Courtenay and Dreux dynasties, to extend Capetian influence into Normandy and Brittany, and northern Burgundy. But he knew that this could lead to dangerous power blocks. As with the Courtenay in northern Burgundy, he tried to counter the danger by demanding heavy pledges and keeping tight control over marriages. When his final illness struck him, he was on his way towards Anet to deal with more baronial unrest.[19]

Many of the aristocracy who felt alienated from Philip Augustus's court left for the Crusade in the east or in the Languedoc. Others had gravitated towards Lord Louis and Blanche. Louis's status as heir presumptive was similar in many ways to other great nobles. His father had not had him crowned and anointed in co-rulership, as most of his predecessors had done; he did not even give Louis the status of king-designate. When Louis was knighted, and when he first determined to take the English crown, Philip insisted that he sign undertakings to do nothing to the disadvantage of the king. Philip used his son's abilities as a diplomat and a soldier, but did not seek his counsel, and kept him at arm's length from real power. Lord Louis and Blanche's court was, with its hunting and its minstrelsy, livelier and more cultured than Philip's, and it is easy to see why it would attract Robert of Courtenay, the Dreux brothers, Stephen of Sancerre and Guy of Châtillon. Besides, Lord Louis offered this group of young men something to do. They fought with him at La Roche-au-Moines; they accompanied him on the slightly half-hearted Albigensian Crusade; and they joined him in the English adventure.

But when Louis came to the throne, he became the ruler, not the ruled. He ruled just like his father. Philip Augustus's chancery clerks led by Guérin (whom Louis made chancellor) and Walter Cornut remained as powerful as ever. The agents of local enforcement, the *baillis* and *prévôts*, remained in place. Louis did

make a cousin, Robert of Courtenay, butler. But otherwise, his firm treatment of Joanna of Flanders suggests that he was just as determined to exploit his seigneurial rights over the great nobles as Philip had been. He controlled the marriages of their daughters and widows.[20] He circumscribed Robert of Dreux's castle building.[21] He made it clear that he would use full rights of wardship if Robert of Courtenay's son succeeded as a minor.[22] He subjected Philip Hurepel's generous endowments to a tight interpretation much in the king's favour.[23] Baronial disappointment was soon apparent. Peter Mauclerc was scheming with Henry III by early 1226. The atmosphere on Louis's Albigensian Crusade was poisonous, with rumours flying that Count Theobald had had an affair with Blanche, and that Louis died because Theobald had poisoned him. Louis's death, leaving the king a minor in the wardship of a foreign queen, simply gave the disaffected barons the opportunity, as they thought, to seize back their proper place at the very heart of the body politic.

The majority of Louis IX made little difference to the baronial attitude. Theobald of Champagne's revolt took place in 1236. Blanche's second regency was almost devoid of baronial problems, but that was because Louis had taken most potential troublemakers with him. The barons were highly critical when Louis forced Enguerrand of Coucy to submit to royal justice in 1259.[24] They were highly critical of Louis's attempts to put an end to their private treaties and private wars.

Private war was not a revolt against the crown. The barons saw it as a rightful privilege. But it did conflict with the king's duty to ensure peace within his realm. In England, there was no right to private war except in the Marches. Louis issued an edict against private warfare in 1258, though probably with limited effect. Philip of Beaumanoir, who was, after all, a royal administrator, regarded private warfare between barons as normal customary practice in the 1280s. The war between the various heirs to the county of Flanders broke out after Blanche's death in the 1250s, while Western France and Burgundy were only finally stabilised in the late thirteenth century.[25]

And so baronial disaffection was a continual problem for the French monarchy throughout the thirteenth century: it was by no means confined to Blanche's regency. It was also not confined to France. Blanche's sister Berengaria struggled with an unruly baronage in Castile. There, indeed, the barons succeeded – as they did not in France – in seizing control of the young king Henry himself. But the French barons must have been more aware of their English counterparts, whom they had allied with or fought against during Louis's invasion, and to whom many of them were related.

The reasons for English baronial disaffection were much the same as in France. The English kings had exploited their lordly rights over their aristocracy with ruthless effectiveness for much of the twelfth century. They were helped by the fact that the English earldom was still in theory, and under most English kings in fact, an office, given at the king's will, and revocable. Tight royal control over the upper levels of the aristocracy was built into the system. King John, desperate to get back his Continental lands, took exploitation to new levels of arbitrariness and viciousness. By 1213 sections of the aristocracy, with the intellectual backing of sections of the Church, had denounced King John as a tyrant who had broken his coronation oath. They invited Philip Augustus, and then Lord Louis, to take the English throne in John's place. In 1215, at Runnymede, they forced John to agree to major limitations on his kingship, especially on his abilities to demand arbitrary reliefs from them. They were able to take advantage of Henry III's minority to ensure that Magna Carta was continually reissued. When Henry III himself began to make what the baronage considered unreasonable demands, they called him to account in great courts, or parliaments. By the late 1250s their leader was Simon de Montfort, earl of Leicester, younger brother of Count Amaury. The English higher aristocracy, like their French counterparts, called themselves 'barons'. As in France, their sense of corporate identity, and their sense of corporate grievance against the king, was expressed in powerful and often satirical political songs.[26]

But English baronial grievances were always more clearly articulated than those of their French counterparts, and their critique of Angevin kingship more intellectually focused. This was partly because King John's rapacity was so arbitrary. Magna Carta was designed to ensure that the king, like everyone else, respected the laws and customs of the land. It was presented as a return to proper kingship, to a kingship that in failing to respect those laws had descended into tyranny. Philip Augustus, Louis VIII and Louis IX and Blanche made the most of royal rights of lordship, but they remained within their customary rights. Indeed, they merely exploited the customary rights that the aristocracy claimed over their vassals, though they did so with increasing competence. To that extent, they remained, like the early Capetians, *primi inter pares*. Only at the very end of the thirteenth century did Philip IV have the administrative and legal capacity to master his aristocracy in the manner of an Angevin king.

Moreover, from the very start the English baronage had the intellectual backing of masters like Stephen and Simon Langton. These churchmen had absorbed the critiques of excessive royal power that were current in the schools of Paris in the

late twelfth century and the early thirteenth. They knew John of Salisbury's *Policraticus*, with its persuasive image of the realm as a body – the body politic – with the king at its head, and with its suggestion that, should the king become a tyrant, it might be necessary to depose him.[27] Armed with this intellectual concept, the English baronage could decide that their king should be dethroned, and could invite Prince Louis and Blanche to take the English throne in his place. The tradition of English churchmen providing a critique of kingship, and thus investing English baronial grievances with real intellectual authority, continued into the late thirteenth century, when Simon de Montfort had the support of the Franciscan Adam Marsh and Robert Grosseteste, bishop of Lincoln.[28] The English baronage, in short, had a philosophy of governance.

The French baronage did not. Their approach was essentially opportunistic. Any succession offered the possibility of obtaining a position of personal influence and power. Robert of Courtenay managed to acquire the butlership in 1223, but Philip Hurepel overreached himself in 1226. The barons' aims, in so far as they had aims, were to protect or further their own interests. There they were limited by the fact that they themselves lived by the same customs of lordship as did the king. They might resent the exploitation of royal rights of lordship, but they could hardly attack the principle. They might try to seize and thus control a minor king, but denying the right of the eldest son to succeed to his father's patrimony could threaten to unravel the fabric of aristocratic society. They could agitate about lack of positions at court, but those remained as they had always been in the gift of the ruler. They could complain that their interests were ignored at court, but, as the baronial poem makes clear, Blanche or any other ruler did indeed just ignore them. Instead, they concentrated on protecting their territories, and trying to expand them if possible by a mixture of marriage alliances and private war. Blanche, like her father-in-law and her husband, succeeded in controlling most of the marriages of the aristocracy. The one marriage that the crown was unable to prevent was that of Theobald of Champagne and Margaret of Bourbon in 1233.[29]

It is surprising that the French baronage did not draw on the critiques of kingship that were widespread in the Paris schools, in the way that the English baronage did. These critiques were well known within French court circles; the moralised bibles commissioned by Blanche and her husband and son are full of them. Peter Mauclerc enticed Parisian students revolting against Blanche and Cardinal Romanus to his court at Nantes.[30] The students obliged with scurrilous and sardonic songs attacking the sexual depravity of the queen and the legate. But there was no

intellectual underpinning for Peter's intrigues with Henry III. Ironically, the very scholars who had supported the baronial uprising against King John, notably Simon Langton, were closely associated with Louis VIII and Blanche.

The closest the French baronage came to taking a theoretical position against Blanche was in their initial attempt to challenge her position as guardian of the realm and of her young son. Even this was never articulated as a legally based challenge. There was no challenge to the validity, or to the fact, of Louis VIII's deathbed provision. There was no real appeal to precedent, to previous arrangements for 'regencies', though Philip Hurepel's attempt to seize the king and the guardianship must have been implicitly based on them. There were grumbles that the guardian was a woman, but no one suggested that the rule of a woman was illegitimate in itself.

•

How did Blanche's rule affect the governance of France in the thirteenth century? In both her regencies, and when she took control in the crisis of 1244–5, she was conscious, as any regent or regency council should properly be, that the role of a regent was to maintain the status quo, and that their rule was essentially provisional. She took care to insert provisional clauses reserving the rights of the king, or stating that the arrangement was to hold until the king reached his majority or returned home.[31] She ensured that acts and judgements were entered into the royal registers, and demanded frequent renderings of accounts for household expenditure.[32] She protected royal rights firmly, sharing the view adumbrated in the Protest of St Louis of the contribution that the Church should make to the welfare of the realm. She received homage on behalf of the king. Like Philip Augustus, she took securities for good behaviour. She was an energetic war leader, if war was necessary to ensure the peace of the realm. The accounts of 1234 capture the complexity of the arrangements required to organise yet another campaign against Peter Mauclerc.[33] Having ordered the fortification of the city and castle of Angers, she is likely to have overseen its construction with the detailed focus that she gave to Maubuisson. The letter from William des Ormes, describing the siege of Carcassonne, was written to a queen who was interested in and understood the technicalities of siege engines and mining, and how one should build to counter them.[34] Having mobilised an army, and produced a show of strength, she was a patient and creative negotiator, persuading Peter Mauclerc to come to terms lest he become an object of derision.[35] As a regent she probably had to buy

co-operation and peace with more generous offers of lands, money and attractive royal marriage prospects than a strong king would have done, but she judged peace worth the price. Both as active ruler and as counsellor to her son, and, in all likelihood, as counsellor to her husband, she acted as diplomat and peacemaker, exploiting family connections and her extensive networks of friendship with both men and women, relationships often enriched by a commonality of interest in matters cultural or religious.

The importance of marriage settlements to ensure peace within the realm, and vital diplomatic alliances without, provided a natural field for action for a queen regent, but also a queen consort or queen dowager, provided she was both trusted and competent. As regent and ruler, Blanche naturally initiated and controlled the entire process. Her marriage policy showed a ruler of France conscious of the need to maintain stable relations with the Empire, concerned to strengthen Capetian influence in Flanders and the northern seaboard, and to establish Capetian influence in the Languedoc, where, during the Albigensian Crusade, 'so much blood had flowed', as the papal dispensation for the marriage of Louis and Margaret of Provence put it. Distrust of Henry III informed her marriage policy. Toulouse not only required stabilising after the Albigensian wars, but also the proximity of Aquitaine laid it open to the blandishments of Henry III. English trade was important for Flanders and the northern seaboard counties, and had led to diplomatic alliances in the recent past.

Blanche was clearly disappointed when Princess Isabella refused to marry Frederick II's heir, Conrad. Both as regent and as dowager queen, Blanche took care to control the marriages of Joanna of Flanders; it was she who insisted that Joanna marry Thomas of Savoy rather than the opportunist Simon de Montfort, with his English earldom, in 1237. The projected marriage of Joanna's heir, Mary, to Robert of Artois would have brought Flanders into direct Capetian family control, in a mirror image of Toulouse. The marriage of Robert and Matilda of Brabant, after Mary's death, would not have such a decisive outcome, but it built diplomatic bridges in the north-east. Blanche took advantage of the fact that the counties of the northern seaboard fell to heiresses to ensure that these counties were in the hands of members of her family. She married her indulged nephew Alphonse of Portugal to Matilda of Boulogne; her irrepressible great-nephew Alphonse of Brienne to Mary of Eu; and her nephew King Ferdinand of Castile to Joanna of Ponthieu, having prevented a planned marriage between Joanna and

Henry III. Most of these marriages were arranged during St Louis's personal rule, but there is no doubt that they were done so on Blanche's initiative.[36]

Alphonse of Poitiers' marriage with Joanna of Toulouse was designed to bring huge tracts of south-west France into the direct rule of a member of the Capetian family. Joanna was brought up at the Capetian court, and the marriage helped Blanche to entice Raymond VII away from his alliance with their mutual cousin, Henry III. But Raymond's attachment to the Capetian cause was not firm. Louis IX's marriage with Margaret of Provence was designed to counterbalance Raymond, as was Charles's with Margaret's youngest sister, Beatrice. Charles's marriage was arranged by Louis IX, but in doing so he was building on his mother's policy. Castilian marriages, like that of Joanna of Ponthieu with Ferdinand III of Castile in 1237, were also planned with a view to keeping an eye on Raymond in Toulouse and Henry III in Gascony. Blanche tried to marry Blanche of Champagne to the future Alfonso X of Castile, and was furious when Theobald of Champagne married his daughter to Count John of Brittany instead. Theobald's succession to the crown of Navarre undoubtedly gave cause for concern: here was another unstable ally bordering Raymond's Toulouse on the one hand and Henry's Aquitaine on the other. Blanche's concern is visible in her household account for 1241: messengers who brought her the news of the first child born to Theobald as king of Navarre were well rewarded.[37]

Again, Louis IX followed his mother's Iberian marriage strategy. He affianced his heir, Louis, to Berengaria of Castile, and his daughter Blanche to Ferdinand, heir presumptive to Alfonso X. He married his son Philip to Isabella of Aragon and his daughter Isabella to Theobald V of Champagne and Navarre. By the late 1250s Louis was developing a rapprochement with Henry III, but he must always have been conscious that Iberian alliances could be helpful to balance the English presence in Gascony.[38]

For most contemporaries, the quintessence of kingship was the doing of justice. The ruler sat in their court in judgement on their people; they must judge with the wisdom of Solomon, for in their action as judge they were a pale prefiguration of the God of the Last Judgement. The word used by the poet to describe Blanche's rule of the whole world was 'justicier'.[39] As regent, she held court in which she sat to judge cases as the king would have done.[40] Adela of Champagne, as Crusade regent for Philip Augustus, had occasionally sat in judgement, so here Blanche was following precedent.[41] She continued to sit in judgement alongside Louis with

some frequency between 1234 and 1238, though, apart from the famous case of the Talmud, much less frequently between 1238 and 1248.[42]

The judging of cases was changing over the thirteenth century. More and more cases were being attracted into the royal court, not least because the king had jurisdiction over a much wider area than had been the case when Philip Augustus became king. The passing of judgement on cases was increasingly a matter for specialists in the law. In the twelfth century judgement in the king's court would have meant judgement delivered by the king himself, advised by his magnates. By the late thirteenth it often meant judgement delivered in the place where things were discussed – the *parlement* – by a group of judges, most of whom had experience of dealing with customary law as *baillis* and *prévôts*.[43] The king's presence, other than in exceptional cases, was not necessary. St Louis liked to be seen to be doing justice, and, especially after his return from Crusade, often interfered with what had become a system, appropriating judgement to himself.[44] Nevertheless, what had not so long ago been the defining manifestation of royal power was becoming to an extent systematised. In this shifting context, it was appropriate to ask any of one's counsellors to sit in judgement. Thus, Blanche and Bartholomew of Roye might judge a case in Normandy; Blanche and Philip Hurepel might sit in judgement together.[45]

For the extraordinary trial of the Talmud in 1240, Louis turned to Blanche. She was supported by a group of bishops; indeed, this case might more appropriately have been tried in an ecclesiastical court, or at least by an ecclesiastical board of inquiry. Louis chose to have it staged as if in a plenary court, and chose the dowager queen to preside in the place of the king. It is as if he felt that this case should come before the full magisterial majesty of the crown, and accepted that Blanche, an anointed queen, provided that. Perhaps, with his reported loathing of the Jews, he thought that she would handle the case more judiciously than he could have done.

At no stage is the slightest surprise expressed that the queen, whether as regent or as counsellor to the reigning king, should sit in judgement. But this is almost certainly an area where the Facinger thesis – that a queen's power was much diminished in the thirteenth century – would hold. By the late thirteenth century judgement was rendered by the king advised by his lawyers in *parlement*, or by the king's lawyers acting on his behalf in *parlement*. There was less need for courts of judgement to be held and judgement to be delivered by ad hoc commissions. But that served to disempower all the counsellors of a king, who might be princes, like

Philip Hurepel, and household officers, like Bartholomew of Roye, as much as the queen. One might note that Eleanor of Provence, for all her active role in English government, does not appear to have sat in judgement.

The giving of counsel and assent is a related issue, in that it was traditionally sought by and given to the king or ruler in his court, often when he had to give judgement. Kings and rulers had probably always found it easier to make decisions with a small cabal of close advisers. This could certainly be described as taking counsel, from counsellors. It was sometimes described as the ruler issuing a judgment *in concilio* – in council. Some courts, especially perhaps the Norman excheq-uer court, inherited from the Angevin kings, were always small affairs, with judgement delivered by professionals.[46] Nevertheless, there were times when the king realised that he must convene the fullest set of those who thought it their role to advise him – his queens, his family, his prelates, his magnates, his castel-lans – to give assent and thus strong legitimacy to his judgements or commands. The use of broad counsel and assent as a legitimating instrument could reflect both strong and challenged kingship. A strong ruler giving judgement or command in full court appears magnanimous and powerful enough to accept advice with grace; a weak ruler may be able to render their judgements or commands effective only with the backing of their full court or council. As Thomas Bisson has shown, the powerful English kings tended to act in full court or council – or at least contem-porary commentators recorded them as doing so. Contemporary French commen-tators showed little interest in recording this aspect of kingship in France. And yet, there is evidence that Philip Augustus convened several full courts to render judge-ments. In 1220 he called a plenary court specifically to take the counsel of his barons: it was called a *parlamentum* – a place to discuss, the first use of the term.[47] Philip was even prepared to assert that in certain circumstances a king's actions would have legitimacy only if they had the assent of his barons, for instance, when King John surrendered England to the pope.[48] Louis VIII made frequent use of such plenary courts at which he would make decisions or deliver judgements or ordinances with the assent of his prelates and magnates. The barons clearly felt, quite rightly, that these great courts were mere showpieces, that the real decisions were made with a few close counsellors. But the great courts were an established mode of governance in early thirteenth-century France.[49]

Blanche as regent certainly did deliver judgements, ordinances and decisions in full *parlaments*. When Peter Mauclerc refused the summons to her great court at Melun in December 1229, it gave her full legal right to attack him: this was the

process that Philip Augustus had used to give legitimacy to his attacks on her uncle, King John, in 1202. The sentence against Peter was delivered at Ancenis a few months later – but essentially in plenary court, with the sealed assent of the bulk of the magnates and prelates of France.[50] The statute against the Jews was issued at another great court held at Melun in December 1230. The ordinance was issued 'de communi consilio baronum nostrorum' – by the common counsel of our barons. 'Volui, consului et juravi' each magnate or prelate declared – 'I will this, I give my counsel for this, and I swear to uphold this'.[51] The accounts of 1234 show the organisation required to convene the magnates and prelates to the *parlamentum* at Saint-Germain-en-Laye to deal with the claims of the queen of Cyprus against Theobald of Champagne.[52]

Did Blanche as regent have to use counsel and assent, the legitimation of decisions in great courts, in *parlament*, in a way that a reigning king of France would not have done? Probably she did. She was, as I have said, well aware of the provisionality of the rule of a regent. Previous regency governments, for instance, that of Abbot Suger a century earlier, had certainly made use of the additional legitimacy that an overt use of rule through counsel and assent could bring.[53] And there are two clear examples from Blanche's first regency. In 1227 Archbishop Theobald of Rouen was first asked to explain his claims over the forest of Louviers at the professional court of the Norman exchequer; then he was called before the king's court at Vernon, presumably a small court consisting of Blanche, Louis and their usual household clerks and counsellors. When the archbishop's answers were unsatisfactory, he was called to answer before a plenary court with the king's barons.[54] When Blanche could not get the viscountess of Châteaudun to return fiefs to the bishop of Chartres by face-to-face discussion, she convened a great council of the barons of France to back up her orders.[55] But her use of *parlament* – of the ruler issuing judgements, commands and ordinances in overt plenary council with the participation of large numbers of barons and prelates – was probably no more frequent than her husband's had been.

And although the image of the king doing justice in a full court was both powerful and pervasive, judgements, particularly arbitrations, might also be delivered in quite informal circumstances and places. Like Philip Augustus and Louis VIII, Blanche did not just use the overt, plenary council that might be called a *parlamentum*; she also made decisions, and issued commands and judgements, with much smaller groups of counsellors, made up of a handful of trusted bishops and

magnates, household officers, clerks and knights. When she is described as giving judgement *in consilio*, this smaller, intimate council is probably what is implied.[56]

Louis IX too used both great courts and more intimate groups of trusted counsellors to render judgement and issue commands. He formally announced his intention to Crusade in Lent 1247: he delivered the ordinance conferring plenary powers to rule in his place on Blanche at a great court in the hospital at Corbeil.[57] But Louis also liked to give judgement beneath an oak at Vincennes.[58] A particularly nice example of the more intimate form of king's court is the judgement rendered in a case between the chapter and the city of Saint-Quentin in 1244 'in the court of the king at Pontoise in the wardrobe of the Queen, down towards the lower garden'. The court comprised Louis, Blanche, Robert of Artois and Alphonse of Poitiers with John of Beaumont, Geoffrey de la Chapelle, Renaud Triecoc and Master William of Sens, Ferry Paste and Peter des Fontaines – household insiders all.[59] There is no evidence that Louis saw the issuing of an ordinance or judgement in either plenary court – *parlamentum* – or in more intimate council as derogation from his kingship. Indeed, it is in that context that Louis wanted the best counsel available to him – that of his mother. As Joinville showed, the king was perfectly capable of calling a plenary council of the prelates and magnates of France, and simply rejecting their considered advice – as he did over the issue of whether to return to France in 1252.[60] But then so was Blanche – at least according to the baronial songs: 'the other day at Compiègne, when the barons could not obtain their rights, and she didn't deign to look at them, or see them'.[61] The concept of the king advised by his counsellors in *parlament* became institutionalised, as those who gave the advice became professionalised. What did not develop in France, even in the minority regency, was the assumption that the king's judgements, commands and decisions required the consent of his barons and prelates in his plenary court, his *parlament*, in way that it did in thirteenth-century England – in spite of Philip Augustus's comment on John's surrender of England to the pope.

•

Historians tend to characterize Blanche's periods of regency as crisis management – following St Louis's hagiographers, for whom Blanche's struggles with the wicked barons made a good story. It is certainly true that when Louis returned from the Crusade he found that the kingdom had fallen into crisis after Blanche's death, and set to work to restore good governance. It is also true that it was Louis

who took the initiative to reform local government before he left on Crusade, setting up the inquisitions of 1247–8 and taking action against the rapacity of local royal agents. The inquisitions unearthed various infractions that had taken place during Blanche's regency (though no more than had taken place at other times within living memory), and Louis's determination to restore good local governance is sometimes interpreted as an attempt to govern with a new morality after the purely political imperatives of his mother's rule.[62]

The scale of St Louis's 'inquisitions', the *enquêtes*, of 1247–8 has persuaded some historians that, for Louis IX, government was about the gathering of knowledge, so that 'a king might govern by knowing the truth'.[63] But I do not think one can invert that statement, attractive though it is. The government of Philip Augustus certainly sought information, and information that was correct. So did the government of Louis VIII.[64] Blanche doubtless wanted to govern by knowing the truth just as much as Louis. The use of small commissions, sometimes of churchmen, sometimes of a household clerk with a household knight, to provide the information on which a judgement might be based, was not new in 1247 – though the scale of Louis IX's inquisitions was. Blanche certainly used 'inquisition' formats frequently in her second regency to inform her judgements and decisions. She would commission a small group of appropriate churchmen, household clerks or knights to report back to her on issues such as disputes between the bishop and burghers of Châlons-sur-Marne, between the countess of Artois and the lord of Béthune, between the lord and citizens of Poix, between the drapers of Paris and the abbey of Saint-Denis. The reports she commissioned were sent back to her, and used as the basis for judgements in the royal court.[65] But this sort of inquiry and judgement was not regularly recorded before the 1260s. The household accounts of the 1230s show members of the household sent on what must have been this type of inquiry. In 1239, for instance, there was an 'inquiry' into an unnamed dispute or issue in the Auvergne.[66] Blanche, like Louis VIII and Philip Augustus, would doubtless have said that government was more just if the ruler had the correct information. What was different about the *enquêtes* instituted by Louis IX in 1247, and then by his brother Alphonse of Poitiers in his lands, was the scale, and the fact that they were for the salvation of the soul of the ruler who instituted them.[67] The great *enquêtes* of 1247–50 were preparations of the soul for Crusade, not attempts to impose good government where the queen had failed to do so.

Like Louis VIII's reign, Blanche's two periods of regency were too brief for her to institute anything resembling the programmes of administrative reorganisation

or reform set in train by the long-reigning Philip Augustus and St Louis – besides, reform was not the role of a regent. But Blanche, along with her husband, must have been inculcated with concepts of – with the importance of the ideal of – good government since her youth. As young adults, Blanche and her husband offered refuge to Simon and Stephen Langton; Simon remained a part of their entourage. Their attempt to depose a tyrant, take the English crown and restore good government on the people of England was at the invitation of the Langtonian clergy who knew the *Policraticus* and the contemporary Parisian critiques of arbitrary royal power. The Paris masters' debates on good governance inform the moralised bibles, reflecting the extent to which these matters were discussed in the court circles of Blanche and Louis VIII.

The influence of the ideals of good governance on Blanche's and Louis VIII's practical rule is evident in their treatment of the Jews. Philip Augustus's approach to the Jews had been pragmatic. When it seemed politic to do so, he expelled them from the kingdom. When it became apparent that the economy of the kingdom, and the king's coffers, would benefit from their economic contribution, he invited them back under royal protection. Both Louis VIII and Blanche clearly believed that allowing the Jews to lend at interest was morally wrong, whatever its economic advantages, and both issued ordinances to stop it. Influenced as they were by reformist churchmen, they would have seen this as good governance. This is particularly clear in Blanche's ordinance of 1230. It was issued for the souls of Louis VIII and his ancestors, 'having thought about the benefit for the entire kingdom'.[68]

Blanche took very seriously the royal responsibility to ensure the peace of the realm. She could probably have allowed her Dreux and Courtenay cousins to attack Theobald of Champagne with impunity, but intervened to impose peace on the warring parties. Her determination to do so prefigured St Louis's attempts to prevent private war altogether in the late 1250s. Her firm reaction to the rioting scholars in Paris in 1227 was driven by the same principles. The students had contravened the law and attacked Church property; the crown must protect the Church and impose peace. She took equally seriously the royal responsibility to protect widows, orphans and the poor – a responsibility accepted by the king at his coronation. She built and funded hospitals; she ensured that there was enough money for young women to marry or to retire into convents. Her extravagant almsgiving, however much it might unsettle St Louis, must have seemed to her the proper fulfilment of the duties she assumed as queen at her coronation. Concern for the poor clouded her judgement over the *pastoreaux*, but underlay her

determination to rescue the captured peasants of Orly from the prisons of the chapter of Notre-Dame.

Louis IX's overt provisions for the good governance of the realm should not been seen as reactions to the rule of his parents. Rather, they, particularly Blanche, provided the inspiration for him. The difference is surely between the ideologically informed 'good' governance of Blanche, her husband and her son, and the more pragmatic governance of Philip Augustus. Philip's government aimed to sustain the crown; Blanche and Louis VIII, influenced by Langton, and followed by Louis IX, saw government as being for the good of the people.

•

The Franciscan who, around 1300, praised Blanche's governance of the kingdom as unrivalled implied too that she had extended the dominion of the kingdom as it had not been before or since.[69] Perhaps Langtonian influence lay behind Blanche's perception of the realm – of what was France. The English kingdom, which Blanche and Lord Louis had struggled so hard to capture, was a clear political entity, its borders well defined – most by the sea. It had a political and cultural integrity that the sprawling kingdom of France lacked. Blanche knew just how sprawling the kingdom of France was: as a child, she had travelled from the Pyrenees to Normandy; like her husband, she possessed substantial properties and connections in the far north-east of France; as queen regent, she campaigned in western Normandy and the Loire; as queen regent and queen mother, she penetrated deep into Burgundy, meeting the pope at Cluny. She came from a political tradition of multiple realms, of empires. She knew all about the great collection of realms ruled by her grandfather Henry II and her uncles Richard and John, and occasionally referred to as an *imperium* – not least because she watched, and contributed to, its slow collapse. She probably knew that her great-grandfather Alfonso VII of Castile-León had styled himself emperor of all the Spains.[70]

Very quickly, she accepted her role as wife of the heir to the kingdom of France. Perhaps she had no choice. She was married to be a diplomatic channel between two great powers, but one of them suffered almost immediately a catastrophic failure. As King John noted bitterly in 1214: 'We remembered how our niece had been given in marriage to Louis, and what the result of that was.'[71] She reinvented herself with remarkable speed as the daughter of the king of Castile, and the future queen of France, not an Angevin princess. Her diplomatic endeavours aimed to ensure that Henry III gained no further foothold in the kingdom of France.

This background, this particular set of experiences, must have informed her conception of the kingdom of France. It was an expansive conception. She contemplated and fought for the construction of a Franco-English *imperium*. Along with her husband, she was determined to incorporate the Languedoc into the direct power of the king, and the county of Toulouse into his indirect power.[72] In 1234 she insisted that all disputes between Provence and the counts of Toulouse should come before the court of the king of France.[73] She was committed to keeping Flanders firmly within the orbit of the French king, for all that parts of Flanders lay within the Empire. She loaned money to her indigent niece, the empress Mary, in order to defend Mary's fortress of Namur, to keep it out of imperial hands.[74] This was a continuation of the strategy developed by Philip Augustus and Louis VIII, but Blanche's property base and networks in this area of north-east France and Flanders gave her the understanding and the means to influence events there. After 1234 a large number of arrangements with the Flemish counts, towns and aristocracy continued to be made in Blanche's, as well as Louis IX's, name; and it was Blanche who ensured that Countess Joanna married Thomas of Savoy, not Simon de Montfort, in 1237.[75] She also knew where to stop. She prevented Robert of Artois responding to papal calls to put himself forward as king of Germany, and she forbad Charles of Anjou to pursue opportunities in Hainault.[76] The extent of her influence in the area is reflected in the fact that the Flemish succession crisis erupted into open war after her death.

Her conception of the powers of the king and kingdom of France was not just expansive. She also thought that, as in England, the powers of the king should run throughout his kingdom, irrespective of the great principalities, the dukedoms and counties that made up the realm. Louis VIII's statute for the Jews of 1223 specified that he had the assent of the barons who had Jews on their lands and of those who did not.[77] But Blanche's statute for the Jews of 1230 is framed to apply throughout the kingdom. It was enacted 'by our sincere will, with the common consent of our barons, bearing in mind the benefit of the whole kingdom' (*utilitate tocius regni*). Nobody 'in the whole of our kingdom' could keep the Jews of another lord. The king would enforce this statute in his own lands – 'in terra nostra'; the barons would enforce it in their own lands. But if any baron did not want to observe the statute, the king would compel him to do so by force. It draws a nice distinction between the lands of the various rulers – the *terrae*, which might be the lands of the king as much as those of the count of Champagne or the count of Flanders – and the kingdom, the *regnum*. But here, both in theory and in

practice, the good, the *utilitas*, of the whole kingdom would override the lordship of its constituent lands.[78] It prefigured St Louis's imposition of a royal coinage throughout the kingdom in 1262. It has been called 'the first measure of effective general legislation' enacted by the Capetian dynasty.[79]

•

Blanche had an astute understanding of the importance of image in the presentation and indeed the realisation of power. This is the area in which she made her most innovative contribution to the governance of the kingdom of France. She did not, and could not, have done this alone. Louis VIII played his part. Between them they introduced a new chivalric tone to the French court, along with a new book culture that was both visually magnificent and engaged in the intellectual currents of the day. The court clergy, who had spent the last two decades trying to present Philip Augustus as the new Charlemagne, must have found their interest in the presentation of image refreshing. The Capetian court under Philip had not been devoid of celebrations of his kingship, but they were not frequent. The two most magnificent occasions had been the knighting of Louis – unwontedly lavish – in 1209, and the triumphal entrance of Philip and Louis into Paris after the victories of Bouvines and La Roche-au-Moines in 1214.[80] Both celebrations concerned Louis, and it may be that his, and his wife's, chivalric sensibilities were behind them. The next grand celebration of kingship was Blanche and Louis's coronation in 1223, which left the archbishop and the city of Reims squabbling over the enormous costs, and their staged entrance, as king and queen, into their capital city afterwards. Such egregious display was not possible in the difficult circumstances of Louis IX's accession in 1226, but from the marriage and coronation at Sens in 1234 Blanche showed herself to be a mistress of ceremonies.[81]

Blanche and Louis VIII had absorbed, in a way that Philip had perhaps not, the obsession of the curial clergy with the position of the Capetian dynasty within the history of the kingdom of France. One of Philip's clerks had copied into Philip's registers a version of the so-called Prophecy of St Valerie, which foretold the return of the kingdom to the line of Charlemagne after seven generations of Capetian kings. This prophecy caused some frisson at the Capetian court in the late twelfth century, for the seventh generation of Capetians was about to run out after Philip Augustus. Fortunately, Louis VIII was descended from Charlemagne through his mother, Isabella of Hainault. The idea that he embodied the fulfilment of the Valerian prophecy was fully developed by the mid-thirteenth century. Vincent of

Beauvais stated it firmly in his *Speculum historiale*, and in the 1260s the royal tombs at Saint-Denis were arranged to make the role of Louis VIII as the direct heir of Charlemagne explicit. But the idea was already crystallising around the king during his lifetime.[82] Louis and Blanche surely showed their awareness in the naming of Philip Dagobert; and Blanche herself, even more overtly, when she named her youngest son Charles.

With the co-operation of Louis VIII, Blanche crafted a new image of the Capetian family, very different from that of Philip Augustus and from her Angevin forbears. Perhaps her Castilian family provided a model. Her parents were devoted to one another and cared deeply for their children, and this was reciprocated.[83] All the evidence suggests that there were strong affective relationships between Blanche and Louis VIII and their children, and among the children themselves. They had no difficulty in projecting their marriage as one of consent and mutual support. But both worked to ensure that they projected an image of a Christian and loving family living in harmony. Louis VIII took care to provide for his younger sons and his daughter in his will. Both before and after his death, Blanche developed a maternal image of herself as the protector and educator of a family. Joinville and Agnes of Harcourt, in her Life of Princess Isabella, show Blanche as a mother deeply involved in the daily life of her children: the image, as the household accounts show, had its basis in reality.[84] As an image, it was noticed by contemporary commentators. Philip Mousquès describes her gathering her children around her to meet her husband returning – in triumph as they thought – from his last Crusade. Matthew Paris shows her sweeping her now-adult children in her train to meet Edmund of Abingdon at Senlis to offer him refuge and hospitality in France.[85] It was noticed by her children themselves, as Charles of Anjou's deposition shows. Of course, Blanche owed her power to her position as the mother of the king. But this was different. The whole family were involved in the image, not just the oldest son and heir. All the brothers helped in the building of Royaumont. The family, not just the king and his mother, was depicted rejoicing at the arrival of the Crown of Thorns in the window in the Sainte-Chapelle. Undoubtedly this strengthened Blanche's position as queen, especially during the first regency. Her role as mother of the royal family was a reflection of the role of the Virgin Mary within the Holy Family. It provided a metaphor for her political role as mother of the people of France. Her children found it a powerful and meaningful image – and the reality behind it attractive. Louis IX, if not always the ideal husband, given Margaret's description of him as 'contrary', was a loving and self-conscious

paterfamilias, addressing fond letters of advice to his children. Charles of Anjou was, by medieval standards, a good husband and a caring father.[86] He made his mother's configuration of the perfect family into a substantive argument for his brother's canonisation.

If Blanche drew on memories of her Castilian family to create a loving and harmonious Capetian family, for other aspects of the image of rulership she was indebted to her Angevin heritage. Philip Augustus's style of rulership was administrative rather than courtly and demonstrative. In this restrained *persona*, Philip set himself within the tradition of his father and grandfather. Louis VI and Louis VII were used to making a virtue of their homespun kingship, circumscribed by relative lack of resources. They were above all conscious of the riches and glamour of the Anglo-Norman kings. Famously, the Angevin courtier Walter Map records a conversation with Louis VII: 'Your king', says Louis, referring to Henry II, 'has everything – horses, rich silks, fighting men, lavish food, a menagerie; but we here in France have nothing but bread, wine and joy.'[87]

The Anglo-Norman and Angevin kings had developed a very different presentation of kingship. They revelled in the wealth and the glamour that magnificent apparel and great buildings as the theatres of their power could bring. Henry II and the empress Matilda eased out founders of impressive religious institutions, insisting they had founded them themselves.[88] They knew and exploited the use of ritual in their rulership – both Richard the Lionheart and King John had themselves inaugurated as duke of Normandy, as well as crowned king of England.[89] Richard was the supreme exponent of staged kingship. In 1190 he made a grand seaborne entry into the harbour at Messina. His painted and caparisoned ships sailed in close formation; the king himself, 'in tanta gloria', stood at the prow of his flagship heralded by the sound of trumpets. It was an unforgettable display of royal majesty – not least for Philip Augustus, who watched it and knew himself outclassed.[90]

Anglo-Norman and Angevin kingship was not just more glamorous, more overtly charismatic, than Capetian kingship; it was also more demonstrative. Perhaps because the Anglo-Norman and Angevin kings could cut such fine figures, they could risk displays of emotion, particularly anger, as political tools.[91] Anger deployed by the less well resourced and the less intrinsically powerful Capetians risked registering merely as petulance, as when the young Philip Augustus hacked down the ancient elm at Gisors, under which the French king and the duke of Normandy had treated since time immemorial.[92] An English king was powerful

enough to stage his own ritual humiliation – as Henry II did at Avranches and then Canterbury in penitential expiation for the death of Thomas Becket. Henry's enemies were defeated as the king suffered the whips of the Canterbury monks; Henry was able to claim that his humiliation brought him victory.[93]

Blanche must have heard stories of these vivid displays of demonstrative kingship from her mother, from her grandmother on the journey from Castile and perhaps from her Angevin cousin Matilda of Perche or her Iberian cousin, Richard's widow, Berengaria of Navarre. She herself was by nature demonstrative: she wept so much they thought she would go mad when her husband died; she fainted away when Louis IX left to go on Crusade. As the Ménestrel of Reims said, 'she knew how to hate and how to love'.[94] At a personal level she introduced a new open emotionalism to the stuffy French court and the phlegmatic Capetian kingship. It is evident too that, like her Angevin relations, she understood how one might use a more demonstrative style as a tool of rulership, and how important the presentation of an image of kingship could be in the construction of royal power.

The outstanding example of her use of royal anger is the occasion when she repaid the monies owed by her great-niece the empress Mary to Greek and Italian shipowners.[95] Mary had pleaded piteously with her aunt to pay off her debts. Blanche finally agreed. But she stipulated that the debts should be paid by Stephen of Montfort, who so often distributed her alms, in the Hôtel-Dieu in Paris – in the great hall that she had built in memory of her husband, who had died in his defence of the True Faith. The shipowners, who demanded payment for their contribution to the defence of Christendom, were handed their pieces of silver surrounded by the poor and sick of the hospital – the poor and sick who in their persons represented Christ, for Christ had said 'I was sick and you visited me, I was poor and you visited me.' It was a powerful display of righteous royal anger, served very cold.

It made sophisticated use of the hospital hall as a theatre of power. Blanche was a great architectural patron, in the Anglo-Norman and Angevin tradition, rather than the Capetian. She had an instinctive understanding of what a building stood for and how a ruler might use the spaces in or around a building, and the buildings themselves, with the sculpture, furnishings, painted glass and walls, to convey the intended image of their rulership. With the help of Bishop Walter of Chartres, she managed to persuade Peter Mauclerc and Philip and Matilda of Boulogne to join her in a great glazed celebration of what looked like Capetian family unity after the Treaty of Vendôme in the transepts of Chartres Cathedral (see pl. 10).[96]

The penitential procession of the three queens to ensure Louis VIII's victory at La Rochelle in 1224 deployed the topography of the city of Paris. Blanche led the people in solemn procession from the mother church, the cathedral of Notre-Dame, out beyond the city walls to the humble Cistercian nunnery of Saint-Antoine, dedicated, like all Cistercian nunneries to the Virgin, but founded for penitent prostitutes. They must have processed out of Notre-Dame through the new west portal, showing the Virgin, crowned as Queen of Heaven – *Santa Maria Regalis* – interceding for mankind with God at the Last Judgement, as now Blanche and her fellow queens were about to do on behalf of Louis VIII and the people of France. Traditionally, the king went to the abbey of Saint-Denis before a military campaign, to take the *oriflamme* from the altar of St Denis, and march to war under the special protection of the saint. This was almost an inversion of that tradition. Here three queens went to a simple Cistercian nunnery rather than a great elaborate Benedictine mausoleum; they went, not as soldiers, but as penitents. Blanche, devoted as she was to Thomas Becket, must have known how her royal grandfather's humility and penitence had brought him victory half a century earlier.

The procession of the three queens undoubtedly inspired the final stages of the reception of the Crown of Thorns in Paris in 1239. Saint-Antoine did not lie on the most direct route between Sens and Paris. But the Cistercian nunnery for reformed prostitutes was the station chosen for the great ostension of the Crown of Thorns (see pl. 13). After that, its processional route into the city, then into the cathedral church of Notre-Dame on the Ile de la Cité, was the precise reverse of the procession of the three queens.[97] Blanche worked closely with Walter Cornut on the reception of the Crown of Thorns. It was received on French lands at Walter's town of Villeneuve-l'Archevêque, and then feted in his cathedral of Sens. Either Walter or Blanche ordered the fine new portal showing the Coronation of the Virgin to be slapped up against the doorway into the modest church at Villeneuve (see pl. 12). Walter had also collaborated with Blanche on the ceremonial for the marriage of Louis and Margaret and Margaret's coronation at Sens in 1234. There the household accounts show the detailed organisation that went into ensuring the success of the ceremony.[98]

The same focus on detail, on the provision of a visually and musically lavish occasion, can be seen in the accounts for the knighting of Robert of Artois, Alphonse of Poitiers and Alphonse of Portugal, reviving memories of the knighting of Lord Louis in 1209. The knighting of Alphonse of Portugal took place at Melun, and was essentially Blanche's affair. Charles was knighted at Blanche's castle of

Melun too, which suggests that the organisation of this event was also handed to Blanche.[99] It is unclear how far the ceremonies and feasts for Robert of Artois and Alphonse of Poitiers were organised by Robert and Alphonse, by Blanche or by Louis himself. Their chivalric exuberance suggests they were not quite what St Louis would have asked for. But they were not just entertainments for the court. They advertised the wealth and thus the power of the French crown in areas that the Capetians had not controlled directly for long. The use of the great hall at Saumur, built by Henry II, for the feast inaugurating his great-grandson Alphonse as count of Poitou must have been deliberate, and discussed at the feast, or Joinville would not have mentioned it. Was it Blanche's idea, or Louis's? If it were the king's, it would show that he had learnt some of his mother's subtle understanding of buildings and ceremonies as signifiers of power.

As, of course, does Louis's commissioning of the Sainte-Chapelle. Blanche might have contributed to this project, but fundamentally it was Louis's. It is a building brimful of meaning – in its forms, in its proportions and dimensions, in arrangements for liturgy and relic display, and in its iconography. All celebrate kingship – the kingship of Solomon and David, the kingship of Christ and the kingship of the Capetians.[100] And Louis, trained by his mother, knew how to make use of the Sainte-Chapelle in his role as *rex imago dei*, in his role as protector of his people, in his role as supporter of the Church, and in his diplomacy.

Louis learnt too from his mother the importance of gesture, and how to use it to compensate for his more retiring, less authoritative personality. Although he eschewed manifestations of courtly festivity, his kingship was highly demonstrative. He gave full reign to his emotions, grieving profoundly for his brother Robert and for Blanche. He signalled his disapproval of the elaborate feast at Saumur with an inappropriate cotton hat amidst the luscious silks. When Louis built a new hospital at Compiègne, he himself helped to carry the first patient into it. When his eldest son died, Louis himself helped to carry the boy's bier to Saint-Denis for burial. He liked to be seen to be doing justice, sitting in the open under an oak at Vincennes, doubtless to the despair of the court officers whose role it was to oversee the king's justice in *parlement*. And he was protective of the image of the king. In 1262 he forbad his magnates to issue coins bearing images of themselves that might imitate those of the king, and thus depreciate royal majesty.[101]

Thus Blanche brought a new tone to Capetian kingship, and a new set of tools – gesture, ceremony, building, imagery – for the expression of Capetian power. It was a contribution in the 'softer', cultural registers of power; but it would

be false to see it as a contribution of exclusively womanly, queenly power. On the contrary. Her understanding of these tools of power almost certainly derived from her ancestors, the Anglo-Norman and Angevin kings. They proved crucial tools of power in the kingship of Louis IX.

Epilogue:
The Image of the Queen

How did blanche see herself? Her tomb, with its bronze effigy, is lost; she probably left its commissioning to her executors anyway. But her seal must indicate how she wanted to be seen (see pl. 22). It is her private seal, not the official seal for royal business that a ruler would use. The inscription identifies her as Blanche, 'by the grace of God, Queen of the Franks' – the words used for her predecessors. The image is slightly surprising. Previous queens of France had stared directly at the viewer, grasping signifiers of queenly authority, usually a fleur-de-lis. Isabelle of Hainault, on the silver seal matrix placed in her tomb, holds a sceptre. Blanche's body sways elegantly, almost provocatively, beneath the soft folds of a long robe, and her face is turned to three-quarter view, like a filmstar in a publicity photo. With one hand, she holds the clasp of her mantle; with the other, she seems to point to, rather than hold, one of the six fleurs-de-lis that decorate the background. This woman of natural authority, who expected, wanted and enjoyed power, who was probably the most successful woman ruler of the Middle Ages, has herself shown on her seal as a woman of fashion and charm. She was the first French queen to use a counterseal. She used this to identify herself not as a wife or mother, but as a daughter. The field is filled by a castle, and the inscription proclaims her 'daughter of the king of Castile' (*Bla[n]cha filia regis Castelle*) (see pl. 23).[1]

In some ways, Blanche's seal image was very 'modern', in comparison to that of her mother-in-law, Isabella of Hainault. Isabella is an icon of power; Blanche has the new Gothic naturalism, appearing as a woman of flesh, blood and excellent dress sense. She was the first queen to use the developing science of heraldry on her seal, with the field of fleur-de-lis, and the castle of Castile on the counterseal. Both trends were followed by subsequent queens of France, but most, including her immediate successor, Margaret, made sure they grasped a sceptre, and it was some time before a queen of France used a counterseal to identify her as her father's daughter. Margaret, for instance, had a fleur-de-lis and the inscription 'Ave Maria Gracia Plena' on hers. Thus she used her seal to express her devotion to the Virgin. And it was Margaret, continually denied the authority and influence proper to a queen, who introduced the sceptre as the accoutrement of the queen on her seal.[2]

Blanche's sense of herself as the daughter of the king of Castile is pervasive. The castles of Castile, gold on a scarlet ground, are stamped over most works of art connected with her. They are on the glass of the transept windows at Chartres; in many of the windows, especially the *Esther* window, of the Sainte-Chapelle; on the choir and transept of Saint-Denis; and on tiles from abbeys, churches and palaces (see pls 1, 13 and illustration on back of jacket). Her children Robert, Charles and, in particular, Alphonse deployed the castles proudly on their arms. The reference to her father, the saviour of Christendom, was very direct: Alfonso VIII was the first king of the land of castles to have them painted in the colours of gold and blood on his shield. He, too, used a castle on his seal. Her mother, Eleanor of England, had castles embroidered onto stoles in the 1190s. Alfonso would be buried in castle-embroidered brocade. The sign was carried into battle with him at the crushing disaster of Alarcos and the glorious victory of Las Navas de Tolosa.[3]

Las Navas de Tolosa transformed Blanche from an Angevin hostage princess, niece of a vicious and defeated English tyrant, into the daughter of an Iberian hero. Perhaps it is not surprising that throughout her life she should have emphasised and drawn strength from her links with the country she had left at the age of twelve. But she did so to a remarkable and remarked-upon extent. It gave easy ammunition to her detractors. Spaniards, especially Spanish women, were apt to be regarded as dangerously exotic, and quick to consort with astrologers, almost like prefigurations of Carmen. William the Breton dismissed Matilda of Portugal, countess of Flanders, as a woman who consulted sorcerers, in the Spanish custom. 'Do you think I am going to rely on dreams and auguries like a Spaniard', asked Simon of Montfort before the battle of Muret.[4] The baronial songs accuse Blanche

of sending monies to Spain, and Walter Cornut of preferring Spanish men to French barons.[5] The household accounts bear out the baronial complaints. Blanche spent huge amounts of royal revenues, as well as her own, on pensions, gifts and alms for Iberians. She sent her sisters painted images, liturgical books and objects, silks and rock crystals – the last likely to have reached France via Spain in the first place. She surrounded herself with Iberians at court, and reserved some of the best marriages in her gift for her Iberian nephews. When Blanche's great-niece Eleanor of Castile arrived in England in 1254 on her marriage to Lord Edward of England, Matthew Paris commented adversely on the Hispanic luxury with which she surrounded herself, especially the carpets.[6] There is no record of similar criticism of Blanche. But the luxuries recorded in the household accounts – the carpets, rich clothes and jewels – were usually acquired for Blanche's use. The books associated with her suggest she liked gold leaf to be thick, and colour to be rich. The two surviving objects that can be associated with her patronage, the crosiers for Maubuisson and Le Lys, sport extraordinarily large and elaborate rock-crystal heads (see pl. 18). The gifts exchanged between Blanche and her sisters are suggestive of exotic, slightly Arabesque Hispanic luxuries too.

Blanche's identification with Castile showed even in her piety, in the many commemorations of her parents and her other relations. The arrangements at both Royaumont and Maubuisson owed much to her parents' foundation of Las Huelgas; and she named Maubuisson 'Santa Maria Regalis', as they had named Las Huelgas. Her patronage of the Dominicans probably owed something to their Spanish origins and connections. They were the brothers of St James – Santiago de Compostela – in France; when Blanche could not undertake a vowed pilgrimage to Santiago itself, she paid for the completion of the Dominican house in Paris instead. She was at the centre of a circle of scholar churchmen who toyed with the new Aristotelian texts; probably both Blanche and the churchmen around her were conscious of the important role played by scholars in Toledo in the transmission of these texts. Whoever designed the opening image of the astronomers in her psalter knew it too, as did the designer of the moralised bible who subverted the image to attack philosophers and those who studied natural sciences (see pls 25 and 26).[7]

The image of Blanche in her psalter is merely conventional (see pl. 4). Made before she was queen, it shows her uncrowned, at prayer before a fine gold cross on an altar, with a substantial devotional book at her feet. The richness of the accoutrements – the gold cross and large devotional book – are certainly

appropriate. She appears in the narrative of the Relic Window at the Sainte-Chapelle, too (see pl. 13). Again, the image itself is unrevealing. She is dressed to resemble the Old Testament queens in the windows, and her role, like that of everyone else involved, is essentially processional. But for Blanche and her sons, to see themselves immortalised in painted glass, taking part in the history of the world from the Creation to the End of Time, caught at a particular time, place and event – the reception of the precious relics in the here and now of France and Paris – must have been extraordinary.

The most famous image of Blanche is that in the Toledo moralised bible, showing her seated, instructing her visibly youthful son Louis IX in the business of kingship (see frontispiece). The image is likely to have been made around 1234 when Louis was about to marry, and thus about to take over personal governance of the realm. It is reasonable to assume that this moralised bible was commissioned by Blanche as a wedding and coronation present for Louis and Margaret; in which case the image of Blanche and Louis was either ordered by Blanche or produced by one of the many painters and book-makers who knew her well, and knew it would please her.

The parallel with images of the Virgin sitting at the right hand of Christ is resonant, and those who saw this image were doubtless intended to notice it (cf. frontispiece and pl. 12). Here is the mother queen following the precept of the Virgin as guide and as intercessor. An anointed king was widely regarded as a reflection, however pale, of Christ. He was the *rex imago dei* – the king in the image of God. This image of the king with his mother at his right hand makes the Christological parallel more overt.

There was another biblical parallel: King Solomon set his mother, Bathsheba, at his right hand too.[8] This was seen by medieval commentators as an Old Testament type for the Virgin and Christ. In his short book on the reception of the Crown of Thorns, Walter Cornut reminded his readers of a verse in the Song of Solomon: 'Enter and see, O daughters of Sion, King Solomon in the diadem with which his mother crowned him.'[9] This passage comes just after Walter has noted that the land of France has recently been honoured by many worthy deeds through the zeal of Louis and the vigilance of his devout mother. When he wrote those words, Walter must surely have had in mind this image of Blanche and young Louis – and the difficult early months of Louis' reign, when Blanche with Walter's help arranged the coronation. Walter's text makes it clear that the Toledo Bible image was not accidental. The image of the queen almost in the guise of the Queen of Heaven – to

whom she dedicated her foundation of Maubuisson – was a powerful statement of the concept of the exalted office of the queen that Blanche and her advisers evidently held.

•

Blanche's own voice comes through sometimes. Her surviving letters are slightly formal and carefully drafted in good Latin, and were probably written by her chancery clerks. Her letter to Henry III, to tell him the good news of the taking of Damietta and of the birth of a nephew to both Margaret and Eleanor of Provence, has none of the spontaneity of the letter sent to her by Robert of Artois, whose contents it transmits.[10] Her letter to her cousin Blanche of Navarre and Champagne is disappointing: it merely transmits sections of the official circular sent out to Christendom by her father.[11] The foundation charters for Maubuisson and Le Lys, with their preambles referring to angels, conversion and the sins of this world – extremely unusual, perhaps unique, among thirteenth-century French lay charters – reflect her direction; but again, the drafting, including the faulty Latin in the Maubuisson act, was due to her clerks. Did she write the songs ascribed to her? The song to the Virgin is short, largely conventional in imagery and concept, but charming and nicely wrought. The invocation to her as queen and the fleur-de-lis suggest that Blanche might indeed have written it. The two-part song is more likely to have been written by Theobald of Champagne alone.

Some of the chroniclers met her and knew her at first hand. William the Breton was oddly uninterested in her – but then he disapproved of the attempt to take the English crown. The author of the 'Histoire des ducs de Normandie' was closely connected with Robert of Béthune and the aristocracy of north-east France; he probably knew her – he uses the possessive, calling her 'my' Lady Blanche rather than 'the' Lady Blanche. Joinville draws a powerful and convincing portrait of a courageous woman who is over-possessive of her son. Her own voice is most unmediated in Rabbi Yehiel's account of the Talmud trial. The queen is unnamed, and the rabbi has no agenda of his own as far as the queen is concerned, but Blanche's natural authority and questioning intelligence come through vividly in his account.

Like her grandmother Eleanor of Aquitaine and her uncle Richard the Lionheart, Blanche became a legend almost in her own lifetime. For Philippe Mousquès, writing within her lifetime, she was a formidable presence: she was the wise queen, whose son loved her more deeply than any other son could love his mother, and

obeyed her in all things.[12] The Ménestrel of Reims wrote in 1262, a mere ten years after her death and long before the image of Blanche became caught up in attempts to declare her son a saint. The Ménestrel has several striking anecdotes featuring Blanche. He tells the story of Blanche blackmailing Philip Augustus into releasing monies to rescue Lord Louis's English campaign by threatening to pawn her children. He tells too the unforgettable story of Blanche disproving the slander that she has been made pregnant by Cardinal Romanus, by jumping on a table in full council and throwing off an enveloping mantle to reveal herself in nothing but a flimsy chemise. 'Lords, look at me, all of you: someone has said I am pregnant with a child', she challenges them, as she twirls on the table to show off her svelte figure.[13] When she died, Matthew Paris called her the 'Lady of the ladies of this world', and compared her to the Persian empress Semiramis. Matthew had developed into one of her most ardent admirers, and it is clear from the context that the highest praise is intended. But Semiramis, who was known to the Middle Ages through the histories of Orosius, Eusebius and Isidore of Seville, was an ambivalent model for female rulership. She too ruled for her minor son. It was said she sometimes wore men's clothes to do so, and she solved the potential problem of a minority by marrying her son. She was believed to have a voracious sexual appetite, and Dante placed her among the lustful in hell. But she also had a more positive reputation. She was admired as an effective ruler of a vast empire, which she expanded to run from India to Ethiopia. Perhaps the ghost of Semiramis informs the comment of the Paris-educated Franciscan, writing around 1300, that under Blanche France was better governed and greater in extent than it had been before or since. Semiramis was often described, as Blanche was, as feminine in sex but masculine in counsel or heart. She was seen as a great architectural patron too – the builder of the hanging gardens of Babylon, a sort of female equivalent to Solomon, the builder of the Temple.[14] So Blanche was the new Semiramis and the new Bathsheba, to whom the new Solomon, St Louis, owed his crown, as Walter Cornut dared to imply in his account of Louis' acquisition of the Crown of Thorns. Bathsheba had been the object of King David's illicit lust. These comparisons, and the Ménestrel's tale of the flinging off of the mantle, suggest that contemporaries sensed a strong sexuality in Blanche, for all that they praised her carefully preserved chastity.

•

Blanche was not a ruler in her own right. She owed her status and power to the fact that she was the wife of Louis VIII and the mother of Louis IX. Her life has to be assessed and understood in relation to both men. Louis VIII's reign was so short that it is usually treated merely as a coda to Philip Augustus's or a prelude to Louis IX's. Louis VIII himself – short, fair, sickly, uxorious, intelligent, bookish, usually gentle but capable of sudden acts of violence, focused and calculating in his organisation of his final Crusade – failed to capture the imagination of his contemporaries, let alone subsequent historians. His wife – intelligent, courageous, determined, intensely devout but also passionate and emotional, and left a widow with a young family, ruling France in a crisis – captured it only too easily. Blanche spent twenty-six years of her life married to Louis VIII. It was a successful and close marriage. The emotional stability, the companionship and the intellectual give and take of the long years with her husband played an important part in making her what she was, as it made him what he was. Her vivid character overshadows him, as it probably did at the time. But his importance in her life and story should not be forgotten.

With her son Louis IX there is almost the opposite problem. Immediately after Louis IX's death on Crusade in 1270, it was obvious that he was a candidate for sainthood. The clergy around him, Franciscan, Dominican and Benedictines from Saint-Denis, began to produce Lives of the king that would demonstrate his sanctity. The canonisation process became official. Those who could remember Louis made their depositions, including Charles of Anjou, Louis's sole remaining sibling. In the very early fourteenth century the long-lived Joinville produced an account of St Louis in French for a lay audience, based in part on the depositions of the canonisation process. With Charles of Anjou's support, there were moves to achieve at least beatitude for Isabella. Isabella's lady, Agnes of Harcourt, produced an account of the princess's attempt to lead a blameless life at court, before founding an order of Franciscan nuns and retiring to her new foundation of Longchamp. The various Lives of Louis IX and the Life of Isabella present an enduring image of the relationship of Blanche with her two saintly children. They stress her importance in her children's lives – the pious root of all their pious branches. They stress, and rightly so, how vital a role Blanche played in governing France during Louis's minority. They became the family's own narrative of their history. Incorporated at Saint-Denis into the *Grandes chroniques de France*, they became the official history of the kingdom.

But they portray Blanche and St Louis in a very particular light. They capture all Louis's sanctimonious and perfervid piety. He emerges as a figure who suffers in Christ-like passivity. There is no doubt that this was an important aspect of his character, as it was Isabella's. But the Lives, even Joinville's, aim to show a saint. And they are written or informed by people like Joinville, or Geoffrey of Beaulieu, who knew Louis in the later stages of his life; few could go back, as Joinville did, as far as the 1240s. It is clear that Louis was changed by his experience on his first Crusade; that his pious penances became more extreme; and that he became more austere, even less comfortable with the demands of the courtly life. It means that certain aspects of Louis's character are underplayed.

The young Louis IX who emerges from accounts written before canonisation became an issue is someone rather different. He had an exalted sense of the God-given nature of his royal authority. Very aware of his kingship, he built magnificent royal chapels. He was knightly and enjoyed war. He was confrontational, especially with the secular Church. In short, the young Louis was very determined to impose himself as king, and may even have tried, rather tentatively, to ensure that his mother was not always at court. Joinville recognised some of these traits; he was certainly aware that Louis was a king who interfered at every level in the business of government. Louis was a more complex and ambivalent character, and a more complex and ambivalent king, than the saint portrayed in the depositions and hagiographies.

The image of Blanche in the hagiographies of her son is that of the mother of a saint.[15] She is pious, severe, almost as austere as her son. Her wisdom, counsel, courage and political achievements are recognised, but not her vitality. But Blanche loved the things of this world too: music and song, rich colours in manuscripts, hunting, pomegranates, ginger and salmon, furs and silks and jewels. She loved and understood the workings of power. She loved the trappings of power, and knew how they should be used in the construction of a regal image. And she knew how important image was in the reality of power. Blanche has to be seen, not just as the mother of St Louis, but as the great-granddaughter of the empress Matilda, the granddaughter of Henry II and Eleanor of Aquitaine, the niece of Richard the Lionheart and the mother of Charles of Anjou. These were the rulers that she herself resembled. They, too, were profoundly pious, with a certain questioning intellectual seriousness. All were great founders and supporters of austerely reformist monasticism or religion. Inner conflict there must have been, but all were strong enough in personality to contain that conflict. So Blanche ate her pomegranates,

chose her jewelled gifts for friends and relations, listened to Melana and Passerele, laughed at the courtly romantic songs of Theobald of Champagne, discussed the new books from Toledo with the urbane Romanus, kept abreast of plots through her agents in La Rochelle and Carcassonne; but she prayed devoutly too, absorbing the meaning of the texts on the sacred pages of her psalters and bibles with her chaplains and religious advisers, planned her abbeys with meticulous care, built hospitals, released prisoners and scattered alms to the poor with lavish abandon. For she knew always that, at the End of Time, someone might point to her and say 'Look – that was once the queen of France'.

Abbreviations

AD	Archives Departmentales
ADVO	Archives Départementales du Val d'Oise
AN	Archives Nationales de France
BL	British Library (London)
BNF	Bibliothèque Nationale de France (Paris)
GC	*Gallia Christiana*, ed. D. Sammarthani et al., 17 vols (Paris, 1715–1865)
LTC	*Layettes du trésor des chartes*, ed. A. Teulet, 5 vols (Paris: H. Plon, 1863–1909)
MGH	*Monumenta Germaniae Historica*
ÖNB	Österreichische Nationalbibliothek (Vienna)
PL	*Patrologiae Latinae Cursus Completus, series Latina*, ed. J.-P. Migne, 221 vols (1844–55)
RHF	*Recueil des historiens des Gaules et de la France*, ed. M. Bouquet et al., 24 vols, new edn, published under the direction of Léopold Delisle (Paris, 1869–1904)

Notes

INTRODUCTION

1 The image is New York, The Morgan Library and Museum, MS M240, f. 8r, from the final section of the Toledo moralised bible. For discussion, see John Lowden, *The Making of the Bibles Moralisées*, 2 vols (University Park, 2000), I, pp. 127–30. It is now generally accepted that the king and queen shown are Blanche and Louis IX.

2 Robert Fawtier, *The Capetian Kings of France: Monarchy and Nation, 987–1328*, trans. Lionel Butler and R. J. Adam (London, 1960), p. 28. The quotation is from the English translation of 1960; for the writing of the original French book in 1940–41, ibid., pp. vii–viii, preface.

3 Ian Wei, *Intellectual Culture in Medieval Paris: Theologians and the University, c.1100–1330* (Cambridge, 2012), pp. 248–50.

4 See, for instance, discussion in Lois Huneycutt, 'Intercession and the High Medieval Queen: The Esther Topos', in *Power of the Weak: Studies on Medieval Women*, ed. Jennifer Carpenter and Sally-Beth MacLean (Urbana, 1995), esp. pp. 200–01.

5 Matthew Paris, *Chronica majora*, ed. H. R. Luard, 7 vols (London, 1872–83), v,

p. 354; Geoffrey of Beaulieu, 'Vita ludovici noni', in *RHF*, xx (1840), p. 4; Geoffrey of Beaulieu, 'Here Begins the Life and Saintly Comportment of Louis, Formerly King of the Franks, of Pious Memory', in *The Sanctity of Louis IX: Early Lives of Saint Louis by Geoffrey of Beaulieu and William of Chartres*, trans. Larry F. Field, ed. M. Cecilia Gaposchkin and Sean L. Field (Ithaca, 2014), p. 74; Guillaume de Saint-Pathus, 'Vie de Saint Louis, par le confesseur de la reine Marguerite', in *RHF*, xx (1840), p. 64.

6 See especially the nuanced discussion of this aspect of commentary on Thatcher in John Campbell, *Margaret Thatcher*, vol. II: *The Iron Lady* (London, 2003), pp. 470–78; p. 472, for Mitterand's famous comment; p. 473, for a female commentator: 'Feminity is what she wears, masculinity is what she admres.'

7 These studies, often collections of papers, include: *Women and Power in the Middle Ages*, ed. Mary Erler and Maryanne Kowalski (Athens, Ga., 1988); *Queens, Regents and Potentates*, ed. Theresa M. Vann (Dallas, 1993); *Medieval Queenship*, ed. John Carmi Parsons (New York, 1993); *Queens and Queenship in Medieval Europe*, ed. Anne J. Duggan (Woodbridge, 1997); more specifically, for

France, see *Capetian Women*, ed. Kathleen Nolan (New York, 2003). The ideas and approaches generated since the 1980s are helpfully and fruitfully reviewed in Theresa Earenfight, *Queenship in Medieval Europe* (Basingstoke, 2013), pp. 5–12, 24–7.

8 Pauline Stafford, 'Emma: The Powers of the Queen in the Eleventh Century', in *Queens and Queenship in Medieval Europe*, p. 11. This article provides a subtle, sustained, but succinct discussion of queenly power.

9 Mary Erler and Maryanne Kowalski, 'Introduction', in *Women and Power in the Middle Ages*, p. 2. See also the more subtle discussion in Stafford, 'Emma', pp. 10–13; and Janna Bianchini, *The Queen's Hand: Power and Authority in the Reign of Berenguela of Castile* (Philadelphia, 2012), p. 5.

10 Janet L. Nelson, 'Early Medieval Rites of Queen-Making and the Shaping of Medieval Queenship', in *Queens and Queenship in Medieval Europe*, pp. 302–5.

11 Notably in the collection entitled *Power of the Weak*, ed. Carpenter and MacLean; see also the illuminating analyses in Gábor Klaniczay, *Holy Rulers and Blessed Princesses: Dynastic Cults in Medieval Central Europe* (Cambridge, 2002). For subtle discussions of gender and power, see *Gendering the Middle Ages*, ed. Pauline Stafford and Anneke B. Mulder-Bakker (Oxford, 2001) [first published as special issue of *Gender and History*, XII/3, 2000].

12 Geoffrey Koziol, *Begging Pardon and Favor: Ritual and Political Order in Early Medieval France* (Ithaca, 1992), esp. pp. 107–73; Geoffrey Koziol, 'Political Culture', in *France in the Central Middle Ages, 900–1200*, ed. Marcus Bull (Oxford, 2002), pp. 43–76; Bernd Schneidmüller, 'Constructing Identities of Medieval France', in *France in the Central Middle Ages*, pp. 15–42, esp. pp. 34–42.

13 Walter Map, *De nugis curialium/ Courtiers' Trifles*, ed. M. R. James, C.N.L.

Brooke and R.A.B. Mynors (Oxford, 1983), esp. pp. 450–51, 452–3, 456–7.

14 The concept of 'hard' and 'soft' powers was developed by Joseph Nye (*Soft Power: The Means to Success in World Politics*, New York, 2004), speculating that modern states should use cultural diffusion as well as military and economic power to obtain their ends. For a stimulating discussion of hard power and soft power in a medieval context, see David Bates, *The Normans and Empire* (Oxford, 2013), pp. 4, 18–19, 81–2.

15 See, among others, John Carmi Parsons, 'The Queen's Intercession in Thirteenth-Century England', in *Power of the Weak*, pp. 147–77; and Huneycutt, 'Intercession'.

16 *Les stratégies matrimoniales, IXe–XIIIe siècle*, ed. Martin Aurell (Turnhout, 2013).

17 See below, p. 38.

18 E.g., Stafford, 'Emma', esp. pp. 5–6, 20.

19 For Margaret of Provence, see below, p. 287; for Isabella of Angoulême, see Nicholas Vincent, 'John's Jezebel: Isabelle of Angoulême', in *King John: New Interpretations*, ed. S. D. Church (Woodbridge, 1999), pp. 165–21; for Eleanor and the revolt of her sons, see Ralph V. Turner, *Eleanor of Aquitaine* (London and New Haven, 2009), pp. 204–30.

20 See discussion, including the problems of this approach, in Stafford and Mulder-Bakker, 'Introduction', in *Gendering the Middle Ages*, pp. 3–4; and Kimberly Lo Prete, 'Historical Ironies in the Study of Capetian Women', in *Capetian Women*, pp. 273–4.

21 Nelson, 'Early Medieval Rites', pp. 304–5.

22 Marjorie Chibnall, *The Empress Matilda: Queen Consort, Queen Mother and Lady of the English* (Oxford, 1991), p. 191.

23 Bianchini, *Queen's Hand*, pp. 5–8. Berengaria is often called Berenguela by historians of medieval Spain. I have used Berengaria – which is what she is called in Blanche's household accounts.

24   Karen Nicholas, 'Countesses as Rulers in Flanders', in *Aristocratic Women in Medieval France*, ed. T. Evergates (Philadelphia, 1999), pp. 129–35; Erin L. Jordan, *Women, Power and Religious Patronage in the Middle Ages* (Basingstoke, 2006).

25   Jacques Le Goff, *Saint Louis* (Paris, 1996), pp. 128, 174.

26   For Philip's administrative kingship, see John W. Baldwin, *The Government of Philip Augustus: Foundations of French Royal Power in the Middle Ages* (Berkeley, Cal., 1986), passim; for its effects on the effective personnel of government, ibid., esp. pp. 104–36.

27   Marion F. Facinger, 'A Study of Medieval Queenship: Capetian France, 987–1237', *Studies in Medieval and Renaissance History*, v (1968), pp. 3–48.

28   Miriam Shadis, 'Blanche of Castile and Facinger's "Medieval Queenship": Reassessing the Argument', in *Capetian Women*, pp. 137–61; and Facinger, 'A Study of Medieval Queenship'. See also comments in Anneke B. Mulder-Bakker, 'Jeanne of Valois: The Power of a Consort', in *Capetian Women*, pp. 253–69; and Lo Prete, 'Historical Ironies', esp. pp. 272–6.

29   Bianchini, *Queen's Hand*, esp. comments on p. 4.

30   John Gillingham, *The Angevin Empire*, 2nd edn (London, 2001), esp. pp. 88–115; Jorg Peltzer, 'The Slow Death of the Angevin Empire', *Historical Research*, LXXXI (2008), pp. 553–84.

31   Richard Kaeuper, *War, Justice and Public Order: England and France in the Later Middle Ages* (Oxford, 1988), pp. 272–4.

32   For an overview, see D. A. Carpenter, *The Struggle for Mastery: Britain, 1066–1284* (Oxford, 2003), pp. 263–99, 338–91. For baronial disaffection in Capetian France under Philip Augustus, see Gabrielle Spiegel, *Romancing the Past: The Rise of Vernacular Prose Historiography in Thirteenth-century France* (Berkeley, Cal., 1993), pp. 11–54; Kaeuper, *War, Justice and Public Order*, esp. pp. 316–25.

33   See below, p. 50–57.

34   'Baron' was originally a technical term for a major landholder below the level of count, but by 1200 it was widely used to mean 'a great man in the kingdom close to the king': see David Crouch, *The Image of Aristocracy in Britain, 1000–1300* (London and New York, 1992), pp. 107–14, esp. p. 113.

35   Baldwin, *Government of Philip Augustus*, pp. 304–28; Lindy Grant, *Abbot Suger of St-Denis: Church and State in Early Twelfth-century France* (London, 1998); Marcel Pacaut, *Louis VII et son royaume* (Paris, 1964), pp. 67–117.

36   For an overview, see John W. Baldwin, *Paris, 1200* (Stanford, Cal., 2010), pp. 175–213 on the schools, esp. pp. 202–3 on the masters in government and society.

37   Though see Quentin Griffiths, 'New Men among the Lay Counsellors of Saint Louis' Parlement', *Medieval Studies*, XXXII (1970), pp. 234–72; and, more recently, William Chester Jordan, *Men at the Center: Redemptive Governance under Louis IX* (Budapest, 2012), esp. p. 12, for his comment on the need to understand the prosopography of the court of Louis IX.

38   Paul Edouard Didier Riant, 'Déposition de Charles d'Anjou pour la canonisation de Saint Louis', in *Notices et documents publiés pour la Société d'histoire de France à l'occasion du cinquantième anniversaire de sa fondation* (Paris, 1884), p. 175.

39   Le Goff, *Saint Louis*, p. 897: 'À la fin, St Louis, a-t-il existé?', and extended discussion, pp. 328–62; M. Cecilia Gaposchkin, *The Making of Saint Louis: Kingship, Sanctity and Crusade in the Later Middle Ages* (Ithaca, 2008), passim. See also the subtle analysis of Louis in William Chester Jordan, '*Persona et gesta*: The Image and Deeds of the Thirteenth-Century Capetians, 2: The Case of Saint Louis', *Viator*, XIX (1988), pp. 208–18.

40   The story is in Geoffrey of Beaulieu, 'Vita ludovici noni', p. 4; Geoffrey of Beaulieu, 'Here Begins the Life', p. 74. The same image

emerges from Guillaume de Saint-Pathus, 'Vie de Saint Louis', pp. 64–5.

41 Terryl Kinder, 'Blanche of Castile and the Cistercians: An Architectural Re-evaluation of Maubuisson Abbey', *Cîteaux: commentarii cistercienses*, XXVII (1976), pp. 161–88; Alexandra Gajewski-Kennedy, 'Recherches sur l'architecture cistercienne et le pouvoir royal: Blanche de Castille et la construction de l'abbaye du Lys', in *Art et architecture à Melun au Moyen âge*, ed. Yves Gallet (Paris, 2000), pp. 223–54; Alexandra Gajewski, 'The Patronage Question under Review: Queen Blanche of Castile (1188–1252) and the Architecture of the Cistercian Abbeys at Royaumont, Maubuisson and Le Lys', in *Reassessing the Roles of Women as 'Makers' of Medieval Art and Architecture*, ed. Therese Martin, 2 vols (Leiden and Boston, Mass., 2012), I, pp. 197–244.

42 Kathleen Nolan, *Queens in Stone and Silver: The Creation of a Visual Imagery of Queenship in Capetian France* (New York, 2009), pp. 121–59.

43 Lowden, *Making of the Bibles Moralisées*; Sara Lipton, *Images of Intolerance: The Representation of Jews and Judaism in the Bible Moralisée* (Berkeley, Cal., 1999); Gerald B. Guest, *Bible moralisée: Codex Vindobonensis 2554, Vienna, Österreichische Nationalbibliothek* (London, 1995). There is a huge bibliography on the moralised bibles.

44 Several papers in *The Cultural Patronage of Medieval Women*, ed. June Hall McCash (Athens, Ga., 1996), notably Madeline H. Caviness, 'Anchoress, Abbess and Queen: Donors and Patrons or Intercessors and Matrons', pp. 105–54. See now also Gajewski, 'Patronage Question'.

45 Elie Berger, *Histoire de Blanche de Castille, reine de France* (Paris, 1895); Miriam Shadis, 'Piety, Politics and Power: The Patronage of Leonor of England and her Daughters, Berenguela of León and Blanche of Castile', in *The Cultural Patronage of Medieval Women*, ed. Hall McCash, pp. 202–27; Shadis

and Constance Hoffman Berman, 'A Taste of the Feast: Reconsidering Eleanor of Aquitaine's Female Descendants', in *Eleanor of Aquitaine, Lord and Lady*, ed. Bonnie Wheeler and John Carmi Parsons (New York, 2002), pp. 177–211; Shadis, 'Blanche of Castile'; Shadis, *Berenguela of Castile (1180–1246) and Political Women in the High Middle Ages* (New York, 2009); Régine Pernoud, *Blanche of Castile*, trans. Henry Noel (London, 1975); Gérard Sivéry, *Blanche de Castille* (Paris, 1990).

46 David Bates, Julia Crick and Sarah Hamilton, 'Introduction', in *Writing Medieval Biography, 750–1250: Essays in Honour of Professor Frank Barlow*, ed. Bates, Crick and Hamilton (Woodbridge, 2006), p. 12, and esp. pp. 9–12 on the possibilities, the limitations and indeed the validity of biography, especially biographies of medieval figures.

47 See the stimulating comments of Pauline Stafford, 'Writing the Biography of Eleventh-century Queens', in *Writing Medieval Biography*, ed. Bates, Crick and Hamilton, pp. 99–109, esp. pp. 100–01, on biography treating the individual as a representative of a group, and 'biography through roles and structures'.

48 Geoffrey of Beaulieu, 'Vita ludovici noni'; Geoffrey of Beaulieu, 'Here Begins the Life'; William of Chartres, 'De vita et actibus inclytae recordationis regis francorum ludovici et de miraculis', in *RHF*, XX (1840), pp. 28–44; William of Chartres, 'On the Life and Deeds of Louis, King of the Franks of Famous Memory, and on the Miracles that Declare his Sanctity', in *Sanctity of Louis IX*, pp. 129–59; Guillaume de Saint-Pathus, 'Vie de Saint Louis'. For discussion of the texts, see Gaposchkin, *Making of Saint Louis*, pp. 33–6, 38–40; Le Goff, *Saint Louis*, pp. 333–44; and Gaposchkin and Field, 'Introduction', in *Sanctity of Louis IX*, pp. 18–57.

49 Agnes of Harcourt, *The Writings of Agnes of Harcourt: The Life of Isabelle of France and the Letter on Louis IX and Longchamp*, ed.

Sean Field (Notre Dame, Ind., 2003); and see Field, *Isabelle of France*, pp. 8–9.

50 For discussion of the text, see Le Goff, *Saint Louis*, pp. 473–98; Gaposchkin, *Making of Saint Louis*, pp. 181–96.

51 Rigord, *Histoire de Philippe Auguste*, ed. Elisabeth Carpentier, Georges Pon and Yves Chauvin (Paris, 2006); William the Breton, 'Gesta Philippi Augusti', in *Oeuvres de Rigord et Guillaume le Breton*, ed. H. Delaborde, 2 vols (Paris, 1882–5), I, pp. 168–333; William the Breton, 'Philippide', ibid., II; for discussion of the texts, see Baldwin, *Government of Philip Augustus*, pp. 396–8.

52 Richard Kay, *The Council of Bourges, 1225: A Documentary History* (Aldershot, 2002), pp. 316–17, on Aubri of Trois-Fontaines, 'Chronica'; ibid., pp. 294–7 on the Chronicle of Tours. The chronicler of Tours is sometimes identified as Pean Gastineau, but not on any convincing evidence. Little is known about Nicholas of Braie.

53 See the introductions to the editions for discussion of these sources.

54 For discussion, see Bianchini, *Queen's Hand*, pp. 14–16.

55 For these chroniclers, see Antonia Gransden, *Historical Writing in England, c.550 to c.1307* (London, 1974), esp. pp. 322–31, 356–79. For Wendover, who died in 1236, and is particularly important for Blanche's first regency, see Kay, *Council of Bourges*, pp. 490–501 and 271–6.

56 Matthew is often very critical of Blanche during her first regency, and until around 1236. However, he is both sympathetic and hugely admiring of her political activities from 1244 in his chronicles and from 1240 in his 'Life of St Edmund of Abingdon'. His earlier critical attitude may reflect that Wendover was his principal source until *circa* 1236.

57 *Histoire des ducs de Normandie et des rois d'Angleterre*, ed. F. Michel (Paris, 1840); Anonymous of Béthune, 'Extrait d'une chronique française des rois de France, par un anonyme de Béthune', in *RHF*, XXIV (1904), pp. 750–75. See discussion in John Gillingham, 'The Anonymous of Béthune, King John and Magna Carta', in *Magna Carta and the England of King John*, ed. Janet S. Loengard (Woodbridge, 2010), pp. 27–44, esp. pp. 29–32; and Spiegel, *Romancing the Past*, pp. 225–36.

58 My italics. The pronounced 'my', as opposed to 'the', seems to suggest a certain closeness. My thanks to John Gillingham for pointing this out to me.

59 See discussion of this text in Kay, *Council of Bourges*, pp. 304–9.

60 See the introduction by Natalis de Wailly in *Récits d'un ménestrel de Reims au treizième siècle*, ed. de Wailly (Paris, 1876), pp. xvii–xxxix.

61 Collected in A.-J.-V. Leroux de Lincy, *Recueil de chants historiques français depuis le XIIe jusqu'au XVIIIe siècle*, vol. I (Paris, 1841). For the English songs, see *Thomas Wright's Political Songs of England*, ed. Peter Coss (Cambridge, 1996), pp. 1–127; and Peter Coss, 'Introduction', ibid., pp. xix–xlii.

62 For general discussion of the French household accounts, see Elisabeth Lalou, 'Introduction', in *Les comptes sur tablettes de cire de Jean Sarrazin, chambellan de Saint Louis*, ed. Lalou (Turnhout, 2003), pp. 14–15.

63 F. Lot and R. Fawtier, *Le premier budget de la monarchie française* (Paris, 1932), pp. clxxiv, clxxxix, and see discussion, pp. 110–11.

64 'Un fragment du compte de l'hôtel du Prince Louis de France pour le terme de la Purification 1213', ed. Robert Fawtier in *Moyen âge*, XLIII (1933), pp. 225–50.

65 Edited in Charles Petit-Dutaillis, *Etude sur la vie et le règne de Louis VIII* (Paris: E. Bouillon, 1894), pièces justificatives, no. xiii, pp. 522–5.

66 Johann Peter von Ludewig, *Reliquiae Manuscriptorum omnis aevi Diplomatum ac Monumentorum ineditorum adhuc*, 12 vols (Frankfurt, 1720–41), vol. XII, book I, pp. 3–5.

67 'Recepta et expensa Anno MCCXXXIIII

inter candelosam et ascensionem', in *RHF*, XXI (1855), pp. 226–51.

68 'Compotus ballivorum et praepositorum Franciae anno Domini 1234 mense Junio de termino ascensionis', in *RHF*, XXII (1865), pp. 565–78.

69 'Expensa militiae comitis Attrebatensis in Penthecoste AD 1237 mense junio', in *RHF*, XXII (1865), pp. 579–83; 'Ea quae distributa fuerunt in milicia Comitis Pictavensis (Die xxiv junio, anno mccxli)', in *RHF*, XXII (1865), pp. 615–22.

70 'Magna recepta de termino Ascensionis, anno Domini MCCXXXVIII mense Mayo et magna expensa', in *RHF*, XXI (1855), pp. 251–60.

71 'Itinera, dona et hernesia AD 1239 inter ascensionem et omnes sanctos', in *RHF*, XXII (1865), pp. 583–615.

72 'Compotus ballivorum'.

73 BL Add. Ch. 4129 and BNF MS lat. 9017, f. 69, the former published in 'Comptes de dépenses de Blanche de Castille', ed. Etienne Symphorien Bougenot in *Bulletin du Comité des travaux historiques et scientifiques: section d'histoire et de philologie* (1889), pp. 86–91, the latter unpublished. Elisabeth Lalou and I are currently working on an edition of the two documents.

74 AN J1030, no. 9, ed. Léopold Delisle in 'Mémoire sur les opérations financières des Templiers', in *Mémoires présentés par divers savantes à l'Académie des inscriptions et belles-lettres*, XXXIII (1889), appendix VIII, pp. 99–102.

75 Now ADVO 72H12. This is partially published in Henri de L'Epinois, 'Comptes relatifs à la fondation de l'abbaye de Maubuisson', *Bibliothèque de l'école des chartes*, XIX (1858), pp. 550–67. Some sections have been published by Constance Berman in *Women and Monasticism in Medieval Europe: Sisters and Patrons of the Cistercian Reform* (Kalamazoo, 2002), pp. 108–11, and Constance Berman is currently working on a full edition, which will be very welcome. Some minor additions and

emendations on f. 2v are in a very similar scribal hand to that of Blanche's accounts of 1241–2 (BL Add. Ch. 4129; BNF MS lat. 9017, f. 69), suggesting that the book was begun almost immediately after the foundation.

76 Monsieur Jean Dufour had been working, before his untimely death, on an edition of the acts of the queens of France, as far as Adela of Champagne, the third wife of Louis VII. Although his edition was not intended to cover Blanche, he had noted her acts where he had found them, and with great generosity he gave me a copy of this list, which proved enormously helpful.

77 Alphonse Dutilleux and Joseph Depoin, *Cartulaire de l'abbaye de Maubuisson (Notre-Dame-la-Royale), I: chartes concernant la fondation de l'abbaye et des chapelles* (Pontoise, 1890); Dutilleux and Depoin, *Cartulaire de l'abbaye de Maubuisson (Notre-Dame-la-Royale), II: contrats* (Pontoise, 1913). See also documents published in Dutilleux and Depoin, *L'abbaye de Maubuisson (Notre-Dame-la-Royale): histoire et cartulaire, III: le trésor et le mobilier* (Pontoise, 1884).

78 See especially AN K190(2) 3^{7a}.

79 There are three copies of the cartulary: BNF MS lat. 5472; BNF MS lat. 9166; ADVO 43H3.

80 Petit-Dutaillis, *Etude*, appendix VI, pp. 449–508.

81 For discussion of the registers, see Baldwin, *Government of Philip Augustus*, pp. 412–18.

82 Both are now in the Musée Lambinet, Versailles, with other objects from the treasury at Maubuisson, including the coconut belonging to Blanche's great-niece, Blanche of Brienne, abbess of Maubuisson.

83 On the increasing wealth, conspicuous consumption, debt and the reaction to them, see Lester K. Little, *Religious Poverty and the Profit Economy in Medieval Europe* (London, 1978), passim.

84 Marjorie Reeves, *Joachim of Fiore and the Prophetic Future* (London, 1976); Alfred J.

Andrea, 'Innocent III, the Fourth Crusade and the Coming Apocalypse', in *The Medieval Crusade*, ed. Susan J. Ridyard (Woodbridge, 2004), pp. 98–101. For apocalypticism in Paris *circa* 1200, see Rigord, *Histoire de Philippe Auguste*, pp. 226–7, 352–3, 351, n. 627.

I   DAUGHTER OF THE KING OF CASTILE

1   'Brevis historia Regum Francorum ad annum MCCXIV' in *RHF*, XVII (1878), p. 426: 'ut esset vinculum pacis, pigneratrix foederis'.

2   William of Poitiers, *The Gesta Guillelmi of William of Poitiers*, ed. and trans. R.H.C. Davis and M. Chibnall (Oxford, 1998), pp. 44–5.

3   Rigord, *Histoire de Philippe Auguste*, ed. Elisabeth Carpentier, Georges Pon and Yves Chauvin (Paris, 2006), pp. 118–19.

4   Roger of Howden, *Chronica magistri Rogeri de Hovedene*, ed. William Stubbs, 4 vols (London, 1868–71), IV, p. 81. Negotiators were sent to Castile in June 1199: Thomas Rymer, *Foedera*, 3 vols (London, 1816–30), I, pt 1, p. 113; and see Theresa Vann, 'The Theory and Practice of Medieval Castilian Queenship', in *Queens, Regents and Potentates*, ed. Vann (Dallas, 1993), p. 138. For the war, see F. M. Powicke, *The Loss of Normandy*, 2nd edn (Manchester, 1961), pp. 95–126; John Gillingham, *Richard I* (London and New Haven, 1999), pp. 301–20.

5   For the text of the treaty, see *Cartulaire normand de Philippe Auguste, Louis VIII, Saint Louis et Philippe-le-Hardi*, ed. Léopold Delisle (Caen, 1852), pp. 280–81, no. 1063; and *LTC*, II, no. 578. For the protracted negotiations of the treaty, see Roger of Howden, *Chronica*, IV, pp. 81, 95, 106–7; Roger of Wendover, *Flores historiarum*, ed. H. G. Hewlett, 3 vols (London, 1886–9), I, p. 294. For discussion of the treaty, see Powicke, *Loss of Normandy*, pp. 134–8. At one point it looked as though the county of Evreux would be the *maritagium*, and Coggeshall, Howden and Wendover report this

as the final arrangement: Ralph of Coggeshall, *Radulphi de Coggeshall Chronicon Anglicanum*, ed. J. J. Stevenson (London, 1875), pp. 100–01; Roger of Howden, *Chronica*, IV, p. 107; Roger of Wendover, *Flores historiarum*, I, p. 284.

6   Roger of Howden, *Chronica*, IV, pp. 95, 106 and 107.

7   Roger of Howden, *Chronica*, IV, pp. 114–15; Roger of Wendover, *Flores historiarum*, I, pp. 293–5; Rigord, *Histoire de Philippe Auguste*, pp. 364–7, ch. 139.

8   Roger of Howden, *Chronica*, IV, p. 114.

9   Vann, 'Theory and Practice', pp. 125–47; and Miriam Shadis, *Berenguela of Castile (1180–1246) and Political Women in the High Middle Ages* (New York, 2009), pp. 23–50, for Eleanor of England. For Eleanor of Aquitaine's role in her sons' governance, see below, pp. 280, 285.

10   Elie Berger, *Histoire de Blanche de Castile, reine de France* (Paris, 1895), p. 8; Shadis, *Berenguela of Castile*, p. 4, n. 5. The sixteenth-century chronicle was the 'Chronica generale de Castila'.

11   E.g., 'Brevis historia Regum Francorum', p. 426: 'commendabilis pulchritudinis puellam'. Philippe Mousket, *Chronique rimée*, ed. Frédéric de Reiffenberg, 2 vols (Brussels, 1836–8), II, p. 444, v. 24,276, describes her as noble – 'gentius et franche'. Cf. the Anonymous of Béthune, 'Extrait d'une chronique française des rois de France, par un anonyme de Béthune', in *RHF*, XXIV (1904), p. 760, who describes Blanche of Navarre as 'molt bele dame', but does not comment on Blanche of Castile's looks.

12   Jean Dunbabin, *Charles I of Anjou: Power, Kingship and State-Making in Thirteenth-century Europe* (London, 1998), p. 22, quoting Villani's description of Charles as large and olive-skinned, with a big nose. For Louis VIII's blond colouring and short stature, see Charles Petit-Dutaillis, *Etude sur la vie et le règne de Louis VIII* (Paris, 1894), p. 12.

13   Marie-Thérèse Morlet, *Les noms de per-*

sonne sur le territoire de l'ancienne Gaul du VIe au XIIe siècle, 3 vols (Paris: CNRS, 1968–85), I, p. 58. My thanks to Kathleen Thompson for the reference and discussion of the name, and to Wendy Davies, who was the first to suggest to me that Blanca was not a Spanish name. For Blanca of Navarre's maternal family, see Kathleen Thompson, *Power and Border Lordship in Medieval France: The County of the Perche, 1000–1226* (Woodbridge, 2002), p. 75.

14 E.g., 'Brevis historia Regum Francorum', p. 426; M. L. Colker, ed., 'The "Karolinus" of Egidius Parisiensis', *Traditio*, XXIX (1973), p. 308; see also Adam of Eynsham, *Magna vita Sancti Hugonis / The Life of St Hugh of Lincoln*, ed. Decima L. Douie and David Hugh Farmer, 2 vols (Oxford, 1985), II, p. 156; and also entries in the Fontevraud Cartulary: BNF MS lat. 5480, vol. II, ff. 106, 125.

15 Berger, *Histoire de Blanche de Castille*, p. 3; Blanche was born before 4 March 1188. For Blanche's siblings, see Shadis, *Berenguela of Castile*, pp. 32–4.

16 For the marriages, see Shadis, *Berenguela of Castile*, p. 70; for Constance, ibid., pp. 4–5.

17 Vann, 'Theory and Practice', pp. 131, 137–8; Shadis, *Berenguela of Castile*, pp. 32–4.

18 Teofilo Ruiz, *From Heaven to Earth: The Reordering of Castillian Society, 1150–1350* (Princeton, 2004), pp. 142–3. For Paris as the capital of France by 1200, see Rigord, *Histoire de Philippe Auguste*, pp. 142–3.

19 Cf. *The Latin Chronicle of the Kings of Castile*, trans. and ed. Joseph F. O'Callaghan (Tempe, Ariz., 2002), p. 72 ('Chronica Latina regum Castellae', in *Chronica hispana saeculi XIII*, ed. L. C. Brea, J. A. Estévez Sola and R. Carande Herrero, Turnhout, 1997, p. 75), which mentions Berengaria and Constance living at Las Huelgas in the early thirteenth century. See comments in Colette Bowie, *The Daughters of Henry II and Eleanor of Aquitaine* (Turnhout, 2014), p. 118.

20 Ruiz, *From Heaven to Earth*, pp. 7–8, 20.

21 'Chronica Latina', p. 48: 'adeo quod nusquam in toto regno vel angulus unus inveniri posset, in quo quisquam securus esset'; *Latin Chronicle*, p. 29.

22 *Latin Chronicle*, pp. 28–33; 'Chronica Latina', pp. 47–51.

23 He invaded in the summers of 1205 and 1206. For the Gascony issue, see *Latin Chronicle*, pp. 33–5; 'Chronica Latina', pp. 50–52; and discussion in Vann, 'Theory and Practice', pp. 129, 138–9; Gillingham, *Richard I*, pp. 149–50; Shadis, *Berenguela of Castile*, pp. 31–2.

24 *Latin Chronicle*, p. 32; 'Chronica Latina', p. 50; Shadis, *Berenguela of Castile*, pp. 61–71.

25 *Latin Chronicle*, p. 36; 'Chronica Latina', pp. 52–3.

26 Gillingham, *Richard I*, pp. 31, 39, 124–5, 306.

27 *Histoire des ducs de Normandie et des rois d'Angleterre*, ed. F. Michel (Paris, 1840), p. 91. For the English drinking the bad wine, see Anonymous of Béthune, 'Extrait d'une chronique française des rois de France', p. 760.

28 John Gillingham, 'At the Deathbeds of the Kings of England, 1066–1216', in *Herrscher- und Fürstentestamente im westeuropäischen Mittelalter*, ed. Brigitte Kasten (Cologne, 2008), pp. 509–30.

29 Rigord, *Histoire de Philippe Auguste*, pp. 364–5, 366–7: 'et post decessum suum totam terram cismarinam si sine herede legitimo ipsium mori contingeret, omni contradictio postposita, eidem Ludovici concessit'. In fact, the treaty limited Louis and Blanche's gains – should John die without an heir – to overlordship of the lands of Hugh of Gournay, the count of Aumale and the count of Perche. Aubri of Trois-Fontaines, 'Chronica Albrici Monachi Trium Fontium', in MGH *Scriptores*, XXIII, ed. Paul Scheffer-Boichorst (Hanover, 1874), p. 882, knew that the French king could claim succession to Normandy through Blanche.

30 Ralph of Coggeshall, *Chronicon Anglicanum*, p. 137.

31 William of Briouze, who knew Arthur's

fate, fled to Paris in 1211: Roger of Wendover, *Flores historiarum*, II, p. 59.

32 Adam of Eynsham, *Magna vita Sancti Hugonis*, II, pp. 136, 149.

33 Adam of Eynsham, *Magna vita Sancti Hugonis*, II, p. 156.

34 Adam of Eynsham, *Magna vita Sancti Hugonis*, II, p. 156: 'illustrissime indolis adholescens'.

35 Mousket, *Chronique rimée*, II, v. 27,687: 'Blons fu et s'ot visage blau/Ausi com li hoir de Hainnau'. See also 'Ex chronico Turonensi: auctore anonymo, S. Martini Turon. canonico', in *RHF*, XVIII (1879), p. 317. See also Petit-Dutaillis, *Etude*, p. 12; Berger, *Histoire de Blanche de Castille*, p. 10.

36 Peter of Les Vaux-de-Cernay, *The History of the Albigensian Crusade*, ed. and trans. W. A. Sibley and M. D. Sibley (Woodbridge, 1998), p. 191, ch. 417; p. 247, ch. 550. Cf. Mousket, *Chronique rimée*, II, p. 343, v. 21,376: 'le preu, le gentil'.

37 'Ex chronico Turonensi', p. 317.

38 Rigord, *Histoire de Philippe Auguste*, pp. 294–7, ch. 84; pp. 396–7, ch. 155.

39 *Récits d'un ménestrel de Reims au treizième siècle*, ed. Natalis de Wailly (Paris, 1876), p. 41.

40 Petit-Dutaillis, *Etude*, appendix I, pp. 435–6; for Isabella's height, see below, note 44.

41 Rigord, *Histoire de Philippe Auguste*, pp. 274–5.

42 Rigord, *Histoire de Philippe Auguste*, pp. 170–77, chs 26–8; John W. Baldwin, *The Government of Philip Augustus: Foundations of French Royal Power in the Middle Ages* (Berkeley, Cal., 1986), p. 18.

43 Aline Hornaday, 'A Capetian Queen as Street Demonstrator: Isabelle of Hainault', in *Capetian Women*, ed. Kathleen Nolan (New York, 2003), pp. 82–6; for the Senlis episode, see Gilbert of Mons, *La chronique de Gilbert de Mons*, ed. L. Vanderkindere (Brussels, 1904), pp. 152–3.

44 For her burial, see Rigord, *Histoire de Philippe Auguste*, pp. 272–3; Kathleen Nolan, *Queens in Stone and Silver: The Creation of a Visual Imagery of Queenship in Capetian France* (New York, 2009), pp. 114–15; for the opening of her coffin, ibid., p. 115; and Hornaday, 'A Capetian Queen', p. 80 and n. 14.

45 For discussion of the marriage, see Baldwin, *Government of Philip Augustus*, pp. 80–86; George Conklin, 'Ingeborg of Denmark, Queen of France, 1193–1223', in *Queens and Queenship in Medieval Europe*, ed. Anne J. Duggan (Woodbridge, 1997), pp. 35–52.

46 Rigord, *Histoire de Philippe Auguste*: see especially his strongly pro-Ingeborg comments on pp. 320–21, and his cursory mention of the marriage with Agnes, pp. 340–41; Colker, 'The "Karolinus"', esp. pp. 308–9, 324.

47 Matthew Paris, *Historia Anglorum*, ed. Sir Frederic Madden, 2 vols (London, 1866), II, p. 259: 'uxorius et delicatus, fluens deliciis, verbis multiplex, action pusillanimous ac infidelis'.

48 Baldwin, *Government of Philip Augustus*, p. 359.

49 Petit-Dutaillis, *Etude*, pp. 4–5. For Amaury of Bène as his tutor, see 'Ex chronico anonymii Laudunensis Canonici', in *RHF*, XVIII (1879), p. 715.

50 'Ex chronico universali anonymi Laudunensis', in *MGH Scriptores*, XXVI, ed. O. Holder-Egger (Hanover, 1882), p. 454.

51 'Ex chronico anonymii', p. 715; 'Ex chronico universali', p. 454.

52 The events are discussed in R. E. Lerner, 'Uses of Heterodoxy: The French Monarchy and Unbelief in the Thirteenth Century', *French Historical Studies*, IV (1965), pp. 189–92; Gary Dickson, 'The Burning of the Amalricians', *Journal of Ecclesiastical History*, XL (1989), pp. 347–69. William the Breton, 'Gesta Philippi Augusti', in *Oeuvres de Rigord et Guillaume le Breton*, ed. H. Delaborde, 2 vols (Paris, 1882–5), I, pp. 231–3, gives an extended account, clearly linking Amaury with

spiritualist and Aristotelian ideas. For the accusations against them, see *Chartularium Universitatis parisiensis: Ex diversis bibliothecis tabulariisque collegit et cum authenticis chartis contulit*, ed. H. Denifle, 4 vols (Paris, 1889–97), I, p.79, no.20; Caesarius of Heisterbach, *Dialogus miraculorum*, ed. Joseph Strange (Cologne, 1851), pp.304–7; and comments by Robert of Auxerre, 'Roberti Canonici S. Mariae Autissiodorensis Chronicon', in MGH *Scriptores*, XXVI, ed. O. Holder-Egger (Hanover, 1882), pp.275–6; and 'Ex chronico anonymii', p.715; 'Ex chronico universali', p.454.

53   For the dedications, see below, pp.232–3, 235. Gerald of Wales dedicated his book 'On the Instruction for Princes' to posterity, but, in a long laudatory passage, says that Louis would be his preferred dedicatee: 'De principis instructione', in *Giraldi Cambrensis opera*, vol.VIII, ed. G. F. Warner (London, 1891), pp.6–7; and see Frédérique Lachaud, 'Le *Liber de principis instructione* de Giraud de Barry', in *Le prince au miroir de la littérature politique de l'antiquité aux lumières*, ed. Lachaud and Lydwine Scordia (Rouen, 2007), p.114. For Louis as the king in ÖNB Cod. Vindob. 1179, see Sara Lipton, *Images of Intolerance: The Representation of Jews and Judaism in the Bible Moralisée* (Berkeley, Cal., 1999), pp.6–8; see also further discussion below, p.240.

54   Sean L. Field, 'Reflecting the Royal Soul: The *Speculum anime* Composed for Blanche of Castile', *Medieval Studies*, LXVIII (2006), pp.1–41; and see below, p.245.

55   Paris, Bibliothèque de l'Arsenal, MS lat.1186; see full discussion below, pp.195–6, 236–9.

56   Leiden, Universiteit Leiden, Bibliotheken, MS Lat.76a. H. Omont, *Le Psautier de Saint Louis de la Bibliothèque de Leyde* (Leiden, 1902), pp.vi, i: a fourteenth-century hand on f.30v claims that St Louis learnt to read from this psalter: 'Cist Psaultiers fu mon seignor saint Looys, qui fu roys de France, ouquel il aprist en s'anfance'. See illustration in *Saint*

Louis, exh. cat., ed. Pierre-Yves Le Pogam (Paris, 2014), p.144, ill. 110.

57   Léopold Delisle, 'Mémoire sur une lettre inédite adressée à la Reine Blanche par un habitant de La Rochelle', *Bibliothèque de l'école des chartes*, 17th year, 4th series, vol.II (1856), text of letter, pp.525–9; for the comment that she could get someone else to read it, see p.525.

58   For Arthur at court in 1200, see Adam of Eynsham, *Magna vita Sancti Hugonis*, II, p.156. For a close friendship between Louis and Arthur, see Mousket, *Chronique rimée*, II, p.313, v.20,575. For Philip Augustus and Count Geoffrey, see Rigord, *Histoire de Philippe Auguste*, pp.218–21, ch.48.

59   For Philip's use of wardship at court, see Baldwin, *Government of Philip Augustus*, pp.197, 198, 203–4, 271.

60   Rigord, *Histoire de Philippe Auguste*, pp.368–71, p.373, n.691.

61   Rigord, *Histoire de Philippe Auguste*, pp.368–9, ch.141.

62   Rigord, *Histoire de Philippe Auguste*, pp.142–3, ch.10.

63   Walter Map, *De nugis curialium/Courtiers' Trifles*, ed. M. R. James, C.N.L. Brooke and R.A.B. Mynors (Oxford, 1983), esp. pp.501–3. On the issue of defining medieval courts and households, see Malcolm Vale, *The Princely Court: Medieval Courts and Culture in North-West Europe* (Oxford, 2001), pp.15–33.

64   Roger of Howden, *Chronica magistri*, IV, p.164.

65   F. Lot and R. Fawtier, *Le premier budget de la monarchie française* (Paris, 1932), discussion, pp.110–11; e.g., p.clxxiv: 440 *livres parisis* for Louis and 50 *livres parisis* for Blanche; p.clxxxix: 630 *livres parisis* for 'Dominus Ludovicus et Domina Blanchia'.

66   *Les registres de Philippe Auguste*, ed. J. W. Baldwin (Paris, 1992), Compoti I, pp.235, 236.

67   *Histoire des ducs de Normandie et des rois d'Angleterre*, p.91.

68 Petit-Dutaillis, *Etude*, p.10; Baldwin, *Government of Philip Augustus*, p.146.

69 'Brevis historia Regum Francorum', pp.426, 427.

70 Petit-Dutaillis, *Etude*, p.331.

71 *Les registres de Philippe Auguste*, p.545; see discussion in Baldwin, *Government of Philip Augustus*, p.361.

72 Mousket, *Chronique rimée*, II, p.317, v.20,718.

73 Anonymous of Béthune, 'Extrait d'une chronique française des rois de France', p.763.

74 *Les registres de Philippe Auguste*, p.502, carte diverse, no.55: 'pro fornienda expensa nostra et uxoris nostre'. See Petit-Dutaillis, *Etude*, p.11.

75 Mousket, *Chronique rimée*, II, p.313, vv.20,593–20,596.

76 *Les registres de Philippe Auguste*, p.502, carte diverse, no.55.

2 THE LORD LOUIS

1 Andrew Lewis, *Royal Succession in Capetian France: Studies on Familial Order and the State* (Cambridge, Mass., 1981), esp. pp.74–7.

2 'Un fragment du compte de l'hôtel du Prince Louis de France pour le terme de la Purification 1213', ed. Robert Fawtier in *Moyen âge*, XLIII (1933), p.234. The account of 1226 is published in Charles Petit-Dutaillis, *Etude sur la vie et le règne de Louis VIII* (Paris, 1894), appendix viii, pièces justicatives, no.xiii, pp.522–5.

3 'Un fragment du compte', p.231, and see p.241, no.37.

4 For Poissy, see 'Un fragment du compte', nos.15, 29, 30, 61, 68, 71; for Lorris, ibid., nos.37, 56, 57, 4; for Boiscommun, ibid., nos.47, 111, 112; for Mantes, ibid., no.77; for Melun, where Louis paid for repairs to the kitchen, ibid., no.52.

5 'Un fragment du compte', nos.37, 113.

6 Jacques Le Goff, *Saint Louis* (Paris, 1996), p.31.

7 For hunting, see 'Un fragment du compte', nos.24, 42, 44, 45, 46, 79, 80, 81, 82, 86, 106, 119; for horses, ibid., nos.71, 76, 114, 115, 117; for robes, ibid., nos.32, 48, 51, 84, 85, 86, 87, 88, 89.

8 'Un fragment du compte', no.20; ibid., no.110; ibid., nos.57, 58; ibid., nos.27, 64, 69; ibid., nos.50, 70.

9 'Un fragment du compte', no.61; ibid., no.60; ibid., no.93; ibid., no.43; ibid., nos.109, 36. For Stephen of Sancerre, see William Mendel Newman, *Les seigneurs de Nesle en Picardie, XIIe–XIIIe siècles: leur chartes et leur histoire*, 2 vols (Paris, 1971), I, p.66; for the Beaumont family, ibid., I, pp.220–24; for the countess of Saint-Pol, ibid., I, p.72. The Courtenays, Stephen of Sancerre and the countess of Saint-Pol were all related to Louis VIII.

10 'Un fragment du compte', nos.108, 62, 67, 77.

11 'Un fragment du compte', no.47. For Theobald in Spain, see Theresa Vann, '"Our Father Has Won a Great Victory": The Authorship of Berenguela's Account of the Battle of Las Navas de Tolosa, 1212', *Journal of Medieval Iberian Studies*, III/I (2011), p.81 and nn.16 and 17; Rodrigo Jiménez De Rada, *Historia de rebus Hispaniae*, ed. Juan Fernández Valverde (Turnhout, 1987), p.266: 'de partibus Pictavie Theobaldus de Blazon, homo nobilis et strenuous et natione Hispanus et genere Castellanus'. See also *The Latin Chronicle of the Kings of Castile*, trans. and ed. Joseph F. O'Callaghan (Tempe, Ariz., 2002), p.46; 'Chronica Latina regum Castellae', in *Chronica hispana saeculi XIII*, ed. L. C. Brea, J. A. Estévez Sola and R. Carande Herrero (Turnhout, 1997), p.58, which says that Theobald was a son of the Guzman family. More work on Theobald and his family is required. See also Elisabeth Verry, 'Les seigneurs d'Anjou au temps de Saint Louis', in *Saint Louis et l'Anjou*, ed. Etienne Vacquet

(Rennes, 2014), p. 49. The name Blaison appears in several forms, especially Blazon and Blasons: I have followed Verry.

12 William Chester Jordan, *Louis IX and the Challenge of the Crusade: A Study in Rulership* (Princeton, 1979), pp. 228, 230.

13 See the comments of Rigord, *Histoire de Philippe Auguste*, ed. Elisabeth Carpentier, Georges Pon and Yves Chauvin (Paris, 2006), pp. 224–7; and Helinand de Froidmont, 'De bono regimine', *PL*, vol. CCXII, col. 735.

14 'Un fragment du compte', no. 13.

15 'Un fragment du compte', no. 102.

16 'Un fragment du compte', no. 38; ibid., nos. 54 and 72; ibid., no. 101; ibid., no. 103.

17 Caesarius of Heisterbach, *Dialogus miraculorum*, ed. Joseph Strange (Cologne, 1851), p. 304.

18 For Stephen Langton as a biblical scholar and moralist, see F. M. Powicke, *Stephen Langton* (Oxford, 1928), esp. pp. 23–74; John W. Baldwin, 'Master Stephen Langton, Future Archbishop of Canterbury: The Paris Schools and Magna Carta', *English Historical Review*, CXXIII (2008), pp. 811–46; Nicholas Vincent, 'Stephen Langton, Archbishop of Canterbury', in *Etienne Langton: prédicateur, bibliste, théologien*, ed. L.-J. Bataillon et al. (Turnhout, 2010), pp. 51–123. For Simon Langton, see Powicke, *Stephen Langton*, pp. 135–6; Baldwin, 'Master Stephen Langton', pp. 844–6; Vincent, 'Stephen Langton', pp. 87–8. For further discussion of the Psalter of Blanche of Castile (Paris, Bibliothèque de l'Arsenal, MS lat. 1186), see below, pp. 326–8.

19 'Un fragment du compte', nos. 16, 23, 49, 124.

20 *RHF*, XIX (1833), pp. 255–6; see discussion in Vann, ' "Our Father Has Won a Great Victory" ', p. 87.

21 Perhaps this is indeed the letter sent by Theobald de Blaison himself, recorded in the household account of 1213. If Berengaria got the poet Theobald to write the letter for her, it would account for oddities that have been noted in it, including a lack of strict chancellery format, some French vocabulary and the reference to Louis as 'our lord'. For the identification of the letter in a manuscript from the abbey of Cambron, see the brilliant detective work of Vann, ' "Our Father Has Won a Great Victory" ', esp. pp. 82–3, 87–8; this article contains an edition and translation, pp. 90–92. See also the discussion in Miriam Shadis, *Berenguela of Castile (1180–1246) and Political Women in the High Middle Ages* (New York, 2009), pp. 129–33; and further discussion below, pp. 165–6.

22 'Un fragment du compte', nos. 14, 15, 17, 18, 19, 72; at Lens, ibid., nos. 17, 18, 19; castle at Lens, ibid., nos. 73, 94–8. For the northern inheritance, see Petit-Dutaillis, *Etude*, pp. 205–16; John W. Baldwin, *The Government of Philip Augustus: Foundations of French Royal Power in the Middle Ages* (Berkeley, Cal., 1986), pp. 81, 340. Philip ensured that Louis ran the lands under Philip's overall control.

23 Ralph of Coggeshall, *Radulphi de Coggeshall Chronicon Anglicanum*, ed. J. J. Stevenson (London, 1875), p. 148.

24 For the marriage, see *Cartulaire normand de Philippe Auguste, Louis VIII, Saint Louis et Philippe-le-Hardi*, ed. Léopold Delisle (Caen, 1852), p. 29, no. 176; for Renaud joining John, see William the Breton, 'Gesta Philippi Augusti', in *Oeuvres de Rigord et Guillaume le Breton*, ed. H. Delaborde, 2 vols (Paris, 1882–5), I, p. 242; and Baldwin, *Government of Philip Augustus*, p. 202.

25 Philippe Mousket, *Chronique rimée*, ed. Frédéric de Reiffenberg, 2 vols (Brussels, 1836–8), II, p. 320, vv. 20,788–20,799 on the marriage: Ferdinand was 'biaus de cors et de vis/ brun ot le cief et s'ot grant nes'.

26 Anonymous of Béthune, 'Extrait d'une chronique française des rois de France, par un anonyme de Béthune', in *RHF*, XXIV (1904), p. 764; Robert of Auxerre, 'Roberti Canonici S. Mariae Autissiodorensis Chronicon', in *MGH Scriptores*, XXVI, ed. O. Holder-Egger (Hanover, 1882), p. 278; *Catalogue des actes de Philippe*

Auguste, ed. Léopold Delisle (Paris, 1856), nos. 1323–7; Patricia Stirneman, 'Catalogue entry no. 45', in *Splendeurs de la cour de Champagne au temps de Chrétien de Troyes*, ed. Thierry Delcourt and Xavier de La Selle (Troyes, 1999), p. 72.

27 Anonymous of Béthune, 'Extrait d'une chronique française des rois de France', p. 764; *Catalogue des actes de Philippe Auguste*, nos. 1349, 1350: Mousket, *Chronique rimée*, II, p. 322, vv. 20,825–20,830.

28 Roger of Wendover, *Flores historiarum*, ed. H. G. Hewlett, 3 vols (London, 1886–9), II, p. 63; William the Breton, 'Gesta Philippi Augusti', p. 244.

29 *Histoire des ducs de Normandie et des rois d'Angleterre*, ed. F. Michel (Paris, 1840), p. 119.

30 William the Breton, 'Gesta Philippi Augusti', p. 240; *Catalogue des actes de Philippe Auguste*, no. 1408.

31 William the Breton, 'Gesta Philippi Augusti', pp. 245–6.

32 *Catalogue des actes de Philippe Auguste*, no. 1437.

33 *Histoire des ducs de Normandie*, pp. 128–30; William the Breton, 'Gesta Philippi Augusti', pp. 249–53.

34 *Histoire des ducs de Normandie*, pp. 137–9; ibid., pp. 140–42; and Mousket, *Chronique rimée*, II, p. 332, vv. 21,068–21,356, for the warfare in the north-east. For Louis's expenditure on his defences in the north-east, see note 22.

35 'Un fragment du compte', no. 90, letters to Flanders. Ibid., no. 66: Louis receives report of the duchess of Louvain, who was Philip Augustus's daughter Mary. She was presumably referring to a stepson, rather than her own son. The *panetarius* or pantler was in charge of the provision of bread for the household, though by 1200 it was merely an honorific title for one of the household officers; see below, p. 171.

36 William the Breton, 'Gesta Philippi Augusti', pp. 254–5, 260; *Histoire des ducs de Normandie*, p. 144.

37 'Brevis historia Regum Francorum ad annum MCCXIV' in *RHF*, XVII (1878), p. 426.

38 William the Breton, 'Gesta Philippi Augusti', pp. 263–5.

39 William the Breton, 'Gesta Philippi Augusti', p. 266.

40 William the Breton, 'Gesta Philippi Augusti', p. 296; for La Victoire, see Continuator of William the Breton, in *Oeuvres de Rigord et Guillaume le Breton*, ed. H. Delaborde, 2 vols (Paris, 1882–5), I, p. 321; for the truce, see William the Breton, 'Gesta Philippi Augusti', p. 298.

41 Peter of Les Vaux-de-Cernay, *The History of the Albigensian Crusade*, ed. and trans. W. A. Sibley and M. D. Sibley (Woodbridge, 1998), pp. 41–2.

42 Peter of Les Vaux-de-Cernay, *History of the Albigensian Crusade*, p. 248. For the Montfort family, see Daniel Power, *The Norman Frontier in the Twelfth and Early Thirteenth Centuries* (Cambridge, 2004), pp. 86, 216, 228–31, 498.

43 Petit-Dutaillis, *Etude*, p. 186.

44 Peter of Les Vaux-de-Cernay, *History of the Albigensian Crusade*, pp. 246–52; William the Breton, 'Gesta Philippi Augusti', p. 300; Petit-Dutaillis, *Etude*, p. 300.

45 Peter of Les Vaux-de-Cernay, *History of the Albigensian Crusade*, pp. 248–9.

46 Daniel Power, 'Who Went on the Albigensian Crusade?', *English Historical Review*, CXXVIII (2013), pp. 1058–69, for the north French contingent.

47 *Catalogue des actes de Philippe Auguste*, nos. 1584, 1585; see discussion in Baldwin, *Government of Philip Augustus*, pp. 270–71.

48 Roger of Wendover, *Flores historiarum*, II, pp. 172 and 178, where Louis is elected 'ratione uxore sui'; William the Breton, 'Gesta Philippi Augusti', p. 305; *Histoire des ducs de Normandie*, p. 160.

49 Roger of Wendover, *Flores historiarum*, II, p. 177; William the Breton, 'Gesta Philippi Augusti', pp. 306–7.

50 *Histoire des ducs de Normandie*, pp. 165–6.

51 *Histoire des ducs de Normandie*, p. 161.

52 Petit-Dutaillis, *Etude*, p. 89; Charles-Victor Langlois, 'Les préparatifs de l'expédition de Louis de France en Angleterre', *Revue historique*, XXXVII (1888), pp. 320–21.

53 William the Breton, 'Gesta Philippi Augusti', pp. 305, 307.

54 But note that Ralph of Coggeshall, *Chronicon Anglicanum*, p. 180, says that Philip refused to listen to John's pleas to stop Louis.

55 For the French arguments, see Roger of Wendover, *Flores historiarum*, II, p. 185; and Charles Bémont, 'Le condamnation de Jean Sans-Terre par la cour des Pairs de France en 1202', *Revue historique*, XXXII (1886), pp. 61–70. Historians are often dismissive of Wendover, but he was well informed on French matters. He was interested in Richard Marshall; see the introduction in Roger of Wendover, *Flores historiarum*, III, p. xxxvi. Marshall had spent time at the French court and had close connections with Peter of Dreux, and it is possible that Wendover received some of his information through Marshall; but one should note that his account of Marshall's final campaign of 1233–4 is very inaccurate.

56 For Louis's first English campaign, see *Histoire des ducs de Normandie*, pp. 168–76; William the Breton, 'Gesta Philippi Augusti', pp. 309–12.

57 *Histoire des ducs de Normandie*, pp. 165–7.

58 E.g., 'Un fragment du compte': Renaud of Amiens, no. 1; Michael of Harnes, no. 14; Robert of Courtenay, no. 62; Guichard of Beaujeu, no. 93, Stephen of Sancerre, no. 108.

59 William the Breton, 'Gesta Philippi Augusti', p. 307; *Histoire des ducs de Normandie*, p. 169.

60 Ralph of Coggeshall, *Chronicon Anglicanum*, pp. 182–3; *Histoire des ducs de Normandie*, pp. 179, 174.

61 This is particularly clear in the writing of the Anonymous of Béthune, esp. *Histoire des ducs de Normandie*.

62 *Histoire des ducs de Normandie*, p. 189.

63 Matthew Paris, *Chronica majora*, ed. H. R. Luard, 7 vols (London, 1872–83), III, p. 28. For the siege of Dover, see Ralph of Coggeshall, *Chronicon Anglicanum*, p. 185.

64 *Histoire des ducs de Normandie*, pp. 184–6.

65 Ralph of Coggeshall, *Chronicon Anglicanum*, p. 185; *Histoire des ducs de Normandie*, p. 177; William the Breton, 'Gesta Philippi Augusti', p. 312.

66 William the Breton, 'Gesta Philippi Augusti', p. 312; *Histoire des ducs de Normandie*, p. 186.

67 *Histoire des ducs de Normandie*, pp. 191–2.

68 *Histoire des ducs de Normandie*, p. 194; William the Breton, 'Gesta Philippi Augusti', p. 313.

69 *Histoire des ducs de Normandie*, pp. 198–200; Roger of Wendover, *Flores historiarum*, II, pp. 220–21; Mousket, *Chronique rimée*, II, p. 390. For Robert's involvement, see William the Breton, 'Gesta Philippi Augusti', p. 314. It is interesting that William the Breton makes much of Philip's opposition to Louis's plans, and makes no specific mention of Blanche's role.

70 For the details of Blanche's fleet, see *Histoire des ducs de Normandie*, pp. 200–01.

71 Roger of Wendover, *Flores historiarum*, II, pp. 220–21; 'Ex Joannis Iperii Chronico Sythensis Sancti-Bertini', in *RHF*, XVIII (1879), pp. 606–7 – this chronicle was produced at the abbey of Saint-Bertin at Saint-Omer, where a chronicler was well placed to be well informed.

72 *Récits d'un ménestrel de Reims au treizième siècle*, ed. Natalis de Wailly (Paris, 1876), pp. 157–8.

73 Ralph of Coggeshall, *Chronicon Anglicanum*, p. 185.

74 *Histoire des ducs de Normandie*, pp.

200–02; William the Breton, 'Gesta Philippi Augusti', p. 314.

75 *Histoire des ducs de Normandie*, pp. 197, 200.

76 *Histoire des ducs de Normandie*, p. 197; Baldwin, 'Master Stephen Langton', pp. 843–4.

77 *Histoire des ducs de Normandie*, pp. 202–5; William the Breton, 'Gesta Philippi Augusti', p. 315.

78 Also Ralph de la Tournelle, Ralph of Estrées, John of Beaumont and William of Barres. See *Catalogue des actes de Philippe Auguste*, pp. 393–4, nos. 1780–88.

79 See below, p. 224; and, for their grief, Mousket, *Chronique rimée*, II, p. 44.

80 Baldwin, *Government of Philip Augustus*, p. 338.

81 William of Puylaurens, *Guillaume de Puylaurens: Chronique, 1145–1275*, ed. and trans. Jean Duvernoy, 2nd edn (Toulouse, 1996), pp. 112–15; Petit-Dutaillis, *Etude*, pp. 197–202.

82 *Histoire des ducs de Normandie*, p. 208.

83 *LTC*, II, no. 1664; and see below, p. 207.

84 *LTC*, II, no. 2221.

85 *Les registres de Philippe Auguste*, ed. J. W. Baldwin (Paris, 1992), securities, p. 429, no. 74; *LTC*, I, nos. 1447–55, 1502–8; Aubri of Trois-Fontaines, 'Chronica Albrici Monachi Trium Fontium', in *MGH Scriptores*, XXIII, ed. Paul Scheffer-Boichorst (Hanover, 1874), p. 912, notes trouble in Burgundy in 1222.

86 *Les registres de Philippe Auguste*, securities, pp. 430–31, nos. 75, 76; *LTC*, I, nos. 1509–12, 1526. Mousket, *Chronique rimée*, II, p. 416, vv. 23,414–23,424.

87 *Les registres de Philippe Auguste*, securities, pp. 434–5, nos. 79 and 80.

88 *Les registres de Philippe Auguste*, securities, p. 435, no. 81.

89 Ralph of Coggeshall, *Chronicon Anglicanum*, p. 195.

90 *LTC*, I, no. 1546.

91 'Annales de Waverleia', in *Annales monastici*, ed. H. R. Luard, 3 vols (London, 1865), II, p. 298. This chronicler was writing

in distant Surrey, but he probably got his information through Cistercian networks, and both Louis and Blanche had close ties to the Cistercians; see below, pp. 210–18.

3 LOUIS VIII AND BLANCHE

1 *LTC*, II, no. 1597.

2 Rigord, *Histoire de Philippe Auguste*, ed. Elisabeth Carpentier, Georges Pon and Yves Chauvin (Paris, 2006), pp. 138–41.

3 Richard A. Jackson, ed., *Ordines coronationis Franciae: Texts and Ordines for the Coronation of the Frankish and French Kings and Queens in the Middle Ages*, 2 vols (Philadelphia, 1995–2000); for discussion of the French orders, ibid., I, pp. 21–8; for the relevant orders, nos. XIX, XXA and XXI, ibid., I, pp. 248–67; II, pp. 291–305, 341–66; Jacques Le Goff et al., *Le sacre royal à l'époque de Saint-Louis* (Paris, 2001), pp. 13–15, 40–41.

4 For the coronation rites for a queen, see Jackson, *Ordines coronationis Franciae*, I, pp. 264–7, II, pp. 303–4, 362–6; Le Goff et al., *Le sacre royal à l'époque de Saint-Louis*: Ordo of Reims, pp. 306–7; Ordo of 1250, pp. 288–9. For the coronation of 1223, see *Récits d'un ménestrel de Reims au treizième siècle*, ed. Natalis de Wailly (Paris, 1876), p. 161. Philippe Mousket, *Chronique rimée*, ed. F. de Reiffenberg, 2 vols (Brussels, 1836–8), II, p. 443, vv. 24,227–24,234, also suggests the use of the same oil for both.

5 'Ex chronico Turonensi: auctore anonymo, S. Martini Turon. canonico', in *RHF*, XVIII (1879), p. 304; Mousket, *Chronique rimée*, II, p. 434, vv. 23,965–23,970. For John of Brienne, see Guy Perry, *John of Brienne: King of Jerusalem, Emperor of Constantinople, c. 1175–1237* (Cambridge, 2013).

6 For the role of Philip Hurepel, see Mousket, *Chronique rimée*, II, p. 443, vv. 24,241–24,244; Charles Petit-Dutaillis, *Etude sur la vie et le règne de Louis VIII* (Paris, 1894), p. 222. For a poem on Louis's consecration,

which refers to his long wait for power, see Léopold Delisle, 'Discours de M. Léopold Delisle, membre de l'Institut, président, et appendice', *Annuaire-bulletin de la Société d'histoire de France* (1885), appendix, p. 132.

7 *LTC*, II, no. 1613; *Récits d'un ménestrel de Reims*, pp. 162–4; Petit-Dutaillis, *Etude*, appendix vi, catalogue des actes, no. 9, p. 450. For a suggestive description of the fabrics, see Mousket, *Chronique rimée*, II, pp. 441–2, vv. 24,190–24,204.

8 Itinerary in Petit-Dutaillis, *Etude*, appendix iii, pp. 438–41.

9 Sean L. Field, *Isabelle of France: Capetian Sanctity and Franciscan Identity in the Thirteenth Century* (Notre Dame, IN, 2006), pp. 176–7, nn. 1, 2; Jean Dunbabin, *Charles I of Anjou: Power, Kingship and State-Making in Thirteenth-century Europe* (London, 1998), p. 10. Dunbabin observes that it is possible that Charles and Stephen were the same child. The Tours Chronicler, 'Ex chronico Turonensi', p. 317, says that Blanche was left with seven live children at Louis's death – Louis, Robert, Alphonse, John, Philip Dagobert, Stephen and Isabella.

10 See discussion in Petit-Dutaillis, *Etude*, p. 331; and the extensive and thoughtful discussion in Miriam Shadis, 'Blanche of Castile and Facinger's "Medieval Queenship": Reassessing the Argument', in *Capetian Women*, ed. Kathleen Nolan (New York, 2003), pp. 137–61. For the subscriptions of queens of France to royal *acta*, see Jean Dufour, 'De l'anneau sigillaire au sceau: évolution du rôle des reines de France jusqu'à la fin du XIIIe siècle', in *Corpus des sceaux français du Moyen âge, tome III: les sceaux des reines et des enfants de France*, ed. Marie-Adélaïde Nielen (Paris, 2011), pp. 11–25, esp. pp. 15–25.

11 Petit-Dutaillis, *Etude*, appendix viii, pièces justicatives, no. xiii, pp. 522–5.

12 Mousket, *Chronique rimée*, II, p. 490, vv. 25,451–25,452: 'Madame Blance l'octroia/ La roine, c'on moult proisa'.

13 Petit-Dutaillis, *Etude*, appendix vi, catalogue des actes, no. 219, p. 479.

14 See below, p. 117.

15 See below, pp. 239–43.

16 *Chartularium Universitatis parisiensis: Ex diversis bibliothecis tabulariisque collegit et cum authenticis chartis contulit*, ed. H. Denifle, 4 vols (Paris, 1889–97), I, pp. 108–9, no. 52: 'regina tenerrime diligit fratres, qui mecum de negociis suis ore proprio satis familiariter loquebatur'. For the establishment of the Dominican house in Paris, see William A. Hinnebusch, *History of the Dominican Order*, 2 vols (New York, 1965–73), I, pp. 58–9, 62–4.

17 *LTC*, II, nos. 1813–21. Janna Bianchini, *The Queen's Hand: Power and Authority in the Reign of Berenguela of Castile* (Philadelphia, 2012), pp. 159–61. This particular revolt is dated to 1223 in *The Latin Chronicle of the Kings of Castile*, trans. and ed. Joseph F. O'Callaghan (Tempe, Ariz., 2002), p. 86/'Chronica Latina regum Castellae', in *Chronica hispana saeculi XIII*, ed. L. C. Brea, J. A. Estévez Sola and R. Carande Herrero (Turnhout, 1997), p. 84.

18 *Latin Chronicle*, p. 87/'Chronica Latina', pp. 84–5; 'Ex chronico Turonensi', p. 305; 'Gesta Ludovici VIII, Francorum Regis', in *RHF*, XVII (1878), p. 303; and discussion in Miriam Shadis, *Berenguela of Castile (1180–1246) and Political Women in the High Middle Ages* (New York, 2009), pp. 111–12.

19 Perry, *John of Brienne*, p. 141.

20 See below, pp. 167–8.

21 Petit-Dutaillis, *Etude*, p. 221.

22 Petit-Dutaillis, *Etude*, pp. 334–7.

23 William the Breton, 'Gesta Philippi Augusti', in *Oeuvres de Rigord et Guillaume le Breton*, ed. H. Delaborde, 2 vols (Paris, 1882–5), I, p. 255. For Peter of Brittany's early career, see Sidney Painter, *The Scourge of the Clergy: Peter of Dreux, Duke of Brittany* (Baltimore, 1937), pp. 6–30.

24 Petit-Dutaillis, *Etude*, pp. 273–4.

25 Matthew Paris, *Historia Anglorum*, ed.

Sir Frederic Madden, 2 vols (London, 1866), II, p. 256.

26 Petit-Dutaillis, *Etude*, p. 259.

27 John W. Baldwin, *The Government of Philip Augustus: Foundations of French Royal Power in the Middle Ages* (Berkeley, Cal., 1986), p. 197.

28 Aubri of Trois-Fontaines, 'Chronica Albrici Monachi Trium Fontium', in MGH *Scriptores*, XXIII, ed. Paul Scheffer-Boichorst (Hanover, 1874), p. 912.

29 Alexis Wällensköld, *Les chansons de Thibaut de Champagne, roi de Navarre: édition critique* (Paris, 1925). See below, p. 247.

30 Baldwin, *Government of Philip Augustus*, pp. 197–8, 279.

31 See above, p. 59.

32 Painter, *Scourge of the Clergy*, pp. 16–17.

33 Mousket, *Chronique rimée*, II, p. 426, vv. 23,700–23,709.

34 *LTC*, II, no. 1629; Petit-Dutaillis, *Etude*, appendix vi, catalogue des actes, no. 71, p. 458. See discussion in Andrew Lewis, *Royal Succession in Capetian France: Studies on Familial Order and the State* (Cambridge, Mass., 1981), pp. 159–61.

35 *LTC*, II, no. 1610. See the detailed analysis and discussion in William Chester Jordan, *The French Monarchy and the Jews: From Philip Augustus to the Last Capetians* (Philadelphia, 1989), pp. 193–204.

36 *LTC*, II, nos. 1612, 1620.

37 Rigord, *Histoire de Philippe Auguste*, pp. 352–3; for Philip and the Jews, see Baldwin, *Government of Philip Augustus*, pp. 230–33.

38 Sara Lipton, *Images of Intolerance: The Representation of Jews and Judaism in the Bible Moralisée* (Berkeley, Cal., 1999), pp. 32–8.

39 *LTC*, II, no. 1610: 'hoc intelligendum est tam de his qui stabilimentum juraverunt quam de illis qui non juraverunt'.

40 *LTC*, II, nos. 1594, 1603; Petit-Dutaillis, *Etude*, appendix vi, catalogue des actes, nos. 20, 21, pp. 451–2.

41 Nicholas Vincent, 'John's Jezebel: Isabelle of Angoulême', in *King John: New Interpretations*, ed. S. D. Church (Woodbridge, 1999), pp. 175–81.

42 *LTC*, II, nos. 1602, 1603.

43 Petit-Dutaillis, *Etude*, appendix vi, catalogue des actes, no. 60, p. 457; *LTC*, II, no. 1631.

44 Petit-Dutaillis, *Etude*, appendix vi, catalogue des actes, no. 103, p. 463; *RHF*, XVII, p. 303.

45 *LTC*, II, no. 1650; Petit-Dutaillis, *Etude*, appendix vi, catalogue des actes, nos. 104, 105, 107, 109, p. 463.

46 Petit-Dutaillis, *Etude*, p. 239.

47 Petit-Dutaillis, *Etude*, appendix vi, catalogue des actes, no. 132, p. 467.

48 Petit-Dutaillis, *Etude*, appendix vi, catalogue des actes, no. 137, p. 468.

49 Petit-Dutaillis, *Etude*, p. 247, n. 2, quoting a letter of the Bayonnais to Henry III in Thomas Rymer, *Foedera*, 3 vols (London, 1816–30), I, pt i, p. 173.

50 Matthew Paris, *Chronica majora*, ed. H. R. Luard, 7 vols (London, 1872–83), III, pp. 83–4.

51 'Ex chronico Turonensi', p. 305. This anecdote is sometimes doubted, but the Tours chronicler was well informed. John of Brienne left for pilgrimage to Santiago from Saint-Martin, taking his staff from there, and returning it there (ibid.), and the Tours chronicler may have heard through John or Berengaria. The story is also in 'Gesta Ludovici VIII', p. 305. For a poem ascribing Louis's victory at La Rochelle to the fact that the beer-drinking English were overcome by the Bacchic French, see Delisle, 'Discours', appendix, pp. 112–13.

52 See below, pp. 115-17. For the foundation of Saint-Antoine, see Rigord, *Histoire de Philippe Auguste*, pp. 350–51.

53 *LTC*, II, no. 1664.

54 Petit-Dutaillis, *Etude*, appendix vi, catalogue des actes, no. 219, p. 479. Louis had organised Ingeborg's dower immediately after

Philip's death in August 1223; ibid., appendix vi, catalogue des actes, no. 12, p. 450.

55   Petit-Dutaillis, *Etude*, appendix vi, catalogue des actes, no. 258, p. 484. For the position of the altar, see Marcel Aubert, *Notre-Dame de Paris*, 2nd edn (Paris, 1929), p. 139, n. 1.

56   *LTC*, II, no. 1710. See comment on his will in Elizabeth A. R. Brown, 'Royal Testamentary Acts from Philip Augustus to Philip of Valois', in *Herrscher- und Fürstentestamente im westeuropäischen Mittelalter*, ed. Brigitte Kasten (Cologne, 2008), pp. 420–21. The daughter, Isabella, is the only named child. The sons are qualified as 'the oldest', 'the second', etc.

57   *RHF*, XIX (1833), p. 760; Petit-Dutaillis, *Etude*, appendix vi, catalogue des actes, no. 242, p. 482; *LTC*, II, no. 1715: homage of Aimery of Thouars, July 1225.

58   Matthew Paris, *Chronica majora*, III, p. 93; Matthew Paris, *Historia Anglorum*, II, pp. 269–70.

59   Petit-Dutaillis, *Etude*, pp. 269–70; Rymer, *Foedera*, I, pt i, pp. 180–81.

60   *LTC*, II, no. 1708; Petit-Dutaillis, *Etude*, appendix vi, catalogue des actes, nos. 249, 250, p. 483.

61   'Ex chronico Turonensi', pp. 316, 320; Petit-Dutaillis, *Etude*, pp. 396–401; Painter, *Scourge of the Clergy*, pp. 36–9.

62   *LTC*, II, nos. 1644, 1645.

63   *LTC*, II, no. 1707.

64   *LTC*, II, no. 1761; Petit-Dutaillis, *Etude*, appendix vi, catalogue des actes, nos. 340–44, p. 495.

65   For the set of conditions that Louis put to the pope in February 1224, see Petit-Dutaillis, *Etude*, pp. 282–4 and appendix vi, catalogue des actes, no. 81, p. 460.

66   Richard Kay, *The Council of Bourges, 1225: A Documentary History* (Aldershot, 2002), pp. 20, 34.

67   For full discussion of the negotiations for Louis's Crusade, and for the full documentary evidence for the twists and turns in the negotiations, see Kay, *Council of Bourges*.

68   Kay, *Council of Bourges*, pp. 39–52; Petit-Dutaillis, *Etude*, pp. 288–9. For his comments on Romanus, see Mousket, *Chronique rimée*, II, pp. 486–7, vv. 25,350–25,379.

69   For Romanus's support of the Dominicans (he dined with them in their refectory), see *Chartularium Universitatis parisiensis*, I, no. 52, p. 109. On his arrogance, 'son orguel', see Mousket, *Chronique rimée*, II, p. 487.

70   Petit-Dutaillis, *Etude*, appendix vi, catalogue des actes, no. 285, p. 488.

71   Petit-Dutaillis, *Etude*, p. 292; Mousket, *Chronique rimée*, II, p. 490, vv. 25,451–25,452: 'Madame Blance l'octroia/ La roine, c'on moult proisa'.

72   Petit-Dutaillis, *Etude*, appendix vi, catalogue des actes, no. 313, p. 491; so did Guy of Montfort: ibid., no. 314.

73   *LTC*, II, no. 1743; Petit-Dutaillis, *Etude*, appendix vi, catalogue des actes, no. 317, p. 492; Matthew Paris, *Historia Anglorum*, II, p. 285; Kay, *Council of Bourges*, pp. 74–5.

74   *LTC*, II, no. 1742; Petit-Dutaillis, *Etude*, appendix vi, catalogue des actes, no. 362, p. 497.

75   Matthew Paris, *Chronica majora*, III, pp. 105–10.

76   Nicholas of Braie, 'Gesta Ludovici VIII, Francorum Regis', in *RHF*, XVII (1878), p. 335.

77   Matthew Paris, *Chronica majora*, III, p. 111.

78   Petit-Dutaillis, *Etude*, pp. 300, 309.

79   Mousket, *Chronique rimée*, II, pp. 519–23, vv. 26,285–26,405; Nicholas of Braie, 'Gesta Ludovici VIII', pp. 343–4; *Récits d'un ménestrel de Reims*, pp. 172–3.

80   Petit-Dutaillis, *Etude*, pp. 314–16.

81   'Ex chronico Turonensi', p. 316.

82   Mousket, *Chronique rimée*, II, p. 516, vv. 26,195–26,218; 'Gesta Ludovici VIII', p. 309.

83   Roger of Wendover, *Flores historiarum*, ed. H. G. Hewlett, 3 vols (London, 1886–9), II, p. 313; Matthew Paris, *Chronica majora*, III,

p. 116. For the suggestions of poison, see Nicholas of Braie, 'Gesta Ludovici VIII', p. 334; Mousket, *Chronique rimée*, II, p. 553, vv. 27, 280–27,287.

84 Petit-Dutaillis, *Etude*, pp. 307–8. For Louis's expedition, see William of Puylaurens, *Guillaume de Puylaurens: Chronique, 1145–1275*, ed. and trans. Jean Duvernoy, 2nd edn (Toulouse, 1996), pp. 124–31.

85 *LTC*, II, no. 1811: 3 November 1226. For Louis's deathbed, see Mousket, *Chronique rimée*, II, pp. 551–2, vv. 27,230–27,260.

86 *LTC*, II, no. 1828. For Miles's relationship to Guy of Châtillon, see Newman, *Les seigneurs de Nesle*, I, p. 193.

87 Mousket, *Chronique rimée*, II, p. 554, vv. 27,293–27,310; 'Gesta Ludovici VIII', p. 310; Matthew Paris, *Chronica majora*, III, p. 117.

4 QUEEN REGENT

1 Philippe Mousket, *Chronique rimée*, ed. F. de Reiffenberg, 2 vols (Brussels, 1836–8), II, p. 554, vv. 27,313–27,314: 'Quar la roine plorait tant/Que tint en firent dementant'; see also *Récits d'un ménestrel de Reims au treizième siècle*, ed. Natalis de Wailly (Paris, 1876), p. 174.

2 *LTC*, II, nos. 1823–7.

3 Jacques Le Goff, *Saint Louis* (Paris, 1996), p. 97.

4 Matthew Paris, *Chronica majora*, ed. H. R. Luard, 7 vols (London, 1872–83), III, p. 118.

5 See the list of those who did attend, and an extensive description, in Mousket, *Chronique rimée*, II, pp. 561–6, vv. 27,504–27,670. Matthew Paris, *Chronica majora*, III, pp. 118–19, exaggerates the non-attendance, and includes the count of Saint-Pol among the list, but Count Guy had just died at Avignon without a son to succeed him, so the countship was probably in temporary abeyance. The Tours Chronicle lists Peter Mauclerc, Theobald of Champagne and Hugh of Lusignan as the non-attenders: 'Ex chronico Turonensi: auctore anonymo, S. Martini Turon. canonico', in *RHF*, XVIII (1879), p. 318. For John of Jerusalem, see Elie Berger, *Histoire de Blanche de Castille, reine de France* (Paris, 1895), p. 66 and n. 1.

6 Andrew Lewis, *Royal Succession in Capetian France: Studies on Familial Order and the State* (Cambridge, Mass., 1981), pp. 46–7. See further discussion of minority and regency below, pp. 276–80.

7 John W. Baldwin, *The Government of Philip Augustus: Foundations of French Royal Power in the Middle Ages* (Berkeley, Cal., 1986), pp. 102–4.

8 Lindy Grant, *Abbot Suger of St-Denis: Church and State in Early Twelfth-century France* (London, 1998), p. 157.

9 *LTC*, II, no. 1828.

10 A.-J.-V. Leroux de Lincy, *Recueil de chants historiques français depuis le XIIe jusqu'au XVIIIe siècle*, vol. 1 (Paris, 1841), no. i, p. 166; no. iii, p. 173.

11 Leroux de Lincy, *Recueil de chants*, nos. i, ii, pp. 171–2; no. iv, pp. 176–8.

12 Introduction to Roger of Wendover, *Flores historiarum*, III, p. xxxvi.

13 William Chester Jordan, *Louis IX and the Challenge of the Crusade: A Study in Rulership* (Princeton, 1979), p. 204. For discussion of private war, see Richard Kaeuper, *War, Justice and Public Order: England and France in the Later Middle Ages* (Oxford, 1988), pp. 231–5; and see below, pp. 295,298.

14 Theobald paid off the claims of Everard and Philippine of Brienne in the summer of 1227: *LTC*, II, nos. 1934, 1941. For the Champagne wars, see Aubri of Trois-Fontaines, 'Chronica Albrici Monachi Trium Fontium', in *MGH Scriptores*, XXIII, ed. Paul Scheffer-Boichorst (Hanover, 1874), pp. 923–4, 936. See also William of Nangis, 'Chronicon Guillelmi de Nangiaco (ab anno 1226 ad 1300)', *RHF*, XX (1840), p. 545; William of Nangis, *Chronique latine de Guillaume de Nangis*, ed. H. Geraud,

2 vols (Paris, 1843), I, pp. 177–8, though he puts this phase under 1228.

15 Jean de Joinville, *Vie de Saint Louis*, ed. Jacques Monfrin (Paris, 2010), pp. 36–7, ch. 72.

16 See, e.g., *LTC*, II, nos. 1915, 1931, 1937.

17 For Michael of Harnes, see Mousket, *Chronique rimée*, II, p. 589, vv. 28,339–28,343.

18 Jordan, *Louis IX and the Challenge of the Crusade*, p. 230; Elisabeth Verry, 'Les seigneurs d'Anjou au temps de Saint Louis', in *Saint Louis et l'Anjou*, ed. Etienne Vacquet (Rennes, 2014), p. 49.

19 *LTC*, II, nos. 1915, 1925; Verry, 'Les seigneurs d'Anjou', pp. 46–7.

20 Joinville, *Vie de Saint Louis*, pp. 36–9, chs 72–4; *Récits d'un ménestrel de Reims*, pp. 176–7.

21 For Robert, see *Cartulaire normand de Philippe Auguste, Louis VIII, Saint Louis et Philippe-le-Hardi*, ed. Léopold Delisle (Caen, 1852), p. 55, no. 361, full text on p. 311; for Philip, see *LTC*, II, no. 1909, including 'feodum comitatus Sancti Pauli quod movere dinoscitur de Bolonesia'.

22 Joinville, *Vie de Saint Louis*, pp. 36–9, chs 72–4.

23 Joinville, *Vie de Saint Louis*, pp. 36–7, ch. 73. This stage in the baronial plotting is sometimes dated to 1229, but it would be surprising if Blanche were so insecure at that stage.

24 *LTC*, II, no. 1761.

25 For the securities and fidelities from the Flemish aristocracy and towns, see *LTC*, II, nos. 1830–94; for the main treaty, ibid., II, no. 1895; for the payment for Ferdinand, ibid., no. 1898. Mousket, *Chronique rimée*, II, pp. 560–61, vv. 27,495–27,503. Matthew Paris, *Chronica majora*, III, p. 118, claims that she was forced to release Ferdinand by the insistence of the barons; in fact, she was implementing a treaty arranged by her husband.

26 *LTC*, II, no. 1899.

27 Leroux de Lincy, *Recueil de chants*, no. i, p. 166; no. ii, p. 171; no. iii, pp. 172–3.

28 See below, pp. 247–8.

29 For baronial hatred of Theobald, see Mousket, *Chronique rimée*, II, p. 578, vv. 27,955–27,960.

30 See the slightly confused chronology in the 'Ex chronico Turonensi', p. 319. Theobald began by plotting with Richard of Cornwall, until Richard tried to capture him. For the treaty, see *LTC*, II, no. 1922.

31 *LTC*, II, no. 1920.

32 Joinville, *Vie de Saint Louis*, pp. 38–9, ch. 75.

33 *LTC*, II, no. 1924.

34 *LTC*, II, nos. 2052, 2065; and see discussion in Sean L. Field, *Isabelle of France: Capetian Sanctity and Franciscan Identity in the Thirteenth Century* (Notre Dame, Ind., 2006), pp. 15–17.

35 *LTC*, II, nos. 1925, 1926.

36 Lindy Grant, 'Representing Dynasty: The Transept Windows of Chartres Cathedral', in *Representing History: Art, Music, History*, ed. Robert A. Maxwell (Philadelphia, 2010), passim.

37 Petit Livre Blanc de Chartres (BNF MS lat. 11062, f. 65), published in Olivier de Romanet, *Géographie du Perche* (Mortagne, 1890–1902), 2 parts in one vol., p. 242, no. 5: 'Vobis pluries mandavisse et etiam viva voce dixisse ut…Quia quod nundum fecistis karissimus filius noster, rex, et nos consilium habuimus cum baronibus Francie ut id fieri faceremus'.

38 *LTC*, II, nos. 1934, 1935, 1941.

39 Matthew Paris, *Chronica majora*, III, pp. 158–9; *LTC*, II, nos. 1967, 1970.

40 *LTC*, II, no. 1968: Hugh of La Marche, June 1228; ibid., no. 1962: Hugh of Thouars, February 1228.

41 *LTC*, II, no. 1969. Joanna of Toulouse's grandmother and Blanche's mother, Alphonse's grandmother, were sisters.

42 *LTC*, II, no. 1946: Comminges, October 1227; ibid., no. 1960: Limoges, March 1228.

43 *LTC*, II, no. 1980; William of Puylaurens, *Guillaume de Puylaurens: Chronique, 1145–1275*, ed. and trans. Jean Duvernoy, 2nd edn (Toulouse, 1996), pp. 132–5.

44 Roger of Wendover, *Flores historiarum*, ed. H. G. Hewlett, 3 vols (London, 1886–9), III, p. 4; Matthew Paris, *Chronica majora*, III, p. 119; Leroux de Lincy, *Recueil de chants*, nos. i, iv.

45 *LTC*, II, no. 1930: Romanus demands payment of tithe from the archbishop of Tours; ibid., no. 1942: Walter Cornut and Walter of Chartres guarantee payments for the Crusade from the chapters in the archdiocese of Sens. See further discussion below, pp. 93–5.

46 *LTC*, II, nos. 1988, 1989.

47 Matthew Paris, *Chronica majora*, III, p. 156.

48 *LTC*, II, nos. 1991, 2008; William of Puylaurens, *Chronique*, pp. 144–5.

49 For Romanus, see *LTC*, II, nos. 2008, 2009; for Peter of Collemezzo, ibid., nos. 1998, 2003, 2004; for Theobald, ibid., nos. 1994, 2008; William of Puylaurens, *Chronique*, pp. 139–41. For the career of Peter of Collemezzo, see *Fasti Ecclesiae Gallicanae, II: le diocèse de Rouen*, ed. Vincent Tabbagh (Turnhout, 1998), pp. 84–6.

50 *LTC*, II, no. 1992; for further concessions, ibid.w, nos. 2010, 2011.

51 *LTC*, II, nos. 2275, 2276; and see below, pp. 123, 127.

52 Roger of Wendover, *Flores historiarum*, II, p. 355; Matthew Paris, *Chronica majora*, III, pp. 164–5.

53 Roger of Wendover, Flores historiarum, III, p. 5.

54 Joinville, *Vie de Saint Louis*, pp. 40–43, chs 80–83.

55 The date of the Champagne invasion is problematic. William of Nangis, 'Chronicon', p. 545; William of Nangis, *Chronique*, I, pp. 177–8, puts it under 1228; Roger of Wendover, *Flores historiarum*, III, pp. 3–4, places it under 1230; Joinville suggests that it happened early in the regency: see Joinville, *Vie de Saint Louis*, pp. 40–43, chs 80–83. But Aubri, 'Chronica', pp. 924, 926, who was best placed to know, says it broke out in summer 1229, after the death of Countess Blanche, and that Theobald continued to have problems along his borders into the 1230s. Documentary evidence supports this: see esp. *LTC*, II, nos. 2016 and 2044. The Ménestrel's entertaining account of the baronial plotting against Blanche focuses as might be expected on the war against Theobald: see *Récits d'un ménestrel de Reims*, pp. 176–81.

56 Aubri, 'Chronica', p. 924; *LTC*, II, no. 2016: July 1229, Louis takes Chablis under his protection, because of war in the area.

57 *LTC*, II, no. 2014: July 1229.

58 *LTC*, II, no. 2044.

59 *LTC*, II, nos. 2038–41: February 1230.

60 Joinville, *Vie de Saint Louis*, pp. 44–5, chs 86–8; and see below, pp. 109–10.

61 Roger of Wendover, *Flores historiarum*, III, p. 3. Aubri, 'Chronica', p. 924, names Philip Hurepel, Count Robert and his brothers, Peter and John of Mâcon, Enguerrand of Coucy, Count Hugh of Saint-Pol and the count of Nevers.

62 Aubri, 'Chronica', p. 926.

63 For the text of his letter, see Sidney Painter, *The Scourge of the Clergy: Peter of Dreux, Duke of Brittany* (Baltimore, 1937), pp. 60–62, and appendix i, pp. 131–2.

64 Roger of Wendover, *Flores historiarum*, III, pp. 5–13; *LTC*, II, nos. 2035–7.

65 For the alliances with Hugh and Andrew, see *LTC*, II, nos. 2052, 2057, 2058, 2059.

66 *LTC*, II, no. 2056.

67 Roger of Wendover, *Flores historiarum*, III, pp. 6–8.

68 *LTC*, II, nos. 2052, 2063, 2065, 2068.

69 For Geoffrey of Argenton and the vis-count of Thouars, respectively, see *LTC*, II, nos. 2052, 2055.

70 Roger of Wendover, *Flores historiarum*, III, p. 13.

71 *LTC*, II, no. 2052: Hugh of La Marche, peace with 'the lady queen while she holds the lord king and his realm in her hand'; ibid., no. 2060: the viscount of Thouars does fidelity to the queen 'until the lord king shall come to the age of legitimacy'.

72 *LTC*, II, nos. 2057, 2052.

73 *LTC*, II, no. 2063.

74 *LTC*, II, no. 2064.

75 Roger of Wendover, *Flores historiarum*, III, p. 8.

76 *LTC*, II, nos. 2128, 2129. The Breton noble Henry of Avagour also joined Blanche and Louis: ibid., nos. 2135, 2136, 2139. See also Daniel Power, *The Norman Frontier in the Twelfth and Early Thirteenth Centuries* (Cambridge, 2004), pp. 464–6.

77 Roger of Wendover, *Flores historiarum*, III, p. 13; *LTC*, II, nos. 2144, 2141.

78 Most of the claims are from summer 1232: *LTC*, II, nos. 2198, 2200, 2201–4, 2215; but works and compensation are still recorded on the officials' accounts for the feast of the Ascension in 1234: 'Compotus ballivorum et praepositorum Franciae anno Domini 1234 mense Junio de termino ascensionis', in *RHF*, XXII (1865), p. 576. See Emmanuel Litoux, 'Un paysage castral dominé par le Château d'Angers', in *Saint Louis et l'Anjou*, pp. 72–80; and François Comte, 'L'enceinte de Saint Louis à Angers: restitution d'une fortification dispa-rue', in *Saint Louis et l'Anjou*, pp. 81–92.

79 *LTC*, II, no. 2021.

80 *LTC*, II, nos. 2182, 2183.

81 *LTC*, II, no. 2266. For a clerk going to Boulogne to receive fealty, see 'Recepta et expensa Anno MCCXXXIIII inter candelosam et ascensionem', in *RHF*, XXI (1855), p. 232. Mousket, *Chronique rimée*, II, p. 582, vv.

28,126–28, 141, says that some suspected Theobald of Champagne of poisoning again, and some blamed Blanche.

82 *LTC*, II, no. 2263. For messengers to Rome, see 'Recepta et expensa', pp. 231, 235.

83 *LTC*, II, no. 2270, February 1234.

84 *LTC*, II, no. 2273. For messengers to Raymond, or support for his household, see 'Recepta et expensa', p. 235, and pp. 230, 232, 233.

85 *LTC*, II, no. 1710.

86 *LTC*, II, no. 1953.

87 Royaumont Cartulary, ADVO MS 43H3, foundation act of Louis IX, 1228, ff. 1–5.

88 *GC*, VIII, col. 1158; Marie-Anselme Dimier, *Saint Louis et Cîteaux* (Paris, 1954), p. 58.

89 Royaumont Cartulary, BNF MS lat. 5472, ff. 102, 111, 143.

90 For Dagobert's death, see Berger, *Histoire de Blanche de Castille*, p. 207; for Royaumont as burial place, see below, p. 224. For the family contributing to building, see Guillaume de Saint-Pathus, 'Vie de Saint Louis, par le confesseur de la reine Marguerite', in *RHF*, XX (1840), p. 87.

91 See above, p. 87; and letter of Romanus to the archbishop of Tours, June 1227: *LTC*, II, no. 1930.

92 *Les registres de Grégoire IX*, ed. Lucien Auvray, 4 vols (Paris, 1890–1955), I, cols 67–76, nos. 130, 131, 133, 134.

93 *LTC*, II, no. 1942.

94 Richard Kay, *The Council of Bourges, 1225: A Documentary History* (Aldershot, 2002), p. 167.

95 For full discussion of the diplomatic moves on both sides, see Kay, *Council of Bourges*, pp. 152–73 and doc. nos. 29–39; *Les registres de Grégoire IX*, I, col. 85, no. 155.

96 *GC*, VIII, col. 203. Philip later became bishop of Châlons-sur-Marne.

97 *Les registres de Grégoire IX*, I, cols 72–6, no. 134; Kay, *Council of Bourges*, pp. 424–5, doc.

no. 32: 'Rege autem defuncto, quicquid dominus legatus cum regina fecerit, quicquid constituerit, quicquid promiserit, requista capitulorum voluntate non est factum ... legatus vellet eos, sicut dicebatur, ad solutionem, ut regine promiserat, compellere, eo dicente quod etiam capas nostras daret ei.'

98 Crucial to an understanding of Blanche's legislation for the Jews are Gavin Langmuir, '*Judaei nostri* and the Beginnings of Capetian Legislation', *Traditio*, XVI (1960), pp. 203–69, esp. pp. 222–31; and William Chester Jordan, *The French Monarchy and the Jews: From Philip Augustus to the Last Capetians* (Philadelphia, 1989), esp. pp. 129–36. For Walter Cornut's Jewish administrators, see below, p. 128.

99 *LTC*, II, no. 2083.

100 Blanche had concluded specific arrangements against harbouring the Jews of other lordships with Theobald of Champagne in April 1229 and with John of Nesle in April 1230, perhaps to lay the groundwork for this statute: see *LTC*, II, nos. 1996, 2049. For further discussion of Blanche's relations with the Jews, see below, pp. 127–9, 197–201.

101 Stephen C. Ferruolo, *The Origins of the University: The Schools of Paris and their Critics, 1100–1215* (Stanford, Cal., 1985), pp. 283–8.

102 *Chartularium Universitatis parisiensis: Ex diversis bibliothecis tabulariisque collegit et cum authenticis chartis contulit*, ed. H. Denifle, 4 vols (Paris, 1889–97), I, pp. 106–7.

103 *Chartularium Universitatis parisiensis*, I, no. 59; *Les registres de Gregoire IX*, I, pp. 117–20, no. 203.

104 Hastings Rashdall, *The Universities of Europe in the Middle Ages*, 3 vols (Oxford, 1936), I, p. 317. Ferruolo, *Origins of the University*, pp. 297–301.

105 *Chartularium Universitatis parisiensis*, I, no. 58.

106 See the very full account in Matthew Paris, *Chronica majora*, III, pp. 166–9; for discussion, see Rashdall, *Universities of Europe*, I,

pp. 334–43; Noël Valois, *Guillaume d'Auvergne, évêque de Paris, 1228–1249: sa vie et ses ouvrages* (Paris, 1880), pp. 50–56.

107 Rashdall, *Universities of Europe*, I, p. 336; Caesar Egassius Bulaeus, *Historia Universitatis parisiensis*, III (Paris, 1666), p. 555. *Chartularium Universitatis parisiensis*, I, p. 64. For Peter's relationship with the Breton clergy, see Painter, *Scourge of the Clergy*, pp. 48–50.

108 Valois, *Guillaume d'Auvergne*, p. 52.

109 Valois, *Guillaume d'Auvergne*, p. 43; *Chartularium Universitatis parisiensis*, I, p. 66.

110 Valois, *Guillaume d'Auvergne*, pp. 53–6, esp. p. 56. 'E libro mortuali Sanctae Catherinae Vallis Scholarum Parisiensis', in *RHF*, XXIII (1876), p. 147.

111 For Gregory's involvement, see *Chartularium Universitatis parisiensis*, I, nos. 69, 70, 71, 74.

112 *Chartularium Universitatis parisiensis*, I, no. 72.

113 William of Nangis, 'Chronicon', p. 546; William of Nangis, *Chronique*, I, pp. 181–2.

114 Matthew Paris, *Chronica majora*, III, p. 169; Leroux de Lincy, *Recueil de chants*, esp. no. i, p. 178.

115 Account of clash in 'E chronico Rotomagensi', in *RHF*, XXIII (1876), pp. 332–3, 334–6. See commentary in Gerard J. Campbell, 'The Attitude of the Monarchy towards the Use of Ecclesiastical Censures in the Reign of Saint Louis', *Speculum*, XXXV (1960), pp. 538–41; J. R. Strayer, *The Administration of Normandy under Saint Louis* (Cambridge, Mass., 1932), pp. 69–80, on forest rights. See also discussion in Lindy Grant, 'Blanche of Castile and Normandy', in *Normandy and its Neighbours, 900–1250*, ed. David Crouch and Kathleen Thompson (Turnhout, 2011), pp. 127–30; and see discussion of Blanche's relations with the church in general below, pp. 182–92.

116 The court was at Vernon in May and July 1227: see *Cartulaire normand*, p. 55, nos. 360, 361, 362.

117 'E chronico Rotomagensi', p. 332: 'Rex

et regina valde irati fuerunt' – which makes explicit Blanche's role in this.

118 *Les registres de Grégoire IX*, I, cols 130–31, no. 216: August 1228.

119 'E chronico Rotomagensi', pp. 334, 337.

120 The Rouen Chronicle suggests that Louis had seized the regalia in summer 1233, but Gregory's letters to Louis, Blanche and the royal councillors are dated November 1232: *Les registres de Grégoire IX*, I, cols 572–3, nos. 967, 968, 969. For the lifting of the interdict, see *Cartulaire normand*, p. 65, no. 405.

121 'E chronico Rotomagensi', pp. 334–6.

122 *Les registres de Grégoire IX*, I, cols 572–3, nos. 967, 969.

123 *Les registres de Grégoire IX*, I, col. 573, no. 968. For John of Montmirail, see Marie-Dominique Chapotin, *Histoire des dominicains de la province de France: le siècle des fondations* (Rouen, 1898), I, p. 226. Master John of Montmirail must have been a relation of John of Oisy, count of Chartres, and the blessed John of Montmirail, a Cistercian who had died at Longpont in 1217. For this family, see Nicolas Civel, *La fleur de France: les seigneurs d'Île-de-France au XIIe siècle* (Turnhout, 2006), pp. 400–02, 454.

124 *Les registres de Grégoire IX*, I, cols 832–7, nos. 1506–10.

125 F. M. Powicke, *The Loss of Normandy*, 2nd edn (Manchester, 1961), pp. 113–17.

126 'E chronico Rotomagensi', p. 333, for the disputed election of 1231; ibid., p. 336, for the dispute in 1234. For the archbishops, their backgrounds and the elections, see *Fasti Ecclesiae Gallicanae: Rouen*, pp. 80–84.

127 *LTC*, III, no. 3853. For these three archbishops, see *Fasti Ecclesiae Gallicanae: Rouen*, pp. 84–9; for Blanche and Eudes Rigaud, see, e.g., *Cartulaire normand*, nos. 478, 502.

128 See below, p. 139.

129 Campbell, 'Attitude of the Monarchy', pp. 537, 551–3; and see below, pp. 191–2.

130 Campbell, 'Attitude of the Monarchy', pp. 546–50.

131 See below, pp. 190–92.

132 For the dispute, see A. Giry, *Documents sur les relations de la royauté avec les villes de France de 1180 à 1314* (Paris, 1885), pp. 66–81; Stephen Murray, *Beauvais Cathedral: Architecture of Transcendence* (Princeton, 1989), pp. 36ff; Odette Pontal Gauthier, 'Le différend entre Louis IX et les évêques de Beauvais et ses incidences sur les Conciles, 1232–1248', *Bibliothèque de l'école des chartes*, CXXIII (1965), pp. 5–34. For the resolution of 1248, see *LTC*, III, no. 3690. For discussion of the age of majority, see below, pp. 276–7.

133 *Récits d'un ménestrel de Reims*, pp. 98–9. The object of the Ménestrel's scorn was Bishop Miles, not the queen. For the relationship between the bishop of Noyon and Bartholomew of Roye, see Aubri, 'Chronica', p. 922.

134 Murray, *Beauvais Cathedral*, p. 37.

135 For the text of the inquiry, see Giry, *Documents*, p. 74: 'respondit rex quod ipsemet emendaret, et idem respondit regina'.

136 *LTC*, II, no. 2280.

137 *LTC*, III, no. 3853.

138 William Mendel Newman, *Les seigneurs de Nesle en Picardie, XIIe–XIIIe siècles: leur chartes et leur histoire*, 2 vols (Paris, 1971), II, pp. 262–3, nos. 162, 163.

5   QUEEN DOWAGER

1 For expenditure on the wedding, see 'Recepta et expensa Anno MCCXXXIIII inter candelosam et ascensionem', in *RHF*, XXI (1855), pp. 241, 243–8.

2 E.g., Philippe Mousket, *Chronique rimée*, ed. F. de Reiffenberg, 2 vols (Brussels, 1836–8), II, p. 601, vv. 28,695–28,696: she was the most 'biele et courtoise' (beautiful and courteous) of young women; ibid., p. 668: 'mout par est lovains et fine' (lovely and elegant without peer).

3 Jacques Le Goff, *Saint Louis* (Paris, 1996), pp. 735–6; Marie-Anselme Dimier, *Saint Louis et Cîteaux* (Paris, 1954), pp. 20–21.

4 Le Goff, *Saint Louis*, p. 369.

5 Jean de Joinville, *Vie de Saint Louis*, ed. Jacques Monfrin (Paris, 2010), pp. 300–03, chs 606–7.

6 Joinville, *Vie de Saint Louis*, pp. 294–5, ch. 594; pp. 314–15, ch. 631.

7 Joinville, *Vie de Saint Louis*, pp. 302–3, ch. 608; pp. 300–02, chs 606–7.

8 Joinville, *Vie de Saint Louis*, pp. 300–01, ch. 605.

9 See especially the comments of William Chester Jordan, *Louis IX and the Challenge of the Crusade: A Study in Rulership* (Princeton, 1979), pp. 142–4, on Louis's interventionist kingship; Le Goff, *Saint Louis*, pp. 864–7, on Louis's ill health. For Louis and the mendicants, there is a huge bibliography, including Lester K. Little, 'Saint Louis' Involvement with the Friars', *Church History*, XXXIII (1963), pp. 125–47; and, more recently, M. Cecilia Gaposchkin and S. Field, 'Introduction', in *The Sanctity of Louis IX: Early Lives of Saint Louis by Geoffrey of Beaulieu and William of Chartres*, trans. Larry F. Field, ed. M. Cecilia Gaposchkin and Sean L. Field (Ithaca, 2014), pp. 1–57.

10 AN L463, no. 34. For other examples, see *LTC*, II, no. 2323, November 1234: a religious issue was 'constituto in presentia Ludovii regis et domine regine matris eius'; ibid., no. 2585: the court held at Compiègne in 1237 was held before Louis and Blanche.

11 Le Goff, *Saint Louis*, pp. 128, 174.

12 Jordan, *Louis IX*, esp. pp. 3–9, 13.

13 Roger of Wendover, *Flores historiarum*, ed. H. G. Hewlett, 3 vols (London, 1886–9), III, pp. 93–5.

14 *LTC*, II, no. 2289; ibid., nos. 2253, 2254, 2255.

15 Daniel Power, *The Norman Frontier in the Twelfth and Early Thirteenth Centuries* (Cambridge, 2004), pp. 251–2; Lindy Grant, 'Blanche of Castile and Normandy', in *Normandy and its Neighbours, 900–1250*, ed. David Crouch and Kathleen Thompson (Turnhout, 2011), pp. 124–5; and *Cartulaire normand de Philippe Auguste, Louis VIII, Saint Louis et Philippe-le-Hardi*, ed. Léopold Delisle (Caen, 1852), p. 65, no. 408.

16 'Recepta et expensa', pp. 236, 237, 240; *LTC*, II, no. 2307.

17 'Recepta et expensa', p. 242.

18 *LTC*, II, nos. 2302; ibid., nos 2303–6.

19 *LTC*, II, nos. 2319, 2320.

20 *LTC*, II, no. 2307.

21 *LTC*, II, no. 2233; and entries in the household account between February and May 1234: 'Recepta et expensa', pp. 229, 238, 241.

22 For the *parlamentum*, see 'Recepta et expensa', pp. 233–4: *LTC*, II, nos. 2310, 2312–14, 2322, 2323. Joinville attaches this arrangement to his narrative of the war of 1229; in fact, it did not occur until five years later. Joinville, *Vie de Saint Louis*, pp. 44–5, chs 86–8.

23 *LTC*, II, no. 2231; Aubri of Trois-Fontaines, 'Chronica Albrici Monachi Trium Fontium', in *MGH Scriptores*, XXIII, ed. Paul Scheffer-Boichorst (Hanover, 1874), p. 930, who says that the marriage alienated some of the baronage.

24 *LTC*, II, no. 2294.

25 *LTC*, II, nos. 2389, 2390, 239L.

26 *Cartulaire normand*, p. 68, no. 421.

27 *LTC*, II, no. 2330.

28 *LTC*, II, no. 2432.

29 Aubri of Trois-Fontaines, 'Chronica', p. 938; negotiations possibly reflected in 'Recepta et expensa', pp. 233, 241, 244.

30 *LTC*, II, no. 2432.

31 *LTC*, II, no. 2443.

32 Matthew Paris, *Chronica majora*, ed. H. R. Luard, 7 vols (London, 1872–83), III, p. 366; Mousket, *Chronique rimée*, II, pp. 616–17, vv. 29,123–29,155; Aubri of Trois-Fontaines, 'Chronica', p. 938, on Theobald's revolt.

33 Mousket, *Chronique rimée*, II, p. 618, vv. 29,160–29,175; *Récits d'un ménestrel de Reims au treizième siècle*, ed. Natalis de Wailly (Paris, 1876), p. 185.

34 *LTC*, II, nos. 2417–19.

35 *LTC*, II, nos. 2705, 2706.

36 *LTC*, II, no. 2446.

37   *LTC*, II, no. 2363.

38   In 1235 Michael of Harnes's brother-in-law did homage for Michael's lands to both Blanche and Louis: *LTC*, II, no. 2356.

39   For the settlement, two parts going to the king, one part to Countess Matilda, see *LTC*, II, nos. 2367, 2368.

40   *LTC*, II, nos. 2335, 2355.

41   *LTC*, II, no. 2473.

42   Matthew Paris, *Chronica majora*, III, p. 327.

43   Miriam Shadis, *Berenguela of Castile (1180–1246) and Political Women in the High Middle Ages* (New York, 2009), p. 108. The documents recording the marriage in Castile are dated March 1238: *LTC*, II, nos. 2699, 2670.

44   *LTC*, II, no. 2387.

45   Mousket, *Chronique rimée*, II, p. 627, vv. 29,423–29,433. *LTC*, II, no. 2492: Joanna renounces marriage to Simon. Aubri of Trois-Fontaines, 'Chronica', p. 940, describes Simon as 'suspect in France'.

46   *LTC*, II, nos. 2611–92, 2697.

47   *LTC*, II, nos. 2538, 2584, 2585.

48   *LTC*, II, no. 2562.

49   For the expenditure, see 'Expensa militiae comitis Attrebatensis in Penthecoste AD 1237 mense junio', in *RHF*, XXII (1865), pp. 580–92. For the knighting and wedding, see Aubri of Trois-Fontaines, 'Chronica', p. 941; for the marriage, see Mousket, *Chronique rimée*, II, p. 623, vv. 29,324–29,339. The wife of Enguerrand of Coucy was Mary of Montmirail, sister of John of Oisy, count of Chartres: see Dominique Barthélémy, *Les deux âges de la seigneurie banale: Coucy, milieu XIe–milieu XIIIe siècle* (Paris, 1984), pp. 408–9, 415.

50   'Itinera, dona et hernesia AD 1239 inter ascensionem et omnes sanctos', in *RHF*, XXII (1865), pp. 589–91.

51   'Itinera, dona et hernesia', p. 609.

52   'Itinera, dona et hernesia': minstrels, pp. 589, 590, 591; wolves, hunters' wages, Alphonse of Portugal/Boulogne's dogs, pp. 591–2.

53   *LTC*, II, no. 2514. Joanna and Alphonse were married in 1237: Aubri of Trois-Fontaines, 'Chronica', p. 941. Raymond was present at the knighting of Robert of Artois: 'Expensa militiae comitis Attrebatensis', p. 582.

54   *LTC*, II, nos. 2729; 2835 and 2836: separate letters to Blanche and Louis.

55   Matthew Paris, *Chronica majora*, III, pp. 624–7; Aubri of Trois-Fontaines, 'Chronica', p. 949.

56   Elie Berger, *Histoire de Blanche de Castille, reine de France* (Paris, 1895), p. 326. Both John of Brienne and his wife Berengaria died in 1237: Aubri of Trois-Fontaines, 'Chronica', p. 941.

57   William of Nangis, *Chronique latine de Guillaume de Nangis*, ed. H. Geraud, 2 vols (Paris, 1843), I, pp. 187–8; 'Itinera, dona et hernesia', pp. 591, 612.

58   *LTC*, II, no. 2577.

59   Aubri of Trois-Fontaines, 'Chronica', p. 946. For this Crusade, see Michael Lower, *The Barons' Crusade: A Call to Arms and its Consequences* (Philadelphia, 2005); for the French noble contingent, ibid., pp. 42–4; for Amaury of Montfort on it, ibid., pp. 43–4.

60   'Itinera, dona et hernesia', pp. 595, 597.

61   Mousket, *Chronique rimée*, II, p. 630, vv. 29,250–29,231; ibid., p. 660, vv. 30,385–30,394. See also Lower, *Barons' Crusade*, pp. 50–51, 93–108.

62   *LTC*, II, nos. 2819, 2776.

63   *LTC*, II, nos. 2705, 2706: April 1238. Many royal gifts to *crucesignati* appear in the account of 1239: 'Itinera, dona et hernesia', pp. 593, 595, 596, 597.

64   'E chronico Sanctae Catherinae de Monti Rotomagi', in *RHF*, XXIII (1876), p. 399.

65   *LTC*, II, no. 2744.

66   Details from Walter Cornut, 'Historia susceptionis Coronae spineae', in *RHF*, XXII (1865), pp. 27–32. See expenditure in 'Itinera, dona et hernesia', pp. 600, 601.

67   For discussion of Walter Cornut's account, see Paul Edouard Didier Riant,

Exuviae sacrae Constantinopolitanae [1877–8], 2 vols (Paris, 2004), I, pp. lxviii–lxxj; and for his edition of the text, ibid., pp. 45–56. For the portal at Villeneuve-l'Archevêque, see Willibald Sauerlander, *Gothic Sculpture in France, 1140–1270*, trans. Janet Sondheimer (London, 1972), pl. 178, pp. 468–9.

68   See Walter Cornut, 'Historia susceptionis', esp. pp. 27–9, 31. For the transport of the Crown of Thorns and the erection of scaffolding at Saint-Antoine by Denis and Peter Pig-Flesh ('Carnporc'), see 'Itinera, dona et hernesia', pp. 601–2. Peter Pig-Flesh obtained pomegranates for Blanche in 1239: ibid., p. 605. Both were definitely in Blanche's household in 1241–2, where they both distributed alms for her: 'Comptes de dépenses de Blanche de Castille', ed. Etienne Symphorien Bougenot in *Bulletin du Comité des travaux historiques et scientifiques: section d'histoire et de philologie* (1889), p. 89; BNF MS lat. 9017, f. 69. For Abbess Agnes Mauvoisin, see below, p. 174.

69   Natalis de Wailly, 'Récit du treizième siècle sur les translations faites en 1239 et en 1241 des saints reliques de la Passion', *Bibliothèque de l'école des chartes*, XXXIX (1878), pp. 401–15.

70   See below, pp. 255–7.

71   *LTC*, II, nos. 2441, 2692; AN J189, nos. 4 and 5.

72   *LTC*, II, no. 2885; AN J189, no. 6.

73   See further discussion below, pp. 225–9. For St Louis's daughter Blanche, see Geoffrey of Beaulieu, 'Vita ludovici noni', in *RHF*, XX (1840), p. 8; Geoffrey of Beaulieu, 'Here Begins the Life and Saintly Comportment of Louis, Formerly King of the Franks, of Pious Memory', in *The Sanctity of Louis IX: Early Lives of Saint Louis by Geoffrey of Beaulieu and William of Chartres*, trans. Larry F. Field, ed. M. Cecilia Gaposchkin and Sean L. Field (Ithaca, 2014), p. 82.

74   For Master Richard at Pontoise, see Eude Rigaud, *Regestrum visitationem archiepiscopi Rothomagensis / Journal des visites pastorales*

d'Eude Rigaud, archevêque de Rouen, ed. T. Bonnin (Rouen, 1852), p. 42. Master Richard had a prebend in the chapter of Saint-Mellon at Pontoise, the collegiate church within the castle. For Master Richard's attestations on the household accounts, see 'Itinera, dona et hernesia', pp. 592, 594, 596–9, 604, 606. See also below, p. 150.

75   The *Achatz d'heritage* is now ADVO MS 72H12. Substantial sections of it have been published by Henri de L'Epinois, 'Comptes relatifs à la fondation de l'abbaye de Maubuisson', *Bibliothèque de l'école des chartes*, XIX (1858), pp. 550–67; and in English translation by Constance Berman in *Women and Monasticism in Medieval Europe: Sisters and Patrons of the Cistercian Reform*, ed. and trans. Berman (Kalamazoo, 2002).

76   For Agnes Mauvoisin, abbess of Saint-Antoine, see William Mendel Newman, *Les seigneurs de Nesle en Picardie, XIIe–XIIIe siècles: leur chartes et leur histoire*, 2 vols (Paris, 1971), I, p. 266; and AN L1015, no. 18, f. 8; for Amicia Briard, see Hippolyte Bonnardot, *L'abbaye royale de Saint-Antoine-des-Champs de l'ordre de Cîteaux* (Paris, 1882), pp. iii, 12; and see further discussion of both abbesses below, p. 174.

77   L'Epinois, 'Comptes relatifs', p. 551. See also Constance Berman, 'Two Medieval Women's Control of Property and Religious Benefactions in France: Eleanor of Vermandois and Blanche of Castile', *Viator*, XLI/2 (2010), pp. 151–82, esp. pp. 172–5.

78   L'Epinois, 'Comptes relatifs', pp. 553, 556.

79   L'Epinois, 'Comptes relatifs', pp. 564–7; for the compensations, ibid., p. 565.

80   ADVO MS 72H80, no. iii for 1243.

81   L'Epinois, 'Comptes relatifs', pp. 553–4; *Achatz d'heritage*, ADVO MS 72H12, f. 21: sales of wood and carbon.

82   L'Epinois, 'Comptes relatifs', pp. 555–6; *Achatz d'heritage*, ADVO MS 72H12, f. 29v.

83   BNF MS lat. 406, f. 389.

84   *Achatz d'heritage*, ADVO MS 72H12, f. 27;
for the excavations, see below, p. 258.

85   L'Epinois, 'Comptes relatifs', pp. 555–64.
For the woods at Cuisy, see *Achatz d'heritage*,
ADVO MS 72H12, ff. 20v–22.

86   Alphonse Dutilleux and Joseph Depoin,
*L'abbaye de Maubuisson (Notre-Dame-la-Royale):
histoire et cartulaire, III: le trésor et le mobilier*
(Pontoise, 1884), p. 154.

87   ADVO MS 72H115; and see below, pp.
217–18.

88   For Alice of Vienne, see below, p. 176.
It is possible that there was another abbess of
Maubuisson, named Mary, who is called abbess
in an act of 1256, though the abbey seems to
have counted Guillemette as the first abbess:
see Alphonse Dutilleux and Joseph Depoin,
*Cartulaire de l'abbaye de Maubuisson (Notre-
Dame-la-Royale), II: contrats* (Pontoise, 1913),
p. 121. It is also possible that the abbess used
both names.

89   Armande Gronier-Prieur, *L'abbaye Notre-
Dame du Lys à Dammarie-lès-Lys* (Verneuil-
l'Etang, 1976), pp. 23, 30.

90   BNF MS lat. 13892, ff. 25–6: Louis's act of
1248, given at Paris; ff. 26–27v: second act of
Louis IX, also given at Paris in 1248.

91   BNF MS lat. 13892, ff. 28v–29: given at
Lyon, 1248; ibid, ff. 29v–30: given by Louis at
Melun, April 1248, confirming Blanche's reve-
nues from the Melun issues.

92   BNF MS lat. 13892, f. 30–30v. For the
emblematic nature of the lily, see Michel
Pastoureau, 'La fleur de lis: emblème royal,
symbole Marial ou thème graphique?', in
*L'hermine et le sinople: études d'héraldique
médiévale* (Paris, 1982), pp. 158–78, esp.
pp. 160–61.

93   ADVO MS 72H6/3, vol. IV, ff. 153–5; and
Achatz d'heritage, ADVO MS 72H12, f. 2–2v.

94   Gronier-Prieur, *Notre-Dame du Lys*,
p. 153.

95   E.g., *LTC*, II, nos. 2768, 2776, both
February 1239; no. 2819, June 1239; nos. 2844,
1239, 2858, March 1240; no. 2980, August 1242.

96   E.g., *LTC*, II, no. 2747, November 1238;
no. 2870, April 1240; no. 2947, November 1241;
no. 2958, February 1242; nos. 3051–3, March
1243: all without reference to Blanche.

97   AN L463, no. 34.

98   Emmanuel Lemaire, *Archives anciennes
de la Ville de Saint-Quentin*, 2 vols (Saint-
Quentin, 1888–1910), I, pp. 42–3, no. 41: 'en la
court le roi…en le warde robe le Roine,
deriere vers le gardin en bas'.

99   Matthew Paris, 'Vita S. Edmundi', in
C. H. Lawrence, *St Edmund of Abingdon: A Study
in Hagiography and History* (Oxford, 1960),
pp. 262–3; Matthew Paris, *The Life of St Edmund
by Matthew Paris*, trans. and ed., with a biography, by C. H. Lawrence (Stroud, 1999), p. 150.

100   For Blanche, Louis and Marguerite at
the chapter at Vézelay, see AN J461.

101   *Statuta Capitulorum generalium ordinis
Cisterciensis ab anno 116 ad annum 1786*, ed.
Joseph Canivez, 8 vols (Louvain, 1935), II,
pp. 275, 276, 277.

102   *LTC*, II, no. 2996: 'quod unquam…data
sit materialem quibusque vestries detractatori-
bus contra bonitatis ac puritatis et discretionis
vestre fama celebrem obloquendi'. For the
context, see below, pp. 126–7.

103   William of Puylaurens, *Guillaume de
Puylaurens: Chronique, 1145–1275*, ed. and trans.
Jean Duvernoy, 2nd edn (Toulouse, 1996),
pp. 180–81.

104   AN J403, nos. 3 and 4; copied into AN
JJ3, f. 58v, xxii and xxiii. *LTC*, II, nos. 2908,
2909.

105   Louis-Claude Doüet d'Arcq, 'Siège de
Carcassonne, 1240', *Bibliothèque de l'école des
chartes*, VII (1845–6), pp. 363–79, esp. pp. 371–5:
'petrariam turquesiam valde bonam' and
'gentes vestre in succursum nostrum, Domina,
veniebant'. See also William of Puylaurens,
Chronique, pp. 162–9.

106   For the knighting and feast, see
Joinville, *Vie de Saint Louis*, pp. 46–51, chs 93–8.
For Alphonse issuing confirmations as count of
Poitou, see *LTC*, II, nos. 2922, 2923, 2927.

107 Joinville, *Vie de Saint Louis*, pp. 48–9, chs 95–6.

108 'Ea quae distributa fuerunt in milicia Comitis Pictavensis (Die xxiv junio, anno mccxli)', in *RHF*, XXII (1865), pp. 617–21.

109 Joinville, *Vie de Saint Louis*, pp. 48–9, ch. 94.

110 'Ea quae distributa', p. 617: 'Quidam homo qui perdidit suum supertunicale subtus reginam ad festum, 20s'.

111 *LTC*, II, no. 2926.

112 'Comptes de dépenses de Blanche de Castille', p. 89.

113 *LTC*, II, no. 2928; and Joinville, *Vie de Saint Louis*, pp. 50–51, ch. 98.

114 Léopold Delisle, 'Mémoire sur une lettre inédite adressée à la Reine Blanche par un habitant de La Rochelle', *Bibliothèque de l'école des chartes*, 17th year, 4th series, vol. II (1856), pp. 513–55. The fact that the correspondent needed to tell Blanche what had happened in such detail shows that the queen with Louis must have been Margaret, not Blanche: ibid., pp. 525–6.

115 Delisle, 'Mémoire sur une lettre inédite', pp. 525–6.

116 Delisle, 'Mémoire sur une lettre inédite', pp. 526–9.

117 Delisle, 'Mémoire sur une lettre inédite', p. 528.

118 William of Puylaurens, *Chronique*, pp. 174–5; *LTC*, II, no. 3367.

119 For Blanche's itinerary, see BNF MS lat. 9017, f. 69: she was in Poitiers by Ascension 1242. For the loan, see Léopold Delisle, 'Mémoire sur les opérations financières des Templiers', *Mémoires présentés par divers savantes à l'Académie des inscriptions et belles-lettres*, XXXIII (1889), p. 101.

120 Joinville, *Vie de Saint Louis*, pp. 50–51, chs 100–01.

121 April 1243, truce between Henry III and Louis: *LTC*, II, no. 3075. Joinville, *Vie de Saint Louis*, pp. 52–3, ch. 103; *LTC*, II, no. 2980.

122 *LTC*, II, no. 2996. He also asked the bishop of Toulouse to negotiate on his behalf: William of Puylaurens, *Chronique*, pp. 180–81.

123 *LTC*, II, nos. 3012, 3013.

124 *LTC*, II, no. 2996: 'tam detractatores vestri quam omnes qui audierint circumspectionem vestram, quia nostra supportastis negocia, benedicent'.

125 *The Trial of the Talmud: Paris, 1240*, ed. and trans. John Friedman, Jean Connell Hoff and Robert Chazan (Toronto, 2012), p. 99: letter of Eudes of Châteauroux to Pope Innocent IV.

126 A. Tuillier, 'La condamnation du Talmud par les maîtres universitaires parisiens, ses causes et ses conséquences politiques et idéologiques', in *Le brûlement du Talmud à Paris, 1242–1244*, ed. Gilbert Dahan (Paris, 1999), p. 74, n. 47.

127 The crucial texts are now available in *The Trial of the Talmud*; for Yehiel's account, see 'The Disputation of Rabbi Yehiel of Paris', trans. John Friedman in *The Trial of the Talmud*, pp. 126–68. For discussion of this incident, see Robert Chazan, 'Trial, Condemnation and Censorship: The Talmud in Medieval Europe', in *The Trial of the Talmud*, pp. 2–92; Jeremy Cohen, *The Friars and the Jews: The Evolution of Medieval Anti-Judaism* (Ithaca, 1982), esp. pp. 60–86; Robert Chazan, 'The Condemnation of the Talmud Reconsidered, 1239–1248', *Proceedings of the American Academy for Jewish Research*, LV (1988), pp. 11–30; William Chester Jordan, *The French Monarchy and the Jews: From Philip Augustus to the Last Capetians* (Philadelphia, 1989); William Chester Jordan, 'Marian Devotion and the Talmud Trials of 1240', in *Religionsgespräche im Mittelalter*, ed. B. Lewis and F. Niewöhner (Wiesbaden, 1992), pp. 61–76; and various articles in *Le brûlement du Talmud à Paris, 1242–1244*, ed. Gilbert Dahan (Paris, 1999).

128 'Disputation of Rabbi Yehiel', p. 130.

129 'Disputation of Rabbi Yehiel', p. 133.

130 'Disputation of Rabbi Yehiel', p. 140.

131 Tuillier, 'La condamnation du Talmud', p. 64.

132 *LTC*, II, nos. 3223, 3224. She did homage to Louis in March 1245: ibid., no. 3340.

133 *LTC*, II, nos. 3231–40, 3243–7.

134 Joinville, *Vie de Saint Louis*, pp. 54–5, chs 106–7. See also a Troubadour song of *circa* 1245 in *The Seventh Crusade, 1244–1254: Sources and Documents*, ed. Peter Jackson (Aldershot, 2007), doc. 2, pp. 18–19.

135 See also *Récits d'un ménestrel de Reims*, pp. 191–2. Though note that Matthew Paris, *Chronica majora*, IV, pp. 397–8, claims that Blanche supported Louis in his decision to go on Crusade. See also discussion of this crucial episode in Jordan, *Louis IX*, pp. 7–9.

6 THE CRUSADE REGENCY

1 *LTC*, II, no. 3352.

2 *LTC*, II, no. 3340.

3 *LTC*, II, no. 3456: February 1246, provision of securities.

4 *LTC*, II, no. 3526.

5 *LTC*, II, no. 3367.

6 William of Nangis, 'Vita Sancti Ludovici'/'Vie de Saint Louis', in *RHF*, XX (1840), pp. 354–5.

7 The fundamental study is William Chester Jordan, *Louis IX and the Challenge of the Crusade: A Study in Rulership* (Princeton, 1979), pp. 35–104.

8 Matthew Paris, *Chronica majora*, ed. H. R. Luard, 7 vols (London, 1872–83), IV, p. 601. *Les registres de Innocent IV: recueil des bulles de ce pape*, ed. Elie Berger, 4 vols (Paris, 1881–1920), I, p. 442, no. 2948: letters from Innocent to both Louis and Blanche.

9 William of Nangis, 'Vita Sancti Ludovici'/'Vie de Saint Louis', pp. 352–3.

10 Matthew Paris, *Chronica majora*, V, p. 70.

11 *LTC*, II, nos. 3559, 3560.

12 *LTC*, III, nos. 3652, 3666. See also Meredith Cohen, 'An Indulgence for the Visitor: The Public at the Sainte-Chapelle of Paris', *Speculum*, LXXXIII (2008), pp. 840–83, esp. p. 866.

13 'Compotus praepositorum et ballivorum Franciae de termino ascensionis, AD MCCXLVIII', in *RHF*, XXI (1855), pp. 261, 262, 284.

14 Matthew Paris, *Chronica majora*, IV, p. 607.

15 For Louis's preparations, see Jordan, *Louis IX*, pp. 65–104. 'Compotus praepositorum', pp. 270–72, 275, 280, shows some of the sums of money raised for the Crusade.

16 Matthew Paris, *Chronica majora*, IV, p. 646.

17 Matthew Paris, *Chronica majora*, IV, pp. 638–9. See discussion of Louis's reforms in Jordan, *Louis IX*, pp. 35–64; for the inquisitions, ibid., pp. 51–8; and Marie Dejoux, 'Mener un enquête', in *Quand gouverner c'est enquêter: les pratiques politiques de l'enquête princière (occident XIIIe–XIVe siècles)*, ed. Thierry Pécout (Paris, 2010), pp. 133–55.

18 *LTC*, III, no. 3604.

19 William of Nangis, 'Vita Sancti Ludovici'/'Vie de Saint Louis', pp. 356–7, says that Alphonse stayed behind to help Blanche 'garder son royaume'.

20 See, e.g., *LTC*, III, no. 3877; and discussion in Jordan, *Louis IX*, p. 117.

21 See 'Comptes de dépenses de Blanche de Castille', ed. Etienne Symphorien Bougenot in *Bulletin du Comité des travaux historiques et scientifiques: section d'histoire et de philologie* (1889), pp. 88, 90; and BNF MS lat. 9017, f. 69.

22 *Ordonnances des roys de France de la troisième race, recueillies par ordre chronologique*, ed. Eusèbe Laurière et al., 21 vols (Paris, 1723–1849), I, p. 60: June 1248.

23 'Compotus praepositorum', p. 274.

24 For Maubuisson, see Alphonse Dutilleux and Joseph Depoin, *Cartulaire de*

l'abbaye de Maubuisson (Notre-Dame-la-Royale), I: chartes concernant la fondation de l'abbaye et des chapelles (Pontoise, 1890), pp. 8–11, nos. ix and x, respectively April and June 1248; for Le Lys Cartulary, BNF MS lat. 13892, ff. 25–6, 26–7, 28v–29.

25 LTC, III, no. 3682.

26 Matthew Paris, Chronica majora, IV, p. 631. See Matthew Paris, 'Vita S. Edmundi', in C. H. Lawrence, St Edmund of Abingdon: A Study in Hagiography and History (Oxford, 1960), p. 263; Matthew Paris, The Life of St Edmund by Matthew Paris, trans. and ed., with a biography, by C. H. Lawrence (Stroud, 1999), p. 150, for Blanche equating Edmund with Becket.

27 Matthew Paris, Chronica majora, V, pp. 2–5.

28 Récits d'un ménestrel de Reims au treizième siècle, ed. Natalis de Wailly (Paris, 1876), pp. 191–2.

29 For inquiries ordered by Blanche, see Edgar Boutaric, Actes du Parlement de Paris, 2 vols (Paris, 1863–7), I, pp. cccx–cccxxi, nos. 24, 27, 28 29, 31, 32, 33. For the agreement between the scholars and citizens of Paris in June 1251, see Chartularium Universitatis parisiensis: Ex diversis bibliothecis tabulariisque collegit et cum authenticis chartis contulit, ed. H. Denifle, 4 vols (Paris, 1889–97), I, pp. 222–4, no. 197.

30 LTC, III, no. 3728.

31 William of Puylaurens, Guillaume de Puylaurens: Chronique, 1145–1275, ed. and trans. Jean Duvernoy, 2nd edn (Toulouse, 1996), pp. 194–5.

32 Jean Dunbabin, Charles I of Anjou: Power, Kingship and State-Making in Thirteenth-century Europe (London, 1998), pp. 41–54, for his rule in Provence; ibid., pp. 27–35, for his rule in Anjou; see also LTC, III, no. 3923.

33 Matthew Paris, Chronica majora, V, p. 51.

34 Letter of Philip the Treasurer in Edgar Boutaric, Saint Louis et Alphonse de Poitiers: études sur la réunion des provinces du Midi et de l'Ouest à la couronne (Paris, 1870), p. 75; LTC, III, no. 3713; Matthew Paris, Chronica majora, V, pp. 96–7, 110–11.

35 LTC, III, no. 3767.

36 Récits d'un ménestrel de Reims, p. 190.

37 LTC, III, no. 3896, September 1250: here Blanche is acting for the absent Charles of Anjou.

38 LTC, III, no. 3978.

39 LTC, III, nos. 3730, 3981. See discussion of the succession in Karen Nicholas, 'Women as Rulers: Countesses Jeanne and Marguerite of Flanders (1212–78)', in Queens, Regents and Potentates, ed. Theresa M. Vann (Dallas, 1993), pp. 85–8; Karen Nicholas, 'Countesses as Rulers in Flanders', in Aristocratic Women in Medieval France, ed. T. Evergates (Philadelphia, 1999), p. 134. For Blanche stopping Charles's intervention, see Jordan, Louis IX, pp. 117, 124; and the implication of Récits d'un ménestrel de Reims, pp. 207, 217.

40 LTC, III, nos. 3971, 3973.

41 LTC, III, no. 3817, also nos. 3812, 3813, 3814, 3815, 3816, 3819.

42 LTC, III, no. 3979.

43 Matthew Paris, Chronica majora, V, p. 90; testament in LTC, III, no. 3802. Letter of Philip the Treasurer in Boutaric, Saint Louis et Alphonse de Poitiers, p. 75. William of Puylaurens, Chronique, pp. 196–7.

44 LTC, III, nos. 3829, 3830, 3831, 3832. See also the letter of Philip the Treasurer in Boutaric, Saint Louis et Alphonse de Poitiers, pp. 69–77.

45 LTC, III, nos. 3833, 3845. Letter of Philip the Treasurer in Boutaric, Saint Louis et Alphonse de Poitiers, pp. 72–5.

46 Letter of Philip the Treasurer in Boutaric, Saint Louis et Alphonse de Poitiers, pp. 72–3.

47 LTC, III, no. 3863.

48 LTC, III, no. 3937.

49   *LTC*, III, no. 3854.

50   For Tours, see *LTC*, III, nos. 3975, 3977; for Clermont, ibid., nos. 3894, 3906; for Soissons, ibid., no. 3976. See also discussion in Gerard J. Campbell, 'Temporal and Spiritual Regalia during the Reigns of St Louis and Philip III', *Traditio*, XX (1964), pp. 351–83, esp. pp. 355, 360, 374–5.

51   *LTC*, III, nos. 3894, 3906.

52   *LTC*, III, no. 3976; and Boutaric, *Actes du Parlement de Paris*, I, p. cccxix, no. 31.

53   *LTC*, III, nos. 3855, 4011; see also Adam J. Davis, *The Holy Bureaucrat: Eudes Rigaud and Religious Reform in Thirteenth-Century Normandy* (Ithaca, 2006), pp. 108, 133.

54   Matthew Paris, *Chronica majora*, V, p. 117; *LTC*, III, no. 3911.

55   On 18 May 1251: *LTC*, III, no. 3924.

56   *Récits d'un ménestrel de Reims*, pp. 225–6.

57   *LTC*, III, nos. 3737, 3740, 374, 3745.

58   *LTC*, III, nos. 3772–5.

59   *Récits d'un ménestrel de Reims*, p. 226. For Mary's journey, see Jean de Joinville, *Vie de Saint Louis*, ed. Jacques Monfrin (Paris, 2010), pp. 68–9, chs 137–40.

60   Robert Lee Wolff, 'Mortgage and Redemption of an Emperor's Son: Castile and the Latin Empire of Constantinople', *Speculum*, XXIX (1954), pp. 45–84, esp. p. 52.

61   Matthew Paris, *Chronica majora*, VI, pp. 152–4.

62   Matthew Paris, *Chronica majora*, VI, pp. 165–7.

63   Matthew Paris, *Chronica majora*, V, pp. 92–3; Joinville, *Vie de Saint Louis*, pp. 194–5, ch. 393.

64   Matthew Paris, *Chronica majora*, V, pp. 134, 153.

65   Joinville, *Vie de Saint Louis*, pp. 106–9, chs 218–19, 244; Matthew Paris, *Chronica majora*, V, pp. 106, 132–3, 147–53. See also *Récits d'un ménestrel de Reims*, pp. 196–9.

66   Joinville, *Vie de Saint Louis*, pp. 194–7, chs 397–9.

67   Matthew Paris, *Chronica majora*, V, p. 169.

68   Issued at Pontoise, November 1250. Transcription by Delisle in Paris, Institut de France, Académie des Inscriptions et Belles-Lettres, Fonds Louis Carolus-Barré, dossier n. 9.

69   Joinville, *Vie de Saint Louis*, pp. 206–11, 214–15, chs 419–27, 436–7, stresses the danger from Henry III. *Récits d'un ménestrel de Reims*, p. 204, writes that Blanche says she is ill, and the princes are fighting one another. She was ill in early 1250. A poem by the Gascon troubadour Bernard of Rovenac, of *circa* 1250, laments Henry's lack of initiative and his failure to attack France: *Thomas Wright's Political Songs of England*, ed. Peter Coss (Cambridge, 1996), pp. 49–51.

70   'Annales de Burton', in *Annales monastici*, ed. H. R. Luard, 3 vols (London, 1864), I, p. 296.

71   *LTC*, III, no. 3956.

72   *LTC*, III, no. 3960.

73   For discussion of this event, see R. E. Lerner, 'Uses of Heterodoxy: The French Monarchy and Unbelief in the Thirteenth Century', *French Historical Studies*, IV (1965), pp. 197–202.

74   William of Nangis, 'Chronicon Guillelmi de Nangiaco (ab anno 1226 ad 1300)', *RHF*, XX (1840), p. 554; William of Nangis, *Chronique latine de Guillaume de Nangis*, ed. H. Geraud, 2 vols (Paris, 1843), I, p. 208; *LTC*, III, no. 3924, dated 18 May 1251; Lerner, 'Uses of Heterodoxy', p. 201.

75   Letter about the *pastoreaux* from the Franciscans of Paris to Adam Marsh in 'Annales de Burton', pp. 290–93. Other contemporary accounts include Matthew Paris, *Chronica majora*, V, pp. 246–8 (esp. p. 248 for the observation that she favoured the *pastoreaux* because she thought they would help Louis), and 'E chronico Rotomagensi', in *RHF*, XXIII (1876), p. 339.

76 For the legend, and the reality behind it, see Bloch, 'Blanche de Castille et les serfs', especially the *pièces justicatives*, pp. 477–90. For Blanche's visit to the church and the exchange between the queen and the castellan, ibid., p. 488: evidence of Petrus de Castris, knight.

77 *Les registres de Innocent IV*, II, pp. 238–9, no. 5329: 'Cum tibi multorum sanus de tua vita dependeat'.

78 Eude Rigaud, *Regestrum visitationem archiepiscopi Rothomagensis / Journal des visites pastorales d'Eude Rigaud, archevêque de Rouen*, ed. T. Bonnin (Rouen, 1852), pp. 140, 142, where Eudes visits Blanche at Pontoise and Melun.

79 *LTC*, III, nos. 4002, 4003, 4030; Boutaric, *Saint Louis et Alphonse de Poitiers*, pp. 86–7.

80 Matthew Paris, *Chronica majora*, V, pp. 311–12, 354.

81 *LTC*, III, no. 4029.

82 *Recueil de chartes et documents de Saint-Martin-des-Champs, monastère Parisien*, ed. J. Depoin, 5 vols (Paris, 1921), IV, no. 1102, pp. 209–11, esp. p. 210.

83 Her will does not survive, but the executors are named in an act recording the fulfilment of one aspect of it in the Fontevraud Cartulary: BNF MS lat. 5480, vol. I, part ii, p. 474.

84 Guillaume de Saint-Pathus, 'Vie de Saint Louis, par le confesseur de la reine Marguerite', in *RHF*, XX (1840), p. 64; see also Paul Edouard Didier Riant, 'Déposition de Charles d'Anjou pour la canonisation de Saint Louis', in *Notices et documents publiés pour la Société d'histoire de France à l'occasion du cinquantième anniversaire de sa fondation* (Paris, 1884), p. 175. The contemporary accounts of Blanche's death and burial come from Charles of Anjou, who was an eyewitness; William of Saint-Pathus, who was Queen Margaret's confessor; and Primat, a monk of Saint-Denis, who was asked to provide an up-to-date history

of the kings of France by St Louis: Primat, 'Chronique de Primat traduite par Jean de Vignay', in *RHF*, XXIII (1876), p. 10. For Primat, see Jacques Le Goff, *Saint Louis* (Paris, 1996), pp. 347–9; M. Cecilia Gaposchkin, *The Making of Saint Louis: Kingship, Sanctity and Crusade in the Later Middle Ages* (Ithaca, 2008), p. 147. William of Saint-Pathus drew heavily on Charles's account, including the murmuring of 'Subvenite sancti Dei'. Charles, however, varies from all other accounts in saying that Blanche's death occurred at Maubuisson.

85 Primat, 'Chronique', p. 10, provides the evidence for this. Since he was a monk of Saint-Denis there is no reason to question it, but for the fact that Charles of Anjou says that Blanche died at Maubuisson.

86 Rigaud, *Regestrum / Journal*, p. 150.

87 Geoffrey of Beaulieu, 'Vita ludovici noni', in *RHF*, XX (1840), p. 17; Geoffrey of Beaulieu, 'Here Begins the Life and Saintly Comportment of Louis, Formerly King of the Franks, of Pious Memory', in *The Sanctity of Louis IX: Early Lives of Saint Louis by Geoffrey of Beaulieu and William of Chartres*, trans. Larry F. Field, ed. M. Cecilia Gaposchkin and Sean L. Field (Ithaca, 2014), pp. 105–6; William of Nangis, 'Vita Sancti Ludovici'/'Vie de Saint Louis', pp. 385–7.

88 Joinville, *Vie de Saint Louis*, pp. 298–301, 302–3, chs 603–5, 610.

89 See full discussion of the rule of the regency council in Jordan, *Louis IX*, pp. 116–25.

90 Dunbabin, *Charles I of Anjou*, pp. 37–8.

91 Matthew Paris, *Chronica majora*, pp. 366, 371–2, 415.

92 'Gesta Sancti Ludovici Noni Francorum regis, auctore monacho Sancti Dionysii anonymo', in *RHF*, XX (1840), p. 56: 'Quod regno Franciae magnum periculum immineret'.

7 FAMILY, FRIENDS AND *FAMILIA*

1   Emmanuel Lemaire, *Archives anciennes de la Ville de Saint-Quentin*, 2 vols (Saint-Quentin, 1888–1910), I, p. 42, no. 41, for the king delivering a judgement in court there in 1244; see above, p. 122. The wardrobe of the king or the queen in France was exactly what its name suggested – the place (in this case, clearly a rather substantial room) in which the robes, and probably other valuable possessions, were kept. It never developed into the private accounting office of the king, as it did in England; see Malcolm Vale, *The Princely Court: Medieval Courts and Culture in North-West Europe* (Oxford, 2001), pp. 65, 78.

2   See above, pp. 22–3.

3   E.g., Doreta and Agnes in 1234: 'Recepta et expensa Anno MCCXXXIIII inter candelosam et ascensionem', in *RHF*, XXI (1855), pp. 238, 239.

4   'Itinera, dona et hernesia AD 1239 inter ascensionem et omnes sanctos', in *RHF*, XXII (1865), pp. 590, 591, 593.

5   E.g., 'Recepta et expensa', p. 235; 'Compotus ballivorum et praepositorum Franciae anno Domini 1234 mense Junio de termino ascensionis', in *RHF*, XXII (1865), pp. 576, 578.

6   Léopold Delisle, 'Mémoire sur les opérations financières des Templiers', in *Mémoires présentés par divers savantes à l'Académie des inscriptions et belles-lettres*, XXXIII (Paris, 1889), p. 101. For Peter of Lissy, see 'Itinera, dona et hernesia', p. 588; 'Comptes de dépenses de Blanche de Castille', ed. Etienne Symphorien Bougenot in *Bulletin du Comité des travaux historiques et scientifiques: section d'histoire et de philologie* (1889), p. 91; BNF MS lat. 9017, f. 69.

7   For Richard's prebends, see Eude Rigaud, *Regestrum visitationem archiepiscopi Rothomagensis / Journal des visites pastorales d'Eude Rigaud, archevêque de Rouen*, ed. T. Bonnin (Rouen, 1852), p. 42; and 'Polyptychum Rotomagensis diocesis', in *RHF*, XXIII (1876),

p. 281. For Master Richard in the royal account of 1239, see 'Itinera, dona et hernesia', pp. 592, 594, 596–9, 604 and 606, where he is mainly concerned with Blanche's expenditure. There are five references to Master Richard in BNF MS lat. 9017, f. 69.

8   See above, pp. 118–19.

9   'Recepta et expensa', pp. 237, 238; 'Itinera, dona et hernesia', p. 594.

10   'Magna recepta de termino Ascensionis, anno Domini MCCXXXVIII mense Mayo et magna expensa', in *RHF*, XXI (1855), p. 259.

11   'Itinera, dona et hernesia', p. 586. This must be Blanche's expenditure; Margaret is still called the 'young queen'.

12   BL Add. Ch. 4129; 'Comptes de dépenses', passim; BNF MS lat. 9017, f. 69; AN J1030, no. 9, ed. in Delisle, 'Mémoire sur les opérations financières des Templiers', appendix VIII, pp. 99–102.

13   Louis-Claude Doüet d'Arcq, *Comptes de l'Hôtel des Rois de France aux XIV au XV siècles* (Paris, 1865), pp. ii–iii; Elisabeth Lalou, 'Le fonctionnement de l'Hôtel du Roi du milieu XIIIe au milieu du XIVe siècle', in *Vincennes aux origines de l'état moderne. Actes du colloque scientifique sur 'Les Capétiens à Vincennes au Moyen âge'*, ed. Jean Chapelot and Elisabeth Lalou (Paris, 1996), pp. 145–55. There is limited discussion of the household before 1261, but see Elisabeth Lalou, 'Introduction', in *Les comptes sur tablettes de cire de Jean Sarrazin, chambellan de Saint Louis*, ed. Lalou (Turnhout, 2003), pp. 14–15. For discussion of household structures and ordinances, though most examples are post-1250, see Vale, *Princely Court*, pp. 34–68. See also C. M. Woolgar, *The Great Household in Late Medieval England* (New Haven and London, 1999), esp. pp. 8–29, though the sources are later and English.

14   See above, pp. 6–7.

15   William of Puylaurens, *Guillaume de Puylaurens: Chronique, 1145–1275*, ed. and trans. Jean Duvernoy, 2nd edn (Toulouse, 1996),

pp. 130–31; Gerald of Wales, 'De principis instructione', in *Giraldi Cambrensis opera*, vol. VIII, ed. G. F. Warner (London, 1891), p. 133.

16 Geoffrey of Beaulieu, 'Vita ludovici noni', in *RHF*, XX (1840), p. 4; Geoffrey of Beaulieu, 'Here Begins the Life and Saintly Comportment of Louis, Formerly King of the Franks, of Pious Memory', in *The Sanctity of Louis IX: Early Lives of Saint Louis by Geoffrey of Beaulieu and William of Chartres*, trans. Larry F. Field, ed. M. Cecilia Gaposchkin and Sean L. Field (Ithaca, 2014), p. 74.

17 Rigord, *Histoire de Philippe Auguste*, ed. Elisabeth Carpentier, Georges Pon and Yves Chauvin (Paris, 2006), pp. 320–21; M. L. Colker, ed., 'The "Karolinus" of Egidius Parisiensis', *Traditio*, XXIX (1973), pp. 308–9, 324; and see above, pp. 39–40.

18 For medieval marriage, see Christopher Brooke, *The Medieval Idea of Marriage* (Oxford, 1989); James Brundage, 'Concubinage and Marriage in Medieval Canon Law', *Journal of Medieval History*, 1 (1975), pp. 6–8; and James Brundage, 'Marriage and Sexuality in the Decretals of Pope Alexander III', in Brundage, *Sex, Law and Marriage in the Middle Ages* (Aldershot, 1993), ch. IX, pp. 61–4, 66–7. On the views of Paris masters on marriage, see Ian Wei, *Intellectual Culture in Medieval Paris: Theologians and the University, c. 1100–1330* (Cambridge, 2012), pp. 258–60. See also Margaret Howell, 'Royal Women in the Mid-Thirteenth Century: A Gendered Perspective', in *England and Europe in the Reign of Henry III, 1216–1272*, ed. Björn K. U. Weiler with Ifor W. Rowlands (Aldershot, 2002), pp. 166–7.

19 Peter of Les Vaux-de-Cernay, *The History of the Albigensian Crusade*, ed. and trans. W. A. Sibley and M. D. Sibley (Woodbridge, 1998), esp. p. 55, ch. 107, and p. 197, ch. 430.

20 See above, p. 44.

21 Jacques Le Goff, *Saint Louis* (Paris, 1996), pp. 735–6; Noël Valois, *Guillaume d'Auvergne, évêque de Paris, 1228–1249: sa vie et ses ouvrages* (Paris, 1880), p. 150. Blanche's mother had produced her first surviving child at the age of nineteen: Miriam Shadis, *Berenguela of Castile (1180–1246) and Political Women in the High Middle Ages* (New York, 2009), pp. 32–3. Margaret went to pray at the tomb of the blessed Theobald of Marly at Les Vaux-de-Cernay in 1239: see Marie-Anselme Dimier, *St Louis et Cîteaux* (Paris, 1954), pp. 20–21.

22 *Les registres de Philippe Auguste*, ed. J. W. Baldwin (Paris, 1992), p. 545; and see above, pp. 44–5.

23 See above, pp. 6–7.

24 For the twin Alphonse, see Alain Erlande-Brandenburg, *Le roi est mort: étude sur les funérailles, les sépultures et les tombeaux des rois de France jusqu'à la fin du XIIIe siècle* (Geneva, 1975), pp. 92–3; *Obituaires de la Province de Sens*, ed. Auguste Molinier and Auguste Longnon, 4 vols in 5 (Paris, 1902–23), II, p. 343; for his joint tomb with his brother John at Poissy, see Kathleen Nolan, *Queens in Stone and Silver: The Creation of a Visual Imagery of Queenship in Capetian France* (New York, 2009), p. 139. The joint tomb has led to suggestions that Alphonse and John were the twins born in 1213. This cannot be the case since John was given the county of Anjou, destined for the third son in Louis VIII's will. Alphonse may have been alive in 1219 when John was named, but dead in 1220, when his name was reused for the next son.

25 I would like to thank Dr Johanna Dale for bringing this to my attention.

26 For the Turpin legends, see Gabrielle Spiegel, *Romancing the Past: The Rise of Vernacular Prose Historiography in Thirteenth-century France* (Berkeley, Cal., 1993), pp. 55–98.

27 *Cartulaire de l'abbaye de Porrois au diocèse de Paris, plus connue sous son nomme*

mystique de Port-Royal, ed. A. de Dion, 2 vols (Paris, 1903), I, p. 253, no. cclxv; Royaumont Cartulary, BNF MS lat. 5472, f. 97.

28 Ralph V. Turner, *Eleanor of Aquitaine* (London and New Haven, 2009), pp. 144–9; Lois Huneycutt, 'Public Lives, Private Ties: Royal Mothers in England and Scotland, 1070–1204', in *Medieval Mothering*, ed. J. C. Parsons and B. Wheeler (New York, 1996), p. 297. But see the reassessment of Eleanor's motherhood of her daughters in Colette Bowie, *The Daughters of Henry II and Eleanor of Aquitaine* (Turnhout, 2014), esp. pp. 33–53.

29 See also the comments of Philippe Mousket, *Chronique rimée*, ed. F. de Reiffenberg, 2 vols (Brussels, 1836–8), II, p. 548, vv. 27,145–27,150; and see below, pp. 312–14.

30 'Un fragment du compte de l'hôtel du Prince Louis de France pour le terme de la Purification 1213', ed. Robert Fawtier in *Moyen âge*, XLIII (1933), p. 245, no. 113. Though the twin Alphonse was buried at Poissy: see below, pp. 224–5.

31 'Recepta et expensa', p. 237: 'de domo puerorum'. It is possible that Alphonse of Poitiers had his own, separate household by 1234. On balance, I think that the references to a large household for 'Lord Alphonse' in the account of 1234 at 'Recepta et expensa', pp. 231, 232, relate to Alphonse of Portugal, since Maundy money was provided for Louis and Robert, Alphonse the nephew – and the other children, which must have included Alphonse; ibid., p. 237.

32 'Recepta et expensa', p. 240.

33 'Itinera, dona et hernesia', p. 600.

34 Guillaume de Saint-Pathus, 'Vie de Saint Louis, par le confesseur de la reine Marguerite', in *RHF*, xx (1840), p. 87 – he makes it clear they are staying at Asnières.

35 Agnes of Harcourt, *The Writings of Agnes of Harcourt: The Life of Isabelle of France and the Letter on Louis IX and Longchamp*, ed. Sean Field (Notre Dame, Ind., 2003), pp. 62–3.

36 'Recepta et expensa', pp. 241, 246.

37 Agnes of Harcourt, *Life of Isabelle of France*, pp. 58–9.

38 'Itinera, dona et hernesia', p. 598; 'Recepta et expensa', p. 242; 'Itinera, dona et hernesia', pp. 611, 595.

39 Agnes of Harcourt, *Life of Isabelle of France*, pp. 58–9.

40 'Itinera, dona et hernesia', p. 606: 'service for Charles'.

41 'Recepta et expensa', p. 236.

42 Saint-Pathus, 'Vie de Saint Louis', p. 65.

43 Jean Dunbabin, *Charles I of Anjou: Power, Kingship and State-Making in Thirteenth-century Europe* (London, 1998), p. 11: Agnes of Harcourt, *Life of Isabelle of France*, pp. 60–61.

44 Leiden Psalter (Leiden, Universiteit Leiden, Bibliotheken, MS Lat. 76a), ff. 30v and 185; f. 30v is illustrated in *Saint Louis*, exh. cat., ed. Pierre-Yves Le Pogam, Conciergerie, Paris (Paris, 2014), p. 144, ill. 110. The psalter remained in the family – Louis gave it to his daughter Agnes of Burgundy; see H. Omont, *Le Psautier de Saint Louis de la Bibliothèque de Leyde* (Leiden, 1902), p. vii; Léopold Delisle, *Notice de douze livres royaux du XIIIe siècle et du XIVe siècle* (Paris, 1902), p. 26. For Blanche's acquisition of this psalter, see below, p. 236.

45 Paul Edouard Didier Riant, 'Déposition de Charles d'Anjou pour la canonisation de Saint Louis', in *Notices et documents publiés pour la Société d'histoire de France à l'occasion du cinquantième anniversaire de sa fondation* (Paris, 1884), p. 175. Cf. also Saint-Pathus, 'Vie de Saint Louis', pp. 24–5, 26. For St Louis's education, see Le Goff, *Saint Louis*, pp. 36, 589–90; for Charles, see Dunbabin, *Charles I of Anjou*, pp. 10–12; for Isabella, see Sean L. Field, *Isabelle of France: Capetian Sanctity and Franciscan Identity in the Thirteenth Century* (Notre Dame, Ind., 2006), p. 21.

46 John W. Baldwin, *The Government of*

Philip Augustus: Foundations of French Royal Power in the Middle Ages (Berkeley, Cal., 1986), pp. 167–8.

47 John Carmi Parsons, 'Mothers, Daughters, Marriage, Power: Some Plantagenet Evidence, 1150–1500', in *Medieval Queenship*, ed. John Carmi Parsons (New York, 1993), pp. 63–78, though this really deals with Eleanor of Castile.

48 See above, p. 57.

49 'Itinera, dona et hernesia', p. 610.

50 See above, p. 131.

51 *LTC*, II, nos. 1922, 1924.

52 See above, pp. 86–7.

53 For Isabella, see Field, *Isabelle of France*; and Field's edition of Agnes of Harcourt, *Life of Isabelle of France*; see also William Chester Jordan, 'Isabelle of France and Religious Devotion at the Court of Louis IX', in *Capetian Women*, ed. Kathleen Nolan (New York, 2003), pp. 209–23.

54 *LTC*, II, no. 1924. See discussion of this episode in Field, *Isabelle of France*, pp. 16–18.

55 Agnes of Harcourt, *Life of Isabelle of France*, pp. 54–5. See discussion in Field, *Isabelle of France*, pp. 27–31.

56 Agnes of Harcourt, *Life of Isabelle of France*, pp. 56–7. Field convincingly links the illness to the pressure to marry Conrad, though it is true that Agnes of Harcourt only places the illness in the 'jeunesse' of Princess Isabella. Field, *Isabelle of France*, pp. 31–3.

57 Riant, 'Déposition de Charles d'Anjou', p. 175.

58 Dimier, *Saint Louis et Cîteaux*, pp. 124–6. For Alphonse's alms, see Edgar Boutaric, *Saint Louis et Alphonse de Poitiers: études sur la réunion des provinces du Midi et de l'Ouest à la couronne* (Paris, 1870), pp. 458–69; for his support of university colleges, ibid., pp. 484–5.

59 For their gambling, see Jean de Joinville, *Vie de Saint Louis*, ed. Jacques Monfrin (Paris, 2010), pp. 198–201 and 206–7, chs 405, 418; for Charles's patronage of minstrels and own

writing of songs, see Dunbabin, *Charles I of Anjou*, p. 11, and below, p. 246. But note also ibid., p. 22, the description of Charles by Tommaso di Pavia in 1267 as moderate and restrained, dressed like a simple knight, not caring for minstrels and hardly ever smiling. For Alphonse's courtly lifestyle, see Boutaric, *Saint Louis et Alphonse de Poitiers*, pp. 338–41. For Louis's hatred of gambling, see Joinville, *Vie de Saint Louis*, pp. 198–201, ch. 405; for his dislike of secular music, see William of Chartres, 'De vita et actibus inclytae recordationis regis francorum ludovici et de miraculis', in *RHF*, XX (1840), p. 29; William of Chartres, 'On the Life and Deeds of Louis, King of the Franks of Famous Memory, and on the Miracles that Declare his Sanctity', in *The Sanctity of Louis IX*, p. 132.

60 Riant, 'Déposition de Charles d'Anjou', p. 175.

61 See above, p. 140.

62 'Recepta et expensa', p. 245: Robert pays for the minstrels for the coronation. Mousket, *Chronique rimée*, II, p. 690, v. 31,230, describes him as 'moult est vallans er cortois'.

63 Mousket, *Chronique rimée*, II, p. 618, vv. 29,160–29,175; Matthew Paris, *Chronica majora*, ed. H. R. Luard, 7 vols (London, 1872–83), V, pp. 133–4 and 147–53, where he attacks the Templars and Hospitallers in 'verbis satiricis et mordacibus'.

64 Joinville, *Vie de Saint Louis*, pp. 198–9, 198–201, 120–21, chs 404, 405, 244.

65 Geoffrey of Beaulieu, 'Vita ludovici noni', p. 4; Geoffrey of Beaulieu, 'Here Begins the Life', p. 74; Saint-Pathus, 'Vie de Saint Louis', p. 64, says that Blanche loved Louis best because he was the king. Agnes of Harcourt, *Life of Isabelle of France*, pp. 52–3, says that Isabella was especially precious as the only daughter.

66 For comments on Isabella's penitential beatings, see Agnes of Harcourt, *Life of Isabelle of France*, pp. 60–61; on Louis, see Saint-Pathus,

'Vie de Saint Louis', pp. 101–3, 106, 107–8; Joinville, *Vie de Saint Louis*, pp. 332–3, 360–61, chs 667, 726. See also Lester K. Little, 'Saint Louis' Involvement with the Friars', *Church History*, XXXIII (1963), pp. 125–47, esp. pp. 125, 141, 143.

67 See the perceptive comments by Jordan, 'Isabelle of France and Religious Devotion'; and Field, *Isabelle of France*, pp. 31–5.

68 Agnes of Harcourt, *Life of Isabelle of France*, pp. 58–9.

69 Joinville, *Vie de Saint Louis*, pp. 120–21, 198–9, 198–201, chs 244, 404, 405.

70 Joinville, *Vie de Saint Louis*, pp. 216–17, ch. 442.

71 Joinville, *Vie de Saint Louis*, pp. 206–7, ch. 418.

72 Joinville, *Vie de Saint Louis*, pp. 198–201, ch. 405.

73 Joinville, *Vie de Saint Louis*, pp. 192–3, 216–17, chs 389, 442.

74 Agnes of Harcourt, *Life of Isabelle of France*, pp. 52–3; Riant, 'Déposition de Charles d'Anjou', esp. pp. 171, 174, 175.

75 Riant, 'Déposition de Charles d'Anjou', p. 175.

76 See the list of witnesses adduced by Saint-Pathus, 'Vie de Saint Louis', pp. 61–3; few could look back before Louis's first Crusade.

77 Geoffrey of Beaulieu, 'Vita ludovici noni', pp. 3–4; Geoffrey of Beaulieu, 'Here Begins the Life', pp. 73–4. See M. Cecilia Gaposchkin and S. Field, 'Introduction', in *The Sanctity of Louis IX*, pp. 44–5.

78 Geoffrey of Beaulieu, 'Vita ludovici noni', p. 4; Geoffrey of Beaulieu, 'Here Begins the Life', p. 74.

79 Agnes of Harcourt, *Life of Isabelle of France*, pp. 54–5, 56–7; 'Itinera, dona et hernesia', p. 610, for silk and gold thread for Isabella in 1239.

80 Blanche's mother died at fifty-three, her sister Berengaria at sixty-six. Eleanor of Provence died at sixty-eight.

81 'Un fragment du compte', p. 243, nos. 74 and 75; 'Recepta et expensa', p. 241.

82 AN L463, no. 34.

83 'Extraits des chroniques de Saint-Denis', in *RHF*, XXI (1855), p. 116, claims that she had heart trouble, but this source dates from *circa* 1300. I would like to thank Rosemary Burch and Dr Max Kelen for discussing Blanche's health with me.

84 See above, p. 38.

85 'Itinera, dona et hernesia', p. 600.

86 Le Goff, *Saint Louis*, pp. 864–7; Saint-Pathus, 'Vie de Saint Louis', pp. 96–9 and 76.

87 'Recepta et expensa', pp. 243, 247.

88 'Itinera, dona et hernesia', p. 605. For St Louis's doctors, see also Dietrich Lohrmann, 'Pierre Lombard, médecin de Saint Louis: un italien à Paris et ses maisons au Quartier Latin', in *Septième centenaire de la mort de Saint Louis. Actes des colloques du Royaumont et de Paris, 21–27 mai 1970* (Paris, 1976), pp. 165–81. For Charles of Anjou and his doctors, see Jean Dunbabin, *The French in the Kingdom of Sicily, 1266–1305* (Cambridge, 2011), pp. 229–30.

89 *Corpus des sceaux français du Moyen Age, III: les sceaux des reines et des enfants de France*, by Marie-Adélaïde Nielen (Paris, 2011), pp. 74–5; Nolan, *Queens in Stone and Silver*, pp. 155–6. Women usually specified their father's name on their seals only if they were heiresses in their own right: see B. Bedos-Rezak, 'Women, Seals and Power in Medieval France', in *Women and Power in the Middle Ages*, ed. Mary Erler and Maryanne Kowalski (Athens, Ga., 1988), p. 68; but ibid., p. 69, fig. 4, showing the counterseal of Matilda of Flanders, which displays the arms of her native Portugal.

90 Lindy Grant, 'Representing Dynasty: The Transept Windows of Chartres Cathedral', in *Representing History: Art, Music, History*, ed. Robert A. Maxwell (Philadelphia, 2010), p. 111.

91 E.g., in 1213: 'Un fragment du compte', p. 241. In 1234: 'Recepta et expensa', pp. 228,

233, 236, 240, 241, 244. In 1248: 'Compotus praepositorum et ballivorum Franciae de termino ascensionis, AD MCCXLVIII', in *RHF*, XXI (1855), p. 262. In 1239: 'Itinera, dona et hernesia', pp. 594, 596, 597, 600, 605. In 1241: BNF MS lat. 9017, f. 69, l. 26: 'qui venit de regina Berengaria'.

92   BNF MS lat. 9017, f. 69. The horses may have been fine Arab palfreys, or solid pack ponies. Eleanor of Castile had both types sent to England: see Thomas Tolley, 'Eleanor of Castile and the Spanish Style in England', in *England in the Thirteenth Century: Proceedings of the 1989 Harlaxton Symposium*, ed. W. M. Ormrod (Stamford, 1991), pp. 173–5; and my thanks to Dr Nicola Coldstream for information on the pack ponies. Either way, the horses were valuable.

93   'Comptes de dépenses', p. 88 for the belt; p. 91 for the camelines and furs; and BNF MS lat. 9017, f. 69, for the chapel contents, and for more clothes to Spain, especially to the queen of Aragón.

94   'Itinera, dona et hernesia', p. 600.

95   AN J1034, no. 8; *LTC*, V, no. 886. It specifies that the gifts were sent by the queen to her sister the queen of Castile – Blanche to Berengaria is the only possibility. The script is very similar to that on Blanche's accounts of 1241–2 (BL Add. Ch. 4129; BNF MS lat. 9017, f. 69) and the Temple audit for 1243 (AN J1030, no. 9). The crystal cross is noted as being from the king.

96   A.-J.-V. Leroux de Lincy, *Recueil de chants historiques français depuis le XIIe jusqu'au XVIIIe siècle*, vol. I (Paris, 1841), no. i, p. 166.

97   See discussion of the relationship between the sisters and the parallels in Shadis, *Berenguela of Castile*, esp. pp. 71–96; see also the assessment of Berengaria's power and position as in effect a queen regnant in Janna Bianchini, *The Queen's Hand: Power and Authority in the Reign of Berenguela of Castile* (Philadelphia, 2012), esp. pp. 125–39, 140–79.

98   'Recepta et expensa', p. 233, messenger from the queen of Castile; pp. 241, 244, gifts to servants and valet of the queen of Castile; BNF MS lat. 9017, f. 69: rewards to messengers from Queen Berengaria.

99   Theresa Vann, ' "Our Father Has Won a Great Victory": The Authorship of Berenguela's Account of the Battle of Las Navas de Tolosa, 1212', *Journal of Medieval Iberian Studies*, III/1 (2011), pp. 79–92, with edition of letter, pp. 90–92. See also discussion of the letter in Shadis, *Berenguela of Castile*, pp. 129–33.

100   See above, p. 49. It is just possible that Theobald wrote this letter at Berengaria's request.

101   For discussion of the letters, see Shadis, *Berenguela of Castile*, p. 104, who dates them to 1217; *LTC*, II, nos. 1813–21, dating them to 1226, before the death of Louis VIII on 8 November. All the letters – the originals are AN J599, no. 1 – are clearly addressed to Louis and Blanche as king and queen of France. See also Bianchini, *Queen's Hand*, pp. 159–61.

102   See above, pp. 110–11.

103   *Statuta Capitulorum generalium ordinis Cisterciensis ab anno 116 ad annum 1786*, ed. Joseph Canivez, 8 vols (Louvain, 1935), II, pp. 260–61, 361. See also discussion in Shadis, *Berenguela of Castile*, pp. 149–50.

104   *Statuta Capitulorum generalium ordinis Cisterciensis*, II, p. 377.

105   'Compotus praepositorum', p. 276.

106   'Recepta et expensa', pp. 235, 236, 237, 241, 247, 248. Note that ibid., pp. 231, 232, 233, probably also refer to Alphonse of Portugal, but could refer to Alphonse of Poitiers.

107   'Itinera, dona et hernesia', pp. 586, 588, 591, 609; 'Ea quae distributa fuerunt in milicia Comitis Pictavensis (Die xxiv junio, anno mccxli)', in *RHF*, XXII (1865), p. 619.

108   *Obituaires de la Province de Sens*, I, part ii, p. 656.

109   *Récits d'un ménestrel de Reims au*

treizième siècle, ed. Natalis de Wailly (Paris, 1876), p. 226; and see above, p. 139–40.

110   Vann, '"Our Father Has Won a Great Victory"'.

111   See below, p. 229. For Mary at Namur, see *Récits d'un ménestrel de Reims*, pp. 227–34.

112   'Itinera, dona et hernesia', pp. 591, 612.

113   Joinville, *Vie de Saint Louis*, pp. 288–91, ch. 583.

114   For the Eu dynasty, see Daniel Power, *The Norman Frontier in the Twelfth and Early Thirteenth Centuries* (Cambridge, 2004), p. 497. The coconut is now in the Musée Lambinet at Versailles; see *Histoire et archéologie à l'abbaye royale et cistercienne de Maubuisson*, ed. Philippe Soulier (Cergy-Pontoise, 1988), p. 51; for the family burials at Maubuisson, see Alexandre Bande, *Le coeur du roi: les Capétiens et les sépultures multiples, XIIIe–XVe siècles* (Paris, 2009), pp. 135–6; Alphonse Dutilleux and Joseph Depoin, *L'abbaye de Maubuisson (Notre-Dame-la-Royale): histoire et cartulaire, II: les bâtiments, l'église et les tombeaux* (Pontoise, 1883), pp. 107, 117.

115   'Recepta et expensa', pp. 238, 239, 246, 249.

116   Shadis, *Berenguela of Castile*, pp. 118–19; Bianchini, *Queen's Hand*, pp. 223–7.

117   'Recepta et expensa', p. 231. He may have been a son of Berengaria's major-domo, García Fernández de Villamayor: see Bianchini, *Queen's Hand*, pp. 149–50.

118   See above, pp. 53–4.

119   *RHF*, XIX (1833), pp. 255–6; Vann, '"Our Father Has Won a Great Victory"', p. 87.

120   *Cartulary of Countess Blanche of Champagne*, ed. Theodore Evergates (Toronto, 2009), pp. 260–61, no. 291.

121   Leroux de Lincy, *Recueil de chants*, no. iii, p. 173.

122   Matthew Paris, *Chronica majora*, V, p. 335.

123   Matthew Paris, *Chronica majora*, VI,

pp. 165–7. For Richard in Paris, see above, p. 136.

124   For the household clerks, see chapter Eight.

125   Doüet d'Arcq, *Comptes de l'Hôtel des Rois de France*, p. ii; Lalou, 'Le fonctionnement de l'Hôtel du Roi'.

126   Baldwin, *Government of Philip Augustus*, pp. 104–5.

127   Quentin Griffiths, 'New Men among the Lay Counsellors of Saint Louis' Parlement', *Medieval Studies*, XXXII (1970), p. 238, and see lists 1 and 2 for the greater and lesser office holders under Louis VIII and Louis IX. For the tables of Louis VIII's officers, see Charles Petit-Dutaillis, *Etude sur la vie et le règne de Louis VIII* (Paris, 1894), appendix V, pp. 445–8.

128   See the lists of those given robes in 1231: Johann Peter von Ludewig, *Reliquiae Manuscriptorum omnis aevi Diplomatum ac Monumentorum ineditorum adhuc*, 12 vols (Frankfurt, 1720–41), XII, bk 1, pp. 3–5. For those given robes in 1239: 'Itinera, dona et hernesia', p. 586. For those given robes in 1241 at the knighting of Alphonse of Poitiers: 'Ea quae distributa', p. 620.

129   'Recepta et expensa', p. 244.

130   For Bartholomew of Roye, see Baldwin, *Government of Philip Augustus*, pp. 109–11. For the family of Ours, often known as the de la Chapelle or of Nemours, ibid., pp. 107–9. The Clément and Nemours families were also intermarried: see *Fasti Ecclesiae Gallicanae, II: le diocèse de Rouen*, ed. Vincent Tabbagh (Turnhout, 1998), p. 86.

131   Griffiths, 'New Men', tables 1 and 2. Note that the various household departments were fully organised only in 1261: see above, p. 170.

132   'Itinera, dona et hernesia', p. 603; BNF MS lat. 9017, f. 69. See also Perrin of the queen's chamber in 1239: 'Ea quae distributa', p. 616.

133   For Adam, see 'Recepta et expensa', pp. 232 and 237.

134 Ludewig, *Reliquiae Manuscriptorum*, XII, bk I, pp. 3–5.

135 'Recepta et expensa', pp. 238, 248.

136 'Ea quae distributa', p. 616.

137 'Itinera, dona et hernesia', p. 597, mentions Roussel of the queen's stable.

138 'Itinera, dona et hernesia', p. 592; BNF MS lat. 9017, f. 69.

139 'Recepta et expensa', p. 241; 'Itinera, dona et hernesia', p. 594.

140 'Itinera, dona et hernesia', pp. 593, 604, 610; BNF MS lat. 9017, f. 69.

141 *Les comptes sur tablettes de cire de Jean Sarrazin*, pp. 94, 100.

142 'Itinera, dona et hernesia', p. 605; BNF MS lat. 9017, f. 69.

143 For Denis the Scutifer and Peter Pig-Flesh, see above, p. 116–17. For Adam's gift, see 'Ea quae distributa', p. 620; for Adam's account, ibid., pp. 609, 619; for the marriage, see William Mendel Newman, *Les seigneurs de Nesle en Picardie, XIIe–XIIIe siècles: leur chartes et leur histoire*, 2 vols (Paris, 1971), I, p. 66.

144 'Itinera, dona et hernesia', pp. 589, 591, 595.

145 'Un fragment du compte', p. 241; 'Recepta et expensa', pp. 236, 238; 'Expensa militiae comitis Attrebatensis in Penthecoste AD 1237 mense junio', in *RHF*, XXII (1865), p. 581; 'Itinera, dona et hernesia', pp. 588, 599, 604.

146 'Un fragment du compte', p. 244; and Delisle, 'Mémoire sur les opérations financières des Templiers', p. 101 for Regina Cornut. 'Itinera, dona et hernesia', p. 588 for Isabel, p. 597 for Agnes. 'Recepta et expensa', pp. 239, 247, for Lady Agnes, and the robes for Agnes and her sister.

147 BNF MS lat. 9017, f. 69; and 'Comptes de dépenses', pp. 90 and 91 for Isabella; BNF MS lat. 9017, f. 69, for Lady Agnes.

148 'Recepta et expensa', pp. 241, 247; 'Compotus ballivorum', p. 566.

149 'Recepta et expensa', p. 246; for John, see 'Ea quae distributa', p. 620.

150 'Itinera, dona et hernesia', p. 610: gift for Joanna. 'Compotus ballivorum', p. 571. See also 'Itinera, dona et hernesia', pp. 590, 602; 'Comptes de dépenses', pp. 88, 91.

151 'Recepta et expensa', pp. 233, 239.

152 'Itinera, dona et hernesia', p. 599; BNF MS lat. 9017, f. 69. For Peter, see Ludewig, *Reliquiae Manuscriptorum*, XII, bk I, pp. 3–5; 'Ea quae distributa', p. 620. Blanche lent him 100 *livres* in 1243: Delisle, 'Mémoire sur les opérations financières des Templiers', p. 101. The family were probably from Vrigny, a few miles away from Blanche's and Lord Louis's properties at Boiscommun and Vitry-aux-Loges.

153 'Comptes de dépenses', pp. 89, 90, 91, for Matilda (de Lorris?), Isabella (Cornut?) and Emellina putting monies in Blanche's coffers. For Agnes giving out gifts, see BNF MS lat. 9017, f. 69.

154 'Recepta et expensa', pp. 238, 239.

155 'Itinera, dona et hernesia', pp. 590, 602, 597, 599.

156 'Recepta et expensa', pp. 246, 247.

157 'Recepta et expensa', p. 233.

158 'Comptes de dépenses', p. 91.

159 See Lindy Grant, 'Blanche of Castile and Normandy', in *Normandy and its Neighbours, 900–1250*, ed. David Crouch and Kathleen Thompson (Turnhout, 2011), pp. 122–5; *Cartulaire normand de Philippe Auguste, Louis VIII, Saint Louis et Philippe-le-Hardi*, ed. Léopold Delisle (Caen, 1852), p. 65, no. 408.

160 'Comptes de dépenses', p. 88.

161 Grant, 'Blanche of Castile and Normandy', p. 122; 'Querimoniae Normannorum', in *RHF*, XXIV (1904), p. 33, no. 255; *Cartulaire normand*, pp. 318–19, no. 1162.

162 'Registrum epistolarum Stephani de Lexington', part II, ed. Fr B. Griesser in *Analecta Sacri Ordinis Cisterciensis*, vol. VIII (1952), p. 252, no. 24.

163 For Robert Mauvoisin, see Peter of Les Vaux-de-Cernay, *History of the Albigensian Crusade*, p. 71, ch. 129.

164 'Itinera, dona et hernesia', pp. 590, 591, 593.

165 'Comptes de dépenses', pp. 89, 90.

166 'Recepta et expensa', p. 230 for Walter; BNF MS lat. 9017, f. 69, for Lady Agnes de Argal and 'puella hispanila de domo'.

167 'Recepta et expensa', pp. 231, 238, 247; 'Itinera, dona et hernesia', p. 604.

168 See below, pp. 185-6.

169 *Statuta Capitulorum generalium ordinis Cisterciensis*, II, p. 362.

170 In spring 1234 the royal household provided a purple pall for the tomb of William of Blaison, presumably one of Theobald's sons, and Blanche loaned the lady of Blaison, presumably Theobald's widow, Valencia, 20 *livres* to attend the marriage of Louis and Margaret: 'Recepta et expensa', pp. 237, 247. The Lady Arviria de Mirabeau was in Blanche's entourage in 1241, and the lord of Mirabeau was indebted to the queen for a substantial loan in 1243: 'Comptes de dépenses', p. 89; AN J1030, no. 9; Delisle, 'Mémoire sur les opérations financières des Templiers', p. 102.

171 For the family, see Newman, *Les seigneurs de Nesle*, I, p. 66.

172 For Simon of Nesle, see William Chester Jordan, *Men at the Center: Redemptive Governance under Louis IX* (Budapest, 2012), pp. 71-5. For the gift of the house, see Newman, *Les seigneurs de Nesle*, II, pp. 262-3, no. 162.

173 'Comptes de dépenses', p. 90; BNF MS lat. 9017, f. 69, for the belt, costing 11 *livres*.

174 'Comptes de dépenses', p. 89. For Gaucher of Nanteuil, see Newman, *Les seigneurs de Nesle*, I, p. 193; he was a brother of Bishop Miles of Beauvais, had married into the Béthune family and had links to the Nesle family.

175 'Itinera, dona et hernesia', p. 603; 'Recepta et expensa', p. 244.

176 *LTC*, II, nos. 3223, 3224.

177 BNF MS lat. 406, f. 400.

178 Miriam Shadis and Constance Hoffman Berman, 'A Taste of the Feast: Reconsidering Eleanor of Aquitaine's Female Descendants', in *Eleanor of Aquitaine, Lord and Lady*, ed. Bonnie Wheeler and John Carmi Parsons (New York, 2002), pp. 177-211, esp. pp. 189-90, 195.

179 'Recepta et expensa', p. 247; 'Ea quae distributa', p. 621.

180 Léopold Delisle, 'Mémoire sur une lettre inédite adressée à la Reine Blanche par un habitant de La Rochelle', *Bibliothèque de l'école des chartes*, 17th year, 4th series, vol. II (1856), pp. 518-23.

181 'Expensa militiae comitis Attrebatensis', p. 581. The count of Saint-Pol was an important vassal of Robert as count of Artois.

182 'Itinera, dona et hernesia', p. 592.

183 'Itinera, dona et hernesia', p. 609.

184 Shadis and Berman, 'A Taste of the Feast', p. 189.

185 *Achatz d'heritage* (ADVO 72H12), ff. 2-2v and 41v-42.

186 For Matilda, see Armande Gronier-Prieur, *L'abbaye Notre-Dame du Lys à Dammarie-lès-Lys* (Verneuil-l'Etang, 1976), p. 153. For Blanche's heart, see below, pp. 225-9.

187 'Itinera, dona et hernesia', p. 601; 'Comptes de dépenses', p. 90.

188 'Recepta et expensa', p. 236; 'Itinera, dona et hernesia', p. 597, the latter authorised by Agnes Cornut. 'Itinera, dona et hernesia', p. 599; 'Comptes de dépenses', p. 88, the former, from the royal household, authorised by Agnes of Livry.

189 *Cartulaire de l'abbaye de Porrois*, I, pp. 244-8, no. cclix. Anselm was married to a member of the Mauvoisin family: see Newman, *Les seigneurs de Nesle*, I, pp. 273-4.

190 'Un fragment du compte', pp. 242, 244, 245.

191 Delisle, 'Mémoire sur les opérations financières des Templiers', pp. 99, 101, 102.

192 BNF, Collection Champagne, vol. XXIV, f. 87. The countess of Ramerupt was Philippa of Brienne, who had caused so many problems for Theobald in the past; her daughter Mary

was married to Gaucher III of Nanteuil: see Newman, *Les seigneurs de Nesle*, I, p. 198.

193 See below, p. 212–15.

194 Newman, *Les seigneurs de Nesle*, II, pp. 262–3, nos. 162, 163.

195 'Recepta et expensa', passim.

196 'Comptes de dépenses', passim; BNF MS lat. 9017, f. 69. For itineration and the logistics involved, see Vale, *Princely Court*, pp. 137–62.

197 For the leeks, see Henri de L'Epinois, 'Comptes relatifs à la fondation de l'abbaye de Maubuisson', *Bibliothèque de l'école des chartes*, XIX (1858), pp. 553, 554; *Achatz d'heritage*, ADVO 72H12, f. 10v.

198 See above, p. 117.

199 The totals for her income are noted on the reverse of the memorandum of 1243: AN J1030, no. 9; see Delisle, 'Mémoire sur les opérations financières des Templiers', p. 102. Note that she was still receiving income from Issoudun in 1243: ibid., p. 102. For her dower properties, see *LTC*, II, nos. 1710, 2562, 2885; for dowry properties, ibid., no. 2692. For the cost of the Sainte-Chapelle, see William Chester Jordan, *Louis IX and the Challenge of the Crusade: A Study in Rulership* (Princeton, 1979), p. 91, n. 180.

200 See, e.g., 'Itinera, dona et hernesia', pp. 590, 607; 'Ea quae distributa', p. 619; 'Comptes de dépenses', p. 91.

201 'Itinera, dona et hernesia', pp. 593, 610; 'Comptes de dépenses', p. 91; BNF MS lat. 9017, f. 69.

202 'Itinera, dona et hernesia', p. 590; 'Comptes de dépenses', p. 91.

203 Saint-Pathus, 'Vie de Saint Louis', pp. 107–8.

204 'Recepta et expensa', p. 235; 'Comptes de dépenses', p. 91; BNF MS lat. 9017, f. 69.

205 'Recepta et expensa', p. 238.

206 'Itinera, dona et hernesia', p. 605; BNF MS lat. 9017, f. 69, l. 9.

207 'Un fragment du compte', no. 110; 'Itinera, dona et hernesia', p. 596. For sugar in the thirteenth century, see Margaret Wade Labarge, *A Baronial Household of the Thirteenth Century* (Brighton, 1980), pp. 95–7.

208 Saint-Pathus, 'Vie de Saint Louis', p. 79; Agnes of Harcourt, *Life of Isabelle of France*, pp. 54–5.

209 For clerical criticism of hunting, see Thomas Szabó, 'Die Kritik der Jagd von der Antike zum Mittelalter', in *Jagd und höfische Kultur im Mittelalter*, ed. Werner Rösenener (Göttingen, 1997), pp. 167–229, esp. pp. 189–211; for hunting as ritualised violence, see Philippe Buc, ' "Principes Gentium dominantur eorum": Princely Powers between Legitimacy and Illegitimacy in Twelfth-Century Exegesis', in *Cultures of Power: Lordship, Status and Process in Twelfth-century Europe*, ed. Thomas Bisson (Philadelphia, 1995), pp. 319–20. For Louis and hunting, see Le Goff, *Saint Louis*, pp. 691–3.

210 See above, pp. 124–5; and 'Ea quae distributa', p. 619.

211 'Un fragment du compte', nos. 24, 42, 44, 45, 46, 79, 80, 81, 82, 86, 106, 119; 'Recepta et expensa', pp. 241, 244; 'Itinera, dona et hernesia', pp. 589, 591, 595.

212 'Itinera, dona et hernesia', pp. 593, 595. Hunting references are more restrained still in the account of 1256; see *Les comptes sur tablettes de cire de Jean Sarrazin*: the hunters' wages are paid, pp. 71, 85; ferreters and partridge hunters, pp. 74, 77, 84.

213 For the custodian of the lion, see 'Compotus praepositorum', p. 261; 'Itinera, dona et hernesia', p. 600. For the distinction between Louis's restrained court and the chivalric, hunting court of Philip III and Mary of Brabant, see Jordan, *Men at the Center*, p. 11.

214 Saint-Pathus, 'Vie de Saint Louis', p. 112.

215 'Un fragment du compte', pp. 242, 243; 'Expensa militiae comitis Attrebatensis', p. 580. See further discussion below, pp. 246–9.

216 'Recepta et expensa', p. 246; 'Itinera, dona et hernesia', p. 592; BNF MS lat. 9017, f. 69.

8 RELIGION, THE CHURCH AND OTHER FAITHS

1 For the political and administrative roles of the household clerks, see below, pp. 185–9.

2 Quentin Griffiths, 'Les collégiales royales et leurs clercs sous le gouvernement capétien', *Francia*, XVIII (1991), p. 102.

3 Johann Peter von Ludewig, *Reliquiae Manuscriptorum omnis aevi Diplomatum ac Monumentorum ineditorum adhuc*, 12 vols (Frankfurt, 1720–41), XII, bk 1, p. 4; and 'Itinera, dona et hernesia AD 1239 inter ascensionem et omnes sanctos', in *RHF*, XXII (1865), p. 588.

4 'Compotus praepositorum et ballivorum Franciae de termino ascensionis, AD MCCXLVIII', in *RHF*, XXI (1855), p. 262. See also Robert Branner, 'The Sainte-Chapelle and the *Capella Regis* in the Thirteenth Century', *Gesta*, X (1971), p. 19; Meredith Cohen, 'An Indulgence for the Visitor: The Public at the Sainte-Chapelle of Paris', *Speculum*, LXXXIII (2008), p. 865. For the little known about Louis VIII's chapel staff, see Charles Petit-Dutaillis, *Etude sur la vie et le règne de Louis VIII* (Paris, 1894), p. 445. For general discussion of usually later court chapels, see Malcolm Vale, *The Princely Court: Medieval Courts and Culture in North-West Europe* (Oxford, 2001), pp. 220–37.

5 For the chaplain of Poissy and the chaplain of Messe, see 'Un fragment du compte de l'hôtel du Prince Louis de France pour le terme de la Purification 1213', ed. Robert Fawtier in *Moyen âge*, XLIII (1933), pp. 239, 245; for Peter, chaplain of Beaumont, see 'Recepta et expensa Anno MCCXXXIIII inter candelosam et ascensionem', in *RHF*, XXI (1855), p. 229; for the chaplain of Etampes, a castle that belonged to Blanche at this stage, see 'Comptes de dépenses de Blanche de Castille', ed. Etienne Symphorien Bougenot in *Bulletin du Comité des travaux historiques et scientifiques: section d'histoire et de philologie* (1889), p. 90.

6 *LTC*, II, no. 2727.

7 For Montargis and Fontainebleau, see 'Compotus praepositorum', p. 274.

8 For Peter as the chaplain of the queen, see *Cartulaire de l'église Notre-Dame de Paris*, ed. B. Guérard, 4 vols (Paris, 1850), II, p. 211, where Peter is given lands by Aubry Cornut, then running the chapter of Notre-Dame. For the campaign of 1231, see 'Compotus Th. De Carnoto et Amarrici Pulli, 1231', in *RHF*, XXI (1855), pp. 220–21.

9 BNF MS lat. 9017, f. 69; 'Comptes de dépenses', p. 89; 'Itinera, dona et hernesia', p. 594.

10 'Itinera, dona et hernesia', p. 591: robes given to Brother Geoffrey, chaplain of the queen, and to Geoffrey, clerk of the young queen.

11 'Recepta et expensa', p. 240.

12 'Magna recepta de termino Ascensionis, anno Domini MCCXXXVIII mense Mayo et magna expensa', in *RHF*, XXI (1855), p. 260; 'Itinera, dona et hernesia', p. 602: Master Terricus, chaplain of Robert of Artois. For Philip the Treasurer, see *LTC*, II, nos. 3796, 3829, 3796; and Edgar Boutaric, *Saint Louis et Alphonse de Poitiers: études sur la réunion des provinces du Midi et de l'Ouest à la couronne* (Paris, 1870), pp. 68–77. He is probably to be identified with Philip of Gometz, treasurer of Poitiers, canon of Notre-Dame of Paris, in *Obituaires de la Province de Sens*, ed. Auguste Molinier and Auguste Longnon, 4 vols in 5 (Paris, 1902–23), I, pp. 114–15.

13 Agnes of Harcourt, *The Writings of Agnes of Harcourt: The Life of Isabelle of France and the Letter on Louis IX and Longchamp*, ed. Sean Field (Notre Dame, IN, 2003), pp. 60–61, 64–5.

14 J. Berlioz, 'La voix de l'évêque: Guillaume d'Auvergne dans les *exempla*, XIIIe–XIVe siècles', in *Autour de Guillaume d'Auvergne*, ed. F. Morenzoni and J.-Y. Tilliette (Turnhout, 2005), pp. 11–12 and 32. This anecdote is often incorrectly ascribed to Stephen of Bourbon, as in Noël Valois, *Guillaume d'Auvergne, évêque de*

Paris, 1228–1249: sa vie et ses ouvrages (Paris, 1880), p. 148. St Louis, Blanche and Margaret were given the right to choose their own confessors in 1243, and St Louis's confessor from 1248 was Geoffrey of Beaulieu: see Xavier de La Selle, *Le service des âmes à la cour: confesseurs et aumôniers des rois de France du XIIIe au XVe siècle* (Paris, 1995), pp. 41, 261; also Xavier de La Selle, 'L'aumônerie royale', in *Vincennes aux origines de l'état moderne. Actes du colloque scientifique sur 'Les Capétiens à Vincennes au Moyen âge'*, ed. Jean Chapelot and Elisabeth Lalou (Paris, 1996), p. 184.

15 In 1231 the almoner was given 12 *livres* 'pro familia sua' and 40 *solidi* for his clerk for the year: Ludewig, *Reliquiae Manuscriptorum*, XII, bk 1, p. 4. For Lucas the clerk of the almonry in 1239, see 'Itinera, dona et hernesia', p. 607. The full functioning of the almonry is apparent only after Louis IX's Ordinance of the Household in 1261: see La Selle, L'aumônerie royale', pp. 183–9; see also La Selle, *Le service des âmes à la cour*, pp. 35–6, 161–91.

16 Ludewig, *Reliquiae Manuscriptorum*, XII, bk 1, p. 4; 'Itinera, dona et hernesia', p. 588.

17 Brother Roger, 'almoner of the court', followed by 'G. Almoner' attesting almsgiving: 'Itinera, dona et hernesia', pp. 593, 604.

18 For the clerk Master William of Bray, attesting alms for Blanche in 1239, see 'Itinera, dona et hernesia', pp. 600, 602; for Master Richard of Tourny attesting alms, ibid., p. 597. For Blanche's ladies attesting alms, see above, p. 173.

19 *LTC*, III, nos. 3772–5. He is clearly the clerk Stephen in her household account of 1241–2: BNF MS lat. 9017, f. 69. For Stephen as one of Blanche's executors witnessing the fulfilment of her arrangements for Fontevraud in 1259, see Fontevraud Cartulary, BNF MS lat. 5480, vol. I, part ii, p. 474; also vol. II, p. 405. For his prebends, see Griffiths, 'Les collégiales royales', p. 102.

20 *LTC*, III, no 4192. For Stephen as a clerk of Louis IX, ibid., no. 4350, and *Les*

comptes sur tablettes de cire de Jean Sarrazin, chambellan de Saint Louis, ed. Elisabeth Lalou (Turnhout, 2003), p. 91. He was a master of the exchequer from 1248 to his death in 1269: Griffiths, 'Les collégiales royales', p. 102; J. R. Strayer, *The Administration of Normandy under Saint Louis* (Cambridge, Mass., 1932), p. 37.

21 Eude Rigaud, *Regestrum visitationem archiepiscopi Rothomagensis/Journal des visites pastorales d'Eude Rigaud, archevêque de Rouen*, ed. T. Bonnin (Rouen, 1852), pp. 477, 503, 535. See also Grant, 'Eudes Rigaud et Saint-Mellon de Pontoise', forthcoming.

22 See above, p. 150. Master Peter received robes as part of the main household in 1239: 'Itinera, dona et hernesia', p. 588.

23 Ludewig, *Reliquiae Manuscriptorum*, XII, bk 1, p. 4; and 'Itinera, dona et hernesia', p. 588. Given their names, Dom Vincent and Master James are likely to have been Iberian; both were already in the royal household in 1224. For Vincent as Louis VIII's chaplain, see *Cartulaire normand de Philippe Auguste, Louis VIII, Saint Louis et Philippe-le-Hardi*, ed. Léopold Delisle (Caen, 1852), p. 307, no. 1129.

24 'Un fragment du compte', p. 241; 'Recepta et expensa', pp. 230, 243; 'Expensa militiae comitis Attrebatensis in Penthecoste AD 1237 mense junio', in *RHF*, XXII (1865), p. 581; 'Itinera, dona et hernesia', p. 587; 'Comptes de dépenses', p. 89.

25 'Recepta et expensa', p. 240; 'Itinera, dona et hernesia', pp. 596, 607.

26 'Itinera, dona et hernesia', pp. 590, 595; 'Comptes de dépenses', pp. 90, 91.

27 'Recepta et expensa', p. 229; 'Itinera, dona et hernesia', p. 590.

28 'Itinera, dona et hernesia', pp. 587, 604.

29 'Recepta et expensa', pp. 235, 236.

30 Griffiths, 'Les collégiales royales', p. 102.

31 'Compotus ballivorum et praepositorum Franciae anno Domini 1234 mense Junio de termino ascensionis', in *RHF*, XXII (1865), p. 566. Simon was also supported by a canonry at Notre-Dame in Paris: *Obituaires de la*

Province de Sens, I, p. 150. He is listed as a clerk of Louis VIII when Archbishop Theobald came before Louis's court in January 1224: *Cartulaire normand*, p. 307, no. 1129.

32   E.g., *LTC*, II, nos. 1327, 2909.

33   For the abbot of Saint-Victor: *LTC*, II, no. 2909; 'Recepta et expensa', p. 236; 'Itinera, dona et hernesia', p. 606; 'Comptes de dépenses', pp. 88, 89, 90; BNF MS lat. 9017, f. 69. For the brothers of Saint-Jacques: 'Recepta et expensa', pp. 230, 234, 238; 'Itinera, dona et hernesia', p. 597; ibid., the prior of Saint-Jacques attests, p. 603, he attests expenses for Maubuisson, p. 607. For the prior of Saint-Jacques travelling with Blanche from Paris to Corbeil; 'Comptes de dépenses', p. 90. For Peter of Collemezzo, see *Fasti Ecclesiae Gallicanae, II: le diocèse de Rouen*, ed. Vincent Tabbagh (Turnhout, 1998), pp. 84–5.

34   'Recepta et expensa', pp. 235, 238, 239, 240. For Walter's ecclesiastical career, see *Fasti Ecclesiae Gallicanae, XI: le diocèse de Sens*, ed. Vincent Tabbagh and Edouard Bouye (Turnhout, 2009), pp. 104–9.

35   Walter Cornut, 'Historia susceptionis Coronae spineae', in *RHF*, XXII (1865), pp. 28–30.

36   *LTC*, II, no. 2896.

37   *LTC*, II, no. 2896.

38   *GC*, VIII, cols 1156–9. He died in 1234.

39   See *LTC*, II, nos. 1824, 2253; Richard Kay, *The Council of Bourges, 1225: A Documentary History* (Aldershot, 2002), p. 20.

40   Ludewig, *Reliquiae Manuscriptorum*, XII, bk 1, p. 4.

41   *GC*, VIII, col. 1158; 'Recepta et expensa', p. 242; *GC*, VIII, instr. col. 363, no. xciii.

42   *GC*, VII, col. 93.

43   Valois, *Guillaume d'Auvergne*, p. 146; Nicholas of Braie, 'Gesta Ludovici VIII, Francorum Regis', in *RHF*, XVII (1878), p. 311.

44   Valois, *Guillaume d'Auvergne*, p. 68.

45   Francesco Santi, 'Guglielmo d'Auvergne e l'ordine dei domenicani tra filosofia naturale e tradizione magica', in *Autour de Guillaume*

d'Auvergne, ed. F. Morenzoni and J.-Y. Tilliette (Turnhout, 2005), pp. 137–53.

46   Berlioz, 'La voix de l'évêque', pp. 11–12.

47   Jean de Joinville, *Vie de Saint Louis*, ed. Jacques Monfrin (Paris, 2010), pp. 22–5, chs 46–9.

48   For Adam of Chambly, see Aubri of Trois-Fontaines, 'Chronica Albrici Monachi Trium Fontium', in *MGH Scriptores*, XXIII, ed. Paul Scheffer-Boichorst (Hanover, 1874), p. 919; *GC*, X, cols 1414–15; *LTC*, II, nos. 2909, 3977; Valois, *Guillaume d'Auvergne*, p. 68. For his robes, see Ludewig, *Reliquiae Manuscriptorum*, XII, bk 1, p. 4, and 'Itinera, dona et hernesia', p. 588. See also *Obituaires de la Province de Sens*, I, part ii, p. 656.

49   For John attesting, see 'Recepta et expensa', pp. 229, 230, 231, 234, 235. For his role as counsellor to Blanche, see *LTC*, III, nos. 3977, 3978. As bishop of Evreux, see *GC*, XI, cols 586–7.

50   Aubri of Trois-Fontaines, 'Chronica', p. 922. Other members of the family had been bishops of Paris, Noyon and Meaux.

51   *Obituaires de la Province de Sens*, I, pp. 3–6, 10, 12, 13.

52   *GC*, XII, col. 245. For memorials to the Clément and Cornut dynasties at Notre-Dame, Paris, see *Obituaires de la Province de Sens*, I, pp. 95, 128, 192, 201.

53   Ludewig, *Reliquiae Manuscriptorum*, XII, bk 1, p. 4; and 'Itinera, dona et hernesia', p. 588. The identification of clerks as Iberian is not always certain: see above, p. 185.

54   For Brother Christian the almoner, see Petit-Dutaillis, *Etude*, p. 445. For the Templars as bankers to the king, see Léopold Delisle, 'Mémoire sur les opérations financières des Templiers', in *Mémoires présentés par divers savantes à l'Académie des inscriptions et belles-lettres*, XXXIII (Paris, 1889), passim.

55   For the prior of Saint-Jacques and Brother Matthew, see pp. 209 and 183; for Stephen the Preacher and Brother John of the Great Bridge (de Magno Ponte), see 'Recepta

et expensa', p. 238; for Brother John, see 'Compotus praepositorum', p. 284.

56 For the relatively limited numbers of masters in Philip's government, see John W. Baldwin, *The Government of Philip Augustus: Foundations of French Royal Power in the Middle Ages* (Berkeley, Cal., 1986), p. 122.

57 Gifts of robes for Pentecost, 1231 (Ludewig, *Reliquiae Manuscriptorum*, XII, bk I, p. 4), include the archbishop of Sens, bishops of Senlis and Chartres, i.e., Walter Cornut, Adam of Chambly and Walter of Chartres, plus the almoner, the dean of Tours (Aubry Cornut), and twenty-two other clerks. For gifts of robes for the household clergy in 1239, see 'Itinera, dona et hernesia', p. 588. For horses, e.g., for the dean of Tours (Aubry Cornut) in 1234, see 'Recepta et expensa', p. 249. For Stephen of Montfort, Blanche's clerk in 1241, see 'Comptes de dépenses', p. 90. For Hugh of Athies, see 'Recepta et expensa', p. 230.

58 E.g., 'Recepta et expensa', p. 235, for Thomas Touquin when ill; BNF MS lat. 9017, f. 69, for the marriage of the niece of Master Robert of Lissy.

59 For their travel with Blanche, see BNF MS lat. 9017, f. 69. For Eudes Rigaud's visitation, see Rigaud, *Regestrum*, p. 42. For Stephen as treasurer of Saint-Mellon in 1249, see *LTC*, III, nos. 3772–5. For further discussion, see Grant, 'Eudes Rigaud et Saint-Mellon de Pontoise'.

60 See below, p. 234.

61 See Aden Kumler, *Translating Truth: Ambitious Images and Religious Knowledge in Late Medieval France and England* (New Haven and London, 2011), pp. 15–40.

62 E.g., *LTC*, II, nos. 2280, 2577, 2729, 2836; *Les registres de Gregoire IX*, ed. Lucien Auvray, 4 vols (Paris, 1890–1955), I, col. 573, no. 969. For Innocent IV, see *Les registres de Innocent IV: recueil des bulles de ce pape*, ed. Elie Berger, 4 vols (Paris, 1881–1920), I, nos. 255, 263, 624, 1056, 1057, 1151, 1152, 1301, 4054, 2948; III, no. 5598.

63 See above, p. 97.

64 See above, pp. 99–104.

65 *LTC*, II, no. 2264.

66 See above, p. 139.

67 *LTC*, II, no. 2404.

68 Matthew Paris, *Chronica majora*, ed. H. R. Luard, 7 vols (London, 1872–83), VI, pp. 99–112, esp. pp. 111–12. The protest of 1247 includes complaints about the papacy appointing to chapters during vacancies: ibid., pp. 103–5. Alexis Charansonnet, 'La révolte des barons de Louis IX: réaction de l'opinion et silence des historiens en 1246–1247', in *Une histoire pour un royaume, XIIe–XVe siècles. Actes du colloque Corpus Regni organisé en hommage à Colette Beaune*, ed. A.-H. Allirot et al. (Paris, 2010), pp. 218–39; Gerard J. Campbell, 'The Protest of Saint Louis', *Traditio*, XV (1959), pp. 405–18.

69 See above, pp. 103–4.

70 *LTC*, II, nos. 2609, 2694, 2698.

71 AN L463, nos. 34–44. For the settlement of 'plusiers querelles' between the king and Notre-Dame of Paris, in the presence of Blanche, the papal legate, the archbishop of Bourges and the bishops John of Evreux and Adam of Senlis in May 1248, see *Cartulaire de l'église Notre-Dame de Paris*, II, pp. 395–8, no. xvii.

72 Joinville, *Vie de Saint Louis*, pp. 336–7, chs 673, 674; *Obituaires de la Province de Sens*, II, p. 29. For Louis's relations with the Church, see Gerard J. Campbell, 'The Attitude of the Monarchy towards the Use of Ecclesiastical Censures in the Reign of Saint Louis', *Speculum*, XXXV (1960), pp. 537, 549–51, 554; Gerard J. Campbell, 'Temporal and Spiritual Regalia during the Reigns of St Louis and Philip III', *Traditio*, XX (1964), pp. 351–83, esp. pp. 354, 358–9, 373, 375–7; and Campbell, 'Protest of St Louis'. See also Jacques Le Goff, *Saint Louis* (Paris, 1996), pp. 782–4.

73 *LTC*, II, no. 3796.

74 *LTC*, II, no. 2731.

75 Lindy Grant, 'Representing Dynasty:

The Transept Windows of Chartres Cathedral', in *Representing History: Art, Music, History*, ed. Robert A. Maxwell (Philadelphia, 2010), p. III.

76 Marie-Dominique Chapotin, *Histoire des dominicains de la province de France: le siècle des fondations* (Rouen, 1898), p. 232.

77 *LTC*, II, no. 2577; 'E chronico Sanctae Catherinae de Monti Rotomagi', in *RHF*, XXIII (1876), p. 399.

78 *Les registres de Grégoire IX*, I, cols 139–41, no. 229.

79 Sara Lipton, *Images of Intolerance: The Representation of Jews and Judaism in the Bible Moralisée* (Berkeley, Cal., 1999), pp. 88–94, esp. p. 89.

80 ÖNB Cod. Vindob. 2554, ff. 30v, 40v. See Gerald B. Guest, *Bible moralisée: Codex Vindobonensis 2554, Vienna, Österreichische Nationalbibliothek* (London, 1995), pp. 88 and 116.

81 See above, p. 126–7; for *Cupientes*, see Campbell, 'Attitude of the Monarchy', pp. 541–2.

82 See above, Chapter One.

83 Recorded in *Chartularium Universitatis parisiensis: Ex diversis bibliothecis tabulariisque collegit et cum authenticis chartis contulit*, ed. H. Denifle, 4 vols (Paris, 1889–97), I, p. 79 n. 20; and Caesarius of Heisterbach, *Dialogus miraculorum*, ed. Joseph Strange (Cologne, 1851), pp. 304–7.

84 William the Breton, 'Gesta Philippi Augusti', in *Oeuvres de Rigord et Guillaume le Breton*, ed. H. Delaborde, 2 vols (Paris, 1882–5), I, pp. 231–3; and see discussion in Chapter One.

85 Caesarius of Heisterbach, *Dialogus miraculorum*, pp. 305–6.

86 Guest, *Bible moralisée* (ÖNB Cod. Vindob. 2554), p. 103, and also images on ff. 3v, 8r, 10v, 29v, 65r, 35v. See also the discussion in Lipton, *Images of Intolerance*, pp. 96–101; and Katherine H. Tachau, 'God's Compass and *Vana Curiositas*: Scientific Study in the Old French *Bible Moralisée*', *Art Bulletin*, LXXX (1998), pp. 7–33, esp. pp. 10–17, 22–7.

87 Rigord, *Histoire de Philippe Auguste*, ed. Elisabeth Carpentier, Georges Pon and Yves Chauvin (Paris, 2006), pp. 226–33 and 352–3; pp. 158–9 for Rigord's condemnation of anxiety about the End of Time; pp. 264–7 for the poem on Philip Augustus as the Last Emperor. Ibid, p. 351, n. 627, the admired Fulk of Neuilly preached in the expectation of the imminent End of Time. For Innocent III, see Alfred J. Andrea, 'Innocent III, the Fourth Crusade and the Coming Apocalypse', in *The Medieval Crusade*, ed. Susan J. Ridyard (Woodbridge, 2004), pp. 97–106.

88 See discussion in Elizabeth A. R. Brown, 'La notion de la légitimité et la prophétie à la cour de Philippe Auguste', in *La France de Philippe Auguste: le temps des mutations. Actes du Colloque international organisé par le CNRS: Paris, 29 septembre–4 octobre 1980*, ed. Robert-Henri Bautier (Paris, 1982), pp. 77–III, esp. pp. 85–96; and Baldwin, *Government of Philip Augustus*, pp. 384–6.

89 For discussion of the various prophecies of the End of Time, see Bernard McGinn, *Visions of the End: Apocalyptic Traditions in the Middle Ages* (New York, 1979), esp. pp. 43–50, 82–7.

90 For discussion of Blanche's psalter, see Harvey Stahl, *Picturing Kingship: History and Painting in the Psalter of St Louis* (University Park, 2008), pp. 143–6; and see below, pp. 236–9.

91 Lindy Grant, 'Saint Michel peseur d'âmes sur les portails gothiques du Jugement dernier vers 1200', in *Rappresentazioni del monte e dell'arcangelo san Michele nella letteratura e nelle arti / Représentations du mont et de l'archange saint Michel dans la littérature et les arts*, ed. Pierre Bouet et al. (Bari, 2011), pp. 135–43. For Amaury's and his followers' denial of the bodily resurrection, see Gary Dickson, 'The Burning of the Amalricians', *Journal of Ecclesiastical History*, XL (1989), p. 359. On the doctrine of the bodily resurrection, see Caroline Bynum, *The Resurrection of*

the Body in Western Christianity, 200–1336 (New York, 1995), esp. pp. 95–153.

92 See further discussion below, p. 242.

93 See above, pp. 141–2. See also the account of this episode in R. E. Lerner, 'Uses of Heterodoxy: The French Monarchy and Unbelief in the Thirteenth Century', French Historical Studies, IV (1965), pp. 197–202.

94 E.g., 'Itinera, dona et hernesia', pp. 593, 595, 596, 597.

95 Jeremy Cohen, The Friars and the Jews: The Evolution of Medieval Anti-Judaism (Ithaca, 1982), p. 14; Robert Chazan, 'Trial, Condemnation and Censorship: The Talmud in Medieval Europe', in The Trial of the Talmud: Paris, 1240, ed. and trans. John Friedman, Jean Connell Hoff and Robert Chazan (Toronto, 2012), pp. 2–92.

96 Lipton, Images of Intolerance, pp. 55–80.

97 Lucy Pick, Conflict and Coexistence: Archbishop Rodrigo and the Muslims and Jews of Medieval Spain (Ann Arbor, 2004), pp. 5–7.

98 Lester K. Little, Religious Poverty and the Profit Economy in Medieval Europe (London, 1978), pp. 179–83; Lipton, Images of Intolerance, pp. 31–8. On attitudes to usury among Paris scholars, see Ian Wei, Intellectual Culture in Medieval Paris: Theologians and the University, c. 1100–1330 (Cambridge, 2012), pp. 306–23.

99 Baldwin, Government of Philip Augustus, pp. 160–61, 230–33.

100 See discussion of Blanche's and Louis VIII's legislation above, pp. 69–70, 95–6. See discussion in William Chester Jordan, The French Monarchy and the Jews: From Philip Augustus to the Last Capetians (Philadelphia, 1989), pp. 94–137, for Louis VIII's and Blanche's policy towards the Jews, and pp. 145–61, for St Louis's policy.

101 Matthew Paris, Chronica majora, V, p. 441; William of Chartres, 'De vita et actibus inclytae recordationis regis francorum ludovici et de miraculis', in RHF, XX (1840), p. 34; William of Chartres, 'On the Life and Deeds of Louis, King of the Franks of Famous Memory, and on the Miracles that Declare his Sanctity', in The Sanctity of Louis IX: Early Lives of Saint Louis by Geoffrey of Beaulieu and William of Chartres, trans. Larry F. Field, ed. M. Cecilia Gaposchkin and Sean L. Field (Ithaca, 2014), p. 142.

102 Pick, Conflict and Coexistence, esp. pp. 138–71, 172–81.

103 For the complex response of the clergy to the trial of the Talmud, see A. Tuillier, 'La condamnation du Talmud par les maîtres universitaires parisiens, ses causes et ses conséquences politiques et idéologiques', in Le brûlement du Talmud à Paris, 1242–1244, ed. Gilbert Dahan (Paris, 1999), esp. pp. 64, 74; and Chazan, 'Trial, Condemnation and Censorship', esp. pp. 22–3.

104 For Rigord's attitude to the Jews, see Rigord, Histoire de Philippe Auguste, pp. 130–33, 144–57. On anti-Judaic imagery in the psalter, see Stahl, Picturing Kingship, pp. 145–6.

105 E.g., Paris, Bibliothèque de l'Arsenal, MS lat. 1186, f. 66: 'De mutatione veteris testamenti in novo ad christum accedamus'; f. 85v: 'contra superbiam iudeorum'; f. 97v: 'Contra iudeos de bonis Christi ut confutet et devotos eccl. redenda moneat'; f. 99: 'De historia veteris testamenti…spiritualiter intelligenda ut novi'. See below, p. 328, for further discussion.

106 Arsenal, MS lat. 1186, f. 168v.

107 See Lipton's sophisticated analysis in Images of Intolerance, esp. pp. 83–111. There is strongly anti-Judaic imagery too in the Christina Psalter, which was commissioned within French royal circles in the 1230s: see Marina Vidas, The Christina Psalter: A Study of the Images and Texts in a French Early Thirteenth-century Illuminated Manuscript (Copenhagen, 2006), pp. 89–90; and William Chester Jordan, 'Anti-Judaism in the Christina Psalter', in Christianity and Culture in the Middle Ages: Essays to Honor John Van Engen, ed. David C. Mengel and Lisa Wolverton (Notre Dame, Ind., 2015), pp. 280–93.

9 PIETY AND DEVOTION

1 Cf. Matthew Paris, *Chronica majora*, ed. H. R. Luard, 7 vols (London, 1872–83), v, p.354, says that she died 'as the devout servant rushing reverently towards her coming Lord Jesus Christ'.

2 See above, pp.73, 117–18.

3 Léopold Delisle, 'Mémoire sur les opérations financières des Templiers', in *Mémoires présentés par divers savantes à l'Académie des inscriptions et belles-lettres*, XXXIII (Paris, 1889), pp.101–2. For Innocent's agreement to her proposal for the loan to Notre-Dame of Paris, see *Les registres de Innocent IV: recueil des bulles de ce pape*, ed. Elie Berger, 4 vols (Paris, 1881–1920), II, p.161, no.4931.

4 *LTC*, II, no.2885; *LTC*, v, no.514; Le Lys Cartulary, BNF MS lat.13892, ff.31v, 32. See discussion in Constance Berman, 'Two Medieval Women's Control of Property and Religious Benefactions in France: Eleanor of Vermandois and Blanche of Castile', *Viator*, XLI/2 (2010), pp.155–6, 169.

5 Louis-Claude Doüet d'Arcq, *Comptes de l'Hôtel des Rois de France aux XIV au XV siècles* (Paris, 1865), pp.v–vi. It is perhaps unfair to compare Blanche's resources as a widow with those of Margaret as queen consort. But even as a widow Margaret does not appear to have been able to rival Blanche's generosity. A full-scale study of Margaret is much needed.

6 E.g., 1234: 'Recepta et expensa Anno MCCXXXIIII inter candelosam et ascensionem', in *RHF*, XXI (1855), p.238, a Spanish *conversa*, 'teste Doreta', must be Blanche's initiative; but ibid., p.230, alms for a poor woman to marry her daughter, 'teste' William of Bray, could be ordered by either Blanche or Louis. 1239: 'Itinera, dona et hernesia AD 1239 inter ascensionem et omnes sanctos', in *RHF*, XXII (1865), pp.590, 591, alms attested by the abbess of Saint-Antoine must be ordered by Blanche, as, clearly, is ibid., p.592, 'pro quadam femina maritate apud Pontisaria de mandato regine,

per M. Richard de Tourny'. Robert-Henri Bautier, 'Les aumônes du roi aux maladreries, Maisons-Dieu et pauvres établissements du royaume', in *Assistance et assistés jusqu'à 1610. Actes du 97e Congrès national des sociétés savantes: Nantes, 1972* (Paris, 1979), pp.37–105, argues convincingly that the surviving fourteenth- and fifteenth-century French royal alms rolls incorporate, and are largely based on, an alms list for Philip Augustus with substantial additions for Blanche of Castile. They correspond very closely to her patterns of occasional almsgiving discussed in this chapter.

7 *Achatz d'heritage*, ADVO 72H12, f.2; Henri de L'Epinois, 'Comptes relatifs à la fondation de l'abbaye de Maubuisson', *Bibliothèque de l'école des chartes*, XIX (1858), p.553; 'Compotus praepositorum et ballivorum Franciae de termino ascensionis, AD MCCXLVIII', in *RHF*, XXI (1855), p.266.

8 'Compotus ballivorum et praepositorum Franciae anno Domini 1234 mense Junio de termino ascensionis', in *RHF*, XXII (1865), p.570; 'Compotus praepositorum', p.266. For the original endowment, see Lindy Grant, *Architecture and Society in Normandy, 1120–1270* (New Haven and London, 2005), p.39.

9 For other, probably Angevin, alms, disbursed from the issues of Chinon and Le Mans, see 'Compotus ballivorum', pp.570–77.

10 'Compotus ballivorum', p.567.

11 For the office of the almonry, see above, pp.184–5. For the functioning of the almonry after 1261, see Xavier de La Selle, 'L'aumônerie royale', in *Vincennes aux origines de l'état moderne. Actes du colloque scientifique sur 'Les Capétiens à Vincennes au Moyen âge'*, ed. Jean Chapelot and Elisabeth Lalou (Paris, 1996); and Bautier, 'Les aumônes du roi'. For almsgiving in general, mainly at later medieval courts, see Malcolm Vale, *The Princely Court: Medieval Courts and Culture in North-West Europe* (Oxford, 2001), pp.236–8.

12 'Recepta et expensa', p.229; BNF MS lat.9017, f.69.

13   For the Annunciation, 1234, see 'Recepta et expensa', p. 233; for Blanche's alms for Christmas and Epiphany, 1241–2, see BNF MS lat. 9017, f. 69; for her alms on Ascension Day at Pontoise, 1241, see 'Comptes de dépenses de Blanche de Castille', ed. Etienne Symphorien Bougenot in *Bulletin du Comité des travaux historiques et scientifiques: section d'histoire et de philologie* (1889), p. 88; for 13 *livres* for Maundy money for Blanche, Louis, Robert, Alphonse the nephew (of Portugal) and the children, see 'Recepta et expensa', p. 237.

14   'Recepta et expensa', pp. 229, 232.

15   BNF MS lat. 9017, f. 69; 'Comptes de dépenses', pp. 91, 89, 91, 90. Note that after 1261 Margaret could feed only thirteen paupers at table: see above, p. 203.

16   'Recepta et expensa', p. 236; 'Comptes de dépenses', pp. 90, 89.

17   Monies for paupers: e.g., 'Recepta et expensa', pp. 229, 231, 234, 238; 'Itinera, dona et hernesia', p. 596; 'Comptes de dépenses', pp. 88, 89, 90, 91. But see bacons for the poor of Lorris: 'Recepta et expensa', p. 232; bread for St Louis and for his alms: 'Ea quae distributa fuerunt in milicia Comitis Pictavensis (Die xxiv junio, anno mccxli)', in *RHF*, XXII (1865), p. 617.

18   'Comptes de dépenses', pp. 88, 91. Note that on p. 88 Bougenot gives xxlviii *livres*, where BL Add. Ch. 4129 has xlviii *livres*.

19   'Recepta et expensa', p. 232; 'Itinera, dona et hernesia', p. 600.

20   'Recepta et expensa', p. 234.

21   Agnes of Harcourt, *The Writings of Agnes of Harcourt: The Life of Isabelle of France and the Letter on Louis IX and Longchamp*, ed. Sean Field (Notre Dame, IN, 2003), pp. 58–9.

22   'Itinera, dona et hernesia', p. 600.

23   E.g., 'Recepta et expensa', p. 234: poor women outside Pontoise; ibid., p. 230: 20 *solidi* for a poor woman to marry her daughter. 'Itinera, dona et hernesia', pp. 592, 597: women of Pontoise, married by order of the queen;

ibid., p. 604: 100 *solidi* for poor girls of Pontoise to marry.

24   'Recepta et expensa', pp. 233, 238. 'Itinera, dona et hernesia', p. 590: for a Norman woman entering Footel, 10 *livres*, attested by the abbess of Saint-Antoine, so definitely on Blanche's initiative; ibid., p. 593: for a girl entering Belleau, 10 *livres*, also attested by the abbess of Saint-Antoine; ibid., p. 597: 20 *livres* to Clairruissel, where Blanche places a nun. 'Comptes de dépenses', p. 90: 7 *livres* for a man entering the Domus Dei at Dourdan.

25   'Recepta et expensa', pp. 238, 245. See also ibid., p. 236: a *conversa* of Paris. 'Itinera, dona et hernesia', p. 589: for converted Saracens; p. 590: for a female Jewish convert, placed in the Domus Dei in Paris; p. 594: Robert the convert of Paris, Peter the convert of Spain; p. 599: a convert of Paris, wife of William the Scribe; p. 607: a *conversa*, baptised at Châteaufort. It is possible that some of these 'converts' had converted from the secular to the religious life: see Anne E. Lester, *Creating Cistercian Nuns: The Women's Religious Movement and its Reform in Thirteenth-century Champagne* (Ithaca, 2011), esp. pp. 22–3, but I think in most cases these are Jewish converts to the Christian faith. There is a close parallel with Henry III's interest in this group: see Robert Stacey, 'Henry III and the Jews', in *Jews in Medieval Christendom*, ed. K. T. Utterback and M. L. Price (Leiden, 2013), pp. 120–44. For the foundation of Henry's Domus Conversorum in London, see Matthew Paris, *Chronica majora*, III, pp. 262–3.

26   'Recepta et expensa', pp. 238, 245; 'Itinera, dona et hernesia', p. 594.

27   'Recepta et expensa', p. 233: merchants of Spain despoiled of goods. 'Itinera, dona et hernesia', p. 590: two poor clerks of Spain in 1239; p. 598: Spanish clerk; p. 599: Spanish cripple to return home; p. 604: two sick Spanish women at Ivry; p. 606: food for a Spanish clerk when a chaplain in Paris, gift to the abbot of Retorta.

28 'Comptes de dépenses', pp. 91, 88.

29 E.g., on Blanche's own account of 1241, to Val-des-Vignes, Longpré, The Paraclete, Molens, Parc-aux-Dames, Chaise-Dieu-du-Theil, Romorantin, Belleau, Clairuissel: 'Comptes de dépenses', pp. 88–90.

30 'Recepta et expensa', pp. 230, 234, 238, 233. Blanche was in the vicinity of Jargeau and Les Andelys when she made these donations. The donation was probably for the church in Grand Andely, rather than Petit Andely.

31 For Le Parc, 30 *livres* to finish the refectory: BNF MS lat. 9017, f. 69. For La Joie, see 'Itinera, dona et hernesia', pp. 600, 607 – note both these gifts are attested by Blanche herself; for the windows, see 'Comptes de dépenses', p. 89. For Le Trésor, see BNF MS lat. 9017, f. 69: four entries for the dormitory and other works; 'Comptes de dépenses', p. 90: to finish the cloister. See discussion of Blanche's architectural patronage below, pp. 249–63.

32 'Itinera, dona et hernesia', p. 602; BNF MS lat. 9017, f. 69: 'Pro beguines crispiaci, 100s'. For St Louis and the Beguines, see Tanya Stabler Miller, *The Beguines of Medieval Paris: Gender, Patronage and Spiritual Authority* (Philadephia, 2014), pp. 14–34.

33 Fontevraud Cartulary, BNF MS lat. 5480, vol. II, f. 105.

34 Fontevraud Cartulary, BNF MS lat. 5480, vol. II, f. 125, specifically links her gifts with her friendship for her 'consanguinea', Abbess Alice. For Alice of Blois as abbess of Fontevraud, see Léopold Delisle, 'Mémoire sur une lettre inédite adressée à la Reine Blanche par un habitant de La Rochelle', *Bibliothèque de l'école des chartes*, 17th year, 4th series, II (1856), pp. 518–23.

35 Fontevraud Cartulary, BNF MS lat. 5480, vol. II, f. 125; *Obituaires de la Province de Sens*, ed. Auguste Molinier and Auguste Longnon, 4 vols in 5 (Paris, 1902–23), IV, p. 193, for Fontaines near Meaux: 'felicis memorie et pie recordationis Blancha regina francie...et quamplurimum aliarum ecclesiarum religionis nostre et maxime matris notre ecclesie Fontis

Ebraldi adjutrix et benefactrix, cujus anima cum electis Dei perenni gaudio perfruantur'. 'Blanche, queen of France of happy and pious memory...helper and benefactor, above all of our mother church of Fontevraud, but also of many of the other churches of our order, whose soul may forever enjoy perpetual joy with the elect of God.'

36 *Obituaires de la Province de Sens*, IV, p. 193.

37 Fontevraud Cartulary, BNF MS lat. 5480, vol. I, part ii, ff. 439, 474. See also Delisle, 'Mémoire sur une lettre inédite', p. 52. The following are gifts to Fontevraudine houses on the accounts. 'Recepta et expensa', p. 231: gifts to four priories of Fontevraud in 1234. 'Compotus ballivorum', p. 567: gifts to Longpré and Fontaines near Meaux in 1234. 'Itinera, dona et hernesia', pp. 592, 593: gifts to Foissy near Troyes and Fontaines near Meaux in 1239; ibid., p. 597: Blanche places a nun in Clairuissel. 'Comptes de dépenses', pp. 88, 90 : gifts to Oursan, Longpré, Clairruissel in 1241. BNF MS lat. 9017, f. 69: for Collinances and Longpré in 1242.

38 *Archives de L'Hôtel-Dieu de Paris, 1157–1300*, ed. L. Brièle and E. Coyecque (Paris, 1894), p. 148, no. 324. On patronage of Hôtels-Dieu, see Lester, *Creating Cistercian Nuns*, esp. pp. 39–42; Lindy Grant, 'Royal and Aristocratic Hospital Patronage in Northern France in the Twelfth and Early Thirteenth Centuries', in *Laienadel und Armenfürsorge im Mittelalter*, ed. Lukas Clemens, Katrin Dort and Felix Schumacher (Trier, 2015), pp. 105–14, esp. pp. 111–14.

39 'Recepta et expensa', pp. 231, 234; 'Itinera, dona et hernesia', p. 602; 'Comptes de dépenses', p. 90; BNF MS lat. 9017, f. 69.

40 'Recepta et expensa', p. 238; 'Itinera, dona et hernesia', p. 590.

41 For lepers in 1234, see 'Recepta et expensa', pp. 231, 234; Blanche gives to the leper house at her dower towns of Melun, Etampes and, probably, Dourdan – the later sections of

BNF MS lat. 9017, f. 69, are difficult to read; see 'Comptes de dépenses', p. 90; BNF MS lat. 9017, f. 69.

42 Alphonse's Cistercian sympathies are clear from his list of alms: Edgar Boutaric, *Saint Louis et Alphonse de Poitiers: études sur la réunion des provinces du Midi et de l'Ouest à la couronne* (Paris, 1870), pp. 460–63. Charles's two foundations, Vittoria and Realvale, were both Cistercian: see Marie-Anselme Dimier, *Saint Louis et Cîteaux* (Paris, 1954), pp. 124–6.

43 *Obituaires de la Province de Sens*, I, p. 603: 'sororis nostre qui... nostram ecclesiam mirabilis affectus sincere dilectionis complectens, multa et magna ei beneficia conferens... quod in ecclesie nostre negociis diligenter promovendis'. 'For our sister who... holding our church in sincere and marvellous love, conferring many and great benefits on it... working diligently to promote the business of our church.'

44 Delisle, 'Mémoire sur les opérations financières des Templiers', p. 101.

45 In 1234: 'Recepta et expensa', p. 236; in 1239: 'Itinera, dona et hernesia', p. 606. On Blanche's own household accounts for 1241–2: 'Comptes de dépenses', pp. 88, 89, 90; BNF MS lat. 9017, f. 69. For the abbot as distributor of alms, see above, p. 205. For Abbot John, see Dom Fourier Bonnard, *Histoire de l'abbaye royale de St Victor et de l'ordre des chanoines réguliers de St-Victor de Paris*, 2 vols (Paris, 1904–8), esp. I, pp. 286–303. He had been one of the executors of Louis VIII's will.

46 *LTC*, II, no. 2909.

47 Fontevraud Cartulary, BNF MS lat. 5480, vol. II, f. 474.

48 *Obituaires de la Province de Sens*, I, pp. 535–603.

49 *Obituaires de la Province de Sens*, I, pp. 598, 540.

50 Lester K. Little, 'Saint Louis' Involvement with the Friars', *Church History*, XXXIII (1963), p. 127. For her gifts to the Franciscan houses, see BNF MS lat. 9017, f. 69. She gave a generous 20 *livres* to each house.

51 E.g., Alphonse of Poitiers named Brother Geoffrey de Virson, Franciscan, as one of the executors of his will in 1249: *LTC*, III, no. 3796.

52 Adam J. Davis, *The Holy Bureaucrat: Eudes Rigaud and Religious Reform in Thirteenth-Century Normandy* (Ithaca, 2006), p. 160. Maubuisson was within the diocese of Rouen, which is perhaps one reason why Eudes officiated.

53 For the early Dominicans, see William A. Hinnebusch, *History of the Dominican Order*, 2 vols (New York, 1965–73), I, pp. 25–109; for Prouille, pp. 96–9. For the Cistercian context from which the early Dominicans emerged, see Beverly Mayne Kienzle, *Cistercians, Heresy and Crusade in Occitania, 1145–1229: Preaching in the Lord's Vineyard* (Woodbridge, 2001), esp. pp. 135–217.

54 Hinnebusch, *History of the Dominican Order*, I, pp. 31, 98; Peter of Les Vaux-de-Cernay, *The History of the Albigensian Crusade*, ed. and trans. W. A. Sibley and M. D. Sibley (Woodbridge, 1998), p. 197, ch. 430.

55 Hinnebusch, *History of the Dominican Order*, I, p. 62; Armelle Bonis and Monique Wabont, 'Cisterciens et Cisterciennes en France du nord-ouest: typologie des fondations, typologie des sites', in *Cîteaux et les femmes*, ed. Armelle Bonis, Sylvie Dechavanne and Monique Wabont (Paris, 2001), pp. 160–61.

56 *The Latin Chronicle of the Kings of Castile*, trans. and ed. Joseph F. O'Callaghan (Tempe, Ariz., 2002), p. 46; 'Chronica Latina regum Castellae', in *Chronica hispana saeculi XIII*, ed. L. C. Brea, J. A. Estévez Sola and R. Carande Herrero (Turnhout, 1997), p. 58, says that he was a member of the Guzmán family, as was Dominic.

57 *Chartularium Universitatis parisiensis: Ex diversis bibliothecis tabulariisque collegit et cum authenticis chartis contulit*, ed. H. Denifle, 4 vols (Paris, 1889–97), I, pp. 108–9, no. 52:

'regina tenerrime diligit fratres, qui mecum de negociis suis ore proprio satis familiariter loquebatur'. For the establishment of the Dominican house in Paris, see Hinnebusch, *History of the Dominican Order*, I, pp. 58–9, 62–4.

58 Walter Cornut, 'Historia susceptionis Coronae spineae', in *RHF*, XXII (1865), p. 29; Marie-Dominique Chapotin, *Histoire des dominicains de la province de France: le siècle des fondations* (Rouen, 1898), p. 309.

59 'Recepta et expensa', p. 236.

60 'Comptes de dépenses', p. 89.

61 Hinnebusch, *History of the Dominican Order*, I, p. 257; Chapotin, *Histoire des dominicains*, pp. 156–9.

62 Given a robe, presumably for wedding/coronation of 1234: 'Recepta et expensa', p. 230; attesting to almsgiving and accompanies Blanche in 1239: 'Itinera, dona et hernesia', pp. 597, 607; with Blanche's household in 1241: 'Comptes de dépenses', p. 90. For Prior Henry, see 'Registrum Epistolarum Stephani de Lexington' (part II), ed. Fr B. Griesser in *Analecta Sacri Ordinis Cisterciensis*, vol. VIII (1952), p. 359.

63 A. Tuillier, 'La condamnation du Talmud par les maîtres universitaires parisiens, ses causes et ses conséquences politiques et idéologiques', in *Le brûlement du Talmud à Paris, 1242–1244*, ed. Gilbert Dahan (Paris, 1999), pp. 67, 70.

64 Noël Valois, *Guillaume d'Auvergne, évêque de Paris, 1228–1249: sa vie et ses ouvrages* (Paris, 1880), p. 148; for the text, see J. Berlioz, 'La voix de l'évêque: Guillaume d'Auvergne dans les *exempla*, XIIIe–XIVe siècles', in *Autour de Guillaume d'Auvergne*, ed. F. Morenzoni and J.-Y. Tilliette (Turnhout, 2005), p. 32.

65 Hinnebusch, *History of the Dominican Order*, I, p. 183. Record of the Dominican general chapter: AN LL1528a, f. 32; Margaret was also included: 'Item pro rege francie matre et uxore...unam missam de Sancto Spiritu et quondam mortem fiat pro eo sicut pro magistro ordinis per totum ordinem'.

66 Hinnebusch, *History of the Dominican Order*, I, pp. 122–8, 145–63; II, pp. 3–14.

67 For Louis's chastity in marriage, see Geoffrey of Beaulieu, 'Vita ludovici noni', in *RHF*, XX (1840), pp. 6–7; Geoffrey of Beaulieu, 'Here Begins the Life and Saintly Comportment of Louis, Formerly King of the Franks, of Pious Memory', in *The Sanctity of Louis IX: Early Lives of Saint Louis by Geoffrey of Beaulieu and William of Chartres*, trans. Larry F. Field, ed. M. Cecilia Gaposchkin and Sean L. Field (Ithaca, 2014), p. 79. For recent discussion of St Louis's response to poverty, see William Chester Jordan, *Men at the Center: Redemptive Governance under Louis IX* (Budapest, 2012), pp. 30–33; Davis, *Holy Bureaucrat*, p. 160; Stabler Miller, *Beguines of Medieval Paris*, pp. 15–25.

68 Delisle, 'Mémoire sur les opérations financières des Templiers', pp. 101–2.

69 See above, p. 174.

70 Original AN J461, no. 4: not noted in *Statuta Capitulorum generalium ordinis Cisterciensis ab anno 116 ad annum 1786*, ed. Joseph Canivez, 8 vols (Louvain, 1935).

71 *Statuta Capitulorum generalium ordinis Cisterciensis*, II, p. 58. For her other memorial petitions, see below, pp. 222–4.

72 *Les registres de Philippe Auguste*, ed. J. W. Baldwin (Paris, 1992), pp. 540–41, Carte diverse, no. 101.

73 Royaumont Cartulary, ADVO 43H3: foundation act of Louis IX, 1228, ff. 1–5.

74 Royaumont Cartulary, BNF MS lat. 5472, ff. 15, 21.

75 Royaumont Cartulary, ADVO 43H3, f. 1.

76 Nothing from Blanche is recorded in the three extant versions of the Cartulary: ADVO 43H3, BNF MS lat. 5472 and BNF MS lat. 9166.

77 BNF MS lat. 5472, ff. 109, 143, 98, 102, 111.

78 For family links among Albigensian Crusaders, especially the extended Montfort-Montmorency families, see Daniel Power, 'Who Went on the Albigensian Crusade?',

English Historical Review, CXXVIII (2013), pp. 1059, 1069. For the piety of the Montfort dynasty, see Alexis Charansonnet, 'Les grands laïcs lèguent-ils leur spiritualité à leur enfants? Le cas des Montfort au XIIIe siècle', in *Expériences religieuses et chemins de perfection dans l'Occident médiéval* (Paris, 2012), pp. 355–74, esp. pp. 363–9. Much of the historiography has focused on women's patronage of Cistercian nuns, and male support of them tends to be overlooked; but for the latter, see Erin L. Jordan, 'Gender Concerns: Monks, Nuns and Patronage of the Cistercian Order in Thirteenth-Century Flanders and Hainault', *Speculum*, LXXXVII (2012), pp. 67, 69. For elite women as patrons, see Constance Berman, 'Noble Women's Power as Reflected in the Foundation of Cistercian Houses for Nuns in Thirteenth-Century Northern France: Port-Royal, Les Clairets, Moncey, Lieu and Eau-lez-Chartres', in *Negotiating Community and Difference in Medieval Europe*, ed. Katherine Allen Smith and Scott Wells (Leiden and Boston, Mass., 2009), pp. 137–49; Lester, *Creating Cistercian Nuns*, pp. 68–72.

79 *Statuta Capitulorum generalium ordinis Cisterciensis*, II, pp. 253, 331.

80 In 1228 the general chapter tried to prevent the foundation of new nunneries: *Statuta Capitulorum generalium ordinis Cisterciensis*, II, p. 68; in 1243 the general chapter tried to insist that abbesses should remain enclosed, to the shock of the abbesses of Parc-aux-Dames and Romorantin: ibid., II, pp. 272–3. See discussion in Armelle Bonis and Monique Wabont, 'Introduction', in *Cîteaux et les femmes*, pp. 7–12; and Lester, *Creating Cistercian Nuns*, esp. pp. 92–116 for a nuanced discussion of the attitude of the order to the incorporation of women religious within it.

81 For the foundations discussed in this and the following paragraph, see Bonis and Wabont, 'Cisterciens et Cisterciennes', esp. pp. 159–63; Berman, 'Noble Women's Power'; Lester, *Creating Cistercian Nuns*, pp. 68–72.

82 William Mendel Newman, *Les seigneurs de Nesle en Picardie, XIIe–XIIIe siècles: leur chartes et leur histoire*, 2 vols (Paris, 1971), I, pp. 48–50.

83 Peter of Les Vaux-de-Cernay, *History of the Albigensian Crusade*, p. 85.

84 *Statuta Capitulorum generalium ordinis Cisterciensis*, II, p. 40.

85 *GC*, III, cols 538–9.

86 *GC*, XII, instr. cols 65–6, no. lxxxiv; *Statuta Capitulorum generalium ordinis Cisterciensis*, I, p. 528. See above, p. 209.

87 *GC*, XII, col. 245, and instr. cols 67–8, no. lxxxix.

88 *GC*, VIII, col. 1591, and instr. col. 535, no. lxxii; *Statuta Capitulorum generalium ordinis Cisterciensis*, II, pp. 54, 115.

89 *Cartulaire de l'abbaye royale de Lieu-Notre-Dame-lès-Romorantin*, ed. E. Plat (Romorantin, 1892), pp. 7–10, for the retrospective foundation charter of May 1247, including, p. 10, a chaplain to celebrate daily Mass for Blanche, Isabella and her husbands; *Statuta Capitulorum generalium ordinis Cisterciensis*, II, p. 54.

90 *GC*, III, cols 185–6.

91 *Statuta Capitulorum generalium ordinis Cisterciensis*, II, pp. 10, 33, 36–7; Lester, *Creating Cistercian Nuns*, pp. 30–33, 112–13. Theodore Evergates, 'Aristocratic Women in the County of Champagne', in *Aristocratic Women in Medieval France*, ed. Theodore Evergates (Philadelphia, 1999), p. 84.

92 E.g., 'Recepta et expensa', p. 239, for La Joie-lès-Nemours; p. 241, for Le Pré near Douai. 'Compotus praepositorum', p. 261: revenues for Villiers-aux-Nonnains and Porret from the Paris issues in 1248. 'Itinera, dona et hernesia', p. 588, for Beaupré. 'Comptes de dépenses', pp. 88, 89, 90, 91, for Val-des-Vignes, Parc-aux-Dames, Romorantin, Villiers-aux-Nonnains, L'Eau, Les Clairets. BNF MS lat. 9017, f. 69, for La Joie-lès-Nemours (three gifts), Romorantin, Les Clairets, Le Verger. For another donation to La Joie-lès-Nemours, see Cartulaire de La Joie-lès-Nemours, Paris, Institut de France,

Académie des Inscriptions et Belles-Lettres, Fonds Louis Carolus-Barré, folder 2, no. clvi.

93 Hippolyte Bonnardot, *L'abbaye royale de Saint-Antoine-des-Champs de l'ordre de Cîteaux* (Paris, 1882), *pièces justificatives*, no. II, pp. 87–8.

94 Bonnardot, *L'abbaye royale*, pp. 12, 21. Peter of Les Vaux-de-Cernay, *History of the Albigensian Crusade*, p. 71, ch. 129, and n. 26. The Mauvoisin family had strong Garlande, Montmorency and Montfort connections: Nicolas Civel, *La fleur de France, les seigneurs d'Ile-de-France au XIIe siècle* (Turnhout, 2006), p. 441. For Adam of Beaumont, see AN L1015, no. 18, f. 7; Bonnardot, *L'abbaye royale*, pp. 21–2.

95 For Petronilla, see Newman, *Les seigneurs de Nesle*, II, p. 342, n. 8; Bonnardot, *L'abbaye royale*, pp. 2–3.

96 For Agnes, see AN L1015, no. 18, f. 8. Her younger son, Robert of Cressonsacq, became bishop of Beauvais, 1238–49: Newman, *Les seigneurs de Nesle*, I, p. 266.

97 Bonnardot, *L'abbaye royale*, pp. iii, 12; for Amicia Briard's family, see Civel, *La fleur de France*, p. 429.

98 Bonnardot, *L'abbaye royale*, p. 2.

99 See above, pp. 72, 116–17.

100 Bonnardot, *L'abbaye royale*, pp. 2–3; sealed original, AN L1015, no. 8.

101 Bonnardot, *L'abbaye royale*, p. 7; original AN L1015, no. 6, indulgence issued by William of Paris and the other bishops to those visiting on the anniversary of the dedication.

102 'Itinera, dona et hernesia', pp. 590, 591, 593; 'Comptes de dépenses', p. 89; Stephen of Lexington, 'Registrum' (part II), p. 252, no. 24; Lindy Grant, 'Etienne de Lexington et l'abbaye de Savigny au treizième siècle', forthcoming; and see above, p. 174.

103 Agnes of Harcourt, *Life of Isabelle of France*, pp. 62–3, 64–5. Perronelle is the vernacular version of Petronilla. For Perronelle/Petronilla, daughter of Count Simon, see Simon Tugwell, ed., *Early Dominicans: Selected Writings* (New York, 1982), p. III, n. 73. The name Petronilla was much used in the Montfort

family, so one cannot be certain that this was Count Simon's daughter.

104 *Statuta Capitulorum generalium ordinis Cisterciensis*, I, pp. 308, 325.

105 For Angevin patronage of the Cistercians, see Grant, *Architecture and Society in Normandy*, esp. pp. 34–5, 38, 115–19.

106 Rose Walker, 'Leonor of England, Plantagenet Queen of Alfonso VIII of Castile, and her Foundation of the Cistercian Abbey of Las Huelgas: In Imitation of Fontevraud?', *Journal of Medieval History*, XXXI (2005), pp. 352–3. See also Miriam Shadis, 'Piety, Politics and Power: The Patronage of Leonor of England and her Daughters, Berenguela of Leon and Blanche of Castile', in *The Cultural Patronage of Medieval Women*, ed. June Hall McCash (Athens, Ga., 1996), pp. 202–27, esp. pp. 203–10; Miriam Shadis, *Berenguela of Castile (1180–1246) and Political Women in the High Middle Ages* (New York, 2009), pp. 39–40; and James D'Emilio, 'The Royal Convent of Las Huelgas: Dynastic Politics, Religious Reform and Artistic Change in Medieval Castile', in *Cistercian Nuns and their World*, ed. M. Parsons Lillich (Kalamazoo, 2005), pp. 191–282. For the authority of its abbess over other Castilian Cistercian houses, see Eva M. Synek, ' "Ex utroque sexu fidelium tres ordines": The Status of Women in Early Medieval Canon Law', in *Gendering the Middle Ages*, ed. Pauline Stafford and Anneke B. Mulder-Bakker (Oxford, 2001), pp. 76–7 [first published as special issue of *Gender and History*, XII/3, 2000]; and the charter of Alfonso VIII and Eleanor of 1199 in Julio González, *El reino de Castilla en la época de Alfonso VIII*, 3 vols (Madrid, 1960), III, pp. 208–10, no. 682.

107 Walker, 'Leonor of England', pp. 361–2.

108 Walker, 'Leonor of England', p. 365.

109 Fontevraud Cartulary, BNF MS lat. 5480, vol. II, f. 105. For their patronage, see Lindy Grant, 'Le patronage architectural d'Henri II et de son entourage', *Cahiers de civilisation médiévale*, XXXVII (1994), pp. 73–84. John and

his sister Joanna, later countess of Toulouse, were both educated there: see Ralph V. Turner, *Eleanor of Aquitaine* (London and New Haven, 2009), pp. 195–6.

110 See above, pp. 166–7.

111 See above, pp. 118–19.

112 Sealed original, ADVO 72H115; Alphonse Dutilleux and Joseph Depoin, *Cartulaire de l'abbaye de Maubuisson (Notre-Dame-la-Royale), I: chartes concernant la fondation de l'abbaye et des chapelles* (Pontoise, 1890), p. 1, no. 1.

113 'Sacro-sancte matris ecclesie doctores asserunt quod beatis angelicis spiritibus cedit ad gaudium si renati fonte baptismatis quos [*sic* – but should probably read 'quia'] difficile est in presenti seculo nequam incursus evadere delictorum suo se creatori affectu erigerunt salutari' (The doctors of Holy Mother Church assert that the blessed angelic spirits give way to joy if someone is reborn at the baptismal font [because?] it is difficult in the present worthless age to evade the incursion of sin, they have raised themselves up to their creator with saving affection). My thanks to Dr Gill Knight for her help with the difficult and slightly defective Latin, which I have checked carefully against the original: ADVO 72H115. See discussion of thirteenth-century interest in Luke 5.10 in David Keck, *Angels and Angelology in the Middle Ages* (Oxford, 1998), pp. 107–9.

114 Le Lys Cartulary, BNF MS lat. 13892, ff. 25–6: Louis's act of 1248, given at Paris. I have not so far found another of Louis's charters with an elaborate preamble. Blanche's parents' charters for Las Huelgas do not have elaborate preambles of this kind, either: see González, *El reino de Castilla*, II, pp. 808–12, no. 472; III, pp. 208–10, no. 682.

115 Le Lys Cartulary, BNF MS lat. 13892, f. 30–30v. For the lily as emblem, see Michel Pastoureau, 'La fleur de lis: emblème royal, symbole Marial ou thème graphique?', in *L'hermine et le sinople: études d'héraldique médiévale* (Paris, 1982), pp. 158–78.

116 This is a rough calculation from 'Comptes de dépenses' and BNF MS lat. 9017, f. 69. Blanche spent approx. 562 *livres* on miscellaneous alms, approx. 341 *livres* on Maubuisson, and approx. 506 *livres* on gifts for building at religious institutions. I have not counted *deniers*. There are lacunae on both manuscripts, and it is not always easy to distinguish gifts to friends from alms. Note that Bougenot mis-transcribed a couple of figures from BL Add. Ch. 4129; 'Comptes de dépenses', p. 88, has 'summa. iiii. c. xvi l. xxii d.' for 'iiii^c lxvi l. xxii d.', and 'xxlviii l.' for 'xlviii l.'; p. 89: 'vi.xx. l. C s.' for 'vi^{xx} l. c s.'

117 See *Corpus des sceaux français du Moyen Age, III: les sceaux des reines et des enfants de France*, by Marie-Adélaïde Nielen (Paris, 2011), pp. 31–2; Jean Dufour, 'De l'anneau sigillaire au sceau: évolution du rôle des reines de France jusqu'à la fin du XIIIe siècle', in ibid., pp. 19–20.

118 For Eleanor of Castile and Eleanor of Provence, see John Carmi Parsons, 'Piety, Power and the Reputation of Two 13th-Century English Queens', in *Queens, Regents and Potentates*, ed. Theresa M. Vann (Dallas, 1993), pp. 118–19; for Eleanor of Provence, see Margaret Howell, *Eleanor of Provence: Queenship in Thirteenth-Century England* (Oxford, 1998), pp. 282–3.

119 Turner, *Eleanor of Aquitaine*, pp. 129, 277–8, 293, 296.

120 For Eleanor of Vermandois, see Berman, 'Two Medieval Women's Control of Property', esp. pp. 157–67.

121 For Joanna of Flanders, see Erin L. Jordan, *Women, Power and Religious Patronage in the Middle Ages* (Basingstoke, 2006), esp. pp. 93–6, 100–09.

122 See the analysis of Louis's expenditure from surviving accounts of February 1256 to February 1257, and February 1257 to November 1257, in Natalis de Wailly, 'Dissertation sur les dépenses et les recettes ordinaires de Saint-Louis', in *RHF*, XXI (1855), p. lxviii, table xiv. Between February 1256 and 1257 Louis's

miscellaneous alms totalled 995 *livres* and his almoner disbursed 5,099 *livres*.

123 For the recluse of Etampes, see 'Comptes de dépenses', p. 89; for the holy woman of Nanterre and Isabella's illness, see Agnes of Harcourt, *Life of Isabelle of France*, pp. 56/7.

124 See below for references, p. 245.

125 Paris, Bibliothèque Mazarine, MS 870, f. 191. This manuscript is famous for its principal text, the 'Somme le roi'.

126 Rodrigo Jiménez de Rada, *Historia de rebus Hispaniae*, ed. Juan Fernández Valverde (Turnhout, 1987), p. 273, for the Virgin and Castile. *Cartulaire de Notre-Dame de Chartres*, ed. Eugène de Lépinois and Lucien Merlet, 3 vols (Chartres, 1862–5), III, p. 213. See above, p. 101, for the humiliation of the Virgin of Rouen.

127 Keck, *Angels and Angelology*, pp. 72–3, 107–9. On the imagery of the fall of the rebel angels, see Nigel Morgan, *Early Gothic Manuscripts, I: 1190–1250* (London, 1982), I, p. 118.

128 Jean de Joinville, *Vie de Saint Louis*, ed. Jacques Monfrin (Paris, 2010), pp. 95–6, ch. 96.

129 Gábor Klaniczay, *Holy Rulers and Blessed Princesses: Dynastic Cults in Medieval Central Europe* (Cambridge, 2002), pp. 202–3 on Elizabeth of Hungary, pp. 235–8 on her impact within the royal families of France, Castile and Portugal.

130 Shadis, *Berenguela of Castile*, pp. 35–7. Anne Duggan, 'The Cult of St Thomas Becket in the Thirteenth Century', in *St Thomas Cantilupe, Bishop of Hereford*, ed. Meryl Jancey (Hereford, 1982), pp. 25–8.

131 'Recepta et expensa', p. 241; BNF MS lat. 9017, f. 69.

132 *LTC*, II, no. 1664.

133 *Obituaires de la Province de Sens*, I, p. 204; *Archives de L'Hôtel-Dieu de Paris*, p. 148, no. 324.

134 *LTC*, II, no. 2221.

135 Matthew Paris, 'Vita S. Edmundi', in C. H. Lawrence, *St Edmund of Abingdon: A Study in Hagiography and History* (Oxford, 1960), pp. 262–3: 'domina Blanchia, domini regis Francorum genitrice, quam constat esse mulierem consilii magni et non muliebris. Que adducens filios suos secum'; 'the lady Blanche, the mother of the lord king of the Francs, who was known to be a woman of great and not womanly counsel. She, taking her sons along with her'. Matthew Paris, *The Life of St Edmund by Matthew Paris*, trans. and ed., with a biography, by C. H. Lawrence (Stroud, 1999), p. 150. For the chasuble, now belonging to Saint-Quiriace at Provins, see *Le Maroc médiéval: un empire de l'Afrique à l'Espagne*, ed. Yannick Lintz, Claire Délery and Bulle Tuil Leonetti (Paris, 2014), cat. no. 17, pp. 96–7.

136 Lawrence, in 'Introduction', *Life of St Edmund by Matthew Paris*, pp. 94–8.

137 Matthew Paris, 'Vita S. Edmundi', p. 286; *Life of St Edmund by Matthew Paris*, p. 167.

138 *Obituaires de la Province de Sens*, I, pp. 603, 540; IV, p. 193; Fontevraud Cartulary, BNF MS lat. 5480, vol. II, f. 125.

139 Original, AN J461, no. 8; *LTC*, II, nos. 2213, 2214.

140 Hinnebusch, *History of the Dominican Order*, I, p. 183.

141 *LTC*, II, nos. 3118, 3119.

142 Vézelay: *LTC*, II, nos. 2461, 3197; Canterbury: ibid., no. 2221.

143 AN J461, no. 13.

144 AN J461, no. 4; *Statuta Capitulorum generalium ordinis Cisterciensis*, II, pp. 57–8.

145 *Statuta Capitulorum generalium ordinis Cisterciensis*, II, p. 103.

146 *Statuta Capitulorum generalium ordinis Cisterciensis*, II, pp. 24, 32.

147 *Statuta Capitulorum generalium ordinis Cisterciensis*, II, pp. 274–7. Joanna of Flanders, the countess of Nevers, the count of Saint-Pol and Stephen of Sancerre were evidently part of the royal entourage: ibid., p. 277.

148 E.g., *Statuta Capitulorum generalium ordinis Cisterciensis*, II, pp. 361, 362, 377.

149 *Obituaires de la Province de Sens*, I, p. 204; and see above, p. 73.

150 For the nineteenth-century discovery of Isabella's burial with her children, see Kathleen Nolan, *Queens in Stone and Silver: The Creation of a Visual Imagery of Queenship in Capetian France* (New York, 2009), p. 115; Aline Hornaday, 'A Capetian Queen as Street Demonstrator: Isabelle of Hainault', in *Capetian Women*, ed. Kathleen Nolan (New York, 2003), p. 87.

151 Jacques Le Goff, *Saint Louis* (Paris, 1996), p. 282.

152 For the tomb, see Willibald Sauerländer, *Gothic Sculpture in France, 1140–1270*, trans. Janet Sondheimer (London, 1972), pl. 159; J. Adhémar, ed., 'Les tombeaux de la collection Gaignières: dessins d'archéologie du xviie siècle' [part I], *Gazette des beaux-arts*, LXXXIV (1974), p. 28, no. 104; Nolan, *Queens in Stone and Silver*, pp. 135–6.

153 Nolan, *Queens in Stone and Silver*, pp. 136–8. The Poissy tombs were drawn for Gaignières, where they were described as the tombs of the princes John and Philip, in yellow copper: see Adhémar, ed., 'Les tombeaux de la collection Gaignières', I, p. 53, no. 258; Nolan, *Queens in Stone and Silver*, fig. 35, p. 139. The seventeenth-century necrology copied into *Obituaires de la Province de Sens*, II, p. 343, records the children as Alphonse and John. On the tomb itself, they are not named, but described as sons of Blanche and Louis (VIII).

154 *Obituaires de la Province de Sens*, I, p. 540.

155 'Chronique de Primat traduite par Jean de Vignay', in *RHF*, XXIII (1876), p. 10. Alain Erlande-Brandenburg, *Le roi est mort: étude sur les funérailles, les sépultures et les tombeaux des rois de France jusqu'à la fin du XIIIe siècle* (Geneva, 1975), pp. 23–6, 77. Le Goff, *Saint Louis*, p. 282, on St Louis's later view that only kings of France should be buried at Saint-Denis.

156 See above, pp. 143–4.

157 Alphonse Dutilleux and Joseph Depoin, *L'abbaye de Maubuisson (Notre-Dame-la-Royale): histoire et cartulaire, II: les bâtiments, l'église et les tombeaux* (Pontoise, 1883), p. 107; For the tomb of Mary, see Nolan, *Queens in Stone and Silver*, pp. 148–9.

158 See above, p. 144. See the thoughtful discussion and full references in Nolan, *Queens in Stone and Silver*, pp. 145–51; and Erlande-Brandenburg, *Le roi est mort*, pp. 95–6.

159 *Testament*, vidimus of 1283, AN J403, no. 10. I would like to thank Xavier Hélary for bringing this document to my attention. Until I saw it, I shared the reservations that most historians have evinced for the seventeenth-century claims. It is also discussed in Alexandre Bande, *Le coeur du roi: les Capétiens et les sépultures multiples, XIIIe–XVe siècles* (Paris, 2009), pp. 59–64, esp. p. 63.

160 For the issue of division of the body burials, see especially Elizabeth A. R. Brown, 'Death and the Human Body in the Later Middle Ages: The Legislation of Boniface VIII on the Division of the Corpse', *Viator*, XII (1981), pp. 221–70; Danielle Westerhof, *Death and the Noble Body in Medieval England* (Woodbridge, 2008), pp. 75–86, on multiple burials; and Bande, *Le coeur du roi*.

161 Roger of Howden, *Chronica magistri Rogeri de Hovedene*, ed. William Stubbs, 4 vols (London, 1868–71), IV, p. 84; John Gillingham, *Richard I* (London and New Haven, 1999), pp. 324–5.

162 Lindy Grant, 'Rouen Cathedral, 1200–1237', in *Medieval Art, Architecture and Archaeology at Rouen*, ed. J. Stratford (Leeds, 1993), p. 66; Grant, *Architecture and Society in Normandy*, p. 41 and pl. 6.

163 Westerhof, *Death and the Noble Body*, pp. 143–4. See the useful appendix 1, listing all multiple burials in England; see also Brown, 'Death and the Human Body', p. 229. For the nobility of the aristocratic heart, see Westerhof, *Death and the Noble Body*, pp. 51–4.

164   Adhémar, ed., 'Les tombeaux de la collection Gaignières', part I, p. 37, no. 160. B. Chauvin and G. Delepierre, 'Le mausolée de la comtesse Jeanne à l'abbaye de Marquette: essai de restitution', *Revue du Nord*, no. 368 (2006), pp. 109–25. Aubri of Trois-Fontaines, 'Chronica Albrici Monachi Trium Fontium', in MGH *Scriptores*, XXIII, ed. Paul Scheffer-Boichorst (Hanover, 1874), p. 933.

165   Philippe Mousket, *Chronique rimée*, ed. Frédéric de Reiffenberg, 2 vols (Brussels, 1836–8), II, pp. 534–5.

166   *Obituaires de la Province de Sens*, II, p. 225; Aubri of Trois-Fontaines, 'Chronica', p. 949.

167   Bande, *Le coeur du roi*, p. 56.

168   Peter of Alençon, Testament, AN J403, no. 10. Peter also made donations to the Dominicans of Provins because Theobald's heart lies there. See also discussion in Bande, *Le coeur du roi*, pp. 59–64, 94. For Theobald's heart tomb, see Sauerländer, *Gothic Sculpture in France*, pp. 292–3.

169   See especially discussion in Brown, 'Death and the Human Body', pp. 221–2.

170   Le Goff, *Saint Louis*, pp. 298–300; Bande, *Le coeur du roi*, pp. 64–6. Geoffrey of Beaulieu, 'Vita ludovici noni', p. 24; Geoffrey of Beaulieu, 'Here Begins the Life', pp. 123–4.

171   Jackie Hall, 'The Legislative Background to the Burial of Laity and Other Patrons in Cistercian Abbeys', in *Sepulturae cistercienses*, ed. Jackie Hall and Christine Kratzke (Forges-Chimay, 2005), pp. 363–72.

172   Dutilleux and Depoin, *L'abbaye de Maubuisson, II: les batiments, l'église et les tombeaux*, pp. 106–7. The tomb was described by Gaignières in the seventeenth century; it was also itemised as being 'of solid copper, supported on a base of copper with columns' in 1790. See also Nolan, *Queens in Stone and Silver*, p. 141.

173   Adhémar, ed., 'Les tombeaux de la collection Gaignières', part I, p. 41: Walter Cornut; p. 49: Peter of Dreux; p. 53: Charles the Bald.

174   Nolan (*Queens in Stone and Silver*, p. 141) argues that Blanche was responsible for the copper effigies for the royal children at Poissy and Royaumont, and thus for her own copper tomb; the argument is plausible, but unproven.

175   Nolan, *Queens in Stone and Silver*, p. 147.

176   Erlande-Brandenburg, *Le roi est mort*, p. 165: 'Pro tumba Blanche regine empta apud Tornacum et pro vectura ejusdem'. See also discussion in Nolan, *Queens in Stone and Silver*, p. 148.

177   Robert Lee Wolff, 'Mortgage and Redemption of an Emperor's Son: Castile and the Latin Empire of Constantinople', *Speculum*, XXIX (1954), pp. 61–2.

178   Nolan, *Queens in Stone and Silver*, pp. 148–9.

10   THE CULTURE OF THE COURT

1   For a nuanced discussion of courts, households and court culture, see Malcolm Vale, *The Princely Court: Medieval Courts and Culture in North-West Europe* (Oxford, 2001), pp. 15–33. For discussion of what it meant to be a patron, see above, p. 16.

2   Patricia Stirnemann, 'Les bibliothèques princières et privées aux xiie et xiiie siècles', in *Histoire des bibliothèques françaises: les bibliothèques médiévales*, ed. A. Verlet (Paris, 1989), pp. 177–8. For the courts of Champagne, see Theodore Evergates, *Henry the Liberal, Count of Champagne, 1127–1181* (Philadelphia, 2016), pp. 35–42, 86–99; Danielle Quéruel, 'Un cour intellectual au xiie siècle', in *Splendeurs de la cour de Champagne au temps de Chrétien de Troyes*, ed. Thierry Delcourt and Xavier de La Selle (Troyes, 1999), pp. 11–18; Xavier Dectot, 'Ou périr ou régner? Les tombeaux des comtes de Champagne à Saint-Etienne de Troyes', in ibid., pp. 22–7 for the Champagne tombs. For the architecture of the Anglo-Normans and

Angevins, see Lindy Grant, *Architecture and Society in Normandy, 1120–1270* (New Haven and London, 2005), pp. 33–5.

3 On the sites of tournaments, see David Crouch, *Tournament* (London, 2005), pp. 6–12. Though one should note that Henry II banned them in England.

4 See especially Patricia Stirnemann, 'Une bibliothèque princière au XIIe siècle', in *Splendeurs de la cour de Champagne*, ed. Delcourt and de La Selle, pp. 36–42. For the books and book culture of the Anglo- Normans and Angevins, see Nicholas Vincent, 'The Great Lost Library of England's Medieval Kings? Royal Users and Ownership of Books, 1066–1272', in *1000 Years of Royal Books and Manuscripts*, ed. Kathleen Doyle and Scot McKendrick (London, 2013), pp. 73–112, esp. pp. 84–112. For the court culture of the Angevins, see Nicholas Vincent, 'The Court of Henry II', in *Henry II: New Interpretations*, ed. Christopher Harper-Bill and Nicholas Vincent (Woodbridge, 2007), pp. 278–334; pp. 308–10 on the wealth of the court, pp. 319–28 on its courtly culture. See also Ian Short, 'Literary Culture and the Court of Henry II', in ibid., pp. 335–61, esp. pp. 356–61.

5 Rigord, *Histoire de Philippe Auguste*, ed. Elisabeth Carpentier, Georges Pon and Yves Chauvin (Paris, 2006), pp. 226–7. There were no *jongleurs* or *histrions*: ibid., pp. 128–9, 224–5.

6 Janna Bianchini, *The Queen's Hand: Power and Authority in the Reign of Berenguela of Castile* (Philadelphia, 2012), p. 20. For Toledo as a cultural centre, see Lynn Thorndike, *Michael Scot* (London, 1965), pp. 12, 22–3; Lucy Pick, *Conflict and Coexistence: Archbishop Rodrigo and the Muslims and Jews of Medieval Spain* (Ann Arbor, 2004), pp. 79–126, esp. pp. 110–15 for the late twelfth century. For Almohad-influenced work at Las Huelgas, see James D'Emilio, 'The Royal Convent of Las Huelgas: Dynastic Politics, Religious Reform and Artistic Change in Medieval Castile', in

Cistercian Nuns and their World, ed. M. Parsons Lillich (Kalamazoo, 2005), pp. 212, 217.

7 On Philip as the new Charlemagne, see John W. Baldwin, *The Government of Philip Augustus: Foundations of French Royal Power in the Middle Ages* (Berkeley, Cal., 1986), pp. 364–7, 371. See also Elizabeth A. R. Brown, 'La notion de la légitimité et la prophétie à la cour de Philippe Auguste', in *La France de Philippe Auguste: le temps des mutations. Actes du Colloque international organisé par le CNRS: Paris, 29 septembre–4 octobre 1980*, ed. Robert-Henri Bautier (Paris, 1982), pp. 77–111.

8 See above, p. 48.

9 Johannes de Hauvilla, *Architrenius*, trans. and ed. Winthrop Wetherbee (Cambridge, 1994), pp. 58–9; William the Breton, 'Gesta Philippi Augusti', in *Oeuvres de Rigord et Guillaume le Breton*, ed. H. Delaborde, 2 vols (Paris, 1882–5), I, pp. 230–31, on Paris as an intellectual centre. See also John W. Baldwin, *Masters, Princes and Merchants: The Social Views of Peter the Chanter and his Circle*, 2 vols (Princeton, 1970); and, more recently, Ian Wei, *Intellectual Culture in Medieval Paris: Theologians and the University, c.1100–1330* (Cambridge, 2012).

10 See above, pp. 48, 189.

11 William the Breton, 'Gesta Philippi Augusti', pp. 231–3; and see above, p. 40.

12 Richard Kay, *The Council of Bourges, 1225: A Documentary History* (Aldershot, 2002), p. 48; Thorndike, *Michael Scot*, pp. 28, 32.

13 Noël Valois, *Guillaume d'Auvergne, évêque de Paris, 1228–1249: sa vie et ses ouvrages* (Paris, 1880), pp. 6, 200, 205; Francesco Santi, 'Guglielmo d'Auvergne e l'ordine dei domenicani tra filosofia naturale e tradizione magica', in *Autour de Guillaume d'Auvergne*, ed. F. Morenzoni and J.-Y. Tilliette (Turnhout, 2005), pp. 140–45.

14 Valois, *Guillaume d'Auvergne*, pp. 56, 147; for the dedication, see Nicholas of Braie, 'Gesta Ludovici VIII, Francorum Regis', in *RHF*, XVII (1878), p. 311.

15 *Chartularium Universitatis parisiensis: Ex diversis bibliothecis tabulariisque collegit et cum authenticis chartis contulit*, ed. H. Denifle, 4 vols (Paris, 1889–97), I, p. 110, n. 54; 'Recepta et expensa Anno MCCXXXIIII inter candelosam et ascensionem', in *RHF*, XXI (1855), pp. 235, 236. Michael did teach in Paris, perhaps in the early 1230s. He died in 1235: see Thorndike, *Michael Scot*, p. 36. See also Pick, *Conflict and Coexistence*, pp. 80–95: Scot held a prebend in the chapter of Toledo Cathedral. He dedicated his 'De caelo' to Master Stephen of Provins (ibid., pp. 94–5), who also attended the marriage and coronation of 1234, with his expenses authorised by Master Martin: 'Recepta et expensa', p. 243.

16 Alfred J. Andrea, 'Innocent III, the Fourth Crusade and the Coming Apocalypse', in *The Medieval Crusade*, ed. Susan J. Ridyard (Woodbridge, 2004), pp. 97–106; Nicholas Vincent, 'Stephen Langton, Archbishop of Canterbury', in *Etienne Langton: prédicateur, bibliste, théologien*, ed. L.-J. Bataillon et al. (Turnhout, 2010), pp. 87–8; Rigord, *Histoire de Philippe Auguste*, pp. 350–51, n. 627.

17 Rigord, *Histoire de Philippe Auguste*, pp. 226–7, 264–7, 352–3.

18 R. E. Lerner, 'Uses of Heterodoxy: The French Monarchy and Unbelief in the Thirteenth Century', *French Historical Studies*, IV (1965), p. 191.

19 Rigord, *Histoire de Philippe Auguste*, pp. 158–9; Valois, *Guillaume d'Auvergne*, p. 201.

20 Brown, 'La notion de la légitimité', pp. 84–96. For the prophecy of Adso of Montier-en-Der, see Jean Dunbabin, 'What's in a Name? Philip, King of France', *Speculum*, LXVIII (1993), pp. 949–68; Bernard McGinn, *Visions of the End: Apocalyptic Traditions in the Middle Ages* (New York, 1979), pp. 44–50 for the Tiburtine Sybil; pp. 75–6 for Pseudo-Methodius on the Last Emperor; pp. 82–7 for Adso of Montier-en-Der.

21 Stirnemann, 'Les bibliothèques', pp. 178–

84; Robert Branner, 'Manuscript Painting in Paris around 1200', in *The Year 1200: A Symposium* (New York, 1975), pp. 175–8; Léopold Delisle, *Notice de douze livres royaux du XIIIe siècle et du XIVe siècle* (Paris, 1902); Robert Branner, 'The Sainte-Chapelle and the Capella Regis in the Thirteenth Century', *Gesta*, X (1971), p. 19.

22 Rigord, *Histoire de Philippe Auguste*, pp. 110–14, with emphasis on Louis's literary accomplishments; William the Breton, 'Philippide', in *Oeuvres de Rigord et Guillaume le Breton*, II, ed. H. Delaborde, pp. 1–4; Gerald of Wales, 'De principis instructione', in *Giraldi Cambrensis opera*, vol. VIII, ed. G. F. Warner (London, 1891), pp. 7–8, on Louis as the ideal literate prince; M. L. Colker, ed., 'The "Karolinus" of Egidius Parisiensis', *Traditio*, XXIX (1973), pp. 324–5 for the dedication.

23 Manchester, John Rylands Library, MS Lat. 22. Delisle, *Notice de douze livres royaux*, pp. 111–15 (Delisle knew it as the Crawford Psalter).

24 For Geoffrey's stormy career, see D. L. Douie, *Archbishop Geoffrey Plantagenet and the Chapter of York* (York, 1960), esp. p. 12. He was in exile in Rouen from 1207. The psalter is now Leiden, Universiteit Leiden, Bibliotheken MS Lat. 76a. H. Omont, *Le Psautier de Saint Louis de la Bibliothèque de Leyde* (Leiden, 1902), pp. vi, i, a fourteenth-century hand on f. 30v claims that St Louis learnt to read from this psalter: 'Cist Psaultiers fu mon seignor saint Looys, qui fu roys de France, ouquel il aprist en s'anfance'. See illustration in *Saint Louis*, exh. cat., ed. Pierre-Yves Le Pogam, Conciergerie, Paris (Paris, 2014), p. 144, ill. no. 110, and catalogue entry no. 40, p. 217. See discussion in Delisle, *Notice de douze livres royaux*, pp. 19–35. See also Nigel Morgan, *Early Gothic Manuscripts, I: 1190–1250* (London, 1982), pp. 13, 60–62.

25 Paris, Bibliothèque de l'Arsenal, MS lat. 1186. The paschal tables of this psalter give computations for Easter from 1216, which sug-

gests that this was the date of its making: see H. Martin, *Les joyaux de l'Arsenal, I: le psautier de Saint Louis et de Blanche de Castille* (Paris, 1909), p. 14. See also Delisle, *Notice de douze livres royaux*, pp. 27–35; Harvey Stahl, *Picturing Kingship: History and Painting in the Psalter of St Louis* (University Park, 2008), pp. 143–6, especially for discussion of the iconography.

26   For the Psalter of Joanna of Flanders (BNF MS lat. 238), see Patricia Stirnemann in *Splendeurs de la cour de Champagne*, catalogue, p. 72; for the Ingeborg Psalter, see Delisle, *Notice de douze livres royaux*, pp. 4–14; Florens Deuchler, *Der Ingeborgpsalter* (Berlin, 1967).

27   For the rarity of this imagery, which probably derives from Anglo-Saxon iconography, see Morgan, *Early Gothic Manuscripts*, p. 118.

28   Paris, Bibliothèque de l'Arsenal, MS lat. 1186, ff. 169v, 170. For the imagery, see Lindy Grant, 'Saint Michel peseur d'âmes sur les portails gothiques du Jugement dernier vers 1200', in *Rappresentazioni del monte e dell'arcangelo san Michele nella letteratura e nelle arti / Représentations du mont et de l'archange saint Michel dans la littérature et les arts*, ed. Pierre Bouet et al. (Bari, 2011), pp. 135–43.

29   Arsenal, MS lat. 1186, f. 168r.

30   Cf. the Tablets of the Law on f. 16 are clearly written in Hebrew characters; this is a very 'literate' manuscript.

31   Joan Diamond Udovitch, 'Three Astronomers in a Thirteenth-century Psalter', *Marsyas: Studies in the History of Art*, XVII (1975), pp. 79, 82; see also discussion in Stahl, *Picturing Kingship*, p. 146.

32   For the Christina Psalter, see below, p. 244. For the only psalters with computational tables listed by Leroquais, see Victor Leroquais, *Les psautiers: manuscrits latins des bibliothèques publiques de France*, 3 vols (Mâcon, 1940–41), II, pp. 53, 125.

33   Udovitch, 'Three Astronomers', esp. p. 81.

34   E.g., penitence, ff. 56, 63v; humanity of

Christ (two natures of Christ), ff. 93, 106, 186v, 134; on Old/New Testaments, ff. 66, 99; on Jews, ff. 39, 85v, 97v; on their conversion, ff. 119v, 72. For the relationship to Lombard's Commentary, e.g., psalm 13 on f. 39, the text is: 'Ut confutet iudeos et contemptores', reflecting Peter Lombard, 'Commentarium in Psalmos', in *PL*, vol. CLXI, col. 162: 'Intentio. Prophetare est confutare Judaeos, Christi contemptores'. For psalm 39 on f. 66, the text is: 'De mutatione veteris testamentum in novum ut ad christum accedamus', reflecting Peter Lombard, 'Commentarium in Psalmos', col. 399: 'quia agit de mutatione veteris testamentum in novum ... monet ad novum testamentum accedere'. For psalm 46 on f. 72, the text is: 'Conversas gentes invitat ad laudem domini', reflecting Peter Lombard, 'Commentarium in Psalmos', col. 454: 'gentes quas in precedenti psalmo vocavit ad fiem iam conversas, in hoc psalmo invitat ad laudem Dei'.

35   Leroquais, *Les psautiers*, I, p. 14, noted the sentences, and said they were unique, as did Delisle, *Notice de douze livres royaux*, pp. 31–2. Delisle gives the first ten sentences. Neither recognised their source in Lombard's Commentary.

36   Now BNF MS lat. 238. Stirnemann in *Splendeurs de la cour de Champagne*, catalogue, p. 72.

37   For Eleanor of Vermandois as commissioner of the volume, see Stirnemann, 'Les bibliothèques', p. 178.

38   Branner, 'Manuscript Painting in Paris', pp. 176–8.

39   See discussion in George Conklin, 'Ingeborg of Denmark, Queen of France, 1193–1223', in *Queens and Queenship in Medieval Europe*, ed. Anne J. Duggan (Woodbridge, 1997), pp. 39–52, esp. pp. 41, 47.

40   For the emphasis on queenship in the imagery of the Ingeborg Psalter, see Stahl, *Picturing Kingship*, p. 143; Kathleen Schowalter, 'The Ingeborg Psalter: Queenship, Legitimacy

and the Appropriation of Byzantine Art in the West', in *Capetian Women*, ed. Kathleen Nolan (New York, 2003), pp. 100, 114–18, though she argues that the book was owned by Ingeborg from the start.

41   See above, p. 51.

42   Conklin, 'Ingeborg of Denmark', pp. 50–51.

43   On these two books, see John Lowden, *The Making of the Bibles Moralisées*, 2 vols (University Park, 2000), esp. I, pp. 11–94; Gerald B. Guest, *Bible moralisée: Codex Vindobonensis 2554, Vienna, Österreichische Nationalbibliothek* (London, 1995), pp. 1–37, which focuses on ÖNB Cod. Vindob. 2554.

44   Sara Lipton, *Images of Intolerance: The Representation of Jews and Judaism in the Bible Moralisée* (Berkeley, Cal., 1999), pp. 6–8, gives a convincing discussion of the verses.

45   See Lowden, *Making of the Bibles Moralisées*, II, pp. 200–01, 207–8.

46   Guest, *Bible moralisée*, pp. 23–4.

47   See discussion in Lowden, *Making of the Bibles Moralisées*, I, pp. 87–8. For the French text, see Guest, *Bible moralisée*, p. 54.

48   Lindy Grant, 'Gold Bezants on the Altar: Coronation Imagery in the Bibles Moralisées', in *Image, Memory and Devotion*, ed. Zoë Opačić and Achim Timmermann (Turnhout, 2011), pp. 55–9.

49   See above, p. 41–2.

50   See above, p. 156.

51   Aden Kumler, *Translating Truth: Ambitious Images and Religious Knowledge in Late Medieval France and England* (New Haven and London, 2011), pp. 15–43.

52   E.g., ÖNB Cod. Vindob. 2554, ff. 19r, 19v, 32v, 33v, 37v, 41v, 46r. See Guest, *Bible moralisée*, p. 26, and see his perceptive comments on the ideological content in general, pp. 27–37.

53   E.g., ÖNB Cod. Vindob. 2554, ff. 23r, 29v, 31r, 33v, 59r.

54   ÖNB Cod. Vindob. 2554, f. 37r.

55   ÖNB Cod. Vindob. 2554, f. 36r.

56   Lipton, *Images of Intolerance*, pp. 88–90. Lipton shows the close relationship between miscreants and Jews in the bibles, but the miscreants have a strong identity of their own. The Albigensians are mentioned by name in ÖNB Cod. Vindob. 2554, f. 40v.

57   E.g., ÖNB Cod. Vindob. 2554, ff. 11v and 12r; ff. 65r, 35v.

58   E.g., ÖNB Cod. Vindob. 2554, f. 10r–v; ÖNB Cod. Vindob. 1179, f. 7. See Katherine H. Tachau, 'God's Compass and *Vana Curiositas*: Scientific Study in the Old French *Bible Moralisée*', *Art Bulletin*, LXXX (1998), pp. 7–33, esp. pp. 10–17, 22–7.

59   ÖNB Cod. Vindob. 2554, f. 3v; also in ÖNB Cod. Vindob. 1179, f. 7; see Lipton, *Images of Intolerance*, p. 99, fig. 70. See also Tachau, 'God's Compass', esp. pp. 13–14 and figs 6–9. The destruction of the astronomers appears in the later moralised bibles.

60   Lipton, *Images of Intolerance*, passim, for a subtle analysis.

61   E.g., Lipton, *Images of Intolerance*, p. 33, fig. 47a; p. 37, fig. 77d; pp. 45–7 and figs 65c and 82d.

62   ÖNB Cod. Vindob. 2554, ff. 22v and 26v. See also discussion in Kumler, *Translating Truth*, pp. 29–31.

63   'Itinera, dona et hernesia AD 1239 inter ascensionem et omnes sanctos', in *RHF*, XXII (1865), p. 608.

64   Now BNF MS lat. 10434; see Marina Vidas, *The Christina Psalter: A Study of the Images and Texts in a French Early Thirteenth-century Illuminated Manuscript* (Copenhagen, 2006), p. 33; Stahl, *Picturing Kingship*, pp. 146–8.

65   'Comptes de dépenses de Blanche de Castille', ed. Etienne Symphorien Bougenot in *Bulletin du Comité des travaux historiques et scientifiques: section d'histoire et de philologie* (1889), p. 88.

66   In 1239, 23 *livres* 3 *deniers* to buy parchment at Lendit Fair: 'Itinera, dona et hernesia', p. 592.

67 BNF MS lat. 9017, f. 69; 'Itinera, dona et hernesia', p. 607.

68 BNF MS lat. 9017, f. 69.

69 'Recepta et expensa', p. 230.

70 AN J1034, no. 8.

71 Vidas, *Christina Psalter*, esp. pp. 49–51, 89–90. Vidas argues that Blanche had this psalter made for herself or for Louis IX, but both Robert and John would have been old enough to have had their own psalter by 1230 (John died in 1232). Alphonse of Portugal is another possibility. For Philip of Castile, who left the Church to marry, see above, p. 186.

72 BNF MS lat. 14397a. *Ex libris* notes on f. 3 and f. 3v say it was given to Saint-Victor by Blanche. See also Robert Branner, 'Saint Louis et l'enluminure parisienne au XIIIe siècle', in *Septième centenaire de la mort de Saint Louis. Actes des colloques du Royaumont et de Paris, 21–27 mai 1970* (Paris, 1976), p. 77 and fig 3.

73 Henri de L'Epinois, 'Comptes relatifs à la fondation de l'abbaye de Maubuisson', *Bibliothèque de l'école des chartes*, XIX (1858), p. 563: 4 *livres* for parchment at Lendit Fair, 1240. October 1239: 'Itinera, dona et hernesia', p. 605.

74 'Comptes de dépenses', p. 90.

75 Recorded in a fifteenth-century inventory: ADVO 72H83, ff. 27v, 32v; Alphonse Dutilleux and Joseph Depoin, *L'abbaye de Maubuisson (Notre-Dame-la-Royale): histoire et cartulaire, III: le trésor et le mobilier* (Pontoise, 1884), pp. 153–4.

76 Lowden, *Making of the Bibles Moralisées*, I, pp. 95–137.

77 Lowden, *Making of the Bibles Moralisées*, II, pp. 127–32. This image is on a detached quire from the bible, New York, The Morgan Library and Museum, MS M240.

78 Lowden, *Making of the Bibles Moralisées*, II, pp. 8–9, 201–2; Tachau, 'God's Compass', pp. 13–14, 17. A fourth moralised bible, now distributed among the Bibliothèque Nationale in Paris (BNF MS lat. 11560), the Bodleian Library in Oxford (MS Bodley 270B) and the British Library (MSS Harley 1526 and 1527), was made almost in tandem with the Toledo Bible: see Lowden, *Making of the Bibles Moralisées*, I, pp. 139–87; ibid., pp. 183–7, arguing that it was commissioned for Margaret of Provence.

79 See the important detective work of Sean L. Field, 'Reflecting the Royal Soul: The *Speculum anime* Composed for Blanche of Castile', *Medieval Studies*, LXVIII (2006), pp. 26–41, which provides an edition of the Latin text, primarily from the earliest Latin version of it, BNF MS lat. 14878, which is probably early fourteenth century. Field (ibid., pp. 5–13) suggests that the author was William of Auvergne or Vincent of Beauvais. See also Léopold Delisle, 'Durand de Champagne, franciscain', *Histoire littéraire de la France*, XXX (1888), pp. 302–33, esp. pp. 325–30.

80 BNF MS lat. 14878, f. 151r, col. b; Field, 'Reflecting the Royal Soul', p. 35: 'Si cogites quid respondebis cum dicetur de te, "Ecce, ista fuit Regina Francie"'.

81 Sean L. Field, *Isabelle of France: Capetian Sanctity and Franciscan Identity in the Thirteenth Century* (Notre Dame, Ind., 2006), pp. 24–6; Delisle, 'Durand de Champagne, franciscain', pp. 326–7. Field has also edited the French text: Sean L. Field, 'From *Speculum anime* to *Miroir de l'âme*: The Origins of Vernacular Advice Literature at the Capetian Court', *Medieval Studies*, LXIX (2007), pp. 59–110. The French text says that it has been translated from Latin to French so that it should be better known, and that because of this the author has had this book written for Blanche and sent to her. Delisle, 'Durand de Champagne, franciscain', p. 326; Paris, Bibliothèque Mazarine, MS 870, f. 192–192v: 'Et pour ce convient il moult de choses metre en scripture, et meismement translater de latin en francois, pour ce que chascune chose soit meuz seue et plus communement. Et pour ce, tres noble et tres puissant dame madame Blanche, par la grace de Dieu royne de France, je vous envoi ce livre... que j'ai fet escrire pour vous.' This used

to be interpreted to imply that Blanche had commissioned the translation into French on the assumption that she could not read Latin, but that is not quite what it says. 'Ce livre…que j'ai fet escrire pour vous' may mean this actual copy, rather than this text. Moreover, the Latin text addresses a queen of France very directly (see previous note). The queen in question can only have been Blanche, and the Latin text must have been written for her: see Field, 'Reflecting the Royal Soul', esp. pp. 21 and 35. The French text incorporated some additions from the Bestiary of Richard of Fournival – another Aristotelian, interested in astronomy: see Field, 'From *Speculum anime* to *Miroir de l'âme*', p. 65.

82   Bibliothèque Mazarine, MS 870, f. 192. Ms 870, ff. 192–207v, is the earliest French version of the text. For the manuscript, which contains mainly a famous copy of the 'Somme le roi', see Kumler, *Translating Truth*, p. 164.

83   Valois, *Guillaume d'Auvergne*, p. 147.

84   E.g., Eleanor of Vermandois commissioned a verse Life of St Geneviève: see Stirnemann, 'Les bibliothèques', p. 178. For the commissions of Eleanor of Provence and women in her entourage, see Margaret Howell, *Eleanor of Provence: Queenship in Thirteenth-century England* (Oxford, 1998), pp. 91–2. For Eleanor of Castile, see John Carmi Parsons, *Eleanor of Castile: Queen and Society in Thirteenth-century England* (New York, 1998), pp. 55–6; and John Carmi Parsons, 'Of Queens, Courts and Books: Reflections on the Literary Patronage of Thirteenth-century Plantagenet Queens', in *The Cultural Patronage of Medieval Women*, ed. June Hall McCash (Athens, Ga., 1996), pp. 177–8.

85   Walter Cornut, 'Historia susceptionis Coronae spineae', in *RHF*, XXII (1865), pp. 27–32. For its use at Matins on the feasts of the Crown of Thorns, see Geoffrey of Beaulieu, 'Vita ludovici noni', in *RHF*, XX (1840), p. 15; Geoffrey of Beaulieu, 'Here Begins the Life and Saintly Comportment of Louis, Formerly King

of the Franks, of Pious Memory', in *The Sanctity of Louis IX: Early Lives of Saint Louis by Geoffrey of Beaulieu and William of Chartres*, trans. Larry F. Field, ed. M. Cecilia Gaposchkin and Sean L. Field (Ithaca, 2014), p. 101. See also discussion in Paul Edouard Didier Riant, *Exuviae sacrae Constantinopolitanae*, 2 vols (Paris, 2004), I, pp. lxviii–lxxi. For further discussion of Cornut's text, see below, pp. 322–3.

86   Field, *Isabelle of France*, pp. 21–6.

87   Edgar Boutaric, *Saint Louis et Alphonse de Poitiers: études sur la réunion des provinces du Midi et de l'Ouest à la couronne* (Paris, 1870), p. 341, quoting BNF MS lat. 9019, f. 1: 'pro romano religando et pro historio de Rencevaux'; Branner, 'Saint Louis et l'enluminure parisienne', pp. 74–5. The text of Alphonse's chronicle is 'Extrait d'un abrégé' in *RHF*, XVII (1878), pp. 429–32.

88   Geoffrey of Beaulieu, 'Here Begins the Life', pp. 99–100; Geoffrey of Beaulieu, 'Vita ludovici noni', p. 15; Branner, 'Saint Louis et l'enluminure parisienne', pp. 69–73; Stirnemann, 'Les bibliothèques', pp. 178–84.

89   Jean Dunbabin, *The French in the Kingdom of Sicily, 1266–1305* (Cambridge, 2011), pp. 230–32, 274; Jean Dunbabin, *Charles I of Anjou: Power, Kingship and State-Making in Thirteenth-century Europe* (London, 1998), pp. 203–4.

90   'Un fragment du compte de l'hôtel du Prince Louis de France pour le terme de la Purification 1213', ed. Robert Fawtier in *Moyen âge*, XLIII (1933), pp. 242, 254, 243. It is interesting to note that between 1205 and 1212 Gace Brulé was given a fief-rent at Mantes – which was where Blanche and Louis heard him – perhaps on their initiative, since Philip lacked interest in this sort of performance: see John W. Baldwin, *Paris, 1200* (Stanford, Cal., 2010), p. 255.

91   'Itinera, dona et hernesia', p. 591.

92   In 1239: 'Itinera, dona et hernesia', p. 592; in 1241: BNF MS lat. 9017, f. 69. I would

like to thank Catherine Leglu for advice on Melana's likely nationality.

93 'Recepta et expensa', p. 245.

94 Dunbabin, *Charles I of Anjou*, pp. 203–8; Dunbabin, *The French in the Kingdom of Sicily*, pp. 269–73.

95 Guillaume de Saint-Pathus, 'Vie de Saint Louis, par le confesseur de la reine Marguerite', in *RHF*, xx (1840), p. 66; William of Chartres, 'De vita et actibus inclytae recordationis regis francorum ludovici et de miraculis', in *RHF*, xx (1840), p. 29; William of Chartres, 'On the Life and Deeds of Louis, King of the Franks of Famous Memory, and on the Miracles that Declare his Sanctity', in *The Sanctity of Louis IX*, trans. Larry F. Field, ed. M. Cecilia Gaposchlin and Sean L. Field, p. 132. See also discussion in William Chester Jordan, *Men at the Center: Redemptive Governance under Louis IX* (Budapest, 2012), pp. 23–9.

96 Guillaume de Saint-Pathus, 'Vie de Saint Louis', p. 112.

97 Stirnemann, 'Les bibliothèques', p. 181.

98 'Recepta et expensa', p. 231; also ibid., pp. 229, 230, 246. A nickname like Malappareillez could be ironic.

99 'Itinera, dona et hernesia', pp. 589, 590, 591.

100 'Itinera, dona et hernesia', pp. 595, 599, 601: minstrels of Alphonse of Portugal, Arnold of Audenarde and John of Nesle.

101 See above, p. 175. For Theobald's career and poetry, see Terence Newcombe, *Les poésies de Thibaut de Blaison* (Geneva, 1978), pp. 15–19; see also the note by Delisle in *RHF*, xxiv, (1904), i, p. 188.

102 For his gifts to Fontevraud, see Fontevraud Cartulary, BNF MS lat. 5480, vol. ii, p. 7.

103 *LTC*, ii, no. 2027: his widow, Valencia, came to do homage.

104 Alexis Wällensköld, *Les chansons de Thibaut de Champagne, roi de Navarre: édition*

critique (Paris, 1925), p. xix; and for Blanche's probable colouring, see above, p. 32.

105 A.-J.-V. Leroux de Lincy, *Recueil de chants historiques français depuis le XIIe jusqu'au XVIIIe siècle*, vol. i (Paris, 1841), no. i, pp. 165–8; no. ii, pp. 169–71. For Wendover's and Matthew Paris' references to these rumours, see above, p. 77.

106 Eglal Doss-Quinby et al., ed. and trans., *Songs of the Women Trouvères* (New Haven and London, 2001), pp. 30–31.

107 BNF MS n.a.fr. 21677, f. 2r. Doss-Quinby et al., *Songs of the Women Trouvères*, no. 36, pp. 167–70.

108 Vatican City, Biblioteca Apostolica Vaticana, MS Regine lat. 1522, f. 169v: Doss-Quinby et al., *Songs of the Women Trouvères*, no. 12, pp. 106–11. The poem is assigned entirely to Theobald in other manuscripts.

109 For the English baronial songs, see *Thomas Wright's Political Songs of England*, ed. Peter Coss (Cambridge, 1996), pp. 1–127.

110 Leroux de Lincy, *Recueil de chants*, no. i, pp. 166–7; no. iv, p. 177; no. iii, pp. 172–5.

111 Leroux de Lincy, *Recueil de chants*, no. i, p. 167.

112 Matthew Paris, *Chronica majora*, ed. H. R. Luard, 7 vols (London, 1872–83), iii, p. 169; and see above, p. 99.

113 Lindy Grant, 'Le patronage architectural d'Henri ii et de son entourage', *Cahiers de civilisation médiévale*, xxxvii (1994), p. 83.

114 Baldwin, *Government of Philip Augustus*, pp. 345–6 on Paris, pp. 296–302 on Philip's castle building. For Philip's castles, see now Meredith Cohen, *The Sainte-Chapelle and the Construction of Sacral Monarchy: Royal Architecture in Thirteenth-century Paris* (New York, 2015), pp. 18–23.

115 'Un fragment du compte', pp. 243–4, for the expenditure and for Master Fulk and his brother Garin; Master Robert the Carpenter; Master Fulk and Garin of Gonesse for the fosse. For Philip's expenditure of 1,200–2,000

livres per new tower, see Baldwin, *Government of Philip Augustus*, p. 300.

116 For Philip's castle builders, see Baldwin, *Government of Philip Augustus*, p. 582, n. 12.

117 See below, pp. 257–8.

118 Lindy Grant, 'Representing Dynasty: The Transept Windows of Chartres Cathedral', in *Representing History: Art, Music, History*, ed. Robert A. Maxwell (Philadelphia, 2010), p. 111.

119 For the building works of Alfonso and Eleanor, see Rodrigo Jiménez De Rada, *Historia de rebus Hispaniae*, ed. Juan Fernández Valverde (Turnhout, 1987), pp. 255, 256. For their very political use of architecture, see D'Emilio, 'Royal Convent of Las Huelgas', pp. 221, 280–81. See also Miriam Shadis, 'Piety, Politics and Power: The Patronage of Leonor of England and her Daughters, Berenguela of León and Blanche of Castile', in *The Cultural Patronage of Medieval Women*, ed. McCash, pp. 202–27; Rose Walker, 'Leonor of England, Plantagenet Queen of Alfonso VIII of Castile, and her Foundation of the Cistercian Abbey of Las Huelgas: In Imitation of Fontevraud?', *Journal of Medieval History*, XXXI (2005), pp. 346–68.

120 Jean de Joinville, *Vie de Saint Louis*, ed. Jacques Monfrin (Paris, 2010), pp. 374–5, ch. 758.

121 *Les gestes des évêques d'Auxerre*, ed. Guy Lobrichon and Michel Sot, 3 vols (Paris, 2002–9), II, pp. 250–53.

122 The classic account of French Gothic remains Jean Bony, *French Gothic Architecture of the Twelfth and Thirteenth Centuries* (Berkeley and Los Angeles, 1983). See the short overview in Grant, *Architecture and Society in Normandy*, pp. 43–61. For Rayonnant, see Robert Branner, *St Louis and the Court Style in Gothic Architecture* (London, 1965). For building in Paris, see Meredith Cohen and Xavier Dectot, *Paris: ville rayonnante* (Paris, 2010); and Cohen, *Sainte-Chapelle*, pp. 14–33. For Rayonnant architecture in Paris, ibid., pp. 33–63.

123 Caroline Bruzelius, 'The Abbey Church of Longpont and the Architecture of the Cistercians in the Early Thirteenth Century', *Analecta Cisterciensia*, XXXV (1979), p. 29 for the dedication, pp. 90–143 for the architecture of Longpont in context. For Saint-Antoine, see above, p. 214.

124 William of Nangis, *Chronique latine de Guillaume de Nangis*, ed. H. Geraud, 2 vols (Paris, 1843), I, p. 183; and see Caroline Bruzelius, *The Thirteenth-century Church at St-Denis* (New Haven and London, 1985), p. 11.

125 Bruzelius, *Thirteenth-century Church at St-Denis*, pp. 1, 153.

126 Bruzelius, *Thirteenth-century Church at St-Denis*, p. 12.

127 Grant, 'Representing Dynasty'; and see above, p. 85.

128 See above, p. 209.

129 See above for the Hôtel-Dieu hall, p. 207. See also Lindy Grant, 'Royal and Aristocratic Hospital Patronage in Northern France in the Twelfth and Early Thirteenth Centuries', in *Laienadel und Armenfürsorge im Mittelalter*, ed. Lukas Clemens, Katrin Dort and Felix Schumacher (Trier, 2015), pp. 113–14; for Le Mans and Angers, see Lindy Grant, 'The Chapel of the Hospital of Saint-Jean at Angers: Acta, Statutes, Architecture and Interpretation', in *Architecture and Interpretation: Essays for Eric Fernie*, ed. Jill Franklin, T. A. Heslop and Christine Stevenson (Woodbridge, 2012), pp. 306–14.

130 For 1232, see *GC*, VIII, col. 1158; for 1236, see Branner, *St Louis and the Court Style*, p. 33.

131 'Magna recepta de termino Ascensionis, anno Domini MCCXXXVIII mense Mayo et magna expensa', in *RHF*, XXI (1855), p. 260.

132 For Royaumont, see Bruzelius, 'Abbey Church of Longpont', pp. 30–39.

133 'Compotus ballivorum et praepositorum Franciae anno Domini 1234 mense Junio de termino ascensionis', in *RHF*, XXII (1865), pp. 576, 578; *LTC*, II, nos. 2200, 2201, 2204. See also François Comte, 'L'enceinte de Saint Louis à Angers: restitution d'une fortification dispa-

rue', in *Saint Louis et l'Anjou*, ed. Etienne Vacquet (Rennes, 2014), pp. 81–92; and Emmanuel Litoux, 'Un paysage castral dominé par le Château d'Angers', in ibid., pp. 67–80, esp. pp. 72–80. For William's letter, see above, p. 124. I would like to thank Emmanuel Litoux for his kindness in discussing the results of recent investigations at Angers on site.

134 'Compotus ballivorum', pp. 567–9, 578.

135 'Compotus ballivorum', p. 567.

136 'Compotus ballivorum', p. 575.

137 'Compotus praepositorum et ballivorum Franciae de termino ascensionis, AD MCCX-LVIII', in *RHF*, XXI (1855), p. 274.

138 'Compotus ballivorum', p. 578.

139 *LTC*, II, no. 2727. Branner, *St Louis and the Court Style*, p. 51, assumed that Louis replaced a new chapel built by Philip Augustus, but see the comments in Claudine Billot, 'Les Saintes Chapelles de Saint-Louis: conditions et signification de ces fondations', in *Vincennes: aux origines de l'état moderne. Actes du colloque scientifique sur 'Les Capétiens à Vincennes au moyen âge'*, ed. Jean Chapelot and Elisabeth Lalou (Paris, 1996), p. 173, who says that Philip merely established daily service there.

140 'Itinera, dona et hernesia', pp. 590, 588.

141 Bruzelius, *Thirteenth-century Church at St-Denis*, pp. 110–13; Branner, *St Louis and the Court Style*, pp. 51–3; Cohen, *Sainte-Chapelle*, pp. 131–5.

142 'Compotus praepositorum', pp. 284, 261, 262.

143 Branner, *St Louis and the Court Style*, pp. 56–65; for the dedication as part of Crusade ceremonial, see William Chester Jordan, *Louis IX and the Challenge of the Crusade: A Study in Rulership* (Princeton, 1979), pp. 108–9.

144 On the architecture of the chapel: Branner, *St Louis and the Court Style*, pp. 61–3; Stephen Murray, 'The Architectural Envelope of the Sainte-Chapelle of Paris', in *Pierre, lumière, couleur: études d'histoire de l'art du moyen âge en honneur d'Anne Prache*, ed. Fabienne Joubert and Dany Sandron (Paris,

1999), pp. 223–30; Meredith Cohen, 'An Indulgence for the Visitor: The Public at the Sainte-Chapelle of Paris', *Speculum*, LXXXIII (2008), pp. 840–83; Cohen, *Sainte-Chapelle*, esp. pp. 92–125.

145 Beat Brenk 'The Sainte-Chapelle as a Capetian Political Programme', in *Artistic Integration in Gothic Buildings*, ed. V. Raguin, K. Brush and P. Draper (Toronto, 1996), pp. 195–213; Daniel H. Weiss, *Art and Crusade in the Age of Saint Louis* (Cambridge, 1998), pp. 11–74. For the glazing programme, see the comprehensive discussion in Alyce Jordan, *Visualising Kingship in the Windows of the Sainte-Chapelle* (Turnhout, 2002), esp. pp. 44–55 for the Esther and Judith windows, and pp. 58–69 for the Relic Window. There are several useful articles in *La Sainte-Chapelle de Paris: royaume de France ou Jérusalem céleste?*, ed. Christine Hediger (Turnhout, 2007), esp. Stephan Gasser, 'L'architecture de la Sainte-Chapelle: état de la question concernant sa datation, son maître d'œuvre et sa place dans l'histoire de l'architecture', pp. 157–80.

146 The total was 680 *livres* 113 *solidi* 9 *deniers*: 'Compotus praepositorum', p. 284.

147 Walter Cornut, 'Historia susceptionis Coronae spineae', in *RHF*, XXII (1865), pp. 27–32, esp. p. 27; and see above, pp. 116–17.

148 For the architecture of Blanche's Cistercian foundations, see Terryl Kinder, 'Blanche of Castile and the Cistercians: An Architectural Re-evaluation of Maubuisson Abbey', *Cîteaux: commentarii cistercienses*, XXVII (1976), pp. 161–88; Alexandra Gajewski-Kennedy, 'Recherches sur l'architecture cistercienne et le pouvoir royal: Blanche de Castille et la construction de l'abbaye du Lys', in *Art et architecture à Melun au Moyen âge*, ed. Yves Gallet (Paris, 2000), pp. 223–54; and now the substantial and richly suggestive article, Alexandra Gajewski, 'The Patronage Question under Review: Queen Blanche of Castile (1188–1252) and the Architecture of the Cistercian Abbeys at Royaumont, Maubuisson and

Le Lys', in *Reassessing the Roles of Women as 'Makers' of Medieval Art and Architecture*, ed. Therese Martin, 2 vols (Leiden and Boston, Mass., 2012), I, pp. 197–244.

149 L'Epinois, 'Comptes relatifs', p. 551; and see above, pp. 118–20.

150 BNF MS lat. 406, f. 389.

151 E.g., L'Epinois, 'Comptes relatifs', p. 556: 'feast of St Andrew (1237), on which day master Richard 'computavit' with the lady queen'.

152 *Achatz d'heritage*, ADVO 72H12. L'Epinois focused on these sections in his publication 'Comptes relatifs', but some information relating to building remains unpublished.

153 Listed three times, including for making the dormitory carpentry: L'Epinois, 'Comptes relatifs', pp. 560, 561.

154 L'Epinois, 'Comptes relatifs', pp. 558 62.

155 L'Epinois, 'Comptes relatifs', pp. 560, 561.

156 L'Epinois, 'Comptes relatifs', pp. 561, 562, where John Morier supplies 100 carved corbels, as well as dealing in timber.

157 L'Epinois, 'Comptes relatifs', p. 60: wood and panels for the side of the cloister; p. 561: beams for the cloister of the infirmary. St Louis gave substantial properties in the forest of Breteuil in the Evreçin to Maubuisson in 1246 (*Cartulaire normand de Philippe Auguste, Louis VIII, Saint Louis et Philippe-le-Hardi*, ed. Léopold Delisle, Caen, 1852, p. 76, no. 462), and in 1248 Blanche gave them property in the area that she had bought in 1246 from Bouchard of Marly (sealed original, ADVO 72H97, also AN K191, no 12/7, f. 126); and see Alphonse Dutilleux and Joseph Depoin, *Cartulaire de l'abbaye de Maubuisson (Notre-Dame-la-Royale), II: contrats* (Pontoise, 1913), p. 118, no. 252. But she was already acquiring wood from the forests of the Evreçin, supplied by Master Geoffrey the Norman and Walter of Vielles-Conches, in the late 1230s. She also obtained a great deal of wood from Cuisy, near

Soissons, in the late 1230s: *Achatz d'heritage*, ADVO 72H12, ff. 20–22.

158 *Achatz d'heritage*, ADVO 72H12, f. 27.

159 L'Epinois, 'Comptes relatifs', p. 560. For an analysis of the highly sophisticated water provision at Maubuisson, see Christophe Toupet and Monique Wabont, 'L'abbaye cistercienne de Maubuisson (Val d'Oise, France): les réseaux hydrauliques du XIIIe au XVIIe siècle', in *L'hydraulique monastique: milieux, réseaux, usages*, ed. L. Pressouyre et al. (Grâne, 1996), pp. 139–48, and pp. 146–59 for the cloister fountain, revealed by Monique Wabont's excavations.

160 For Marquette, see B. Chauvin and G. Delepierre, 'Le mausolée de la comtesse Jeanne à l'abbaye de Marquette: essai de restitution', *Revue du Nord*, no. 368 (2006), pp. 109–25.

161 For Le Lys, see Gajewski-Kennedy, 'Recherches'; Gajewski, 'Patronage Question'; and Armande Gronier-Prieur, *L'abbaye Notre-Dame du Lys à Dammarie-lès-Lys* (Verneuil-l'Etang, 1976).

162 *Statuta Capitulorum generalium ordinis Cisterciensis ab anno 116 ad annum 1786*, ed. Joseph Canivez, 8 vols (Louvain, 1935), II, p. 331.

163 Le Lys Cartulary, BNF MS lat. 13892, ff. 25–6.

164 Le Lys Cartulary, BNF MS lat. 13892, ff. 28v–29.

165 Act making a gift to Nemours issued by Blanche at Le Lys, October 1251: Institut de France, Académie des Inscriptions et Belles-Lettres, Fonds Louis Carolus-Barré, no. 2, Cartulaire de La Joie-lès-Nemours, no. clvi. See also a mandate to the constable of Carcassonne issued in October 1251 at Le Lys: BNF, Collection Doat, vol. 154, f. 97.

166 'Comptes de dépenses', p. 89; BNF MS lat. 9017, f. 69.

167 *Statuta Capitulorum generalium ordinis Cisterciensis*, II, pp. 167, 225. Armelle Bonis and Monique Wabont, 'Cisterciens et Cisterciennes en France du nord-ouest: typologie des fonda-

tions, typologie des sites', in *Cîteaux et les femmes*, ed. Armelle Bonis, Sylvie Dechavanne and Monique Wabont (Paris, 2001), p. 162.

168 'Itinera, dona et hernesia', pp. 600, 607; 'Comptes de dépenses', p. 89; BNF MS lat. 9017, f. 69.

169 *Statuta Capitulorum generalium ordinis Cisterciensis*, II, p. 156.

170 BNF MS lat. 9017, f. 69; 'Comptes de dépenses', p. 90.

171 Grant, *Architecture and Society in Normandy*, pp. 207–8.

172 BNF MS lat. 9017, f. 69; 'Comptes de dépenses', pp. 89, 90. Bougenot did not identify all expenditure on Corbeil in his edition of BL Add. Ch. 4129.

173 'Compotus ballivorum', p. 567. For the water systems at Royaumont and Maubuisson, see Toupet and Wabont, 'L'abbaye cistercienne de Maubuisson', pp. 139–48; Marc Viré, 'Le système hydraulique de l'abbaye cistercienne de Royaumont du XIIIe au XVIIIe siècles', in *L'hydraulique monastique*, ed. L. Pressouyre et al., pp. 257–69; Bonis and Wabont, 'Cisterciens et Cisterciennes', pp. 165–7. For the works at Vincennes, see Jean Chapelot, 'L'eau dans le manoir et le château', in *Vincennes: du manoir capétien à la résidence de Charles V* ([Dijon], 2004), pp. 28–30.

174 'Compotus ballivorum', p. 575; 'Compotus praepositorum', p. 274.

175 Branner, *St Louis and the Court Style*, p. 39. But see the discussion in Gajewski, 'Patronage Question'.

176 Bruzelius, 'Abbey Church of Longpont', p. 97.

177 See also the important contributions to this discussion of Bruzelius, *Thirteenth-century Church at St-Denis*, esp. pp. 162–5; and Bruzelius, 'Abbey Church of Longpont'.

178 For building in Paris, see Cohen and Dectot, *Paris: ville rayonnante*; and Cohen, *Sainte-Chapelle*, pp. 92–105.

179 For Henry III and the Sainte-Chapelle, see *Thomas Wright's Political Songs of England*,

p. 67: 'Song of the Peace with England' – 'Paris fout vil mult grant/Il i a .i. chapel don't je fi coetant/Je le ferra portier, a .i. charrier rollant,/ a Saint Amont a Londres toute droit en estant.'

For the influence of the moralised bibles in England, see Lowden, *Making of the Bibles Moralisées*, I, p. 187.

180 Bruzelius, *Thirteenth Century Church at St-Denis*, p. 163.

181 Stirnemann, 'Les bibliothèques', pp. 181–4.

11   LEGITIMACY AND AUTHORITY

1 The definition is from Mary Erler and Maryanne Kowalski, 'Introduction', in *Women and Power in the Middle Ages*, ed. Mary Erler and Maryanne Kowalski (Athens, Ga., 1988), p. 2; and see above, pp. 4–5.

2 Ivo of Chartres, 'Decretum', *PL*, vol. CLXI, col. 912, ch. 39, and cols 913–14, ch. 42.

3 Suger, *Vie de Louis VI le Gros*, ed. and trans. Henri Waquet (Paris, 1929), esp. pp. 100–02; and see Lindy Grant, *Abbot Suger of St-Denis: Church and State in Early Twelfth-century France* (London, 1998), p. 17.

4 Beryl Smalley, *The Becket Conflict and the Schools: A Study of Intellectuals in Politics* (Oxford, 1973).

5 For the episode, see John W. Baldwin, *The Government of Philip Augustus: Foundations of French Royal Power in the Middle Ages* (Berkeley, Cal., 1986), pp. 185–6.

6 Grant, *Abbot Suger of St-Denis*, p. 17; Suger, *Œuvres complètes de Suger, recueillies, annotées et publiées d'après les manuscrits*, ed. A. Lecoy de la Marche (Paris, 1867), p. 278.

7 John of Salisbury, *Policraticus, sive De nugis curialium et vestigiis philosophorum*, ed. C.C.J. Webb, 2 vols (Oxford, 1909), II, Book VIII, pp. 709–822 on dealing with tyrants; for Judith and other positive Old Testament examples, ibid., II, pp. 794–7; on the body politic,

ibid., I, pp. 540–42. For discussion, see Richard H. Rouse and Mary A. Rouse, 'John of Salisbury and the Doctrine of Tyrannicide', *Speculum*, XLII (1967), pp. 693–709; Cary Nedermann, 'A Duty to Kill: John of Salisbury's Theory of Tyrannicide', *Review of Politics*, L (1988), pp. 365–89. The concept of the body politic could have been derived from, e.g., Honorius of Autun's metaphor of the Church as Christ's body: see Caroline Bynum, *The Resurrection of the Body in Western Christianity, 200–1336* (New York, 1995), p. 141. For the influence of *Policraticus*, see Julie Barrau, 'Ceci n'est pas un miroir; ou, le *Policraticus* de Jean de Salisbury', in *Le prince au miroir de la littérature politique de l'antiquité aux lumières*, ed. Frédérique Lachaud and Lydwine Scordia (Rouen, 2007), pp. 108–9.

8   Philippe Buc, *L'ambigüité du livre: prince, pouvoir et peuple dans les commentaires de la Bible au moyen âge* (Paris, 1994), passim, but esp. pp. 36–9, 350–78; Philippe Buc, '"Principes Gentium dominantur eorum": Princely Powers between Legitimacy and Illegitimacy in Twelfth-century Exegesis', in *Cultures of Power: Lordship, Status and Process in Twelfth-century Europe*, ed. Thomas Bisson (Philadelphia, 1995), pp. 310–28.

9   See the firmness of Louis IX's claims as protector of the Church in his Protest of 1247, in Matthew Paris, *Chronica majora*, ed. H. R. Luard, 7 vols (London, 1872–83), VI, pp. 99–112, esp. p. 110. See also above, pp. 191–2.

10   For Louis VII asleep beneath the tree, see Walter Map, *De nugis curialium/Courtiers' Trifles*, ed. M. R. James, C.N.L. Brooke and R.A.B. Mynors (Oxford, 1983), pp. 452–3.

11   F. M. Powicke, *Stephen Langton* (Oxford, 1928), pp. 102–8; Nicholas Vincent, 'Stephen Langton, Archbishop of Canterbury', in *Etienne Langton: prédicateur, bibliste, théologien*, ed. L.-J. Bataillon et al. (Turnhout, 2010), esp. pp. 73–7 and p. 84, n. 115.

12   See, e.g., ÖNB Cod. Vindob. 2554, in Gerald B. Guest, *Bible moralisée: Codex Vindobonensis 2554, Vienna, Österreichische National-*

bibliothek (London, 1995), f. 19r and p. 73; f. 41v and p. 118: bad counsellors; f. 28v and pp. 85, 86: bad *prévôts*.

13   Buc, '"Principes Gentium dominantur eorum"', pp. 316–21; Buc, *L'ambigüité du livre*, esp. pp. 147–70. Gerald of Wales, 'De principis instructione', in *Giraldi Cambrensis opera*, vol. VIII, ed. G. F. Warner (London, 1891), pp. 8–9. See also discussion above, pp. 194–5.

14   ÖNB Cod. Vindob. 2554 in Guest, *Bible moralisée*, for bad clergy: f. 19v and p. 73, f. 23r and p. 79, ff. 28v and 29r and p. 86, f. 29v and p. 87, and see discussion in introduction, pp. 32–3; for sodomy and pederasty: f. 36r and p. 109; and see Robert Mills, 'Seeing Sodomy in the *Bible Moralisée*', *Speculum*, LXXXVII (2012), pp. 413–68. John of Salisbury, *Policraticus*, II, pp. 690–96.

15   For general discussion of coronation orders, especially the French ones, see Janet L. Nelson, 'The Lord's Anointed and the People's Choice: Carolingian Royal Ritual', in Nelson, *The Frankish World, 750–900* (London, 1996), pp. 99–131; Richard A. Jackson, ed., *Ordines coronationis Franciae: Texts and Ordines for the Coronation of the Frankish and French Kings and Queens in the Middle Ages*, 2 vols (Philadelphia, 1995–2000), esp. I, pp. 21–8; Jacques Le Goff et al., *Le sacre royal à l'époque de Saint-Louis* (Paris, 2001). See also above, pp. 61–2.

16   See discussion in John W. Baldwin, *Masters, Princes and Merchants: The Social Views of Peter the Chanter and his Circle*, 2 vols (Princeton, 1970), I, p. 173; Buc, *L'ambigüité du livre*, pp. 314–33.

17   Bjorn Weiler, 'Kingship, Usurpation and Propaganda in Twelfth-century Europe: The Case of Stephen', *Anglo-Norman Studies*, XXIII (2001), pp. 303–5.

18   Walter Map, *De nugis curialium/ Courtiers' Trifles*, pp. 442–51; Gerald of Wales, 'De principis instructione', pp. 57ff.

19   Baldwin, *Masters, Princes and Merchants*, I, p. 174.

20   For Capetian succession strategy, see Andrew Lewis, *Royal Succession in Capetian*

France: Studies on Familial Order and the State (Cambridge, Mass., 1981).

21 *Les registres de Philippe Auguste*, ed. J. W. Baldwin (Paris, 1992), p. 352: 'Hugo Capetus electus a baronibus'.

22 Weiler, 'Kingship, Usurpation and Propaganda'.

23 John Gillingham, 'At the Deathbeds of the Kings of England, 1066–1216', in *Herrscher- und Fürstentestamente im westeuropäischen Mittelalter*, ed. Brigitte Kasten (Cologne, 2008), pp. 509–30: Gillingham notes that in England up to *circa* 1200 the wishes of the dying king conferred legitimacy; by 1220 election or inheritance had become the crucial element: ibid., pp. 515–17.

24 *Les registres de Philippe Auguste*, p. 545: 'Blancha...optato partu Francis dominum dat et Anglis'.

25 Roger of Wendover, *Flores historiarum*, ed. H. G. Hewlett, 3 vols (London, 1886–9), II, p. 178: 'ratione uxore sui'. See narrative above, pp. 50–57.

26 Roger of Wendover, *Flores historiarum*, II, p. 177.

27 William the Breton, 'Gesta Philippi Augusti', in *Oeuvres de Rigord et Guillaume le Breton*, ed. H. Delaborde, 2 vols (Paris, 1882–5), I, p. 170: 'electus a baronibus'; *Les registres de Philippe Auguste*, pp. 351–2: 'per conspectum baronum Francie'; 'electus a baronibus'.

28 Gerald of Wales, 'De principis instructione', p. 133.

29 Roger of Wendover, *Flores historiarum*, II, p. 185.

30 *Les registres de Philippe Auguste*, pp. 554–5.

31 Roger of Wendover, *Flores historiarum*, II, p. 185, and see above, pp. 54–5.

32 See above, pp. 2–11.

33 Marc Bloch, *Les rois thaumaturges*, 2nd edn (Paris, 1961), pp. 199–200.

34 For the queen's coronation liturgy in thirteenth-century French orders, see Jackson, ed., *Ordines coronationis Franciae*, I, pp. 264–7; II, pp. 303–4, 362–6; Le Goff et al., *Le sacre royal*, pp. 288–91, 306–7. See discussion in Janet L. Nelson, 'Early Medieval Rites of Queen-Making and the Shaping of Medieval Queenship', in *Queens and Queenship in Medieval Europe*, ed. Anne J. Duggan (Woodbridge, 1997), pp. 302–5.

35 See text for the rod and sceptre of the king in Le Goff et al., *Le sacre royal*, pp. 282–3; Jackson, ed., *Ordines coronationis Franciae*, II, pp. 358–9.

36 Le Goff et al., *Le sacre royal*, pp. 260–61, 266–7; Jackson, ed., *Ordines coronationis Franciae*, II, pp. 346, 351.

37 'Regnique sui consortium' and 'regnique sui participium'. For these phrases in the 'Ordo of 1250', see Le Goff et al., *Le sacre royal*, pp. 292–3; Jackson, ed., *Ordines coronationis Franciae*, II, p. 364; for these phrases in the 'Ordo of 1200', ibid., I, p. 265.

38 George Conklin, 'Ingeborg of Denmark, Queen of France, 1193–1223', in *Queens and Queenship in Medieval Europe*, ed. Anne J. Duggan, pp. 39–52, esp. pp. 41–4, 46. See Ingeborg's letter to Pope Celestine of 1194 (*RHF*, XIX, 1833, p. 314), saying that she has been 'regali solio sublimata'; and *RHF*, XIX (1833), pp. 322–3, her letter to the dean and chapter of the cathedral of Amiens, reminding them that she received 'the unction of royal dignity' there, and the dean's agreement that she 'received the unction of sacred benediction and the crown of the kingdom'. See also ibid., p. 315, a letter to Ingeborg from Abbot William of the Paraclete, saying that God has the power to set her back again in full power, so that her sublimity would command at the head of the people and would hold the throne of glory: 'quia potens est Dominus statuere vos iterum in plenitudinem potestatis, ut vestra sublimitas in caput gentium imperet populis et solium gloriae teneat'.

39 Grant, *Abbot Suger of St-Denis*, p. 157, for the arrangements for the regency; pp. 174–6, for Adela during the regency.

40 Rigord, *Histoire de Philippe Auguste*, ed. Elisabeth Carpentier, Georges Pon and Yves Chauvin (Paris, 2006), pp. 274–5; pp. 276–85 for the text of the ordinance. Baldwin, *Government of Philip Augustus*, pp. 102–4. For a broad view of Capetian queens as regents, see Jean Poulet, 'Capetian Women and the Regency: The Genesis of a Vocation', in *Medieval Queenship*, ed. John Carmi Parsons (New York, 1993), pp. 93–116.

41 *Ordonnances des roys de France de la troisième race, recueillies par ordre chronologique*, ed. Eusèbe Laurière et al., 21 vols (Paris, 1723–1849), I, pp. 60–61. See discussion above, p. 134. *LTC*, v, no. 514; and see William Chester Jordan, *Louis IX and the Challenge of the Crusade: A Study in Rulership* (Princeton, 1979), p. 92.

42 Lewis, *Royal Succession in Capetian France*, pp. 45–7.

43 Baldwin, *Government of Philip Augustus*, esp. p. 15.

44 D. A. Carpenter, *The Minority of Henry III* (London, 1990), pp. 123–4.

45 Carpenter, *Minority of Henry III*, pp. 123–4.

46 Achille Luchaire, *Manuel des institutions françaises: période des Capétiens directs* (Paris, 1892), p. 171.

47 Baldwin, *Government of Philip Augustus*, pp. 278–9.

48 Luchaire, *Manuel des institutions françaises*, p. 468.

49 Lewis, *Royal Succession in Capetian France*, pp. 45–7.

50 Carpenter, *Minority of Henry III*, pp. 13–19, 123–4, 240–41; Gillingham, 'At the Deathbeds of the Kings of England', pp. 520–21. For brief discussion of the minorities of St Louis, Henry VII of Germany and James I of Aragón, see also Christian Hillen and Frank Wiswall, 'The Minority of Henry III in the Context of Europe', in *The Royal Minorities of Medieval and Early Modern England*, ed.

Charles Beem (New York and Basingstoke, 2008), pp. 17–66.

51 Theresa Vann, 'The Theory and Practice of Medieval Castilian Queenship', in *Queens, Regents and Potentates*, ed. Theresa Vann (Dallas, 1993), pp. 139–40.

52 Miriam Shadis, *Berenguela of Castile (1180–1246) and Political Women in the High Middle Ages* (New York, 2009), pp. 86–95; Janna Bianchini, *The Queen's Hand: Power and Authority in the Reign of Berenguela of Castile* (Philadelphia, 2012), pp. 105–22.

53 Shadis, *Berenguela of Castile*, pp. 98–107, 125–39.

54 *LTC*, II, nos. 1813–21; and see above, pp. 64–5.

55 For Blanche of Navarre's rule, see *Littere baronum: The Earliest Cartulary of the Counts of Champagne*, ed. Theodore Evergates (Toronto, 2003), introduction by Evergates, esp. pp. 11–12, 16–17.

56 Lois Huneycutt, *Matilda of Scotland: A Study in Medieval Queenship* (Woodbridge, 2003), esp. pp. 78–93; Ralph V. Turner, *Eleanor of Aquitaine* (London and New Haven, 2009), pp. 150–55, 174; Marjorie Chibnall, *The Empress Matilda: Queen Consort, Queen Mother and Lady of the English* (Oxford, 1991), p. 161.

57 Jane Martindale, 'Eleanor of Aquitaine: The Last Years', in *King John: New Interpretations*, ed. S. D. Church (Woodbridge, 1999), pp. 137–64; and see further below, p. 285.

58 Jean de Joinville, *Vie de Saint Louis*, ed. Jacques Monfrin (Paris, 2010), pp. 36–7, ch. 72.

59 For further analysis of Blanche's supporters, see below, p. 293–4.

60 For the issue of private war in France and England, see Richard Kaeuper, *War, Justice and Public Order: England and France in the Later Middle Ages* (Oxford, 1988), pp. 225–67, esp. pp. 231–5; John Hudson, 'Feud, Vengeance and Violence in England from the Tenth to the Twelfth Centuries', in *Feud, Violence and Practice: Essays in Medieval Studies in Honour of*

Stephen D. White, ed. Belle S. Tuten and Tracey L. Ballado (Farnham, 2010), pp. 45–7. For de Beaumanoir, see *The Coutumes de Beauvaisis of Philippe de Beaumanoir*, ed. and trans. F.R.P. Akehurst (Philadephia, 1992), ch. 59, pp. 610–18.

61 E.g., *LTC*, III, no. 3978.

62 *LTC*, III, no. 3915.

63 *LTC*, III, no. 3914.

64 *LTC*, III, no. 3975.

65 *LTC*, III, no. 3976.

66 Matthew Paris, *Chronica majora*, V, p. 354. The force of 'dominarum saecularium domina' is lost in the translation 'Lady'.

67 Guillaume de Saint-Pathus, 'Vie de Saint Louis, par le confesseur de la reine Marguerite', in *RHF*, XX (1840), p. 64.

68 *Statuta Capitulorum generalium ordinis Cisterciensis ab anno 116 ad annum 1786*, ed. Joseph Canivez, 8 vols (Louvain, 1935), I, p. 325. For Isabella of Angoulême at Poitiers, see p. 125.

69 *Corpus des sceaux français du Moyen Age, III: les sceaux des reines et des enfants de France*, by Marie-Adélaïde Nielen (Paris, 2011), p. 33: in particular, Blanche used seals and corroborative clauses when an act aimed to have perpetual effect, but neither when an act would have immediate or short-term effect.

70 Jacques Le Goff, *Saint Louis* (Paris, 1996), pp. 128, 174.

71 See discussion in Shadis, *Berenguela of Castile*, esp. pp. 55–6, 60.

72 Andrew Lewis, 'Anticipatory Association of the Heir in Early Capetian France', *American Historical Review*, LXXXIII (1978), pp. 906–27; Lewis, *Royal Succession in Capetian France*, esp. pp. 39–41, 74–7.

73 Carpenter, *Minority of Henry III*, p. 389.

74 Lois Huneycutt, 'The Creation of a Crone: The Historical Reputation of Adelaide of Maurienne', in *Capetian Women*, ed. Kathleen Nolan (New York, 2003), pp. 27–43.

75 Chibnall, *Empress Matilda*, p. 161.

76 Chibnall, *Empress Matilda*, esp. pp. 158–73; for Matilda and the Becket controversy, ibid., esp. pp. 169–73.

77 Martindale, 'Eleanor of Aquitaine'; Turner, *Eleanor of Aquitaine*, pp. 256–98.

78 William the Breton, 'Gesta Philippi Augusti', p. 256; Jacques Krynen, *L'empire du roi: idées et croyances politiques en France, XIIIe–XVe siècle* (Paris, 1993), p. 55.

79 See above, p. 151.

80 Joinville, *Vie de Saint Louis*, pp. 194–7, chs 397–9; ibid., pp. 320–23, 312–15, 298–9, chs 645–7, 630–33, 601.

81 Louis-Claude Doüet d'Arcq, *Comptes de l'Hôtel des Rois de France aux XIV au XV siècles* (Paris, 1865), pp. v–vi.

82 Edgar Boutaric, 'Marguerite de Provence, femme de Saint Louis: son caractère, son rôle politique', *Revue des questions historiques*, III (1867), pp. 417–58 (article reprinted Paris, 1867, pp. 10–12); Jordan, *Louis IX*, p. 6.

83 Elizabeth A. R. Brown, 'The Prince is the Father of the King: The Character and Childhood of Philip the Fair of France', in *The Monarchy of Capetian France and Royal Ceremonial* (Aldershot, 1991), article II, pp. 304–6 [reprinted from *Medieval Studies*, XL, 1987]; Charles T. Wood, *The French Apanages and the Capetian Monarchy, 1224–1328* (Cambridge, Mass., 1966), p. 58.

84 D. A. Carpenter, *The Struggle for Mastery: Britain, 1066–1284* (Oxford, 2003), p. 468. For Eleanor of Provence's position as regent, with the custody of the kingdom and the heir, see Margaret Howell, *Eleanor of Provence: Queenship in Thirteenth-century England* (Oxford, 1998), pp. 111, 112, 114–15.

85 Guillaume de Saint-Pathus, 'Vie de Saint Louis', p. 65.

86 For Margaret's extensive diplomacy during the Barons' War, see Edgar Boutaric, *Saint Louis et Alphonse de Poitiers: études sur la réunion des provinces du Midi et de l'Ouest à la couronne* (Paris, 1870), pp. 98–111; Boutaric, 'Marguerite de Provence', reprint pp. 15–26.

87 Jean Dunbabin, *Charles I of Anjou: Power, Kingship and State-Making in Thirteenth-century Europe* (London, 1998), p. 54; Boutaric,

'Marguerite de Provence', reprint pp. 9–10, 33–43.

88 Marion F. Facinger, 'A Study of Medieval Queenship: Capetian France, 987–1237', *Studies in Medieval and Renaissance History*, v (1968), pp. 3–48. See the thoughtful discussion in Miriam Shadis, 'Blanche of Castile and Facinger's "Medieval Queenship": Reassessing the Argument', in *Capetian Women*, ed. Nolan, pp. 137–61.

89 E.g., *LTC*, iii, no. 3863.

90 See the astute comments by Howell, *Eleanor of Provence*, pp. 255–86, on Eleanor as queen consort, and pp. 287–312, on Eleanor's relationship with Edward i.

12 RULER AND COUNSELLOR

1 Guillaume de Saint-Pathus, 'Vie de Saint Louis, par le confesseur de la reine Marguerite', in *RHF*, xx (1840), pp. 65, 64; Geoffrey of Beaulieu, 'Vita ludovici noni', in *RHF*, xx (1840), p. 4; Geoffrey of Beaulieu, 'Here Begins the Life and Saintly Comportment of Louis, Formerly King of the Franks, of Pious Memory', in *The Sanctity of Louis IX: Early Lives of Saint Louis by Geoffrey of Beaulieu and William of Chartres*, trans. Larry F. Field, ed. M. Cecilia Gaposchkin and Sean L. Field (Ithaca, 2014), pp. 74, 105. On the meaning of 'preudomme' and 'preude femme' – in this case, 'wise woman', or 'woman of courtesy and good counsel', or even 'model woman', see David Crouch, *The Birth of Nobility: Constructing Aristocracy in England and France, 900–1300* (Harlow, 2005), pp. 30–37, esp. p. 37 for the use of *preudomme* at St Louis's court.

2 Aubri of Trois-Fontaines, 'Chronica Albrici Monachi Trium Fontium', in *MGH Scriptores*, xxiii, ed. Paul Scheffer-Boichorst (Hanover, 1874), p. 949.

3 Matthew Paris, *Chronica majora*, ed. H. R. Luard, 7 vols (London, 1872–83), v, p. 354.

4 A.-J.-V. Leroux de Lincy, *Recueil de chants historiques français depuis le XIIe jusqu'au XVIIIe siècle*, vol. i (Paris, 1841), no. i, p. 167.

5 University of Birmingham, MSS 6/iii/19, f. lv, cols a–b: 'Unde usque hodie dicitur quod domina Brancha regina Francie adeo bene rexit regnum Francie et dominium eius auxit, quod nullus alius melius post eam rexit.' From a 'collatio de muliere bona'. I would like to thank David D'Avray for providing me with this text, and its context.

6 AN J461, no. 4; and see above, p. 223.

7 See above, pp. 63–4.

8 Philippe Mousket, *Chronique rimée*, ed. Frédéric de Reiffenberg, 2 vols (Brussels, 1836–8), ii, p. 490, vv. 25,451–25,452: 'Madame Blance l'octroia/La roine, c'on moult proisa'.

9 Jean de Joinville, *Vie de Saint Louis*, ed. Jacques Monfrin (Paris, 2010), pp. 36–7, ch. 72.

10 For Philip and the city merchants and trade, see John W. Baldwin, *Paris, 1200* (Stanford, Cal., 2010), pp. 47–50.

11 For these families, see Nicolas Civel, *La fleur de France: les seigneurs d'Ile-de-France au XIIe siècle* (Turnhout, 2006), esp. pp. 23–79.

12 *LTC*, ii, no. 2063.

13 Joinville, *Vie de Saint Louis*, pp. 36–7, 40–43, chs 72, 81–3.

14 Leroux de Lincy, *Recueil de chants*, no. ii, p. 171: 'Bien est France abastardie/ [Signeur baron, entendés]/Quant feme l'a em Baillie'; ibid., no. ii, p. 167: 'L'autre jour a Compaigne, Quant li baron ne porent droit avoir/ Ne ne.s deigna esguarder ne veoir'. See also *Chansons des trouvères, chanter m'estuet*, ed. Samuel N. Rosenberg, Hans Tischler and Marie-Geneviève Grossel (Paris, 1995), pp. 576–7, 572–3.

15 John W. Baldwin, *The Government of Philip Augustus: Foundations of French Royal Power in the Middle Ages* (Berkeley, Cal., 1986), p. 262; *Les registres de Philippe Auguste*, ed. J. W. Baldwin (Paris, 1992), pp. 327–35: 'État des ducs et comtes; État des barons du roi; État des chastellains; État des vavasseurs'.

16 Baldwin, *Government of Philip Augustus*,

esp. pp. 259–94; Gabrielle Spiegel, *Romancing the Past: The Rise of Vernacular Prose Historiography in Thirteenth-century France* (Berkeley, Cal., 1993), pp. 11–54; Richard Kaeuper, *War, Justice and Public Order: England and France in the Later Middle Ages* (Oxford, 1988), pp. 272–4, 316–25; *The Coutumes de Beauvaisis of Philippe de Beaumanoir*, ed. and trans. F.R.P. Akehurst (Philadephia, 1992), p. 363; Jean Dunbabin, 'The Political World of France, *c.*1200–*c.*1336', in *France in the Later Middle Ages, 1200–1500*, ed. David Potter (Oxford, 2002), pp. 35–7.

17 Baldwin, *Government of Philip Augustus*, pp. 104–6.

18 See below, pp. 305-7. For the English evidence, see David Crouch, *The English Aristocracy, 1072–1272: A Social Transformation* (London and New Haven, 2011), pp. 65–83, and esp. pp. 74–83 for conciliar rule under the Angevin kings, and the increasing exclusion of the magnates from counsel and policy.

19 See above, p. 59.

20 E.g., *LTC*, II, nos. 1595, 1713.

21 *LTC*, II, no. 1708.

22 Charles Petit-Dutaillis, *Etude sur la vie et le règne de Louis VIII* (Paris, 1894), appendix vi, catalogue des actes, no. 373, p. 499.

23 See discussion in Andrew Lewis, *Royal Succession in Capetian France: Studies on Familial Order and the State* (Cambridge, Mass., 1981), pp. 158–61.

24 William Chester Jordan, *Louis IX and the Challenge of the Crusade: A Study in Rulership* (Princeton, 1979), pp. 208–9, n. 156.

25 For the issue of endemic private warfare, see Kaeuper, *War, Justice and Public Order*, esp. pp. 225–67: on St Louis and private warfare, pp. 231–5; see also Jordan, *Louis IX*, p. 204. *Coutumes de Beauvaisis of Philippe de Beaumanoir*, pp. 610–18.

26 For the English political songs, see Peter Coss, 'Introduction', in *Thomas Wright's Political Songs of England*, ed. Peter Coss (Cambridge, 1996), pp. xi–lxvii, esp. p. xxii. The bibliography for the baronial rebellions in

thirteenth-century England is huge. D. A. Carpenter, *The Struggle for Mastery: Britain, 1066–1284* (Oxford, 2003), pp. 272–99, 352–61, 369–82, provides a magisterial overview. For the baronial perspective, see also David Crouch, 'Baronial Paranoia in King John's Reign', in *Magna Carta and the England of King John*, ed. Janet S. Loengard (Woodbridge, 2010), pp. 45–62; and Crouch, *English Aristocracy*, pp. 84–96.

27 See above, pp. 267–8. John W. Baldwin, 'Master Stephen Langton, Future Archbishop of Canterbury: The Paris Schools and Magna Carta', *English Historical Review*, CXXIII (2008), pp. 811–46; and Nicholas Vincent, 'Stephen Langton, Archbishop of Canterbury', in *Etienne Langton: prédicateur, bibliste, théologien*, ed. L.-J. Bataillon et al. (Turnhout, 2010), pp. 51–123, for discussion of the Langtons and the master's contribution to the baronial movement.

28 John Maddicott, *Simon de Montfort* (Cambridge, 1994), pp. 79–84, 84–105.

29 See above, p. 110.

30 See above, p. 97.

31 E.g., treaties of the 1230s: *LTC*, II, nos. 2052, 2060. In the arrangements of the Boulogne inheritance, February 1252: *LTC*, III, no. 3978; AN J390, no. 1.

32 E.g., a judgement of September 1252 is 'mise en Registre le Roi' on Blanche's orders: Edgar Boutaric, *Actes du Parlement de Paris*, 2 vols (Paris, 1863–7), I, cccxx, no. 32. The accounts of 1234 show computing of the account occurring at two-weekly intervals: 'Recepta et expensa Anno MCCXXXIIII inter candelosam et ascensionem', in *RHF*, XXI (1855), p. 228.

33 'Recepta et expensa', pp. 240–42, for all the messengers sent on missions to summon the host in 1234.

34 See above, p. 253.

35 'Ex chronico Turonensi: auctore anonymo, S. Martini Turon. canonico', in *RHF*, XVIII (1879), p. 319; and see above, p. 85.

36 See the comments of Matthew Paris, *Chronica majora*, III, p. 327; Mousket, *Chronique rimée*, II, p. 627; and see above, p. 112–13.

37 'Comptes de dépenses de Blanche de Castille', ed. Etienne Symphorien Bougenot in *Bulletin du Comité des travaux historiques et scientifiques: section d'histoire et de philologie* (1889), p. 91.

38 For Louis's rapprochement with Henry III, see Jacques Le Goff, *Saint Louis* (Paris, 1996), pp. 257–64; for the marriages, ibid., pp. 737–8. See also David Carpenter, 'The Meetings between Kings Henry III and Louis IX', in *Thirteenth Century England, X: Proceedings of the Durham Conference, 2003*, ed. M. Prestwich, R. Britnell and R. Frame (Woodbridge, 2005), pp. 1–30.

39 Leroux de Lincy, *Recueil de chants*, no. i, p. 167.

40 E.g., in the first regency, the freeing of Cadurc on tight terms was settled in the presence of Blanche and Louis: *LTC*, II, no. 1937; the archbishop of Rouen was called to judgement before Blanche in 1227–8: see above, p. 100; the cathedral of Angers appealed to Blanche and Louis in 1232 for compensation for the building of the castle: ibid., no. 2200. See also below the cases in note 41. The Boulogne inheritance arrangement act of February 1252, issued by Blanche, says that the case was settled by 'nos in consilio': *LTC*, III, no. 3978; AN J390, no. 1. The case of the inheritance of Amaury of Meulan, also 1252, was adjudged 'coram dominam reginam': AN JJ26, f. 323v, col. 2.

41 Boutaric, *Actes du Parlement de Paris*, I, p. ccxcvii, no. 2: a judgement issued by Adela and William, archbishop of Reims, 'dum vices regias gereremus'.

42 E.g., November 1234, a case between the bishops of Laon and Châlons-sur-Marne is heard 'in presentia' of Louis and the lady queen his mother: *LTC*, II, no. 2323. December 1237, arrangements due to Joanna of Flanders' second marriage are made in the court held at Compiègne, 'coram' Louis and Blanche:

ibid., no. 2585. See also in 1237, the case between Ralph of Fougères and Guy Mauvoisin is heard in Blanche's presence: ibid., nos. 2390, 2389.

43 Quentin Griffiths, 'New Men among the Lay Counsellors of Saint Louis' Parlement', *Medieval Studies*, XXXII (1970), pp. 234–72; Jean Hilaire, *La construction de l'état de droit dans les archives judiciaires de la cour de France au XIIIe siècle* (Paris, 2011), pp. 22–36.

44 See Joinville, *Vie de Saint Louis*, pp. 30–31, chs 59–60, on Louis doing justice beneath the oak at Vincennes; and the comments in Jordan, *Louis IX*, pp. 142–4.

45 For Blanche and Bartholomew of Roye in judgement, between 1228 and 1237, see 'Querimoniae Normannorum', in *RHF*, XXIV (1904), p. 45, no. 19; and see Lindy Grant, 'Blanche of Castile and Normandy', in *Normandy and its Neighbours, 900–1250*, ed. David Crouch and Kathleen Thompson (Turnhout, 2011), p. 125; for Blanche and Philip Hurepel sitting in judgement at Beaumont (?sur-Oise) in 1233 over the Alençon inheritance, see *Cartulaire normand de Philippe Auguste, Louis VIII, Saint Louis et Philippe-le-Hardi*, ed. Léopold Delisle (Caen, 1852), p. 314, no. 1149.

46 J. R. Strayer, *The Administration of Normandy under Saint Louis* (Cambridge, Mass., 1932), pp. 17–19, 92–3.

47 Thomas Bisson, *The Crisis of the Twelfth Century: Power, Lordship and the Origins of European Government* (Princeton, 2009), pp. 566–7, 544–5. For the English tradition of the giving of counsel in full court, see also Crouch, *English Aristocracy*, pp. 65–83.

48 See above, p. 271.

49 Petit-Dutaillis, *Etude*, appendix iv, pp. 442–4, lists twenty-five 'political assemblies' during Louis's short reign; and see discussion, ibid., pp. 342–51.

50 See above, p. 89–90.

51 *LTC*, II, no. 2083; sealed original AN J427 Juifs, no. II.2.

52 'Recepta et expensa', pp. 229, 233, 234.

53 Lindy Grant, *Abbot Suger of St-Denis:*

Church and State in Early Twelfth-century France (London, 1998), p. 178.

54 'E chronico Rotomagensi', in *RHF*, XXIII (1876), pp. 332–6; and see above, p. 100.

55 Petit Livre Blanc de Chartres, Paris, BNF MS lat. 11062, f. 65; and see above, p. 85–6.

56 The Boulogne inheritance arrangement, February 1252, issued by Blanche, 'nos in consilio': *LTC*, III, no. 3978; AN J390, no. 1.

57 Matthew Paris, *Chronica majora*, IV, p. 607; *Ordonnances des roys de France de la troisième race, recueillies par ordre chronologique*, ed. Eusèbe Laurière et al., 21 vols (Paris, 1723–1849), I, p. 60.

58 Joinville, *Vie de Saint Louis*, pp. 30–31, chs 59–60.

59 Emmanuel Lemaire, *Archives anciennes de la Ville de Saint-Quentin*, 2 vols (Saint-Quentin, 1888–1910), I, p. 42, no. 41: 'tot cist furent au jugement ki fu rendus en la cort le Roi au Pontoise en la ward robe le Roine, deriere vers le gardin en bas... Il hi fu li Roi Louis, li Roinne sa mere', plus Robert of Artois, Alphonse of Poitiers, John of Beaumont, Geoffrey de la Chapelle, Renaud Triecoc, Master William of Sens, who read out letters of Philip Augustus, the bishops of Beauvais and Clermont, Ferry Paste, the marshal, and Peter des Fontaines. See above, p. 122.

60 Joinville, *Vie de Saint Louis*, pp. 208–15, chs 422–35.

61 Leroux de Lincy, *Recueil de chants*, no. i, p. 167.

62 Most elegantly and generously expressed by Jordan, *Louis IX*, p. 47: 'If Blanche is not known as a great reformer, it is because she is known as a great saviour.'

63 Claude Garaud, 'Introduction', in *Quand gouverner c'est enquêter: les pratiques politiques de l'enquête princière (occident, XIIIe–XIVe siècles)*, ed. Thierry Pécout (Paris, 2010), p. 11.

64 For Louis VIII's *enquêtes*, see Petit-Dutaillis, *Etude*, appendix vii, pp. 509–10.

65 Boutaric, *Actes du Parlement de Paris*, I, pp. cccx–cccxxi, nos. 24, 27, 28, 29, 33.

66 'Itinera, dona et hernesia AD 1239 inter ascensionem et omnes sanctos', in *RHF*, XXII (1865), p. 600.

67 Marie Dejoux, 'Mener un enquête', in *Quand gouverner c'est enquêter*, ed. Thierry Pécout, pp. 133–55; Gaël Chenard, 'Les enquêtes administratives dans les domaines de Alphonse de Poitiers', in ibid., p. 157.

68 *LTC*, II, no. 2083; AN J427 Juifs, no. 11.2.

69 See above, note 5.

70 John Gillingham, *The Angevin Empire*, 2nd edn (London, 2001), pp. 3–4, on the use of the word *imperium*; Teofilo Ruiz, *From Heaven to Earth: The Reordering of Castillian Society, 1150–1350* (Princeton, 2004), p. 5, on the idea of the *imperium* of all the Spains.

71 Roger of Wendover, *Flores historiarum*, ed. H. G. Hewlett, 3 vols (London, 1886–9), I, p. 100, in a letter from Poitou.

72 See discussion in Charles T. Wood, *The French Apanages and the Capetian Monarchy, 1224–1328* (Cambridge, Mass., 1966), pp. 72–3.

73 *LTC*, II, no. 2270; and see above, p. 92.

74 *Récits d'un ménestrel de Reims au treizième siècle*, ed. Natalis de Wailly (Paris, 1876), pp. 225–6.

75 See above, pp. 112–13.

76 Aubri of Trois-Fontaines, 'Chronica', p. 949; Jordan, *Louis IX*, pp. 113, 124.

77 *LTC*, II, no. 1610.

78 *LTC*, II, no. 2083. Sealed original, AN J427 Juifs, no. 11.2.

79 Gavin Langmuir, '*Judaei Nostri* and the Beginnings of Capetian Legislation', *Traditio*, XVI (1960), p. 235.

80 Baldwin, *Paris, 1200*, pp. 215–16.

81 See below, p. 106.

82 Gabrielle Spiegel, 'The *Reditus Regni ad Stirpem Karoli Magni*: A New Look', *French Historical Studies*, VII (1971), pp. 145–74; Elizabeth A. R. Brown, 'La notion de la légitimité et la prophétie à la cour de Philippe Auguste', in *La France de Philippe Auguste: le temps des mutations. Actes du Colloque international organisé par le CNRS: Paris, 29 septembre–4*

octobre 1980, ed. Robert-Henri Bautier (Paris, 1982), pp. 77–111; Georgia Sommers Wright, 'A Royal Tomb Program in the Reign of St Louis', *Art Bulletin*, LVI (1974), pp. 224–43; Lewis, *Royal Succession*, esp. pp. 107–15.

83   Rodrigo Jiménez De Rada, *Historia de rebus Hispaniae*, ed. Juan Fernández Valverde (Turnhout, 1987), pp. 280–81; and Colette Bowie, *The Daughters of Henry II and Eleanor of Aquitaine* (Turnhout, 2014), p. 118; and see above for Blanche's relationship with her natal family, pp. 164–8 The dysfunctional nature of the family of Henry II and Eleanor of Aquitaine was well known to contemporaries: see Ralph V. Turner, *Eleanor of Aquitaine* (London and New Haven, 2009), p. 295.

84   See above, p. 38.

85   Mousket, *Chronique rimée*, II, p. 548, vv. 27,137–27,140, and vv. 27,145–27,150, on the mutual love between the parents and their children; Matthew Paris, 'Vita S. Edmundi', in C. H. Lawrence, *St Edmund of Abingdon: A Study in Hagiography and History* (Oxford, 1960), pp. 262–3: 'Domina Blanchia…que adducens filios suos in praesencia sua'. See also *The Life of St Edmund by Matthew Paris*, trans. and ed., with a biography, by C. H. Lawrence (Stroud, 1999), p. 150.

86   Geoffrey of Beaulieu, 'Here Begins the Life and Saintly Comportment of Louis, Formerly King of the Franks, of Pious Memory', in *The Sanctity of Louis IX*, pp. 82–6; Geoffrey of Beaulieu, 'Vita ludovici noni', in *RHF*, XX (1840), pp. 8–9, for Louis's letters of advice to his son and heir, Philip, and to his daughter Blanche. For Louis's inadequacy as a husband, at least as perceived by Margaret and Joinville, see Joinville, *Vie de Saint Louis*, pp. 294–5, ch. 594, and pp. 314–15, ch. 631, and see above, p. 107. For Charles, see Jean Dunbabin, *Charles I of Anjou: Power, Kingship and State-Making in Thirteenth-century Europe* (London, 1998), pp. 181–6.

87   Walter Map, *De nugis curialium/ Courtiers' Trifles*, ed. M. R. James, C.N.L.

Brooke and R.A.B. Mynors (Oxford, 1983), pp. 450–51.

88   Lindy Grant, 'Le patronage architectural d'Henri II et de son entourage', *Cahiers de civilisation médiévale*, XXXVII (1994), pp. 80–83.

89   Roger of Howden, *Chronica magistri Rogeri de Hovedene*, ed. William Stubbs, 4 vols (London, 1868–71), III, p. 3; see Lindy Grant, *Architecture and Society in Normandy, 1120–1270* (New Haven and London, 2005), p. 122.

90   Roger of Howden, *Chronica*, III, p. 55. See also John Gillingham, *Richard I* (London and New Haven, 1999), p. 131. For Richard's use of propaganda, see John Gillingham, 'Royal Newsletters, Forgeries and English Historians: Some Links between Court and History in the Reign of Richard I', in *La cour Plantagenet, 1154–1204*, ed. Martin Aurell (Poitiers, 2000), pp. 171–86.

91   See the extended comparison of Capetian and Angevin kingship in Gerald of Wales, 'De principis instructione', in *Giraldi Cambrensis opera*, vol. VIII, ed. G. F. Warner (London, 1891), rewritten to draw the distinction between the two dynasties for, Gerald hoped, the future Louis VIII. See also the astute comments of Ralph V. Turner, 'England in 1215: An Authoritarian Dynasty Facing Multiple Threats', in *Magna Carta and the England of King John*, ed. Janet S. Loengard (Woodbridge, 2010), pp. 17–19; see also on royal anger: Paul Hyams, 'What Did Henry III of England Think in Bed (and in French) about Kingship and Anger?', in *Anger's Past: The Social Uses of Emotion in the Middle Ages*, ed. B. H. Rosenwein (Ithaca, 1998), pp. 92–125, esp. pp. 99–112; and Nicholas Vincent, 'The Court of Henry II', in *Henry II: New Interpretations*, ed. Christopher Harper-Bill and Nicholas Vincent (Woodbridge, 2007), pp. 311–16.

92   Roger of Howden, *Chronica*, II, p. 345.

93   Roger of Howden, *Chronica*, II, pp. 61–2; W. L. Warren, *Henry II*, paperback edn (London, 1977), p. 135.

94 *Récits d'un ménestrel de Reims*, p. 181.

95 See above, pp. 139–40.

96 Lindy Grant, 'Representing Dynasty: The Transept Windows of Chartres Cathedral', in *Representing History: Art, Music, History*, ed. Robert A. Maxwell (Philadelphia, 2010), passim.

97 Note that Mousquès conflated the two processions, saying that three queens were present at the reception of the Crown of Thorns – Blanche, Margaret and Ingeborg (who had died three years earlier): Mousket, *Chronique rimée*, II, pp. 668–9.

98 'Recepta et expensa', pp. 241, 243–8.

99 William of Nangis, 'Vita Sancti Ludovici'/'Vie de Saint Louis', in *RHF*, xx (1840), p. 355. There are no surviving household accounts for this ceremony.

100 Daniel H. Weiss, *Art and Crusade in the Age of Saint Louis* (Cambridge, 1998); Meredith Cohen, 'An Indulgence for the Visitor: The Public at the Sainte-Chapelle of Paris', *Speculum*, LXXXIII (2008), pp. 840–83; Beat Brenk, 'The Sainte-Chapelle as a Capetian Political Programme', in *Artistic Integration in Gothic Buildings*, ed. V. Raguin, K. Brush and P. Draper (Toronto, 1996), pp. 195–213; Meredith Cohen, *The Sainte-Chapelle and the Construction of Sacral Monarchy: Royal Architecture in Thirteenth-century Paris* (New York, 2015), esp. pp. 113–25; and articles in *La Sainte-Chapelle de Paris: royaume de France ou Jérusalem céleste?*, ed. Christine Hediger (Turnhout, 2007).

101 For the hospital at Compiègne, see Guillaume de Saint-Pathus, 'Vie de Saint Louis', p. 98: 'sus un drap de soye porterent et mistrent le premier malade qui onques fus mis en la meson-Dieu nouvelement fete'; for justice beneath the oak, see Joinville, *Vie de Saint Louis*, pp. 30–31, chs 59–60; for the burial of the heir, Louis, in 1260, see Carpenter, 'Meetings', pp. 19–20. For a subtle and rounded discussion of Louis's use of ideology and image in his kingship, see Jordan, *Louis*, pp. 182–213.

EPILOGUE

1 *Corpus des sceaux français du Moyen Age, III: les sceaux des reines et des enfants de France*, by Marie-Adélaïde Nielen (Paris, 2011), pp. 74–5.

2 *Corpus des sceaux français*, pp. 76–7 for Margaret; pp. 71–2 for Isabella of Hainault. See also discussion in Kathleen Nolan, *Queens in Stone and Silver: The Creation of a Visual Imagery of Queenship in Capetian France* (New York, 2009), esp. pp. 94–8, 152–7.

3 For the use of the castles by her sons, see *Corpus des sceaux français*, pp. 155–74. For the use of the castle as the arms of Castile by Alfonso VIII, see Faustino Menéndez Pidal de Navascués, 'L'essor des armes en Castille d'après les sources du XIIIe siècle', in *Sources de l'héraldique en Europe occidentale. Actes du 4e colloque international d'héraldique* (Brussels, 1985), pp. 92–103, esp. pp. 95–6. For Eleanor's castle-decorated stoles, see José Manuel Cerda, 'The Marriage of Alfonso VIII of Castile and Leonor Plantagenet: The First Bond between Spain and England in the Middle Ages', in *Les stratégies matrimoniales, IXe–XIIIe siècle*, ed. Martin Aurell (Turnhout, 2013), p. 114 and n. 10.

4 William the Breton, 'Gesta Philippi Augusti', in *Oeuvres de Rigord et Guillaume le Breton*, ed. H. Delaborde, 2 vols (Paris, 1882–5), I, p. 295; Peter of Les Vaux-de-Cernay, *The History of the Albigensian Crusade*, ed. and trans. W. A. Sibley and M. D. Sibley (Woodbridge, 1998), ch. 449, p. 205.

5 A.-J.-V. Leroux de Lincy, *Recueil de chants historiques français depuis le XIIe jusqu'au XVIIIe siècle*, vol. 1 (Paris, 1841), no. i, p. 166; no. iii, p. 173.

6 Matthew Paris, *Chronica majora*, ed. H. R. Luard, 7 vols (London, 1872–83), v, p. 513. See also John Carmi Parsons, *Eleanor of Castile: Queen and Society in Thirteenth-century England* (New York, 1998), p. 64.

7 See above, pp. 237–8, 242.

8   1 Kings 2.19, in both the Vulgate and the Revised Standard Version.

9   Song of Solomon 3.11 (in both Vulgate and Revised Standard Version): 'Go forth O daughters of Sion and behold King Solomon with the crown with which his mother crowned him.' Walter continues with a complex typology: 'This speaks of the mother Synagogue, from which Christ, the true Solomon, that is the peaceful, comes forth according to the origin of flesh': Walter Cornut, 'Historia susceptionis Coronae spineae', in *RHF*, XXII (1865), p. 28.

10   Matthew Paris, *Chronica majora*, VI, pp. 165–7, 152–4.

11   *RHF*, XIX (1833), pp. 255–6.

12   Philippe Mousket, *Chronique rimée*, ed. Frédéric de Reiffenberg, 2 vols (Brussels, 1836–8), II, pp. 601, 668.

13   *Récits d'un ménestrel de Reims au treizième siècle*, ed. Natalis de Wailly (Paris, 1876), p. 98: 'la bonne roine sage...elle se despouilla en pure chemise, s'afulbla d'un mantel...elle monta sur une table dormant a dues piez, et dist, "Seigneurs, esgardeiz moi

tuit: aucuns dit que je sui enceinte d'enfant", et lait cheoir son mantel...et se tourne devant et derriere'; ibid., pp. 157–8, for Blanche and Philip Augustus.

14   Matthew Paris, *Chronica majora*, V, p. 354. See Irene Samuel, 'Semiramis in the Middle Ages: The History of a Legend', *Medievalia et humanistica*, II (1944), pp. 32–44, who argues that the largely positive classical image of Semiramis as a great empress and a builder was lost in the Middle Ages, which concentrated on her lust, until Chaucer and Boccaccio revived her classical reputation. But Matthew Paris is very clearly using the comparison as praise, which suggests that the positive, classical image of Semiramis was by no means unknown then.

15   See also comments on the developing legend of Blanche as the mother of the saint in Anne-Hélène Allirot, 'Une *beata stirps* au féminine? Autour de quelques saintes reines et princesses royales', in *Une histoire pour un royaume, XIIe–XVe siècles. Actes du colloque Corpus Regni organisé en hommage à Colette Beaune*, ed. Allirot et al. (Paris, 2010), pp. 144–5.

Bibliography

Note: I have not divided primary from secondary sources in this bibliography, because so many primary sources are in fact published within books or articles. Conversely, important secondary literature is often contained within the introductions to primary sources. Listed here are the sources – primary, secondary, published and manuscript – that are cited in the Notes. It does not include everything that was consulted during the course of my research.

Within the Notes, I have occasionally used number references rather than page references, where this has seemed appropriate. These are indicated, except in the case of *Layettes du trésor des chartes*, where, like most historians, I have used number rather than page references throughout. For Joinville, I have used the edition by Monfrin, but have given chapter as well as page references, so that those who will use Joinville in the excellent new Penguin Classics edition ('John of Joinville, "The Life of Saint Louis"', in *Joinville and Villehardouin Chronicles of the Crusades*, ed. and trans. Caroline Smith, London: Penguin Classics, 2008, pp. 137–336) will be able to find the appropriate reference. Some frequently cited sources are cited in abbreviated form: see 'Abbreviations', p. 328.

UNPUBLISHED MANUSCRIPTS AND DOCUMENTARY SOURCES

Birmingham, University Library
  University of Birmingham MSS 6/iii/19
Cambridge, Corpus Christi College
  MS 16 II (Matthew Paris, *Chronica majora*)

Cergy-Pontoise, Archives Départementales du Val d'Oise (ADVO)

43H3 (Royaumont Cartulary)

72H12 (*Achatz d'heritage*)

72H80, 72H6/3, 72H115, 72H83, 72H97 (Maubuisson series)

Chantilly, Musée Condé

MS 9 olim 1695 (Ingeborg Psalter)

Copenhagen, Det Kongelige Bibliotek

GKS 1606 (Christina Psalter)

Leiden, Universiteit Leiden, Bibliotheken

MS Lat. 76a

London, British Library (BL)

Add. Ch. 4129 (household accounts for 1241)

Manchester, John Rylands Library

MS Lat. 22 (Crawford Psalter/Psalter of Joanna of Navarre)

New York, The Morgan Library and Museum

MS M240

Paris

Archives Nationales (AN)

J189, nos. 4 and 5; J189, no. 6

J390, no. 1

J403, nos. 3 and 4; J403, no. 10 (Testament of Peter of Alençon, vidimus of 1283)

J427 Juifs, no. 11.2

J461, no. 4; J461, no. 8; J461, no. 13

J599, no. 1

J1030, no. 9 (Candlemas audit at the Temple, 1243)

J1034, no. 8

JJ3

JJ26 (Register E)

K190(2)

K191, no. 12/7

L463, nos. 34–44 (Paris, Notre-Dame)

L1015 (Sainte-Antoine)

LL1528a (record of the Dominican general chapter)

Bibliothèque de l'Arsenal

MS lat. 1186 (Psalter of Blanche of Castile)

Bibliothèque Mazarine

MS 870, ff. 191–207v ('Miroir de l'âme') [Also includes 'Somme le roi']

Bibliothèque Nationale de France (BNF)

Collection Champagne

Collection Doat, vol. 154

MS Est. Rés. Pe 11c (Gaignières Collection)

MS fr. 5700 ('Chronique des Rois')

MS lat. 238 (Psalter of Joanna of Flanders)

MS lat. 406 (Psalter for Maubuisson)

MS lat. 5472, MS lat. 9166 (Royaumont Cartulary – two copies)

MS lat. 5480 (Fontevraud Cartulary, 2 vols)

MS lat. 6191 (Karolinus)

MS lat. 9017, f. 69 (household account for 1241/2)

MS lat. 10434 (Psalter of Saint-Germain-en-Laye)

MS lat. 11062 (Petit Livre Blanc de Chartres)

MS lat. 13892 (Le Lys Cartulary)

MS lat. 14397a (Bible of Saint-Victor)

MS lat. 14878 ('Audi domina', or the 'Speculum anime')

MS n.a.fr. 21677

Institut de France, Académie des Inscriptions et Belles-Lettres, Fonds Louis Carolus-Barré

Fonds Louis Carolus-Barré, no. 2 (Cartulaire de La Joie-lès-Nemours)

Rome, Vatican City, Biblioteca Apostolica Vaticana

MS Regine lat. 1522

Toledo, Tesoro de la Catedral

Biblia de San Luis

Vienna, Österreichische Nationalbibliothek

Codex Vindobonensis 1179

Codex Vindobonensis 2554

PUBLISHED SOURCES: PRIMARY AND SECONDARY

L'abbaye parisienne de Saint-Victor au moyen âge, ed. Jean Longère, Bibliotheca Victorina, 1 (Turnhout: Brepols, 1991)

'Abrégé de l'histoire de France', in *RHF*, XVII (1878), pp. 428–32

Adam of Eynsham, *Magna vita Sancti Hugonis / The Life of St Hugh of Lincoln*, ed. Decima L. Douie and David Hugh Farmer, 2 vols (Oxford: Clarendon Press, 1985)

Adhémar, J., ed., 'Les tombeaux de la collection Gaignières: dessins d'archéologie du xviie siècle' [part 1], *Gazette des beaux-arts*, LXXXIV (1974), pp. 11–191

Agnes of Harcourt, *The Writings of Agnes of Harcourt: The Life of Isabelle of France and the Letter on Louis IX and Longchamp*, ed. Sean Field (Notre Dame, Ind.: University of Notre Dame Press, 2003)

Allirot, Anne-Hélène, 'Une *beata stirps* au féminine? Autour de quelques saintes reines et princesses royales', in *Une histoire pour un royaume, XIIe–XVe siècles. Actes du colloque Corpus Regni organisé en hommage à Colette Beaune*, ed. Allirot et al. (Paris: Perrin, 2010), pp. 142–51

Andrea, Alfred J., 'Innocent III, the Fourth Crusade and the Coming Apocalypse', in *The Medieval Crusade*, ed. Susan J. Ridyard (Woodbridge: Boydell Press, 2004), pp. 97–106

'Annales de Burton', in *Annales monastici*, ed. H. R. Luard, 3 vols, Rolls Series (London: Longman, Green, 1864), I, pp. 183–500

'Annales de Waverleia', in *Annales monastici*, ed. H. R. Luard, 3 vols, Rolls Series (London: Longman, Green, 1865), II, pp. 129–411

Anonymous of Béthune, 'Extrait d'une chronique française des rois de France, par un anonyme de Béthune', in *RHF*, XXIV (1904), pp. 750–75

Archives de L'Hôtel-Dieu de Paris, 1157–1300, ed. L. Brièle and E. Coyecque (Paris: Champion, 1894)

Aubert, Marcel, *Notre-Dame de Paris*, 2nd edn (Paris: Laurens, 1929)

Aubri of Trois-Fontaines, 'Chronica Albrici Monachi Trium Fontium', in MGH *Scriptores*, XXIII, ed. Paul Scheffer-Boichorst (Hanover, 1874), pp. 631–950

Autour de Guillaume d'Auvergne, ed. F. Morenzoni and J.-Y. Tilliette (Turnhout: Brepols, 2005)

Baldwin, John W., *Masters, Princes and Merchants: The Social Views of Peter the Chanter and his Circle*, 2 vols (Princeton: Princeton University Press, 1970)

—, *The Government of Philip Augustus: Foundations of French Royal Power in the Middle Ages* (Berkeley: University of California Press, 1986)

—, 'Master Stephen Langton, Future Archbishop of Canterbury: The Paris Schools and Magna Carta', *English Historical Review*, CXXIII (2008), pp. 811–46

—, *Paris, 1200* (Stanford, Cal.: Stanford University Press, 2010)

Bande, Alexandre, *Le coeur du roi: les Capétiens et les sépultures multiples, XIIIe–XVe siècles* (Paris: Tallandier, 2009)

Barrau, Julie, 'Ceci n'est pas un miroir; ou, le *Policraticus* de Jean de Salisbury', in *Le prince au miroir de la littérature politique de l'antiquité aux lumières*, ed. Frédérique Lachaud and Lydwine Scordia (Rouen: Publications des universités de Rouen et du Havre, 2007), pp. 87–111

Barthélémy, Dominique, *Les deux âges de la seigneurie banale: Coucy, milieu XIe–milieu XIIIe siècle* (Paris: Sorbonne, 1984)

Bataillon, Louis-Jacques, Nicola Bériou, Gilbert Dahan and Riccardo Quinto, eds, *Etienne Langton: prédicateur, bibliste, théologien* (Turnhout: Brepols, 2010)

Bates, David, *The Normans and Empire* (Oxford: Oxford University Press, 2013)

—, Julia Crick and Sarah Hamilton, 'Introduction', in *Writing Medieval Biography, 750–1250: Essays in Honour of Frank Barlow*, ed. Bates, Crick and Hamilton (Woodbridge: Boydell Press, 2006), pp. 1–13

Bautier, Robert-Henri, 'Les aumônes du roi aux maladreries, Maisons-Dieu et pauvres établissements du royaume', in *Assistance et assistés jusqu'à 1610. Actes du 97e Congrès national des sociétés savantes: Nantes, 1972* (Paris: Bibliothèque nationale, 1979), pp. 37–105

Bedos-Rezak, B., 'Women, Seals and Power in Medieval France', in *Women and Power in the Middle Ages*, ed. Mary Erler and Maryanne Kowalski (Athens, Ga.: University of Georgia Press, 1988), pp. 61–82

Bémont, Charles, 'Le condamnation de Jean Sans-Terre par la cour des Pairs de France en 1202', *Revue historique*, XXXII (1886), pp. 33–72, 290–311

Berger, Elie, *Histoire de Blanche de Castille, reine de France* (Paris: Thorin, 1895)

Berlioz, J., 'La voix de l'évêque: Guillaume d'Auvergne dans les *exempla*, XIIIe–XIVe siècles', in *Autour de Guillaume d'Auvergne*, ed. F. Morenzoni and J.-Y. Tilliette (Turnhout: Brepols, 2005), pp. 9–34

Berman, Constance, 'Noble Women's Power as Reflected in the Foundation of Cistercian Houses for Nuns in Thirteenth-century Northern France: Port-Royal, Les Clairets, Moncey, Lieu and Eau-lez-Chartres', in *Negotiating Community and Difference in Medieval Europe*, ed. Katherine Allen Smith and Scott Wells (Leiden and Boston, Mass.: Brill, 2009), pp. 137–49

—, 'Two Medieval Women's Control of Property and Religious Benefactions in France: Eleanor of Vermandois and Blanche of Castile', *Viator*, XLI/2 (2010), pp. 151–82

Bianchini, Janna, *The Queen's Hand: Power and Authority in the Reign of Berenguela of Castile* (Philadelphia: University of Pennsylvania Press, 2012)

Billot, Claudine, 'Les Saintes Chapelles de Saint-Louis: conditions et signification de ces fondations', in *Vincennes: aux origines de l'état moderne. Actes du colloque scientifique sur 'Les Capétiens à Vincennes au moyen âge'*, ed. Jean Chapelot and Elisabeth Lalou (Paris: Presses de l'Ecole normale supérieure, 1996), pp. 171–81

Bisson, Thomas, *The Crisis of the Twelfth Century: Power, Lordship and the Origins of European Government* (Princeton: Princeton University Press, 2009)

Bloch, Marc, *Les rois thaumaturges*, 2nd edn (Paris: Colin, 1961)

—, 'Blanche de Castille et les serfs du chapitre de Paris', *Mélanges historiques*, I (1963), pp. 462–90

Bonis, Armelle, and Monique Wabont, 'Cisterciens et Cisterciennes en France du nord-ouest: typologie des fondations, typologie des sites', in *Cîteaux et les femmes*, ed. Armelle Bonis, Sylvie Dechavanne and Monique Wabont (Paris: Créaphis, 2001), pp. 151–75

Bonnard, Dom Fourier, *Histoire de l'abbaye royale et de l'ordre des chanoines réguliers de St-Victor de Paris*, 2 vols (Paris: Savaète, 1904–8)

Bonnardot, Hippolyte, *L'abbaye royale de Saint-Antoine-des-Champs de l'ordre de Cîteaux* (Paris, 1882)

Bony, Jean, *French Gothic Architecture of the Twelfth and Thirteenth Centuries* (Berkeley and Los Angeles: University of California Press, 1983)

Boutaric, Edgar, *Actes du Parlement de Paris*, 2 vols (Paris: Plon, 1863–7)

—, 'Marguerite de Provence, femme de Saint Louis: son caractère, son rôle politique', *Revue des questions historiques*, III (1867), pp. 417–58 [article reprinted Paris: Victor Palme, 1867]

—, *Saint Louis et Alphonse de Poitiers: études sur la réunion des provinces du Midi et de l'Ouest à la couronne* (Paris: Plon, 1870)

Bowie, Colette, *The Daughters of Henry II and Eleanor of Aquitaine* (Turnhout: Brepols, 2014)

Branner, Robert, *St Louis and the Court Style in Gothic Architecture* (London: Zwemmer, 1965)

—, 'The Sainte-Chapelle and the *Capella Regis* in the Thirteenth Century', *Gesta*, X (1971), pp. 19–22

—, 'Manuscript Painting in Paris around 1200', in *The Year 1200: A Symposium* (New York, 1975), pp. 173–85

—, 'Saint Louis et l'enluminure parisienne au XIIIe siècle', in *Septième centenaire de la mort de Saint Louis. Actes des colloques du Royaumont et de Paris, 21–27 mai 1970* (Paris: CNRS/ Les Belles Lettres, 1976), pp. 69–84

Brenk, Beat, 'The Sainte-Chapelle as a Capetian Political Programme', in *Artistic Integration in Gothic Buildings*, ed. V. Raguin, K. Brush and P. Draper (Toronto: University of Toronto Press, 1996), pp. 195–213

'Brevis historia Regum Francorum ad annum MCCXIV' in *RHF*, XVII (1878), pp. 423–8

Brooke, Christopher, *The Medieval Idea of Marriage* (Oxford: Oxford University Press, 1989)

Brown, Elizabeth A. R., 'Death and the Human Body in the Later Middle Ages: The Legislation of Boniface VIII on the Division of the Corpse', *Viator*, XII (1981), pp. 221–70

—, 'La notion de la légitimité et la prophétie à la cour de Philippe Auguste', in *La France de Philippe Auguste: le temps des mutations. Actes du Colloque international organisé par le CNRS: Paris, 29 septembre–4 octobre 1980*, ed. Robert-Henri Bautier (Paris: CNRS, 1982), pp. 77–111

—, 'The Prince is the Father of the King: The Character and Childhood of Philip the Fair of France', in *The Monarchy of Capetian France and Royal Ceremonial* (Aldershot: Variorum, 1991), article II, pp. 282–334 [reprinted from *Medieval Studies*, XL, 1987, pp. 282–334]

—, 'Royal Testamentary Acts from Philip Augustus to Philip of Valois', in *Herrscher- und Fürstentestamente im westeuropäischen Mittelalter*, ed. Brigitte Kasten (Cologne: Böhlau, 2008), pp. 415–30

Le brûlement du Talmud à Paris, 1242–1244, ed. Gilbert Dahan (Paris: Cerf, 1999)

Brundage, James, 'Concubinage and Marriage in Medieval Canon Law', *Journal of Medieval History*, I (1975), pp. 1–17

—, 'Marriage and Sexuality in the Decretals of Pope Alexander III', in Brundage, *Sex, Law and Marriage in the Middle Ages* (Aldershot: Ashgate, 1993), article IX, pp. 59–83

Bruzelius, Caroline, 'The Abbey Church of Longpont and the Architecture of the Cistercians in the Early Thirteenth Century', *Analecta Cisterciensia*, XXXV (1979), pp. 3–204

—, *The Thirteenth-century Church at St-Denis* (New Haven and London: Yale University Press, 1985)

Buc, Philippe, *L'ambigüité du livre: prince, pouvoir et peuple dans les commentaires de la Bible au moyen âge* (Paris: Beauchesne, 1994)

—, ' "Principes Gentium dominantur eorum": Princely Powers between Legitimacy and Illegitimacy in Twelfth-century Exegesis', in *Cultures of Power: Lordship, Status and Process in Twelfth-century Europe*, ed. Thomas Bisson (Philadelphia: Pennsylvania University Press, 1995), pp. 310–28

Bulaeus, Caesar Egassius, *Historia Universitatis parisiensis*, III (Paris: Franciscus Noel, 1666)

Bynum, Caroline, *The Resurrection of the Body in Western Christianity, 200–1336* (New York: Columbia University Press, 1995)

Caesarius of Heisterbach, *Dialogus miraculorum*, ed. Joseph Strange (Cologne: J. M. Heberle, 1851)

Campbell, Gerard J., 'The Protest of Saint Louis', *Traditio*, XV (1959), pp. 405–18

—, 'The Attitude of the Monarchy towards the Use of Ecclesiastical Censures in the Reign of Saint Louis', *Speculum*, XXXV (1960), pp. 535–55

—, 'Temporal and Spiritual Regalia during the Reigns of St Louis and Philip III', *Traditio*, XX (1964), pp. 351–83

Campbell, John, *Margaret Thatcher*, vol. II: *The Iron Lady* (London: Jonathan Cape, 2003)

Capetian Women, ed. Kathleen Nolan (New York: Palgrave Macmillan, 2003)

Carolus-Barré, Louis, 'La grande ordonnance de 1254 sur la réforme de l'administration et la police du royaume', in *Septième centenaire de la mort de Saint Louis. Actes des colloques du Royaumont et de Paris, 21–27 mai 1970* (Paris: CNRS/Les Belles Lettres, 1976), pp. 85–96

—, *Le procès de canonisation de Saint-Louis, 1272–1297: essai de reconstitution* (Rome: Ecole française de Rome, 1994)

Carpenter, D. A., *The Minority of Henry III* (London: Methuen, 1990)

—, *The Struggle for Mastery: Britain, 1066–1284* (Oxford: Oxford University Press, 2003)

—, 'The Meetings between Kings Henry III and Louis IX', in *Thirteenth Century England, X: Proceedings of the Durham Conference, 2003*, ed. M. Prestwich, R. Britnell and R. Frame (Woodbridge: Boydell & Brewer, 2005), pp. 1–30

Cartulaire de l'abbaye de Porrois au diocèse de Paris, plus connue sous son nomme mystique de Port-Royal, ed. A. de Dion, 2 vols (Paris: Picard, 1903)

Cartulaire de l'abbaye royale de Lieu-Notre-Dame-lès-Romorantin, ed. E. Plat (Romorantin, 1892)

Cartulaire de l'église Notre-Dame de Paris, ed. B. Guérard, 4 vols (Paris, 1850)

Cartulaire de Notre-Dame de Chartres, ed. Eugène de Lépinois and Lucien Merlet, 3 vols (Chartres: Garnier, 1862–5)

Cartulaire normand de Philippe Auguste, Louis VIII, Saint Louis et Philippe-le-Hardi, ed. Léopold Delisle (Caen: Société des antiquaires, 1852)

Cartulary of Countess Blanche of Champagne, ed. Theodore Evergates (Toronto: University of Toronto Press, 2009)

Catalogue des actes de Philippe Auguste, ed. Léopold Delisle (Paris: Durrand, 1856)

Caviness, Madeline H., 'Anchoress, Abbess and Queen: Donors and Patrons or Intercessors and Matrons', in *The Cultural Patronage of Medieval Women*, ed. June Hall McCash (Athens, Ga.: University of Georgia Press, 1996), pp. 105–54

Cerda, José Manuel, 'The Marriage of Alfonso VIII of Castile and Leonor Plantagenet: The First Bond between Spain and England in the Middle Ages', in *Les stratégies matrimoniales, IXe–XIIIe siècle*, ed. Martin Aurell (Turnhout: Brepols, 2013), pp. 143–53

Chansons des trouvères, chanter m'estuet, ed. Samuel N. Rosenberg, Hans Tischler and Marie-Geneviève Grossel (Paris: Livre de Poche, 1995)

Chapelot, Jean, 'L'eau dans le manoir et le château', in *Vincennes: du manoir capétien à la résidence de Charles V*, Dossiers d'archéologie, 289 ([Dijon: Faton], 2004), pp. 28–30

Chapotin, Marie-Dominique, *Histoire des dominicains de la province de France: le siècle des fondations* (Rouen, 1898)

Charansonnet, Alexis, 'La révolte des barons de Louis IX: réaction de l'opinion et silence des historiens en 1246–1247', in *Une histoire pour un royaume, XIIe–XVe siècles. Actes du colloque Corpus Regni organisé en hommage à Colette Beaune*, ed. A.-H. Allirot et al. (Paris: Perrin, 2010), pp. 218–39

—, 'Les grands laïcs lèguent-ils leur spiritualité à leur enfants? Le cas des Montfort au XIIIe siècle', in *Expériences religieuses et chemins de perfection dans l'Occident médiéval* (Paris: Boccard, 2012), pp. 355–74

Chartularium Universitatis parisiensis: Ex diversis bibliothecis tabulariisque collegit et cum authenticis chartis contulit, ed. H. Denifle, 4 vols (Paris, 1889–97)

Chauvin, B., and G. Delepierre, 'Le mausolée de la comtesse Jeanne à l'abbaye de Marquette: essai de restitution', *Revue du Nord*, no. 368 (2006), pp. 109–25

Chazan, Robert, 'The Condemnation of the Talmud Reconsidered, 1239–1248', *Proceedings of the American Academy for Jewish Research*, LV (1988), pp. 11–30

—, 'Trial, Condemnation and Censorship: The Talmud in Medieval Europe', in *The Trial of the Talmud: Paris, 1240*, ed. and trans. John Friedman, Jean Connell Hoff and Robert Chazan (Toronto: Pontifical Institute of Medieval Studies, 2012), pp. 2–92

Chenard, Gaël, 'Les enquêtes administratives dans les domaines de Alphonse de Poitiers', in *Quand gouverner c'est enquêter: les pratiques politiques de l'enquête princière (occident, XIIIe–XIVe siècles)*, ed. Thierry Pécout (Paris: De Boccard, 2010), pp. 157–68

Chibnall, Marjorie, *The Empress Matilda: Queen Consort, Queen Mother and Lady of the English* (Oxford: Blackwell, 1991)

'Chronica Latina regum Castellae', in *Chronica hispana saeculi XIII*, ed. L. C. Brea, J. A. Estévez Sola and R. Carande Herrero (Turnhout: Brepols, 1997)

Cîteaux et les femmes, ed. Armelle Bonis, Sylvie Dechavanne and Monique Wabont (Paris: Créaphis, 2001)

Civel, Nicolas, *La fleur de France: les seigneurs d'Ile-de-France au XIIe siècle* (Turnhout: Brepols, 2006)

Cohen, Jeremy, *The Friars and the Jews: The Evolution of Medieval Anti-Judaism* (Ithaca: Cornell University Press, 1982)

Cohen, Meredith, 'An Indulgence for the Visitor: The Public at the Sainte-Chapelle of Paris', *Speculum*, LXXXIII (2008), pp. 840–83

—, *The Sainte-Chapelle and the Construction of Sacral Monarchy: Royal Architecture in Thirteenth-century Paris* (New York: Cambridge University Press, 2015)

—, and Xavier Dectot, *Paris: ville rayonnante* (Paris: Réunion des musées nationaux, 2010)

Colker, M. L., ed., 'The "Karolinus" of Egidius Parisiensis', *Traditio*, XXIX (1973), pp. 199–325

'Compotus ballivorum et praepositorum Franciae anno Domini 1234 mense Junio de termino ascensionis', in *RHF*, XXII (1865), pp. 565–78

'Compotus praepositorum et ballivorum Franciae de termino ascensionis, AD MCCXLVIII', in *RHF*, XXI (1855), pp. 260–84

'Compotus Th. De Carnoto et Amarrici Pulli, 1231', in *RHF*, XXI (1855), pp. 220–26

'Comptes de dépenses de Blanche de Castille', ed. Etienne Symphorien Bougenot in *Bulletin du Comité des travaux historiques et scientifiques: section d'histoire et de philologie* (1889), pp. 86–91

Les comptes sur tablettes de cire de Jean Sarrazin, chambellan de Saint Louis, ed. Elisabeth Lalou, Monumenta Palaeographica Medii Aevii (Turnhout: Brepols, 2003)

Comte, François, 'L'enceinte de Saint Louis à Angers: restitution d'une fortification disparue', in *Saint Louis et l'Anjou*, ed. Etienne Vacquet (Rennes: Presses universitaires de Rennes, 2014), pp. 81–92

Conklin, George, 'Ingeborg of Denmark, Queen of France, 1193–1223', in *Queens and Queenship in Medieval Europe*, ed. Anne J. Duggan (Woodbridge: Boydell Press, 1997), pp. 39–52

Continuator of William the Breton, in *Oeuvres de Rigord et Guillaume le Breton*, ed. H. Delaborde, 2 vols (Paris: Société de l'Histoire de France, 1882–5), I, pp. 321–7

Corpus des sceaux français du Moyen Age, III: les sceaux des reines et des enfants de France, by Marie-Adélaïde Nielen (Paris: Service interministériel des Archives de France, 2011)

Coss, Peter, 'Introduction', in *Thomas Wright's Political Songs of England*, ed. Coss (Cambridge: Cambridge University Press, 1996), pp. xi–lxvii

The Coutumes de Beauvaisis of Philippe de Beaumanoir, ed. and trans. F.R.P. Akehurst (Philadephia: University of Pennsylvania Press, 1992)

Crouch, David, *The Image of Aristocracy in Britain, 1000–1300* (London and New York: Routledge, 1992)

—, *The Birth of Nobility: Constructing Aristocracy in England and France, 900–1300* (Harlow: Pearson, 2005)

—, *Tournament* (London: Hambledon, 2005)

—, 'Baronial Paranoia in King John's Reign', in *Magna Carta and the England of King John*, ed. Janet S. Loengard (Woodbridge: Boydell Press, 2010), pp. 45–62

—, *The English Aristocracy, 1072–1272: A Social Transformation* (London and New Haven: Yale University Press, 2011)

The Cultural Patronage of Medieval Women, ed. June Hall McCash (Athens, Ga.: University of Georgia Press, 1996)

Davis, Adam J., *The Holy Bureaucrat: Eudes Rigaud and Religious Reform in Thirteenth Century Normandy* (Ithaca: Cornell University Press, 2006)

Dectot, Xavier, 'Ou périr ou régner? Les tombeaux des comtes de Champagne à Saint-Etienne de Troyes', in *Splendeurs de la cour de Champagne au temps de Chrétien de Troyes*, ed. Thierry Delcourt and Xavier de La Selle (Troyes: Association Champagne historique, 1999), pp. 22–9

Dejoux, Marie, 'Mener un enquête', in *Quand gouverner c'est enquêter: les pratiques politiques de l'enquête princière (occident, XIIIe–XIVe siècles)*, ed. Thierry Pécout (Paris: De Boccard, 2010), pp. 133–55

Delisle, Léopold, 'Mémoire sur une lettre inédite adressée à la Reine Blanche par un habitant de La Rochelle', *Bibliothèque de l'école des chartes*, 17th year, 4th series, vol. II (1856), pp. 513–55

—, 'Discours de M. Léopold Delisle, membre de l'Institut, président, et appendice', *Annuaire-bulletin de la Société d'histoire de France* (1885), pp. 82–139

—, 'Durand de Champagne, franciscain', *Histoire littéraire de la France*, XXX (1888), pp. 302–33

—, 'Mémoire sur les opérations financières des Templiers', *Mémoires présentés par divers savantes à l'Académie des inscriptions et belles-lettres*, XXXIII (1889), part II, pp. 1–248

—, *Notice de douze livres royaux du XIIIe siècle et du XIVe siècle* (Paris: Imprimerie nationale, 1902)

D'Emilio, James, 'The Royal Convent of Las Huelgas: Dynastic Politics, Religious Reform and Artistic Change in Medieval Castile', in *Cistercian Nuns and their World*, ed. M. Parsons Lillich, Studies in Cistercian Art and Architecture, 6 (Kalamazoo: Cistercian Publications, 2005), pp. 191–282

De Rada, Rodrigo Jiménez, *Historia de rebus Hispaniae*, ed. Juan Fernández Valverde (Turnhout: Brepols, 1987)

Deuchler, Florens, *Der Ingeborgpsalter* (Berlin: Walter de Gruyter, 1967)

Dickson, Gary, 'The Burning of the Amalricians', *Journal of Ecclesiastical History*, XL (1989), pp. 347–69

Dimier, Marie-Anselme, *Saint Louis et Cîteaux* (Paris, 1954)

'The Disputation of Rabbi Yehiel of Paris', trans. John Friedman in *The Trial of the Talmud: Paris, 1240*, ed. and trans. Friedman, Jean Connell Hoff and Robert Chazan (Toronto: Pontifical Institute of Medieval Studies, 2012), pp. 126–68

Doss-Quinby, Eglal, et al., ed. and trans., *Songs of the Women Trouvères* (New Haven and London: Yale University Press, 2001)

Doüet d'Arcq, Louis-Claude, 'Siège de Carcassonne, 1240', *Bibliothèque de l'école des chartes*, 7th year, 2nd series, vol. II (1845–6), pp. 363–79

—, *Comptes de l'Hôtel des Rois de France aux XIV au XV siècles* (Paris: Société de l'histoire de France, 1865)

Douie, D. L., *Archbishop Geoffrey Plantagenet and the Chapter of York* (York: St Anthony's Press, 1960)

Dufour, Jean, 'De l'anneau sigillaire au sceau: évolution du rôle des reines de France jusqu'à la fin du XIIIe siècle', in *Corpus des sceaux français du Moyen âge, tome III: les sceaux des reines et des enfants de France*, ed. Marie-Adélaïde Nielen (Paris: Archives de France, 2011), pp. 11–25

Duggan, Anne, 'The Cult of St Thomas Becket in the Thirteenth Century', in *St Thomas Cantilupe, Bishop of Hereford*, ed. Meryl Jancey (Hereford: Dean and Chapter of Hereford Cathedral, 1982), pp. 21–44

Dunbabin, Jean, 'What's in a Name? Philip, King of France', *Speculum*, LXVIII (1993), pp. 949–68

—, *Charles 1 of Anjou: Power, Kingship and State-Making in Thirteenth-century Europe* (London: Longman, 1998)

—, 'The Political World of France, *c*.1200–*c*.1336', in *France in the Later Middle Ages, 1200–1500*, ed. David Potter (Oxford: Oxford University Press, 2002), pp. 23–46

—, *The French in the Kingdom of Sicily, 1266–1305* (Cambridge: Cambridge University Press, 2011)

Dutilleux, Alphonse, and Joseph Depoin, *L'abbaye de Maubuisson (Notre-Dame-la-Royale): histoire et cartulaire, I: histoire de l'abbaye et des abbesses* (Pontoise, 1882)

—, and —, *L'abbaye de Maubuisson (Notre-Dame-la-Royale): histoire et cartulaire, II: les bâtiments, l'église et les tombeaux* (Pontoise, 1883)

—, and —, *L'abbaye de Maubuisson (Notre-Dame-la-Royale): histoire et cartulaire, III: le trésor et le mobilier* (Pontoise, 1884)

—, and —, *L'abbaye de Maubuisson (Notre-Dame-la-Royale): histoire et cartulaire, IV: analyse du cartulaire et annexes* (Pontoise, 1885)

—, and —, *Cartulaire de l'abbaye de Maubuisson (Notre-Dame-la-Royale), I: chartes concernant la fondation de l'abbaye et des chapelles* (Pontoise, 1890)

—, and —, *Cartulaire de l'abbaye de Maubuisson (Notre-Dame-la-Royale), II: contrats* (Pontoise: Société historique du Vexin, 1913)

'E chronico Rotomagensi', in *RHF*, XXIII (1876), pp. 331–43

'E chronico Sanctae Catherinae de Monti Rotomagi', in *RHF*, XXIII (1876), pp. 397–410

'E libro mortuali Sanctae Catherinae Vallis Scholarum Parisiensis', in *RHF*, XXIII (1876), p. 147

'Ea quae distributa fuerunt in milicia Comitis Pictavensis (Die XXIV junio, anno MCCXLI)', in *RHF*, XXII (1865), pp. 615–22

Earenfight, Theresa, *Queenship in Medieval Europe* (Basingstoke: Palgrave Macmillan, 2013)

Eleanor of Aquitaine, Lord and Lady, ed. Bonnie Wheeler and John Carmi Parsons (New York: Palgrave Macmillan, 2002)

Emery, R. W., *The Friars in Medieval France: A Catalogue of French Mendicant Convents, 1200–1550* (New York: Columbia University Press, 1962)

Erlande-Brandenburg, Alain, *Le roi est mort: étude sur les funérailles, les sépultures et les tombeaux des rois de France jusqu'à la fin du XIIIe siècle* (Geneva: Droz, 1975)

Erler, Mary, and Maryanne Kowalski, 'Introduction', in *Women and Power in the Middle Ages*, ed. Erler and Kowalski (Athens, Ga.: University of Georgia Press, 1988), pp. 1–17

Etienne Langton: prédicateur, bibliste, théologien, ed. L.-J. Bataillon et al. (Turnhout: Brepols, 2010)

Eude Rigaud, *Regestrum visitationem archiepiscopi Rothomagensis / Journal des visites pastorales d'Eude Rigaud, archevêque de Rouen*, ed. T. Bonnin (Rouen, 1852)

Evergates, Theodore, 'Aristocratic Women in the County of Champagne', in *Aristocratic Women in Medieval France*, ed. Evergates (Philadelphia: University of Pennsylvania Press, 1999)

—, *Henry the Liberal, Count of Champagne, 1127–1181* (Philadelphia: Penn, 2016)

'Ex chronico anonymii Laudunensis Canonici', in *RHF*, XVIII (1879), pp. 702–20

'Ex chronico Turonensi: auctore anonymo, S. Martini Turon. canonico', in *RHF*, XVIII (1879), pp. 290–320

'Ex chronico universali anonymi Laudunensis', in MGH Scriptores, XXVI, ed. O. Holder-Egger (Hanover, 1882), pp. 442–57

'Ex Joannis Iperii Chronico Sythensis Sancti-Bertini', in RHF, XVIII (1879), pp. 594–610

'Expensa militiae comitis Attrebatensis in Penthecoste AD 1237 mense junio', in RHF, XXII (1865), pp. 579–83

'Extrait d'un abrégé de l'histoire de France', in RHF, XVII (1878), pp. 429–32

'Extraits des chroniques de Saint-Denis', in RHF, XXI (1855), pp. 103–23

Facinger, Marion F., 'A Study of Medieval Queenship: Capetian France, 987–1237', Studies in Medieval and Renaissance History, V (1968), pp. 3–48

Fasti Ecclesiae Gallicanae, II: le diocèse de Rouen, ed. Vincent Tabbagh (Turnhout: Brepols, 1998)

Fasti Ecclesiae Gallicanae, XI: le diocèse de Sens, ed. Vincent Tabbagh and Edouard Bouye (Turnhout: Brepols, 2009)

Fawtier, Robert, The Capetian Kings of France: Monarchy and Nation, 987–1328, trans. Lionel Butler and R. J. Adam (London: Macmillan, 1960)

Ferruolo, Stephen C., The Origins of the University: The Schools of Paris and their Critics, 1100–1215 (Stanford, Cal.: Stanford University Press, 1985)

Field, Sean L., Isabelle of France: Capetian Sanctity and Franciscan Identity in the Thirteenth Century (Notre Dame, Ind.: University of Notre Dame Press, 2006)

——, 'Reflecting the Royal Soul: The Speculum anime Composed for Blanche of Castile', Medieval Studies, LXVIII (2006), pp. 1–41

——, 'From Speculum anime to Miroir de l'âme: The Origins of Vernacular Advice Literature at the Capetian Court', Medieval Studies, LXIX (2007), pp. 59–110

'Un fragment du compte de l'hôtel du Prince Louis de France pour le terme de la Purification 1213', ed. Robert Fawtier in Moyen âge, XLIII (1933), pp. 225–50

La France de Philippe Auguste: le temps des mutations. Actes du Colloque international organisé par le CNRS: Paris, 29 septembre–4 octobre 1980, ed. Robert-Henri Bautier (Paris: CNRS, 1982)

Gajewski, Alexandra, 'The Patronage Question under Review: Queen Blanche of Castile (1188–1252) and the Architecture of the Cistercian Abbeys at Royaumont, Maubuisson and Le Lys', in Reassessing the Roles of Women as 'Makers' of Medieval Art and Architecture, ed. Therese Martin, 2 vols (Leiden and Boston, Mass.: Brill, 2012), I, pp. 197–244

Gajewski-Kennedy, Alexandra, 'Recherches sur l'architecture cistercienne et le pouvoir royal: Blanche de Castille et la construction de l'abbaye du Lys', in Art et architecture à Melun au Moyen âge, ed. Yves Gallet (Paris: Picard, 2000), pp. 223–54

Gaposchkin, M. Cecilia, The Making of Saint Louis: Kingship, Sanctity and Crusade in the Later Middle Ages (Ithaca: Cornell University Press, 2008)

——, and S. Field, 'Introduction', in The Sanctity of Louis IX: Early Lives of Saint Louis by Geoffrey of Beaulieu and William of Chartres, trans. Larry F. Field, ed. M. Cecilia Gaposchkin and Sean L. Field (Ithaca: Cornell University Press, 2014), pp. 1–57

Garaud, Claude, 'Introduction', in Quand gouverner c'est enquêter: les pratiques politiques de l'enquête princière (occident, XIIIe–XIVe siècles), ed. Thierry Pécout (Paris: De Boccard, 2010), pp. 9–19

Gasser, Stephan, 'L'architecture de la Sainte-Chapelle: état de la question concernant sa datation, son maître d'œuvre et sa place dans l'histoire de l'architecture', in *La Sainte-Chapelle de Paris: royaume de France ou Jérusalem céleste?*, ed. Christine Hediger (Turnhout: Brepols, 2007), pp. 157–80

Gendering the Middle Ages, ed. Pauline Stafford and Anneke B. Mulder-Bakker (Oxford: Blackwell, 2001) [first published as special issue of *Gender and History*, XII/3, 2000]

Geoffrey of Beaulieu, 'Vita ludovici noni', in *RHF*, XX (1840), pp. 1–27

—, 'Here Begins the Life and Saintly Comportment of Louis, Formerly King of the Franks, of Pious Memory', in *The Sanctity of Louis IX: Early Lives of Saint Louis by Geoffrey of Beaulieu and William of Chartres*, trans. Larry F. Field, ed. M. Cecilia Gaposchkin and Sean L. Field (Ithaca: Cornell University Press, 2014), pp. 69–128

Gerald of Wales, 'De principis instructione', in *Giraldi Cambrensis opera*, vol. VIII, ed. G. F. Warner, Rolls Series (London: HMSO/Eyre and Spottiswoode, 1891)

'Gesta Ludovici VIII, Francorum Regis', in *RHF*, XVII (1878), pp. 302–11

'Gesta Sancti Ludovici Noni Francorum regis, auctore monacho Sancti Dionysii anonymo', in *RHF*, XX (1840), pp. 45–57

Les gestes des évêques d'Auxerre, ed. Guy Lobrichon and Michel Sot, 3 vols (Paris: Les Belles Lettres, 2002–9)

Gilbert of Mons, *La chronique de Gilbert de Mons*, ed. L. Vanderkindere (Brussels, 1904)

Gillingham, John, *Richard I* (London and New Haven: Yale University Press, 1999)

—, 'Royal Newsletters, Forgeries and English Historians: Some Links between Court and History in the Reign of Richard I', in *La cour Plantagenet, 1154–1204*, ed. Martin Aurell (Poitiers: Université de Poitiers, 2000), pp. 171–86

—, *The Angevin Empire*, 2nd edn (London: Arnold, 2001)

—, 'At the Deathbeds of the Kings of England, 1066–1216', in *Herrscher-und Fürstentestamente im westeuropäischen Mittelalter*, ed. Brigitte Kasten (Cologne: Böhlau, 2008), pp. 509–30

—, 'The Anonymous of Béthune, King John and Magna Carta', in *Magna Carta and the England of King John*, ed. Janet S. Loengard (Woodbridge: Boydell Press, 2010), pp. 27–44

Giry, A., *Documents sur les relations de la royauté avec les villes de France de 1180 à 1314* (Paris, 1885)

González, Julio, *El reino de Castilla en la época de Alfonso VIII*, 3 vols (Madrid: CSIC, 1960)

Gransden, Antonia, *Historical Writing in England, c.550 to c.1307* (London: Routledge and Kegan Paul, 1974)

Grant, Lindy, 'Rouen Cathedral, 1200–1237', in *Medieval Art, Architecture and Archaeology at Rouen*, ed. J. Stratford, British Archaeological Association Conference Transactions, 12 (Leeds: W. S. Maney, 1993), pp. 60–68

—, 'Le patronage architectural d'Henri II et de son entourage', *Cahiers de civilisation médiévale*, XXXVII (1994), pp. 73–84

—, *Abbot Suger of St-Denis: Church and State in Early Twelfth-century France* (London: Longman, 1998)

—, *Architecture and Society in Normandy, 1120–1270* (New Haven and London: Yale University Press, 2005)

—, 'Blanche of Castile and Normandy', in *Normandy and its Neighbours, 900–1250*, ed. David Crouch and Kathleen Thompson (Turnhout: Brepols, 2011), pp. 117–31

—, 'Gold Bezants on the Altar: Coronation Imagery in the Bibles Moralisées', in *Image, Memory and Devotion*, ed. Zoë Opačić and Achim Timmermann (Turnhout: Brepols, 2011), pp. 55–9

—, 'Representing Dynasty: The Transept Windows of Chartres Cathedral', in *Representing History: Art, Music, History*, ed. Robert A. Maxwell (Philadelphia: University of Pennsylvania Press, 2010), pp. 109–14

—, 'Saint Michel peseur d'âmes sur les portails gothiques du Jugement dernier vers 1200', in *Rappresentazioni del monte e dell'arcangelo san Michele nella letteratura e nelle arti / Représentations du mont et de l'archange saint Michel dans la littérature et les arts*, ed. Pierre Bouet et al. (Bari: Edipuglia, 2011), pp. 135–43

—, 'The Chapel of the Hospital of Saint-Jean at Angers: *Acta*, Statutes, Architecture and Interpretation', in *Architecture and Interpretation: Essays for Eric Fernie*, ed. Jill Franklin, T. A. Heslop and Christine Stevenson (Woodbridge: Boydell Press, 2012), pp. 306–14

—, 'Royal and Aristocratic Hospital Patronage in Northern France in the Twelfth and Early Thirteenth Centuries', in *Laienadel und Armenfürsorge im Mittelalter*, ed. Lukas Clemens, Katrin Dort and Felix Schumacher, Trierer historische Forshungen, 71 (Trier: Kliomedia, 2015), pp. 105–14

—, 'Eudes Rigaud et Saint-Mellon de Pontoise', forthcoming

—, 'Etienne de Lexington et l'abbaye de Savigny au treizième siècle', forthcoming

Griffiths, Quentin, 'New Men among the Lay Counsellors of Saint Louis' Parlement', *Medieval Studies*, XXXII (1970), pp. 234–72

—, 'Les collégiales royales et leurs clercs sous le gouvernement capétien', *Francia*, XVIII (1991), pp. 93–110

Gronier-Prieur, Armande, *L'abbaye Notre-Dame du Lys à Dammarie-lès-Lys* (Verneuil-l'Etang: Amis des monuments et des sites de Seine-et-Marne, 1976)

Guest, Gerald B., *Bible moralisée: Codex Vindobonensis 2554, Vienna, Österreichische Nationalbibliothek* (London: Harvey Miller, 1995)

Guillaume de Saint-Pathus, 'Vie de Saint Louis, par le confesseur de la reine Marguerite', in *RHF*, XX (1840), pp. 58–121

Hall, Jackie, 'The Legislative Background to the Burial of Laity and Other Patrons in Cistercian Abbeys', in *Sepulturae cistercienses*, ed. Hall and Christine Kratzke, Cîteaux: commentarii Cistercienses, 56 (Forges-Chimay: Cîteaux, 2005), pp. 363–72

Helinand de Froidmont, 'De bono regimine principis', *PL*, CCXII, cols 735–46

Henry II: New Interpretations, ed. Christopher Harper-Bill and Nicholas Vincent (Woodbridge: Boydell & Brewer, 2007)

Hilaire, Jean, *La construction de l'état de droit dans les archives judicaires de la cour de France au XIIIe siècle* (Paris: Dalloz, 2011)

Hillen, Christian, and Frank Wiswall, 'The Minority of Henry III in the Context in Europe', in *The Royal Minorities of Medieval and Early Modern England*, ed. Charles Beem (New York and Basingstoke: Palgrave Macmillan, 2008), pp. 17–66

Hinnebusch, William A., *History of the Dominican Order*, 2 vols (New York: Alba House, 1965–73)

Histoire et archéologie à l'abbaye royale et cistercienne de Maubuisson, ed. Philippe Soulier (Cergy-Pontoise: Conseil Général du Val d'Oise, 1988)

Histoire des ducs de Normandie et des rois d'Angleterre, ed. F. Michel (Paris: Société de l'Histoire de France, 1840)

Hornaday, Aline, 'A Capetian Queen as Street Demonstrator: Isabelle of Hainault', in *Capetian Women*, ed. Kathleen Nolan (New York: Palgrave Macmillan, 2003), pp. 77–97

Howell, Margaret, *Eleanor of Provence: Queenship in Thirteenth Century England* (Oxford: Blackwell, 1998)

—, 'Royal Women in the Mid-Thirteenth Century: A Gendered Perspective', in *England and Europe in the Reign of Henry III, 1216–1272*, ed. Björn K. U. Weiler with Ifor W. Rowlands (Aldershot: Ashgate, 2002), pp. 163–81

Hudson, John, 'Feud, Vengeance and Violence in England from the Tenth to the Twelfth Centuries', in *Feud, Violence and Practice: Essays in Medieval Studies in Honour of Stephen D. White*, ed. Belle S. Tuten and Tracey L. Ballado (Farnham: Ashgate, 2010), pp. 29–53

Huneycutt, Lois, 'Intercession and the High Medieval Queen: The Esther Topos', in *Power of the Weak: Studies on Medieval Women*, ed. Jennifer Carpenter and Sally-Beth MacLean (Urbana: University of Illinois Press, 1995), pp. 126–46

—, 'Public Lives, Private Ties: Royal Mothers in England and Scotland, 1070–1204', in *Medieval Mothering*, ed. J. C. Parsons and B. Wheeler (New York: Garland, 1996), pp. 295–311

—, 'Female Succession and the Language of Power in the Writings of Twelfth-century Churchmen', in *Medieval Queenship*, ed. John Carmi Parsons, 2nd edn (Stroud: Alan Sutton, 1998), pp. 189–201

—, 'The Creation of a Crone: The Historical Reputation of Adelaide of Maurienne', in *Capetian Women*, ed. Kathleen Nolan (New York: Palgrave Macmillan, 2003), pp. 27–43

—, *Matilda of Scotland: A Study in Medieval Queenship* (Woodbridge: Boydell Press, 2003)

Hyams, Paul, 'What Did Henry III of England Think in Bed (and in French) about Kingship and Anger?', in *Anger's Past: The Social Uses of Emotion in the Middle Ages*, ed. B. H. Rosenwein (Ithaca: Cornell University Press, 1998), pp. 92–125

'Itinera, dona et hernesia AD 1239 inter ascensionem et omnes sanctos', in *RHF*, XXII (1865), pp. 583–615

Ivo of Chartres, 'Decretum', *PL*, CLXI, cols 47–1036

Jackson, Richard A., ed., *Ordines coronationis Franciae: Texts and Ordines for the Coronation of the Frankish and French Kings and Queens in the Middle Ages*, 2 vols (Philadelphia: University of Pennsylvania Press, 1995–2000)

Johannes de Hauvilla, *Architrenius*, trans. and ed. Winthrop Wetherbee (Cambridge: Cambridge University Press, 1994)

John of Salisbury, *Policraticus, sive De nugis curialium et vestigiis philosophorum*, ed. C.C.J. Webb, 2 vols (Oxford: Clarendon Press, 1909)

Joinville, Jean de, *Vie de Saint Louis*, ed. Jacques Monfrin (Paris: Classiques Garnier, 2010)

Jordan, Alyce, *Visualising Kingship in the Windows of the Sainte-Chapelle* (Turnhout: Brepols, 2002)

Jordan, Erin L., *Women, Power and Religious Patronage in the Middle Ages* (Basingstoke: Palgrave Macmillan, 2006)

—, 'Gender Concerns: Monks, Nuns and Patronage of the Cistercian Order in Thirteenth Century Flanders and Hainault', *Speculum*, LXXXVII (2012), pp. 62–94

Jordan, William Chester, *Louis IX and the Challenge of the Crusade: A Study in Rulership* (Princeton: Princeton University Press, 1979)

—, '*Persona et gesta*: The Image and Deeds of the Thirteenth-century Capetians, 2: The Case of Saint Louis', *Viator*, XIX (1988), pp. 208–18

—, *The French Monarchy and the Jews: From Philip Augustus to the Last Capetians* (Philadelphia: University of Pennsylvania Press, 1989)

—, 'Marian Devotion and the Talmud Trials of 1240', in *Religionsgespräche im Mittelalter*, ed. B. Lewis and F. Niewöhner (Wiesbaden: Harrassowitz, 1992), pp. 61–76

—, 'Isabelle of France and Religious Devotion at the Court of Louis IX', in *Capetian Women*, ed. Kathleen Nolan (New York: Palgrave Macmillan, 2003), pp. 209–23

—, *Men at the Center: Redemptive Governance under Louis IX* (Budapest: Central European University Press, 2012)

—, 'Anti-Judaism in the *Christina Psalter*', in *Christianity and Culture in the Middle Ages: Essays to Honor John Van Engen*, ed. David C. Mengel and Lisa Wolverton (Notre Dame, Ind.: University of Notre Dame Press, 2015), pp. 280–93

Kaeuper, Richard, *War, Justice and Public Order: England and France in the Later Middle Ages* (Oxford: Clarendon Press, 1988)

Kay, Richard, *The Council of Bourges, 1225: A Documentary History* (Aldershot: Ashgate, 2002)

Keck, David, *Angels and Angelology in the Middle Ages* (Oxford: Oxford University Press, 1998)

Kienzle, Beverly Mayne, *Cistercians, Heresy and Crusade in Occitania, 1145–1229: Preaching in the Lord's Vineyard* (Woodbridge: York Medieval Press/Boydell, 2001)

Kinder, Terryl, 'Blanche of Castile and the Cistercians: An Architectural Re-evaluation of Maubuisson Abbey', *Cîteaux: commentarii cistercienses*, XXVII (1976), pp. 161–88

King John: New Interpretations, ed. S. D. Church (Woodbridge: Boydell, 1999)

Klaniczay, Gábor, *Holy Rulers and Blessed Princesses: Dynastic Cults in Medieval Central Europe* (Cambridge: Cambridge University Press, 2002)

Koziol, Geoffrey, *Begging Pardon and Favor: Ritual and Political Order in Early Medieval France* (Ithaca: Cornell University Press, 1992)

—, 'Political Culture', in *France in the Central Middle Ages, 900–1200*, ed. Marcus Bull (Oxford: Oxford University Press, 2002), pp. 43–76

Krynen, Jacques, *L'empire du roi: idées et croyances politiques en France, XIIIe–XVe siècle* (Paris: Gallimard, 1993)

Kumler, Aden, *Translating Truth: Ambitious Images and Religious Knowledge in Late Medieval France and England* (New Haven and London: Yale University Press, 2011)

Lachaud, Frédérique, 'Le *Liber de principis instructione* de Giraud de Barry', in *Le prince au miroir de la littérature politique de l'antiquité aux lumières*, ed. Lachaud and Lydwine Scordia (Rouen: Publications des universités de Rouen et du Havre, 2007), pp. 113–42

Lalou, Elisabeth, 'Le fonctionnement de l'Hôtel du Roi du milieu xiiie au milieu du xive siècle', in *Vincennes aux origines de l'état moderne. Actes du colloque scientifique sur 'Les Capétiens à Vincennes au Moyen âge'*, ed. Jean Chapelot and Elisabeth Lalou (Paris: Presses de l'Ecole normale supérieure, 1996), pp. 145–55

—, 'Introduction', in *Les comptes sur tablettes de cire de Jean Sarrazin, chambellan de Saint Louis*, ed. Lalou, Monumenta Palaeographica Medii Aevii (Turnhout: Brepols, 2003), pp. 3–29

Langlois, Charles-Victor, 'Les préparatifs de l'expédition de Louis de France en Angleterre', *Revue historique*, xxxvii (1888), pp. 318–22

Langmuir, Gavin, '*Judaei nostri* and the Beginnings of Capetian Legislation', *Traditio*, xvi (1960), pp. 203–69

La Selle, Xavier de, *Le service des âmes à la cour: confesseurs et aumôniers des rois de France du XIIIe au XVe siècle* (Paris: Ecole des chartes, 1995)

—, 'L'aumônerie royale', in *Vincennes aux origines de l'état moderne. Actes du colloque scientifique sur 'Les Capétiens à Vincennes au Moyen âge'*, ed. Jean Chapelot and Elisabeth Lalou (Paris: Presses de l'Ecole normale supérieure, 1996), pp. 183–9

The Latin Chronicle of the Kings of Castile, trans. and ed. Joseph F. O'Callaghan (Tempe, Ariz.: Medieval and Renaissance Text Society, 2002)

Lawrence, C. H., *St Edmund of Abingdon: A Study in Hagiography and History* (Oxford: Clarendon Press, 1960)

Layettes du trésor des chartes, ed. A. Teulet, 5 vols (Paris: H. Plon, 1863–1909)

Le Goff, Jacques, *Saint Louis* (Paris: Gallimard, 1996)

—, et al., *Le sacre royal à l'époque de Saint-Louis* (Paris: Gallimard, 2001)

Lemaire, Emmanuel, *Archives anciennes de la Ville de Saint-Quentin*, 2 vols (Saint-Quentin, 1888–1910)

L'Epinois, Henri de, 'Comptes relatifs à la fondation de l'abbaye de Maubuisson', *Bibliothèque de l'école des chartes*, xix (1858), pp. 550–67

Lerner, R. E., 'Uses of Heterodoxy: The French Monarchy and Unbelief in the Thirteenth Century', *French Historical Studies*, iv (1965), pp. 189–202

Leroquais, Victor, *Les psautiers: manuscrits latins des bibliothèques publiques de France*, 3 vols (Mâcon: Protat, 1940–41)

Leroux de Lincy, A.-J.-V., *Recueil de chants historiques français depuis le XIIe jusqu'au XVIIIe siècle*, vol. i (Paris: Gosselin, 1841)

Lester, Anne E., *Creating Cistercian Nuns: The Women's Religious Movement and its Reform in Thirteenth-century Champagne* (Ithaca: Cornell University Press, 2011)

Lewis, Andrew, 'Anticipatory Association of the Heir in Early Capetian France', *American Historical Review*, lxxxiii (1978), pp. 906–27

—, *Royal Succession in Capetian France: Studies on Familial Order and the State* (Cambridge, Mass.: Harvard University Press, 1981)

Lipton, Sara, *Images of Intolerance: The Representation of Jews and Judaism in the Bible Moralisée* (Berkeley: University of California Press, 1999)

Litoux, Emmanuel, 'Un paysage castral dominé par le Château d'Angers', in *Saint Louis et l'Anjou*, ed. Etienne Vacquet (Rennes: Presses universitaires de Rennes, 2014), pp. 67–80

Littere baronum: The Earliest Cartulary of the Counts of Champagne, ed. Theodore Evergates (Toronto: Medieval Academy of America/University of Toronto Press, 2003)

Little, Lester K., 'Saint Louis' Involvement with the Friars', *Church History*, XXXIII (1963), pp. 125–47

—, *Religious Poverty and the Profit Economy in Medieval Europe* (London: Elek, 1978)

Lohrmann, Dietrich, 'Pierre Lombard, médecin de Saint Louis: un italien à Paris et ses maisons au Quartier Latin', in *Septième centenaire de la mort de Saint Louis. Actes des colloques du Royaumont et de Paris, 21–27 mai 1970* (Paris: CNRS/Les Belles Lettres, 1976), pp. 165–81

Lo Prete, Kimberly, 'Historical Ironies in the Study of Capetian Women', in *Capetian Women*, ed. Kathleen Nolan (New York: Palgrave Macmillan, 2003), pp. 271–86

Lot, F., and R. Fawtier, *Le premier budget de la monarchie française* (Paris, 1932)

Lowden, John, *The Making of the Bibles Moralisées*, 2 vols (University Park: Pennsylvania State University Press, 2000)

Lower, Michael, *The Barons' Crusade: A Call to Arms and its Consequences* (Philadelphia: University of Pennsylvania Press, 2005)

Luchaire, Achille, *Manuel des institutions françaises: période des Capétiens directs* (Paris: Hachette, 1892)

Ludewig, Johann Peter von, *Reliquiae Manuscriptorum omnis aevi Diplomatum ac Monumentorum ineditorum adhuc*, 12 vols (Frankfurt, 1720–41)

McCash, June Hall, 'The Cultural Patronage of Medieval Women: An Overview', in *The Cultural Patronage of Medieval Women*, ed. McCash (Athens, Ga.: University of Georgia Press, 1996), pp. 1–49

McGinn, Bernard, *Visions of the End: Apocalyptic Traditions in the Middle Ages* (New York: Columbia University Press, 1979)

Maddicott, John, *Simon de Montfort* (Cambridge: Cambridge University Press, 1994)

Magna Carta and the England of King John, ed. Janet S. Loengard (Woodbridge: Boydell Press, 2010)

'Magna recepta de termino Ascensionis, anno Domini MCCXXXVIII mense Mayo et magna expensa', in *RHF*, XXI (1855), pp. 251–60

Le Maroc médiéval: un empire de l'Afrique à l'Espagne, ed. Yannick Lintz, Claire Déléry and Bulle Tuil Leonetti (Paris: Hazan/Musée du Louvre, 2014)

Martin, H., *Les joyaux de l'Arsenal, I: le psautier de Saint Louis et de Blanche de Castille* (Paris: Berthaud Frères, 1909)

Martindale, Jane, 'Eleanor of Aquitaine: The Last Years', in *King John: New Interpretations*, ed. S. D. Church (Woodbridge: Boydell, 1999), pp. 137–64

Matthew Paris, *Chronica majora*, ed. H. R. Luard, 7 vols, Rolls Series (London: Longman, 1872–83)

—, *Historia Anglorum*, ed. Sir Frederic Madden, 2 vols, Rolls Series (London: Longmans, Green, Reader and Dyer, 1866)

—, 'Vita S. Edmundi', in C. H. Lawrence, *St Edmund of Abingdon: A Study in Hagiography and History* (Oxford: Clarendon Press, 1960), pp. 222–89

—, *The Life of St Edmund by Matthew Paris*, trans. and ed., with a biography, by C. H. Lawrence (Stroud: Sandpiper, 1999)

Medieval Queenship, ed. John Carmi Parsons (New York: St Martin's Press, 1993)

Menéndez Pidal de Navascués, Faustino, 'L'essor des armes en Castille d'après les sources du xiiie siècle', in *Sources de l'héraldique en Europe occidentale. Actes du 4e colloque international d'héraldique* (Brussels: Archives générales du Royaume, 1985), pp. 92–103

Mills, Robert, 'Seeing Sodomy in the *Bible Moralisée*', *Speculum*, LXXXVII (2012), pp. 413–68

Morgan, Nigel, *Early Gothic Manuscripts, I: 1190–1250* (London: Harvey Miller, 1982)

Morlet, Marie-Thérèse, *Les noms de personne sur le territoire de l'ancienne Gaul du VIe au XIIe siècle*, 3 vols (Paris: CNRS, 1968–85)

Mousket, Philippe, *Chronique rimée*, ed. Frédéric de Reiffenberg, 2 vols (Brussels: M. Hayez, 1836–8)

Mulder-Bakker, Anneke B., 'Jeanne of Valois: The Power of a Consort', in *Capetian Women*, ed. Kathleen Nolan (New York: Palgrave Macmillan, 2003), pp. 253–69

Murray, Stephen, *Beauvais Cathedral: Architecture of Transcendence* (Princeton: Princeton University Press, 1989)

—, 'The Architectural Envelope of the Sainte-Chapelle of Paris', in *Pierre, lumière, couleur: études d'histoire de l'art du moyen âge en honneur d'Anne Prache*, ed. Fabienne Joubert and Dany Sandron (Paris: Presses de l'Université de Paris-Sorbonne, 1999), pp. 223–30

Nedermann, Cary, 'A Duty to Kill: John of Salisbury's Theory of Tyrannicide', *Review of Politics*, L (1988), pp. 365–89

Nelson, Janet L., 'Early Medieval Rites of Queen-Making and the Shaping of Medieval Queenship', in *Queens and Queenship in Medieval Europe*, ed. Anne J. Duggan (Woodbridge: Boydell Press, 1997), pp. 301–15

—, 'The Lord's Anointed and the People's Choice: Carolingian Royal Ritual', in Nelson, *The Frankish World, 750–900* (London: Hambledon, 1996), pp. 99–131

Newcombe, Terence, *Les poésies de Thibaut de Blaison* (Geneva: Droz, 1978)

Newman, William Mendel, *Les seigneurs de Nesle en Picardie, XIIe–XIIIe siècles: leur chartes et leur histoire*, 2 vols (Paris: Picard, 1971)

Nicholas of Braie, 'Gesta Ludovici VIII, Francorum Regis', in *RHF*, XVII (1878), pp. 311–45

Nicholas, Karen, 'Women as Rulers: Countesses Jeanne and Marguerite of Flanders (1212–78)', in *Queens, Regents and Potentates*, ed. Theresa M. Vann (Dallas: Academia Press, 1993), pp. 73–89

—, 'Countesses as Rulers in Flanders', in *Aristocratic Women in Medieval France*, ed. T. Evergates (Philadelphia: University of Pennsylvania Press, 1999), pp. 111–37

Nolan, Kathleen, *Queens in Stone and Silver: The Creation of a Visual Imagery of Queenship in Capetian France* (New York: Palgrave Macmillan, 2009)

Nye, Joseph, *Soft Power: The Means to Success in World Politics* (New York: Public Affairs, 2004)

Obituaires de la Province de Sens, ed. Auguste Molinier and Auguste Longnon, 4 vols in 5 (Paris, 1902–23)

Oeuvres de Rigord et Guillaume le Breton, ed. H. F. Delaborde, 2 vols (Paris: Société de l'Histoire de France, 1882–5)

Omont, H., *Le Psautier de Saint Louis de la Bibliothèque de Leyde* (Leiden: A. W. Sijthoff, 1902)

Ordonnances des roys de France de la troisième race, recueillies par ordre chronologique, ed. Eusèbe Laurière et al., 21 vols (Paris, 1723–1849)

Pacaut, Marcel, *Louis VII et son royaume* (Paris: SEVPEN, 1964)

Painter, Sidney, *The Scourge of the Clergy: Peter of Dreux, Duke of Brittany* (Baltimore: Johns Hopkins Press, 1937)

Parsons, John Carmi, 'Mothers, Daughters, Marriage, Power: Some Plantagenet Evidence, 1150–1500', in *Medieval Queenship*, ed. Parsons (Stroud: Alan Sutton, 1998), pp. 63–78

——, 'Piety, Power and the Reputation of Two 13th-century English Queens', in *Queens, Regents and Potentates*, ed. Theresa M. Vann (Dallas: Academia Press, 1993), pp. 107–23

——, 'The Queen's Intercession in Thirteenth Century England', in *Power of the Weak: Studies on Medieval Women*, ed. Jennifer Carpenter and Sally-Beth MacLean (Urbana: University of Illinois Press, 1995), pp. 147–77

——, 'Of Queens, Courts and Books: Reflections on the Literary Patronage of Thirteenth-century Plantagenet Queens', in *The Cultural Patronage of Medieval Women*, ed. June Hall McCash (Athens, Ga.: University of Georgia Press, 1996), pp. 175–201

——, *Eleanor of Castile: Queen and Society in Thirteenth-century England* (New York: St Martin's Press, 1998)

Pastoureau, Michel, 'La fleur de lis: emblème royal, symbole Marial ou thème graphique?', in *L'hermine et le sinople: études d'héraldique médiévale* (Paris: Léopard d'or, 1982), pp. 158–78

Peltzer, Jorg, 'The Slow Death of the Angevin Empire', *Historical Research*, LXXXI (2008), pp. 553–84

Pernoud, Régine, *Blanche of Castile*, trans. Henry Noel (London: Collins, 1975) [French original: *La Reine Blanche*, Paris: Albin Michel, 1972]

Perry, Guy, *John of Brienne: King of Jerusalem, Emperor of Constantinople, c.1175–1237* (Cambridge: Cambridge University Press, 2013)

Peter of Les Vaux-de-Cernay, *The History of the Albigensian Crusade*, ed. and trans. W. A. Sibley and M. D. Sibley (Woodbridge: Boydell Press, 1998)

Peter Lombard, 'Commentarium in Psalmos', *PL*, CXCI, cols 35–1296

Petit-Dutaillis, Charles, *Etude sur la vie et le règne de Louis VIII* (Paris: E. Bouillon, 1894)

Pick, Lucy, *Conflict and Coexistence: Archbishop Rodrigo and the Muslims and Jews of Medieval Spain* (Ann Arbor: University of Michigan Press, 2004)

'Polyptychum Rotomagensis diocesis', in *RHF*, XXIII (1876), pp. 229–331

Pontal Gauthier, Odette, 'Le différend entre Louis IX et les évêques de Beauvais et ses incidences sur les Conciles, 1232–1248', *Bibliothèque de l'école des chartes*, CXXIII (1965), pp. 5–34

Poulet, Jean, 'Capetian Women and the Regency: The Genesis of a Vocation', in *Medieval Queenship*, ed. John Carmi Parsons (New York: St Martin's Press, 1993), pp. 93–116

Power of the Weak: Studies on Medieval Women, ed. Jennifer Carpenter and Sally-Beth MacLean (Urbana: University of Illinois Press, 1995)

Power, Daniel, *The Norman Frontier in the Twelfth and Early Thirteenth Centuries* (Cambridge: Cambridge University Press, 2004)

—, 'Who Went on the Albigensian Crusade?', *English Historical Review*, CXXVIII (2013), pp. 1047–85

Powicke, F. M., *Stephen Langton* (Oxford: Clarendon Press, 1928)

—, *The Loss of Normandy*, 2nd edn (Manchester: Manchester University Press, 1961)

Primat, 'Chronique de Primat traduite par Jean de Vignay', in *RHF*, XXIII (1876), pp. 5–106

Quand gouverner c'est enquêter: les pratiques politiques de l'enquête princière: occident, XIIIe–XIVe siècles, ed. Thierry Pécout (Paris: De Boccard, 2010)

Queens and Queenship in Medieval Europe, ed. Anne J. Duggan (Woodbridge: Boydell Press, 1997)

Queens, Regents and Potentates, ed. Theresa M. Vann (Dallas: Academia Press, 1993)

'Querimoniae Normannorum', in *RHF*, XXIV (1904), pp. 1–73

Quéruel, Danielle, 'Un cour intellectual au xiie siècle', in *Splendeurs de la cour de Champagne au temps de Chrétien de Troyes*, ed. Thierry Delcourt and Xavier de La Selle (Troyes: Association Champagne historique, 1999), pp. 11–18

Ralph of Coggeshall, *Radulphi de Coggeshall Chronicon Anglicanum*, ed. J. J. Stevenson, Rolls Series (London, 1875)

Rashdall, Hastings, *The Universities of Europe in the Middle Ages*, 3 vols (Oxford: Clarendon Press, 1936)

Reassessing the Roles of Women as 'Makers' of Medieval Art and Architecture, ed. Therese Martin, 2 vols (Leiden and Boston, Mass.: Brill, 2012)

'Recepta et expensa Anno MCCXXXIIII inter candelosam et ascensionem', in *RHF*, XXI (1855), pp. 226–51

Récits d'un ménestrel de Reims au treizième siècle, ed. Natalis de Wailly (Paris: Société de l'histoire de France/Renouard, 1876)

Recueil de chartes et documents de Saint-Martin-des-Champs, monastère Parisien, ed. J. Depoin, 5 vols, Archives de la France monastique, XXI (Paris: Picard, 1921)

Reeves, Marjorie, *Joachim of Fiore and the Prophetic Future* (London: SPCK, 1976)

Les registres de Philippe Auguste, ed. J. W. Baldwin (Paris: Imprimerie nationale, 1992)

Les registres de Gregoire IX, ed. Lucien Auvray, 4 vols (Paris: Fontemoing, 1890–1955)

Les registres de Innocent IV: recueil des bulles de ce pape, ed. Elie Berger, 4 vols (Paris: E. Thorin, 1881–1920)

Riant, Paul Edouard Didier, 'Déposition de Charles d'Anjou pour la canonisation de Saint Louis', in *Notices et documents publiés pour la Société d'histoire de France à l'occasion du cinquantième anniversaire de sa fondation* (Paris, 1884), pp. 155–76

—, *Exuviae sacrae Constantinopolitanae* [1877–8], 2 vols (Paris: Editions du CTHS, 2004)

Rigord, 'Gesta Philippi Augusti', in *Oeuvres de Rigord et de Guillaume le Breton, historiens de Philippe-Auguste*, ed. H. F. Delaborde, 2 vols (Paris: Société de l'Histoire de France, 1882–5), I, pp. 1–167

—, *Histoire de Philippe Auguste*, ed. Elisabeth Carpentier, Georges Pon and Yves Chauvin, Sources d'Histoire Médiévale, 33 (Paris: CNRS, 2006)

Robert of Auxerre, 'Roberti Canonici S. Mariae Autissiodorensis Chronicon', in MGH *Scriptores*, XXVI, ed. O. Holder-Egger (Hanover, 1882), pp. 219–87

Roger of Howden, *Chronica magistri Rogeri de Hovedene*, ed. William Stubbs, 4 vols, Rolls Series (London: Longmans, 1868–71)

Roger of Wendover, *Flores historiarum*, ed. H. G. Hewlett, 3 vols, Rolls Series (London, 1886–9)

Romanet, Olivier de, *Géographie du Perche* (Mortagne: Le Perche, Documents sur la Province du Perche, 1890–1902), 2 parts in one vol.

Rouse, Richard H., and Mary A. Rouse, 'John of Salisbury and the Doctrine of Tyrannicide', *Speculum*, XLII (1967), pp. 693–709

Ruiz, Teofilo, *From Heaven to Earth: The Reordering of Castillian Society, 1150–1350* (Princeton: Princeton University Press, 2004)

Rymer, Thomas, *Foedera*, 3 vols (London, 1816–30)

La Sainte-Chapelle de Paris: royaume de France ou Jérusalem céleste?, ed. Christine Hediger (Turnhout: Brepols, 2007)

Saint Louis, exh. cat., ed. Pierre-Yves Le Pogam, Conciergerie, Paris (Paris: Editions du patrimoine, Centre des monuments nationaux, 2014)

Saint Louis et l'Anjou, ed. Etienne Vacquet (Rennes: Presses universitaires de Rennes, 2014)

Samuel, Irene, 'Semiramis in the Middle Ages: The History of a Legend', *Medievalia et humanistica*, II (1944), pp. 32–44

The Sanctity of Louis IX: Early Lives of Saint Louis by Geoffrey of Beaulieu and William of Chartres, trans. Larry F. Field, ed. M. Cecilia Gaposchkin and Sean L. Field (Ithaca: Cornell University Press, 2014)

Santi, Francesco, 'Guglielmo d'Auvergne e l'ordine dei domenicani tra filosofia naturale e tradizione magica', in *Autour de Guillaume d'Auvergne*, ed. F. Morenzoni and J.-Y. Tilliette (Turnhout: Brepols, 2005), pp. 137–53

Sauerlander, Willibald, *Gothic Sculpture in France, 1140–1270*, trans. Janet Sondheimer (London: Thames and Hudson, 1972)

Schowalter, Kathleen, 'The Ingeborg Psalter: Queenship, Legitimacy and the Appropriation of Byzantine Art in the West', in *Capetian Women*, ed. Kathleen Nolan (New York: Palgrave Macmillan, 2003), pp. 99–135

Schneidmüller, Bernd, 'Constructing Identities of Medieval France', in *France in the Central Middle Ages, 900–1200*, ed. Marcus Bull (Oxford: Oxford University Press, 2002), pp. 15–42

The Seventh Crusade, 1244–1254: Sources and Documents, ed. Peter Jackson (Aldershot: Ashgate, 2007)

Septième centenaire de la mort de Saint Louis. Actes des colloques du Royaumont et de Paris, 21–27 mai 1970 (Paris: CNRS/Les Belles Lettres, 1976)

Sepulturae cistercienses, ed. Jackie Hall and Christine Kratzke, Cîteaux: commentarii Cistercienses, 56 (Forges-Chimay: Cîteaux, 2005)

Shadis, Miriam, 'Piety, Politics and Power: The Patronage of Leonor of England and her Daughters, Berenguela of León and Blanche of Castile', in *The Cultural Patronage of*

Medieval Women, ed. June Hall McCash (Athens, Ga.: University of Georgia Press, 1996), pp. 202–27

—, 'Blanche of Castile and Facinger's "Medieval Queenship": Reassessing the Argument', in *Capetian Women*, ed. Kathleen Nolan (New York: Palgrave Macmillan, 2003), pp. 137–61

—, *Berenguela of Castile (1180–1246) and Political Women in the High Middle Ages* (New York: Palgrave Macmillan, 2009)

—, and Constance Hoffman Berman, 'A Taste of the Feast: Reconsidering Eleanor of Aquitaine's Female Descendants', in *Eleanor of Aquitaine, Lord and Lady*, ed. Bonnie Wheeler and John Carmi Parsons (New York: Palgrave Macmillan, 2002), pp. 177–211

Short, Ian, 'Literary Culture and the Court of Henry II', in *Henry II: New Interpretations*, ed. Christopher Harper-Bill and Nicholas Vincent (Woodbridge: Boydell & Brewer, 2007), pp. 335–61

Sivéry, Gérard, *Blanche de Castille* (Paris: Fayard, 1990)

Smalley, Beryl, *The Becket Conflict and the Schools: A Study of Intellectuals in Politics* (Oxford: Blackwell, 1973)

Spiegel, Gabrielle, 'The *Reditus Regni ad Stirpem Karoli Magni*: A New Look', *French Historical Studies*, VII (1971), pp. 145–74

—, *Romancing the Past: The Rise of Vernacular Prose Historiography in Thirteenth-century France* (Berkeley: University of California Press, 1993)

Splendeurs de la cour de Champagne au temps de Chrétien de Troyes, ed. Thierry Delcourt and Xavier de La Selle (Troyes: Association Champagne historique, 1999)

Stabler Miller, Tanya, *The Beguines of Medieval Paris: Gender, Patronage and Spiritual Authority* (Philadephia: University of Pennsylvania Press, 2014)

Stacey, Robert, 'Henry III and the Jews', in *Jews in Medieval Christendom*, ed. K. T. Utterback and M. L. Price (Leiden: Brill, 2013), pp. 117–27

Stafford, Pauline, 'Emma: The Powers of the Queen in the Eleventh Century', in *Queens and Queenship in Medieval Europe*, ed. Anne J. Duggan (Woodbridge: Boydell Press, 1997), pp. 3–26

—, 'Writing the Biography of Eleventh-century Queens', in *Writing Medieval Biography, 750–1250: Essays in Honour of Frank Barlow*, ed. David Bates, Julia Crick and Sarah Hamilton (Woodbridge: Boydell Press, 2006), pp. 99–109

Stahl, Harvey, *Picturing Kingship: History and Painting in the Psalter of St Louis* (University Park: Pennsylvania State University Press, 2008)

Statuta Capitulorum generalium ordinis Cisterciensis ab anno 116 ad annum 1786, ed. Joseph Canivez, 8 vols (Louvain, 1935)

Stephen of Lexington, 'Registrum epistolarum Stephani de Lexington', ed. Fr B. Griesser in *Analecta Sacri Ordinis Cisterciensis*, vol. II (1946), pp. 1–118 [part I]; vol. VIII (1952), pp. 181–378 [part II]

Stirnemann, Patricia, 'Une bibliothèque princière au XIIe siècle', in *Splendeurs de la cour de Champagne au temps de Chrétien de Troyes*, ed. Thierry Delcourt and Xavier de La Selle (Troyes: Association Champagne historique, 1999), pp. 36–42

—, 'Les bibliothèques princières et privées aux XIIe et XIIIe siècles', in *Histoire des bibliothèques françaises: les bibliothèques médiévales*, ed. A. Verlet (Paris: Editions du Cercle de la librairie, 1989), pp. 173–91

Les stratégies matrimoniales, IXe–XIIIe siècle, ed. Martin Aurell (Turnhout: Brepols, 2013)

Strayer, J. R., *The Administration of Normandy under Saint Louis* (Cambridge, Mass.: Medieval Academy of America, 1932)

Suger, *Œuvres complètes de Suger, recueillies, annotées et publiées d'après les manuscrits*, ed. A. Lecoy de la Marche (Paris: Société de l'histoire de France, 1867)

—, *Vie de Louis VI le Gros*, ed. and trans. Henri Waquet (Paris: H. Champion, 1929)

Synek, Eva M., ' "Ex utroque sexu fidelium tres ordines": The Status of Women in Early Medieval Canon Law', in *Gendering the Middle Ages*, ed. Pauline Stafford and Anneke B. Mulder-Bakker (Oxford: Blackwell, 2001), pp. 65–91 [first published as special issue of *Gender and History*, XII/3, 2000]

Szabó, Thomas, 'Die Kritik der Jagd von der Antike zum Mittelalter', in *Jagd und höfische Kultur im Mittelalter*, ed. Werner Rösenener (Göttingen: Vandenhoeck and Ruprecht, 1997), pp. 167–229

Tachau, Katherine H., 'God's Compass and *Vana Curiositas*: Scientific Study in the Old French *Bible Moralisée*', *Art Bulletin*, LXXX (1998), pp. 7–33

Thomas Wright's Political Songs of England, ed. Peter Coss (Cambridge: Cambridge University Press, 1996)

Thompson, Kathleen, *Power and Border Lordship in Medieval France: The County of the Perche, 1000–1226* (Woodbridge: Boydell Press/Royal Historical Society, 2002)

Thorndike, Lynn, *Michael Scot* (London: Nelson, 1965)

Tolley, Thomas, 'Eleanor of Castile and the Spanish Style in England', in *England in the Thirteenth Century: Proceedings of the 1989 Harlaxton Symposium*, ed. W. M. Ormrod, Harlaxton Medieval Studies (Stamford: Paul Watkins, 1991), pp. 167–92

Toupet, Christophe, and Monique Wabont, 'L'abbaye cistercienne de Maubuisson (Val d'Oise, France): les réseaux hydrauliques du XIIIE au XVIIE siècle', in *L'hydraulique monastique: milieux, réseaux, usages*, ed. L. Pressouyre et al. (Grâne: Creaphis, 1996), pp. 135–55

The Trial of the Talmud: Paris, 1240, ed. and trans. John Friedman, Jean Connell Hoff and Robert Chazan (Toronto: Pontifical Institute of Medieval Studies, 2012)

Tugwell, Simon, ed., *Early Dominicans: Selected Writings* (New York: Paulist Press, 1982)

Tuillier, A., 'La condamnation du Talmud par les maîtres universitaires parisiens, ses causes et ses conséquences politiques et idéologiques', in *Le brûlement du Talmud à Paris, 1242–1244*, ed. Gilbert Dahan (Paris: Cerf, 1999), pp. 59–78

Turner, Ralph V., *Eleanor of Aquitaine* (London and New Haven: Yale University Press, 2009)

—, 'England in 1215: An Authoritarian Dynasty Facing Multiple Threats', in *Magna Carta and the England of King John*, ed. Janet S. Loengard (Woodbridge: Boydell Press, 2010), pp. 10–26

Udovitch, Joan Diamond, 'Three Astronomers in a Thirteenth-century Psalter', *Marsyas: Studies in the History of Art*, XVII (1975), pp. 79–83

Vale, Malcolm, *The Princely Court: Medieval Courts and Culture in North-West Europe* (Oxford: Oxford University Press, 2001)

Valois, Noël, *Guillaume d'Auvergne, évêque de Paris, 1228–1249: sa vie et ses ouvrages* (Paris: A. Picard, 1880)

Vann, Theresa, 'The Theory and Practice of Medieval Castilian Queenship', in *Queens, Regents and Potentates*, ed. Vann (Dallas: Academia Press, 1993), pp. 125–47

—, '"Our Father Has Won a Great Victory": The Authorship of Berenguela's Account of the Battle of Las Navas de Tolosa, 1212', *Journal of Medieval Iberian Studies*, III/I (2011), pp. 79–92

Verry, Elisabeth, 'Les seigneurs d'Anjou au temps de Saint Louis', in *Saint Louis et l'Anjou*, ed. Etienne Vacquet (Rennes: Presses universitaires de Rennes, 2014), pp. 40–54

Vidas, Marina, *The Christina Psalter: A Study of the Images and Texts in a French Early Thirteenth-century Illuminated Manuscript* (Copenhagen: Museum Tusculanum Press, 2006)

Vincennes aux origines de l'état moderne. Actes du colloque scientifique sur 'Les Capétiens à Vincennes au Moyen âge', ed. Jean Chapelot and Elisabeth Lalou (Paris: Presses de l'Ecole normale supérieure, 1996)

Vincent, Nicholas, 'John's Jezebel: Isabelle of Angoulême', in *King John: New Interpretations*, ed. S. D. Church (Woodbridge: Boydell, 1999), pp. 165–21

—, 'The Court of Henry II', in *Henry II: New Interpretations*, ed. Christopher Harper-Bill and Nicholas Vincent (Woodbridge: Boydell & Brewer, 2007), pp. 278–334

—, 'Stephen Langton, Archbishop of Canterbury', in *Etienne Langton: prédicateur, bibliste, théologien*, ed. L.-J. Bataillon et al. (Turnhout: Brepols, 2010), pp. 51–123

—, 'The Great Lost Library of England's Medieval Kings? Royal Users and Ownership of Books, 1066–1272', in *1000 Years of Royal Books and Manuscripts*, ed. Kathleen Doyle and Scot McKendrick (London: British Library, 2013), pp. 73–112

Viré, Marc, 'Le système hydraulique de l'abbaye cistercienne de Royaumont du XIIIE au XVIIIE siècles', in *L'hydraulique monastique: milieux, réseaux, usages*, ed. L. Pressouyre et al. (Grâne: Créaphis, 1996), pp. 257–69

Wabont, Monique, *Maubuisson au fil de l'eau: les réseaux hydrauliques de l'abbaye du XIIIe au XVIIIe siècle*, Notice d'Archéologie du Val-d'Oise, 3 (Saint-Ouen-l'Aumône: Service départemental d'archéologie du Val-d'Oise, 1992)

Wade Labarge, Margaret, *A Baronial Household of the Thirteenth Century* (Brighton: Harvester Press, 1980)

Wailly, Natalis de, 'Récit du treizième siècle sur les translations faites en 1239 et en 1241 des saints reliques de la Passion', *Bibliothèque de l'école des chartes*, XXXIX (1878), pp. 401–15

—, 'Dissertation sur les dépenses et les recettes ordinaires de Saint-Louis', in *RHF*, XXI (1855), pp. liii–lxxxvii

Walker, Rose, 'Leonor of England, Plantagenet Queen of Alfonso VIII of Castile, and her Foundation of the Cistercian Abbey of Las Huelgas: In Imitation of Fontevraud?', *Journal of Medieval History*, XXXI (2005), pp. 346–68

Wällensköld, Alexis, *Les chansons de Thibaut de Champagne, roi de Navarre: édition critique* (Paris: Société des anciens textes français, 1925)

Walter Cornut, 'Historia susceptionis Coronae spineae', in *RHF*, XXII (1865), pp. 27–32

Walter Map, *De nugis curialium/Courtiers' Trifles*, ed. M. R. James, C.N.L. Brooke and R.A.B. Mynors (Oxford: Clarendon Press, 1983)

Warren, W. L., *Henry II*, paperback edn (London: Eyre Methuen, 1977)

Wei, Ian, *Intellectual Culture in Medieval Paris: Theologians and the University, c.1100–1330* (Cambridge: Cambridge University Press, 2012)

Weiler, Bjorn, 'Kingship, Usurpation and Propaganda in Twelfth-century Europe: The Case of Stephen', *Anglo-Norman Studies*, XXIII (2001), pp. 299–326

Weiss, Daniel H., *Art and Crusade in the Age of Saint Louis* (Cambridge: Cambridge University Press, 1998)

—, 'Architectural Symbolism and the Decoration of the Sainte-Chapelle', *Art Bulletin*, LXXVII (1995), pp. 308–20

Westerhof, Danielle, *Death and the Noble Body in Medieval England* (Woodbridge: Boydell Press, 2008)

William the Breton, 'Gesta Philippi Augusti', in *Oeuvres de Rigord et Guillaume le Breton*, ed. H. Delaborde, 2 vols (Paris: Société de l'Histoire de France, 1882–5), I, pp. 168–333

—, 'Philippide', in *Oeuvres de Rigord et Guillaume le Breton*, ed. H. Delaborde, 2 vols (Paris: Société de l'Histoire de France, 1882–5), II, pp. 1–385

William of Chartres, 'De vita et actibus inclytae recordationis regis francorum ludovici et de miraculis', in *RHF*, XX (1840), pp. 28–44

—, 'On the Life and Deeds of Louis, King of the Franks of Famous Memory, and on the Miracles that Declare his Sanctity', in *The Sanctity of Louis IX: Early Lives of Saint Louis by Geoffrey of Beaulieu and William of Chartres*, trans. Larry F. Field, ed. M. Cecilia Gaposchkin and Sean L. Field (Ithaca: Cornell University Press, 2014), pp. 129–59

William of Nangis, 'Chronicon Guillelmi de Nangiaco (ab anno 1226 ad 1300)', in *RHF*, XX (1840), pp. 543–82

—, *Chronique latine de Guillaume de Nangis*, ed. H. Geraud, 2 vols, Société de l'Histoire de France (Paris: Jules Renouard, 1843)

—, 'Vita Sancti Ludovici'/'Vie de Saint Louis', in *RHF*, XX (1840), pp. 309–465

William of Poitiers, *The Gesta Guillelmi of William of Poitiers*, ed. and trans. R.H.C. Davis and M. Chibnall (Oxford: Clarendon Press, 1998)

William of Puylaurens, *Guillaume de Puylaurens: Chronique, 1145–1275*, ed. and trans. Jean Duvernoy, 2nd edn (Toulouse: Le Pérégrinateur, 1996)

Wolff, Robert Lee, 'Mortgage and Redemption of an Emperor's Son: Castile and the Latin Empire of Constantinople', *Speculum*, XXIX (1954), pp. 45–84

Women and Monasticism in Medieval Europe: Sisters and Patrons of the Cistercian Reform, ed. and trans. Constance Berman (Kalamazoo: Western Michigan University, 2002)

Women and Power in the Middle Ages, ed. Mary Erler and Maryanne Kowalski (Athens, Ga.: University of Georgia Press, 1988)

Wood, Charles T., *The French Apanages and the Capetian Monarchy, 1224–1328* (Cambridge, Mass.: Harvard University Press, 1966)

Woolgar, C. M., *The Great Household in Late Medieval England* (New Haven and London: Yale University Press, 1999)

Wright, Georgia Sommers, 'A Royal Tomb Program in the Reign of St Louis', *Art Bulletin*, LVI (1974), pp. 224–43

Writing Medieval Biography, 750–1250: Essays in Honour of Professor Frank Barlow, ed. David Bates, Julia Crick and Sarah Hamilton (Woodbridge: Boydell Press, 2006)

Index

Photograph Credits